COMPREHENSION PROCESSES
IN READING

edited by

D. A. Balota

G. B. Flores d'Arcais

K. Rayner

LEA LAWRENCE ERLBAUM ASSOCIATES, PUBLISHERS
1990 Hillsdale, New Jersey   Hove and London

Lawrence Erlbaum Associates, Inc., Publishers
365 Broadway
Hillsdale, New Jersey 07642

Library of Congress Cataloging-in-Publication Data

Comprehension processes in reading / edited by David A. Balota,
    Giovanni B. Flores d'Arcais, Keith Rayner.
        p. cm.
    Includes bibliographical references.
    ISBN 0-8058-0653-9. -- ISBN 0-8058-0654-7 (pbk.)
    1. Reading comprehension. 2. Dyslexia. I. Balota, David A.
    II. Flores D'Arcais, Giovanni B.   III. Rayner, Keith,
    LB1050.45.C73   1990
    428.4'3--dc20   90-31318
                                                         CIP

Printed in the United States of America
10 9 8 7 6 5 4 3 2 1

TABLE OF CONTENTS

5. The locus of the associative-priming effect in the mental lexicon 101

A. M. B. de Groot

6. Lexical processing, morphological complexity and reading 125

R. Schreuder, M. Grendel, N. Poulisse, A. Roelofs & M. van de Voort

SECTION 2: SYNTACTIC PROCESSES IN COMPREHENSION

22. Referential processing in reading: Focusing on roles and individuals **465**

S. Garrod & A. Sanford

23. A connectionist model of text comprehension **487**

N. E. Sharkey

COMMENTARY ON SECTION 3:

**SECTION 4: COMPREHENSION FAILURES AND
          READING**

28. Comprehension problems in dyslexia
J. Rispens

COMMENTARY ON SECTION 4:

29. Comprehension failures
A. van der Leij

GENERAL COMMENTARY

CONTRIBUTORS

David A. Balota, Washington University, St. Louis.

Derek Besner, University of Waterloo.

Paul van den Broek, University of Minnesota.

Charles Clifton Jr., University of Massachusetts, Amherst.

Frances A. Conners, University of Colorado.

Stephen Crain, University of Connecticut, Storrs and Haskins Laboratories.

Fernando Cuetos, University of Oviedo.

Marica De Vincenzi, University of Massachusetts, Amherst.

Giovanni Flores d'Arcais, Max Planck Institute, Nijmegen and University of Leiden.

Lyn Frazier, University of Massachusetts, Amherst.

Simon Garrod, University of Glasgow.

Jonathan M. Golding, University of Kentucky.

Marjon Grendel, University of Nijmegen.

Annette M. B. de Groot, University of Amsterdam.

Patrick Hudson, University of Leiden.

Tracy M. Jennings, University of Denver.

Janice M. Keenan, University of Denver.

Aryan van der Leij, Free University Amsterdam.

James L. McClelland, Carnegie-Mellon University.

Gail McKoon, Northwestern University.

Jerome L. Myers, University of Massachusetts, Amherst.

Don C. Mitchell, University of Exeter.

Odmar Neumann, University of Bielefeld.

Leo G.M. Noordman, University of Tilburg.

Dennis Norris, MRC Applied Psychology Unit, Cambridge.

Richard K. Olson, University of Colorado.

Charles A. Perfetti, University of Pittsburgh.

Alexander Pollatsek, University of Massachusetts, Amherst.

George R. Potts, University of Denver.

Nanda Poulisse, University of Nijmegen.

Roger Ratcliff, Northwestern University.

Keith Rayner, University of Massachusetts, Amherst.

Jan Rispens, University of Leiden.

Ardi Roelofs, University of Nijmegen.

Anthony J. Sanford, University of Glasgow.

Robert Schreuder, University of Nijmegen.

Mark S. Seidenberg, McGill University.

Philip H.K. Seymour, University of Dundee.

Noel E. Sharkey, University of Exeter.

Donald Shankweiler, University of Connecticut, Storrs and Haskins Laboratories.

Roman Taraban, Carnegie-Mellon University.

Wietske Vonk, Max Planck Institute for Psycholinguistics, Nijmegen and University of Nijmegen.

Marlies van de Voort, University of Nijmegen.

Daniel Zagar, University of Dijon.

PREFACE

Research on reading has made enormous progress during the last twenty years. Many books and journal articles have been devoted to the study of reading and various subcomponents of the reading process. The central focus of this volume is the process of reading comprehension. Clearly, there are many processes involved in reading, but no one would deny that understanding comprehension during reading is the most important goal of reading research. The present book contains chapters by many distinquished researchers on some central topics relevant to understanding the processes associated with comprehending text.

The present volume contains papers that were presented at a Conference held at the Netherlands Institute for Advanced Studies (NIAS) in Wassenaar and at the Netherlands Royal Academy of Sciences in Amsterdam in June, 1988. The conference was organized as the culmination of the work of a year-long study group on Reading, Word Recognition, and Dyslexia at the NIAS. The planning and organization of the study group was co-ordinated by Giovanni B. Flores d'Arcais. Members of the study group were: David A. Balota, G.B. Flores d'Arcais, Simon Garrod, Odmar Neumann, Charles A. Perfetti, Keith Rayner, Jan Rispens, Andre van Dongen, and Aryan van der Leij. In addition to the year-end conference, a number of workshops were held at various universities throughout the Netherlands.

The theme of the Conference was Comprehension Processes in Reading. In organizing the Conference, we attempted to deal with a number of aspects of reading processes that are relevant to this theme. Since one of us had recently completed a textbook on reading, our intial discussion focused on what aspects of reading were not well-understood. We found that our early discussions centered on the topic of reading comprehension processes and it was our sense that there was not much interaction between researchers working on different aspects of reading that are relevant to comprehension. Thus, it was our impression that researchers in the fields of word recognition, sentence parsing, discourse comprehension, and reading problems rarely have the opportunity to interact together, even though there are clear overlaps in their respective interests. Therefore, our goal was to bring together scientists working on these different topics, as well as to have something of an international and inter- disciplinary flavor to the conference. In attendance were experimental psychologists, cognitive scientists, linguists, and educators. This volume reflects the structure and the content of the conference. It is intended as an up-to-date overview of topics relevant to understanding the processes associated with reading comprehension. The conference itself was vigorous, stimulating, and highly productive. The discussion periods at the end of most presentations were extremely interesting. We hope that much of the excitement that was present in the meeting is captured in the pages of this volume.

As Fellows of the NIAS, we would like to express our sincere appreciation for the support and hospitality we received during our stay at NIAS. A year free from any type of academic or teaching responsibility was greatly appreciated, as was the opportunity to interact freely with a number of colleagues with mutual interests. The peace and tranquility of NIAS was greatly missed once we returned to our own universities. However, we would also like to note our appreciation to our home institutions (Washington University, the Max Planck Institute for Psycholinguistics and the University of Leiden, and the University of Massachusetts) for making the year possible.

We would also like to thank the Foundation Psychon of the Netherlands Pure Research Organization (NWO), the Netherlands Royal Academy of Arts and Sciences (KNAW), and the NIAS for their financial assistance that made the Conference possible. Support for the organization of the Conference was also given by the Max Planck Institute and the University of Leiden. We would particularly like to thank Professor Dirk van de Kaa, the Director of the NIAS, for his support and encouragement throughout the planning stages and during the Conference. We also thank the various staff members of the NIAS for their assistance. In particular, we wish to thank Rita Buis and Pilar Breda for their help in the preparation and execution of the conference. We are most grateful to Edith Sjoerdsma of the Max Planck Institue for her skilled assistance in the preparation of the conference and of the programs, abstracts and papers, and to Li-Lian Brak of the University of Leiden for her help in the organization of the hospitality of the participants and of the social events.

We would also like to thank the Max Planck Institute for generously supporting the preparation of this volume. Special thanks and appreciation go to Edith Sjoerdsma, who cheerfully and extremely competently handled all stages of the manuscript processing associated with preparing the volume up to the final layout of the book. Judith Henstra carefully checked all the references, prepared the index, and was helpful throughout the many stages of manuscript preparation; her contribution is also very gratefully acknowledged. We also thank Inge Tarim for preparing or adapting many of the figures.

We appreciate the support we received from Judith Suben Amsel, our Editor at Lawrence Erlbaum Associates. And, of course we would like to thank the authors of the chapters for their excellent contributions. Finally, we would like to acknowledge the support that we received from our families during the time that we were editing the chapters in the volume.

Wassenaar, December 1989.   D. A. Balota
                                             G. B. Flores d'Arcais
                                             K. Rayner

1 COMPREHENSION PROCESSES: INTRODUCTION

Keith Rayner

University of Massachusetts, Amherst

INTRODUCTION

During the past 15 years, there has been considerable interest among experimental psychologists, educational psychologists, child psychologists, linguists, and others in the process of reading. In the past couple of years, two textbooks (Just & Carpenter, 1987; Rayner & Pollatsek, 1989) have surveyed research on the psychology of reading. In addition, numerous other edited volumes (e.g., Coltheart, 1987) have appeared that deal with the reading process. Although a considerable amount of information has been learned about reading since 1975, there are many gaps in our knowledge and understanding of the process of skilled reading. In particular, our understanding of moment-to-moment comprehension processes still seems quite limited.

The chapters appearing in the present volume represent an attempt to provide reviews of current research on topics relevant to on-line comprehension processes. It should be noted that the primary focus is on the process of comprehension and not on the product of comprehension (or what people remember from what they have read). What people remember from what they have read is certainly an important topic, but it is not unique to reading. Although some of the chapters in this volume deal with the product of reading, the primary concern is with how readers comprehend written text on a moment-to-moment basis. Accordingly, the four sections of the book are: (a) comprehension of words, (b) syntactic processes in comprehension, (c) comprehension of discourse, and (d) comprehension failures manifested in dyslexia and

1

poor reading. Each section consists of a number of presentations followed by one or two commentary chapters. Whereas some of the commentary chapters deal with specific points made by the authors, others deal more globally with general topics relevant to the section.

COMPREHENSION OF WORDS

When we read, it is necessary to recognize the individual words that are printed on the page. There is a very large literature within experimental psychology dealing with the recognition of printed words (Rayner & Pollatsek, 1989). In many cases, researchers studying word recognition are not really interested in reading per se. Rather, printed letters and words are merely a convenient way to study perceptual processes because they represent a stimulus set in which variables such as frequency, visual angle, legibility, and so on, can readily be controlled. As a result of this fact, the relevance of studies of word recognition to understanding the reading process is often questioned. In addition, the particular tasks used to study word recognition are sometimes considered unrelated to what happens during fluent silent reading. For example, lexical decision, categorization, and naming tasks are typically used to study word-recognition processes, and it can be argued that such tasks are somewhat removed from what happens in normal reading. Likewise, threshold-identification tasks, in which words are degraded by brief tachistoscopic presentations, seem somewhat unlike normal reading. Despite these criticisms, it is clearly the case that in order to read fluently, individual words must be comprehended. In fact, a considerable amount of the variance in reading rate and how long readers look at individual words is accounted for by variables that also influence simple word recognition tasks (such as word length, word frequency, etc., Just & Carpenter, 1980). Hence, it does seem to be the case that understanding how individual words are comprehended is directly related to processes that occur in reading. Lately, there has been considerable interest in this issue (as opposed to the earlier and more frequent interest in perceptual issues related to word recognition).

The chapters in Section 1 address a number of important topics related to lexical access and the processes whereby word recognition occurs. The initial chapter by Balota deals with a somewhat controversial topic, namely is there a magical moment wherein lexical access occurs? More precisely, his issue is: Are there any tasks that psychologists typically use to investigate lexical access that can tap into this magical moment (if it exists)? The chapters by Seidenberg and by Besner are interesting because they highlight current debates in the field over the utility of connectionist models in understanding word recognition processes. The chapters by de Groot and by Schreuder, Grendel, Poulisse, Roelofs, and van de Voort deal with the structure of the mental lexicon. Finally, the chapter by Pollatsek and Rayner deals with the relationship between lexical access and eye movements in reading.

SYNTACTIC PROCESSES IN COMPREHENSION

When we read text, there is an underlying grammatical structure that influences the ease (or difficulty) of understanding. Whereas some approaches to understanding comprehension processes are based on the assumption that readers go from individual words to a more global semantic internal representation of the text (without any involvement of syntactic parsing processes), recent research clearly documents the important role that syntax plays in reading. It is the case that most work on syntactic processing merely uses reading as the context for the research. That is, the questions asked are very much the same whether the subjects in the research are reading or listening to discourse. However, I suspect that understanding the way that individual words are parsed into their appropriate syntactic constituents is vitally relevant to understanding how moment-to-moment comprehension processes occur.

Currently, there are a number of interesting debates concerning parsing strategies. These debates revolve around the extent to which parsing is a modular process that is unaffected by contextual information and real-world knowledge. All theorists realize that context and plausibility factors influence sentence processing. The critical question is when these types of information have their influence. Research by Rayner, Carlson, and Frazier (1983) and Ferreira and Clifton (1986) has suggested that initially the parser does not rely on such information in making syntactic parsing decisions but relies on procedures related to underlying grammatical principles. Thus, the impact of these types of information (context and world knowledge) is on reanalysis procedures. However, other researchers (Altmann, 1988; Altmann & Steedman, 1988; Taraban & McClelland, 1988) have argued that these types of information have an effect on early parsing decisions. The chapters in Section 2 largely deal with this issue and with a second general issue: To what extent are there general syntactic principles that are generalizable across different language systems? In one way or another, the chapters in Section 2 by Perfetti, Taraban and McClelland, Clifton and DeVincenzi, Mitchell, Cuetos, and Zagar, and Frazier all deal with these two issues.

COMPREHENSION OF DISCOURSE

There are many studies in the literature dealing with what people remember from what they have read. Although there are often debates about the most appropriate measure of retention (recall vs. recognition, for example), the general conclusions are quite similar across many studies. It is only in the past few years that there has been a serious attempt to understand moment-to-moment comprehension processes. As a result, there is now much interest in topics like anaphoric reference, causal inferences, elaborative inferences, instrumental inferences, and backward inferences. Much of the current research seems to focus on when anaphoric processes and inferences take place. It isn't enough to know that such processes have or have not taken place, researchers now want to know when they take place (if, indeed they do take place). The chapters in Section 3 focus on the general issue of on-line comprehension processes.

In addition to dealing with on-line comprehension processes, there are some interesting themes running through the chapters in Section 3. One thing that is very central to the section is the extent to which different types of models can account for comprehension processes. Although the Kintsch and van Dijk (1978; van Dijk & Kintsch, 1983) model received a great deal of notoriety, one could argue that, although it's interesting at a global level, the specifics are not well worked out. To be sure, the Kintsch and van Dijk model may still serve as a useful framework for researchers interested in comprehension processes, and many of the ideas that they initially proposed still have some currency. However, as the chapters in Section 3 make clear, researchers are now providing models that are much more specific about certain aspects of the comprehension process during reading. Thus, the chapters by Myers, van den Broek, Garrod and Sanford, and Vonk and Noordman deal with rather specific models and aspects of reading comprehension. The chapter by Sharkey, on the other hand, presents more of a global model of comprehension based on connectionist principles.

A second general theme running through the chapters in Section 3 has to do with the appropriate methods to use in assessing on-line comprehension processes. This topic is addressed very clearly by Keenan, Potts, Golding, and Jennings and is also dealt with by McKoon and Ratcliff (who also address the issue of appropriate models of the comprehension process). The chapter by Keenan et al. ties in very nicely with issues touched upon in Section 1 by Balota and others.

COMPREHENSION FAILURES AND DYSLEXIA

Dyslexia is a topic of considerable practical interest. As a result, there has been much recent research dealing with reading disability. Like the work on word recognition, much of the early research focused on perceptual issues related to dyslexia. More recently, the view has emerged that dyslexia reflects various types of language processing deficits (as opposed to a perceptual deficit). However, most of the work has not dealt with language processing per se, and a great deal of recent research has focused on the debate over whether developmental dyslexia represents an extreme point along a continuum of reading ability and on the extent to which there are distinct subtypes of developmental dyslexia.

Although not much attention has been paid to the relationship between reading disability and comprehension processes, it does seem that examining potential relationships might be important. After all, whereas reading rates of dyslexic readers are often quite slow, the primary characteristic of a dyslexic is that he or she does not understand written language. In the past few years, there have been some very interesting proposals concerning the relationship between word recognition failures and dyslexia, between syntactic parsing failures and dyslexia, and between comprehension monitoring failures and dyslexia. The chapters in Section 4 by Crain and Shankweiler, Conners and Olson, Seymour, and Rispens all deal with these issues.

GLOBAL THEMES

As you read the various chapters in the different sections, certain themes that cross the sections will be apparent to you. These themes are especially interesting because they provide a basis of common ground for discussion for workers interested in slightly different topics.

One obvious theme across the different sections relates to the need to determine when on-line processes are occurring. Thus, there is considerable interest in knowing when a particular process (be it lexical access or word recognition, parsing, or inferencing) occurs in real time during reading. The desire for this type of information leads to a second general theme, which concerns the appropriate measures to use to index on-line processes. The chapters by Balota and by Pollatsek and Rayner in Section 1, by Keenan et al. in Section 3, and many of the chapters in Section 2 all address the issue of how best to measure the processes one is interested in studying.

A third general theme crossing many of the sections deals with appropriate models of the processes one is interested in studying. Many of the chapters deal with this issue and it is one that is addressed in many of the commentary chapters. Although such a concern has been with us for some time, the fourth general theme is something of a new development (though obviously very much related to the third theme I have identified). This fourth theme concerns the relevance of connectionist models in studying processes like word recognition, parsing, and discourse comprehension. Some of the chapters (see Seidenberg, Taraban and McClelland, and Sharkey) represent a very pro-connectionist viewpoint, whereas other chapters (see Besner and Norris) take very anti-connectionist viewpoints. It seems that few issues have attracted the attention of so many scientists in different areas (all perhaps under the general umbrella of Cognitive Science) as have the claims of the connectionists, and many of the chapters in this volume reflect both the zeal and the apprehension associated with the enterprise.

A final general theme which I will touch on here doesn't really cross many of the sections but rather is reflected primarily in Section 4. Although basic researchers often do not realize it, their work has practical implications. In the study of reading, basic research often has relevance for how reading is taught to children and for the development of remedial programs for people who do not read very well. Hence, because understanding the skilled reading process has significant implications for understanding why some people don't read well, Section 4 has been included in the hope of stimulating further thought on the relationship between word processing, parsing, and comprehension processes on the one hand, and reading problems on the other.

In the final chapter the various issues and general themes that have been described in this chapter will be addressed again. My primary goal in the present chapter has been to set the stage for the different topics discussed in the four sections of this volume.

REFERENCES

Altmann, G. (1988). Ambiguity, parsing strategies, and computational models. *Language and Cognitive Processes, 3*, 73 - 98.

Altmann, G., & Steedman, M. (1988). Interaction with context during human sentence parsing. *Cognition, 30*, 191 - 238.

Coltheart, M. (Ed.). (1987). *Attention and performance XII: The psychology of reading.* Hillsdale, NJ: Lawrence Erlbaum Associates.

Ferreira, F., & Clifton, C. (1986). The independence of syntactic processing. *Journal of Memory and Language, 25*, 348 - 368.

Just, M. A., & Carpenter, P. A. (1980). A theory of reading: From eye fixations to comprehension. *Psychological Review, 87*, 329 - 354.

Just, M. A., & Carpenter, P. A. (1987). *The psychology of reading and language comprehension.* Boston: Allyn & Bacon.

Kintsch, W., & Van Dijk, T. A. (1978). Toward a model of text comprehension and production. *Psychological Review, 85*, 363 - 394.

Rayner, K., Carlson, M., & Frazier, L. (1983). The interaction of syntax and semantics during sentence processing: Eye movements in the analysis of semantically biased sentences. *Journal of Verbal Learning and Verbal Behavior, 22*, 358 - 374.

Rayner, K., & Pollatsek, A. (1989). *The psychology of reading.* Englewood Cliffs, NJ: Prentice-Hall.

Taraban, R., & McClelland, J. L. (1988). Constituent attachment and thematic role assignment in sentence processing: Influences of content-based expectations. *Journal of Memory and Language, 27*, 597 - 632.

Van Dijk, T. A., & Kintsch, W. (1983). *Strategies of discourse comprehension.* New York: Academic Press.

COMPREHENSION
OF WORDS

2 THE ROLE OF MEANING IN WORD RECOGNITION

David A. Balota

Washington University

INTRODUCTION

The goal of the present discussion is to bring into focus a number of implicit assumptions in the area of word recognition research (see also Seidenberg, this volume). These assumptions revolve around what will here be referred to as the magic moment in word processing. The magic moment refers to that point in time where the subject has recognized the word but has yet to access meaning. Researchers have argued that they can both collect data and develop adequate models of this crucial point in word processing. The outline for this chapter is as follows: First, the empirical support for a magic moment is evaluated. The thrust of this discussion is that the major tasks used to provide data regarding the magic moment entail characteristics that question their utility as pure reflections of this crucial point in word processing. Second, an alternative framework is presented that emphasizes the functional utility of words in language processing, that is, to convey meaning. Third, empirical evidence is presented that suggests that meaning can contribute to components involved in early word processing. Finally, there is a brief discussion of how meaning might be incorporated into the current theoretical accounts of word processing.

THE MAGIC MOMENT IN WORD PROCESSING

If one considers the classic models of word recognition proposed by Becker (1980), Forster (1979), and Morton (1969), among others (e.g., Norris, 1986), there is consistent emphasis on a point in time where there is sufficient overlap between stimulus-driven information and some internal lexical representation that the subject recognizes the word. For example, within Morton's logogen model this magic moment is the point in time where a logogen's threshold is surpassed. Within Becker's verification model, this magic moment is when there is sufficient overlap with a sensory-defined internal representation and the information residing in sensory memory about the stimulus word. In Forster's bin model, the magic moment refers to the point in time where there is a sufficient match between an orthographic representation derived from operations on the stimulus word and a representation in an orthographically defined access bin. In each of these models, it is only after this magic moment in word processing that the subject can access the goodies associated with the word, for example, meaning and syntactic class.

It should be noted that the description just given primarily involves isolated word recognition and cases where words are presented in unrelated contexts. When words are presented in related contexts, meaning of a word may become available before the word is recognized, via priming from related representations. Although meaning may actually contribute to word recognition when relevant context is preactivated, meaning of a word that is not preactivated by related context will not contribute to word recognition within these models. Moreover, even in cases where relevant meaning is preactivated, word recognition in each of the earlier mentioned models still involves a magic moment in word processing.

Psychologists have relied heavily on the lexical decision task (LDT) and the pronunciation task to tap this crucial point in word processing. Based on the arguments made from the data obtained from these tasks, it would appear that researchers in the area of word recognition are in the comfortable position of having tasks available that decouple word recognition from meaning access. Unfortunately, this comfortable position is deceptive.

Surface-Level Descriptions

On the surface, both the LDT and the pronunciation task seem to be faithful reflections of the magic moment. For example, making a lexical decision seems to involve the point in time when an internal representation has been matched by stimulus-driven information, and, therefore, the meaning of the word seems unnecessary. Thus, the button press in the LDT appears to be a reasonable reflection of the magic moment. In addition, it appears that naming a word simply involves a match between stimulus-driven processing of the word and some lexical representation. Once this match is completed, the appropriate sequence of motor codes is engaged for output. Thus, onset of pronunciation, on the surface, also appears to be a reasonable reflection of the magic moment.

Before turning to a more detailed discussion of these tasks, it might be worthwhile to ask whether the use of a response latency measure helps to promote the notion of a measurable magic moment in word processing. That is, the magic moment is that point in time when the subject decides to press a button or begins vocalization. Thus, the researcher has a characteristic of performance that can be mapped onto a temporally defined stage in processing. The availability of response latency measures might mislead one into accepting isolable stages in processing instead of a more cascadic processing framework (McClelland, 1979).

One of the major goals of the present discussion is to look beyond the surface-level descriptions of lexical decision and pronunciation performance. It is important to note here that the present arguments are primarily aimed at the relevance of these tasks to the magic moment hypothesis in word processing and not at their general relevance to research addressing issues involved in pattern recognition, word processing, and attention. Thus, the intention is not to dismiss all data from these tasks but simply to question the purity of these tasks as reflections of the magic moment.

Beyond the Surface in Lexical Decision Performance

First, let us consider a deeper analysis of the LDT. The literature is now replete with concerns about its utility as a measure of the magic moment (e.g., Balota & Chumbley, 1984; Balota & Lorch, 1986; Besner & McCann, 1987; Chumbley & Balota, 1984; De Groot, 1983; Keefe & Neely, in press; Lorch, Balota, & Stamm, 1986; Neely & Keefe, 1989; Neely, Keefe, & Ross, 1989; Seidenberg, Waters, Sanders, & Langer, 1984; West & Stanovich, 1982). The major problem with this task is that the surface-level account ignores the fact that this task is not simply an identification task but rather is a discrimination task in which subjects are forced to discriminate words from nonwords. Subjects can rely on any source of information that is available to make such discriminations. The present discussion simply emphasizes the fact that some variables that presumably influence processing up to the magic moment also could reflect the influence of a confounding between the manipulated variable and the discrimination the subject is required to make.

Isolated Lexical Decisions

First, let us consider lexical decision trials on which only a single word is presented. There are at least two sources of information that would appear to be especially useful in discriminating words from nonwords (Balota & Chumbley, 1984; Besner & McCann, 1987; Chumbley & Balota, 1984): familiarity and meaningfulness. Very simply, words are more familiar and meaningful than nonwords.

With respect to the familiarity dimension, Balota and Chumbley (1984) reported the results of a series of experiments that directly compared the size of the frequency (an obvious correlate of familiarity) effect in lexical decision, category verification, and pronunciation performance for the same set of stimuli. The authors argued that all of these tasks, as viewed by the extant theories, should involve lexical access. Therefore, if word frequency modulates only lexical access processing, then these tasks should produce a similar impact of frequency. However, the results of Balota and Chumbley's study (also see Chumbley & Balota, 1984) indicated that the category verification task produced a significantly smaller influence of frequency than the LDT. The relatively small impact of frequency in the category verification task was not simply due to idiosyncratic characteristics of the Balota and Chumbley study, because similar small influences of frequency have been reported in other experimental situations where performance a priori should be influenced by variables that influence lexical access (e.g., Anderson & Reder, 1974; Brown, Carr, & Chaderjian, 1987; De Groot, 1989; Forster, 1985; Günther, Gfroerer, & Weiss, 1984; Kliegl, Olson, & Davidson, 1982; Manelis, 1977; Millward, Rice, & Corbett, 1975).

Why is the frequency effect so large in the lexical decision task? Basically, there is a confounding between the manipulated variable, frequency/familiarity, and the word/nonword discrimination demanded by the task. Low-frequency words are more similar to nonwords on the relevant familiarity dimension than are high-frequency words. Thus, low frequency words are more difficult to discriminate from nonwords than are high-frequency words. This increased difficulty in discrimination slows response latency. It is important to note here that Balota and Chumbley did not argue that word frequency did not influence early operations in word processing. The major point made in their study is that one cannot unequivocally argue that the impact of frequency in lexical decision performance is only due to processes leading up to and including the magic moment in word processing.

The impact of the discrimination component on the size of the frequency effect is further supported by data from Duchek and Neely (1989) and James (1975). These studies provide evidence that the frequency effect is decreased when the nonwords become less "word-like," for example, making the nonwords unpronounceable. This, of course, would be expected if recognition of low-frequency words is slowed down by their similarity to the nonword distractors. When this similarity is decreased, via the presentation of unpronounceable nonwords, one finds that the low-frequency words benefit more than the high-frequency words from this increased ease in discrimination. The major point here is that the discrimination is modulating the frequency effect, not simply lexical access.

Finally, it should be noted that although familiarity values are available to subjects, it does not *necessarily* follow that in the LDT they modulate lexical access processes. In order to further illustrate this point, consider the hypothesis that subjects are faster to recognize words printed in red compared to words printed in purple. To test this hypothesis, red and purple words along with blue nonwords are presented in a LDT. The results support the hypothesis. The words printed in red produce faster response latencies than the words printed in purple. The

obvious interpretive problem here is that the purple words are more difficult to discriminate from the blue nonwords than the red words. Thus,
the obtained pattern does not necessarily reflect the fact that color is
influencing lexical access but rather that color is a dimension available
to subjects and this dimension is influencing the decision process. We
are simply making a similar argument with respect to familiarity.

Priming Lexical Decisions

Turning to the priming paradigm, here two letter strings are typically presented. The first string is often a word and the second string
is either a word or a nonword. The experimenter manipulates the relationship between the first word and the second string. For example, in
a semantic priming experiment, subjects might receive semantically related prime-target pairs (e.g., *dog - cat*) or unrelated prime-target pairs
(e.g., *pen - cat*). The basic finding here is that subjects are faster to
recognize words (i.e., press the word button) that are primed by related
words compared to words primed by unrelated words (e.g., Meyer &
Schvaneveldt, 1971; Neely, 1977). This priming effect has been viewed
as supportive of the notion that the related prime preactivates or directs
the search to the target's lexical representation, thereby decreasing the
time taken to recognize that word (see, however, Ratcliff & McKoon,
1988). Priming effects have been the focus of considerable attention
in virtually all models of word recognition (e.g., Becker, 1980; Forster,
1981; Norris, 1986).

Unfortunately, it has become clear that there are influences of prime-
target relationships in the LDT that do not necessarily reflect the direc-
tional impact of the prime on target processing (e.g., Balota & Lorch,
1986; De Groot, 1983; Forster, 1981; Keefe & Neely, in press; Lorch et
al., 1986; Lupker, 1984; McNamara & Altarriba, 1988; Neely & Keefe,
1989; Neely et al., 1989; Seidenberg et al., 1984; West & Stanovich,
1982). There again appears to be a simple confounding in this task
between the manipulation (prime–target relatedness) and the discrimination (word - nonword) that the subject is making. The argument
is that subjects could rely on finding a relationship between the prime
and target to bias a "word" response. If the subject finds a relationship
between the prime and target, then the target must be a word, because
nonwords cannot be related to the primes. However, if no relationship
is found between the prime and target, then the target could either be a
nonword or an unrelated target. Thus, on unrelated prime-target trials,
subjects are faced with a more difficult word - nonword discrimination
than on related prime-target trials. Hence, it appears that checking
for a relationship after the magic moment may influence the priming
effects found in the LDT. It is somewhat encouraging that researchers
have recently begun to develop procedures to address this problem and
modulate the reliance on such checking processes (see Keefe & Neely, in
press; McNamara & Altarriba, 1988; Neely et al., 1989).

In sum, the major point to note concerning the LDT is that there is often a confounding between the manipulation of interest and the information that the subject can use to make the word - nonword discrimination. Subjects are very sensitive to such confoundings (see Chumbley & Balota, 1984), and these confoundings can produce exaggerated influences of variables, thereby misdirecting theories of word recognition. Most importantly, for the present discussion, these confoundings question the utility of the LDT to measure the magic moment in word processing.

Beyond the Surface in Pronunciation

On the surface it would appear that pronunciation is more straightforward. Here, the subject is not asked to make a discrimination between words and nonwords and therefore there should be little contribution of a potentially contaminated decision process on overall response latency. Thus, the magic moment of matching stimulus-driven information with an internal lexical representation might be better reflected in this task. However, even in the pronunciation task a variable could potentially play a role at many different loci in this task, thereby also questioning the utility of this task for providing unequivocal evidence concerning processes leading up to the magic moment.

Isolated Pronunciation

The basic concern with the pronunciation task was voiced originally by Cattell (1886). In pronouncing a word, the subject not only has to recognize the stimulus but also has to output the recognized word. Thus, a variable could have an impact on recognition processes and/or on processes after recognition that are tied to the output of the response. Consider the impact of word frequency. Balota and Chumbley (1985) used a delayed-pronunciation task to tease apart the impact of frequency on word recognition from its impact on output processes. In the delayed-pronunciation task, subjects are given sufficient time to recognize the word and then are presented a cue to pronounce the word aloud. If frequency only influences the recognition stage in this task, then one should not find a frequency effect after subjects have had sufficient time to recognize the stimulus. Balota and Chumbley found that subjects still produced a significant frequency effect in this task, even though they were given up to 1400 ms to recognize the stimulus. Because 1400 ms should clearly be sufficient time to recognize a word, they argued that frequency must play at least some role in processing after word recognition. More recently, Balota and Shields (1988) have replicated this pattern with a new set of stimuli that were better equated on (a) beginning and ending phonemes, (b) number of phonemes, (c) number of syllables, and (d) syntactic class. Interestingly, not only did Balota and Shields replicate the delayed pronunciation frequency effect, but they also provided evidence for an impact of frequency on the production durations of these stimuli. Low-frequency words produced longer production durations than high-frequency words.

The impact of word frequency on output processes should not be surprising. If frequency of usage has an impact on the perception of words, it is unclear why frequency of usage would not also have an impact on processes involved in the production of words. Balota and Chumbley (1985) argued that because of the time constraints in producing speech versus writing, the range of frequency in producing speech might actually be smaller than the range of frequency in print. Because speakers have temporal constraints in production, they might be less likely to take the necessary time to search for an obscure word to perfectly convey a given meaning, whereas, writers, because they don't have the same temporal constraints, can pause to complete the search for a relatively obscure word to convey a given meaning. Moreover, finding such a perfect word in writing may be more important because there is not interactive feedback from the recipient of the message, as there is in speech. Thus, because of these potential differences in the range of frequency in speech production versus writing, one might actually expect a larger frequency effect in the output processes involved in pronunciation compared to the word recognition processes involved in pronunciation. Unfortunately, because of the current paucity of detailed production frequency norms, this argument can only take the form of a functional assessment of the temporal constraints in writing and producing speech.

Priming Pronunciations

Now, consider the impact of prime-target manipulations on pronunciation performance. Recently, Balota et al. (1989) have demonstrated that prime-target associations can influence both onset latencies and production durations in a delayed-pronunciation task. For example, in one of their experiments, they reported that subjects were faster to begin their production of two related words, compared to two unrelated words, even though they had 1400 ms to recognize the stimuli (also see Dallas & Merikle, 1976; Midgley-West, 1979). Moreover, they found that the production durations were shorter for related words than unrelated words. Because 1400 ms should be sufficient to recognize two words, it is unclear how one can unequivocally attribute the priming effect in pronunciation performance to the magic moment. The theoretical implication of this finding is that any extra activation due to the relationship between two words can influence performance throughout the processing system (also see Shields & Balota, 1988).

In sum, the important point for the present discussion is that because variables appear to influence processes after subjects have sufficient time to recognize the stimulus, one cannot unequivocally attribute the influence of a variable in the pronunciation task to processes leading up to the magic moment in word processing.

Other Measures

The emphasis in the present discussion addresses the utility of the pronunciation task and the LDT as windows into the magic moment. The emphasis on these tasks is necessary because they have provided the primary source of data for models of word recognition. However, it should be noted that there are other measures of the magic moment available. For example, some have argued that threshold identification can provide a window to the magic moment (e.g., Broadbent, 1967; Humphreys, Evett, Quinlan, & Besner, 1987; Tulving & Gold, 1963). Although such research has provided some intriguing findings, there is the potential problem that in an untimed paradigm subjects can rely on domains of knowledge in a sophisticated-guessing fashion to identify the degraded stimuli. These domains may not be the same domains that are used in fluent reading. Hence, one must also question the utility of the threshold identification task as a window to the magic moment in word processing (see Catlin, 1969, 1973).

A better window to the magic moment might entail on-line measures (fixation and gaze durations) during reading. Here, the subject is engaged in a more natural task that does not have the problem of directing the processing system to a domain of knowledge that is in some sense peculiar to the task demands. This is an important advantage. However, even in this task, one cannot use the data to support the magic moment hypothesis. It is clear from the work of Rayner and colleagues that meaning and integration processes can occur very early in word processing and can carry over into subsequent fixations (Balota, Pollatsek, & Rayner, 1985; Ehrlich & Rayner, 1983; Frazier & Rayner, 1982; Rayner, Carlson, & Frazier, 1983). Thus, fixation duration on a given word cannot be used as a pure indicant of the magic moment. Pollatsek and Rayner (this volume) and Rayner and Balota (1989) provide a more detailed discussion of the use of fixation times as a measure of word recognition processes.

WHAT'S THE ALTERNATIVE?

The major thrust of the discussion just presented is that superficial descriptions of the major tasks used to provide data concerning the magic moment in word processing can be misleading. In particular, a deeper consideration of the two major tasks, lexical decision and pronunciation, indicates that both tasks involve components that clearly question their utility as windows into the magic moment.

However, what's the alternative? It would appear that at some level there must be a lexical identification process that leads to meaning analysis. How could one analyze the meaning of a stimulus without knowing the identity of the stimulus? Thus, again on the surface level, there appears to be a necessary step of word recognition prior to meaning access.

Although it is clear that some level of visual analysis must precede meaning access, it does not necessarily follow that word recognition in the sense emphasized in the models of word recognition is a logical prerequisite for meaning analysis. It is possible that meaning analysis occurs relatively early in word processing and in fact might contribute to word recognition in the sense emphasized by the models. If this were the case, then one might argue for a more prominent role of meaning in word recognition.

There are two general arguments in favor of a more prominent role for meaning in models of word recognition. The first argument emphasizes the functional role of words in language, and the second is based on empirical evidence that suggests that meaning can play an early role in word processing.

THE FUNCTIONAL ROLE OF WORDS IN LANGUAGE

Obviously, the functional role of words in language is to convey meaning. However, in tasks used to investigate word recognition processes (lexical decision and pronunciation), meaning presumably plays little functional role. This difference in emphasis on meaning between tasks that are used to investigate word recognition and the task of more natural language processing may be quite important. This is especially noteworthy in light of arguments concerning transfer-appropriate processing (Durgunoğlu & Roediger, 1987; Jacoby & Witherspoon, 1982; Kolers & Brison, 1984; Kolers & Paradis, 1980; Kolers & Roediger, 1984; Morris, Bransford, & Franks, 1977). According to the transfer-appropriate processing framework, a stimulus may be coded in many different forms based on an individual's expectations, available skills, and the particular task demands. Specific tasks may differentially emphasize different subsets of these codes. Thus, the representations that play a functional role in speeded lexical decision and pronunciation may not be the same representations that play a functional role in more natural language processing.

The importance of the transfer-appropriate processing approach has been nicely illustrated by Durgunoğlu and Roediger (1987). These authors addressed the evidence concerning the debate over language-independent and language-dependent representational systems in bilinguals. In reviewing the literature, they suggested that one typically finds evidence for language-independent performance in conceptually-driven tasks such as free recall, whereas one finds evidence for language-dependent performance in more data-driven tasks such as lexical decision and fragment completion. In the past, researchers have simply been led to different conclusions across these studies regarding single-versus dual-code representations. Durgunoğlu and Roediger replicated this basic pattern in a single experiment. They found that the language of an earlier presentation of a word (i.e., either English or Spanish) was crucial in determining later fragment completion performance (in English), whereas this had no impact on later recall performance. In addition, they found that conceptual processing of a word (e.g., forming an image or translating a word into a different language) had a substantial impact on free recall performance but had very little impact on fragment-completion performance. Thus, based on the fragment completion results, one would argue for a language-dependent representational model, whereas, based on the free-recall results, one would argue for a language-independent representational model.

In accounting for their data, Durgunoğlu and Roediger made a distinction between tasks that tap conceptually-driven operations and tasks that tap data-driven operations. The distinction between conceptually-driven and data-driven tasks and transfer-appropriate processing is clearly relevant to the present discussion. Very simply, the tasks (i.e., LDT and pronunciation) used to build models of word recognition are more data-driven, whereas the task of comprehending words in language processing is more conceptually driven. As the Durgunoğlu and Roediger results nicely illustrate, a variable can have quite different impacts across such domains of tasks. Thus, if one wishes to develop adequate models of word recognition, then the tasks that are used to build such models should contain a functional role for meaning analysis. This is precisely why eye-tracking records during reading for meaning may eventually provide the best window into word processing.

EMPIRICAL EVIDENCE

In addition to the functional appeal for a more prominent role of meaning in word recognition, there is also empirical evidence that suggests that meaning can influence early perceptual processing. This evidence takes two forms. First, there is evidence which will be referred to as decoupling evidence. The basic form of this evidence is that meaning can influence performance even though the subject cannot, in some sense, recognize the stimulus. The second line of evidence is more direct. In this research, there is evidence that meaning can directly influence early perceptual operations in word processing. It is important to point out here, however, that there may be alternative accounts of aspects of this evidence for the notion that meaning can influence early processing in words.

Decoupling Meaning from Word Recognition

The research discussed in this section suggests that meaning can influence performance even though the subject cannot recognize the stimulus word, at least as indicated by correctly naming the stimulus word aloud. Thus, the strict serial dependency on word recognition, as indicated by accurate naming, before the access of meaning is called into question. As to be described, there are two distinct lines of research that provide evidence for meaning access without explicit recognition of the stimulus word.

Threshold Priming

First, consider the threshold priming literature. Here, one finds that even though subjects cannot make above-chance presence/absence detection decisions about a prime word, there is still evidence of meaning access (Balota, 1983; Fowler, Wolford, Slade, & Tassinary, 1981; Marcel, 1983). That is, subjects are faster to recognize the word *dog* when it follows *cat* than when it follows *pen* even under masking conditions that yield chance presence/absence detection performance on the prime items. One possible account for this pattern of data is that there may be multiple codes that are activated upon word presentation. These codes might involve at least the three basic types of information that subjects have available for a visual stimulus word, that is, its meaning, its sound, and its visual form. The threshold-priming experiments could be viewed as indicating that the visual form code can be disrupted by a pattern mask even though the meaning code is still accessed. The importance of the visual form code is that without such a code the subject cannot consciously report that a visual stimulus was presented. The threshold-priming situation suggests that meaning can be accessed in situations where the subject cannot provide direct evidence of word recognition. Hence, it appears that meaning may be available very early on in word processing.

It should be noted that there is some debate in the literature concerning threshold priming. This debate centers around the issue of whether researchers have obtained an accurate estimate of presence/absence detection thresholds (see Holender, 1986, for a detailed discussion). Even if subjects were not at a detection level threshold in the already cited studies, it is unlikely that subjects were at a level of visual analysis that would yield accurate lexical decision or pronunciation performance. That is, if subjects have difficulty indicating whether something or nothing was presented on a given trial, then it is unlikely that they could make a lexical decision or correctly pronounce the word aloud. If this analysis is correct, then these results suggest that meaning can be accessed before sufficient information is obtained to produce lexical access as measured by lexical decision and pronunciation performance. This obviously runs counter to the suggestion that these tasks are a reflection of a premeaning access component of word recognition. It appears that meaning can be accessed very early and without the full visual record of the stimulus available for conscious report.

Deep Dyslexia

A second line of research suggesting that meaning can be accessed even though subjects do not have sufficient information available for accurate identification is the evidence from aphasic individuals exhibiting the syndrome referred to as *deep dyslexia*. Deep dyslexics are individuals that produce an interesting type of semantic error in output. For example, when presented with the word *dog*, such individuals might produce the word "cat" instead of the appropriate response "dog." Other types of errors are also produced. For example, these individuals exhibit (a) derivational errors (e.g., *mercy* for *merciful*), (b) visual errors (e.g., *puddle* for *puppy*), and (c) considerable difficulty producing nonsense strings.

For the present purposes, we focus on the semantic errors. As a number of researchers have argued (e.g., Marshall & Newcombe, 1980; Shallice & Warrington, 1980), such effects can be accounted for by arguing that there is a breakdown in a nonlexical grapheme-to-phoneme output system. The notion is that there is a direct route to the lexical/semantic system and also routes that correspond to visual-to-grapheme correspondences and grapheme-to-phoneme correspondences. Presumably, the direct route is intact and therefore activates lexical/semantic representations. These representations produce a spread of activation to related areas in the system. Assuming some noise in the system, it is possible that a lexical representation that is semantically related to the letter string is sometimes output instead of the actual letter string. Newcombe and Marshall argue that the extra feedback from the grapheme-to-phoneme correspondence route serves to eliminate such errors in output. However, because this system is deficient for the deep dyslexics, there is no extra stabilization from these routes to minimize such errors. Thus, one finds on some trials the output of a semantically related word, even though that word is not visually related to the target word.

What's the relevance of this finding to the present discussion? First, such semantic output errors again provide a situation where there is a decoupling of meaning from recognition, as indicated by accurate naming. In some sense, the subject has accessed meaning but cannot identify the presented word. Second, the pattern of errors produced by these individuals also reflects syntactic-class distinctions. For example, these individuals are more likely to read concrete nouns correctly, followed by verbs, adjectives, and abstract nouns. Function words produce the greatest number of errors. The importance of these differences is that it appears that at some level the syntactic characteristics (along with other meaning-level differences such as concreteness) influence the probability that the word is correctly output. These patterns of errors are difficult to reconcile with a pre-meaning, pre-syntactic magic moment in word processing.

Direct Influences of Meaning on Perception

Recently, there have appeared a series of experiments that could be viewed as suggesting that the meaning available for a stimulus can influence lower-level perceptual processes. First, consider a recent series of experiments by Whittlesea and Cantwell (1987). For the present purposes, we focus on their third experiment. In this experiment, the materials consisted of 24 pronounceable five-letter nonwords. Half of these nonwords were assigned meaning, whereas the remaining half were presented in a perceptual letter-checking task to equate simple visual processing. The items that were assigned meaning corresponded to lexical gaps. That is, the meanings were such that there was no common word that already involved the proposed meaning, for example, *walen* was defined as "the sound that a dam makes before breaking." After the visual-processing and meaning-assignment tasks, the nonwords were presented in a Reicher (1969) letter-detection paradigm in which the stimuli were presented for 30 ms followed by a pattern mask. After the mask, subjects attempted to report the letters from the display. The results indicated that subjects produced considerably more letters from the nonwords that were assigned a definition compared to the nonwords that were given extra visual processing at encoding. Thus, the meaning of the words appeared to influence letter-level perceptual processes. Moreover, comparisons across experiments indicated that mere exposure to the stimuli was not influencing the "meaning superiority effect."

Of course, there are alternative accounts of this finding. One might simply be that the meaning assignment to the nonwords provided more integration of the letters in encoding and this produced the higher recall. A more tempting account from the present perspective is that meaning-level analyses reinforced the lexical-level representation and this in turn influenced the letter-level representations. That is, the meaning of a stimulus word also influences the perceptibility of the individual letters in addition to its lexical-level representation. As noted later, a simple extension of the McClelland and Rumelhart (1981) framework to include meaning-level representations could easily accommodate this finding.

The effect of meaning on letter recognition is similar to the research by Balota et al. (1989) described earlier. As noted, Balota et al. provided evidence that conceptual-level relationships influenced the speed of accessing the phonemes that are included in the production of a given word. Thus, a higher-level relationship involving the meaning between words appears to influence the access of relatively lower-level codes. In the case of the Whittlesea and Cantwell study, this meaning-level input influenced the speed of accessing the letter-level representations, whereas, in the case of the Balota et al. study, this meaning-level input influenced the speed of accessing the phonological codes used to pronounce the word aloud.

A second study that appears to provide evidence for an impact of meaning on perception has been reported by Forster (1985). Consider the results from his first experiment. Forster presented obsolete words such as *holimonth* in a masked-repetition priming LDT. Forster was using the masked repetition effect as a metric of accessing lexical representations. That is, masked repetition priming presumably reflects facilitation in accessing a lexical representation that is still activated via a recent access. The importance of the mask is that it insures that the priming effects reflect pure repeated access effects, as opposed to episodic influences from their earlier presentation. Forster argued that because the obsolete words used in the experiment were unknown to the subjects, they should not be contained in the subject's lexicon and, therefore, should not exhibit a masked repetition priming effect. This

is precisely what Forster found in Phase One of his first experiment.
There was no masked-repetition priming effect for the obsolete words.
However, after Phase One, subjects were provided information about
the nature of the obsolete words, and their corresponding definitions.
Forster found in Phase Two that the same obsolete items that earlier
produced no evidence for a masked-repetition priming effect now immediately produced a large effect. Moreover, because items were repeated
five times for a given subject, and there was no evidence for a change in
the size of the priming effect, it appeared that the effect was not dependent upon episodic exposure of the obsolete words during the definition
aspect of the experiment. The important point to note here is that the
same strings that did not produce a masked-repetition priming effect
now produced an effect when these items were given meaning. It would,
of course, be interesting to address whether the meaning is actually the
crucial factor here or whether simply indicating to subjects that these
items deserve a "word" response would be sufficient. Unfortunately,
such an experiment has yet to be conducted.

A third set of experiments that should be noted here are experiments
that address the impact of semantic variables on isolated lexical decision performance. For example, James (1975), Kroll and Merves (1986),
and Schwanenflugel, Harnishfeger, and Stowe (1988) have produced evidence indicating that concrete words produce faster lexical decisions
than abstract words. Hence, an apparent semantic dimension, concreteness of the referent of the word, appears to influence a major task that
presumably reflects the magic moment in word processing. In addition,
Chumbley and Balota (1984) found that associative response latency
was a strong predictor of lexical decision performance, and Balota and
Chumbley (1984) found instance dominance (as defined by Battig &
Montague, 1969) was a strong predictor of lexical decision performance
(also see Whaley, 1978). In these latter studies, the influence of lexical
variables were presumably partialled out. Finally, Jastrzembski (1981)
and Millis and Button (1989) found that the number of meanings available for a word is a strong predictor of lexical decision performance
above-and-beyond the impact of word frequency. Thus, these experiments suggest that if one uses lexical decision as a reflection of word
recognition performance, meaning variables clearly play a role in word
recognition.

Some Caveats

Before leaving the empirical support for meaning-level influences on
word recognition, it is important to note some obvious alternative accounts of the present discussion. First, it is possible that the threshold priming effects might simply reflect intralexical-priming effects. As
noted in De Groot (this volume), there is considerable debate concerning
whether priming effects occur within the lexical system and/or within
the semantic system. Second, as noted, the data presented on deep

dyslexia can also be interpreted as indicating a breakdown in the phonological output lexicon. Third, both the Forster (1985) results and the Whittlesea and Cantwell (1987) results could be interpreted as suggesting influences at the lexical level instead of the meaning level. Although one can provide alternative explanations of the available data, the important point to note here is that meaning-level interpretations of these results appear just as viable at the present point in time. Hopefully, this potential interpretation should at least serve as a catalyst for more direct investigations of the impact of meaning-level information on word recognition.

A POSSIBLE FRAMEWORK

The present discussion has emphasized a number of distinct theoretical and empirical positions. First, it was suggested that the lexical decision and pronunciation tasks are insufficient data sources to localize effects of variables leading up to and including the magic moment. Second, it was noted that one major deficiency in the available models and the interpretation of the available data on word recognition is an emphasis on nonmeaning analyses of words. Thus, the important functional utility of words (i.e., to convey meaning) may be underemphasized in the available models. Third, empirical data were presented that suggest that recognition, at some level, may not always precede meaning analysis, and meaning in some tasks can contribute to what appear to be perceptual operations.

Two Possible Accounts of the Early Influence of Meaning

There are two obvious theoretical frameworks that one could use to account for a more direct influence of meaning on word recognition. First, as noted earlier, one might consider a slight modification of the highly interactive system proposed by McClelland and Rumelhart (1981). In their framework, there are featural-level representations, letter-level representations, and word-level representations. Activation spreads bidirectionally across levels with inhibitory pathways within a level. For example, when the word *dog* is presented, the letter *d* in *dog* receives some additional activation from the word-level representation *dog*. (This is how the model accounts for the word-superiority effect.) Thus, the higher-level lexical representations contribute to the lower-level letter representations. This is due to the cascadic nature of the processing system. That is, information from one level can influence higher and lower levels in the system without the completion of processing at any of the individual levels (McClelland, 1979). To incorporate meaning-level analyses on performance, one might simply add a meaning-level representation above the lexical-level representation. In addition, one would need to incorporate both bottom-up and top-down pathways from this level of analysis. Such a framework is presented in Figure 2.1.

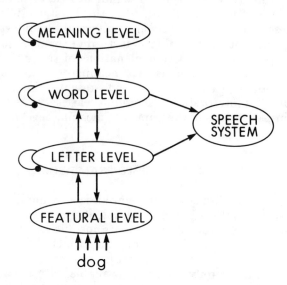

FIGURE 2.1. Potential interactive activation framework for word recognition including meaning-level influences.

An alternative framework that is more in the tradition of the flow-diagram models used to describe lexical performance is displayed in Figure 2.2. This framework is very similar to suggestions made by Allport (1977), Marcel and Patterson (1978), Morton and Patterson (1980), and Newcombe and Marshall (1980). The basic notion is that when a visual stimulus is presented, it is coded in multiple ways. One route of coding is a direct picture-level access route to the lexicon. A second route involves graphemic analyses. A third route involves grapheme-to-phoneme conversions. For most high-frequency words, the direct route to the lexicon has the strongest impact on word recognition. The graphemic and phonological routes also play a role, but their impact is relatively diminished for skilled reading. The impact of meaning here again involves the cascadic influence from the lexicon to the semantic system and back to the lexicon. Moreover, as the lexical representations become activated, they also reinforce the graphemic and phonological systems. Thus, the meaning-level analysis helps to tune and stabilize the perception of consistent elements.

The major difference between the two accounts displayed in Figures 2.1 and 2.2 seems to be in the routes to the lexicon. In the interactive activation framework, displayed in Figure 2.1, the notion is that the lexicon is always accessed via featural and orthographic information. The alternative framework, displayed in Figure 2.2, suggests that there are both direct routes to the lexicon and indirect routes to the lexicon via graphemic and phonological information. Thus, these different routes would appear to have a more distinct representation in the latter framework. Moreover, the direct route in Figure 2.2 is only part of the general system for recognizing objects. Thus, the same mechanisms involved in general pattern recognition are viewed as being involved in word processing, even though they might feed into different representations.

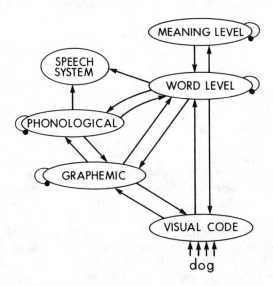

FIGURE 2.2.   Potential flow-diagram framework for word recognition including meaning-level influences.

· Interestingly, there has been some recent evidence for a more direct lexical route. Howard (1987) has reported evidence concerning an acquired dyslexic patient who was at chance at matching a lower-case target letter (e.g., *b*) to an upper-case target in a four-alternative forced-choice procedure (e.g., *K, B, D, L*). Thus, this individual does not appear to have an intact abstract letter code. Interestingly, however, this individual could still read aloud 30 - 40% of the isolated words presented to him. Howard argued that this was possible via the more direct route to the lexical system. Similar arguments have been made based on the phenomena of word-form or spelling dyslexia (Kinsbourne & Warrington, 1962; Warrington & Shallice, 1980) in which subjects can only read by spelling out the words letter by letter. Here, the argument has been that the direct access route to the lexicon is disrupted, but the abstract letter route is intact. Because of the importance of the direct route, these patients read only very slowly and laboriously.

In sum, it should be noted that the theoretical frameworks displayed in Figures 2.1 and 2.2 are not novel. Moreover, the frameworks could be easily modified so that they make isomorphic predictions. It is unclear how one could provide a strong test to distinguish between these two classes of models, although one could distinguish between these two particular instantiations. Currently, one might prefer the framework that is in the vein of that displayed in Figure 2.2 because of the distinction between different access routes. It would seem that the masked-priming effects and the evidence from deep dyslexia suggest that one can block one of the access routes while leaving other access routes intact.

Meaning Representation: An Alternative Approach

A major issue that has not been discussed is what meaning representation might involve. This is a very difficult issue that has produced considerable psychological and philosophical debate. For example, one consistent problem that has occurred in the literature on word meaning is whether it should be attributed to a single prototype representation or whether it should be attributed to a list of semantic features. In both approaches, the meaning of a stimulus word is viewed as representing some core set of information.

An interesting alternative approach to meaning representation follows from suggestions made by Hintzman (1986, also see Medin & Schaffer, 1978; Schwanenflugel & Shoben, 1983). Hintzman has developed an instance based model of prototype development that does a very good job of accounting for some of the core data supporting prototype representations. For example, consider the classic study by Posner and Keele (1968). These authors presented subjects a set of instances that were formed by pseudorandom permutations of a single random dot prototype. The actual prototype that the instances were based upon was not directly presented to the subjects. The results indicated that, after some delay, subjects were more confident in recognizing the prototype that was not directly presented than the instances that were directly presented. Posner and Keele argued that this pattern supports the notion that subjects abstract the prototype from the individual instances and store the abstracted prototype directly in memory. In contrast to this interpretation, Hintzman argued that each of the episodic experiences with the instances produces a unique episodic memory trace that consists of a list of primitive features. The higher recognition memory for the prototype reflects the fact that the test stimulus in some sense partially activates all of the episodic traces. In fact, the partial overlap with many of these traces produces a stronger match (echo) than the stronger overlap with a single instance-based trace. Thus, the culmination of many different, but related, episodic memory traces produces the higher recognition confidence for a stimulus (i.e., the prototype) that was never directly presented.

The relevance of this approach to meaning representation is quite straightforward. Meaning of a given word is not simply represented as a list of isolable semantic features or a prototype but rather should be conceived as a cumulation of individual episodic experiences with that word. Each of the experiences (i.e., the word and its embedded context) contributes to the evolving meaning that we attribute to a given word.

One advantage of this approach is that it very nicely accommodates the large degree of context dependency in word meaning. This dependency follows from this framework because the precise trace that is retrieved by the stimulus will depend on the context in which the word is embedded. Different contexts will yield different combinations of episodic traces that are activated.

Obviously, this brief discussion poses more questions than it provides answers. For example, it is crucial to specify what are the primitive features of word meaning that might contribute to the episodic memory traces. Moreover, it is crucial to specify how context contributes to the retrieval of episodic representations. The contribution of this discussion is simply to consider meaning of words as the combinatorial action of individually encoded episodic traces as opposed to distinct semantic representations. This approach may lead to a more fruitful functional account of word meaning.

SUMMARY

The goal of the present discussion is simply to bring meaning back into word recognition. It has been argued that there is no unequivocal evidence that suggests that one can empirically tap the word-recognition stage without meaning analysis. Moreover, even if one could develop a task that is sensitive to pure meaning-free lexical access, one would then have to be concerned about the relevance of performance in that task for linguistic processing. At this level, it is necessary to remind ourselves that the functional value of words is to convey meaning, not to convey orthography, phonology, or lexicality.

ACKNOWLEDGEMENTS

The author expresses his gratitude to the Netherlands Institute for Advanced Study for their generous support while the present chapter was written. Thanks are also extended to Simon Garrod, Ino Flores d'Arcais, Odmar Neumann, Keith Rayner, and Paula Schwanenflugel for their helpful comments on an earlier version of this chapter.

REFERENCES

Allport, D. A. (1977). On knowing the meaning of words we are unable to report: The effects of visual masking. In S. Dornic (Ed.), *Attention and performance VI* (pp. 505 - 533). Hillsdale, NJ: Lawrence Erlbaum Associates.

Anderson, J. R., & Reder, L. M. (1974). Negative judgments in and about semantic memory. *Journal of Verbal Learning and Verbal Behavior, 13,* 664 - 681.

Balota, D. A. (1983). Automatic semantic activation and episodic memory encoding. *Journal of Verbal Learning and Verbal Behavior, 22,* 88 - 104.

Balota, D. A., Boland, J., & Shields, L. W. (1989). Priming in pronunciation: Beyond pattern recognition and onset latency. *Journal of Memory and Language, 28,* 14 - 36.

Balota, D. A., & Chumbley, J. I. (1984). Are lexical decisions a good measure of lexical access? The role of word frequency in the neglected decision stage. *Journal of Experimental Psychology: Human Perception and Performance, 10,* 340 - 357.

Balota, D. A., & Chumbley, J. I. (1985). The locus of word-frequency effects in the pronunciation task: Lexical access and/or production? *Journal of Memory and Language, 24,* 89 - 106.

Balota, D. A., & Lorch, R. F. (1986). Depth of automatic spreading activation: Mediated priming effects in pronunciation but not in lexical decision. *Journal of Experimental Psychology: Learning, Memory and Cognition, 12,* 336 - 345.

Balota, D. A., Pollatsek, A., & Rayner, K. (1985). The interaction of contextual constraints and parafoveal visual information in reading. *Cognitive Psychology, 17,* 364 - 390.

Balota, D. A., & Shields, L. W. (1988). Localizing word-frequency effects in pronunciation. Paper presented at the Psychonomic Society Meeting, Chicago.

Battig, W. F., & Montague, W. E. (1969). Category norms for verbal items in 56 categories: A replication and extension of the Connecticut category norms. *Journal of Experimental Psychology Monograph, 80,* 1 - 46.

Becker, C. A. (1980). Semantic context effects in visual word recognition. An analysis of semantic strategies. *Memory & Cognition, 8,* 493 - 512.

Besner, D., & McCann, R. S. (1987). Word frequency and pattern distortion in visual word identification and production: An examination of four classes of models. In M. Coltheart (Ed.), *Attention and performance XII: The psychology of reading* (pp. 201 - 219). Hillsdale, NJ: Lawrence Erlbaum Associates.

Broadbent, D. E. (1967). Word-frequency effect and response bias. *Psychological Review, 74,* 1 - 15.

Brown, T. L., Carr, T. H., & Chaderjian, M. (1987). Orthography, familiarity, and meaningfulness reconsidered: Attentional strategies may affect the lexical sensitivity of visual code formation. *Journal of Experimental Psychology: Human Perception and Performance, 13,* 127 - 139.

Catlin, J. (1969). On the word-frequency effect. *Psychological Review, 76,* 504 - 506.

Catlin, J. (1973). In defense of sophisticated-guessing theory. *Psychological Review, 80,* 412 - 416.

Cattell, J. M. (1886). The time taken up by cerebral operations. *Mind, 11,* 230 - 242.

Chumbley, J. I., & Balota, D. A. (1984). A word's meaning affects the decision in lexical decision. *Memory & Cognition, 12,* 590 - 606.

Dallas, M., & Merikle, P. M. (1976). Response processes and semantic-context effects. *Bulletin of the Psychonomic Society, 8,* 441 - 444.

De Groot, A. M. B. (1983). The range of automatic spreading activation in word priming. *Journal of Verbal Learning and Verbal Behavior, 22,* 417 - 436.

De Groot, A. M. B. (1989). Concreteness and word-frequency effects in producing word associations. *Journal of Experimental Psychology: Learning, Memory and Cognition, 15,* 824 - 845.

Duchek, J. M., & Neely, J. H. (1989). A dissociative word-frequency X levels-of-processing interaction in episodic recognition and lexical decision tasks. *Memory & Cognition, 17,* 148 - 162.

Durgunoğlu, A. Y., & Roediger, H. L. III (1987). Test differences in accessing bilingual memory. *Journal of Memory and Language, 26*, 377 - 391.

Ehrlich, K., & Rayner, K. (1983). Pronoun assignment and semantic integration during reading: Eye movements and immediacy of processing. *Journal of Verbal Learning and Verbal Behavior, 22*, 75 - 87.

Forster, K. I. (1979). Levels of processing and the structure of the language processor. In W. E. Cooper & E. C. T. Walker (Eds.), *Sentence processing: Psycholinguistic studies presented to Merrill Garrett* (pp. 27 - 85). Hillsdale, NJ: Lawrence Erlbaum Associates.

Forster, K. I. (1981). Priming and the effects of sentence and lexical contexts on naming time: Evidence for autonomous lexical processing. *Quarterly Journal of Experimental Psychology, 33A*, 465 - 495.

Forster, K. I. (1985). Lexical acquisition and the modular lexicon. *Language and Cognitive Processes, 1*, 87 - 108.

Fowler, C. A., Wolford, G., Slade, R., & Tassinary, L. (1981). Lexical access with and without awareness. *Journal of Experimental Psychology: General, 110*, 341 - 362.

Frazier, L., & Rayner, K. (1982). Making and correcting errors during sentence comprehension: Eye movements in the analysis of structurally ambiguous sentences. *Cognitive Psychology, 14*, 178 - 210.

Günther, H., Gfroerer, S., & Weiss, L. (1984). Inflection, frequency, and the word superiority effect. *Psychological Research, 46*, 261 - 281.

Hintzman, D. L. (1986). "Schema abstraction" in a multiple-trace memory model. *Psychological Review, 93*, 411 - 428.

Holender, D. (1986). Semantic activation without conscious identification in dichotic listening, parafoveal vision, and visual masking: A survey and appraisal. *Behavioral and Brain Sciences, 9*, 1 - 66.

Howard, D. (1987). Reading without letters? In M. Coltheart, G. Sartori, & R. Job (Eds.), *The cognitive neuropsychology of language* (pp. 27 - 58). Hillsdale, NJ: Lawrence Erlbaum Associates.

Humphreys, G. W., Evett, L. J., Quinlan, P. T., & Besner, D. (1987). Orthographic priming: Qualitative differences between priming from identified and unidentified primes. In M. Coltheart (Ed.), *Attention and performance XII: The psychology of reading* (pp. 105 - 125). London: Lawrence Erlbaum Associates.

Jacoby, L. L., & Witherspoon, D. (1982). Remembering without awareness. *Canadian Journal of Psychology, 36*, 300 - 324.

James, C. T. (1975). The role of semantic information in lexical decisions. *Journal of Experimental Psychology: Human Perception and Performance, 1*, 130 - 136.

Jastrzembski, J. E. (1981). Multiple meanings, number of related meanings, frequency of occurrence, and the lexicon. *Cognitive Psychology, 13*, 278 - 305.

Keefe, D. E., & Neely, J. H. (in press). Semantic priming in the pronunciation task: The role of prospective prime-generated expectancies. *Memory & Cognition.*

Kinsbourne, M., & Warrington, E. K. (1962). A disorder of simultaneous form perception. *Brain, 85*, 461 - 486.

Kliegl, R., Olson, R. K., & Davidson, B. J. (1982). Regression analyses as a tool for studying reading processes: Comment on Just and Carpenter's eye fixation theory. *Memory & Cognition, 10*, 287 - 296.

Kolers, P. A., & Brison, S. J. (1984). Commentary: On pictures, words, and their mental representation. *Journal of Verbal Learning and Verbal Behavior, 23*, 105 - 113.

Kolers, P. A., & Paradis, M. (1980). Psychological and linguistic studies of bilingualism. *Canadian Journal of Psychology, 34*, 287 - 303.

Kolers, P. A., & Roediger, H. L. (1984). Procedures of mind. *Journal of Verbal Learning and Verbal Behavior, 23*, 425 - 449.

Kroll, J. F., & Merves, J. S. (1986). Lexical access for concrete and abstract words. *Journal of Experimental Psychology: Learning, Memory, and Cognition, 12*, 92 - 107.

Lorch, R. F., Balota, D. A., & Stamm, E. G. (1986). Locus of inhibition effects in the priming of lexical decision: Pre- or post-lexical access? *Memory & Cognition, 14*, 95 - 103.

Lupker, S. J. (1984). Semantic priming without association: A second look. *Journal of Verbal Learning and Verbal Behavior, 23*, 709 - 733.

Manelis, L. (1977). Frequency and meaningfulness in tachistoscopic word recognition. *American Journal of Psychology, 90*, 269 - 280.

Marcel, A. J. (1983). Conscious and unconscious perception: Experiments on visual masking and word recognition. *Cognitive Psychology, 15*, 197 - 237.

Marcel, A. J., & Patterson, K. E. (1978). Word recognition and production: Reciprocity in clinical and normal studies. In J. Requin (Ed.), *Attention and performance VII* (pp. 209 - 226). Hillsdale, NJ: Lawrence Erlbaum Associates.

Marshall, J. C., & Newcombe, F. (1980). The conceptual status of deep dyslexia: An historical perspective. In M. Coltheart, K. Patterson, & J. C. Marshall (Eds.), *Deep dyslexia* (pp. 1 - 21). London: Routledge & Kegan Paul.

McClelland, J. L. (1979). On the time relations of mental processes: An examination of systems of processes in cascade. *Psychological Review, 86*, 287 - 330.

McClelland, J. L., & Rumelhart, D. E. (1981). An interactive activation model of context effects in letter perception: Part 1. An account of basic findings. *Psychological Review, 88*, 375 - 407.

McNamara, T. P., & Altarriba, J. A. (1988). Depth of spreading activation revisited: Semantic mediated priming occurs in lexical decisions. *Journal of Memory and Language, 27*, 545 - 559.

Medin, D. L., & Schaffer, M. M. (1978). Context theory of classification learning. *Psychological Review, 85*, 207 - 238.

Meyer, D., & Schvaneveldt, R. (1971). Facilitation in recognizing pairs of words: Evidence of a dependence between retrieval operations. *Journal of Experimental Psychology, 90*, 227 - 234.

Midgley-West, L. (1979). *Phonological encoding and subject strategies in skilled reading.* Unpublished doctoral thesis, University of London, Birkbeck College.

Millis, M. L., & Button, S. B. (1989). The effect of polysemy on lexical decision time: Now you see it, now you don't. *Memory & Cognition, 17*, 141 - 147.

Millward, R. B., Rice, G., & Corbett, A. (1975). Category production measures and verification times. In A. Kennedy & A. Wilkes (Eds.), *Studies in long-term memory* (pp. 219 - 252). New York: Wiley.

Morris, C. D., Bransford, J. D., & Franks, J. J. (1977). Levels of processing versus transfer appropriate processing. *Journal of Verbal Learning and Verbal Behavior, 16*, 519 - 533.

Morton, J. (1969). The interaction of information in word recognition. *Psychological Review, 76*, 165 - 178.

Morton, J., & Patterson, K. (1980). A new attempt at an interpretation, or, an attempt at a new interpretation. In M. Coltheart, K. Patterson, & J. C. Marshall (Eds.), *Deep dyslexia* (pp. 91 - 118). London: Routledge & Kegan Paul.

Neely, J. H. (1977). Semantic priming and retrieval from lexical memory: Roles of inhibitionless spreading activation and limited capacity attention. *Journal of Experimental Psychology: General, 106*, 226 - 254.

Neely, J. H., & Keefe, D. E. (1989). Semantic context effects on visual word processing: A hybrid prospective/retrospective processing theory. In G. H. Bower (Ed.), *The psychology of learning and motivation: Advances in research and theory* (Vol. 24, pp. 207 - 248). New York: Academic Press.

Neely, J. H., Keefe, D. E., & Ross, K. L. (1989). Semantic priming in the lexical decision task: Roles of prospective prime-generated expectancies and retrospective semantic matching. *Journal of Experimental Psychology: Learning, Memory, and Cognition, 15*, 1003 - 1019.

Newcombe, F., & Marshall, J. C. (1980). Transcoding and lexical stabilization in deep dyslexia. In M. Coltheart, K. Patterson, & J. C. Marshall (Eds.), *Deep dyslexia* (pp. 176 - 188). London: Routledge & Kegan Paul.

Norris, D. (1986). Word recognition: Context effects without priming. *Cognition, 22*, 93 - 136.

Posner, M. I., & Keele, S. W. (1968). On the genesis of abstract ideas. *Journal of Experimental Psychology, 77*, 353 - 363.

Ratcliff, R., & McKoon, G. (1988). A retrieval theory of priming in memory. *Psychological Review, 95*, 385 - 408.

Rayner, K., & Balota, D. A. (1989). Parafoveal preview effects and lexical access during eye fixations in reading. In: W. Marslen-Wilson (Ed.), *Lexical representation and process* (pp. 261 - 290). Cambridge, MA: MIT Press.

Rayner, K., Carlson, M., & Frazier, L. (1983). The interaction of syntax and semantics during sentence processing: Eye movements in the analysis of semantically biased sentences. *Journal of Verbal Learning and Verbal Behavior, 22*, 358 - 374.

Reicher, G. M. (1969). Perceptual recognition as a function of meaningfulness of stimulus material. *Journal of Experimental Psychology, 81*, 275 - 310.

Schwanenflugel, P. J., Harnishfeger, K. K., & Stowe, R. W. (1988). Context availability and lexical decisions for abstract and concrete words. *Journal of Memory and Language, 27*, 499 - 520.

Schwanenflugel, P. J., & Shoben, E. J. (1983). Differential context effects in the comprehension of abstract and concrete verbal materials. *Journal of Experimental Psychology: Learning, Memory, and Cognition, 9*, 82 - 102.

Seidenberg, M. S., Waters, G. S., Sanders, M., & Langer, P. (1984). Pre- and post-lexical loci of contextual effects on word recognition. *Memory & Cognition, 12*, 315 - 328.

Shallice, T., & Warrington, E. K. (1980). Single and multiple component central dyslexic syndromes. In M. Coltheart, K. Patterson, & J. C. Marshall (Eds.), *Deep dyslexia* (pp. 119 - 145). London: Routledge & Kegan Paul.

Shields, L. W., & Balota, D. A. (1988). The influence of associative priming in sentence production. Paper presented at the Midwestern Psychological Association, Chicago.

Tulving, E., & Gold, C. (1963). Stimulus information and contextual information as determinants of tachistoscopic recognition of words. *Journal of Experimental Psychology, 66*, 319 - 327.

Warrington, E. K., & Shallice, T. (1980). Word-form dyslexia. *Brain, 103*, 99 - 112.

West, R. F., & Stanovich, K. E. (1982). Source of inhibition in experiments on the effect of sentence context on word recognition. *Journal of Experimental Psychology: Learning, Memory, and Cognition, 8*, 385 - 399.

Whaley, C. P. (1978). Word-nonword classification time. *Journal of Verbal Learning and Verbal Behavior, 17*, 143 - 154.

Whittlesea, B. W. A., & Cantwell, A. L. (1987). Enduring influence of the purpose of experiences: Encoding - retrieval interactions in word and pseudoword perception. *Memory & Cognition, 15*, 465 - 472.

3 LEXICAL ACCESS: ANOTHER THEORETICAL SOUPSTONE?[1]

Mark S. Seidenberg
McGill University

INTRODUCTION

Over the past 20 years, research on the role of lexical processing in language comprehension has focused on three central issues:
- How is knowledge of words represented in memory?
- How is this information accessed in the course of comprehension?
- How is the accessed information used in developing an understanding of a text or discourse? [1]

As this summary suggests, the concept of lexical access has played a central role in thinking about these issues. Although the term lexical access is ubiquitous, it is very rarely explicitly defined, and its meaning seems to vary as a function of the theoretical context in which it occurs. The general idea, however, is something like this. Identifying the words in a text or discourse is an important part of the comprehension process. A person who knows a language has acquired a vocabulary of many thousands of words; several types of knowledge are associated with each word form (e.g., its spelling, pronunciation(s), meaning(s), syntactic and thematic functions, etc.). Thus, the processing of words in the course of language comprehension involves accessing some of this stored information. In many cases, lexical access is used as a synonym for accessing the meaning of a word. However, the term affords other usages, insofar as the orthographic and phonological entries for words are also lexical and said to be accessed. For example, Balota and Chumbley

---

[1] The first theoretical soupstone, of course, was "resources" (Navon, 1984).

(1985) distinguish lexical access from access of meaning. In their usage, lexical access refers to accessing an entry in memory corresponding to the written or spoken form of a word; Monsell, Doyle and Haggard (1989) term this *lexical identification*. Additional processing is then required to use this code to access other information, such as a word's meaning or syntactic category.

The lexical access way of thinking has set the agenda for research on lexical processing over the past two decades. Several theories have been proposed within this general framework (e.g., Coltheart, 1978; Forster, 1976; Morton, 1969). Although the theories differ in detail, they share the basic assumption that the units of representation in the mental lexicon correspond to the perceptual units in question, namely words. In Morton's (1969) model, for example, each word is represented by an entry termed a *logogen*. Forster's (1976) model consists of a master file, containing entries for all the words in a person's vocabulary, and slave files, containing entries for their spellings, pronunciations, and meanings. Hence, knowledge of a word is represented in terms of entries that correspond to its different codes. Similarly, there is a class of models (see, e.g., Allport & Funnell, 1981; Patterson & Shewell, 1987) in which knowledge of words is represented in terms of a set of orthographic, phonological, and semantic lexicons. The number of separate lexicons has proliferated, with recent models distinguishing between input lexicons used in perception and output lexicons used in production. For example, there are separate representations of the orthographic codes for words used in reading and spelling (Miceli, Silveri & Caramazza, 1985; Monsell, 1987). Finally, the models proposed by Glushko (1979) and McClelland and Rumelhart (1981) also assumed that each word has a corresponding entry in memory.

In sum, models of lexical knowledge have uniformly held to what might be termed a principle of *perceptual-representational isomorphism*: the units of representation in the mind correspond to the basic perceptual units in speech and reading. Given this assumption, it is easy to see why the metaphor of accessing a lexical entry has played such an important role in theorizing.

The lexical access framework has generated a large amount of research and a deeper understanding of a broad range of phenomena. My own view is that word recognition research, much of it motivated by the lexical access framework, is among the most sophisticated in cognitive psychology, that it has progressed to the point where very refined issues can be addressed, and that these issues bear on basic questions about thinking, learning, and perception. At the same time, I think it might be time to take a hard look at the metaphor of accessing a lexical entry. In this chapter, I explore an alternative view that does not entail a traditional notion of lexical access. This view has recently emerged from the connectionist or parallel distributed processing approach to understanding cognition. The core assumptions of the traditional approach – that lexical knowledge consists of entries in memory that are accessed in the course of processing – are not retained by models that employ what are termed *distributed representations.* The goal of the present chapter is to consider how several basic questions, which have been construed as issues concerning lexical access, can be framed within such a theory. The issues to be considered are (a) does word naming require lexical access? (b) is lexical access direct or phonologically mediated? (c) do lexical decisions require lexical access? and (d) what is the role of lexical access in semantic processing? Very little consensus has emerged concerning these issues despite a large amount of research. This lack of resolution may be due in part to limitations of the lexical access metaphor.

PARALLEL DISTRIBUTED PROCESSING MODELS OF THE LEXICON

Parallel distributed processing models are a subset of the connectionist models that are currently the focus of considerable attention in cognitive science and in neuroscience. The properties of these models have been described elsewhere (e.g., Rumelhart & McClelland, 1986) and will not be exhaustively reviewed here. The basic concept is that behavior is seen as the result of interactions among simple, neuronlike processing elements. Knowledge in a given domain (say, the lexicon) is encoded by the weights on connections between units. Learning involves setting the weights on the basis of experience. Biological constraints on learning are realized in terms of assumptions about the architecture of the network. Perhaps the distinguishing characteristic of PDP models, as opposed to others within the general connectionist framework, is the use of distributed, rather than local, representations (see Hinton, McClelland, & Rumelhart, 1986, for discussion). In brief, models that employ distributed representations do not entail the principle of perceptual-representational isomorphism mentioned earlier. A perceptual entity (e.g., a word or object) is represented as a pattern of activation over a set of units. The same units are reused to encode different entities. The units themselves are thought to represent components or features of perceptual wholes; this has been termed the *subsymbolic* level of representation (Smolensky, 1988).

As an example, consider the system used to encode spelling patterns in the Seidenberg and McClelland (1989) model of word recognition. The representation of each spelling pattern (word or nonword) in this system corresponds to a pattern of activation across 400 orthographic units. That is, each input string corresponds to a unique pattern of *on*s and *off*s across a vector of 400 units. This single set of units is used to encode every string; all that differs is which units happen to be on or off. The scheme that is used to determine the on/off patterns ensures that words with similar spellings will produce similar, overlapping patterns of activation; words with different spellings will activate different patterns (see Seidenberg & McClelland, 1989, for details).

The relevance of distributed representations to theories of lexical processing should be obvious: Here is an alternative to the idea that the mental lexicon consists of entries corresponding to the codes of words. Because there are no such entries, they cannot be accessed as part of the recognition process. It is for this reason that the model cannot be said to incorporate a traditional notion of lexical access. Rather, the codes for a word (spelling, pronunciation, meaning, perhaps others) must be *computed* each time the word is perceived, producing different patterns of activation over sets of units used to represent these types of information. These patterns are jointly determined by (a) the stimulus input (i.e., the pattern that is initially presented to the network) and (b) the structure of the network, particularly the weights on connections between units in the network, which are determined on the basis of experience (typically, in simulation models, a learning algorithm that modifies the weights on the basis of feedback). Similarly, issues as to how the entries in the lexicon are organized (e.g., by frequency or similarity) do not arise; the organization of the lexicon is also entailed by the weights on connections between units.

Several PDP models of the lexicon have been developed in recent years (e.g., Kawamoto, 1988; Golden, 1985; Lacouture, 1989; Sejnowski & Rosenberg, 1986). Perhaps the most fully realized model is one by Seidenberg and McClelland (1989). I will use this model as a framework for considering how lexical knowledge and processing could be captured within a PDP system. The goal is not to celebrate the merits of this particular simulation program, which is limited in scope and inadequate in detail. Rather, it is to use this framework to rethink a number of traditional issues thought to involve lexical access, with an eye toward trying to reconcile some seemingly opposing theoretical viewpoints.

The Seidenberg and McClelland Model

Seidenberg and McClelland (1989) presented a general theory of lexical representation and process, part of which has been implemented as a simulation model. The lexicon is assumed to have a structure roughly like the one in Figure 3.1. Each large ellipse represents a set of simple processing units; there are separate pools for orthography, phonology, and semantics. These units correspond to representational primitives of each type. For example, the semantic units might represent semantic microfeatures that recur in different words (see Hinton et al., 1986; Kawamoto, 1988). Each of the codes of a word is assumed to correspond to a pattern of activation over the appropriate units and each unit participates in many words. Hence, the representations of lexical codes are distributed. Each small ellipse represents a set of interlevel hidden units. Processing involves the spread of activation between units. Accessing the meaning of a word from print, for example, corresponds to encoding the stimulus as an orthographic pattern and computing a pattern of activation over the semantic nodes. Similarly, accessing phonology involves a computation from orthographic input to phonological output.

The characteristics of these computations are a function of the weights on connections between units, which are determined by experience.

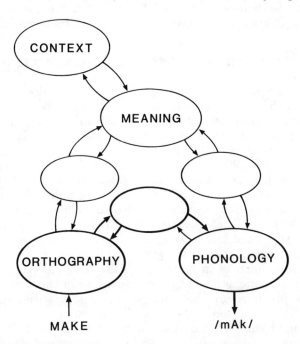

FIGURE 3.1. Structure of a general model of lexical processing.

The implemented model is more limited. It takes letter strings as input and produces two types of output: a phonological code and a recreation of the input orthographic code. Seidenberg and McClelland then specify how these codes are used in performing tasks such as lexical decision and naming, and use quantitative measures of the model's performance to simulate various behavioral phenomena. The model was trained on a corpus of about 2,900 monosyllabic words. During the training phase, the model was given feedback about the correct orthographic and phonological codes for words. The weights on connections were adjusted using the backpropagation learning algorithm (Rumelhart, Hinton & Williams, 1986). The algorithm corrects the weights in a manner that reduces the discrepancies between the computed codes and the correct target codes. As Seidenberg and McClelland show, the model simulates a broad range of findings concerning human performance on simple lexical processing tasks. The generalization that accounts for the model's performance, and appears to apply to humans as well, concerns facts about the distribution of spelling patterns in the lexicon and about the correspondences between spelling and pronunciation that are picked up by the learning algorithm and encoded by the weights on connections.

It can be seen that the traditional notion of lexical access does not relate well to the types of knowledge representations and processes employed in the Seidenberg and McClelland model. We now consider how several basic issues can be construed within this framework.

DOES WORD NAMING REQUIRE LEXICAL ACCESS?

The first issue is whether naming a word aloud requires lexical access. Written English is an alphabetic system; the orthographic representations of words systematically encode information about their pronunciations. It is standardly assumed that readers' knowledge of spelling-sound correspondences is encoded by a set of rules (see Hanna, Hanna, Hodges, & Rudorf, 1966; Venezky, 1970; and Wijk, 1966, for attempts at listing them). For example, there might be a rule governing the correspondence -ust → /ust/. That the orthography encodes this correspondence is suggested by the fact that all monosyllabic words that end in -ust rhyme. That readers have formulated a rule stating this regularity is suggested by the fact that they can easily pronounce unfamiliar stimuli such as nust. It is equally clear, however, that the spelling - sound correspondences in many words are irregular (e.g., have, give, said, were, was, done, etc.). The pronunciations of these words will not be correctly predicted by the rules governing regularities elsewhere in the corpus. The intuition underlying all previous proposals concerning spelling - sound knowledge is that the pronunciations of these words – call them exceptions – must be listed in a phonological store. Whereas the pronunciation of regular words and nonwords might be accomplished using nonlexical spelling - sound correspondence rules, exception words can only be pronounced by accessing their entries in lexical memory. Hence, the pronunciation of at least some words requires lexical access or lexical identification; the letter string have cannot be pronounced without determining that it is an instance of the word have, which, in this framework, corresponds to accessing one of its entries in memory.

The assumptions laid out in the previous paragraph are the central tenets of so-called dual-route models of naming (Coltheart, 1978; Patterson, Marshall & Coltheart, 1985). What I have termed the central dogma of dual-route models (Seidenberg, 1988) is that at least two separate naming mechanisms are needed in order to generate the pronunciations of letter strings in English, because no single mechanism could accommodate regular words, regular nonwords, and exceptions. The lexical naming process relevant to exception words seems to strongly implicate a notion of access to stored lexical entries or lexical access. This notion follows as a consequence of the assumption that knowledge of spelling - sound regularities is represented in the form of rules. By definition, the rules will fail in the case of irregular words; hence a second mechanism involving listed pronunciations is necessary. It should be noted that this rules-and-exceptions approach has been applied to other types of linguistic knowledge. For example, morphological theories typically entail rules governing word formation that generate regular cases; words for which the rules make incorrect predictions are thought to be listed in the lexicon (see Aronoff, 1976). The theories of verb morphology very strongly defended by Pinker and Prince (1988) in their critique of connectionism also have this character. Similarly, theories of the rules governing stress assignment (e.g., Liberman & Prince, 1977) also employ the strategy of listing irregular cases. In each of these areas there has been considerable debate as to the correct formulation of the rules, producing uncertainties as to exactly which exceptions must be listed. The same issues have arisen in connection with attempts to define the rules governing spelling - sound correspondences. Is *done* an irregular word which must be listed, or is its pronunciation determined by a minor rule that also applies to *none*?

Things work somewhat differently in the Seidenberg and McClelland (1989) model. There is a single naming mechanism that takes orthographic strings as input and computes phonological codes as output. The computed phonological codes are then translated into articulatory-motor commands used in overt naming. The simulation model performs the first of these computations; Lacouture (1989) presents an extension of the model that is relevant to producing articulatory output. Seidenberg and McClelland show that their mechanism is able to generate plausible phonological codes for both regular and irregular words and nonwords. Moreover, the model makes quantitative predictions about the relative ease of pronouncing different types of letter strings, which, in general, provide a good fit to a broad range of behavioral data. Thus, the weights on connections between units encode both the fact that *have* is pronounced /hav/ and the fact that *gave* is pronounced /gAv/; when presented with the nonword *mave* it produces the pattern /mAv/. Exactly the same knowledge representations and processing mechanisms are employed in all of these cases.

Why the model performs this way is explained in detail in Seidenberg and McClelland (1989). Knowledge of spelling - sound correspondences is encoded by the weights on connections between units implementing distributed representations. In the simulation model, the values of the weights reflect the aggregate effects of training on the corpus of words. The effects of each learning experience are superimposed on the weights. In a sense, then, the pronunciation of any given word is affected by the model's (or reader's) knowledge of *all* words. In sum, the model shows that one mechanism can support the pronunciation of both regular and irregular words, and nonwords; it employs distributed representations rather than lexical entries; and the pronunciations of words are computed rather than accessed. The key idea is that the lexical pronunciation mechanism in dual-route models can be abandoned because the correspondences between spelling and pronunciation are encoded not by rules but by weights on connections between units.

To this point I have argued that a PDP network can encode knowledge of spelling - sound correspondences previously thought to require pronunciation rules and lists of exceptions. However, this type of knowledge representation is not merely *sufficient*; Seidenberg and McClelland argue that something like it is *necessary* in order to capture empirical facts about human performance. Dual-route models distinguish between rule-governed words such as *must* and irregular, listed words such as *have*. Thus, regularity of pronunciation is treated as a dichotomous variable. In Seidenberg and McClelland's model, in contrast, regularity is a matter of degree (see also Shallice, Warrington, & McCarthy, 1983). The weights are determined by the aggregate effects of training on all words; the degree to which a word is regular or irregular depends on properties of the training corpus. Thus, the model predicts the existence of intermediate degrees of consistency. Glushko (1979), for example, examined a class of words he termed regular inconsistent. These are regular words, such as *gave*, that have irregular neighbors, such as *have*. Other examples are *dive* (*give*) and *paid* (*said*). According to the rules-and-exceptions framework, words such as *gave* should act like entirely regular words because their pronunciations are correctly specified by the rules. In our model, however, the pronunciation of *gave* could be affected by experience in reading *have* because of the way learning affects the weights. Such intermediate cases of inconsistency do exist (although they are somewhat different than Glushko envisioned; Seidenberg, McRae, & Jared, 1988), and the model provides a proper account of them. There is no natural account of these intermediate degrees of inconsistency within a rules-and-exceptions framework because the distinction between rule-governed words and exceptions is simply not rich enough.

These intermediate cases are extremely important. If attention is restricted to the regular and irregular cases, it is difficult to distinguish between dual-process models and the connectionist alternative. Within a given domain, it is always possible to formulate a set of rules governing a subset of cases if there is a second mechanism to deal with cases where the rules fail. In the case of spelling-sound correspondences, our model shows that a single mechanism – employing a different type of knowledge representation – can handle both regular and irregular cases. It is a further consequence of this approach that intermediate degrees of regularity should exist, and careful empirical studies suggest that they do.[2]

---

[2] One could ask whether it would not be possible to formulate a set of pronunciation rules that produce the entire range of consistency effects. What I have observed is that consistency effects are not congruent with everyday assumptions about what rules are and how they operate. However, in the absence of any constraints on what is meant by rule of pronunciation or on the processes by which rules are applied, it might be possible to develop a rule-based system that exhibits the appropriate characteristics. This conclusion should not be surprising; it is often possible to develop notational variants of theories. Note, however, that this would involve investing the rule-based system with properties identified on the basis of a connectionist learning model. This represents the inverse of a situation foreseen by Pinker and Prince (1988). They note that it is trivial to develop connectionist models that implement rule-based systems; that is, to assign to the connectionist model properties known to be necessary on the

Frequency, Lexical Access, and Naming

The conclusion that word naming does not involve a distinct lexical access stage can be taken seriously only if it squares with all naming phenomena, not merely those associated with knowledge of spelling-sound correspondences. Although I cannot consider all of the relevant phenomena here, it is worth considering briefly some other important evidence thought to support the lexical access idea. In particular, a good deal of attention has recently focused on questions concerning frequency effects. Word frequency, as estimated by norms such as Kučera and Francis (1967) or subjective ratings of familiarity (e.g., Gernsbacher, 1984), affects performance on a wide variety of tasks, including naming (e.g., Forster & Chambers, 1973), lexical decision (e.g., Frederiksen & Kroll, 1976), and semantic and syntactic categorization (e.g., Monsell, 1985) and influences fixation durations as well (Rayner & Duffy, 1986). Because frequency has pervasive effects on performance, accounting for this factor has played an important role in the development of models of word recognition and naming.

The standard view is that frequency affects processes that result in lexical access (see Henderson, 1982, for review). For example, frequency might influence the rate at which information accrues at a logogen (Morton, 1969), or it could affect the order in which entries in an orthographic or phonological lexicon are searched (Forster, 1976). According to this general approach, once lexical access is accomplished, the information that becomes available can be used in performing different tasks, such as overt naming or lexical decision. Several researchers have recently observed that frequency also has an impact on these postlexical or postaccess processes. For example, the information that becomes available as a result of lexical access can be used to make a word/nonword decision. Balota and Chumbley (1984) and Gordon (1983) have shown how frequency information enters into the decision process. Thus, frequency effects in simple tasks such as lexical decision are potentially ambiguous as to their source; they could derive from processes leading to lexical access, or from postaccess processing.

A number of recent studies have attempted to identify the locus or loci of frequency effects in word naming. The naming process is often viewed as involving the access of information about a word stored in lexical memory, using this information to generate an articulatory-motor program, and executing this program. Frequency could influence all of

---

[2] (cont.) basis of studies of higher-level, symbolic systems. Their point is that the important generalizations about various types of behavior (e.g., morphology) are captured at the level of rules and symbols. Connectionist models are interesting only insofar as they provide a plausible neurological realization of the rules. In the case I envision, we assign to a rule-based system the properties independently known to be relevant on the basis of a connectionist model. The important generalizations derive from understanding how this model works, particularly how learning is achieved. With this understanding in hand, one could try to develop a rule-based notational variant.

these stages. It might influence lexical access for reasons already mentioned. Frequency could also influence processes involved in generating an articulatory-motor response. It may be easier to generate the articulatory codes for common words because they tend to be shorter, because they tend to contain phonemes that are easier to pronounce, or because they are simply more practiced (Jared & Seidenberg, in press; Landauer & Streeter, 1973). These factors could also influence the latency to initiate an articulatory-motor response; for example, the articulatory-motor programs for higher frequency words may be shorter or less complex than those for lower frequency words, and the time to initiate a motoric response is related to its complexity (Sternberg, Monsell, Knoll, & Wright, 1978). As in the lexical decision task, the frequency effects that are obtained in naming could derive from several sources, only one of which is lexical access.

One strategy used in attempts to isolate the locus of frequency effects in naming is to compare performance on immediate and delayed naming tasks (Balota & Chumbley, 1985; Forster & Chambers, 1973; Monsell et al., 1989). In the immediate naming task, the subject names a word aloud as soon as it is presented. The dependent measures are the time required to initiate the vocal response, measured from the onset of the stimulus, and the number of mispronunciation errors. In delayed naming, the subject does not begin to initiate pronunciation until a signal to respond occurring several hundred milliseconds after stimulus presentation. The logic of the task is as follows. It is assumed that lexical access is completed within 100 to 300 ms of stimulus presentation, an estimate derived from studies of fixation durations during reading (Rayner, 1978) and performance on other tasks (Gough & Cosky, 1977). If the subject is not signaled to respond until after a much longer delay, lexical access should be completed; therefore, any residual effects of a variable such as frequency must be due to postaccess processes involved in producing the articulatory-motor response.

In the Forster and Chambers (1973) experiment, for example, subjects named higher frequency words 71 ms more rapidly than lower frequency words in immediate naming (i.e., at a zero ms delay). When subjects were cued to begin naming the words after a delay of two seconds, the frequency effect was eliminated entirely. Thus, Forster and Chambers concluded that the frequency effect was due to differences in lexical access time, not processes involved in producing the articulatory-motor response.

Balota and Chumbley (1985) reported somewhat different results in a careful series of studies employing 72 high frequency and 72 low frequency words. The experiments used multiple delay intervals (e.g., zero, 150, 400, 650, 900, 1150, and 1400 ms). Although the frequency effect decreased in size over delay intervals, significant effects still obtained at long delays. In one study, for example, the frequency effect dropped from 58 ms in immediate naming to 19 ms at a 1400 ms delay. The significant residual effects at delays well over the estimated latency of lexical access were taken as evidence that word frequency influences postaccess production processes.

Balota and Chumbley concluded that "a major portion of the word-frequency effect in the pronunciation task cannot be unequivocally attributed to success, but rather, appears more likely to be due to processes occurring after lexical access" (p. 104). McCann and Besner (1987) present a stronger version of this hypothesis. They retain the notion that word recognition involves lexical access but suggest that this process is not frequency sensitive. In their view, all frequency effects in naming are due to postlexical processes involved in assembling the articulatory-motor response.

How are these results to be reconciled with a model, such as Seidenberg and McClelland's, which does not involve a distinct lexical access stage? When delay intervals range from 150 to 1400 ms (as in Balota and Chumbley's, 1985, Experiment 2, for example), the signal to respond occurs at different points in the process of assembling a pronunciation. In immediate naming, latencies typically average 500 - 600 ms; in the Balota and Chumbley study, they have averaged approximately 500 ms for higher frequency words and 550 ms for lower frequency words. These latencies provide an estimate of the amount of time needed to compute the pronunciations of familiar words and initiate overt responses. A short delay interval such as 400 ms requires subjects to respond before they are completely prepared on many trials, because the signal to respond occurs before the subject has completed pronunciation assembly. This will occur more often for lower frequency words because it takes longer to assemble their pronunciations. With longer delay intervals, more of the process of assembling a pronunciation will have been completed for more items. With sufficient time to complete the assembly process, the computation of the phonological and articulatory codes will have been completed for all words, and naming latencies will only reflect differences between words in terms of the amount of time needed to initiate the overt articulatory-motor response. If high and low frequency stimuli are equated in terms of phonemic inventory (e.g., number and distribution of phonemes), no residual frequency effects are predicted.

In sum, the delayed naming paradigm has been used as a way to partition frequency effects into lexical access and postaccess components. Balota and Chumbley's main point is that whereas researchers had often assumed that frequency primarily influences lexical access, there appears to be effects associated with assembling and executing the articulatory-motor response. Their paper is not concerned with validating the notion of lexical access as applied to naming; it emphasizes the role of frequency in production. The Seidenberg and McClelland (1989) model merely goes one step further: insofar as there is no lexical access stage in their model, *all* effects of frequency on naming are due to processes involved in going from print to sound. The effects of the delay manipulation depend on when the signal to respond occurs relative to the finishing times for this process, which differ for high and low frequency words.

McRae, Jared, and Seidenberg (in press) report four experiments bearing on these issues. They replicated the Balota and Chumbley delayed naming studies with two changes in methodology. First, they utilized high and low frequency stimuli that are closely equated in terms of articulatory characteristics. The stimuli were high and low frequency homophones (e.g., *main, mane*), high and low frequency rhymes (e.g., *must, dust*), and word/pseudohomophone pairs such as *tame, taim*. The stimuli are similar or identical in terms of articulatory codes; hence they provide a strong test of the role of frequency per se in naming. Second, the delay intervals were calibrated on a subject-by-subject basis. College student subjects vary in their naming abilities. Mean naming latencies for common words range from about 350 ms for the fastest subjects to 750 ms for the slowest. McRae et al. obtained baseline naming latencies for each subject and used delay intervals that were 200, 400, or 600 ms over baseline. The studies yielded the following results. First, there were significant frequency effects in immediate naming (i.e., naming with a zero ms delay). Second, there were smaller, less robust frequency effects at intermediate delay intervals (e.g., 200 ms); third, the frequency effects were eliminated at the longest delay intervals. McRae et al. provide evidence from an analysis of the reaction time distributions that the small frequency effects obtained in the delay conditions were related to the amount of time subjects needed to complete the generation of a pronunciation. When subjects had sufficient time to prepare their responses, no frequency effect obtained. On trials when the response signal appeared before they were fully prepared, frequency affected response latencies.

To summarize, McRae et al.'s data replicate many aspects of the Balota and Chumbley findings; however, they also suggest that frequency effects in delayed naming can be explained in terms of the timing of the response signal relative to the finishing times for the process of assembling a pronunciation. Computing a phonological code and converting it into a set of articulatory-motor commands are processes that occur in real time. The signal to respond occurs at different points in this process, depending on the delay interval, the speed of the subject, and the difficulty of the item. If the signal occurs after the articulatory code has been assembled, no frequency effect results. The effects are smaller at intermediate delay intervals because they reflect a mix between items for which the assembly process has finished, and ones for which it has not. This account is consistent with data from studies such as Balota and Chumbley (1985) and Monsell et al. (1989) and with a model in which naming does not involve a discrete lexical access stage.

I do not have space here to consider all of the issues concerning the naming process that are raised by the model illustrated in Figure 3.1, but one other should be mentioned. The model implies that there is a second, indirect way to compute the pronunciations of words: by means of a computation first from orthography to semantics, and then from semantics to phonology. This indirect, semantic route has played an important role in discussions of phonological dyslexia, a type of reading impairment observed following brain injury (Patterson et al., 1985). It is clear that this route plays a role in normal performance. Consider, for example, how the reader identifies the contextually appropriate pronunciation of a homograph such as *wind*. Presumably, the correct pronunciation is determined in part by identifying the relevant meaning; this effect could be realized by feedback from the semantic units to the phonological units. Consider, too, the following observation. College student subjects who are good readers often mispronounce low frequency irregular words such as *viscount* or *manger* (Jared & Seidenberg, in press), despite the fact that they do know these words and how they are pronounced. If these words are then placed in context (e.g., *The Queen introduced me to the viscount*), fewer errors will be made. Presumably, this reflects the contribution of the semantics-to-phonology route. Understanding how this route contributes to normal naming will require developing a more explicit computational account of the subprocesses involved (the computations from orthography to semantics, and from semantics to phonology).

Of course, insofar as the Figure 3.1 model entails two naming mechanisms, it is a dual-route model. However, it has to be stressed that the processes hypothesized within this model are not isomorphic with those in standard dual-route models; the models are not notational variants. What is important is not the number of routes, but their computational properties: What types of knowledge representations and processes do they involve? What kinds of strings do they apply to? What kinds of output do they yield? In each of these respects, the models differ (see Seidenberg, 1989, for discussion).

PHONOLOGY AND LEXICAL ACCESS

A large amount of research has been directed at determining whether readers use phonological information to access the meanings of words from print. This is one of the most well-studied, not to say well-worn, issues in reading research. The basic idea is that readers of an alphabetic orthography such as the one for English could access the meanings of words in two ways: directly from the orthography or indirectly by first computing the phonological code for a word and then using this code to search for an entry. The first alternative has been termed direct access and the second phonologically-mediated access (e.g., Baron, 1979; Meyer, Schvaneveldt, & Ruddy, 1974; Rubenstein, Lewis, & Rubenstein, 1971). The empirical question concerns which of these processes is actually used by readers. A secondary question is whether the extent to which each process occurs depends on the skill of the reader or the type of orthography being read. For example, it has been argued that only relatively poor readers use phonological mediation (e.g., Doctor & Coltheart, 1980). Similarly, it has been argued that phonological mediation is characteristically used in reading orthographies, such as Serbo-Croatian, in which the correspondences between spelling and pronunciation are simple and direct (Katz & Feldman, 1981).

The direct versus phonologically-mediated pendulum has swung back and forth with remarkable regularity over the past 25 years; see Carr and Pollatsek (1985), Perfetti and McCutchen (1982), and Henderson (1982) for reviews. At the moment, it appears to be moving into the phonologically mediated phase again. It has always been a fairly simple matter to show that phonological information is accessed in silent reading (e.g., Besner & Davelaar, 1982; Kleiman, 1975). The issue of phonological access to meaning has proven more difficult to resolve, however. The fact that phonological information influences performance on a silent reading task such as lexical decision does not itself establish that phonology was used to access meaning. It is quite possible, for example, that phonological and semantic codes for words are accessed in parallel. In general, it has been difficult to obtain evidence that clearly distinguishes between *activation* of phonology and phonologically mediate *access* of meaning.

Recently there have been some fairly clear demonstrations that phonological mediation does occur under at least some conditions. Consider, for example, experiments using pseudohomophones – nonwords such as *brane* that sound like words. Van Orden, Hale, and Johnston (1988) showed that on a significant proportion of trials, subjects falsely classified nonwords such as *sute* as members of categories such as *article* or *clothing*. The rate of false positive responses was higher than for nonpseudohomophone controls such as *sart*. The apparent explanation for this result is that subjects phonologically recoded the nonword stimuli; the phonological code for a pseudohomophone such as *sute* was used to access the meaning associated with the base word *suit*, and the activation of this semantic information supported the incorrect *yes* response on the categorization task. Van Orden et al.'s study replicates essential aspects of the Rubenstein et al. (1971) lexical decision experiment.

Van Orden et al. concluded that meaning is always accessed from a phonological representation (i.e., that phonological mediation is obligatory). However, it is not clear from their results how often phonological mediation occurs in normal reading. The studies simply do not address the range of conditions under which phonological effects obtain. The claim that access to meaning is always phonologically mediated is also difficult to reconcile with other findings in the literature. For example, Shulman, Hornak, and Sanders (1978) reported a study in which there was a dissociation between semantic and phonological priming effects. Semantic priming occurred when a prime word facilitated the lexical decision to a semantically related target (e.g., *doctor-nurse*). Phonological priming was indicated by the conjunction of two effects: pairs such as *gave-save* producing facilitation and pairs such as *paid-said* producing interference. One study (utilizing orthographically illegal nonwords) produced semantic priming but not phonological. This dissociation between the effects is inconsistent with the claim that access to meaning is necessarily phonologically mediated. We know that subjects accessed the meanings of target words because there was facilitation on semantically related trials. If meaning access were phonologically mediated, rhyme priming should also have obtained, but it did not.

Findings such as these have suggested to many (e.g., Perfetti & McCutchen, 1982) that both direct and phonologically mediated routes to meaning are used in reading. What is needed, then, is a principled account of why one or another of these processes is used in any given case. Consider again the model outlined in Figure 3.1. The model assumes that the meanings of words are computed, either from orthographic input (in reading) or from phonological input (in listening). Meanings are themselves represented as patterns of activation over units representing semantic primitives (discussed later). According to the model, there is a computation from orthographic input to meaning, corresponding to the traditional notion of a direct route. There is also a computation from orthography to phonology. We assume that readers attempt to compute both semantic and phonological codes in parallel; the computed phonological code may be responsible for the omnipresent voice in the head experienced during reading. The model presented in Figure 3.1 also includes a computation from phonology to meaning, relevant to spoken word recognition. Given this architecture, it follows that there is also an indirect route to meaning, involving a computation from orthography to phonology and a second computation from phonology to meaning. Phonological mediation, then, refers to feedback from the computed phonological code to the meaning units.

This conception of phonological mediation differs from the traditional one in several respects. In earlier models, phonological mediation involved either deriving the phonological code of a word by rule or accessing its entry in a phonological lexicon. This derived code could then be used to access the meaning of a word, represented as an entry in a semantic lexicon. In the Seidenberg and McClelland model, the codes for words are represented as patterns of activation over relevant types of units. This type of representation affords the possibility of *partial* activation of a code. This partially activated code may be sufficient to produce phenomena such as phonological priming effects (e.g., Meyer et al., 1974; Shulman et al., 1978); moreover, it may result in partial activation of semantic nodes that is sufficient to produce the false positives in the Van Orden et al. experiments.

A second point is that we can now see why the notion of lexical access is unnecessary. In previous accounts it was assumed that accessing the meaning of a word required a preliminary identification of the input (i.e., access to an entry in an orthographic or phonological lexicon, or activation of a logogen). Intuitively, the meaning of the input *book* could not be determined until it was identified as an instance of the word *book*. This is simply a variant of the argument presented earlier concerning the need for lexical access in naming exception words. In the Seidenberg and McClelland model, determining the meaning of a word does not require accessing a stored orthographic or phonological code;

meanings are simply computed, either directly or indirectly. The input is encoded and activation spreads through the system.[3]

Within the framework illustrated in Figure 3.1, the key question concerns the time course of processing, that is, the rate at which different types of output units are activated. Several computations – from orthography to phonology, from orthography to semantics, from phonology to meaning – are assumed to occur in parallel. The characteristics of these computations are determined by the weights on connections between units. Seidenberg and McClelland's simulation model is quite limited in that only the computation from orthography to phonology is implemented; there is no representation of meaning. Moreover, the implemented model is not a real time system; orthographic and phonological output are computed in a single step rather than in the cascaded manner we assume is true in reality. Hence, very little can be said about the time course of processing, specifically how much feedback from phonology to semantics would occur for different words. The clear prediction, however, is that there should be more of this feedback when the computation from orthography to meaning is itself very slow. This might occur, for example, when the input word is low in frequency. Some time ago I proposed that phonological mediation is associated with lower frequency words (Seidenberg, 1985; see also McCusker, Hillinger, & Bias, 1981), and we now have the beginnings of a computational account of why this might be so. Perhaps the limiting case is provided by pseudohomophones such as *sute*, for which the computation from orthography to meaning will produce very little semantic output. Similar effects may obtain if the reader's decoding skills are poor. By hypothesis, the poor reader computes meanings from orthography very slowly, allowing more time for feedback from the indirect orthography-phonology-meaning route.

This framework provides a useful context for understanding the Van Orden et al. (1988) results. Recall that they found a significant number of false positive responses on a classification task when the target stimuli were homophones (e.g., *family relative: sun*) or pseudohomophones (e.g., *article of clothing: sute*). Within the model we have been considering, various types of information are computed over time: orthographic, phonological, semantic, possibly others. The subject's task is to find a reliable basis for deciding whether the target is a member of a prespecified category. Performance on the task must be characterized in terms of how the computed information contributes to the decision process. Several types of information could be used: Does the stimulus

---

[3] It might be asked whether the initial encoding of a word as a pattern of activation over the input, orthographic nodes, corresponds to the notion of accessing an entry in an orthographic lexicon. The two ideas really aren't the same. Aside from the contrast between using distributed rather than local lexical representations, there is the fact that the encoding process in the Seidenberg and McClelland model applies to both words and nonwords. Insofar as the process applies to nonwords, it does not correspond to accessing entries in an orthographic lexicon; nonwords don't have any.

look like a word, sound like a word, look like an exemplar of the category, sound like an exemplar of the category, have the correct meaning? As in the lexical decision task, subject performance is likely to depend on the properties of the stimuli in the experiment: their orthographic and phonological characteristics and frequencies, the properties of the stimuli on the catch trials, the specificity of the category and predictability of the target, and so forth. In sum, the conditions in experiments like Van Orden et al.'s create a classic constraint satisfaction problem. The subject makes the response that is most consistent with a large set of intersecting constraints. If this is in fact how the classification task is performed, it is very difficult to conclude from a particular set of results that access to meaning is always phonologically mediated, because it implies that very different results will obtain if the constraints are modified.

Differences Among Orthographies

To this point the discussion of the pronunciation process has been motivated by facts about English. It is well known, however, that orthographies differ in the extent to which they encode phonological information (see Henderson, 1982, for an interesting discussion of orthographies). Like other alphabetic orthographies, written English systematically encodes information about the pronunciation and sound of words. However, it is perhaps unusual in the extent to which it exhibits irregular spelling-sound correspondences. Spanish, French, vowelized Hebrew, and many other orthographies exhibit fewer of the irregularities at the level of grapheme-phoneme correspondences that are so prominent in English. We now consider how these differences among orthographies relate to the framework developed here on the basis of English.

There have been many cross-linguistic studies using tasks such as lexical decision and pronunciation. The general consensus that has emerged from this research is that readers adjust their processing strategies in response to the properties of writing systems. Serbo-Croatian, for example, exhibits very consistent correspondences between graphemes and phonemes, and is said to be a shallow alphabetic orthography; English is the quintessential example of a deep alphabetic orthography, exhibiting many inconsistencies (Turvey, Feldman, & Lukatela, 1984). Orthographies with very simple and direct correspondences between written and spoken forms are thought to encourage the use of phonological information in reading; orthographies with irregular or inconsistent spelling-sound correspondences are thought to discourage the use of phonological recoding. Based on studies of reading in Serbo-Croatian, Turvey et al. (1984) have argued that in this language, access to meaning is always phonologically mediated: "The Serbo-Croatian orthography constrains the reader to a phonologically analytic strategy". Most studies of reading in Serbo-Croatian have emphasized the greater reliance on phonological mediation in reading this language (e.g., Lukatela, Feldman, Turvey, Carello, & Katz, 1989). Paradoxically, Van Orden et al.

(1988) now make the same claim about English, the writing system thought to discourage the use of phonological information.

We can again try to construe these issues within the framework presented in Figure 3.1. Facts about the correspondences between orthography and phonology are encoded by the weights on connections. The weights are determined by an error-correcting learning algorithm, which picks up on orthographic-phonological regularities during training; in essence, words with similar spelling-sound correspondences push the weights in similar directions. We have argued that this way of encoding orthographic - phonological correspondences is felicitous given the properties of the English orthography and facts about naming performance (e.g., consistency effects). However, writing systems such as those for Serbo-Croatian and Spanish are different. Though it has proven difficult to formulate the spelling-sound correspondences of English in terms of a set of rules mapping between graphemes and phonemes, it is easy to do this in Serbo-Croatian. It might be asked, then, whether learning to pronounce words aloud is fundamentally different in Serbo-Croatian. It might be sufficient for the child to simply learn the grapheme-phoneme correspondence rules. Similarly, a child learning to read Japanese Kana, a syllabary, would simply have to learn the association between each symbol and its entirely regular pronunciation. This would simply imply that there are very basic differences in the types of knowledge and processes relevant to reading different orthographies.

It should be noted, however, that the mechanism illustrated in Figure 3.1 could be utilized in learning *any* alphabetic orthography, regardless of the degree to which graphemes and phonemes correspond. The learning algorithm will pick up on regularities in the training corpus where they exist. Whether the orthography is deep or shallow does not have to be stipulated; the learning algorithm simply goes to work. To the extent that orthographies vary in terms of spelling-sound correspondences, these differences will be reflected in the weights. According to this view, the same types of knowledge representations and processes underlie reading in different orthographies; the differences among them merely influence the weights, which are determined on the basis of experience.

Several other considerations recommend this approach to orthographic differences. The facts about spelling-sound correspondences are rarely as simple as they might appear from existing empirical studies, which have tended to focus on monosyllabic words. Orthographies have several structural characteristics and there appear to be trade-offs among them in terms of complexity. For example, Serbo-Croatian is relatively simple at the level of grapheme-phoneme correspondences (the only complication is the fact that there are both Roman and Cyrillic versions of the orthography, and several letters appear, with different pronunciations, in both of them). Except in the case of monosyllabic words, however, pronunciation is not simply a matter of assigning phonemes to graphemes. In multisyllabic words there is the problem of stress assignment, and here Serbo-Croatian is enormously complex, a fact that is often ignored. Thus, pronunciation in Serbo-Croatian is shallow only if attention is restricted to graphemes and phonemes. It remains to be determined whether a more complete account of pronunciation in this language – one that took into account stress assignment – sustain the conclusion that words are easier to pronounce in Serbo-Croatian.

In comparing Serbo-Croatian and English we see a good illustration of the trade-offs in terms of design features that were mentioned previously. Serbo-Croatian appears to have relatively fewer short, monosyllabic words than does English. In part this is because the language employs an elaborate set of inflections for case and gender. In English, the words with irregular spelling-sound correspondences are not randomly distributed throughout the lexicon. Rather, they tend to be short, monosyllabic, and high in frequency; that is, they are words like *said, give, have, done, love,* and *shoe.* Importantly, in the Seidenberg and McClelland model, irregular spelling-sound correspondences have little impact on the processing of such high frequency words; the model performs as well on these words as on comparable regular ones because repeated exposure to the irregular items themselves swamp the effects of exposure to inconsistent neighbors. And, of course, readers perform in a similar manner: They read short, monosyllabic, high frequency regular and exception words equally well. Two facts emerge from these considerations. First, in English, effects of irregular spelling-sound correspondences are modulated by the fact that they tend to appear in words for which this structural variable has little impact. This fact should be kept in mind when considering the extent to which English differs from other orthographies in terms of difficulty of pronunciation. Second, Serbo-Croatian has fewer short, monosyllabic words and more of the longer words for which stress assignment is an issue. It could be speculated that these trade-offs among structural factors such as length, syllabic structure, and transparency at the level of grapheme-phoneme correspondences yield a situation in which both orthographies are roughly similar in terms of difficulty of acquisition and processing.

It is likely that there is a more general principle at work here. Languages exhibit inconsistencies at many structural levels. Taking English again as an example, there are many inconsistencies at the level of morphology; consider, for example, the celebrated case of the past tense of verbs (Bybee & Slobin, 1982; Pinker & Prince, 1988; Rumelhart & McClelland, 1986). It is because of such cases that morphological theories have distinguished between word forms that are generated by rule and those that are listed. In general, English can be seen as structured at many levels simultaneously; at each level, however, there are cases that depart from the rules describing these regularities. This prompts the following conjecture:

Seidenberg's Razor: Irregularities in linguistic structure tend to cluster among the high frequency cases in which they have little impact on processing.

This conjecture appears to be correct in regard to the grapheme-phoneme correspondences of English. It is also consistent with the observation that the irregular past tense forms tend to be high frequency words and to derive from high frequency bases. Moreover, there is some evidence that the diachronic processes that are, in part, responsible for irregularities at the lexical level tend to affect higher frequency words more than low (Hooper, 1976; Wang, 1979). It remains to be determined, of course, whether this conjecture will prove to be robust.

Returning now to the question of direct versus phonologically mediated access of meaning in different orthographies, within the framework illustrated in Figure 3.1, this issue concerns the properties of the computations from orthography to meaning, from orthography to phonology, and from phonology to meaning. The empirical question concerns the time course of processing: Is meaning activated more rapidly directly from the orthography or indirectly through phonology? Differences between orthographies would be realized in terms of the properties of these computations. If the correspondences between orthography and phonology are consistent, the computation along this route will be more rapid, allowing more time for activation to spread from phonology to meaning. Other factors being equal, then, we would expect to observe more phonological mediation – more activation of semantic units on the basis of feedback from phonology – in shallow orthographies. Note, however, that the force of the preceding discussion is that when it comes to orthographies, other factors may not in fact be equal. Facts about graphemes and phonemes cannot be isolated from other knowledge relevant to pronunciation.

One final point should be noted. Within this framework, the extent to which phonology influences the activation of meaning will depend on the properties of *both* the direct and indirect routes to meaning. In principle, if the direct computation is itself rapid enough, there will be little opportunity for phonological feedback to develop. It seems likely that such a direct process is available in reading Serbo-Croatian. The Serbo-Croatian reader is not "constrained to a phonologically analytic process" in naming familiar objects; why should they be so constrained in reading familiar objects that happen to be words? Surely there is an acquired dyslexic patient somewhere in Yugoslavia who is able to read words for meaning but not pronounce them aloud. If there are in fact two routes to meaning in Serbo-Croatian, then the system is fundamentally like that for English and it is simply an empirical question whether the phonological route contributes more to the activation of meaning in one orthography than the other.

Summary

The main features of this account can be summarized as follows. The first is the architecture of the proposed system – the pathways from orthography to meaning, from orthography to phonology, and from phonology to meaning. It is a consequence of this architecture that there are, potentially, two ways to compute the meanings of words from print. This aspect of the model is very closely related to previous accounts. Second, there is the idea that each of these pathways involves the computation of distributed representations rather than access to lexical entries. This affords the possibility of partial activation of a code. Hence, phonological mediation does not necessarily involve deriving a complete phonological code (phonological recoding). Finally, there are issues concerning the nature of these computations: They are determined by the weights on connections between units which are determined by experience. These weights – which are different, of course, in the three cases – determine the time course of processing. It is the timing of the various activation processes that determines whether access of meaning is direct or phonologically mediated. Differences between orthographies may simply relate to which of the processes is more efficient.

DO LEXICAL DECISIONS REQUIRE LEXICAL ACCESS?

As we have noted, the Seidenberg and McClelland model computes orthographic and phonological codes of words. These computed codes are then used in performing tasks such as naming a word aloud or making a lexical decision. Much of the Seidenberg and McClelland paper is concerned with characterizing how these tasks are performed. We have suggested that the model provides an account of word naming that does not involve a lexical access stage in processing. We turn now to performance on the lexical decision task, which presents a strong challenge to the model because standard accounts suggest that the task is performed by accessing the kinds of lexical representations our model lacks. The basic question is whether a model employing distributed representations – and therefore lacking entries for individual words – can support performance of this task.

The lexical decision task – in which the subject is presented with a string of letters and must decide if they form a word or not – is probably the most widely used task in psycholinguistics. The task appears to have been introduced by Rubenstein, Garfield, and Millikan (1970) as a way of studying processes involved in identifying the meanings of words. The logic of the task was as follows: The subject is asked to discriminate between words (such as *book*) and nonwords (such as *sook*). As in this example, nonwords are typically constructed so as to be orthographically and phonologically well-formed; there could have been a lexical item *sook* in English and it is an accident of history that there is not. As the words and nonwords are similar in terms of their orthographic and phonological properties, the lexical decision can only be made by determining whether the letter strings have associated meanings or not. Hence, latencies on word trials should reflect processes involved in accessing meanings. The task could then be used to examine how properties of words, such as frequency, influence access of meaning. It was thought to contrast with a task such as naming, which could be performed nonlexically (i.e., on

the basis of rules governing spelling-sound correspondences). This view
of the task is still widely accepted; for example, Theios and Amrhein
(1989) observed in a recent paper, "Lexical decision tasks by their very
nature require access to meaning" (p. 6).

Although it has been widely assumed that lexical decisions require
access to meaning, there is now a growing body of evidence that decisions can be based on other types of information. The task requires
subjects to discriminate between words and nonwords. As in a signal
detection task, the subject must establish decision criteria that allow
fast responses with acceptable error rates. Perhaps the primary conclusion from extensive use of the task is that these criteria vary as a
function of the properties of the stimuli in an experiment. As subjects'
response criteria vary, so do the effects of variables such as frequency,
orthographic-phonological regularity, and contextual congruence (e.g.,
Forster, 1981; Neely, 1977; Seidenberg, Waters, Barnes, & Tanenhaus,
1984; Stanovich & West, 1981).

Words and nonwords differ along several dimensions, each of which
could provide the basis for making lexical decisions depending on the
properties of the stimuli in a given experiment. Specifically, words tend
to be more familiar orthographic patterns; they have more familiar pronunciations; and they have meanings. If the stimuli in an experiment
consist of words and orthographically illegal nonwords (e.g., *bskl*), orthographic information may provide a reliable basis for making responses.
If the stimuli consist of words and orthographically legal nonwords (such
as *rone*), the decision might be made by determining if the stimulus has
a familar sound or meaning. If the nonwords are pseudohomophones
(such as *brane*), it may be difficult to make the decision on the basis of
either orthography or phonology, forcing the subject to use meaning.

Exact predictions about which types of information will be used in
making lexical decisions depend on knowing just how similar the words
and nonwords are in terms of orthography and phonology. Consider, for
example, the use of orthographic information. Given a word or nonword
as input, our model produces a pattern of activation across the orthographic nodes as output. We can then interpret this pattern of activation
by computing various error scores – comparing the output to different
target patterns. Typically we find that the best fit to the computed
output (smallest error score) is provided by the pattern corresponding
to the input. Thus, the model recreates the input pattern as output.
The error scores vary in magnitude, indicating that the model performs
better on some items than on others. In most cases, words produce
smaller error scores than nonwords because the model has been trained
on the words but not the nonwords. In many cases, the distributions will
overlap very little. The word/nonword decision, then, could be made
by establishing a cutoff: Scores below the cutoff correspond to words,
above the cutoff, nonwords. We think, in fact, that when the stimuli
have these characteristics, subjects make lexical decisions in exactly this
way. They compute orthographic output, perform a comparison to the

encoded stimulus, calculate something like the error score, and use this to make the decision.

There are several important aspects of this account of lexical decision performance. The error scores provide a general measure of familiarity or degree of lexicality. Items that are familiar to the model (e.g., because they are high in frequency and have been presented many times during training) produce low error scores; hence they are very clearly words. Items that are unfamiliar to the model (e.g., because they are nonwords and never presented during training) produce larger error scores; hence they are very clearly nonwords. The model still produces plausible output for many of these nonword items because they are similar to words in the training corpus. They fare somewhat worse, however, because they are never themselves presented during training. We think, then, that subjects perform the lexical decision by judging how wordlike the stimuli are, and that the error scores provide rough quantitative basis for this decision. Note the contrast to the idea that decisions are made by accessing entries in lexical memory. Our claim is that subjects make their decisions by judging the properties of the patterns of activation that words and nonwords produce over the output nodes. In effect, the error scores provide a basis for the familiarity judgment hypothesized by Balota and Chumbley (1984) in their account of lexical decision.

It is important to acknowledge that the error scores computed by the model are by no means perfect. They derive from the effects of the training regime on the values of the weights, and the model was only trained on 2,897 monosyllabic words. In reality, of course, readers know many more words, including multisyllabic items, and these would also have an impact on the weights. Hence, the error scores will fail to account for the variance associated with the effects of this larger pool of items. Moreover, error scores depend on relatively arbitrary aspects of the implemented model, such as the number of units. Still, the error scores do surprisingly well; for example, using the distributions of error scores for the stimuli in actual experiments one can establish decision criteria (cutoffs) that produce error rates comparable to the ones that were observed (Seidenberg & McClelland, 1989).

It should be clear from this simple example that the model provides a basis for making lexical decisions even though it lacks entries of words. In fact the model is somewhat more interesting than this because it accounts for some more subtle aspects of subjects' performance on the task. Subjects vary their decision criteria in response to the properties of the stimuli in a given experiment; the model provides a basis for understanding why such criterion shifts occur. Seidenberg and McClelland (1989) work through a simple case in which subjects base their decisions on phonological information rather than orthographic. It turns out that there are cases in which words and nonwords produce overlapping distributions of orthographic error scores. This occurs when the word stimuli include items such as *aisle* or *beige*, which contain unusual spelling patterns, and the nonwords are very wordlike items such as *nust* or *mave*. In this case, the orthographic error scores do not provide a basis for responding, predicting that subjects must use other types of information. Empirically, it is observed that when these stimuli are used, lexical decision latencies are influenced by phonological factors, such as spelling-sound regularity (Waters & Seidenberg, 1985). Thus, there is a shift in subjects' decision criteria conditioned by the properties of the stimuli in the experiment. The error scores correctly predict when orthographic information does and does not provide a sufficient basis for responding.

The lexical decision paradigm affords many possibilities other than the simple ones simulated by Seidenberg and McClelland. There may be conditions under which phonology does not provide a reliable basis for responding either. Imagine a case in which the nonwords include pseudohomophones such as *brane* or *pruve*. Perhaps when the nonwords actually sound like words, subjects cannot use phonology as a basis for responding. In this case, subjects might have to consult a third source of information, the pattern of activation produced by the computation from orthography to meaning. When words appear in meaningful contexts, subjects may use other kinds of information, such as a judgment of the congruence of context and target.

To conclude, lexical decision performance is fairly complex. At this point we have a general theory of the task and simulations of some specific cases. The computed information is used in a decision stage, with response criteria varying in response to properties of the stimuli. These assumptions follow earlier proposals about the lexical decision task. What the model contributes is the idea that decision criteria vary because stimuli produce different patterns of activation in the lexical network. By looking at the properties of the computed patterns of activation, we gain independent evidence as to why one or another type of information is or is not sufficient in a given case. I should stress that although this account is fairly detailed, it is by no means complete. First, it is clear that readers can ultimately determine that words have meanings and nonwords do not, information that would be provided by the pattern of activation over the semantic units. The model in its current stage does not address the use of this type of information. Second, we do not have a complete account of the decision process: how different types of information are weighed when the simple orthographic strategy cannot be used.

LEXICAL ACCESS AND MEANING

The final issue to be considered concerns lexical access and meaning. The discussion to this point has focused on the use of orthographic and phonological information in performing tasks such as naming a word aloud and making a lexical decision. The basic point was that, at least in these limited though interesting domains, we can account for performance within a theory which, because it employs distributed representations, does not entail the standard notion of lexical access. When we turn to meaning, similar questions can be raised: Will an adequate theory of access to meaning involve the standard notion of lexical access? Is it useful to think of meanings being accessed at all? How does the use of distributed representations affect our thinking about reading for meaning? This section is necessarily much more speculative than previous parts of the chapter. For one thing, the issues are much more complex, lying at the intersection of linguistics, philosophy, psychology, and artificial intelligence. I cannot hope to even review the main issues thoroughly, let alone attempt to resolve any of them in a serious way. For another, there aren't as yet any PDP models with sufficiently broad scope to draw upon. There have been several interesting first attempts at implementing models with semantic representations (e.g., Hinton et al., 1986; Kawamoto, 1988), but they have dealt with fairly narrow phenomena and serve mostly to introduce the approach and its intuitive appeal. My goal here is merely to make some suggestive observations that might eventually contribute to a more rigorous and sustained attack on the issues.

Lexical access is often used as a synonym for access of meaning. The standard view is that word meanings are stored in memory, as in a dictionary, perhaps; the entries are accessed by first identifying the input string as a token of a particular type. This identification process involves locating an entry for a word in memory (e.g., a logogen or an entry in an orthographic or phonological lexicon). Figure 3.1 suggests an alternative account, which has two main assumptions. First, the meanings of words are represented by semantic units that encode conceptual primitives or features. A word's meaning is represented as a pattern of activation across the relevant set of units. Second, access to meaning (in reading) involves a computation from orthography to semantics, analogous to the orthography-to-phonology computation discussed earlier. As before, there are no entries corresponding to individual words or meanings to be accessed.

Perhaps the most problematic aspect of this proposal is the assumption that word meanings are represented in terms of features. Featural representations of meaning have had a bad reputation since the demise of the Katz and Fodor (1963) theory some time ago. For a cogent discussion of the limitations of traditional feature theories, see Smith and Medin (1981). Among the limitations are: (a) the proposed sets of features seem ad hoc, there being no way to independently establish what they are; (b) sets of binary features such as $+/-$ animate or $+/-$ heavy seem incapable to handling the entire range of semantic phenomena (e.g., accounting for subtle differences in meaning); (c) feature theories have not provided an adequate account of psychological phenomena such as graded effects of category structure. In light of earlier research, one would have to greet a new featural account with considerable skepticism.

Though mindful of what happens to people who fail to remember history, I nonetheless think the proposal has some interesting features, so to speak. First of all, the scheme I envision relaxes the assumption that the features are binary. The features are represented by units, which are activated in different degrees. This analogue notion might be better suited to capturing subtle differences among related words such as *black*, *ebony*, and *onyx*. Differences in meaning might be associated with differences in the levels of activation associated with one or more units; these different levels of activation might not themselves be coded by words in the language. In sum, many problems with featural theories have to do with the assumption that they are binary and it is not clear whether they obtain when this restriction is removed. I would also note that this approach has the potential to account for the graded effects of category structure that motivated prototype theories, the main alternative to featural theories. Prototypes simply reflect properties of the aggregate set of learning experiences (Rumelhart, Smolensky, McClelland, & Hinton, 1986). To the extent that the members of a category share semantic features, they will tend to push the weights in a similar direction. The prototype, then, shares a large number of features with members of the category. A nonprototypical member of a category may actually share more features with members of other categories (e.g., *tomato* may share more features with vegetables than fruits).

A second attractive characteristic of this approach is that meanings are not represented as fixed packets that are stored with each word. Perhaps because there has not been very much progress toward a comprehensive theory of meaning, there has been a tendency to write as though meanings were discrete, fixed entities. For example, within the subfield of lexical ambiguity research, the question, "how many meanings of an ambiguous word are accessed in context?" is well-formed and suitable for seemingly endless study. The question appears to presuppose that meanings are countable entities. Many people have remarked upon the inadequacy of this conception (e.g., Gerrig, 1986). For example, it has a terrible time with polysemy. The problem isn't simply that words differ slightly in terms of meaning; it's that each word itself has many slightly different meanings. Moreover, the meanings cannot comprise a fixed inventory, because new ones are invented frequently and effortlessly (e.g., Clark & Clark, 1979; Glucksberg & Keysar, in press). In fairness to the people who studied lexical ambiguity resolution (e.g., me!), I don't think that it was ever seriously proposed that meanings have this discrete, packetlike quality. Ambiguity research has been concerned with some fairly general processing issues that are neutral with respect to the theory of semantic representation. Still, there *is* the tyranny of metaphors; the notion of accessing one or more meanings has perhaps even less appeal than that of accessing pronunciations.

A third issue, related to the second, is that the alternative theory holds out the prospect of a nice account of contextual effects on the activation of meaning. According to this theory, the meanings of words are computed each time they are encountered. For a given word, different patterns of activation will result if contextual information feeds into the system. Consider again the model presented in Figure 3.1. When an orthographic input is processed, two types of output are computed:

patterns of activation over pools of phonological and semantic nodes, respectively. When a word is presented in isolation, the computed output pattern will simply depend on the weights on connections between units. Imagine now that there is a set of context units feeding into the system. Assume for the moment that these units simply encode the pattern over the hidden units produced by a prior input word. The computed pattern of activation, then, will depend on both the input from the orthographic units and the input from the context units. For example, the word *cat*, in isolation, might activate features related to *fur* and *claws*. The word *cat* plus the context *scratch* might activate *claws* more strongly; *cat* plus *petted* might activate *fur* more strongly. These are simplified examples meant to illustrate how the mechanism should work; I am not committed to the idea that *claws* and *fur* are primitive features. Still, the idea should be clear. Something like this type of mechanism seems to be demanded by the large number of studies showing such context effects. For example, Merrill, Sperber and McCauley (1981) showed that different features of *cat* are activated in the contexts "John was scratched by the cat" and "John petted the cat". For demonstrations of other such effects, see Anderson and Ortony (1975), Barsalou (1982), and Schwanenflugel and Shoben (1985). It is more difficult to account for such effects within a theory in which meanings are entries that are accessed.

What we have here, of course, is a potential account of semantic priming. It is well known that the processing of a target word is facilitated by a semantically-related context word. What has been lacking, however, is a theory of the underlying semantics. In the absence of an account of what it means for two words to be semantically related, it has been hard to assess the scope of semantic priming effects. The suggestion here is that priming results from the structure of the semantic portions of the network, specifically the values of the weights on connections. One word primes another in virtue of activating some of the target word's features.[4]

There are other ways of thinking about semantic priming within this general framework. Consider, for example, the architecture presented in Figure 3.2, in which contextual information is coded by a set of plan or context units, as in Jordan (1986). We present the word *doctor* to the system and let it compute phonological and semantic output. We copy the pattern of activation from the hidden units over to the context units. When we present a subsequent word (e.g., *nurse*), the computed semantic output will depend jointly on the word itself and the input from the context units. Facilitation would result if the conjoint input caused the semantic units to be activated more rapidly. This might occur, for example, if *doctor* and *nurse* themselves tend to activate some units in

---

[4] This account of priming can be seen as one way of realizing the Ratcliff and McKoon (1988) "cue contiguity" explanation of these phenomena. My remarks are only intended to be suggestive; see their paper for a more substantive analysis of priming.

common, or if the model is trained to expect that *doctor* will be followed by *nurse*.[5]

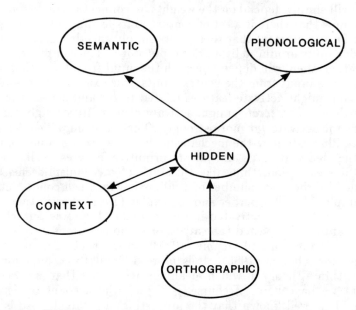

FIGURE 3.2. Example of an architecture for generating contextual effects. The context produces a pattern of activation over the hidden units. The output computed for a new pattern (e.g., a target word) then depends jointly on the input from the context units and the input from the orthographic units.

A fourth issue concerns acquisition. From the proposed point of view, learning the meanings of words amounts to learning to activate appropriate semantic units based on orthographic (or phonological) input. This approach has several interesting implications. First, it may account for facts about the acquisition of word meanings. There is a large amount

---

[5] This discussion is relevant to some findings reported by Keenan, Potts, Golding, and Jennings (this volume). They found that naming latencies to a target word such as *break* are facilitated in contexts such as "The angry husband threw the vase against the wall". Control conditions suggest that the priming effect is not due to an associative relationship between any word in the context and the target. Hence, the effects cannot be intralexical (Forster, 1981) and therefore show that lexical processing is not modular (Fodor, 1983). It would be interesting to determine whether such facilitation would occur within a model employing the architecture sketched in Figure 3.2. The question is really whether the conjunction of *throw* on the context units and *vase* as the input would activate sufficient semantic features relevant to *break* to facilitate naming. Note that these effects would undoubtedly depend on the order in which words were presented; hence, it would not be surprising if the effect did not occur if, for example, several words intervened between *throw* and *vase*. The main point is that lexical priming effects in a network such as this may be more subtle than expected under earlier conceptions of semantic and associative priming. In the absence of a theory of what kinds of semantic relations do and do not cause priming, it cannot be unambiguously determined whether they violate modularity in the way Keenan et al. suggest.

of evidence concerning how children acquire word meanings, focussing on the kinds of errors they initially make and seeming discontinuities in or reorganizations of semantic knowledge (e.g., Keil, 1981). It would be interesting to determine whether a model that was trained using an algorithm such as backpropagation would exhibit similar developmental trends. In a model of the proposed sort, the hidden units will come to encode different things as a function of experience. Over time, for example, units may encode interesting conjunctions or co-occurrences of features. Given that the effects of experience are again superimposed on the weights, the kinds of spontaneous generalizations that would arise in such a system could be quite subtle and unpredictable.

It should also be noted that the proposed framework is not inconsistent with proposals concerning the role of biological constraints in the acquisition of word meanings. If it is indeed the case that some (possibly all; Fodor, 1983) concepts are innate, it would be possible to model this in terms of the initial configuration of semantic nodes. There may be units (or, more realistically, pools of units) that, as a consequence of evolution, innately encode certain conceptual primitives. What is learned, then, is merely how these units, at different levels of activation, are associated with orthographic or phonological patterns. It is also widely observed that children's acquisition of word meanings seems to conform to certain principles or constraints (Keil, 1981). Some of these may arise from outside the semantic system (for example, they may be secondary to facts about perception or action), but some may arise from the behavior of the network itself. For example, what a network learns depends in part on its architecture. Seidenberg and McClelland provide a simple illustration of this fact. When their model was trained using 200 hidden units, it was able to learn to produce the correct phonological codes for both regular words and exceptions. When the model was configured with only 100 hidden units, it was able to encode regular spelling-sound correspondences but performed miserably on the irregular cases. Given the constraints imposed by the architecture, it simply could not encode all of the relevant generalizations. Clearly, it would be interesting to determine whether aspects of what the child does and does not know at any given point in time could be explained in terms of this type of constraint on learning. In sum, what is learned depends on three factors, among others: the biological endowment of the organism, its capacity to learn, and its experience. Within the framework I have described, biological constraints are realized in terms of the initial architecture of the system, and learning is characterized by the properties of one or another algorithm. The goal, then, would be to explain the complex set of facts about the acquisition of word meanings (and other learning phenomena) in terms of this set of constraints.

I realize that these observations are entirely speculative. My own belief, however, is that this framework has the potential to provide a unified account of a range of phenomena concerning the meanings of words. It seems likely that this approach, or something very much like it, will be the focus of considerable attention in the immediate future.

CONCLUSIONS

The purpose of this chapter has been to explore the idea that lexical knowledge does not involve lexical representations. The idea is somewhat counterintuitive, and so it is not obvious how it could be reconciled with the many and varied phenomena that have been uncovered in studies of lexical access. The conclusions to be drawn from this discussion are fairly modest and, I hope, not excessively controversial. One can see how many of the phenomena can be recast in the new terms; one can see some areas in which this recasting might provide the basis for reconciling some opposing views (concerning, for example, direct vs. phonologically mediated access of meaning). These preliminary explorations have not uncovered any obvious limitations of this approach; even something like lexical decision performance, which seems to demand a notion of accessing a lexical entry, can be coherently formulated in these terms. Of course, nothing that has been said militates decisively in favor of the new view. Moreover, the lexical access approach has led to a deeper understanding of phenomena not touched upon in this chapter; for example, the alternative approach does not, as yet, contribute much to the understanding of acquired dyslexias, an area in which the lexical access view has been notably successful (see Patterson, Seidenberg, & McClelland, 1989, for some preliminary work on this issue).

In light of these observations, it is worth considering briefly the status of a model such as Seidenberg and McClelland's. As I noted earlier in the text, my goal here has not been so much to promote this particular model as the general approach it represents. The model – specifically, the successful simulation of a broad range of behavioral phenomena – establishes the plausibility of the approach and suggests that it would be productive to explore it further. I hope it is obvious that the particular model we have implemented is very limited in scope and, like all other simulation models, simply incorrect in detail. The scope limitations are discussed in Seidenberg (1989) and Seidenberg and McClelland (1989), and they should be apparent. The model is restricted to monosyllabic words; the model has no semantics; the model does not incorporate procedures for actually generating articulatory output; the scheme used for representing phonology is inadequate; and so on. It is clear that because of these limitations, which are characteristic of simulation models, Seidenberg and McClelland's model will prove to be false, in the sense that it will not correctly predict all behavioral phenomena in the intended domain of application. We can see this already. For example, the model does not perform as well on nonwords as do people; the model predicts much larger differences between word and nonword latencies (e.g., in naming) than are actually observed. This limitation of the model is important but difficult to interpret without further research. It may derive from a trivial aspect of the simulation (e.g., the wrong number of units or training trials, the wrong encoding of frequency or phonology, the size of the training corpus), or it may reflect a deeper, theoretically important limitation (e.g., the absence of nodes representing individual words). It is possible (though, as I have argued elsewhere, unlikely; Seidenberg, 1989) that the model performs as well as it does in simulating various aspects of human performance merely because of these limitations in scope. In light of these considerations, however, a healthy degree of caution is certainly warranted in assessing what has and has not been achieved.

The issues that arise in connection with our model are characteristic of simulations in general and can be illustrated as follows. In the Seidenberg and McClelland model, two types of output are computed: a phonological code and an orthographic code. As noted earlier, the computed orthographic code plays an important role in our account of lexical decision. The general *theory* here is that the computation of this code is affected by knowledge concerning the frequency and distribution of letters in the lexicon. In the simulation *model*, this information is encoded by the weights on connections, particularly those between hidden units and orthographic output units. One of the important theoretical implications of this approach is that it provides an account of orthographic redundancy. The distribution of letters in words is obviously not random; see Adams (1981) for an informative discussion of this issue. An important issue concerns how readers utilize this information in reading words. Until now, researchers have attempted to characterize orthographic redundancy in terms of summary statistics, such as bigram frequencies or positional letter frequencies. Each of these summary statistics captures only a small part of the orthographic structure of the lexicon. The Seidenberg and McClelland model represents a different approach to this issue. Rather than using summary statistics, the model actually encodes information about orthographic structure directly. The model says that readers' knowledge of orthographic structure is determined by their aggregate experience in reading words, which affects the weights in specifiable ways. From this perspective, a statistic such as bigram frequency merely partials out a small – and theoretically uninteresting – part of the information encoded in the lexical network.

It follows from this approach that we can now develop a new kind of measure of orthographic redundancy. The orthographic error scores generated by the model are themselves determined by the weights. A word with a common orthographic pattern produces a small error score; a word with an uncommon orthographic pattern produces a larger error score. Empirically, we find that the error scores do a good job in capturing some very general differences among words in terms of processing difficulty. For example, under conditions where lexical decisions can be based on orthographic information, words with higher error scores (e.g., strange words like *aisle*) produce longer decision latencies than words with lower scores (e.g., regular words).

The limitation of the implemented model, of course, is that it is trained on only 2,897 words. In a more complete model, the relevant weights would be affected by knowledge of many other words as well. Apparently, training on only a subset of words is sufficient to capture some basic differences among words in terms of processing difficulty.

However, it is likely that the model will not capture more subtle differences among words – those attributable to knowledge of the other 50,000 or so words that the average reader knows. Thus, although error scores will be correlated with reaction times, there will be variance that is not accounted for.

These observations are relevant to results reported by Besner (this volume). Besner shows that there is variance in naming latencies that is not explained by the model's error scores. Some residual variance is correlated with a statistical measure termed Coltheart's N. Since this measure is derived by counting words (it equals the number of words that can be formed from a given word by changing one letter), Besner concludes that there must be entries for individual words in memory. Hence the model is incorrect because it has no such entries. This logic is not persuasive, however. The amount of residual variance explained by N is remarkably small, about 6%. Moreover, the N measure itself is correlated with error scores; thus, it does not reflect an independent factor outside the domain of the existing model. One way to view the data is that the model fails to pick up some fairly subtle differences between words because it was only trained on 2897 words. It is part of our theory that performance on a given word depends on the entire ensemble of learning experiences. Restricting this ensemble therefore should have detectable effects on performance. According to this view, the kinds of effects that Besner observed are not surprising; they are *build into* the simulation; it is, after all, a model, not a complete implementation of everything a person knows about words. In light of the limitations of the implemented model, the surprising thing is that the error scores do so well in accounting for regularity and frequency effects and the like, not that there is unexplained variance. The fact that the error scores do well despite obvious limitations of the simulation gives us some confidence that our theory is on the right track.

Here we reach limitations of the implemented model that can only be addressed by further research. Do results like Besner's reflect uninteresting limits on the scope of the implemented model -- for example, exposure to a relatively small set of words – or do they reflect a deeper limitation of the more general theory on which the implemented model is based – for example, the absence of a level of structure at which words and nonwords differ? It seems to me that there are two ways to approach such questions. One is to develop new simulations, incorporating the same basic architecture as ours, that deal with a broader range of cases. The other is to develop computationally explicit alternative theories that account for the phenomena. For example, one might try to develop an alternative theory that utilizes a different type of knowledge representation; for example, nodes for individual lexical items rather than distributed representations. The alternative theory would have to be developed to the point where it accounted for the same range of phenomena as ours but incorporated additional ones as well. There is nothing in this approach that is particular to connectionism or to simulation models; this is just good science, in my view.[6]

In sum, the simulation model entails certain theoretical claims (e.g., concerning the representation of orthographic knowledge, the inadequacy of summary statistics such as bigrams, how the computed code is used in performing different tasks, etc.). The implemented model accounts for a surprisingly broad range of phenomena despite the limitations in scope. However, the scope limitations introduce a window of uncertainty. They guarantee that the model will fail to account for at least some phenomena, and it will not be immediately clear whether this reflects a trivial limitation of the implementation or a more basic problem with the approach. This is true of every simulation model. This uncertainty necessitates further research dealing with a broader range of phenomena.

I think that the strategy of developing very explicit computational models in fairly broad, though limited, domains is a good one, and, as noted in Seidenberg (1989) and Seidenberg and McClelland (1989), I think there is good reason to believe that substantive conclusions can be drawn from the existing model despite its limitations. Still, there is a daunting amount of work yet to be done.

ACKNOWLEDGMENTS

I thank Debra Jared, Ken McRae, and Jonathon Cohen for helpful discussions. This research was supported by grants from the Natural Science and Engineering Council of Canada and the Quebec Ministry of Education. My thinking on the issues discussed in this chapter was stimulated by David Balota's presentation at the NIAS conference on reading held in 1988. I realized then that the Seidenberg and McClelland model was an example of a theory of lexical processing without the "magical moment" of lexical access that he critiqued. The approach I have taken here is therefore in very much the same spirit as his paper in this volume.

---

[6] There is also the question as to whether Besner's results are correct. Gloria Waters and I have recently completed the preliminary analysis of a corpus of naming latencies for 3000 monosyllabic words based on responses from 30 subjects. the corpus includes data concerning measures such as Coltheart's N, bigram frequency, Kucera and Francis (1967) frequency, and the like. The overall correlation between Coltheart's N and naming latency is -.27. However, this measure is also correlated with length in letters (-.57) and with the phonological error scores generated by the model (-.28). The net result is that when length in letters and phonological error score are entered in a stepwise regression, there is no residual effect due to Coltheart's N. Hence, Besner's results do not replicate with this much larger corpus of stimuli. Note that the reason the model does not account for the effect of length in letters is trivial: each processing trial is initiated with the encoding of a word across the set of orthographic units. Error scores do not reflect this initial encoding process. In sum, the model misses the length effect because we did not attempt to simulate it.

REFERENCES

Adams, M. (1981). What good is orthographic redundancy? In O. J. L. Tzeng & H. Singer (Eds.), *Perception of print: Reading research in experimental psychology* (pp. 197 - 221). Hillsdale, NJ: Lawrence Erlbaum Associates.

Allport, D. A., & Funnell, E. (1981). Components of the mental lexicon. *Philosophical transactions of the Royal Society of London, B295*, 397 - 410.

Anderson, R. C., & Ortony, A. (1975). On putting apples into bottles - A problem of polysemy. *Cognitive Psychology, 7*, 167 - 180.

Aronoff, M. (1976). *Word formation in generative grammar* (Linguistic Inquiry Monograph No. 1). Cambridge, MA: MIT Press.

Balota, D. A., & Chumbley, J. I. (1984). Are lexical decisions a good measure of lexical access? The role of word frequency in the neglected decision stage. *Journal of Experimental Psychology: Human Perception and Performance, 10*, 340 - 357.

Balota, D. A., & Chumbley, J. I. (1985). The locus of word-frequency effects in the pronunciation task: Lexical access and/or production? *Journal of Memory and Language, 24*, 89 - 106.

Baron, J. (1979). Orthographic and word-specific mechanisms in children's reading of words. *Child Development, 50*, 60 - 72.

Barsalou, L. W. (1982). Context-independent and context-dependent information in concepts. *Memory & Cognition, 10*, 82 - 93.

Besner, D., & Davelaar, E. (1982). Basic processes in reading: Two phonological codes. *Canadian Journal of Psychology, 36*, 701 - 711.

Bybee, J. L., & Slobin, D. I. (1982). Rules and schemas in the development and use of the English past tense. *Language, 58*, 265 - 289.

Carr, T. H., & Pollatsek, A. (1985). Recognizing printed words: A look at current models. In D. Besner, T. G. Waller, & G. E. MacKinnon (Eds.), *Reading research: Advances in theory and practice* (Vol. 5, pp. 1 - 82). New York: Academic Press.

Clark, E. V., & Clark, H. H. (1979). When nouns surface as verbs. *Language, 55*, 767 - 811.

Coltheart, M. (1978). Lexical access in simple reading tasks. In G. Underwood (Ed.), *Strategies of information processing* (pp. 151 - 216). New York: Academic Press.

Doctor, E. A., & Coltheart, M. (1980). Children's use of phonological encoding when reading for meaning. *Memory & Cognition, 8*, 195 - 209.

Fodor, J. A. (1983). *Modularity of mind.* Cambridge, MA: MIT Press.

Forster, K. I. (1976). Accessing the mental lexicon. In R. J. Wales & E. Walker (Eds.), *New approaches to language mechanisms* (pp. 257 - 287). Amsterdam: North-Holland.

Forster, K. I. (1981). Priming and the effects of sentence and lexical contexts on naming time: Evidence for autonomous lexical processing. *Quarterly Journal of Experimental Psychology, 33A*, 465 - 495.

Forster, K. I., & Chambers, S. M. (1973). Lexical access and naming time. *Journal of Verbal Learning and Verbal Behavior, 12*, 627 - 635.

Frederiksen, J. R., & Kroll, J. F. (1976). Spelling and sound: Approaches to the internal lexicon. *Journal of Experimental Psychology: Human Perception and Performance, 2*, 361 - 379.

Gernsbacher, M. A. (1984). Resolving 20 years of inconsistent interactions between lexical familiarity and orthography, concreteness, and polysemy. *Journal of Experimental Psychology: General, 113*, 256 - 281.

Gerrig, R. J. (1986). Process and products of lexical access. *Language and Cognitive Processes, 1*, 187 - 195.

Glucksberg, S., & Keysar, B. (in press). Understanding metaphoric comparisons: Beyond similarity. *Psychological Review.*

Glushko, R. J. (1979). The organization and activation of orthographic knowledge in reading aloud. *Journal of Experimental Psychology: Human Perception and Performance, 5*, 674 - 691.

Golden, R. M. (1985). A developmental neural model of word perception. *Proceedings of the seventh annual meeting of the Cognitive Science Society.* Hillsdale, NJ: Lawrence Erlbaum Associates.

Gordon, B. (1983). Lexical access and lexical decision: Mechanisms of frequency sensitivity. *Journal of Verbal Learning and Verbal Behavior, 22*, 24 - 44.

Gough, P. B., & Cosky, M. J. (1977). One second of reading again. In N. J. Castellan, Jr., D. B. Pisoni, & G. R. Potts (Eds.), *Cognitive Theory* (Vol. 2, pp. 271 - 288). Hillsdale, NJ: Lawrence Erlbaum Associates.

Hanna, P. R., Hanna, J. S., Hodges, R. E., & Rudorf, E. H. (1966). *Phoneme-grapheme correspondences as cues to spelling improvement.* Washington, DC: US Department of Health, Education and Welfare.

Henderson, L. (1982). *Orthography and word recognition in reading.* London: Academic Press.

Hinton, G. E., McClelland, J. L., & Rumelhart, D. E. (1986). Distributed representations. In D. E. Rumelhart, J. L. McClelland, & the PDP research group (Eds.), *Parallel distributed processing: Explorations in the microstructure of cognition: Vol. 1. Foundations* (pp. 77 - 109). Cambridge, MA: MIT Press.

Hooper, J. B. (1976). Word frequency in lexical diffusion and the source of morphophonological change. In W. M. Christie (Ed.), *Current progress in historical linguistics* (pp. 95 - 105). Amsterdam: North-Holland.

Jared, D., & Seidenberg, M. S. (in press). Naming multisyllabic words. *Journal of Experimental Psychology: Human Perception and Performance.*

Jordan, M. I. (1986, May). *Serial order: A parallel distributed processing approach.* Institute for Cognitive Science Report 8604. University of California, San Diego.

Katz, J. J., & Fodor, J. A. (1963). The structure of a semantic theory. *Language, 39*, 170 - 210.

Katz, L., & Feldman, L. B. (1981). Linguistic coding in word recognition: Comparisons between a deep and a shallow orthography. In A. M. Lesgold & C. A. Perfetti (Eds.), *Interactive processes in reading* (pp. 85 - 106). Hillsdale, NJ: Lawrence Erlbaum Associates.

Kawamoto, A. (1988). Distributed representations of ambiguous words and their resolution in a connectionist network. In S. Small, G. Cottrell, & M. K. Tanenhaus (Eds.), *Lexical ambiguity resolution: Perspectives from psycholinguistics, neuropsychology, and artificial intelligence* (pp. 195 - 228). San Mateo, CA: Morgan Kauffman.

Keil, F. C. (1981). Constraints on knowledge and cognitive development. *Psychological Review, 88*, 197 - 227.

Kleiman, G. M. (1975). Speech recoding in reading. *Journal of Verbal Learning and Verbal Behavior, 14,* 323 - 339.

Kučera, H., & Francis, W. N. (1967). *Computational analysis of present-day American English.* Providence, RI: Brown University Press.

Lacouture, Y. (1989). From mean square error to reaction time: A connectionist model of word recognition. In D. Touretsky, G. Hinton, & T. Sejnowski (Eds.), *Proceedings of the 1988 Connectionist Models Summer School* (pp. 178 - 187). San Mateo, CA: Morgan Kauffman.

Landauer, T. K., & Streeter, L. A. (1973). Structural differences between common and rare words: Failure of equivalence assumptions for theories of word recognition. *Journal of Verbal Learning and Verbal Behavior, 12,* 119 - 131.

Liberman, M., & Prince, A. (1977). On stress and linguistic rhythm. *Linguistic Inquiry, 8,* 249 - 336.

Lukatela, G., Feldman, L. B., Turvey, M. T., Carello, C., & Katz, L. (1989). Context effects in bi-alphabetical word perception. *Journal of Memory and Language, 28,* 214 - 236.

McCann, R. S., & Besner, D. (1987). Reading pseudohomophones: Implications for models of pronunciation assembly and the locus of word-frequency effects in naming. *Journal of Experimental Psychology: Human Perception and Performance, 13,* 14 - 24.

McClelland, J. L., & Rumelhart, D. E. (1981). An interactive activation model of context effects in letter perception: Part 1. An account of basic findings. *Psychological Review, 88,* 375 - 407.

McCusker, L. X., Hillinger, M. L., & Bias, R. G. (1981). Phonological recoding and reading. *Psychological Bulletin, 89,* 217 - 245.

McRae, K., Jared, D., & Seidenberg, M. S. (1990). On the roles of frequency and lexical access in word naming. *Journal of Memory and Language, 29,* 43 - 65.

Merrill, E. C., Sperber, R. D., & McCauley, C. (1981). Differences in semantic encoding as a function of reading comprehension skill. *Memory & Cognition, 9,* 618 - 624.

Meyer, D. E., Schvaneveldt, R. W., & Ruddy, M. G. (1974). Functions of graphemic and phonemic codes in visual word-recognition. *Memory & Cognition, 2,* 309 - 321.

Miceli, G., Silveri, M. C., & Caramazza, A. (1985). Cognitive analysis of a case of pure dysgraphia. *Brain and Language, 25,* 187 - 212.

Monsell, S. (1985). Repetition and the lexicon. In A. W. Ellis (Ed.), *Progress in the psychology of language* (Vol. 2, pp. 147 - 195). Hillsdale, NJ: Lawrence Erlbaum Associates.

Monsell, S. (1987). On the relation between lexical input and output pathways for speech. In A. Allport, D. G. MacKay, W. Prinz, & E. Scheerer (Eds.), *Language perception and production: Relationships between listening, speaking, reading, and writing* (pp. 273 - 312). London: Academic Press.

Monsell, S., Doyle, M. C., & Haggard, P. N. (1989). Effects of frequency on visual word recognition tasks: Where are they? *Journal of Experimental Psychology: General, 118,* 43 - 71.

Morton, J. (1969). The interaction of information in word recognition. *Psychological Review, 76,* 165 - 178.

Navon, D. (1984). Resources: A theoretical soupstone? *Psychological Review, 91,* 216 - 234.

Neely, J. H. (1977). Semantic priming and retrieval from lexical memory: Roles of inhibitionless spreading activation and limited-capacity attention. *Journal of Experimental Psychology: General, 106,* 226 - 254.

Patterson, K. E., Marshall, J. C., & Coltheart, M. (1985). *Surface dyslexia: Neuropsychological and cognitive studies of phonological reading.* London: Lawrence Erlbaum Associates.

Patterson, K. E., Seidenberg, M. S., & McClelland, J. L. (1989). Connections and disconnections: Dyslexia in a computational model of reading. In P. Morris (Ed.), *Parallel distributed processing: Implications for psychology and neuroscience.* Oxford: Oxford University Press.

Patterson, K., & Shewell, C. (1987). Speak and spell: Dissociations and word-class effects. In M. Coltheart, G. Sartori, & R. Job (Eds.), *The cognitive neuropsychology of language* (pp. 273 - 294). London: Lawrence Erlbaum Associates.

Perfetti, C. A., & McCutchen, D. (1982). Speech processes in reading. In N. J. Lass (Ed.), *Speech and language: Advances in basic research and practice* (Vol. 7, pp. 238 - 269). New York: Academic Press.

Pinker, S., & Prince, A. (1988). On language and connectionism: Analysis of a parallel distributed processing model of language acquisition. *Cognition, 28,* 73 - 193.

Ratcliff, R., & McKoon, G. (1988). A retrieval theory of priming in memory. *Psychological Review, 95,* 385 - 408.

Rayner, K. (1978). Eye movements in reading and information processing. *Psychological Bulletin, 85,* 618 - 660.

Rayner, K., & Duffy, S. A. (1986). Lexical complexity and fixation times in reading: Effects of word frequency, verb complexity, and lexical ambiguity. *Memory & Cognition, 14,* 191 - 201.

Rubenstein, H., Garfield, L., & Millikan, J. A. (1970). Homographic entries in the internal lexicon. *Journal of Verbal Learning and Verbal Behavior, 9,* 487 - 494.

Rubenstein, H., Lewis, S. S., & Rubenstein, M. A. (1971). Evidence for phonemic recoding in visual word recognition. *Journal of Verbal Learning and Verbal Behavior, 10,* 645 - 657.

Rumelhart, D. E., Hinton, G. E., & Williams, R. J. (1986). Learning internal representations by error propagation. In D. E. Rumelhart, J. L. McClelland, & the PDP research group (Eds.), *Parallel distributed processing: Explorations in the microstructure of cognition: Vol. 1. Foundations* (pp. 318 - 362). Cambridge, MA: MIT Press.

Rumelhart, D. E., & McClelland, J. L. (1986). On learning the past tenses of English verbs. In J. L. McClelland, D. E. Rumelhart, & the PDP research group (Eds.), *Parallel distributed processing: Explorations in the microstructure of cognition: Vol. 2. Psychological and biological models* (pp. 216 - 271). Cambridge, MA: MIT Press.

Rumelhart, D. E., Smolensky, P., McClelland, J. L., & Hinton, G. E. (1986). Schemata and sequential thought processes in PDP models. In J. L. McClelland & D. E. Rumelhart (Eds.), *Parallel distributed processing: Explorations in the microstructure of cognition: Vol. 2. Psychological and biological models* (pp. 7 - 57). Cambridge, MA: MIT Press.

Schwanenflugel, P. J., & Shoben, E. J. (1985). The influence of sentence constraint on the scope of facilitation for upcoming words. *Journal of Memory and Language, 24,* 232 - 252.

Seidenberg, M. S. (1985). The time course of information activation and utilization in visual word recognition. In D. Besner, T. G. Waller, & G. E. MacKinnon (Eds.), *Reading research: Advances in theory and practice.* (Vol. 5, pp. 199 - 252). New York: Academic Press.

Seidenberg, M. S. (1988). Cognitive neuropsychology and language: The state of the art. *Cognitive Neuropsychology, 5,* 413 - 426.

Seidenberg, M. S. (1989). Visual word recognition and naming: A computational model and its implications. In W. D. Marslen-Wilson (Ed.), *Lexical representation and process* (pp. 25 - 74). Cambridge, MA: MIT Press.

Seidenberg, M. S., & McClelland, J. L. (1989). A distributed, developmental model of visual word recognition and naming. *Psychological Review, 96,* 523 - 568.

Seidenberg, M. S., McRae, K., & Jared, D. (1988, November). *Frequency and consistency effects in naming.* Paper presented at the meeting of the Psychonomic Society, Chicago, IL.

Seidenberg, M. S., Waters, G. S., Barnes, M. A., & Tanenhaus, M. K. (1984). When does irregular spelling or pronunciation influence word recognition? *Journal of Verbal Learning and Verbal Behavior, 23,* 383 - 404.

Sejnowski, T. J., & Rosenberg, C. R. (1986). *NETtalk: A parallel network that learns to read aloud.* (Technical Report JHU/EECS - 86/01). Baltimore, MD: Johns Hopkins University.

Shallice, T., Warrington, E. K., & McCarthy, R. (1983). Reading without semantics. *Quarterly Journal of Experimental Psychology, 35A,* 111 - 138.

Shulman, H. G., Hornak, R., & Sanders, E. (1978). The effects of graphemic, phonetic, and semantic relationships on access to lexical structures. *Memory & Cognition, 6,* 115 - 123.

Smith, E. E., & Medin, D. (1981). *Categories and concepts.* Cambridge, MA: Harvard University Press.

Smolensky, P. (1988). On the proper treatment of connectionism. *Behavioral and Brain Sciences, 11,* 1 - 74.

Stanovich, K. E., & West, R. F. (1981). The effect of sentence context on ongoing word recognition: Tests of a two-process theory. *Journal of Experimental Psychology: Human Perception and Performance, 7,* 658 - 672.

Sternberg, S., Monsell, S., Knoll, R. L., & Wright, C. E. (1978). The latency and duration of rapid movement sequences: Comparisons of speech and typing. In G. E. Stelmach (Ed.), *Information processing in motor control and learning* (pp. 117 - 152). New York: Academic Press.

Theios, J., & Amrhein, P. C. (1989). Theoretical analysis of the cognitive processing of lexical and pictorial stimuli: Reading, naming, and visual and conceptual comparisons. *Psychological Review, 96,* 5 - 24.

Turvey, M. T., Feldman, L. B., & Lukatela, G. (1984). The Serbo-Croatian orthography constrains the reader to a phonologically analytic strategy. In L. Henderson (Ed.), *Orthographies and reading* (pp. 81 - 90). London: Lawrence Erlbaum Associates.

Van Orden, G. C., Johnston, J. C., & Hale, B. L. (1988). Word identification in reading proceeds from spelling to sound to meaning. *Journal of Experimental Psychology: Learning, Memory, and Cognition, 14,* 371 - 386.

Venezky, R. L. (1970). *The structure of English orthography.* The Hague: Mouton.

Wang, W. S.-Y. (1979). Language change: A lexical perspective. *Annual Review of Anthropology, 8,* 353 - 371.

Waters, G. S., & Seidenberg, M. S. (1985). Spelling-sound effects in reading: Time course and decision criteria. *Memory & Cognition, 13*, 557 - 572.
Wijk, A. (1966). *Rules of pronunciation of the English language.* Oxford: Oxford University Press.

4

DOES THE READING SYSTEM NEED A LEXICON?

Derek Besner
University of Waterloo

INTRODUCTION

Every field has its sacred cows, and visual word recognition is no exception. Two such sacred cows are the assumptions that the mind contains several lexica of word forms and that there are a number of routines that make use of these word forms in various ways to read aloud, make lexical decisions, and access meaning. These assumptions are common to what otherwise are a number of quite different word recognition models (e.g., Balota & Chumbley, 1984; Becker, 1976, 1979; Besner & Johnston, 1989; Besner & McCann, 1987; Forster, 1976; Meyer & Schvaneveldt, 1971; Morton, 1969, 1979; Norris, 1986; Paap, McDonald, Schvaneveldt, & Noel, 1987; Paap, Newsome, McDonald, & Schvaneveldt, 1982; Rubenstein, Lewis, & Rubenstein, 1971; Treisman, 1960). Moreover, these basic assumptions have gone unchallenged – until recently. The parallel distributed processing model (PDP) developed by McClelland and his colleagues (e.g., Patterson, Seidenberg, & McClelland, in press; Seidenberg & McClelland, 1989) is unique in that it has no lexicon. Reading aloud, accessing semantics, and making lexical decisions to different types of alphabetic letter strings are all processes that are accomplished without a lexicon.

In what follows I first briefly review some of the evidence that has traditionally been taken to support both the concept of a lexicon and the use of multiple routines, and then I briefly describe how the PDP model handles these data. Other data are then presented that this particular PDP model cannot account for at its present level of development. I conclude that it is still useful to suppose that the reading system incorporates some form of lexicon and associated multiple routines. If this view is correct, then *lexical* access is a necessary preliminary to word comprehension.

THE LEXICAL MODEL OF VISUAL WORD IDENTIFICATION AND PRODUCTION: SOME STANDARD ASSUMPTIONS

The lexical model of visual word recognition and oral reading refers to a class of models (e.g., Coltheart, 1980; Morton & Patterson, 1980) containing a number of assumptions that are useful to recapitulate for the present discussion.

The lexical system is responsible for word recognition and production and consists of two main components: an orthographic lexicon and a phonological lexicon. The orthographic lexicon contains lexical entries for the spellings of all the words that a reader knows, whereas the phonological lexicon contains lexical entries for the sounds of all the words that a reader knows. In contrast to the lexical systems, which are linguistic in nature and represent the words of a language, the semantic system is conceptual in nature. The lexical and semantic systems are highly interactive, such that the orthographic lexicon and the phonological lexicon both address and receive inputs from the semantic system, as well as each other (see Figure 4.1).

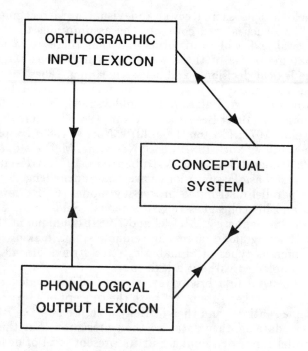

FIGURE 4.1. Architecture of the lexical-semantic system.

Producing a Phonological Representation

The phonological representation of a printed word can be produced in two ways: First, the phonology corresponding to a printed word can be produced by *assembling* phonology from orthographic segments smaller than a word. Current controversy concerns whether this is done by recourse to rules, lexical analogies, or some combination of both, but the details of this particular controversy need not concern us here. Interested readers may wish to consult Humphreys and Evett (1985), Patterson and Coltheart (1987) and Brown and Besner (1987) for a variety of views. Second, the phonology corresponding to a printed word can also be produced by first locating the whole word entry in the orthographic input lexicon. The whole word form in the phonological output lexicon is then *addressed* through lexical–lexical connections. (Phonology may also be obtained via a semantic route, but that additional routine need not concern us at present.)

These assumptions form the kernel of what is commonly referred to as *two route theory* or *dual routines* (see Patterson and Coltheart, 1987, for a review). These routines can be used for purposes such as lexical decision, phonological lexical decision, oral reading, and as a preliminary to the retrieval of semantic knowledge. Evidence for the distinction between these two routines comes from two principal sources: studies of acquired dyslexias and experiments with intact college students.

The Addressed-Assembled Distinction: Evidence from Acquired Dyslexia

In so-called *phonological dyslexia* (e.g., Patterson, 1982), the patient is severely impaired at reading aloud nonwords but retains the ability to read aloud words that were known prior to the onset of the dyslexia. The most common explanation is that the assembled routine is impaired, leaving the addressed routine intact. As nonwords do not have word-level entries in the orthographic lexicon, they cannot be read via the addressed routine. The assembled routine provides the only basis for the oral reading of nonwords. Because the assembled routine is impaired, there is a deficit in nonword reading. In contrast, words, which do have lexical entries, can be read aloud correctly using the intact addressed routine.

In so-called *surface dyslexia* (e.g., Patterson, Marshall, & Coltheart, 1985), the dissociation is manifested in the opposite direction: Patients can read aloud both nonwords and words that are regular in terms of their spelling to sound correspondences, but they have difficulty with words that are irregular in this regard. This deficit suggests that the addressed routine is impaired and the assembled routine intact, if we are prepared to assume that (a) irregular words are difficult to read aloud using the assembled routine (imagine trying to read *chaos* or *yacht* via this routine), and (b) some proportion of the entries in the orthographic lexicon are impossible to access, or, having been accessed, fail to allow access to the phonological-semantic system. As there is no reason why these difficulties should differentially impair regular and irregular words when reading aloud via the addressed routine, the fact that regular words are less impaired than irregular words is ascribed to the assembled routine's difficulty with irregular words.

It is beyond the scope of this chapter to discuss these reading disorders in any detail. Interested readers may wish to peruse the reviews and original investigations contained in Coltheart, Patterson, and Marshall (1980), Patterson et al. (1985) and Coltheart, Sartori, and Job (1987), among others. For present purposes, the important point is that oral reading by the dyslexic patients described here has typically been explained in terms of two separable routines. In phonological dyslexia the assembled routine is held to be impaired with the addressed routine intact. Surface dyslexia presents the mirror image: the addressed routine is impaired, whereas the assembled routine is intact.

The Addressed-Assembled Distinction:
Evidence from Oral Reading by Intact Subjects

Another approach that provides evidence compatible with the addressed-assembled distinction comes from oral reading studies carried out with intact college students. Two findings are relevant to the present discussion:

1. Subjects read words aloud faster than nonwords (e.g., Forster & Chambers, 1973) even when the nonword sounds like a real word (McCann & Besner, 1987). The correct pronunciations for words (provided they are regular) can be produced by either the addressed or assembled routine. However, as there are no lexical representations for nonwords in the orthographic lexicon, nonwords must of necessity use the assembled routine. If we assume that the addressed routine is on average faster than the assembled routine, this would explain why words are named faster than nonwords.

2. The naming of high- and low-frequency words is differentially affected by regularity. High-frequency words are named faster than low-frequency words, but high-frequency words are unaffected by regularity, whereas lower-frequency words are slower to name if they are irregular as compared to regular (cf. Seidenberg, Waters, Barnes, & Tanenhaus, 1984; Waters & Seidenberg, 1985). One explanation is that high frequency words, regardless of regularity, are always read by the addressed routine because this routine produces an output more rapidly than the assembled routine. In contrast, low-frequency words are processed sufficiently slowly by the addressed routine that output from the assembled routine is also available. When the output from these two routines is different, as is the case with irregular words, it takes time to resolve the conflict. This conflict results in the slower naming for irregular words.

Hence, considerable data on oral reading collected from both neurologically impaired and intact subjects can readily be interpreted within a common framework that holds that there are two distinct ways of producing phonology from a printed letter string.

AN ALTERNATIVE ACCOUNT OF ORAL READING AND LEXICAL DECISION: A PDP MODEL

Seidenberg and McClelland (1989) have developed a parallel distributed processing model of visual word recognition that purports to provide an account of oral reading and lexical decision. This model is described in detail elsewhere (see Patterson et al., in press; Seidenberg & McClelland, 1989). Space limitations preclude more than a brief sketch of the bare bones of the model.

The model consists of three levels of units. A visually presented letter string first makes contact with a set of orthographic units. These units feed forward to a set of hidden units, which in turn project to a layer of units that correspond to phonetic patterns. When the model is at steady state, there is feedback from the hidden units to the orthographic level, but not from the phonetic level to the hidden units. Each unit at the orthographic level is connected to every hidden unit, and every hidden unit is connected back to every unit at the orthographic level. Similarly, every hidden unit is connected to every unit at the phonetic level.

The orthographic units are, essentially, distributed letter pattern detectors. When a letter string is presented, it is coded at the orthographic level by a pattern of activation across the entire set of units. Activation then spreads to the hidden units. This pattern of activation across all the hidden units is mediated by variations in the strength of individual connections between levels. These connection strengths are adjusted during training so as to minimize the difference between the pattern of activation at the orthographic level consequent to presentation of the letter string, and the pattern of activation at the orthographic level following feedback from the hidden units.

The hidden units also feed forward to the phonetic level to create a pattern of activation across all these units. The weights on the connections from the hidden units to the phonetic level are also adjusted during training so as to minimize the difference between the pattern of activation across the phonetic level resulting from input from the hidden units, and the pattern of activation externally imposed upon the phonetic level to represent a target item during training.

These differences in the patterns of activation can be converted into error scores. The *smaller* the error score, the better the performance (see Seidenberg & McClelland, 1989, for a discussion of the assumptions that suppose that these error scores are monotonically related to Response time and accuracy).

There are two error scores: the orthographic error score and the phonological error score. The orthographic error score represents how closely the pattern of activation produced over the orthographic units following feedback from the hidden units approximates the original pattern of activation over the same units when a letter string is presented to the model. The phonological error score represents the similarity of the pattern of activation across the phonological units produced by presentation of a letter string, as compared to the pattern of activation across these same phonological units when the desired output, specified in terms of phonemes, is fed directly to the phonological units. Naming performance is therefore assessed by presenting a letter string to the model and examining the magnitude of the error score it produces at the phonological level. Lexical-decision performance is discussed at length in the second section of the discussion on phonology and the PDP model.

For present purposes, the important elements of the model are that it functions without any lexicon or multiple routines. The addressed-assembled distinction does not exist in the context of this model; regular words, irregular words, and nonwords are all read aloud via the same single routine. Despite this minimal architecture, the model is able to simulate the pattern of performance described earlier. Oral reading performance is better with words than with nonwords, and better with high-frequency words than low-frequency words. Regularity of spelling-sound correspondence affects low- but not high-frequency words. Given the model's success, it can be argued that the oral reading data obtained from intact human subjects simply do not demand an explanation couched in terms of word-level representations and multiple routines.

What about the neuropsychological evidence suggesting a dissociation between addressed and assembled phonology? Clearly, there is a dissociation between the reading of words and nonwords and between regular and irregular words. The difficulty is that it is unclear whether such data can be interpreted only within a framework that assumes a distinction between assembled and addressed routines. The fairest conclusion at present may be that the relation between the neuropsychological evidence associated with oral reading and the performance of the single routine PDP model is currently an unsettled issue. This is hardly surprising, given that the attempt to simulate brain damaged performance is in its infancy (see Patterson et al., in press). Nonetheless, a model capable of explaining performance by both intact and brain-damaged readers is preferable to a model explaining only one or the other. It is hoped that Seidenberg and McClelland will address this issue in the near future.

ON THE PSYCHOLOGICAL REALITY OF THE ADDRESSED-ASSEMBLED DISTINCTION: SOME OLD AND NEW EVIDENCE

Given the PDP model's success in utilizing only a single routine to simulate data that previously had been interpreted as reflecting at least two separable routines, it seems clear that more powerful evidence is needed to reject the single-process view. One such line of evidence is offered in the following discussion. I first consider the occurrence of regularity effects in lexical decision and naming, and I adopt the traditional view that the presence or absence of regularity effects provides an index of whether addressed or assembled routines are involved. I then review evidence that cAsE aLtErNaTiOn and word frequency differentially affect the two routines. More specifically, these two factors have *additive* effects on reaction time performance when the addressed routine is operative but *interactive* effects when the assembled routine makes a contribution to performance. These data seem problematic for the single routine PDP model, because they suggest *qualitative* differences in performance between two classes of words.

Regularity Effects in Naming and Lexical Decision

In the lexical-decision task, locating an entry in the orthographic lexicon is a sufficient basis for a correct response. In contrast, the naming task requires the output of a phonological code. This difference results in differential effects of regularity in the two tasks.

As already noted, regularity affects the *naming* of low- but not high-frequency words (Seidenberg, 1985; Seidenberg et al., 1984; Waters & Seidenberg, 1985). Lexical decision, on the other hand, is typically unaffected by regularity in college level readers, arguably because the addressed routine is able to locate a lexical entry in the orthographic lexicon before the assembled routine can make any contribution to performance (e.g., Coltheart, Besner, Jonasson, & Davelaar, 1979; Seidenberg et al., 1984). However, regularity effects may appear for low frequency words in lexical decision when some proportion of the stimuli are composed of unusual spelling (operationalized as low bigram frequency by Seidenberg et al., 1984; e.g., *aisle*). Unusual spelling makes it harder to discriminate words from nonwords, thus slowing the decision process and allowing the assembled routine time to exert its influence (Waters & Seidenberg, 1985).

It is also interesting to note that phonological effects in lexical decision are also present for low frequency words in younger readers (cf. Frederiksen, 1978), even without unusually spelled words in the background context. I suggest that this occurs because these low-frequency words have not been encountered sufficiently often in print for the addressed routine to function efficiently enough to escape the effects of competition from the assembled routine.

Two Effects of Case Alternation: Letter and Multiletter Unit Identification

Case alternating a letter string slows performance in both lexical decision and naming (e.g., Besner, 1983). According to one explanation, there are two separate loci for this effect: preliminary-letter identification and identification of adjacent multiletter visual units that correspond to a phoneme (see Besner & Johnston, 1989, for a review and extended discussion). The impairment of individual letter identification could arise because (a) the search set is larger (one out of 52 instead of one out of 26) or (b) because certain letters are harder to discriminate from each other when both cases are used (e.g., *I* and *l*). Either or both of these possibilities can account for why the letter identification process is impaired.

It is assumed that use of the addressed route relies upon preliminary-letter identification, whereas use of the assembled route relies on preliminary letter recognition and/or multiletter visual units that correspond to a phoneme. Case alternation thus has a more deleterious impact upon assembled than addressed phonology, because when an attempt to use adjacent multiletter visual information is foiled, the reader must restart the process from scratch, this time by identifying individual letters.

On the Interaction of Case Alternation, Word Frequency, and the Addressed-Assembled Distinction

Given the stated interpretation of regularity and case alternation effects in terms of the operation of addressed and assembled routines, several predictions follow naturally.

1. *Case alternation and word frequency should have additive effects in the context of lexical decision when the subjects are college level or good readers.* The absence of regularity effects in lexical decision for good readers has been argued to reflect use of the addressed routine only (Coltheart et al., 1979; Seidenberg et al., 1984; Waters & Seidenberg, 1985). Under these circumstances, the only effect of case alternation is to delay letter identification. As letter identification is a preliminary to word identification, and word frequency exerts its influence at or beyond the word-identification stage, case alternation and word frequency can be seen as factors influencing separate, successive stages. The results of three studies are consistent with this analysis. Frederiksen (1978), Kinoshita (1987), and Besner and McCann (1987) have all reported experiments in which case alternation and word frequency have additive effects upon response time in the context of lexical decision.

2. *Case alternation should affect low frequency words more than high frequency words in lexical decision when the subjects are young readers.* For word-recognition skills, the developmental sequence is one in which a contribution from assembled phonology is more likely in younger rather than older readers, and for low- rather than high-frequency words (e.g., see Seidenberg, 1985). The interaction of case alternation and word frequency will therefore arise for the same reasons given for this interaction in the context of oral reading by college students (see 3). Frederiksen (1978, Experiment 3) reported that case alternation and word frequency are strongly interacting factors provided that the subjects were high school readers of lower ability. If we assume that lower ability high school readers can be considered equivalent to young readers, the data are consistent with the prediction.

3. *Naming: Case alternation should affect low-frequency words more than high-frequency words, and nonwords more than words.* As argued for skilled readers, high-frequency words depend upon the addressed routine only, whereas low frequency words also draw upon the contribution of the assembled routine. When the addressed routine is used, case alternation exercises its effect upon letter identification alone. Both parsing into multiletter units and letter identification are disrupted when the assembled routine is employed. Consequently, case alternation effects are greater for low- as compared to high-frequency words, as can be seen in Besner and McCann (1987). Because the assembled routine is *always* used to name nonwords, but only makes a contribution to word naming *some* of the time, case alternation impairs the naming of nonwords more than words, as can be seen in Besner and Johnston (1989).

4. *Cross task and cross reader type comparisons when the stimulus set is held constant.* The data are even more compelling when we consider the *same* stimulus set across *reader type.* Frederiksen (1978) reported that case alternation and word frequency were additive factors in lexical decision when the subjects were good high school readers, (i.e., when only that component of the addressed routine is used which locates an entry in the orthographic lexicon), but interacting factors when the subjects were high school readers of lower ability (i.e., when the assembled routine makes a contribution to performance).

When a constant stimulus set is utilized with college level readers, the predicted *task* differences emerge. Besner and McCann (1987) found that case alternation and word frequency are additive factors in lexical decision (as expected because only the addressed routine is typically operative), but interacting factors in the context of naming (as expected because the assembled routine makes a contribution for low frequency words).

A New Prediction

What other predictions follow from the analysis presented here? One prediction is that the interaction between case alternation and word frequency in the naming task should disappear – provided that all the items are *irregular* in terms of their spelling-sound correspondence, thereby forcing the use of the addressed routine regardless of word frequency. If subjects are able to restrict themselves to utilizing the output of the addressed routine alone, the only effect of case alternation will be a constant delay to letter identification. The results of such an experiment are shown in Table 4.1. Both case alternation and word frequency produce large and statistically reliable main effects, but there is no trace of an interaction between these two factors. When all the stimuli in the experiment are irregular, case alternation and word frequency have additive effects in the naming task.

TABLE 4.1

Mean Response Latencies (ms) and Error Rate
for Naming High-and Low-Frequency Words
with Irregular Spelling-Sound Correspondences
(N = 32, with 24 observations per cell per subject).

	Lower Case		Case Alternated	
	Latencies	Percent Errors	Latencies	Percent Errors
High	490	1.0	524	8.8
Low	549	0.9	584	7.8

Conclusions

The standard view is that dual routines are operative in visual word identification, particularly naming. This view has been challenged by Seidenberg and McClelland (1989) on the grounds that their single routine PDP model successfully simulates data that have typically been interpreted in terms of these dual routines.

I argued that the traditional dual routine model, when coupled with some assumptions about how case alternation impairs letter identification and parsing of adjacent multiletter visual units, makes some new and straightforward predictions about how performance will vary as a function of lexical class (high-frequency words, low-frequency words, nonwords), stimulus type (regular words, irregular words), task (naming, lexical decision), and reader level (expert, inexpert). A review of the literature and the results of a new experiment confirm these predictions. It will be interesting to see whether a single routine PDP model can simulate these data.

I conclude that these data are consistent with the traditional assumption that at least two lexicons (an orthographic lexicon and a phonological lexicon) and two routines (addressed and assembled) are operative in visual word identification and production. The traditional view, which supposes that these representation-process pairs are a preliminary to meaning access, is therefore still a viable working assumption, as I can see no reason that they should have evolved only to subserve processes such as lexical decision and naming.

PHONOLOGY AND THE PDP MODEL: SOME FORMAL TESTS

The next section takes a different approach toward trying to examine the adequacy of the single routine PDP model. Simply put, will the model produce effects that are seen in the literature if the stimuli from published experiments are run through the simulation? To this end I first briefly review results from several standard experiments in which subjects either name a letter string or make a lexical decision to it. I then discuss the results produced by the PDP model when the stimuli from these experiments are submitted to the simulation and discuss the implications.

Oral Reading of Nonwords

Standard dual routine theory has it that nonwords are always read aloud via the use of assembled phonology, a process held to be distinct from addressed phonology, the process that produces the oral reading of familiar words. In contrast, the PDP model holds that both words and nonwords are read aloud through the use of the exact same process. A straightforward question concerns how well the model does on the oral reading of nonwords relative to words. Seidenberg and McClelland have already demonstrated that, in the case of words which the model has been trained on, the pattern of activation produced across the phonological level almost always fits the desired phonological target better than it fits any other candidate. However, they report remarkably little data on the reading of nonwords. I therefore examined the model's performance on a tightly matched set of 79 words, pseudohomophones, and control items because (a) we already know how well real subjects perform on this stimulus set (McCann & Besner, 1987) and (b) over 95% of the real word counterparts of these pseudohomophones belong to the corpus of words that Seidenberg and McClelland's model is trained on.

The data can be seen in Table 4.2. The critical point concerns what the pattern of activation produced across the phonological units best corresponds to. For the pseudohomophones, 41% of the phonological patterns fit an alternative phonological target better than the desired target (i.e., the alternative target produces a smaller phonological error score than the desired target). For the control strings this figure is 49%.[1] In contrast, when college-level readers pronounce these same items under speed pressure, the error rate is five times smaller than the values produced by the model. Although the model does very well with the *properly spelled* words, its performance with the nonwords is very poor.

In this regard, the model behaves more like a phonological dyslexic than it does like a normal reader (cf. Patterson, 1982). It is tempting to suppose that what Seidenberg and McClelland have done is model a *lexical route*, although it is not labeled as such, and there are no *individuated* lexical entries.

---

[1] This analysis is based upon McClelland's BEATENBY program which lists all the phonological sequences that differ from the target by one phoneme and that yield smaller error scores than the phonological sequence designated as the correct target.

It is unclear at this juncture precisely why the model does so poorly with these nonwords. One possibility is that details of the model's implementation need tinkering with. For example, there may be too many hidden units in the model and/or the encoding scheme is too crude. Another possibility is that a separate routine for dealing with nonwords may have to be incorporated into the model.

TABLE 4.2

*Proportion of "Correct" Pronunciations by the Model
and by Normal Subjects under Speed Pressure.*

	Words	Pseudo-homophones	Controls
Model	.987	.590	.510
Humans	.978	.943	.886

Can the Model do Lexical Decision Without a Lexicon? The Case of Regularity Effects

How does the model do lexical decision? Seidenberg and McClelland (1989) assume that what the reader does is compute the *orthographic* error score, and subject it to a familiarity assessment much like that described by Balota and Chumbley (1984) and Atkinson and Juola (1973). The subject compares the error score to a criterion value adopted on the basis of experience with prior word and nonword error scores, the relative frequency of words and nonwords, and instructional factors, as standardly assumed in signal detection experiments. If the error score is below a criterion, the subject treats it as evidence that the stimulus is sufficiently familiar that it is likely to correspond to a word and responds *yes*. If the error score is above the criterion, then the subject treats it as a nonword and responds *no*. The placement of the criterion is chosen so as to yield an acceptable error rate. When the distributions of error scores for words and nonwords overlap considerably, as is the case when the nonwords consist of familiar spelling patterns (e.g., *slint*) but the words consist of unusual spelling patterns (e.g., *aisle, chaos, mauve*), assessing the orthographic error score leads to an unacceptably high error rate. Seidenberg and McClelland therefore assumed that under these conditions "subjects assess the familiarity of the stimuli in terms of the computed phonological output." Phonological effects (e.g., the regularity effect) will therefore emerge when the familiarity assessment is carried out at the phonological level, not when this assessment is carried out at the orthographic level.

Seidenberg and McClelland are concerned to demonstrate that the model can do lexical decision, because standard accounts of the task assume that it is performed by accessing the kinds of lexical entries that the model lacks. When the model is successful, their main point is that distributed representations provide a basis for making lexical decisions. Hence, their claim: "The simulations are concerned with cases in which orthographic and phonological information provide a basis for making lexical decisions." This claim bears examination; I therefore consider the model in the context of the data from Waters and Seidenberg (1985), because Seidenberg and McClelland considered that the model successfully simulates these data.

The first piece of data from Waters and Seidenberg (1985) is as follows. There is no regularity effect in lexical decision when orthographically strange words are excluded from the stimulus set. According to Seidenberg and McClelland, under these conditions the orthographic error scores from the model have distributions for words and nonwords that allow a decision criterion to be established that yields an error rate similar to that observed in the actual experiment. The second piece of data is that when orthographically strange words are added to the stimulus set, low-frequency words are now affected by regularity.[2]

Seidenberg and McClelland argued that, under these circumstances, the orthographic error score distributions for words and nonwords overlap so much that an acceptable error rate cannot be achieved upon the basis of an orthographic familiarity assessment. Instead, subjects now conduct a familiarity assessment based upon phonology. Because phonology is being assessed, a regularity effect follows.

The question which Seidenberg and McClelland did not address, however, is whether an assessment of the *phonological* error scores will actually lead to an acceptable error rate. This issue can be addressed in a very straightforward manner, as all we need to do is look at the overlap in the phonological error score distributions for words and nonwords. In Figure 24 of their report, Seidenberg and McClelland plotted the *orthographic* error score distributions for both the words (regular, exception, and strange) and the nonwords from the lexical decision experiment by Waters and Seidenberg (1985). This figure shows that there is considerable overlap in the word and nonword distributions when strange words are included in the stimulus set. These data are displayed in Figure 4.2. The corresponding phonological error scores were obtained from the model and are also plotted in Figure 4.2. It is clear that there is

---

[2] It should be noted, however, that 50% of Waters and Seidenberg's low-frequency "strange" words are also homophones (e.g., *chute, sword, heir, aisle, corps, seize*). This turns out to be problematic for the PDP model because a regularity effect *is* observed when homophones which are *not* orthographically strange are present in the background. Since under these conditions there is minimal overlap in the orthographic error scores for words and nonwords, the PDP model predicts *no* regularity effect (see Besner et al., in press).

considerable overlap in these distributions as well. This means that lexical decisions based upon a familiarity assessment of the phonological error scores will also lead to an unacceptably high error rate. When there are strange words in the set, it does not appear that the *implemented* model can simulate the lexical decision results reported by Waters and Seidenberg (1985), contrary to the claims by Seidenberg and McClelland.

Of course, in principle, regularity effects in lexical decision may result from a familiarity assessment of *semantic* patterns, following the activation of phonological patterns, as Seidenberg and McClelland themselves

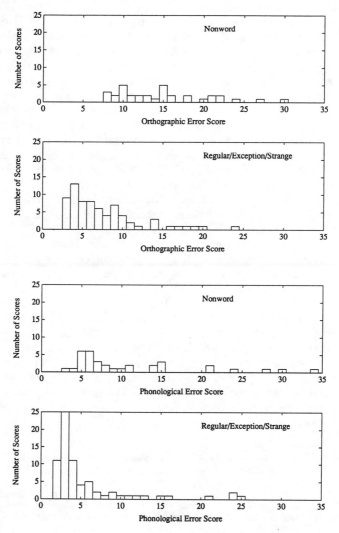

FIGURE 4.2. Orthographic and phonological error scores from Seidenberg's and McClelland's PDP model for the Waters and Seidenberg (1985) stimulus set.

acknowledge. It is unfortunate that it is impossible to assess this, given that the semantic system is not implemented in Seidenberg and McClelland's model at the present time. An alternative explanation, of course, is the traditional one which posits that regularity effects in lexical decision reflect the use of a phonological lexicon.

Pseudohomophone Effects in Lexical Decision and Naming

A stimulus such as *brane* is often referred to as a pseudohomophone in the word-recognition literature because it sounds like a real word despite the fact that it does not spell one. A common finding is that subjects in the lexical-decision task are slower to respond no to pseudohomophones like *brane* than to control items like *frane* (Besner & Davelaar, 1983; Besner, Dennis & Davelaar, 1985; Coltheart, Davelaar, Jonasson, & Besner, 1977; McCann, Besner, & Davelaar, 1988; see also Dennis, Besner, & Davelaar, 1985, for a review of this literature). A related finding is seen in the naming task, except that the direction of the effect is reversed. Pseudohomophones like *brane* are named faster than control items like *frane* (McCann & Besner, 1987).

Pseudohomophones have also been used to explore differences between good and poor young readers (Barron, 1978), differences between left and right hemisphere processing (Cohen & Freeman, 1978), subtyping of young readers (Mitterer, 1982), mechanisms of spelling-to-sound-translation (Pring, 1981), dyslexic reading (Patterson & Marcel, 1977), types of phonological codes (Besner, 1987; Besner & Davelaar, 1982; Besner, Davies, & Daniels, 1981) and to identify the locus of word frequency effects in word recognition, identification and production (McCann & Besner, 1987; McCann et al., 1988).

The standard explanation for these effects assumes that assembled phonology makes contact with lexical entries in the phonological lexicon. In the case of the lexical-decision task, this impairs performance because the output from the phonological lexicon signals the presence of a word (the phonological representation of *brain*) while the output from the orthographic lexicon signals that it is not a word, because there is no orthographic entry corresponding to *brane*. Resolving this conflict takes time. In naming, the process of assembling phonology for a visually presented nonword letter string that corresponds to a real word in the phonological domain is more efficient because of the interaction with a whole word representation in the phonological lexicon; nonwords that do not sound like a real word are denied this benefit (Brown & Besner, 1987; McCann & Besner, 1987).

Before discussing the results of the simulation, a few remarks about Seidenberg and McClelland's views about pseudohomophone effects are in order. Seidenberg and McClelland (1989) stated quite clearly that the model can not produce a *phonologically* based pseudohomophone effect in either naming or lexical decision: "Pseudohomophone effects would appear to be a problem for our model because it lacks word level representations; there does not seem to be a way for the spelling or pronunciation of *brain* to directly influence *brane* because there is no lexical entry for *brain*."

Because the presence of pseudohomophone effects in naming and lexical decision is embarrassing to a model which purports to give an account of these tasks, the tack they pursue is that pseudohomophone effects, when they are present in experiments, are not phonological in nature but simply reflect the fact that pseudohomophones are orthographically more similar to real words known to the reader than are the control items. Seidenberg and McClelland therefore predicted that if pseudohomophones and control items are matched in terms of the orthographic and phonological error scores produced by the model, there will be no pseudohomophone effect in either naming or lexical decision. Indeed, this is the result they reported in one of their experiments. I offer several observations in response to this argument.

First, the experiment they reported in which they failed to find a pseudohomophone in either naming or lexical-decision response times is badly flawed because casual inspection of the stimulus set shows that a number of their control nonwords are actually pseudohomophones (e.g., *hoan* [hone]; *boad* [bode]; *loap* [lope]; *birl* [burl])! Accepting the null hypothesis is a risky business when the stimulus set is as small as theirs (n = 23); inclusion of such items makes it even more suspect.

As I have noted before, Seidenberg and McClelland have repeatedly argued that phonological effects in lexical decision (e.g., a regularity effect) occur only when the orthography of the words is sufficiently unusual that the orthographic scores for words and nonwords overlap considerably. This overlap prevents decisions being made correctly upon the basis of orthography; under these circumstances lexical decisions are based instead upon a familiarity assessment of the *phonological* error scores. Given Seidenberg and McClelland's explicit claims as to how phonological effects arise, one would therefore expect them to test for the presence of a pseudohomophone effect in lexical decision under conditions where the words are orthographically unusual. As Seidenberg and McClelland never specified that the words in this experiment were orthographically unusual, it is unclear to me exactly what the null effect they obtained in this experiment is meant to demonstrate.

I am also inclined to the view that simply matching pseudohomophones and controls on the basis of the orthographic and phonological error scores produced by the model is inadequate because it ignores the fact that (a) in at least one corpus of 80 items, the error scores account for less than 5% of the variance to nonwords in lexical decision (the corpus from McCann et al., 1988); (b) in the model, the phonological pattern of activation produced by Seidenberg and McClelland's pseudohomophone stimulus set actually fits an alternative target better than the intended one in approximately 25% of the cases; and (c) several other factors contribute to whether a pseudohomophone effect will be manifest or not (see Dennis et al., 1985; McCann & Besner, 1987, and McCann et al., 1988, for extended discussion). These points have yet to be addressed by Seidenberg and McClelland.

More generally, Seidenberg and McClelland's account of "lexical decision" is again problematic when they assume that decisions are made *upon the basis of the error scores produced by the implemented model.* Consider the phonological lexical-decision task (e.g., Besner et al., 1981; McCann et al., 1988) in which subjects are presented with a letter string such as *brane* or *frane* and asked to decide whether the letter string sounds like a real word or not (i.e., *brane*-yes; *frane*-no). Because this task requires a phonological judgement, it is presumably carried out at the phonological level. But if the orthographic and phonological error scores for the two stimulus conditions are matched, *then the implemented model has no basis for producing anything better than chance performance.* At the risk of belaboring the point, this is not what happens with real subjects; readers can judge for themselves. The following stimulus pairs are, according to Seidenberg and McClelland, matched for orthographic and phonological error scores: GURST – FURST; GESS – DESS; GLEW – PLEW; HAZZ – CAZZ; CRUVE – PRUVE; TAIP – LAIP; FENT – MENT.

Seidenberg and McClelland have an obvious move available to them in response to this problem. They could argue that *phonological* lexical decision involves the use of *semantic* information. On this argument, pseudohomophones such as WAIK would evoke a pattern of activation across the phonological units, which would in turn provoke activation across semantic units corresponding to WAKE. The discrimination between WAIK and DAIK *could* then be mediated by the semantic system, following phonological access.

There are two observations I would make in response to the suggestion that phonological lexical decision will be mediated by the semantic system:

1. On this theory, it should be *impossible* to find a patient with impaired semantic access who, in terms of accuracy, is as good as normal subjects at phonological lexical decision. Patients such as those described by Whitaker (1976) and Schwartz, Marin, and Saffran (1979) may be good candidates for such a test.

2. We need to know, given a letter string like WAIK, whether the pattern of activation across the phonological units would actually result in a pattern of activation across the semantic units that is indistinguishable from the pattern of activation across the semantic units consequent to the presentation of the letter string WAKE. If the pattern of activation is not highly similar in these cases, the model will not be able to do phonological lexical decision. Some skepticism as to whether these patterns of activation will be sufficiently similar seems natural, given that (a) the phonological error score for a stimulus such as WAIK is 10 times as large as the phonological error score for WAKE, and (b) WAIK, as a phonological target, is beaten by 21 other alternative phonological sequences despite the fact that WAIK is the orthographic string presented to the model (see footnote 1).

Implementation of the semantic system in Seidenberg and McClelland's model will have to come sooner rather than than later if these issues are to be addressed.

Simulation Results

We now turn to the results of this simulation exercise. Does the model produce better performance (i.e., smaller phonological error scores) for the pseudohomophones when confronted with the stimulus set that produced a pseudohomophone effect in the naming and lexical-decision experiments reported by McCann and Besner (1987) and McCann et al. (1988)? Or, as Seidenberg and McClelland would have it, is the pseudohomophone effect seen in the data entirely attributable to differences between pseudohomophones and controls in terms of an orthographic error score difference?

The stimulus set from the naming and lexical decision experiments reported by McCann and Besner (1987) and McCann et al. (1988) were submitted to Seidenberg and McClelland's computational model. Stimuli were presented one at a time to the model and the resulting error scores were examined. These error scores can be seen in Table 4.3, averaged across individual items (n = 79).

TABLE 4.3

Orthographic and Phonological Error Scores
for Pseudohomophones and Controls Produced
by Seidenberg and McClelland's PDP Model.

	Pseudo-homophones	Controls
Orthographic	21.5	23.5
Phonological	16.7	18.1
Phonological* (adjusted)	17.5	17.3

*These values correspond to phonological error scores with orthographic error scores partialled out.

The first fact to note is that the orthographic error score produced by the model is significantly smaller for the pseudohomophones than for the controls ($p < .01$) This result raises the possibility that Seidenberg and McClelland are correct in supposing that the pseudohomophone effects reported by McCann and Besner (1987) and McCann et al. (1988) reflect an orthographic basis to the pseudohomophone effects they observed, rather than a phonological one.

Fortunately, this possibility is easy to assess. If the pseudohomophone effect seen in the human data is entirely orthographic, then partialling out the orthographic contribution to performance by regression techniques using the orthographic error scores from the model against the reaction times from the human data should lead to a total elimination of the pseudohomophone effect. This does not happen; when the orthographic scores are partialled out of the human performance data, a substantial pseudohomophone effect remains in both the naming and lexical-decision data ($p < .001$). *This result strongly supports the standard assumption that the pseudohomophone effect reported in the literature includes a phonological component* (cf. Besner & Davelaar, 1983; Besner et al. 1985).

The problem that remains for the PDP model is more serious. Although the model also produces a pseudohomophone advantage in terms of the phonological error scores (see Table 4.3), these scores are highly correlated with the orthographic errors scores ($r = .78$, $p < .001$). This suggests that the phonological pseudohomophone effect produced by the *model* derives from the fact that the model does better with the pseudohomophones at the orthographic level. This interpretation is supported by the results of an analysis of covariance that partials the orthographic scores out of the phonological error scores. The adjusted phonological error score shows no trace of a pseudohomophone advantage. These data are displayed in the bottom line of Table 4.3.

The conclusion is straightforward: After the orthographic contribution is partialled out, a phonologically based pseudohomophone effect can be observed in the lexical decision and naming data with human subjects. In contrast, the current instantiation of this particular PDP model does not produce a difference between pseudohomophones and controls in the phonological error scores once the orthographic contribution is partialled out.

I conclude that, at it current level of development, the *implemented* version of *this* PDP model does not offer an account of pseudohomophone effects in naming and lexical decision, nor can it provide an account of phonological lexical decision or lexical decision when orthographically strange words are included in the stimulus set.[3] It remains to be seen what kinds of modifications to the model are necessary to allow it to produce such effects and whether the model can be tailored to *these* predictions, while continuing to make presently successful predictions.

---

[3] Seidenberg and McClelland (1989) claimed that "studies of pseudohomophone effects have yielded inconsistent results" and they cite Dennis et al. (1985) and Coltheart et al. (1977) as evidence of this. If by "inconsistent" they mean that Coltheart et al. found a pseudohomophone effect, whereas Dennis et al. failed to find one in one of their experiments, then this claim is difficult to understand. The latter reviewed this literature at length and concluded that the presence/absence of the pseudohomophone effect depends upon the presence/absence of homophones in the stimulus set.

I end this chapter by briefly discussing two other aspects of the simulation's performance with the stimuli from the McCann and Besner (1987) experiment, which present further problems for the model.

MEASURES OF ORTHOGRAPHY

Yet another central claim made by Seidenberg and McClelland (1989) is that their PDP model captures aspects of orthography not well reflected in standard measures and that their model captures *all* aspects of this variation in the pattern of activation across the orthographic units as reflected in the orthographic error scores:

"In effect, the orthographic error scores provide a measure of orthographic familiarity... This measure is also interesting because it derives from everything that the model has encoded about the frequency and distribution of letter patterns in the lexicon. Error scores are a function of the input stimulus and the weights on connections that derive from the entire training experience. *Other measures of orthographic familiarity have been used in word recognition experiments (e.g., positional letter frequencies, bigram frequencies, Coltheart's N measure), with mixed results.* These inconsistent results, we suggest, may be due to the fact that orthographic familiarity as it is reflected in the performance of the adult reader *is better captured by the overlaid effects of the full range of experiences with the structure of words, as in our model,* than by these *other measures,* which reflect only part of the information that is acquired through experience (p. 552, italics mine)."

Given these remarks, it interesting to inquire whether any *other* measure of orthography referred to earlier captures variance *unaccounted* for by the model. I chose to look at Coltheart et al.'s (1977) N measure because (a) Seidenberg and McClelland had already made some specific claims about N, (b) N is often thought of as a measure of *lexical* density – a property that does not exist in the context of this PDP model, and (c) McCann and Besner (1987) reported data concerning the effect of N upon the naming of pseudohomophones and controls.

N (for *Neighbors*) is standardly taken to be a simple measure of lexical density; the number of real-word neighbors that a letter string has (cf. Coltheart et al., 1977; McCann & Besner, 1987; McCann et al., 1988). This measure is calculated by simply totaling up the number of words that can be produced from a target letter string when a single letter at a time is exchanged for any letter that could transform the letter string into another word.

Seidenberg and McClelland have already shown that they can simulate *some* of the effects of N in that the model provides "a very good fit" to Andrews's (1989) observation that as the frequency of a word increases, the effect of neighboring words diminishes. In other words, the model again simulates the effect of a variable without recourse to a lexicon, despite the claim that N is a measure of lexical density.

This cannot be the whole story however. Andrews also found that N effects are the same size for low-frequency words in naming and lexical decision, despite the fact that the word-frequency effect is much smaller in naming than in lexical decision. This seems problematic for the PDP model, because word frequency effects and orthographic effects fall out of the same process: Connection strength. My suspicion is that this version of the implemented model cannot accommodate such dissociations.

Another prediction about the effects of N is as follows. If the PDP account is *sufficient*, the straightforward prediction is that once orthographic error scores are partialled out of the data from an experiment, N ought not to account for *any* variance. This is not what happens. When the orthographic error scores are partialled out, N captures a significant amount of variance (6% in the nonword RT data from McCann & Besner's, 1987, naming experiment). It is true that 6% is not a lot of variance, but it can be put in perspective by pointing out that the orthographic error scores from the model account for only 8% of the variance in McCann et al.'s (1988) nonword data from the lexical decision task. Clearly, there is variation in the human data attributable to N which is not captured by the pattern of activation across *any* of the currently implemented units in the PDP model.

N purports to offer a measure of *lexical* density, a property which does not exist in this PDP model. Taken at face value, the fact that N accounts for a significant proportion of variance after the orthographic error scores are partialled out of the data may be understood as a need for a lexical level of representation in the PDP model. What other data might buttress such a claim? Table 4.4 shows the correlations between several measures and the reaction time data from the McCann and Besner naming study. The first thing to note is that N fails to account for any variance in the pseudohomophone condition. It does account for variance in the control condition; the more neighbors, the faster the response. This result is not surprising from a lexical point of view, since the "nearest" phonological neighbor for a pseudohomophone is its real word counterpart, and one would therefore not expect much in the way of an additional contribution from other neighbors. For the controls however, any assistance rendered by neighbors is gratefully acknowledged. This contrast between pseudohomophones and controls in terms of the effect of N again suggests a lexical contribution to performance.

The last point to be made here is that remaining data from Table 4.4 present another problem for the PDP model. The phonological error scores from the model account for significantly *more* variance in the reaction time data from the control condition as compared to the pseudohomophone condition. That is, in a regression analysis, the slopes for the two conditions are significantly different ($p < .05$). What does this difference reflect?

The suggestion advanced here is that this finding is not understandable in the context of the current version of this PDP model, but it can be understood in the context of the view that what the model lacks is a lexicon. Simply put, the errors scores from the model correlate better with the control condition than with the pseudohomophones because there is a larger lexical contribution to performance in the case of the pseudohomophones (cf. McCann & Besner, 1987).

TABLE 4.4

Correlation Coefficients between the Naming Latencies from the McCann and Besner (1987) Experiment, and the Orthographic and Phonological Error Scores obtained from Seidenberg and McClelland's Model, and the Number of Neighbors.

	Pseudo-homophones	Controls
Orthographic	.27*	.41*
Phonological	.21*	.42*
Neighbors	−.11	−.34*

*p < .05

SUMMARY

The results of the simulation exercise are summarized in the following points.

1. Although the PDP model is very good at producing phonological patterns for words that the model was trained on, it performs extremely poorly with a large set of nonwords that real subjects read with little difficulty.

2. Seidenberg and McClelland's account of lexical decision produces an unacceptably high error rate when tested with Waters and Seidenberg's (1985) stimulus set which includes orthographically strange words. At least for this stimulus set then, the *implemented* model cannot provide an account of regularity effects in lexical decision by appealing to the notion of a familiarity assessment carried out at the phonological level.

3. The implemented model produces chance performance on phonological lexical decision (does this letter string sound like a real word?) when the stimulus set from McCann et al. (1988) is used, as well as the balanced nonword stimulus set that Seidenberg and McClelland used to explore pseudohomophone effects.

4. The PDP model is unable to produce the phonologically based pseudohomophone effect observed in the lexical decision task with human subjects (*slower* performance with pseudohomophones as compared to controls) because the model does not produce a difference in the

phonological error scores for pseudohomophones and control items once the orthographic error scores are partialled out.

5. The model does not simulate the pseudohomophone effect seen in naming by human subjects (*faster* performance with pseudohomophones as compared to controls) since the model does not produce smaller phonological error scores for pseudohomophones than controls once the orthographic error scores are partialled out.

6. The PDP model has no account to offer for the fact that, in speeded naming of nonwords, the number of neighbors accounts for variance that is orthogonal to variance captured by the orthographic error scores produced by the model, or that for words, the neighbor effect maintains its size across lexical decision and naming while the magnitude of the word frequency effect changes.

7. The PDP model has no explanation to offer for the fact that, in speeded naming, the phonological error scores from the model account for *less* variance in the response time data for pseudohomophones than it does for the control items.

CONCLUSIONS

The currently implemented version of Seidenberg and McClelland's PDP model fails to account for a number of facts concerning how human subjects read aloud and carry out lexical decisions, despite the fact that these tasks are central to the performance domain which the model purports to give an account of. The challenge is whether this PDP model *can* be tailored to deal with these data while continuing to make presently successful predictions.

How much violence does a PDP framework do to the concept of a lexicon? My suspicion is that it does very little. Representations in the connectionist framework can be distributed rather than individuated, but they are functionally equivalent in that they represent information about the spelling and sound of words, and act as an interface between the sensory surface and semantics.

ACKNOWLEDGMENTS

This work was supported by Grant #A0998 from the Natural Sciences and Engineering Research Council of Canada to the author. A number of the arguments and additional data can be seen in an expanded version of the present chapter (Besner, Twilley, McCann, and Seergobin, in press). I am grateful to Karalyn Patterson, Max Coltheart, Rob McCann, and Pierre Jolicoeur for discussion, and to Dave Balota and Keith Rayner and particularly Leslie Henderson and Marilyn Smith for their comments on an early version of the manuscript. My discussion of the Seidenberg and McClelland model is based upon the revised version of the manuscript published in *Psychological Review*, 1989. I am particularly grateful to Jay McClelland for providing me with a copy of the model and to Ken Seergobin for assistance in running the simulations.

REFERENCES

Andrews, S. (1989). Frequency and neighborhood effects on lexical access: Activation or search? *Journal of Experimental Psychology: Learning, Memory and Cognition, 15*, 802 - 814.

Atkinson, R. C., & Juola, J. F. (1973). Factors influencing speed and accuracy of word recognition. In S. Kornblum (Ed.), *Attention and performance IV* (pp. 583 - 612). New York: Academic Press.

Balota, D. A., & Chumbley, J. I. (1984). Are lexical decisions a good measure of lexical access? The role of word frequency in the neglected decision stage. *Journal of Experimental Psychology: Human Perception and Performance, 10*, 340 - 357.

Barron, R. W. (1978). Reading skill and phonological coding in lexical access. In M. M. Gruneberg, P. E. Morris, & R. N. Sykes (Eds.), *Practical aspects of memory* (pp. 468 - 475). London: Academic Press.

Becker, C. A. (1976). Allocation of attention during visual word recognition. *Journal of Experimental Psychology: Human Perception and Performance, 2*, 556 - 566.

Becker, C. A. (1979). Semantic context and word frequency effects in visual word recognition. *Journal of Experimental Psychology: Human Perception and Performance, 5*, 252 - 259.

Besner, D. (1983). Basic decoding components in reading: Two dissociable feature extraction processes. *Canadian Journal of Psychology, 37*, 429 - 438.

Besner, D. (1987). Phonology, lexical access in reading, and articulatory suppression: A critical review. *Quarterly Journal of Experimental Psychology, 39A*, 467 - 478.

Besner D., & Davelaar, E. (1982). Basic processes in reading: Two phonological codes. *Canadian Journal of Psychology, 36*, 701 - 711.

Besner, D., & Davelaar, E. (1983). Seudohomofoan effects in visual word recognition: Evidence for phonological processing. *Canadian Journal of Psychology, 37*, 300 - 305.

Besner, D., Davies, J., & Daniels, S. (1981). Reading for meaning: The effects of concurrent articulation. *Quarterly Journal of Experimental Psychology, 33A*, 415 - 437.

Besner, D., Dennis, I., & Davelaar, E. (1985). Reading without phonology? *Quarterly Journal of Experimental Psychology, 37A*, 477 - 491.

Besner, D., & Johnston, J. (1989). Reading and the mental lexicon: On the uptake of visual information. In W. Marslen-Wilson (Ed.), *Lexical representation and process* (pp. 291 - 316). Cambridge, MA: MIT Press.

Besner, D., & McCann, R. S. (1987). Word frequency and pattern distortion in visual word identification and production: An examination of four classes of models. In M. Coltheart (Ed.), *Attention and performance XII: The psychology of reading* (pp. 201 - 219). Hillsdale, NJ: Lawrence Erlbaum Associates.

Besner, D., Twilley, L. C., McCann, R. S., & Seergobin, K. (in press). On the connection between connectionism and data: Are a few words necessary? *Psychological Review.*

Brown, P., & Besner, D. (1987). The assembly of phonology in oral reading: A new model. In M. Coltheart (Ed.), *Attention and performance XII: The psychology of reading* (pp. 471 - 489). Hillsdale, NJ: Lawrence Erlbaum Associates.

Cohen, G., & Freeman, R. (1978). Individual differences in reading strategies in relation to cerebral asymmetry. In J. Requin (Ed.), *Attention and performance VII* (pp. 411 - 426). Hillsdale, NJ: Lawrence Erlbaum Associates.

Coltheart, M. (1980). Reading, phonological recoding and deep dyslexia. In M. Coltheart, K. E. Patterson, & J. C. Marshall (Eds.), *Deep dyslexia* (pp. 197 - 226). London: Routledge & Kegan Paul.

Coltheart, M., Besner, D., Jonasson, J. T., & Davelaar, E. (1979). Phonological recoding in the lexical decision task. *Quarterly Journal of Experimental Psychology, 31*, 489 - 507.

Coltheart, M., Davelaar, E., Jonasson, J. T., & Besner, D. (1977). Access to the internal lexicon. In S. Dornic (Ed.), *Attention and performance VI* (pp. 535 - 555). Hillsdale, NJ: Lawrence Erlbaum Associates.

Coltheart, M., Patterson, K. E., & Marshall, J. C. (Eds.). (1980). *Deep dyslexia*. London: Routledge & Kegan Paul.

Coltheart, M., Sartori, G., & Job, R. (Eds.). (1987). *The cognitive neuropsychology of language*. London: Lawrence Erlbaum Associates.

Dennis, I., Besner, D., & Davelaar, E. (1985). Phonology in visual word recognition: Their is more two this than meats the I. In D. Besner, T. G. Waller, & G. E. MacKinnon (Eds.), *Reading research: Advances in theory and practice* (Vol. 5, pp. 167 - 197). Toronto: Academic Press.

Forster, K. I. (1976). Accessing the mental lexicon. In R. J. Wales & E. W. Walker (Eds.), *New approaches to language mechanisms* (pp. 257 - 287). Amsterdam: North-Holland.

Forster, K. I., & Chambers, S. M. (1973). Lexical access and naming time. *Journal of Verbal Learning and Verbal Behavior, 12*, 627 - 635.

Frederiksen, J. R. (1978). Assessment of perceptual, decoding, and lexical skills and their relation to reading proficiency. In A. M. Lesgold, J. W. Pellegrino, S. D. Fokkema, & R. Glaser (Eds.), *Cognitive psychology and instruction* (pp. 153 - 169). New York: Plenum.

Humphreys, G. W., & Evett, L. J. (1985). Are there independent lexical and nonlexical routes in word processing? An evaluation of the dual route theory of reading. *Behavioral and Brain Sciences, 8*, 689 - 740.

Kinoshita, S. (1987). Case alternation effect: Two types of word recognition? *Quarterly Journal of Experimental Psychology, 39A*, 701 - 720.

McCann, R. S., & Besner, D. (1987). Reading pseudohomophones: Implications for models of pronunciation and the locus of word-frequency effects in word naming. *Journal of Experimental Psychology: Human Perception and Performance, 13*, 14 - 24.

McCann, R. S., Besner, D., & Davelaar, E. (1988). Word recognition and identification: Do word-frequency effects reflect lexical access? *Journal of Experimental Psychology: Human Perception and Performance, 14*, 693 - 706.

Meyer, D., & Schvaneveldt, R. (1971). Facilitation in recognizing pairs of words: Evidence of a dependence between retrieval operations. *Journal of Experimental Psychology, 90*, 227 - 234.

Mitterer, J. O. (1982). There are at least two kinds of poor readers: Whole-word poor readers and recoding poor readers. *Canadian Journal of Psychology, 36*, 445 - 461.

Morton, J. (1969). The interaction of information in word recognition. *Psychological Review, 76*, 165 - 178.

Morton, J. (1979). Facilitation in word recognition: Experiments causing change in the logogen model. In P. A. Kolers, M. E. Wrolstad, & H. Bouma (Eds.), *Processing of visible language* (Vol. 1, pp. 259 - 268). New York: Plenum.

Morton, J., & Patterson, K. (1980). A new attempt at an interpretation, or, an attempt at a new interpretation. In M. Coltheart, K. Patterson, & J. C. Marshall (Eds.), *Deep dyslexia* (pp. 91 - 118). London: Routledge & Kegan Paul.

Norris, D. (1986). Word recognition: Context effects without priming. *Cognition, 22*, 93 - 136.

Paap, K. R., McDonald, J. E., Schvaneveldt, R. W., & Noel, R. W. (1987). Frequency and pronounceability in visually presented naming and lexical decision tasks. In M. Coltheart (Ed.), *Attention and performance XII: The psychology of reading* (pp. 221 - 243). Hillsdale, NJ: Lawrence Erlbaum Associates.

Paap, K. R., Newsome, S. L., McDonald, J. E., & Schvaneveldt, R. W. (1982). An activation-verification model for letter and word recognition: The word superiority effect. *Psychological Review, 89*, 573 - 594.

Patterson, K. E. (1982). The relation between reading and phonological coding: Further neuropsychological observations. In A. W. Ellis (Ed.), *Normality and pathology in cognitive functions* (pp. 77 - 111). New York: Academic Press.

Patterson, K., & Coltheart, V. (1987). Phonological processes in reading: A tutorial review. In M. Coltheart (Ed.), *Attention and performance XII: The psychology of reading* (pp. 421 - 447). Hillsdale, NJ: Lawrence Erlbaum Associates.

Patterson, K. E., & Marcel, A. J. (1977). Aphasia, dyslexia and the phonological coding of written words. *Quarterly Journal of Experimental Psychology, 29*, 307 - 318.

Patterson, K. E., Marshall, J. C., & Coltheart, M. (1985). *Surface dyslexia.* London: Lawrence Erlbaum Associates.

Patterson, K. E., Seidenberg, M. S., & McClelland, J. L. (in press). Word recognition and dyslexia: A connectionist approach. In P. Morris (Ed.), *Connectionism: The Oxford Symposium.* Cambridge: Cambridge University Press.

Pring, L. (1981). Phonological codes and functional spelling units: Reality and implications. *Perception & Psychophysics, 30*, 573 - 578.

Rubenstein, H., Lewis, S. S., & Rubenstein, M. A. (1971). Homographic entries in the internal lexicon: Effects of systematicity and relative frequency of meanings. *Journal of Verbal Learning and Verbal Behavior, 10*, 57 - 62.

Schwartz, M. F., Marin, O. S. M., & Saffran, E. M. (1979). Dissociations of language function in dementia: A case study. *Brain and Language, 7*, 277 - 306.

Seidenberg, M. S. (1985). The time course of phonological code activation in two writing systems. *Cognition, 19*, 1 - 30.

Seidenberg, M. S., & McClelland, J. L. (1989). A distributed, developmental model of word recognition and naming. *Psychological Review, 96*, 523 - 568.

Seidenberg, M. S., Waters, G. S., Barnes, M. A., & Tanenhaus, M. K. (1984). When does irregular spelling or pronunciation influence word recognition? *Journal of Verbal Learning and Verbal Behavior, 23*, 383 - 404.

Treisman, A. M. (1960). Contextual cues in selective listening. *Quarterly Journal of Experimental Psychology, 12*, 242 - 248.

Waters, G. S., & Seidenberg, M. S. (1985). Spelling-sound effects in reading: Time course and decision criteria. *Memory & Cognition, 13*, 557 - 572.

Whitaker, H. (1976). A case of the isolation of the language function. In H. Whitaker & H. A. Whitaker (Eds.), *Studies in Neurolinguistics* (Vol. 2, pp. 1 - 58). London: Academic Press.

5

THE LOCUS OF THE ASSOCIATIVE-PRIMING EFFECT IN THE MENTAL LEXICON

Annette M.B. de Groot
University of Amsterdam

INTRODUCTION

Although it is beyond dispute that contextual information plays an important role in reading (and, for that matter, in speech perception), there is much debate about what processing stage or stages it can affect. The major question is whether or not context can influence word recognition. According to the autonomy view, context cannot affect word processing before the processes that lead to recognition of the word have finished. Instead, context is exploited later on, for instance, when the recognized word is to be integrated in the representation of the preceding text. In contrast, the interactive view claims that context does affect the processes leading up to recognition. It may do so by allowing a more cursory or less complete analysis of the information comprised in the stimulus word (e.g., Morton, 1969).

Originally, the main impetus for the type of research reported on here, word-context priming, was to help resolve this dispute. (Hereafter, word-context priming refers to a situation where the test words are preceded by a single word that serves as context.) Subsequently, in numerous word-context experiments a context effect on the recognition of visually presented words has been observed, but these experiments have also shown that the effects are largely due to processes that under more natural reading conditions are not effective (see Mitchell, 1982, for an extensive discussion). So, these data are not crucial with respect to the discussion on autonomous versus interactive word recognition. A second goal of word-context studies, obviously also of relevance to the study of reading, has been to provide insight into the structure of the mental lexicon. The word-context studies to be reported on here fit in best with this goal. In pursuing this goal, an attempt is made to determine the loci in the memory system of one particular type of word-context effect.

Localizing the Associative-Priming Effect

In a number of word recognition tasks, including the popular lexical decision and word pronunciation tasks, responding to a target word is generally faster when that word is preceded by an associatively related word rather than an unrelated word. I regard two words as associatively related when they occur as stimulus and response terms in a corpus of word associations. It appears that some form of semantic relationship (e.g., synonymy, antonymy, or class inclusion) exists between the two words in the majority of stimulus-response combinations of such a corpus. In explaining the described priming effect, this semantic relationship is often regarded as somehow causing the effect, a view that is reflected in its most common name: *semantic priming*. The major goal of this chapter is to question the role of semantic processing (and of the memory system where such processing occurs) in this priming effect. I use the term *associative-priming effect* to refer to the effect occurring with pairs of words that co-occur as stimulus and response terms in word association norms, and that *at the same time* include some semantic relation. In all experiments to be reported, this type of word pairs served as stimuli in the related conditions. For the time being, the term is meant to be neutral with respect to the origin of the effect, semantic or not, this being the unresolved issue to be investigated here.

A number of processes have been suggested as causes of the associative-priming effect. For instance, in their seminal study Meyer and Schvaneveldt (1971, p. 232) suggested two, namely *automatic (attention-free) spreading activation* in long-term memory and *location-shifting*. Neely (1976) similarly distinguished between a process of automatic-spreading activation in memory and a process that depletes the resources of the attentional mechanism. More recently, a further associative-priming process has been suggested that, unlike the others, is thought to affect word processing postlexically (e.g., de Groot, Thomassen, & Hudson, 1982; Lupker, 1984; Seidenberg, Waters, Sanders, & Langer, 1984). This process is mostly called *meaning integration*. The associative-priming effect observed in a particular experiment may be caused by a single priming process or it may be the combined effect of the contributions of two or more processes. Whether just one or more than one processes contribute to the effect depends upon particular characteristics of the experiment, an important one being the task that is used. The focus of this chapter is the process of automatic spreading activation as a source of associative priming, although only in a subset of the experiments to be reported care has been taken to prevent the other priming processes from operating.

An associative-priming effect due to automatic-spreading activation presupposes some network structure in memory in which the nodes for associatively related words are connected to each other. The activation that arises in one of the nodes in this network in response to the presentation of the corresponding word spreads along the paths in the network, activating the nodes that it encounters en route. If a word represented in one of these preactivated nodes is subsequently presented (and if accessing this particular node is indeed part and parcel of word processing in the particular task being used), this prior activation will influence its processing. Depending upon the task, responding is accelerated (e.g., in lexical decision and in word pronunciation) or slowed down (e.g., in a Stroop task). The network structure involved in the effect is generally regarded to be semantic memory (e.g., Collins & Loftus, 1975).

An important characteristic of this spreading-activation view of associative priming, acknowledged by Meyer and Schvaneveldt in their seminal 1971 article, is that it is thought to arise from the structure of memory: The effect is presumably due to the existence of a link between the nodes for associatively related words. The semantic content of the nodes connected by these links does not have to be accessed for the effect to occur.

The plausibility of a structural interpretation of the effect allows one to go further than to doubt that semantic analysis underlies the effect. It also becomes questionable whether the semantic level of representation is indeed the (only) place where the effect occurs. Collins and Loftus's (1975) often-cited memory model includes a second level of representation in addition to the semantic level. This level has been typically ignored in the associative-priming literature. They call it the *lexical* level, but for reasons that need not concern us here I refer to it as the *word* level. Whereas the nodes at the semantic level are organized according to semantic similarity, the nodes at the word level are organized according to orthographic and acoustic similarity. In word processing tasks, access of the semantic level proceeds via the word level.

It is plausible that, in addition to the connections between nodes for orthographically and acoustically similar words, the word level also contains links between nodes for associatively-related words (irrespective as to whether these words are orthographically or acoustically similar). Such links may have come about through past spatiotemporal contiguity of the corresponding words, for instance, through their verbal contiguity (in both inner thought and outer speech) during concept acquisition: Acquiring the concept CALF may not only result in the formation of a relationship (link) between the concepts CALF and COW, but because language undoubtedly is an important means via which concepts are learned, a link may also be formed between the *words* that refer to these concepts. In other words, at the semantic level of representation a connection may exist between the concepts COW and CALF, and additionally, at the word level a connection may exist between the words referring to these concepts. Assuming that links at all representational levels give rise to an automatic spread of activation from a node activated by a word input, such a word level of representation could then be an additional locus of the associative-priming effect. A priming effect originating at this level would again be a structural effect, but now the structure concerned would be nonsemantic by nature. In tasks that do not necessitate semantic processing of the stimuli, the word level could under certain circumstances be the primary or even the only locus of the effect.

The present research addresses the question of where to localize the associative-priming effect in the mental lexicon. In spirit, it is very similar to studies by Fischler (1977) and Lupker (1984), but the approach is different. Fischler was the first to question the assumption that the underlying semantic relation in pairs of associatively related words is responsible for what was typically referred to as semantic priming, and to suggest that the accidental association between these words was responsible for the effect (Fischler, 1977). He approached this question by comparing, in a lexical decision experiment (wherein subjects categorize letter strings as words or nonwords), the priming effect for two sets of word pairs. One set was both associatively and semantically related (AS-pairs; the type of related word pairs exclusively used in the present study); the other set consisted of word pairs not occurring as stimulus-response combinations in norms of word association but judged nevertheless to be semantically related to one another (S-pairs). Fischler observed a small difference between the size of the priming effects for AS-pairs and S-pairs (the latter effect being somewhat smaller), but the difference was not significant. Thus, he concluded that the same type of relationship (i.e., the semantic relationship) presumably underlies the effect on both types of material.

Lupker (1984) also compared performance on AS- and S-pairs (using a different type of S-pairs), in both lexical decision and in word pronunciation. In contrast to Fischler's results he obtained a significantly larger priming effect for AS-pairs than for S-pairs in the lexical decision task. Furthermore, in word pronunciation he found a much smaller priming effect on AS-pairs than in lexical decision, and the effect on S-pairs lessened to 6 ms Lupker (1984) argued that this residual effect on S-pairs in pronunciation may best be regarded as a null effect, and that the priming effect on AS-pairs in pronunciation is solely due to the associative links between primes and targets. He attributed the larger priming effects in lexical decision, rather than in pronunciation, to post-lexical processing.

The present study builds on those by Fischler and Lupker by focusing on the level(s) in the memory system where the priming effect originates. This study did not compare priming effects on both AS- and S-materials in lexical decision and/or naming, that is, in tasks that per se do not require access of the semantic level of representation (but see Balota, this volume, for ample indications that at some stage in lexical decision, semantic processing of at least some of the test words occurs). Rather, the general approach here was to compare the effect on (only) AS-test words in lexical decision with the effect on these same words in two tasks in which access of the semantic level is compulsory. One of the semantic tasks was animateness categorization, in which the referents of the test words were categorized as animate or inanimate. The second was size categorization, in which the test words were categorized according to the size of their referents. More specifically, subjects decided whether the test words referred to entities larger or smaller than an average-sized, nonportable TV set.

Although similar in that they both require the retrieval of semantic information, categorization on animateness and (the present) categorization on size appear to require quite different processing. For instance, size categorization may involve imagery, whereas this is less likely to be the case for animateness categorization. A more marked difference is that the size categorization task presumably generally requires an additional processing stage: Upon accessing the test word's node in semantic memory, all information relevant for animateness categorization is available in this very node, whereas it is likely that only part of the relevant information, namely, the size of the test word's referent, is available there in the case of size categorization. A second piece of information relevant for size categorization, the size of the standard of comparison, here the TV set, has to be accessed in the TV set's semantic node, and subsequently a comparison has to be made between the sizes of the test word's referent and the standard. Occasionally, the subject may skip this comparison stage when a test word's semantic representation, in addition to information about the actual size of the referent, explicitly contains the information that it concerns a large (*elephant; whale*) or a small (*needle; ant*) entity. Upon accessing this information, the subject may directly use it to categorize the test word. However, such a strategy may cause errors. The examples given are all entities that are large or small relative to most other entities that surround us, including TV sets, and skipping the comparison stage would not lead to an error. But now consider *hut* and *cottage*. The semantic representations of these words are also likely to contain the information 'small', because this information is crucial in distinguishing them from *house*. Yet, huts and cottages are larger than TV sets, and the comparison stage would thus be necessary if a correct response is to be output. It is not clear for which concepts "large" or "small" is explicitly represented, but the fact that, unlike "animate" and "inanimate," they are relative terms (a small building and a large spoon are not small or large in absolute sense) suggests that this is the exception rather than the rule. This, as well as the discussed risk of producing errors, suggests that on most trials the size comparison between a TV set and the target's referent will indeed have to be made.

As a starting point, the working hypothesis is that if associative connections exist at both the word and the semantic representational levels, the associative-priming effect may be expected to be smaller in lexical decision than in semantic classification. This prediction is based on the notion that in the latter type of task the categorization process would benefit from preactivation in nodes at both levels on relatively many trials. This prediction holds under either of two different states of affairs (of which the first is unlikely, given the evidence that at some stage in lexical decision semantic processing of the test words occurs; see also the earlier discussion): (a) The subjects may execute control over what levels of representation to access and adapt themselves to the task requirements. Thus, in lexical decision the subjects may decide to switch off the semantic level so that their lexical categorizations will only be affected by the activation spread from the prime's word node to the target's word node. (b) No such control over processing levels can be exerted. Instead, activation in the system takes its natural course, and a classificatory response is made as soon as the information critical for classification has been gathered. Concentrating on the lexical decision task again, if at that moment preactivation in the target's semantic node has had time to spread back to the target's word node, the priming effect, accumulating from two levels, will be relatively large. If not, it will be small, attributable to prior activation spreading from the prime's word node only. Note that the complete route of activation that is assumed here is as follows: Prime presentation results in activation of the prime's word node. From this node, activation spreads to the test word's word node as well as to the prime's semantic node. From the latter, it subsequently spreads, among others, to the semantic node of the test word. From there, activation spreads back to the test word's word node at the word level of representation, where, in case the classification has not been made yet, it will affect the response.

Unlike in lexical decision, in semantic classification the exploitation of semantic information and, hence, accessing the semantic node, is obligatory. This fact underlies the prediction that, if associative connections exist at both levels, the associative-priming effect should be larger in semantic classification than in lexical decision. In the case of (a) above, in lexical decision only spreading activation at the word level will cause priming. However, in semantic classification this effect is augmented by the priming that results from all trials where at the time of access, the test word's semantic node has already received preactivation from the prime's semantic node. Because semantic classification necessitates the retrieval of semantic information, response latency in this task may be expected to be longer than in lexical decision. This is why also in the case of (b) above, larger priming effects may be expected in semantic classification than in lexical decision: More often than in lexical decision, there will be sufficient time for activation from the prime's semantic node to spread to the test word's semantic node in time to affect responding. In sum, according to both schemes, more associative priming should occur in semantic classification than in lexical decision.

Note that in both accounts, I have ignored the possibility of a contribution to the priming effect of processes other than automatic spreading activation. I will make up for this later.

METHOD

Materials

Lexical Decision versus Animateness Categorization

Five experiments were run in which associative-priming effects in lexical decision and animateness categorization were compared. In all these experiments, the set of critical stimuli consisted of the same 92 pairs of Dutch nouns, the first noun of each pair serving as prime, the second as target (the stimulus to which the subjects had to respond). In half of these stimuli, the target was either the primary (in 43 cases) or secondary (in 3 cases) response to the prime in a corpus of Dutch association norms (de Groot, 1980), in which the latter occurred as the stimulus word. The remaining half of the stimuli consisted of a pair of words not associatively related to one another. They were formed by dissociating and recombining primes and targets of the associated stimuli. Half of the targets of the related stimuli had an animate refer-ent and half had an inanimate referent. Similarly, half of the targets of the unrelated stimuli had an animate referent and half had an inanimate referent. The overall associative strength of targets to primes in the con-dition with prime-related targets referring to animate entities was about the same as that in the condition with prime-related targets referring to inanimate entities (46.9% and 49.3%, respectively, with corresponding standard deviations of 16.4 and 14.4).

In selecting materials from the association norms it turned out that in the majority of stimulus/primary response combinations the two words either both referred to animate beings or they both referred to inanimate entities. Consequently, this was also the case with the present experi-mental materials. In fact it was true for all of them. In order to prevent the subjects discovering the systematic relation between animateness of prime and target, and strategically using the (in)animateness of the prime as a cue to category membership of the target, 46 filler prime-target pairs were constructed in which category membership of prime and target differed. Half of these included primes and targets that were associatively related, as judged by the author and three of her colleagues. The remaining half were unrelated. The latter were formed by recom-bining primes and targets of the associated filler stimuli. Half of the targets in the filler stimuli had an animate referent and were preceded by an inanimate prime. For the remaining half of the fillers, animate-ness of prime and target were reversed. Finally, a further 92 stimuli were added to the set of materials for the lexical decision part of the ex-periments. For these stimuli the primes were words and the targets were pseudowords, that is, nonwords conforming to the sound and spelling rules of Dutch. An example set of these stimulus materials is presented in Table 5.1.

TABLE 5.1

*Lexical Decision versus Animateness Categorization
(Sample Stimuli).*

| Target referent | Related | | Unrelated | |
	Prime	Target	Prime	Target
Animate	robber	thief	hare	thief
	lady	gentleman	goose	gentleman
	goose	duck	robber	duck
	hare	rabbit	lady	rabbit
Inanimate	boot	shoe	table	shoe
	tea	coffee	boot	coffee
	fork	knife	tea	knife
	table	chair	fork	chair
Fillers	school	pupil	crown	pupil
	crown	king	school	king
	pilot	plane	writer	plane
	writer	book	pilot	book

Lexical Decision versus Size Categorization

Two experiments were run in which associative-priming effects in lexical decision and in size categorization were compared. In both experiments, the set of critical materials consisted of 104 pairs of Dutch nouns. Half of these items included targets that were the primary response to the prime in a corpus of word associations (de Groot, 1980). The remaining half of the stimuli were word pairs consisting of words not associatively related to one another, formed as before. Of both the related and the unrelated stimuli, half had a target referring to an entity larger than the standard TV set and half had a target referring to an entity smaller than this standard. The overall associative strength of targets to primes in the related condition with target referents larger than the standard was about the same as that in the related condition with target referents smaller than the standard (45.3% and 45.1%, respectively, with corresponding standard deviations of 18.3 and 19.1).

In selecting materials from the association norms it turned out that the size of the referents of the stimulus words and that of their primary responses were often about the same, and only few pairs could be selected in which the referents of stimulus and primary response belonged to different size categories. In other words, on the relevant dimension once again a systematic relation existed between prime and target that could come to be used strategically by the subjects (see earlier discussion). In order to prevent this, a set of filler stimuli, now consisting of 52 word pairs (26 related and 26 unrelated), was again constructed in which category membership of prime and target differed, so that subjects could not strategically use size of the prime's referent as a cue to target classification. Finally, 104 prime-target pairs with a word as prime and a pseudoword as target were added to the set of materials for the lexical decision part of the experiments. An example set of the stimulus materials is presented in Table 5.2.

TABLE 5.2

Lexical Decision versus Size Categorization
(Sample Stimuli).

	Related		Unrelated	
	Prime	Target	Prime	Target
Target Referent				
Larger	monk	monastery	branch	monastery
	branch	tree	monk	tree
	harbour	ship	foal	ship
	foal	horse	harbour	horse
Smaller	fork	knife	thumb	knife
	thumb	finger	vase	finger
	vase	flower	hammer	flower
	hammer	nail	fork	nail
Fillers	head	body	pill	body
	pill	doctor	head	doctor
	ditch	frog	sink	frog
	sink	tap	ditch	tap

Subjects, Apparatus, and Procedure

In each of the five lexical decision versus animateness categorization experiments and in both lexical decision versus size categorization experiments, 40 students of the University of Nijmegen participated as subjects. Different subjects participated in each experiment. In each experiment, 20 subjects performed the lexical decision task and 20 performed the semantic categorization task. Of each of these groups, half indicated their word/animate/larger decisions by pushing the right one of two buttons and nonword/inanimate/smaller decisions by pushing the left button. The response-to-button assignment was reversed for the remaining 10 subjects within each group of 20.

The same apparatus was used in all experiments. Stimuli were presented on a TV monitor. Individual stimulus presentation and the recording of response times and errors were under program control. Prime and target were always presented pairwise, that is, without intervening stimuli, and successively, and the subjects only responded overtly to the target. The target remained on the screen until the subject responded or until a deadline had expired. Apart from the variation in the type of semantic classification to be made, the various experiments varied on two dimensions, namely, the stimulus-onset-asynchrony (SOA) between prime and target and the unmasked versus masked presentation of the prime. In the experiments with unmasked primes, the prime was always clearly visible. In the masked-prime experiments, conscious identification of the prime was prevented. The reason for the masking manipulation is given later.

UNMASKED-PRIME EXPERIMENTS

Lexical Decision versus Animateness Categorization

The outcome of the first three experiments comparing lexical decision with animateness categorization is presented in Table 5.3 (collapsed across the two response-to-button-assignment conditions). Experiments 1 and 2 were exact replications of one another. Prime-target SOA in these experiments was 440 ms (prime duration: 400 ms; interval between prime offset and target onset: 40 ms). Experiment 3 differed from Experiments 1 and 2 in that the prime-target SOA was 240 ms (prime duration 200 ms; interval between prime offset and target onset: 40 ms).

The main goal was to determine whether or not there is more priming in animateness categorization than in lexical decision. In Experiments 1 and 2 the relevant interaction, that between task and relatedness, was significant in the item analysis ($p < .05$ in both cases), but only marginally so in the subject analysis ($.05 < p < .10$ in both cases). In Experiment 3 it was nonsignificant in both analyses ($F < 1$ in both cases). Consistent with the prediction of the priming-at-two-levels view, the overall associative-priming effect in Experiments 1 and 2 was larger in animateness categorization than in lexical decision. But, as can be seen in Table 5.3, the priming effect was only larger in animateness categorization than in lexical decision in the condition wherein target referents are animate. This result is reflected by a significant second-order interaction between task, relatedness, and animateness of the target ($p < .05$ or better in both the subject and the item analysis in all three experiments). A further relevant outcome is that in all analyses but one (the subject analysis of Experiment 3 being the exception), animateness categorization took significantly longer than lexical decision ($p < .05$ or better).

TABLE 5.3

Mean Response Times (RT) in ms and Error Rates (ER) for all Task by Relatedness by Target-Animateness Conditions of Experiments 1, 2 and 3 (Unmasked Primes).

		Animateness Categorization					
Experiment		1		2		3	
		RT	ER	RT	ER	RT	ER
Animate	Related	472	1.5%	476	2.4%	485	0.9%
	Unrelated	560	5.0%	558	5.4%	561	5.9%
Priming effect		88		82		76	
Inanimate	Related	553	1.8%	536	2.6%	545	2.2%
	Unrelated	579	3.5%	575	2.4%	572	2.6%
Priming effect		26		39		27	

		Lexical Decision					
Experiment		1		2		3	
		RT	ER	RT	ER	RT	ER
Animate	Related	468	1.3%	474	1.1%	486	0.5%
	Unrelated	511	4.1%	521	2.4%	531	2.0%
Priming effect		43		47		45	
Inanimate	Related	480	1.3%	487	1.1%	494	1.1%
	Unrelated	522	4.2%	526	2.0%	537	2.2%
Priming effect		42		39		43	

Lexical Decision versus Size Categorization

The data of the two experiments comparing lexical decision with size categorization are summarized in Table 5.4 (again collapsed across the response-to-button-assignment conditions). These experiments (Experiments 4 and 5) were exact replications of one another. As in Experiments 1 and 2, prime-target SOA was 440 ms (prime duration: 400 ms; interval between prime offset and target onset: 40 ms).

In Experiment 4 the interaction between task and relatedness was significant ($p < .05$ and $p < .01$ in the subject and item analyses, respectively), but the direction of the effect was unexpected: More priming was observed with lexical decision than with size categorization. However, as can be seen in Table 5.4, this was only the case when targets referred to entities smaller than the standard. The second-order interaction between task, relatedness, and size was statistically reliable in the item analysis ($p < .05$) but only marginally so in the subject analysis ($.05 < p < .10$). Finally, the main effect of task was significant ($p < .001$ in both the subject and the item analyses), size categorization taking 90 ms longer overall than lexical decision.

TABLE 5.4

Experiments 4 and 5: Mean Response Times (RT) in ms and Error Rates (ER) as a Function of Task, Relatedness and of Target-Size (Unmasked Primes).

		Size Categorization				Lexical Decision			
Experiment		4		5		4		5	
		RT	ER	RT	ER	RT	ER	RT	ER
Larger	Related	583	5.8%	534	4.8%	485	2.2%	490	2.3%
	Unrelated	608	5.8%	584	4.8%	514	2.1%	520	2.3%
	Priming Effect	25		50		29		30	
Smaller	Related	582	3.5%	537	5.6%	482	1.9%	496	0.6%
	Unrelated	606	6.2%	582	4.1%	536	5.4%	553	6.4%
	Priming Effect	24		45		54		57	

In Experiment 5 the interaction between task and relatedness failed to approach significance ($F < 1$ in both the analysis by subjects and by items), but the second-order interaction was statistically reliable in the subject analysis ($p < .05$), and marginally significant in the item analysis ($.05 < p < .10$). The main effect of task was also again significant, with size categorization now taking 46 ms longer than lexical decision ($p < .05$ in the analysis by subjects and $p < .001$ in the analysis by items). As in Experiment 4, in size categorization the associative-priming effects on larger and smaller targets were equally large, whereas in lexical decision more priming occurred on the smaller targets. The only difference between the two experiments was that in Experiment 5 the priming effects in the size categorization conditions were larger than in Experiment 4. In an overall analysis of Experiments 4 and 5, the task by relatedness interaction was not significant ($p > .10$ in both the subject and the item analyses). The task by relatedness by size interaction was significant both by subjects ($p < .01$) and by items ($p < .05$). The overall priming effects in the larger and smaller size categorization conditions and in the larger and smaller lexical decision conditions were 38 ms, 35 ms, 30 ms, and 56 ms, respectively.

The finding that in lexical decision more priming occurs on smaller targets was not anticipated, but in hindsight it is not all that surprising. It may be due to a contamination of the size variable with word frequency. When targets in the larger and smaller word groups were checked on word frequency, it turned out that the frequency values of the targets with referents smaller than the standard were reliably ($p < .05$) smaller than those with referents larger than the standard (this contamination did not occur in the experiments comparing lexical decision with animateness categorization). Becker (1979) has shown the priming effect in lexical decision to be larger for low-frequency words than for high-frequency words. The present data show a tendency in the same direction: A small, marginally significant negative correlation occurred ($r = -.19$, $.05 < p < .10$) between the frequency of the targets in the critical (nonfiller) stimuli and the amount of priming observed for these words (collapsed across the two experiments) with lexical decision. Interestingly, there is no hint of any such correlation with size classification ($r = .03$, $p = .42$).

Discussion

The data so far seem to warrant the dismissal of the two-level view of associative priming introduced earlier: It is not *generally* the case that semantic categorization produces more associative priming than lexical decision. There is, however, one semantic categorization condition that consistently shows far more priming than any of the other experimental conditions, namely, the one in which targets referring to animate beings are categorized according to animateness. What is so special about this condition? The conclusion that only in this condition two levels in the memory system contribute to the priming effect appears to be wrong, as in terms of potential memory levels contributing to the effect, this condition is no different than the other semantic categorization conditions.

Thus, I looked for an interpretation in terms of the different sources of information that the subjects may have been using in the various experimental conditions. More sources of facilitatory information may have been available in the related condition with animate targets in animateness categorization than in any of the other experimental conditions. In animateness categorization, the outcome of a categorization of the *prime* on animateness may have been an additional source of information used by the subjects (recall that in all critical stimuli the referents of *both* prime and target were animate or they were *both* inanimate). As mentioned earlier, the *strategic* use of such information was prevented by including filler stimuli in which prime and target belonged to different animateness categories. (That the inclusion of these filler stimuli has indeed had the effect of preventing such strategy is clear from the low error rate for these stimuli in the error-prone animateness-categorization conditions. In Experiments 1, 2, and 3, the overall error rates in the animateness-categorization *filler* conditions were 3.5%, 2.9%, and 5.0%, respectively.) But a categorization of the prime on animateness may have come about automatically, and the output of this process may *automatically* have cued the response. Information about the *size* of the prime's referent may also become available automatically during prime processing, but in contrast to prime animateness in the animateness-categorization task, this information per se is presumably not a valid cue for responding in size categorization. What *would* have been useful prior information for classifying the target in size categorization is prime size in relation to the size of a TV set (recall that most of the time the referents of prime and target were on the same side of the TV set on the size dimension), but this information would certainly not become available automatically, it has to be computed on the spot (see the discussion on size categorization in the Introduction).

The postlexical associative-priming process of meaning integration, briefly alluded to in the introduction, may also have influenced responding in animateness categorization. The process entails that the subjects exploit their recognition of the relationship or non-relationship between prime and target in target classification. Verbal reports of the subjects strongly suggest that in categorizing targets on animateness they transform the *animate* and *inanimate* responses to *yes* and *no* responses, respectively. These positive and negative decisions may be differentially affected by a given output of meaning integration, a related (= positive) output speeding up responses to animate targets by a response bias in the right direction but slowing down responses to inanimate targets by biasing the wrong response. Conversely, an unrelated (= negative) output of meaning integration may slow down responses to animate targets and it may speed up responses to inanimate targets. It has been argued (e.g., de Groot, 1985) that, similarly, in lexical decision related and unrelated outputs of meaning integration speed up and slow down, respectively, responding to words. In general, meaning integration may be assumed to affect processing in all binary tasks in which the two responses, as the two different outputs of meaning integration themselves, are quite naturally associated with *yes* and *no*.

In sum, there is reason to believe that responding in the condition wherein animate targets that are associatively related to their primes have to be categorized on animateness, was favored by the operation of a number of processes confounding the effects of automatic spreading activation. These processes may have been differentially operative or altogether inoperative in the remaining experimental conditions, causing the priming effects in those conditions to be smaller. The purpose of the following experiments, in which the primes were masked such that they could not be identified by the subjects, was to try to prevent the workings of these confounding processes in order to obtain a purer assessment of the magnitude of the associative-priming effect due to spreading activation.

MASKED-PRIME EXPERIMENTS

In a number of lexical decision studies (Balota, 1983; de Groot, 1983; Fowler, Wolford, Slade, & Tassinary, 1981; Marcel, 1983) an associative-priming effect has been reported on targets preceded by masked primes. The masked-prime technique has been used for various reasons. For the present purposes it is used to render postlexical meaning integration inoperative (see de Groot, 1983). If, as suggested here, the effects of this process boost the associative-priming effect in animateness categorization on prime-related targets with animate referents, this effect should decrease when the primes are masked. Of course, rendering meaning integration inoperative should also affect the associative-priming effects in the lexical decision part of the experiment. Thus, the associative-priming effect should *generally* be smaller under masked-prime presentation than in Experiments 1-5. Furthermore, if it is assumed that exploiting a categorization of the prime on animateness also requires conscious prime identification, such a process should also be rendered inoperative by the masking manipulation, and the associative-priming effect should decrease further in the animate, related condition in that task. The total decrease of the priming effect should thus be larger in animateness categorization than in lexical decision. Thus, because a number of other sources of priming have been removed, the resulting priming effects should more purely reflect priming due to automatic-spreading activation in the memory system than those obtained when the primes were not masked.

A further remark concerning the masked-prime technique is due here. As anybody who has worked with it realizes, this is not the easiest and most dependable of experimental techniques. Yet it is assigned a crucial role in this study. The problems with the technique are especially tedious when the purpose of an investigation is to find out whether or not priming occurs under *perfect* masking conditions, that is, when none of the subjects can identify any of the primes (see Holender, 1986, for an extensive discussion). I would like to stress that here the technique is merely used as a tool to get rid of processes obscuring the workings of spreading activation, without claiming that the prime was always perfectly masked (in fact, some subjects reported that they had occasionally identified a prime). The data themselves indicate whether or not this goal is fulfilled.

The prime-masking manipulation that was used here is based on the technique used by Forster and Davis (1984), who had the prime preceded by a stimulus serving as a forward mask and followed by the target, serving as a backward mask. In the present two masking experiments (Experiments 6 and 7) the forward mask consisted of a string of 11 hashes (#). It was presented for 480 ms. Twenty ms after its offset, the prime appeared and remained on the screen for 40 ms. Twenty ms after prime offset, the target appeared and remained on the screen for 500 ms. In both experiments, associative priming in lexical decision and in semantic classification was compared, with animateness categorization being used as the semantic-classification task.

Results and Discussion

Table 5.5 summarizes the results of Experiments 6 and 7. Consistent with the view that masking the prime has the effect of rendering inoperative a number of processes that contribute to the associative-priming effect, the priming effects turned out to be smaller on the whole than in the experiments with unmasked prime presentation. Most interesting for our present purpose is the finding that there is hardly any trace left of the task by relatedness by animateness interaction that occurred before ($p > .10$ in both the analysis by subjects and the analysis by items in both Experiments 6 and 7). The task by relatedness interaction was also nonsignificant ($F < 1$ in both analyses in both experiments). Yet, the main effect of relatedness was statistically reliable in both experiments ($p < .01$ or better in both analyses in both experiments). In short, in all experimental conditions an equally reliable priming effect

TABLE 5.5

Experiments 6 and 7: Mean Response Times (RT) in ms and Error Rates (ER) as a Function of Task, Relatedness and of Target-Animateness (Masked Primes).

		Task						
		Animateness Categorization				Lexical Decision		
Experiment		6		7		6		7
		RT	ER	RT	ER	RT	ER	RT	ER
Animate	Related	528	3.5%	524	5.0%	516	2.6%	513	2.6%
	Unrelated	552	3.9%	535	7.2%	530	3.9%	516	5.5%
	Priming Effect	24		11		14		3	
Inanimate	Related	566	1.5%	545	2.6%	521	2.6%	513	2.2%
	Unrelated	584	3.5%	550	2.8%	542	3.5%	532	5.3%
	Priming Effect	18		5		21		19	

was now observed. Finally, in Experiment 6 the main effect of task was again significant, animateness categorization producing longer RTs than lexical decision ($p < .05$ in the subject analysis, and $p < .001$ in the item analysis). Also, in Experiment 7 animateness categorization took longer than lexical decision, but here the effect was only significant in the item analysis ($p < .001$).

All of these findings are consistent with the view that, with unmasked prime presentation, the priming effect on related, animate targets in animateness classification is boosted by the use of animateness information about the prime. This process, together with another, that with unmasked prime presentation is an effective source of priming in both animateness categorization and lexical decision (postlexical meaning integration), is rendered inoperative by the masking manipulation.

GENERAL DISCUSSION

Contrary to the predictions of the two-level view of associative priming, in Experiments 1 through 5, all with unmasked-prime presentation, the priming effect was not consistently larger in the semantic categorization tasks than in lexical decision. Semantic categorization only showed more priming than lexical decision when animate prime-related targets were categorized for animateness. The relatively large priming effect in this condition was attributed to a number of processes that operate in addition to automatic spreading activation. In the masked-prime experiments (Experiments 6 and 7), these processes were rendered ineffective. In these experiments, equally large priming effects were obtained for both animate and inanimate targets in lexical decision *and* animateness categorization. A further important result is that the data generally indicate semantic categorization takes longer than lexical decision (only in the subject analyses of Experiments 3 and 7 was the effect of task not reliable). This finding is important because longer processing time in semantic classification than in lexical decision may be a prerequisite in testing the two-level view of associative priming. According to the more likely of the two processing accounts of two-level priming (alternative (b) in the Introduction), a larger priming effect should be obtained in semantic classification than in lexical decision, because in the former more often than in the latter the priming effect arising at the semantic level can join the word level priming effect in time to affect responding. If semantic classification and lexical decision would take equally long, both levels could contribute to the overall priming effect equally often in both tasks, and hence there would be no grounds for expecting more priming in semantic classification. In other words, the present finding of equally large associative-priming effects in lexical decision and semantic classification would not refute the two-level view of priming. However, because semantic categorization indeed appears to take longer than lexical decision, the finding that the two tasks produce equally large priming effects suggests that the two-level view of priming is incorrect and that associative priming originates at one level only.

The reason semantic classification was assumed to take longer than lexical decision (see the Introduction) was that in the former task the response *always* has to await an output from the semantic-representational level, whereas in lexical decision on a subset of trials (the number of which will vary with stimulus characteristics that affect processing time, such as length and frequency) all information relevant for response selection may already be available and the response can be executed prior to access of the semantic level. However, there are other possible causes for a longer overall response time in semantic classification than in lexical decision. One is that word/nonword discrimination is an easier task than semantic classification. Yet another is the possibility of differential postlexical priming influences in the two types of tasks. In order to rule out the latter interpretation, an additional experiment was conducted, in which responses were collected to the targets from the earlier lexical decision versus animateness-categorization studies (Experiments 1, 2, 3, 6, and 7), but now these targets were not preceded by their primes. It turned out that also *unprimed* RT was faster (by 67 ms) in lexical decision than in animateness categorization ($p < .001$ on both the subject and the item analyses). This finding rules out an interpretation of the difference in overall RT between the two tasks under priming conditions in terms of differential postlexical priming effects.

To recapitulate, the findings that larger associative-priming effects were not obtained in the semantic classification tasks than in lexical decision and that overall RT was generally larger in semantic classification than in lexical decision together suggest that the priming effect in both types of tasks originates at a single representational level. That the level concerned is the semantic level (cf. Collins & Loftus, 1975) is strongly suggested by two lexical decision experiments that I conducted together with Gerard Nas of the University of Utrecht. The purpose of those experiments was to investigate the lexical structure of Dutch-English compound (Ervin & Osgood, 1954) bilinguals. We did so by looking at both the associative-priming effect and the repetition-priming effect in two within-language and two between-language conditions. In the within-language conditions, prime and target were either both Dutch words or they were both English words (e.g., associative priming: *kalf–koe* or *calf–cow*; repetition priming: *kalf–kalf* or *calf–calf*). In the between-language conditions, primes were presented in Dutch and targets in English or vice versa (e.g., associative priming: *kalf–cow* or *calf–koe*; repetition priming: *kalf–calf* or *calf–kalf*). In one of the experiments the primes were clearly visible. In the second they were masked, using the same masking technique as in the two masking experiments here. As materials we only used pairs of Dutch-English cognates, that is, words of which the Dutch form and its English equivalent are perceptually similar, both in sound and in spelling (*kalf–calf*, but not *dak–roof*).

In both experiments, we obtained about the same pattern of results: Overall, the repetition-priming effects were larger than the associative-priming effects. The analyses further showed that the repetition-priming effects tended to be larger in the within-language conditions than in the between-language conditions, whereas the associative-priming effects were equally large within and between languages. A full explanation of these results is provided elsewhere (de Groot & Nas, 1989). For the moment I'll concentrate on the finding of equally large associative-priming effects within and between languages, because that finding appears to be particularly relevant to the present research.

The assumption of connections between associatively related words at the word level of representation is only plausible *within* a language system. As mentioned earlier, such connections would be the result of contiguity of associatively related words during concept acquisition. But such contiguous associatively related words will typically be words from the same language (e.g., some English person may be told that a *calf* is a young *cow* but not that a *calf* is a young *koe*). So, if associative links at the word level would come to be formed during concept learning, this would only be the case within a language system. (Note that it is very plausible that at the word level between-language connections do exist between *repeated* words, e.g., between *cow* and *koe*, because in school second languages are typically learned in a paired-associate paradigm. If these between-language connections do indeed exist, then at the word level associatively related words from different languages may be linked indirectly, e.g., *calf–cow–koe*. This possibility is not elaborated here.) In other words, the word level of representation can only be a locus of the associative-priming effect in the within-language conditions. Following my earlier reasoning, in case of the appropriateness of the two-level view (rejected earlier), this additional level of associative priming should have resulted in larger associative-priming effects in the within-language conditions than in the between-language conditions. The single-level view that would localize all of the effect at the *word* level of representation should have predicted an associative-priming effect only to be obtained in the within-language conditions. That the associative-priming effects were in fact equally large within and between languages (see earlier discussion) thus suggests that the semantic level of representation is the only locus of the effect. A relevant implication of this conclusion is that, also *within* a language system, there appear to be no links between nodes representing associatively related words at the word level of representation. Had they existed, they would have unconditionally led to spreading activation and, hence, to a priming effect.

The conclusion that at the word level no connections exist between associated words is surprising, as undoubtedly words referring to related concepts co-occur during concept acquisition. How can the formation of a link at the word level be prevented? One possibility is that the formation of links between nodes anywhere in the memory system requires a certain minimal amount of attention to be paid to the corresponding elements. We may furthermore assume that during concept acquisition attention is primarily focused on the semantic relation between the to-be-learned concept on the one hand and related concepts on the other, and not to the words that name them. It may then be that there's simply too little attention left for the formation of links between the word nodes. The suggestion that the formation of links is an attentional process converges with my interpretation of the finding that word frequency hardly affects word association RT (de Groot, 1989). There, I concluded that the *strengthening* of a link between two nodes appears to require attention to be drawn to these nodes. A more radical solution would be to give up the present notion of a stratified lexical memory, with separate levels representing words and concepts, and to assume integrated lexical representations with links departing from one and the same node to nodes related to it on various dimensions, acoustically, orthographically, associatively, and semantically. The associative links in these amalgamated representations may then solely be responsible for the associative-priming effect in both lexical decision and semantic categorization (under conditions that prevent priming processes other than automatic spreading activation to operate), and equally large effects should thus indeed be obtained across tasks.

How do the present data fit in with those of Fischler (1977) and Lupker (1984)? As mentioned before, their studies were concerned with very much the same issue as the one investigated here, although they were not aimed at localizing the priming effect in the underlying memory structure. To recapitulate, unlike Fischler, Lupker obtained more priming for targets that were associatively and semantically related to their primes (AS-targets) than for targets that were only semantically related to their primes (S-targets) in lexical decision. In word pronunciation, both effects decreased considerably, and Lupker argued that the residual (6-ms) effect on S-targets in pronunciation might best be regarded as a null effect. He suggested that the relatively small (as compared to lexical decision) but reliable AS-effect in pronunciation is solely due to the associative links between prime and target and that the effects in lexical decision are larger than in pronunciation because only in the former does postlexical processing contribute to them. Consistent with Lupker's findings, in an unpublished experiment Hudson, Thomassen, and I also obtained more priming on AS-targets than on S-targets in lexical decision. (It should be noted that Lupker's and our S-materials were different in that the words in his S-pairs both referred to [nonassociated] members of the same semantic category, e.g, body parts, clothing, whereas our S-pairs were typically not taken from common semantic categories, although for the members of these pairs *ad-hoc* categories [Barsalou, 1983] could be created [*mud–pudding; pepper–sand; pin–thorn*].)

These data suggest that an association component in related word pairs causes priming prelexically, for instance, through spreading activation along links in the memory system, and that a semantic component causes priming postlexically, for instance, through meaning integration, but only in tasks that can tap the output of this postlexical process.

In other words, the priming effect on AS-targets in lexical decision is a compound effect composed of a prelexical associative component and a postlexical semantic component; the priming effect on AS-targets in word pronunciation is a simple prelexical associative effect; the priming effect on S-targets in lexical decision is a simple postlexical semantic effect; and finally, the null effect of priming on S-targets in word pronunciation suggests that no priming process is effective under these particular experimental conditions.

In Lupker's (1984) study, both primes and targets were clearly visible. In the present study, postlexical meaning integration was argued to be inoperative (so that the prelexical component could be isolated) when the primes are masked. If the analysis presented is correct, the priming effect on S-targets in lexical decision, attributed solely to meaning integration here, should disappear under masked-prime presentation conditions. Such a result would have an interesting consequence for the underlying memory model (cf. Lupker, 1984): As already mentioned, in case of a link between two nodes, activation from the first unconditionally spreads to the second, and a priming effect on the word represented by this node should occur. A null effect of priming on S-targets under masked-prime conditions would thus indicate that in the memory system no (direct) links exist between nodes for semantically related words that are not at the same time associatively related to one another (*mud–pudding*). Considering this, the label *associative-priming effect* for the effect occurring on AS-pairs now seems very appropriate. Of course, the memory nodes of the words in these S-pairs may come to be connected (and a priming effect under masked-prime conditions *should* subsequently occur) when attention is drawn to their semantic relation, and an association is thus formed. (For instance, when at the time I set out to construct pairs of words that are semantically but not associatively related, I first thought up [incomplete] featural descriptions of the concept referred to by a word, e.g., *pepper*: yellow/brownish and gritty, and then actively searched memory for the presence of a second word matching this description, e.g., *sand*. This procedure may have caused the two words to become linked in my memory.) Finally, the present data indicate that, as suggested by the masked-prime data, the links that *do* exist, namely, those connecting AS-words, are localized at the semantic-representational level.

ACKNOWLEDGMENTS

Most of the experiments reported here were run when I was at the University of Nijmegen and were supported by the Netherlands Organization for the Advancement of Pure Research (ZWO: Grant H56-279). I am grateful to both ZWO and to the Department of Experimental Psychology at the University of Nijmegen for their invaluable support.

REFERENCES

Balota, D. A. (1983). Automatic semantic activation and episodic memory encoding. *Journal of Verbal Learning and Verbal Behavior, 22,* 88 - 104.

Barsalou, L. W. (1983). Ad hoc categories. *Memory & Cognition, 11,* 211 - 227.

Becker, C. A. (1979). Semantic context and word frequency effects in visual word recognition. *Journal of Experimental Psychology: Human Perception and Performance, 5,* 252 - 259.

Collins, A. M., & Loftus, E. F. (1975). A spreading-activation theory of semantic processing. *Psychological Review, 82,* 407 - 428.

De Groot, A. M. B. (1980). *Mondelinge woordassociatienormen.* [Verbal word association norms]. Lisse: Swets & Zeitlinger.

De Groot, A. M. B. (1983). The range of automatic spreading activation in word priming. *Journal of Verbal Learning and Verbal Behavior, 22,* 417 - 436.

De Groot, A. M. B. (1985). Word context effects in word naming and lexical decision. *Quarterly Journal of Experimental Psychology, 37A,* 281 - 297.

De Groot, A. M. B. (1989). Representational aspects of word imageability and word frequency as assessed through word association. *Journal of Experimental Psychology: Learning, Memory, and Cognition, 15,* 824 - 845.

De Groot, A. M. B., & Nas, G. L. J. (1989). *The bilingual mental lexicon: Some within- and between-language connections between lexical representations.* Manuscript submitted for publication.

De Groot, A. M. B., Thomassen, A. J. W. M., & Hudson, P. T. W. (1982). Associative facilitation of word recognition as measured from a neutral prime. *Memory & Cognition, 10,* 358 - 370.

Ervin, S. M., & Osgood, C. E. (1954). Second-language learning and bilingualism. *Journal of Abnormal Social Psychology, Supplement,* 139 - 146.

Fischler, I. (1977). Semantic facilitation without association in a lexical decision task. *Memory & Cognition, 5,* 335 - 339.

Forster, K. I., & Davis, C. (1984). Repetition priming and frequency attenuation in lexical access. *Journal of Experimental Psychology: Learning, Memory, and Cognition, 10,* 680 - 698.

Fowler, C. A., Wolford, G., Slade, R., & Tassinary, L. (1981). Lexical access with and without awareness. *Journal of Experimental Psychology: General, 110,* 341 - 362.

Holender, D. (1986). Semantic activation without conscious identification in dichotic listening, parafoveal vision, and visual masking: A survey and appraisal. *Behavioral and Brain Sciences, 9,* 1 - 66.

Lupker, S. J. (1984). Semantic priming without association: A second look. *Journal of Verbal Learning and Verbal Behavior, 23,* 709 - 733.

Marcel, A. J. (1983). Conscious and unconscious perception: Experiments on visual masking and word recognition. *Cognitive Psychology, 15,* 197 - 237.

Meyer D. E., & Schvaneveldt, R. W. (1971). Facilitation in recognizing pairs of words: Evidence of a dependence between retrieval operations. *Journal of Experimental Psychology, 90,* 227 - 234.

Mitchell, D. C. (1982). *The process of reading: A cognitive analysis of fluent reading and learning to read.* Chichester: Wiley.

Morton, J. (1969). The interaction of information in word recognition. *Psychological Review, 76,* 165 - 178.

Neely, J. H. (1976). Semantic priming and retrieval from lexical memory: Evidence for facilitatory and inhibitory processes. *Memory & Cognition, 4*, 648 - 654.

Seidenberg, M. S., Waters, G. S., Sanders, M., & Langer, P. (1984). Pre- and postlexical loci of contextual effects on word recognition. *Memory & Cognition, 12*, 315 - 328.

6 LEXICAL PROCESSING, MORPHOLOGICAL COMPLEXITY AND READING

Robert Schreuder
Marjon Grendel
Nanda Poulisse
Ardi Roelofs
Marlies van de Voort

University of Nijmegen

INTRODUCTION

One of the basic processes involved in reading is word recognition. This process is a very efficient one considering the fact that the normal reading rate is around five to eight words a second. This process involves looking up a word and retrieving the associated information in the very short time span of 125 - 200 ms. This is fast considering estimations of passive vocabulary size of approximately seventy thousand lemma's (Oldfield, 1963). The number of access representations could be dramatically higher if one would assume that every inflected form of such a lemma would have its own access representation. Thus, a theory of word recognition has to take into account the morphological status of access representations. Some aspects of this issue also have consequences, as we argue presently, for word recognition as it occurs during reading, that is, when word recognition takes place as part of processing a larger linguistic structure than the single word.

Questions about the role of morphology in word recognition can be summarized as follows (Henderson, 1985):

1. To what extent are words decomposed into their constituent morphemes prior to lexical access? (e.g., Taft & Forster, 1975).

125

2. Does the mental lexicon contain separate lexical entries for morphological variants of words and for the constituent morphemes of compounds? (e.g., MacKay, 1978; Murrell & Morton, 1974).

3. Is there any evidence for the existence of morphological rules, and if so, what is their nature?

It is obvious that these questions are closely related. In this chapter, however, we focus on the second question. We attempt to shed some light on the problem of the mental representation of morphological variants. With respect to this issue, three main hypotheses have been distinguished.

One has been referred to as the full listing hypothesis (Butterworth, 1983). According to the full listing hypothesis words are stored in and retrieved from the mental lexicon as full forms. This implies that all the individual forms of a word have independent representations. Thus, *read, reader, reads* and *reread* each has a separate lexical entry.

The second hypothesis holds that words are represented in the lexicon only by their stems (or base forms) and that the full forms are to be derived by the application of morphological rules (see MacKay, 1978, for a related view). According to this hypothesis, the mental lexicon has independent lexical entries READ, -ER (meaning AGENT), -S (meaning THIRD PERSON SINGULAR PRESENT TENSE), and RE- (meaning DO AGAIN), plus some specifications as to which morphemes can be combined with each other.

The third (and weaker) hypothesis claims that both full forms and morphemes are listed in the lexicon (e.g., Caramazza, Laudanna, & Romani, 1988, the so-called augmented addressed morphology [AAM] model). Such models are in fact a combination of the first two types of models.

In this chapter, we present some data bearing on the role of inflectional and derivational morphological structures during word recognition. On the one hand, the experiments presented here test some aspects of the AAM model for inflected forms. However, these experiments also explore a particular subset of morphologically complex words that are of special interest for the process of word recognition during reading. These are complex verbs consisting of a particle (often a preposition or an adverb) and a verb such as *aan + vallen* 'attack' or *weg + lopen* 'walk away'. Both in Dutch and in German, the particle of these complex verbs can appear much later in the sentence than the accompanying verb parts, as can be seen in Example 2.

1. *De soldaten mogen niet aanvallen.*
   The soldiers are not allowed to attack.

2. *De soldaten vielen die nacht aan.*
   The soldiers attacked that night.

This introduces interesting problems for the processing system, to be argued later.

Before presenting a review of some of the crucial studies that have been conducted on the role of morphology in word recognition, we discuss briefly the distinction between inflectional and derivational morphology. Inflectional morphemes, such as the suffix -s in the English form *rereads*, are rule governed. These rules generally apply to all members of a grammatical class. As such, they are semantically predictable, which means that they do not radically change the meaning of the word stem to which they are added nor do they change its grammatical category. Derivational morphemes, on the other hand, can be used to express special meanings that are not reliably predictable from the meaning of the component morphemes. An example given by Henderson (1985) is the word pair *to generate–generation*. Although *generation* is clearly derived from *to generate*, the meaning of the stem is not the same in these two words, and there is a change in grammatical category. In contrast to inflectional morphemes, derivational morphemes combine with only a relatively small subset of words. Hence, derivational processes are not necessarily productive. Given the notion of predictability, one could assume that decomposition for inflected forms is more probable than decomposition for derived forms, because the meaning of a derived word is not always a simple function of the meaning of its parts. Or, in linguistic terminology, derived forms are not fully compositional whereas inflected forms are.

EMPIRICAL EVIDENCE FOR A DECOMPOSED LEXICON

Prefix Stripping

Much of the research on the internal representation of morphologically complex words was inspired by Taft and Forster's (1975) theory of prelexical morphological decomposition. Taft and Forster presented a model of word recognition which combined a decomposed lexicon with a prelexical decomposition process, and hence their model is relevant to the first two questions mentioned at the beginning of this chapter. Their model consists of several stages. In the first, possible affixes are detected and stripped off the word form. In the second, the lexicon is searched for an entry corresponding to the word stem. If this entry is not found, a search is started for the entry of the whole word. If, however, the entry for the stem is found, the next step is to check if stem plus affix form a word.

Taft and Forster's decomposition model predicts longer latencies in lexical decision tasks for pseudo-affixed words, such as *premium* and *sublime*, than for truly affixed words such as *subnormal*). In both cases, prelexical decomposition takes place, but in the case of a pseudo-affixed word, more tests are required to decide on its being a real word. This prediction was supported by the results of Taft and Forster's (1975) investigations, in which they utilized a lexical-decision task (see also Taft, 1981). Manelis and Tharp (1977), however, and Henderson, Wallis, and Knight (1984) failed to find evidence for morphological decomposition when (derivationally) suffixed rather than prefixed words were used. They found no differences in the lexical decision times for pseudo-suffixed and truly suffixed words. Thus, there appears to be a difference between suffixes and prefixes.

In line with these last findings, Bergman, Hudson, and Eling (1988) obtained similar effects using Dutch words with pseudoprefixes, but not for Dutch words with pseudosuffixes. These authors argue for a model where the basic access representation is the stem. The prefix in this model is not stripped, but its access is a by-product of stem extraction.

Other investigators tested the prelexical decomposition model by means of a paradigm which exploits the fact that words are recognized more easily when they are presented for a second time (repetition priming). The interpretation of the (often conflicting) results obtained with repetition priming is not without problems, however. It is often claimed that evidence for the role of morphology in repetition priming arises due to morphological analyses performed *after* lexical access (e.g., Bergman, 1988, Henderson, 1985). That is, morphological structures might become available as a result of lexical access, without playing a role in the process of access itself. For this reason, we do not discuss this line of evidence here.

The AAM Model

Recently, Caramazza et al. (1988) investigated the issue of the level of morphological decomposition in the mental lexicon studying the Italian inflectional system for verbs. They assumed that a letter string activates both whole-word representations (for known word forms) as well as the morphemes that comprise a word. The stimulus *walked* will activate the access representations WALKED, WALK-, and -ED (as well as orthographically similar representations). Because the model stipulates that the whole word representations for known words will always reach their thresholds before the associated morpheme representations reach theirs, it is assumed that the decomposed access units only play a role when the letter string forms a word seen for the first time. In a number of lexical decision experiments, Caramazza et al. varied the morphological structure of nonword stimuli. The pattern of results was both inconsistent with a fully decomposed lexicon and with a lexicon of full forms only.

One problem with this study is that it crucially depends on pseudoword processing in a lexical-decision task. The reason for this is that the AAM model predicts that morphological complexity of existing word forms does *not* influence lexical access time as long as these word forms have an access representation. Caramazza et al. claimed that their model could only be tested by varying inflectional structures of pseudowords. Lexical-decision experiments, however, may encourage subjects to use special strategies (Balota & Chumbley, 1984). For this reason, such experiments may tap task-related rather than natural behavior. Furthermore, there is the question whether processing of non-words can give essential information about the processing of real words. Fortunately, there is a technique that allows one to test some of the properties of the AAM model while using existing words. This same technique can also be used for testing prefix stripping theories using a naming task rather than a lexical-decision task.

THE SHORT SOA PRIMING TASK

Inflection

Jarvella, Job, Sandström, and Schreuder (1987)[1] adopted a priming technique from Eriksen and Eriksen (1974) that avoids many of the problems just noted. They showed some of the letters of a word as a prime, while the remaining letters were momentarily withheld. After a very short SOA (30 to 60 ms), the remaining letters were filled in, making the whole word visible. In a nonpriming trial, the word was presented all at once. The idea behind this technique is that presenting some parts of the word first (e.g., the stem) will affect lexical access more than presenting other parts first.

The study by Jarvella et al. indicated that this method is potentially fruitful for studying the effects of morphological structure in early stages of lexical processing. Their results indicated that inflected verb forms in Italian had decomposed entries, whereas the Dutch verb forms seemed to have a full listing. The results are as yet inconclusive because precise controls in that study were lacking. The rationale for our using the task they employed to investigate the AAM model is as follows. Assume that a lexicon is organized as described by the AAM model and consider the Dutch verb form *helpt* (2nd and 3rd person singular, present tense; 'to help'). According to AAM the lexicon contains the entries HELPT, HELP-, and -T. We present the string *help* for 60 ms and then add the final *t*. Both HELPT and HELP- will become activated (presumably HELP- will get a higher activation). As, according to Caramazza et al., the phonological output lexicon is also organized in a morphologically decomposed form, both access representations will start to preactivate the phonological output representation HELP-. This then predicts that, if we present the form *help* with the final *t* presented 60 ms later, the naming latency for *helpt* will be faster than when we present *helpt* in the no-priming condition. The earlier studies of Jarvella et al. suggest that 60 ms is enough to trigger the access representation of a given form. However, controls are crucial to show that this is an effect of morphological information and is not caused by orthographic priming only. Therefore the same conditions will be used with a control noun like *helft* ('half') of the same length but without an internal morphological

---

[1] The technique used in the experiments presented in this article was developed by Bob Jarvella and Remo Job.

structure. That is, *helf* is *not* a word stem like *help*. The AAM model predicts that the amount of priming should be larger when a string with morphemic status is given as a prime (*help* for the form *helpt*) than with a nonmorphemic prime (*helf* for the form *helft*).

Of course, a full listing theory does not predict a difference. We return to the issue of a fully decomposed lexicon in the discussion. A fully decomposed lexicon is, at least for a language like Dutch, on purely linguistic grounds very improbable, as we argue.

Because we used complex verbs of two morphemes, it is possible also to use the *second* morpheme as a prime. It is not clear what the AAM model would predict here, but again the full entry theory does not predict a difference between morphologically defined strings and strings that have no morphological status.

Derivationally Complex Words

Taft and Forster's (1975) prefix-stripping model and the left-to-right parsing model of Bergman (1988) and Bergman et al. (1988) both suggest that access of the prefix and access of the stem occur separately. It seems reasonable to assume that to present these parts asynchronously in time would be helpful in the identification of these substructures. Therefore, both models predict priming effects for the first morpheme used as a prime and for the second morpheme used as a prime. That is, in both cases a separation in time helps to identify the two components that have to be accessed separately.

MORPHOLOGICAL PROPERTIES
OF THE MATERIALS USED

This study consisted of four different parts. In two of these, the experimental items were inflected verb forms, as in the experiments run by Caramazza et al. (1988). The other two parts involved verb forms with derivational prefixes and complex verbs with a separable, preposed particle. Here, we address the difference between separable and inseparable verb particles. The Dutch language distinguishes between verbs with separable derivational prefixes and verbs with separable particles, often prepositions or adverbs. In the case of separable particles the particle that is attached to the stem in the infinitive verb form (*aannemen*) is separated from the stem in the inflected verb forms. Consider the following examples:

3. *Zullen we dat cadeautje AANNEMEN?*
    (Shall we accept that present?)
4. *Ik NEEM dat cadeautje niet AAN.*
    (I do not accept that present.)

Inseparable prefixes are always attached to the stem, whether they occur in infinitive verb forms or inflected verb forms. This is illustrated in Examples 5 and 6.

5. *Je had dat feit moeten VERMELDEN.*
   (You should have mentioned that fact.)
6. *Ik VERMELD dat feit niet.*
   (I do not mention that fact.)

The reason to include verbs with separable particles is that they have the important property of generally being noncompositional. As an example consider the verb *vallen* ('to fall') in complex verbs with a preposition like *aanvallen* ('to attack'), *afvallen* ('to lose weight'), *omvallen* ('to fall over'), *invallen* ('to invade'). In these cases, knowing the meaning of the verb *vallen* and knowing the meaning of the preposition does not help much in predicting the meaning of the combination of the two. The noncompositionality of the verbs with a separable particle poses some interesting problems for lexical access during reading, because after having accessed *vallen* there can be a stretch of several words before the associated particle appears, for example, *aan*. But the meaning of the sentence cannot be computed on the basis of the separate entries of *aan* and *vallen* alone! Rather, these two have to be combined in some way so that the entry for their combination becomes available. That is, it seems as if the morphological structure of this type of complex verb has to be represented in some way in the lexicon. If we expect evidence for morphological structures in the access lexicon for Dutch verbs at all, we expect it in the case of these verbs. Neither the left-to-right parsing theory nor the prefix stripping theory make a distinction between different types of preposed particles, and thus both models predict the same amount of priming for the different types of verbs.

METHOD

Subjects

The subjects were 51 native speakers of Dutch, all students at the University of Nijmegen. They were paid for their participation.

Materials and Design

The words were selected from lists of potential stimuli that were generated from the CELEX data base (cf. Schreuder & Kerkman, 1987). This data base, which was constructed for linguistic research, contains lexical information for approximately 110,000 Dutch headwords (i.e., stems or lemmas). This is nearly exhaustive for the Dutch language.[2]

---

[2] Because we posed many constraints on our materials, they are almost exhaustive for the Dutch language. That is, it would not be possible to run the same experiment again using other materials. For this reason, we did not compute statistics across materials. There are two possibilities to overcome the generalization problem in this case. One is that other experiments using other methods and/or designs should be run looking at the same issues. The other is to study other languages that have the same phenomenon. German is such a language. We are currently pursuing both approaches.

The four parts of the experiment were conducted in one combined design. There were two inflection and two derivation subexperiments. The stimuli for each part were different. Within each subexperiment the stimuli were divided into two equal groups of items: experimental items and control items.

For the first subexperiment, dealing with inflectional suffixes, 48 word pairs were found that fulfilled our requirements. The experimental items were verbs with the following inflectional endings: -*t* (2nd and 3rd person singular present tense) and -*te* (2nd and 3rd person singular past tense). The control items were nouns ending in noninflectional -*t* or -*te*. These nouns differed from the verbs in only one letter, as shown in Examples 7 and 8.

	Experimental	Control
7.	*beeft* 'trembles' -	*beest* 'beast'
8.	*hoopte* 'hoped' -	*hoogte* 'height'

The second part, dealing with inflectional prefixes, consisted of 39 word pairs. The experimental items were past participles, starting with *ge-*. The control items were nouns, also starting with *ge-*. Again the difference between the experimental and the control items was that the string *ge-* has a morphological status in the experimental items but not in the control items as shown in Examples 9 and 10.

	Experimental	Control
9.	*gelucht* 'aired' -	*gehucht* 'hamlet'
10.	*gerafeld* 'frayed' -	*geranium* 'geranium'

In the third part, dealing with separable particles (again, 39 word pairs), the experimental items were verbs in the infinitive form beginning with one of the following separable particles: *uit-, aan-, toe-, op-, in-, af-, om-*. The control items were nouns beginning with one of these seven letter strings, but this time the letter strings did not function as prefixes, that is, they were pseudoprefixes, as shown in Examples 11 and 12.

	Experimental	Control
11.	*indrukken* 'press' -	*industrie* 'industry'
12.	*omkeren* 'turn round' -	*omelet* 'omelet'

In the fourth subexperiment, dealing with derivational inseparable prefixes, 39 word pairs were used. Four inseparable prefixes occurred: *be-, ge-, ver-,* and *ont-*. The control items were nouns starting with the same letter strings, but, as in the second subexperiment, these strings did not function as prefixes but as pseudoprefixes as shown in Examples 13 and 14.

	Experimental	Control
13.	*betonen* 'show' -	*begonia* 'begonia'
14.	*verteren* 'digest' -	*verkering* 'courtship'

All groups of experimental and control words were matched for frequency, number of syllables, word length, and stress pattern as far as possible in order to obtain comparable naming latencies in the baseline conditions. All items were presented in three conditions:

1. Without an SOA, that is, with all letters shown at once (the NO-PRIMING condition).

2. With the first morpheme, or the corresponding part of the control items, appearing 60 ms before the remainder of the word (the M1 condition, respectively C1 condition).

3. With the second morpheme, or the corresponding part of the control items, appearing 60 ms before the remainder of the word (the M2 condition, resp. C2 condition).

Each subject was presented with each item in only one of the three conditions. For each item, the three conditions were rotated across subjects. For each subject, the items of the four subexperiments were completely randomized.

Procedure

All subjects were tested individually. Their task was to name the stimuli as fast as possible. The words were displayed on a CRT screen attached to a BBC computer system. They were presented in lowercase letters of 3 mm height. The subjects were seated in front of the screen at a distance of approximately 30 cm. Each trial was preceded by a fixation point that appeared on the screen 600 ms before the stimulus was shown. The words disappeared as soon as the subjects vocalization triggered the voice key.

To familiarize the subjects with the procedure, a practice session consisting of 54 trials was run before the actual experiment. The stimuli in the practice session were representative of those used in the four subexperiments. Before the experimental session started, the subjects were given a short break. They were given another break during the experimental session when they had completed 200 of the 330 trials. Altogether, the session lasted approximately 35 minutes.

RESULTS

The naming latencies of incorrectly pronounced words were discarded from analysis, as were latencies outside the range of a subject's grand mean plus or minus two times the standard deviation for that subject. Nine subjects were excluded from analysis because their error percentage exceeded 5%. The rotation of materials across subjects was complete.

The mean naming latencies for the baseline condition (NO-PRIMING) of the different subparts are reported in Table 6.1. There was no difference between the experimental and the control items in the baseline conditions of the inflectional suffix, the separable particle, and inseparable prefix subexperiments: respectively $t(82) = 0.814$, $MSE = 175.66$, $t(82) = 1.379$, $MSE = 301.94$, and $t(82) = 0.820$, $MSE = 308.83$, $p > 0.05$. In the inflectional prefix part, however, the control items were named significantly faster than the experimental items ($t(82) = 5.532$, $MSE = 388.92$, $p < 0.05$).

TABLE 6.1

Mean Naming Latencies (ms) for the No-priming Condition of the Inflectional Suffix, Inflectional Prefix, Separable Particle, and Inseparable Prefix Parts.

	Experimental	Control
Inflectional Suffix	521	518
Inflectional Prefix	564	543
Separable Particle	505	510
Inseparable Prefix	538	534

For all parts of the experiment, a priori contrasts were carried out to test whether the amount of facilitation obtained by priming the target word by part of it differed between the experimental and the control items. The amount of facilitation is the difference between a priming condition (M1, M2, C1, C2) and its baseline condition (NO-PRIMING).

Means for the conditions of the inflectional suffix part are shown in Table 6.2. The M1 condition showed no difference in facilitation between the experimental and the control items ($t(82) = 1.22$, $MSE = 175.66$, $p > 0.05$). Also, the difference in facilitation between the experimental and the control items in the M2 condition failed to reach significance ($t < 1$). Thus, providing an inflectional suffix gave the same amount of priming as a nonmorphological control string.

Means for the conditions of the inflectional prefix part are presented in Table 6.3. The amount of priming was not significantly greater for the experimental items than for the control items in both the M1 condition and the M2 condition ($t < 1$). Again, there is no evidence for a morphological priming effect.

TABLE 6.2

Means for the Conditions of the Inflectional Suffix.[a]

	Experimental			Control		
	No-priming	M1	M2	No-priming	C1	C2
Example	(hapte)	(hap)	(te)	(halte)	(hal)	(te)
	521	474	523	518	476	517
		[47]	[-2]		[42]	[1]

[a] Mean naming latencies (ms) for the experimental and the control words without a prime (No-priming) or primed by either their first morpheme (M1) or the second morpheme (M2), or primed by a nonmorphemic string in the control conditions (C1 and C2, respectively). Square brackets indicate the amount of facilitation in ms.

TABLE 6.3

Means for the Conditions of the Inflectional Prefix.[a]

	Experimental			Control		
	No-priming	M1	M2	No-priming	C1	C2
Example	(gewed)	(ge)	(wed)	(gewei)	(ge)	(wei)
	564	539	543	543	519	527
		[25]	[21]		[24]	[16]

[a] Mean naming latencies (ms) for the experimental and the control words without a prime (No-priming) or primed by either their first morpheme (M1) or second morpheme (M2), or primed by a nonmorphemic string in the control conditions (C1 and C2, respectively). Square brackets indicate the amount of facilitation in ms.

Means for each condition of the derivational separable prefix part are presented in Table 6.4. The facilitation was significantly greater for the experimental items than for the control items in the M1 condition and in the M2 condition (respectively, $t(82) = 1.84$, $MSE = 308.83$, $p < 0.05$ and $t(82) = 4.98$, $p < 0.05$). For the experimental words, the M2 priming was significantly greater than the M1 priming ($t(82) = 3.008$, p

< 0.05). Thus, in this case it does appear that a morphological priming effect has been obtained.

TABLE 6.4

Means for the Conditions of the Derivational Separable Particle.[a]

	Experimental			Control		
	No-priming	*M1*	*M2*	*No-priming*	*C1*	*C2*
Example	*(inenten)*	*(in)*	*(enten)*	*(intentie)*	*(in)*	*(tentie)*
	505	479	467	510	494	499
		[26]	[38]		[16]	[11]

[a] Mean naming latencies (ms) for the experimental and the control words without a prime (No-priming) or primed by either their first morpheme (M1) or second morpheme (M2), or primed by a nonmorphemic string in the control conditions (C1 and C2, respectively). Square brackets indicate the amount of facilitation in ms.

TABLE 6.5

Means for Conditions of the Inseparable Prefix.[a]

Experimental			Control		
No-priming	*M1*	*M2*	*No-priming*	*C1*	*C2*
(betonen)	*(be)*	*(tonen)*	*(begonia)*	*(be)*	*(gonia)*
538	515	512	534	508	512
	[23]	[26]		[26]	[22]

[a] Mean naming latencies (ms) for the experimental and the control words without a prime (No-priming) or primed by either their first morpheme (M1) or second morpheme (M2), or primed by a nonmorphemic string in the control conditions (C1 and C2, respectively). Square brackets indicate the amount of facilitation in ms.

The mean naming latencies for the conditions of the inseparable prefix part are shown in Table 6.5. No difference was found in facilitation between the experimental and the control items in the M1 condition ($t < 1$) = 0.49, $MSE = 388.92$, $p > 0.05$). The difference between the experimental and the control items in the M2 condition also failed to reach significance ($t < 1$) = 0.66, $p > 0.05$).

DISCUSSION

Before discussing the pattern of data we first briefly mention some general methodological aspects of the experiment. The design of this study used experimental and control groups of words. As can be seen in Table 6.1 these groups were fairly well matched for naming time in the nonpriming condition. Only in the inflectional prefix subexperiment was a significant difference in naming time obtained. The effect of priming is calculated by subtracting *within* either the experimental or the control group of words, so the absolute size of the nonpriming condition is not very crucial. However, the amount of priming obtained could well be a function of the response time (RT) in the nonpriming condition in that words that have relatively slow naming times would show more priming. In the inflectional prefix condition, the RTs in the NO-PRIMING condition are higher in the experimental group, which means that the priming effect in this group might be overestimated. The data analysis, however, shows no significant difference. This suggests that the interpretation of the results of the inflectional prefix subexperiment as showing no morphological priming is justified.

Our results can be briefly summarized as follows. First, there were only effects of morphological structure for derivationally complex verbs with separable particles, both when priming involved the preposed particle and when priming involved the verb part of the complex verb. This indicates that our task is in principle sensitive enough to show effects of morphological structures and allows us to interpret the results of the other three subexperiments as not simply due to a lack of sensitivity. Second, the morphological priming occurred for verbs with separable particles. In the introduction we have claimed that it seemed necessary that especially those verbs should have their morphological structure reflected in the lexicon. Our finding is in line with this.

Inflectionally Complex Forms

The AAM model of Caramazza et al. (1988) predicts priming effects for the inflectionally complex verb forms used in two of the four subparts of our experiment. However, all priming effects obtained in those two parts were not larger than the priming obtained with similar strings without morphological status.

Caramazza et al. (1988) used as their materials Italian inflected verb forms (and nonwords with varying morphological structure, using Italian verb stems and affixes). They found evidence for a decomposed lexicon for these forms whereas we did not. This outcome is somewhat similar to that of Jarvella et al. (1987), whose results also suggested a decomposed lexicon for Italian inflected verb forms. However, they found no evidence for the existence of the complete full form as an entry. For Dutch, the results showed a pattern similar to that which the AAM model would have predicted. This latter study, however, still lacked controls with nonmorphological parts of words as priming strings.

Although not totally conclusive, their results show decomposition in the lexicon for Italian and not for Dutch inflected verb forms. It is possible that this is due to the different properties of the verb inflectional systems of these languages. The Italian language has a much more complicated verb inflectional system than the Dutch language. This means that the amount of storage saved by only storing stems and affixes of verbs and not storing all full forms would be much larger for Italian than for Dutch. Thus, if a difference emerges when these languages are investigated in psycholinguistic experiments, then one would expect effects indicating a decomposed lexicon for Italian verbs but not for Dutch verbs. The opposite finding would be rather counterintuitive. In other words, the AAM model might be the right one for some languages but not for all languages. This clearly points to the importance of cross-linguistic comparisons in psycholinguistic research (see also Mitchell, Cuetos, and Zagar, this volume).

Derivationally Complex Verb Forms

Our results are problematic for models that assume prefix stripping or left-to-right parsing. Both type of models predict morphological priming effects for both of the types of derivationally complex verbs we used. Our results, however, showed significant morphological priming only in the case of verbs with a preposed, separable particle. We have postponed, so far, further discussion of problems associated with a fully decomposed lexicon, that is, a lexicon where the only access units are the simple morphemes, both bound and free. As stated before, we think that for a language like Dutch (and presumably also for English, cf. Henderson, 1985) this is simply not a realistic option. First, there is the problem of noncompositionality. Many of the derivational complex forms are noncompositional, and even when they seem to be compositional they often still have idiosyncratic meaning aspects. But there is also a computational issue. A fully decomposed lexicon entails processes like affix stripping. That is, a complex word form should be disassembled in order to access the different morphemes. But in many cases something will be stripped that was not a prefix after all, in the case of so-called pseudoprefixes like *premium* and *sublime*. We have begun some computational research on the relative occurrences of prefixes and pseudoprefixes in Dutch using the CELEX lexicon containing 110,000 lemmas with frequency information based on a 44-million-word corpus. Preliminary results show that for Dutch, prefix stripping is not a very attractive option (Schreuder & Kusters, in preparation). In approximately 75% of the cases that a prefix would be stripped from a word in our corpus, it turns out to be a pseudoprefix. Therefore, from a computational point of view, prefix stripping should be avoided, making a fully decomposed lexicon unattractive for Dutch.

Morphological Priming in a Nondecomposed Lexicon?

This leaves us with a Dutch lexicon that is not decomposed. Remember that the verbs for which we did find effects of morphological structure consisted of a preposed particle and a verb. Both the particle and the verb part of these verbs occur as free morphemes in Dutch and need to have their own access representation in the lexicon by definition. They have to be represented in the access lexicon according to *any* theory. Therefore, we would suggest that our results are consistent with a full listing hypothesis (e.g., Butterworth, 1983). We still have to explain, then, why we found an effect of morphological priming for verbs with separable particles.

Our account of this finding is as follows. We assume that all free-occurring particles like prepositions and all (inflected) forms of simple verbs are connected with the entry of the corresponding complex form if it exists in the language. That is, we assume that the entry for the preposition *aan* is connected with *aanvallen*, 'to attack', *aanpassen*, 'to adapt', *aankijken* 'to look at', and so on. Similarly the entry for *vallen* is connected with *aanvallen* but also with *afvallen* 'to lose weight' and all other complex verb forms that contain the verb part *vallen*. Earlier, we stated that a particle (e.g., a preposition) of a complex verb can appear many words later in the sentence than the verb stem. When the preposition is recognized it still has to be combined with the verb part to look for the meaning of the combination that is most often noncompositional. Compare *Zij viel ondanks alle problemen uiteindelijk aan*, 'Despite all problems she finally attacked', and *Zij viel ondanks alle problemen uiteindelijk af*, 'Despite all problems she finally lost weight'.

According to our proposal, access representations of simple verbs and those of free-occurring particles like prepositions and adverbs are connected with the access representations of the complex verbs that contain their combination. When such a simple verb or a particle is accessed, activation will spread to the access representations of the complex verbs to which they are connected. When, separated in time, both are accessed, their combined influence on the access representation of the complex form should be enough to trigger it and so make available the idiosyncratic information that is unique for *this* particular combination of verb and particle.

This account entails the following critical prediction. Because there is no connection between simple verbs and complex verbs with a nonseparable prefix, we predict that the verb *vallen* will activate the complex verb *aanvallen* (preposition) but not *bevallen* which contains the same verb but now with an inseparable prefix. The reason for this is that during reading, the verb *vallen* never needs to be recombined with a prefix like *be* coming later in the sentence. This prefix is *always* attached to the verb and therefore no links between prefix, verb, and complex verb access representations are necessary. Currently, we are exploring these aspects of our account of this interesting process that we would like to call *distributed lexical access*.

CONCLUSION

In this chapter, lexical access of morphologically complex verbs was studied. Both inflectionally and derivationally complex verb forms were used. A naming task was used in which a part of a word could be given a very short headstart. When reaction times to words presented in this way are compared with the naming times of the same words presented all at once, a priming effect can be obtained. To control for graphemic priming, exactly the same or very graphemically similar subparts were presented twice: Once when they had a morphological status in a given verb and once when they did not. Only in the case of verbs with separable preposed particles did we find a significant morphological priming effect. The results are discussed with respect to existing theories of access of morphologically complex words. Also, morphological differences between languages and some computational issues are taken into account. It seems that, at least for Dutch, the full listing hypothesis is still tenable.

It is argued, furthermore, that verbs of the type that produced significant morphological priming effects pose special problems for lexical access in reading. Their subparts can be separated by a large amount of intervening verbal material, yet often their meaning cannot be computed on the basis of the meaning of the subparts alone. We offer the hypothesis that the morphological subparts of these verbs have access representations that are connected to the access representation of the complex form. These connections make it possible to retrieve the meaning information associated with the complex form when both of its subparts are presented asynchronously in time. These connections most likely produced the priming effects observed in our experiment.

REFERENCES

Balota, D. A., & Chumbley, J. I. (1984). Are lexical decisions a good measure of lexical access? The role of word frequency in the neglected decision stage. *Journal of Experimental Psychology: Human Perception and Performance, 10,* 340 - 357.

Bergman, M. W. (1988). *The visual recognition of word structure: Left-to-right processing of derivational morphology.* Unpublished doctoral dissertation. University of Nijmegen.

Bergman, M. W., Hudson, P. T. W., & Eling, P. A. T. M. (1988). How simple complex words can be: Morphological processing and word representations. *Quarterly Journal of Experimental Psychology, 40A,* 41 - 72.

Butterworth, B. (1983). Lexical representation. In B. Butterworth (Ed.), *Language production* (Vol. 2, pp. 257 - 294). London: Academic Press.

Caramazza, A., Laudanna, A., & Romani, C. (1988). Lexical access and inflectional morphology. *Cognition, 28,* 297 - 332.

Eriksen, B. A., & Eriksen, C. W. (1974). The importance of being first: A tachistoscopic study of the contribution of each letter to the recognition of four-letter words. *Perception & Psychophysics, 15*, 66 - 72.

Henderson, L. (1985). Toward a psychology of morphemes. In A. W. Ellis (Ed.), *Progress in the psychology of language* (Vol. 1, pp. 15 - 72). London: Lawrence Erlbaum Associates.

Henderson, L., Wallis, J., & Knight, D. (1984). Morphemic structure and lexical access. In H. Bouma & D. G. Bouwhuis (Eds.), *Attention and performance X* (pp. 211 - 227). London: Lawrence Erlbaum Associates.

Jarvella, R. J., Job, R., Sandström, G., & Schreuder, R. (1987). Morphological constraints on word recognition. In A. Allport, D. G. MacKay, W. Prinz, & E. Scheerer (Eds.), *Language perception and production: Relationships between listening, speaking, reading, and writing* (pp. 245 - 265). London: Academic Press.

MacKay, D. G. (1978). Derivational rules and the internal lexicon. *Journal of Verbal Learning and Verbal Behavior, 17*, 61 - 71.

Manelis, L., & Tharp, D. A. (1977). The processing of affixed words. *Memory & Cognition, 5*, 690 - 695.

Murrell, G. A., & Morton, J. (1974). Word recognition and morphemic structure. *Journal of Experimental Psychology, 102*, 963 - 968.

Oldfield, R. C. (1963). Individual vocabulary and semantic currency: A preliminary study. *British Journal of Social and Clinical Psychology, 2*, 122 - 130.

Schreuder, R., & Kerkman, H. (1987). On the use of a lexical data base in psycholinguistic research. In W. Meys (Ed.), *Corpus linguistics and beyond* (pp. 295 - 302). Amsterdam: Rodopi.

Schreuder, R., & Kusters, D. (in preparation). Prefix stripping: Some lexical statistics.

Taft, M. (1981). Prefix stripping revisited. *Journal of Verbal Learning and Verbal Behavior, 20*, 289 - 297.

Taft, M., & Forster, K. I. (1975). Lexical storage and retrieval of prefixed words. *Journal of Verbal Learning and Verbal Behavior, 14*, 638 - 647.

7 EYE MOVEMENTS AND LEXICAL ACCESS IN READING

Alexander Pollatsek and Keith Rayner

University of Massachusetts, Amherst

INTRODUCTION

We suspect that virtually everyone would agree that we can learn about reading from the pattern of eye movements and duration of eye fixations (see Rayner & Pollatsek, 1989). However, there is still a good deal of controversy over what kinds of inferences about cognitive processes can be made from the eye-movement record. In this chapter, we discuss what is known about the relationship between eye movements in reading and comprehension processes in order to explore the legitimacy of various types of inferences drawn from eye movement data.

To focus our discussion, we begin with two well-known examples of eye-movement research. First, consider the following two sentences.

Even though Jay usually jogs a mile seems very long to him.
Even though Jay usually jogs a mile this seems long to him.

Two possible grammatical structures are possible up to the point of disambiguation (*seems* or *this* in the two sentences, respectively). It has been shown that readers fixate longer on the word *seems* in the first sentence than on the word *this* in the second sentence, whereas there is no discriminable difference in the eye-movement record in the two sentences up to that point (Frazier & Rayner, 1982). In other words, there is a disruption in processing the first sentence that appears within a couple of hundred milliseconds after the reader fixates on *seems*, or in less than a second after the first point at which processing could have begun on *seems* (given our knowledge of the perceptual span). Hence, we can conclude that the lexical encoding of *seems* and the discovery of difficulty in fitting it into a syntactic structure are accomplished (at least some of the time) in less than a second and that the syntactic structure of the sentence is being constructed on-line. In addition, the fact that disruption only occurs in the first sentence (and not until the point of disambiguation) allows us to discriminate among theories of parsing (see Section 2 of this book).

A second example of the use of eye-movement records to make inferences about cognitive processes in reading is the use of multiple regression analyses on fixation times during reading (Just & Carpenter, 1980). Just and Carpenter employed gaze duration (the total time spent fixating on a word before another word was fixated) and assumed that it represents the time to do all processing on a word: lexical access, adding it to the syntactic structure, integration into the meaning of the sentence, and so on. Using this assumption (called the immediacy assumption), they attempted to test a model of reading by examining how well gaze duration could be predicted from various linguistic indices (such as word frequency, part of speech, etc.) via a regression analysis.

Clearly, the latter method is making stronger assumptions about the eye movement record than the former. It assumes that the gaze duration on a word represents the processing time for that word, and furthermore, that it can be decomposed into the sum of component effects due to various linguistic variables. Much of what we discuss argues that this interpretation of gaze duration is wrong and thus that the regression analysis is unjustified. Even so, we shouldn't despair. The alternative use of eye movements is quite powerful and has allowed us to say quite a bit about the process of reading. However, its logic is ordinal: All we know is that some part of sentence X takes longer to process than the corresponding part of sentence Y. Hence, in order to understand which cognitive operation takes longer, it is usually necessary to use perfectly controlled sentence materials, with a possible cost in ecological validity.

In sum, the examples given (and others to follow) indicate that the eye movement record is reflecting cognitive processes in reading. However, other data indicate that the relationship between fixation times and cognitive processes is far more complex than that assumed by Just and Carpenter in making the immediacy assumption. As most conclusions from the eye-movement record assume some implicit theory of eye-movement control, it would be best if this theory was at least close to the truth. Our agenda is as follows. We first review some data on the relationship of eye movements to the text being processed. We then consider a model of eye-movement control during reading that we view as the simplest one that is remotely plausible. We next present some data which imply that reality cannot be quite this simple and finally ponder what a more complex model would look like. Our exploration of the simpler model allows us to discuss implications for drawing inferences about cognitive processes during reading. We touch on syntax and sentence integration; however, our focus is on lexical access and how it relates to the progress of the eyes across the page. This is because understanding the relationship between lexical access and eye-movement control is central to making any kind of inference about on-line comprehension processes in reading.

Before going on, we need to clarify what we mean by *lexical access*. The conception we rely on in this chapter is that there is an internal lexicon in which representations of individual words are stored at different nodes. When sufficient excitation occurs at one of these nodes (or possibly when the difference between the excitation at the appropriate node and excitation at other nodes exceeds threshold), lexical access occurs. At this moment, presumably there is recognition that the stimulus is a word, and access of other information (such as the meaning of the word, its syntactic class, its sound, and its spelling) would be rapid if not immediate. There is currently controversy over whether such a "magic moment" exists (see Balota, this volume) or whether the access of lexical and other types of information are incremental processes. At present, the issue is not decided, although there is certainly no magic measure of lexical access time from reaction time measures if the construct of lexical access is valid. We persevere in maintaining a relatively simple conception of lexical access, however, because a more complex conception would make models of eye movements in reading dangerously unconstrained.

BACKGROUND:
THE PERCEPTUAL SPAN IN READING

It would clearly be difficult to relate eye movements to cognitive processing if readers extracted information from a wide area of the page. Fortunately, this is not the case. The moving window technique (McConkie & Rayner, 1975) has established that the area from which readers extract visual information is quite limited. The logic of the method is as follows. Subjects read text displayed on a cathode ray tube (CRT) while their eye movements are being recorded. A computer is interfaced with both the eye-movement recording system and the CRT and displays text contingent upon where the subject is fixated. The major finding from such studies is that when readers are given a window of normal text extending from about 4 characters to the left of fixation to about 15 characters to the right of fixation, reading speed and comprehension are the same as if no window were present (see Rayner & Pollatsek, 1987, for a summary of this work). However, if the window is restricted to the fixated word, reading is slowed down to about 60% of the normal rate although comprehension is unaltered (Rayner, Well, Pollatsek, & Bertera, 1982).

Hence, although readers are extracting useful visual information from a restricted area, it is significantly larger than the fixated word. Although this ability to extract parafoveal information is beneficial to readers and allows them to read faster, it is somewhat unfortunate for cognitive psychologists; if the perceptual span were a single word, we would know exactly which word was being processed on each fixation, and the relation between cognitive processing and eye movements would be far simpler. The next simplest possibility is that readers extract a variable number of words on a fixation: often just one, but sometimes two or even three. If this were the case (and readers skipped to the first word not encoded), making inferences about lexical access from eye movements would still be fairly simple. The data, unfortunately, indicate that the situation is more complex and that some words are processed on more than one fixation (see Rayner & Pollatsek, 1987).

There are now many lines of evidence that indicate that information is combined across fixations in reading. We cite two. First, whereas the perceptual span extends 15 characters to the right of fixation, the size of the average saccade in reading is only about 7 - 9 characters; thus the perceptual span on successive fixations overlaps. However, this argument is loose; because the perceptual span is the maximum region from which information is extracted, the average region might be appreciably less. More convincing data come from a study by Rayner et al. (1982), in which the window presented to the subject was the fixated word (word n) plus three characters of the following word (word $n + 1$). The major finding was that reading speed was appreciably faster when these extra characters were presented, even though precautions were taken never to expose the entire next word. In fact, in some conditions, reading speed was almost as fast in these conditions as when the entire word $n + 1$ was exposed.

Rayner et al.'s (1982) experiments thus indicate that partial information about a word can be extracted from one fixation and used to facilitate processing of the word on the next fixation (we refer to this as the preview effect). This conclusion is supported by the finding that naming time for a word is speeded when there is a parafoveal preview on the prior fixation (Balota & Rayner, 1983; Rayner, McConkie, & Ehrlich, 1978; Rayner, McConkie, & Zola, 1980). Space does not permit going into the details, but the pattern of data that emerges from these experiments is that the partial information that is crucial for facilitation is the first two or three letters of the parafoveal word. In addition, the available evidence indicates that the integration involves relatively abstract codes, because changing the case of the letters has no effect on the size of the preview effect. Furthermore, there is at present no positive evidence indicating that morphemic codes are involved in the integration process.

To summarize, extraction of visual information is related to where the eye is fixating. At worst, the reader is extracting the visual information from the word two to the right of the fixated word, and much of the time may be processing no more than the fixated word. Thus, the effects of cognitive processes on eye movements are likely to be reasonably immediate. For example, in the sentence discussed at the beginning of the chapter, one can conclude that visual processing of the word *seems* begins no earlier than two fixations before it is fixated, so that the disruptive effect observed when fixating *seems* is registered no more than about 750 ms after the beginning of visual information extraction on *seems* (and probably appreciably less than 750 ms after). However, other disruptive effects occur after *seems* is fixated, making the task of inferring cognitive processes from fixation times more complex.

MORE BACKGROUND:
IMMEDIACY OF EYE-MOVEMENT CONTROL

So far, we have reviewed data bearing on how visual information is extracted from text. However, the previous discussion says little about how cognitive events during reading are expressed in the eye-movement record. There are two ways to approach the issue of eye control: correlational and experimental. First, let us consider the correlational evidence.

When the eyes move through text, the pattern of fixations is in fact not random but bears certain relations to the text being read. One illustration is the example discussed at the beginning: Disruption due to inappropriate syntactic parsing was reflected fairly immediately in the eye-movement record (sometimes right on the disambiguating word). Variables directly related to the extraction of visual information also have an effect on the eye-movement record. Word frequency affects the first fixation duration[1] on a word (Inhoff & Rayner, 1986; Rayner & Duffy, 1986) and it also affects the gaze duration (Inhoff & Rayner, 1986; Just & Carpenter, 1980; Rayner & Duffy, 1986). Although word length is highly confounded with word frequency in English and most languages (and probably contributes to the previously mentioned frequency effect), word frequency influences both of these fixation time measures even when word length is controlled (Inhoff & Rayner, 1986; Rayner & Duffy, 1986). Furthermore, the predictability of a word from the prior sentence context influences both the first fixation duration (Zola, 1984) and gaze duration on the word (Balota, Pollatsek, & Rayner, 1985) and also the probability that a word is skipped (Balota et al., 1985; Ehrlich & Rayner, 1981). The most parsimonious explanation for these results is that lexical access is influencing eye movements (at least some of the time) and that predictability influences the speed of lexical access.

In contrast, the effects of higher-order variables such as inferential processes may often be delayed or smeared over a number of fixations (Rayner & Duffy, 1988). For example, when subjects attempt to look up the antecedent for a pronoun, the process is often revealed in the eye-movement record a word or two downstream from the pronoun (Ehrlich & Rayner, 1983); when the difficulty of finding the antecedent is varied by manipulating the gender relationship between the pronoun and noun (e.g., when *he* or *she* may refer to *doctor*), the effect often is both

---

[1] The first fixation duration is defined as the duration of the first fixation on a word if there are multiple fixations or the duration of the fixation if there is only one fixation on a word. The mean first fixation (and mean gaze duration) is usually computed conditional on there being a fixation on a word (i.e., when the word is skipped, that is not counted as a zero ms fixation).

delayed beyond the initial fixation on which the pronoun was plausibly encoded and smeared out over a series of fixations on the phrase following the pronoun (Ehrlich & Rayner, 1983; Carroll & Slowiaczek, 1987). It thus appears that some comprehension processes are slower than lexical access and their expression in the eye-movement record may be more complex.

The subsequent discussion focuses on the question of how lexical access affects eye movements. One reason for this is that the multiple regression analyses mentioned earlier (Just & Carpenter, 1980; Kliegl, Olson, & Davidson, 1982) found that most of the variability in eye movements can be explained by word frequency and/or word length. A second is that (as we have just argued) the effects of comprehension processes may be registered on the eye-movement record in a more complex manner. As to be shown, understanding how lexical access relates to eye movements is difficult enough.

STILL MORE BACKGROUND:
THE TIMING OF EVENTS ON A FIXATION

One reason that people were skeptical that there could be a close relation between cognitive operations during reading and eye movements was a belief that there wasn't enough time during a fixation for cognitive events occurring during that fixation to influence the decisions of when and where to move the eye next. The argument was made most strongly about lexical access and goes something like this. A typical fixation in reading is about 225 ms or so. Certain experiments indicate that the latency of an eye-movement being programmed to a known target is about 175 ms (Arnold & Tinker, 1939; Rayner, Slowiaczek, Clifton, & Bertera, 1983; Salthouse & Ellis, 1980), suggesting that lexical access of the fixated word would have to be completed within the first 50 ms or so of the fixation in order to have any effect on how long it is fixated. Because it is usually assumed that lexical access takes at least about 150 - 200 ms, this appears to rule out lexical access as an important influence on eye movements.

There may be problems with this argument, however. First, 175 ms may be an overestimate of the time in reading between when the appropriate visual information has been extracted and when an eye-movement is executed. One assumption made in the experiments mentioned is that no visual information needs to be extracted on a fixation, as the position of the target is known beforehand. However, the subjects may still have waited for visual information on each fixation in order to program an eye movement (perhaps some sort of double-checking operation). In addition, the latency of the eye movements in such experiments may have been slowed down by the implicit requirement that they be made relatively accurately to the spatial location of the target. In contrast, eye movements in reading appear to be fairly variable – they appear to be programmed to the middle of a word but with a considerable amount of variability (McConkie, Kerr, Reddix, & Zola, 1988; O'Regan, 1981; Rayner, 1979) – and thus may be able to be programmed more quickly. Second, lexical access may take less than 150 - 200 ms (especially if partial information has been extracted on a prior fixation). Thus, there is no strong plausability argument against the assertion that lexical access of the fixated word can guide the eye on that fixation.

In addition, there is conclusive evidence that at least some visual events on a fixation can influence both the duration of that fixation and the length of the ensuing saccade. Rayner and Pollatsek (1981; see also Morrison, 1984) demonstrated that when the text in central vision was delayed, the duration of the fixation was lengthened, even when the delay of text was randomly varied from fixation to fixation. Similarly, when the size of the window of text was varied randomly from fixation to fixation, the size of the saccade was a function of the size of the window. Thus, visual events on a fixation can influence both the timing and location of the ensuing saccade. As we shall see, however, it is still far from clear what the relationship between lexical access and the pattern of eye movements is.

A Simple Model of Eye-Movement Control

A relatively simple model of eye-movement control in reading has been proposed by Morrison (1984). Although there are problems with it, it has promise for being a good basis for developing an adequate theory. In addition, if it were true, the relationship between cognitive processes and eye movements would be relatively simple. As a result, we discuss the model in some depth and then see what additional assumptions need to be made (which will complicate the relationship between cognitive processes and eye movements). We warn you in advance that it accounts for eye movements solely in terms of lexical access, which our prior discussion indicates cannot be true. However, before worrying about that complication, let's see how far it can be pushed.

Morrison's model has five key assumptions. The first is that there is an internal attention mechanism that jumps ahead word by word. The second is that the signal to move attention to the next word is lexical access of the current word. The third is that each new "fixation" of attention on a word produces a motor program to move the eyes to that word. There is a latency between when the motor program is created and the saccade is executed – let us call it the motor program latency to distinguish it from the total fixation duration – which is assumed to have a mean and variability determined by the oculomotor system and unrelated to processing of text. There is evidence that such a covert visual attention mechanism exists and is related to eye movements (Posner, 1980; Wurtz, Goldberg, & Robinson, 1982), but whether it moves forward in a word-by-word fashion and whether there is such a direct link between visual attention and eye movements are still open questions.

Given these three assumptions, the eye-movement record would have a fairly simple relation to lexical access times. Lexical access of the first word on a line (which would not be seen before it was fixated) would begin when the word was fixated, would be completed, and then an eye movement would occur on average X ms afterwards (where X is the mean motor program latency). Thus, mean fixation time would equal mean lexical access time plus X. For subsequent words on the line, however, lexical access would start when attention shifted so that lexical access would start on average X ms before the word was fixated and – if we assumed this speeded lexical access by X ms – the Xs would cancel so that lexical access time would equal mean fixation time (see Figure 7.1).

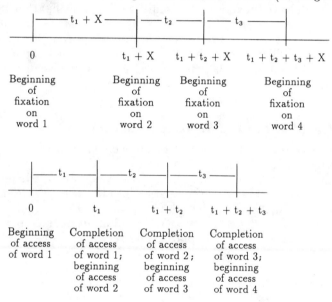

FIGURE 7.1. A diagram of a hypothetical temporal sequence of events according to Morrison's model.[a]

[a] The top panel represents the observed pattern of eye movements (the duration of the saccade is not represented in order to simplify the picture). The lower panel represents the sequence of cognitive operations driving the eye movement in the upper panel. The time scale in both panels is the same. Notice that the sequence of observed events lags behind lexical access by a fixed amount X. (Actually, X would be a random variable.) Thus, the fixation times on words 2 and 3 would equal the lexical access times for those words, but the fixation time on word 1 would be equal to the lexical access time plus X.

To summarize, so far we have assumed something close to the immediacy assumption for lexical access but assumed that processing begins in the parafovea. From that, we have gotten a simple relation (equality) between fixation times and lexical access times for all but the first word on a line of text. Let us emphasize that this simplicity follows only if we assume that the processing of words is completely serial (i.e., no processing of word $n + 1$ begins before processing of word n is complete). In addition, we have to realize that the total lexical access time includes X ms of processing in the parafovea, and thus might be different if the entire processing of the word was foveal.

Things are not so simple, however. Most importantly, we know that many words in reading are skipped. This phenomenon is accounted for in Morrison's model by the fourth and fifth assumptions. The fourth assumption is that eye movements can be programmed in parallel. That is, when the eye is fixated on word n, it is possible that the reader can make two jumps of attention – to word $n + 1$ and then to word $n + 2$ – before the eye actually moves to word $n + 1$. If so, then two eye movements are programmed on word n and each executed an average of X ms after attention shifted. Thus, the fixation time on word $n + 1$ might be quite short, as the saccade to end it was programmed sometime during the fixation on word n. The fifth assumption is based on the work of Becker and Jurgens (1979). Morrison assumed that if two attention shifts (and hence two eye-movement programs) occur within a certain time window, then the second program cancels the first; this is backward masking in the motor domain. Sometimes the first motor program will leave absolutely no trace, whereas sometimes the resulting eye movement will be intermediate in location between where the two eye-movement programs were directed (Becker & Jurgens, 1979).

These two assumptions provide an elegant way to explain word skipping without having to invoke a complex decision mechanism. That is, if the word to the right of the fixated word (word $n + 1$) is encoded quickly, attention will move to word $n+2$ soon after it moved to word $n + 1$ and hence the eye-movement program to word $n + 1$ is likely to be cancelled and word $n + 1$ skipped. Because high-frequency and/or predictable words (such as function words) are likely to be encoded rapidly, Morrison's model provides an account of why they are frequently skipped. Moreover, it explains another interesting phenomenon: When a word is skipped, the fixation time on the preceding word is lengthened (Hogaboam, 1983; Pollatsek, Rayner, & Balota, 1986). This follows from the model because skipping involves cancelling an earlier eye-movement program and replacing it with a later one.

Before proceeding to explore problems with Morrison's model, let's briefly take stock of what implications it would have for inferring lexical access times from the eye-movement record. First, the parallel programming assumption adds no complication to the analysis when there is no cancellation of eye movements (see Figure 7.2). However, when words are skipped, the lexical access time for word $n + 1$ is added to the fixation time on word n (see Figure 7.3). The previous argument indicates that if Morrison's model were correct, the relation between fixation times and lexical access times would be relatively simple. There would be some problem in knowing how to relate parafoveal encoding times and foveal encoding times. In addition, one would have to figure out how to partition the time on a word prior to a skipped word into lexical access time for the fixated word and lexical access time for the skipped word, or else avoid analysis of regions in which skipping occurred. Unfortunately, there is evidence from several sources indicating that the story isn't so simple. We have already mentioned an important one: Higher-order processes are involved and hence lexical access is not the sole cause of eye movements.

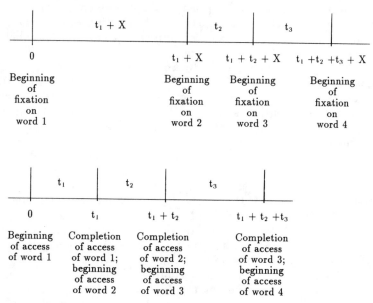

FIGURE 7.2. A diagram of a hypothetical sequence of events according to Morrison's model. The representation is the same as in Figure 7.1.[a]

[a] Note that lexical access of words 1 and 2 are both completed before the beginning of fixation 2. Nonetheless, the same logic applies as in Figure 7.1, and the relationship between fixation durations and lexical access times is as in Figure 7.1.

Discourse comprehension effects clearly need to be accounted for by a mechanism beyond the five already given. The simplest such mechanism would be one in which the normal processes driven by lexical access are interrupted when higher-order processes signal that something does not compute, and others take over while the reader is reanalyzing the sentence until the problem is resolved. The work of Frazier and Rayner (1982), among others, demonstrates that the pattern of eye movements is fairly variable when such reanalysis occurs, including maintaining fixation at the region of disambiguation, regressing to the region of ambiguity, or going back to the beginning of the sentence. Attempting to account for such patterns is well beyond the scope of this chapter, so we slough over higher-level intervention in eye-movement control. Instead, we concentrate on evidence that appears to be unrelated to such higher-level intervention that does not appear to be easily accounted for by the five assumptions. Let us consider this evidence, the problems it raises for a model of eye-movement control, and the implications for interpreting eye movements in reading.

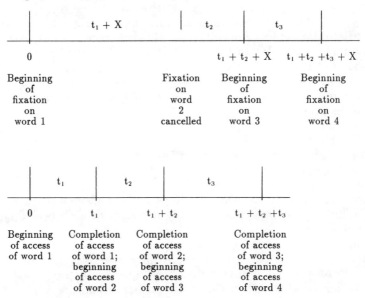

FIGURE 7.3. A diagram of a hypothetical sequence of events according to Morrison's model. The representation is the same as in Figures 7.1 and 7.2.[a]

[a] The representation is the same as in Figures 7.1 and 7.2. However, here lexical access of word 2 is so rapid that the program to move to word 3 cancels the program to move to word 2. Thus, the lexical access time of word 2 is added to the fixation time on word 1. In this case, the first fixation time also includes X. However, if word 3 were skipped instead of word 2, the fixation time on word 2 would have been $t2 + t3$.

Refixations of Words

There are two types of refixations on words: those in which a regression is made back to a word from a subsequent word and those in which the subject moves from one point in a word to another point in the same word (usually in a forward direction) before moving on to another word. We assume that the first kind of regression can be explained by syntactic and semantic miscomputations and concentrate on the latter (which we call consecutive fixations on the same word). They present a clear problem for Morrison's model because, on the face of it, the model has no mechanism for predicting such consecutive fixations.

One mechanism that could explain consecutive fixations without any major modification of Morrison's model is error in directing the eye. That is, the reader may intend to place the next fixation on word $n + 1$, but undershoot some fraction of the time and land again on word n instead. This is a plausible explanation for some consecutive fixations, as there is appreciable random variability in the programming of eye movements. As there is undoubtedly a Fitts' Law underlying all motor movements – a trade-off between speed and accuracy – this variability may be necessary in order to allow the eyes to move rapidly enough to read at 300 words per minute. McConkie et al. (1988) found that the distribution of fixations on words are truncated normal distributions whose means are a bit to the left of center of the word, suggesting that there is both random variability and a bias to undershoot in sending the eye in reading. Moreover, there is no reason to believe that there is a magic mechanism that truncates the tails of the distributions (which would be either refixations or skips).

In other words, it appears that at least part of the story with consecutive fixations is uninteresting: Some are undoubtedly due merely to inaccuracy in eye-movement programming. Even so, the presence of this motor noise introduces a complication in our analysis of fixations. To obtain estimates of lexical access times, our observations will have to be adjusted in some way. Perhaps if the parameters estimated by McConkie et al. (1988) are relatively invariant over texts and subjects, the corrections will not be too difficult.

Random error in eye guidance is not the sole source of consecutive fixations, however, because the probability of refixating a word can be shown to be a function of text variables. Specifically, Inhoff and Rayner (1986) showed that (when there was no parafoveal preview of a word) word frequency did not affect the first fixation duration on the word but did affect the gaze duration on it. As the increased gaze duration in these conditions is primarily due to a greater probability of refixating the word, that means that word frequency did not affect the decision of how long to stay in the first fixation (i.e., a decision of when to go) but did affect whether the next fixation was on the same word or on a different word (i.e., a decision of where to go). Similarly, Balota et al. (1985) showed that gaze duration (but not first fixation duration) was affected by the predictability of a target word in the sentence. Thus, we need to introduce some additional mechanism that accounts for intelligent refixations.

One option would be to change the unit of analysis and posit that the unit processed in one attentional fixation is smaller than a word: perhaps a syllable or morpheme. However, both of the cited experiments used fairly short target words, many of them monosyllabic, making the smaller unit hypothesis a fairly implausible explanation for the phenomena discussed. Thus, Morrison's model appears to need a more basic revision.

The alternative that changes the model least is to explain consecutive fixations as a compromise between a command to move on to the next word and a command to stay on the same word. That could conceivably occur if some signal tells the eye to move on that is closely followed by a signal to remain on the fixated word. As we argued before, Becker and Jurgens' work indicates that if two such commands occur in close temporal contiguity, the resulting eye movement can be an average of the two locations (in this case, a refixation on the word further into the word). Although this explanation seems plausible (and would be a minimal expansion of the theory), a major obstacle is to specify a cognitive operation that would produce a command to stay that could operate quickly enough. Perhaps a little background is needed to explain the problem.

Morrison's model was inspired by an earlier model by McConkie (1979) which had the basic mechanism of an internal attentive process preceding and controlling the eye movements. However, the signal that McConkie posited for moving the eyes was that there was difficulty extracting information in a region and that the eyes should go to the region of difficulty. The problem with such a mechanism is that "difficulty" is a negative computation: A failure to compute something sufficiently rapidly that would only be detected after a certain amount of time has elapsed and no computation has emerged. Thus, it would seem to be too slow to be driving eye movements whose mean latency is a little over 200 ms. Although one could conceivably build a difficulty detector (e.g., something that computed the derivative of lexical excitation with respect to time for visual information at a given spatial location and decided there was difficulty if the derivative was too small), difficulty does not seem like an attractive candidate for something to drive eye movements in reading.

The alternative is that the signal to stay on a word is a decision that something doesn't compute. Some candidates include: (a) An incorrect word has been accessed, (b) more than one word or meaning has been accessed, and/or (c) the word accessed does not compute in either the syntactic or semantic structure of the sentence being constructed. We have already seen evidence from garden path sentences that detection of such failures of computation can influence what happens after the first fixation on a word. Thus, if two signals occur in close proximity that say (a) "word accessed, move on to word $n + 1$" or (b) "something didn't compute so fixate word n again," the model as it now stands may be adequate to explain consecutive fixations. The key question, of course, is exactly what signal (b) is. Before exploring that, let us first examine the relationship between where to move and when to move in a bit more detail.

A problem with positing a different source of information underlying the decision to refixate (i.e., where to move) from that controlling the first fixation duration (i.e., when to move) is that Inhoff and Rayner's data suggest that word frequency affected them similarly. That is, if there was a parafoveal preview of a word, then both first fixation duration and gaze duration on a word were influenced by word frequency, whereas (as already discussed) if there was no preview, only gaze duration (and hence the probability of refixating) was affected. This suggests that lexical access can influence both, but that the decision of where to move can be affected later than the decision when to move. That is, if there is a preview, lexical access is occurring rapidly enough to control the first fixation duration on a word, whereas if there is no preview, lexical access appears only able to affect the decision of where to move the eye (see Rayner & Balota, 1989; Rayner & Pollatsek, 1987). Although this explanation sounds reasonable, it is not at all clear how to incorporate it into the model.

Inhoff and Rayner's data raise another problem for the model. When there is no preview of the word, the first fixation duration is not affected by the frequency of the word. Hence, the duration of this first fixation does not appear to be controlled by lexical access, contrary to one of the basic assumptions of Morrison's model. Thus, it appears that some signal prior to lexical access drives the eye to move forward in at least some circumstances. One possibility is a clock (i.e., if N ms have elapsed since the beginning of the fixation, move the eye forward regardless of whether lexical access is complete). A second is that there is a signal related to lexical access but prior to it. We consider such a mechanism in the next section. However, we wish to briefly discuss evidence against a clock mechanism being a major factor in reading.

In an experiment by Blanchard, Pollatsek, and Rayner (1989), the size of the window was varied from fixation to fixation during reading. There was little evidence that fixation times were controlled by any global measures such as the average window size (which would presumably affect the setting of the clock). Instead, fixation times appeared to be almost completely controlled by the size of the window on the prior fixation (i.e., whether there was a preview of the fixated word or not). This suggests that whatever is controlling fixation time is related to the ongoing processing of text even if it may not be lexical access.

Lower-Level Signals to Drive the Eye

Inhoff and Rayner's data indicate that, at least in some circumstances, the eye doesn't wait for lexical access to start to move. One possibility is that this occurs only in unnatural situations, such as in their experiment, where there is a restricted window. Perhaps in normal reading, lexical access always drives the eye. There are other data, however, which indicate that lexical access and higher-order processes such as text comprehension may not be the only drivers of the eyes. An experiment by Lima and Inhoff (1985) varied the orthography of target words, holding the frequency of the words and the predictability constant. Thus, in a target location, the target word might either be *dwarf* or *clown*. The difference between the target words is the amount of constraint on what the word could be given the first three letters: few words start with *dwa*, whereas many start with *clo*. The finding was that both first fixation duration and gaze duration were affected by this constraint manipulation, even when there was no parafoveal preview; the less constrained words were fixated for a shorter time than the more constrained words.

This makes sense if one thinks of the less constrained words as being more orthographically regular and hence more "normal." However, because word frequency was equated, there is no reason from anything we have said so far to expect normality to affect lexical access time. If one broadens the concept of lexical access, however, in the direction of current theorizing (McClelland & Rumelhart, 1981; Paap, Newsome, McDonald, & Schvaneveldt, 1982), then the pattern of data can be explained. That is, if words excite not only their own lexical entry but those of close neighbors, then a word that is highly constrained (and has few close neighbors in the lexicon) may produce less total excitation in the lexicon than a word that is less constrained. If we further postulate that a signal to move attention (and hence the eyes) is that a certain total level of excitation in the lexicon has been reached, then we can explain why orthographic regularity of a word can affect fixation time.

Ecologically, such a signal to move both attention and the eyes may make a good deal of sense. If lexical access is not always fast enough to move the eyes efficiently, then one would like a signal that would reliably indicate that lexical access is imminent. The computation that the level of excitation in the lexicon has crossed some threshold may be relatively easy, and it may signal that lexical access will occur with a high enough probability to be useful in signaling the eyes to move forward in reading. In addition, if there is some signal (which we have not specified) that can redirect a second fixation on the same word if there is trouble, then problems due to lexical access not being complete before the next word is fixated may be minimized. We hasten to point out, however, that the word-frequency effect discussed earlier is not merely an artifact of the orthographic effect; Rayner and Duffy (1986) obtained a substantial word-frequency effect on first fixation duration even with various letter bigram and trigram frequencies controlled for. Thus, this global lexical excitation mechanism would have to coexist somehow with a a more specific lexical access mechanism.

To summarize, there is work indicating that signals that are lower-level than lexical access can drive the eyes during reading. One possibility is that a certain level of total excitation has been reached in the lexicon. However, to the extent that such lower-level signals drive the eyes, we have obviously lost a direct connection between fixation times and lexical access times.

Changing Perceptual Span

A key assumption of Morrison's model is that attention moves ahead from word to word, with the eyes following X ms later. Thus, according to the model, each word should be processed for X ms in the parafovea, plus or minus some random error in the oculomotor system. The constancy of this preview benefit was one of the factors allowing a relatively simple translation between mean fixation times and mean lexical access times (until we started worrying about other things). Another way to view the constant preview assumption is that it assumes that the perceptual span is constant from fixation to fixation.

Although there are data that indicate that this assumption is relatively robust, it does not always hold. For example, Rayner (1986) found

that when text difficulty increased for children, the size of the perceptual span decreased. In another experiment (Inhoff, Pollatsek, Posner,
& Rayner, 1989) in which unusual text materials were used (the text
was rotated and twisted in various ways), the perceptual span changed
with the type of textual materials. For example, when words in the
text were rotated 180 degrees, then the perceptual span appeared to
be at most the fixated word when subjects began to read and extended
beyond the fixated word only after 4 days of practice. However, when
the words themselves were normal, but the order of the words on the
page was right-to-left, the preview benefit was as large as with normal
text. These two findings suggest that preview benefit may be constant
as long as the difficulty of accessing individual words is held constant.
Of course, Inhoff et al.'s experiment presents an extreme case, as the
difficulty of the text is manipulated in a way that goes far beyond what
is experienced in normal reading. In addition, the difficulty of the text
in the fovea and parafovea is confounded, so that one can't say for sure
whether information from word $n + 1$ is hard to extract because word
$n + 1$ is rotated or because word n is rotated (or both).

An experiment has been conducted, however, which demonstrates
that more ordinary types of difficulty appear to control preview benefit and hence the perceptual span. Henderson and Ferreira (in press),
varied the frequency of a target word (word n) and whether there was
a preview of word $n + 1$. They found that there was a preview benefit for word $n + 1$ only when word n was high frequency; there was
virtually no preview benefit when word n was low frequency. These
data cannot be explained by Morrison's model, because (as argued earlier) eye movements would lag a constant amount of time behind the
attention movements. According to Morrison's model, low-frequency
words should produce longer fixation times, but when lexical access is
completed, there should be the same amount of time to process the
parafoveal word before the eyes move.

This result appears to call for a fairly drastic revision of Morrison's
model, as it appears to call for at least some decoupling of attention and
eye movements. One possibility is that the coupling of attention and eye
movements postulated by the model is only statistical and that they are
driven by correlated, rather than identical, signals. There are several
possibilities; we have space for one. Part of the word-frequency effect
may be lexical access and part may be a text-integration effect: Lower
frequency words are harder to integrate into the sentence context than
are higher frequency words. Perhaps lexical access drives the eye movements, but attention does not move until the word has been successfully
integrated into the sentence. In the case of lower frequency words (if
text integration takes longer for them), there will then be a greater slip-
page between the movement of the eyes and that of attention and thus
there will be a reduced preview effect. Such a mechanism would also
explain the lack of a preview effect observed in another condition of the
Henderson and Ferreira experiment when the prior word was difficult to
process because it was hard to fit into the structure of the sentence.

To summarize, there are several findings that are difficult for Morrison's model to explain: (a) refixations on words, (b) occasional lack of frequency effects on first fixation durations, and (c) variable preview effects. In all cases, the simplicity of Morrison's model would have to be compromised in order to explain the phenomena. The solutions we proposed involved positing events other than lexical access to help guide the eyes. These processes included a process lower than lexical access – achieving a sufficient general level of excitation in the lexicon – and a higher level one – fitting the word into the current sentence structure. In addition, it appears that the assumption that eye movements and attention are tightly coupled is in error. All of these complications imply that lexical access times cannot be computed from fixation durations as simply as indicated in Figures 7.1 - 7.3.

IMPLICATIONS FOR UNDERSTANDING READING

We have used Morrison's model as a framework to explain why certain findings are hard to integrate into a coherent theory of eye-movement control. We close by discussing some implications for making inferences about reading from eye movements.

It is now clear, as we stated at the outset of this chapter, that a great deal can be learned about reading by examining the eye-movement record. Many of the experiments that we discussed here have clearly illuminated our thinking concerning the reading process. Where specific target words or regions of text can be identified for examination, resulting eye-movement data have shed light not only on word recognition and lexical access processes but also on processes such as (a) the resolution of lexical ambiguity (Duffy, Morris, & Rayner, 1988; Rayner & Duffy, 1986; Rayner & Frazier, 1989), (b) syntactic parsing strategies (Ferreira & Clifton, 1986; Frazier & Rayner, 1982, 1987; Rayner, Carlson, & Frazier, 1983; Rayner & Frazier, 1987), and (c) comprehension processes (Duffy & Rayner, 1989; O'Brien, Shank, Myers, & Rayner, 1988). In all three of these areas, eye-movement data have proved to be extremely important indicants of moment-to-moment text processing. However, the most obvious and important conclusion to be drawn from this chapter is that the eye-movement record needs to be interpreted with great caution. We are far from being able to use fixation times to derive estimates of lexical access times (or the times of any other component processes of reading). Clearly, we can pick up ordinal effects, such as finding greater disruption at a key target word in sentence A than in sentence B (if everything is carefully controlled). Because words can be processed in the parafovea, however, we have to exercise a bit of caution in making temporal estimates of how immediate effects are.

At several points in this chapter, we raised the possibility that word frequency effects observed in the eye-movement record may not be due to lexical access. In some sense, this is not particularly scandalous, as similar concerns have been raised about other putative measures of lexical access, such as naming time (Coltheart, 1978) and lexical decision time (Balota & Chumbley, 1984). In particular, we suggested that at least some of the effects thought to be due to access of a specific entry in the lexicon may be due either to prelexical effects, such as total excitation in the lexicon, or postlexical effects such as text integration. There are ways to try to pull these apart. One strategy is controlling for other factors, as in Rayner and Duffy (1986). A second, following Balota et al. (1985), is to vary the visual quality of the preview and to see whether it acts interactively or additively with something like predictability. If interactive, then Sternberg's additive factors logic suggests that predictability is affecting some aspect of visual information extraction, be it lexical or prelexical. A third is to use converging operations, such as determining whether a text manipulation affects fixation time and naming time similarly (Schustack, Ehrlich, & Rayner, 1987). Assuming that naming time merely taps lexical access, one can separate lexical and postlexical effects.

Perhaps a less obvious point that needs to be made concerns the interpretation of spillover effects. That is, it is tempting to conclude that if a manipulation on word n has effects on fixations on succeeding words, then the effects must be on postlexical processes, as lexical access on the word should be complete after the eye has left it. Henderson and Ferreira's experiment suggests another possible interpretation for some spillover effects, however. If word n was difficult to process, then word $n + 1$ may be deprived of an effective preview so that lexical access of word $n + 1$ is also slowed. A similar effect could be transmitted further down the line in the sentence. At present, we see no easy way to distinguish between the two explanations of spillover.

In sum, one has to exercise great caution in interpreting eye movements, but eye movements clearly do provide a reasonably good reflection of the cognitive processes in reading. We suggest that the best approach is to have one's test of theories merely based on ordinal properties of the data. In addition, the more the theory can specify where ordinal distinctions are to be found and where they are not, the better off one will be. Such an approach, however, may require understanding quite a bit of the technical detail about eye movements. The alternative is a method where some sort of algorithm can distill lexical access time and other processing times from the eye-movement record. As this chapter indicates, we are still a long way from having such an algorithm.

ACKNOWLEDGMENTS

Preparation of this chapter was supported by Grant #BNS86-09336 from the National Science Foundation. We thank David Balota and Ino Flores d'Arcais for their comments.

REFERENCES

Arnold, D. C., & Tinker, M. A. (1939). The fixational pause of the eyes. *Journal of Experimental Psychology, 25*, 271 - 280.

Balota, D. A., & Chumbley, J. I. (1984). Are lexical decisions a good measure of lexical access? The role of word frequency in neglected decision stage. *Journal of Experimental Psychology: Human Perception and Performance, 10*, 340 - 357.

Balota, D. A., Pollatsek, A., & Rayner, K. (1985). The interaction of contextual constraints and parafoveal visual information in reading. *Cognitive Psychology, 17*, 364 - 390.

Balota, D. A., & Rayner, K. (1983). Parafoveal visual information and semantic contextual constraints. *Journal of Experimental Psychology: Human Perception and Performance, 9*, 726 - 738.

Becker, W., & Jurgens, R. (1979). An analysis of the saccadic system by means of double-step stimuli. *Vision Research, 19*, 967 - 983.

Blanchard, H. E., Pollatsek, A., & Rayner, K. (1989). The acquisition of parafoveal word information in reading. *Perception & Psychophysics, 46*, 85 - 94.

Carroll, P., & Slowiaczek, M. L. (1987). Modes and modules: Multiple pathways to the language processor. In J. Garfield (Ed.), *Modularity in knowledge representation and natural language processing* (pp. 221 - 247). Cambridge, MA: MIT Press.

Coltheart, M. (1978). Lexical access in simple reading tasks. In G. Underwood (Ed.), *Strategies of information processing* (pp. 151 - 216). London: Academic Press.

Duffy, S. A., Morris, R. K., & Rayner, K. (1988). Lexical ambiguity and fixation times in reading. *Journal of Memory and Language, 27*, 429 - 446.

Duffy, S. A., & Rayner, K. (1989). *Eye movements and antecedent search: The effects of antecedent typicality and distance.* Manuscript submitted for publication.

Ehrlich, S. F., & Rayner, K. (1981). Contextual effects on word perception and eye movements during reading. *Journal of Verbal Learning and Verbal Behavior, 20*, 641 - 655.

Ehrlich, K., & Rayner K. (1983). Pronoun assignment and semantic integration during reading: Eye movements and immediacy of processing. *Journal of Verbal Learning and Verbal Behavior, 22*, 75 - 87.

Ferreira, F., & Clifton C. (1986). The independence of syntactic processing. *Journal of Memory and Language, 25*, 348 - 368.

Frazier, L., & Rayner, K. (1982). Making and correcting errors during sentence comprehension: Eye movements in the analysis of structurally ambiguous sentences. *Cognitive Psychology, 14*, 178 - 210.

Frazier, L., & Rayner, K. (1987). Resolution of syntactic category ambiguities: Eye movements in parsing lexically ambiguous sentences. *Journal of Memory and Language, 26*, 505 - 526.

Henderson, J. M., & Ferreira, F. (in press). The effects of foveal processing difficulty on the perceptual span in reading: Implications for eye movement control. *Journal of Experimental Psychology: Learning, Memory, and Cognition.*

Hogaboam, T. W. (1983). Reading patterns in eye movement data. In K. Rayner (Ed.), *Eye movements in reading* (pp. 309 - 332). New York: Academic Press.

Inhoff, A. W., Pollatsek, A., Posner, M. I., & Rayner, K. (1989). Covert attention and eye movements in reading. *Quarterly Journal of Experimental Psychology, 41A*, 63 - 89.

Inhoff, A. W., & Rayner, K. (1986). Parafoveal word processing during eye fixations in reading: Effects of word frequency. *Perception & Psychophysics, 40*, 431 - 439.

Just, M. A., & Carpenter, P. A. (1980). A theory of reading: From eye fixations to comprehension. *Psychological Review, 87*, 329 - 354.

Kliegl, R., Olson, R. K., & Davidson, B. J. (1982). Regression analyses as a tool for studying reading processes: Comment on Just and Carpenter's eye fixation theory. *Memory & Cognition, 10*, 287 - 296.

Lima, S. D., & Inhoff, A. W. (1985). Lexical access during eye fixations in reading: Effects of word-initial letter sequence. *Journal of Experimental Psychology: Human Perception and Performance, 11*, 272 - 285.

McClelland, J. L., & Rumelhart, D. E. (1981). An interactive activation model of context effects in letter perception: Part 1. An account of basic findings. *Psychological Review, 88*, 375 - 407.

McConkie, G. W. (1979). On the role and control of eye-movements in reading. In P. A. Kolers, M. E. Wrolstad, & H. Bouma (Eds.), *Processing of visible language* (Vol. 1, pp. 37 - 48). New York: Plenum.

McConkie, G. W., Kerr, P. W., Reddix, M. D., & Zola, D. (1988). Eye movement control during reading: 1. The location of eye fixations on word. *Vision Research, 28*, 1107 - 1118.

McConkie, G. W., & Rayner, K. (1975). The span of the effective stimulus during a fixation in reading. *Perception & Psychophysics, 17*, 578 - 586.

Morrison, R. E. (1984). Manipulation of stimulus onset delay in reading: Evidence for parallel programming of saccades. *Journal of Experimental Psychology: Human Perception and Performance, 10*, 667 - 682.

O'Brien, E. J., Shank, D. M., Myers, J. L., & Rayner, K. (1988). Elaborative inferences during reading: Do they occur on-line? *Journal of Experimental Psychology: Learning, Memory, and Cognition, 14*, 410 - 420.

O'Regan, K. (1981). The "convenient viewing position" hypothesis. In D. F. Fisher, R. A. Monty, & J. W. Senders (Eds.), *Eye movements: Cognition and visual perception* (pp. 289 - 298). Hillsdale, NJ: Lawrence Erlbaum Associates.

Paap, K. R., Newsome, S. L., McDonald, J. E., & Schvaneveldt, R. W. (1982). An activation-verification model for letter and word recognition: The word superiority effect. *Psychological Review, 89*, 573 - 594.

Pollatsek, A., Rayner, K., & Balota, D. A. (1986). Inferences about eye movement control from the perceptual span in reading. *Perception & Psychophysics, 40*, 123 - 130.

Posner, M. I. (1980). Orienting of attention. *Quarterly Journal of Experimental Psychology, 32*, 3 - 25.

Rayner, K. (1979). Eye guidance in reading: Fixation locations within words. *Perception, 8*, 21 - 30.

Rayner, K. (1986). Eye movements and the perceptual span in beginning and skilled readers. *Journal of Experimental Child Psychology, 41*, 211 - 236.

Rayner, K., & Balota, D. A. (1989) Parafoveal preview and lexical access during eye fixations in reading. In W. Marslen-Wilson (Ed.), *Lexical representation and process* (pp. 261 - 290). Cambridge, MA: MIT Press.

Rayner, K., Carlson, M., & Frazier, L. (1983). The interaction of syntax and semantics during sentence processing: Eye movements in the analysis of semantically biased sentences. *Journal of Verbal Learning and Verbal Behavior, 22*, 358 - 374.

Rayner, K., & Duffy, S. A. (1986). Lexical complexity and fixation times in reading: Effects of word frequency, verb complexity, and lexical ambiguity. *Memory & Cognition, 14*, 191 - 201.

Rayner, K., & Duffy, S. A. (1988). On-line comprehension processes and eye movements in reading. In M. Daneman, G. E. MacKinnon, & T. G. Waller (Eds.), *Reading Research* (Vol. 6, pp. 13 - 66). New York: Academic Press.

Rayner, K., & Frazier, L. (1987). Parsing temporarily ambiguous complements. *Quarterly Journal of Experimental Psychology, 39A*, 657 - 673.

Rayner, K., & Frazier, L. (1989). Selection mechanisms in reading lexically ambiguous words. *Journal of Experimental Psychology: Learning, Memory, and Cognition, 15*, 779 - 790.

Rayner, K., McConkie, G. W., & Ehrlich, S. (1978). Eye movements and integrating information across fixations. *Journal of Experimental Psychology: Human Perception and Performance, 4*, 529 - 544.

Rayner, K., McConkie, G. W., & Zola, D. (1980). Integrating information across eye movements. *Cognitive Psychology, 12*, 206 - 226.

Rayner, K., & Pollatsek, A. (1981). Eye movement control during reading: Evidence for direct control. *Quarterly Journal of Experimental Psychology, 33A*, 351 - 373.

Rayner, K., & Pollatsek, A. (1987). Eye movements in reading: A tutorial review. In M. Coltheart (Ed.), *Attention and performance XII: The psychology of reading* (pp. 327 - 362). Hillsdale, NJ: Lawrence Erlbaum Associates.

Rayner, K., & Pollatsek, A. (1989). *The psychology of reading.* Englewood Cliffs, NJ: Prentice-Hall.

Rayner, K., Slowiaczek, M. L., Clifton, C., & Bertera, J. H. (1983). Latency of sequential eye movements: Implications for reading. *Journal of Experimental Psychology: Human Perception and Performance, 9*, 912 - 922.

Rayner, K., Well, A. D., Pollatsek, A., & Bertera, J. H. (1982). The availability of useful information to the right of fixation in reading. *Perception & Psychophysics, 31*, 537 - 550.

Salthouse, T. A., & Ellis, C. L. (1980). Determinants of eye fixation duration. *American Journal of Psychology, 93*, 207 - 234.

Schustack, M. W., Ehrlich, S., & Rayner, K. (1987). Local and global sources of contextual facilitation in reading. *Journal of Memory and Language, 26*, 322 - 340.

Wurtz, R. H., Goldberg, M. E., & Robinson, D. L. (1982). Brain mechanisms of visual attention. *Scientific American, 246(6)*, 100 - 107.

Zola, D. (1984). Redundancy and word perception during reading. *Perception & Psychophysics, 36*, 277 - 284.

8 LEXICAL ACCESS: SOME COMMENTS ON MODELS AND METAPHORS

Odmar Neumann

University of Bielefeld

INTRODUCTION

The chapters that make up this section reflect a most interesting stage of scientific inquiry. They all draw upon findings and models from a line of research that was initiated about 20 years ago. Yet, some of them question basic notions of this research tradition; and almost all are critical of some of the assumptions that used to be regarded as conventional wisdom during these two decades. This tendency is apparent throughout this section, albeit in various degrees and with respect to different problems. Sure enough, much more can be found in each contribution than a critical attitude toward previous research. But the picture as whole – at least the picture as I interpret it – is one of a research field in transition rather than in a phase of consolidation.

The most articulate chapter in this respect is that of Seidenberg, who forcefully argues for a connectionist alternative to the classical view of the mental lexicon, whereas Besner points out some difficulties of this alternate approach as it stands presently. However, the doubts about the standard concepts of the lexicon and lexical access are not merely the repercussion of the connectionist revolution. Balota, who is not arguing from a connectionist point of view (although he does not seem unsympathetic to the PDP approach) develops his argument against some standard assumptions about lexical access out of a careful analysis of empirical findings. The chapters by Schreuder, Grendel, Paulisse, Roelofs, and van de Voort and by de Groot are centered around specific experimental investigations, but still both contain many critical reflections on standard assumptions, for example, about mechanisms of priming. Pollatsek and Rayner's chapter is particular in that it is based on findings from eye movement rather than RT research; that is, on data from an experimental situation that is both more complex and more natural than the tasks typically used in research on word recognition. It is interesting to note that, although Pollatsek and Rayner also caution against methodological pitfalls, they seem to be less worried about the basic assumptions underlying their research field than most of the other authors.

The aims of this commentary are two-fold. My first purpose is to put together, and to comment upon, the various worries about traditional assumptions voiced by these authors. I start by sketching the standard model and then discuss these worries (plus some of my own) under four headings: First, does lexical decision RT really reflect the time needed to access the lexicon? Second, a more radical question: Is there at all a point in time at which lexical access takes place? Third, do priming effects really reflect the structure of the lexicon? And finally, the most radical of these worries: Is there a lexicon at all?

In the second part of the chapter I put these questions into a slightly more general context. It seems that many of the current theoretical problems are related to assumptions that date back to the computer hardware metaphor and that seem unwarranted as soon as this metaphor is abandoned. I argue that, given the current upsurge of connectionism, the time may indeed be ripe for such a step.

THE STANDARD MODEL

By "standard model" I mean a set of assumptions that have been shared by most accounts of lexical access between the early 1970s and very recently. Of course, the various models that have been suggested (e.g., Becker, 1976; Forster, 1979; Norris, 1986; Seidenberg, 1985) differ in important details. Interest was naturally focused on these details as long as the common framework was more or less generally accepted. Under the present perspective, the similarities among the different models stick out more clearly.

The first and perhaps most general assumption of the standard model is that word recognition -- and, for that matter, the recognition of any stimulus -- consists in the activation of an internal representation. Treisman (1960) introduced the term *dictionary units* for these internal representations of words. Treisman's dictionary units were among the ancestors of Morton's (1969) *logogens*, which in turn were the ancestors of the *nodes* and *entries* of the later models.

The notion of dictionary units suggests a similarity between representations of words in the human processing system and entries in a dictionary or lexicon. This metaphor has subsequently found wide acceptance or, more exactly, it has mixed with two other metaphors into a common notion, whose metaphorical character seems to have sometimes been overlooked. One of these other ingredients has been the metaphor of accessing information stored in a computer memory. *Looking up a lexical entry* and *accessing an address in computer memory* merged into the hybrid metaphor of *lexical access*. The other ingredient has been the metaphor of a network in which activation can spread to neighboring units similar to an electrical charge spreading in a cable network.

Thus, the idea of the internal representation of words was elaborated into the idea of representational systems or lexica. This entailed several interesting questions. For example, how many lexica does the system encompass? How are they organized, that is, based on which properties are entries stored close together versus far apart? Via which routes are these lexica accessed?

To investigate these and similar questions, several promising tools were developed. One was the lexical decision task (Rubenstein, Garfield, & Millikan, 1970), that seemed to provide a direct means for measuring the time needed for lexical access. Another was the priming technique (Meyer & Schvaneveldt, 1971). If a prime facilitates the processing of a target word that follows it, then -- so the reasoning went -- this is evidence that their respective entries in the lexicon are linked or located close together, so that activation can spread between them. Thus, priming offered itself as a powerful technique for disclosing the internal structure of the lexicon. Further methods, such as measuring pronunciation latency (Meyer, Schvaneveldt, & Ruddy, 1975), completed the methodological inventory.

In summary, until recently the investigation of the internal lexicon and lexical access has looked like a healthy, coherent, and well-founded field of research – at least at the surface level, to use Balota's term. But as this section's chapters show, there are disturbances beyond the surface. It seems that none of the basic assumptions of the standard model is any longer undisputed. In the next section, I look into what I regard as the four major challenges against the standard model, as they appear in the foregoing chapters.

DOUBTS ABOUT THE STANDARD MODEL

The four questions to be discussed in this section carry different weight. The first addresses problems with research methodology that may not be unsolvable, whereas the last strikes at the root of the standard model. The other two are more severe than the first but probably less severe than the last.

First Challenge: Does Lexical Decision RT Really Reflect the Time Needed to Access the Lexicon?

At least in one sense, it seems now to be clear that the answer is no: lexical decision RT does not reflect access time in the sense that effects of independent variables on RT can unequivocally be attributed to differences in access time. Lexical decision RT may, however, reflect lexical access time in the sense that access time is one component of RT and that there are ways and means of separating this component from other components.

As has been assumed since the times of Donders (1868) and Wundt (e.g., 1903), response latency is composed of several components, often called stages. Hence, if an independent variable influences RT, this may in principle be due to its affecting any of, or any combination of, these components. The lexical decision task, which is a choice RT experiment, is, of course, no exception. However, until recently, most researchers who used this task seem to have worked on the tacit assumption that the variables of interest, such as word frequency, orthographic regularity, or priming, have their effect exclusively on the lexical access stage.

Unfortunately, this assumption is wrong. As Balota and Seidenberg point out, subjects in a lexical decision experiment are confronted with a discrimination task. Not surprisingly, it seems that they behave in much the same way as subjects in other discrimination tasks: They use the available cues, their performance depends on stimulus discriminability, and they select a decision criterion, all that will vary depending on task requirements. Balota and Seidenberg provide ample evidence that variables which were thought to affect exclusively lexical access (e.g., word frequency) act at the decision stage by providing additional cues, by influencing the discriminability of words and nonwords, and/or by changing the subjects' decision criterion.

Of course, this does not imply that these variables do not also affect lexical access. The (re)discovery of the neglected decision stage (Balota & Chumbley, 1984) poses a problem for using the lexical decision task as an operationalization of lexical access time, but this problem need not be unsurmountable. Indeed, this research field now finds itself in exactly the situation that RT research in general has been faced with from the beginning. Methods have been invented to deal with the problem of identifying the locus or loci at which a variable acts; most notably, of course, the additive factors method (Sanders, 1980; Sternberg, 1969). Another, potentially powerful method whose potential has not yet been fully explored is to compare different tasks as well as different output variables (e.g., RT and evoked potential latency) within a task. Some of these possibilities are discussed by Pollatsek and Rayner. De Groot's chapter contains a most interesting example of cross-tasks comparisons.

In principle, these methods could serve to disentangle the effects of a given variable on lexical access versus other stages of processing. However, Balota is nevertheless probably right in bringing up this problem in connection with his doubts about the concept of a magical moment. Although this concept is not incompatible with findings that some of the effects that have been attributed to lexical access are actually located at some other stage, the notion of a magical moment itself may well owe part of its popularity to the contrary assumption. It is, of course, not uncommon that the availability of a well-suited experimental paradigm drives theorizing. The oversimplified interpretation of the lexical decision paradigm may have nurtured the tacit assumption that lexical access as a discrete event is not a theoretical construct but an observable fact.

Second Challenge: Is There a Point in Time at Which Lexical Access Takes Place?

Within the standard model, the notion of lexical access has usually implied several assumptions. The most basic is that reading comprehension presupposes word recognition. Second, it has been assumed that word recognition takes place at some discrete moment in time (Balota's magical moment). Third, there has usually been the assumption that word recognition consists of at least two components, namely lexical access (finding the appropriate headword in the lexicon) and access to meaning (retrieving the information stored under the headword). (The model of Collins and Loftus, 1975, as discussed by de Groot, provides a good illustration.) A corollary of the last assumption is that lexical access and retrieval of meaning are not only separate events but that the former logically precedes the latter: You cannot possibly know what is stored under a headword before you know this headword in the first place.[1]

These assumptions have not always been made explicit and have rarely been questioned, during the reign of the standard model. This is not surprising, as they are all inherent in the logic of this model. If word comprehension is similar to accessing information stored under the word's address in a computer file, or to looking up the entry under the corresponding headword in a lexicon, then these assumptions follow quite naturally. On the other hand, there is not much to justify them independently of these metaphors. This is what Balota shows from an empirical point of view for two of these assumptions, and what Seidenberg demonstrates for all of them by presenting an alternative, connectionist view of lexical access.

Balota's two main points regard the magical moment and the assumed priority of lexical access relative to the retrieval of meaning. His alternative to both assumptions is an interactive, continuous processing view of lexical and semantic processing: As lexical processing is going on, its intermediate results feed into the semantic system in a cascade-like manner and receive in turn input from there. Because of the system's cascadic character, (some) meaning becomes available while

---

[1] There is less unanimity about whether this logical order also implies a temporal sequence. Whereas Balota and de Groot tend to this interpretation of the standard model, Seidenberg cites theories that equate lexical access with meaning access. Perhaps Pollatsek and Rayner capture both views in their formulation that, once lexical access has occurred, meaning access is supposed to be "rapid if not immediate". Indeed, the difference may be more one of degree than one of principle. If there is an automatic and very fast retrieval of meaning as a consequence of lexical access, it may be said that lexical access encompasses meaning analysis. If the retrieval of meaning is believed to be less automatic and more time consuming, it may be viewed as a separate, subsequent processing step.

lexical processing is still under way, and because of its interactive character, meaning can influence lexical processing via a top-down linkage. As Balota shows, both characteristics are in line with a host of empirical findings, for example, on threshold priming and on differences between the processing of meaningful an meaningless letter sequences.

As I interpret Balota's argument, its main thrust is not that there is no moment in time at which lexical access may be said to be accomplished but rather that (a) such a moment, if it exists, is not very interesting, because it is not the gateway to meaning, and (b) that it may be difficult to assess as it is not directly reflected in dependent measures such as lexical decision RT. It seems that Pollatsek and Rayner reach a somewhat similar conclusion in a different context. They discuss evidence that lexical access drives eye movements, but that under certain conditions a saccade to the next target is triggered before lexical access has been completed for the previously fixated word. This, they suggest, can be explained by assuming that a certain level of total excitation in the lexicon (prior to lexical access but indicating to the system that lexical access is imminent) is sufficient to trigger the eye movement. This proposal converges with Balota's line of argument in the conclusion that what happens during lexical access may be functionally more important than the moment at which the word's entry is found.

On the other hand, it is clear from Pollatsek and Rayner's analysis that continuous processing cannot be the whole story. At some discrete moment in time, the system must decide that sufficient lexical information has accrued to trigger an eye movement. Generally speaking, although input analysis may have a continuous character, motor control requires a threshold mechanism that dichotomizes the output of continuous processing for a *go/no go* decision.

Whereas Balota's chapter may be classified as revisionist with respect to the standard model, Seidenberg's is blatantly revolutionary. Its most revolutionary assumptions are discussed later under the question whether there is a lexicon at all. As to the construct of lexical access, Seidenberg suggests that what happens when a word is recognized is not access but computation. That is, recognition is not the activation of an entry that is already part of the lexicon. Rather, it is the creation of a new pattern of activity over a network's units that depends jointly on the state of the network prior to stimulus presentation and on the impact of the stimulus on the network.

This connectionist view of the recognition process diverges radically from the standard model. The issue is not restricted to lexical access. It bears upon the whole concept of recognition, in perception as well as in higher cognitive processes (see, e.g., the discussion of the schema concept in Rumelhart, Smolensky, McClelland, & Hinton, 1987). According to the traditional view, of which the standard model is just one example, recognition is essentially the access to, or the activation of, a structural entity (a node, an entry, a logogen, a schema, etc.) that was preexistent in memory prior to stimulus presentation, albeit in an inactive state. In a way, it is not the stimulus input that is represented as a result of the recognition process, but this memory entity. The input activates it, but it does not modify it.

Although it is not difficult to point out the shortcomings of such a static view of the recognition process - How are the memory entities created in the first place? How can novel stimuli be represented? and so on – its early critics (e.g., Gibson, 1979; Neisser, 1976) did not offer a formally attractive alternative. Connectionism does, which, in my view, is one of its main attractions in this area. In Seidenberg's chapter, the advantage of the connectionist view of recognition is perhaps most apparent in his discussion of meaning. As Seidenberg shows, many of the problems of the traditional static concept of meaning (for an extensive discussion see Hörmann, 1976) are no longer present in a connectionist approach that views meaning as emerging from an interaction between input and context rather than as a fixed entry that is simply accessed by the input. Unfortunately, the present version of the Seidenberg and McClelland (1989) model does not yet contain an explicit account of the semantic component. So the final success of this approach cannot yet be judged, but the principles are certainly promising.

Third Challenge: Do Priming Effects Really Reflect the Structure of the Lexicon?

Besides the lexical decision task itself, the priming technique has probably been the most widely used instrument in research on lexical access. The reason is obvious: It was expected that, by studying the interaction between several (usually two) lexical entries, light could be shed on the structure of the lexicon. The notion that priming depends on the lexical distance between the entries of the prime and the target was already suggested by Meyer and Schvaneveldt (1971), who introduced the priming paradigm (see de Groot, this volume). They considered two ways how this distance could be bridged: the location shift of a readout mechanism and spreading activation. Subsequently, due to the influence of articles such as Collins and Loftus (1975), the spreading activation idea developed into the standard assumption. Most of the empirical work was done with either semantic or associative priming (see de Groot, this volume, for a clarification of these terms), though priming based on other characteristics (e.g., phonology; Humphreys, Evett, & Taylor, 1982) has also been explored.

In the late 1970s, it became clear that not all priming effects could be accounted for by spreading activation. In 1975, Posner and Snyder (1975) had introduced the distinction between automatic and controlled processing, and soon after Neely (1977) demonstrated its relevance for the lexical decision task by showing that, besides priming based on semantic relatedness, which was attributed to automatic spreading activation, there was a priming effect that seemed to be due to the subject's conscious expectation of the target's semantic category.

In itself, this finding did not challenge the spreading activation account of priming, as Neely's (1977) data indicated functional differences between the two types of priming (different shapes of the priming function, absence vs. presence of inhibition with invalid primes) that seemed to make a distinction easy. However, as this section's chapters show, the situation has become much less distinct in the decade since Neely's (1977) work. It seems now likely that there are postlexical sources that may contribute to priming effects. As discussed earlier, it is probable that factors such as word familiarity have their impact not only on lexical access but also on postlexical decision processes. Balota and de Groot discuss evidence that the same holds for the effect of semantic relatedness, which may bias subjects toward a yes response in the lexical decision task.

Thus, if priming is to serve as a tool for revealing lexical structure, then these contaminating effects need to be eliminated or controlled. De Groot's chapter illustrates one potentially powerful approach, the comparison between the effects of unmasked and masked primes. Her evidence indicates that masking indeed disposes of priming effects that are likely to be located postlexically, possibly laying bare the remaining, truly structural effects. There is, however, at least one caveat: We do not know the effect that masking may in turn have on these assumed true priming effects. The assumption that these effects are completely resistant to masking is one possibility, but masking may also interfere with them, and there still seems to be little hard evidence against Holender's (1986) suspicion that, with appropriate controls for awareness, priming may disappear altogether if masking is complete. Thus, masking may eliminate postlexical effects but at the price of possibly also affecting the lexical effects that are of interest.

Let us now have a closer look at these lexical effects, supposing that it is possible to isolate them from effects that are due to other sources of priming. The standard model says that they are basically different from these other effects. Whereas meaning integration, response cueing, and so forth, are processes that depend on the task context, truly lexical priming is believed to be based on activation spreading along structural linkages that are part of the lexicon's organization. This assumption (to which I refer as the structural interpretation) is, of course, basic to the logic of using the priming method to investigate the structure of a lexicon that is conceived as consisting of nodes and linkages. It also corresponds to the notion of automatic processing as passive pathway activation, as it was suggested, for example, by Posner and Snyder (1975).

Two of this section's chapters (de Groot and Schreuder et al.) explore this logic for investigating the structure of the lexicon. Both report most intriguing findings and contain new theoretical suggestions. Interestingly, they suggest interpretations that seem to transcend the logic of the structural interpretation.

Consider the chapter by Schreuder et al. The overarching problem is a structural one: Does the mental lexicon comprise separate entries for all morphophonological variants of words, or does it contain entries only for root morphemes? Or are there both kinds of entries? To investigate the latter alternative, Schreuder et al. used a priming technique in

which the root morpheme of Dutch verbs was presented briefly before
the onset of the whole (inflected or prefixed) word. The logic of this
method is based on the structural interpretation: If there are entries
both for the root morpheme and the inflection or derivation, then both
should be activated by this manipulation, resulting in a facilitation effect
on pronunciation latency.

Schreuder et al. investigated four different kinds of inflections and
derivations, which turned out to be a fortunate decision. Generally,
there was no facilitation. The exceptions were verbs with separable
prepositions, that is, complex verbs where the preposition can be de-
tached from the verb part and appear in the sentence many words after
it. Schreuder et al. offer an interesting interpretation of this finding.
With these verbs, they argue, meaning becomes available only by combining the verb part of the word with the preposition over the distance
that separates them in the sentence. This is why there are, in these
cases, connections between the representations of the simple words and
prepositions on the one hand, and the complex verbs to which they
belong on the other. It is by virtue of these connections that the representation of the complex verb can be accessed via the representations of
its two components, and activation spreading along these connections
brings about the observed facilitation.

The interesting thing about this suggestion is that the connection
that is assumed to produce priming is not part of the structure of the
lexicon as such; rather, it exists because it serves a particular function, namely, to integrate the components of a particular type of verb
across the distance that separates them in the sentence. With respect
to meaning, orthography, or any other potential organizing dimension
of the lexicon, there is no difference between these complex verbs and
other lexical entries. Thus, Schreuder et al.'s explanation of this priming effect is basically different from the the structural interpretation.
Spread of activation is viewed as serving a specific functional purpose
rather than resulting from leakage of excitation along pathways that are
given by the structure of the lexicon.

Perhaps less obviously, de Groot also goes beyond the structural
interpretation. The result of her investigation into the locus of seman-
tic/associative priming is somewhat paradoxical. She concludes from
her data and a review of the literature that (a) priming (i.e., the true
priming as discussed earlier, excluding postlexical effects) is located at
a semantic rather than at a lexical level, yet (b) it is based on an associative rather than on a purely semantic relation. To integrate these
two seemingly contradictory conclusions, she assumes that a semantic
relation as such is insufficient to form a link between two nodes along
which activation can spread. Such a link, she suggests, is only established when attention is directed to the relation, forming an association
between the related representations.

This implies that, contrary to the structural interpretation, priming data do not reflect the structure of the lexicon. Instead, they are
based on a record of the semantic relations that have previously been

attended to. This suggests a kind of memory that is somewhere in between semantic and episodic memory. As in Schreuder et al.'s chapter, the relation between structure and function is reversed as compared to the structural interpretation. It is not the structure of the lexicon that has the functional consequence of producing priming; rather, there is some function (integrating the components of a complex verb, attending to a semantic relation) that produces the structural connections on which priming is based.

Fourth Challenge: Is There a Lexicon at all?

As Besner remarks, the notion of a mental lexicon – embodied in several specialized lexica such as an orthographic and a phonological lexicon – has been among the holy cows of modern research on word recognition. Seidenberg presents a connectionist alternative to this aspect of the standard model, based on the work of Seidenberg and McClelland (1989). As Besner's thorough discussion shows, there are many findings that this model cannot yet handle adequately. Besner and Seidenberg seem to agree, however, that it is presently difficult to decide whether such shortcomings are due to the current implementation or whether they point to more basic inadequacies of the approach. Whereas Besner emphasizes the problematic aspects of the implementation, Seidenberg stresses the explanatory potential of the general approach.

As the debate stands currently, it seems that none of Besner's criticisms is a fatal blow to the Seidenberg and McClelland (1989) approach as such, although hardly any of them leaves the present implementation unhurt. So we will have to wait and see how the Seidenberg and McClelland model develops in the future, based on constructive criticisms such as Besner's. Probably the biggest challenge is to elaborate the model in such a way that improvements in one respect (e.g., producing the correct phonological output for nonwords) will not deteriorate the model's performance in some other respect (e.g., discriminating between words and nonwords in a lexical decision task).

Whatever the outcome of such a – highly desirable – attempt to better adapt the model to the data, it is likely to produce interesting insights. One of the most exciting aspects of connectionism is that it permits what might be called experimental modeling, that is, using a model not only to implement a set of theoretical ideas but also to explore which changes in the implemented assumptions lead to which changes in the model's output, and to just empirically find out how the model has to be modified to produce certain desired outputs. I comment further on this perspective of connectionist modeling in the final section.

What is the basic difference between the standard model and Seidenberg's view? At first sight, it seems simply to be whether or not we need to assume a lexicon. But things are not quite that simple. Although the titles of Seidenberg's and Besner's chapters suggest such a dichotomy, a closer look indicates more subtle differences.

To begin with, Seidenberg does not deny the existence of a lexicon in the sense of an internal representation of lexical knowledge. His account of the macrostructure of what he explicitly calls the lexicon is indeed remarkably similar to the standard model's assumption of different subsystems or modules for orthographic, phonological, and semantic knowledge (compare Seidenberg's Figure 3.1 with Besner's Figure 4.1 and Balota's Figure 2.1). Trivially, any account of word recognition must encompass structures that represent orthographic, phonetic, and semantic knowledge about words and that are sufficiently different for words and nonwords to enable the system to discriminate between them in, say, a lexical decision experiment. In this sense, the Seidenberg and McClelland model does have a lexicon.

The difference is not in the notion of mental lexicon as a macrostructure, but in the conception of how this macrostructure is implemented at the microstructural level. According to the standard model, lexical knowledge is incorporated in something like a list of all words that the person knows, each with its individual address, similar to how a file in computer memory is organized. By contrast, according to the Seidenberg and McClelland model, lexical knowledge is incorporated in the pattern of weights between the units at each level (e.g., orthographic) and the hidden units that mediate between levels.

The representations of all words use the same set of units, and encoding a word is equivalent to producing a pattern of activation over these units. This means, of course, a highly distributed representation of lexical knowledge. But more important than distributed representation as such is the consequence that such a system, by its very nature, is able to encode nonwords as well as words. Even a nonword that the system has never before encountered will produce some pattern of activation over the units, that is, be encoded. In this respect there is no difference between words and nonwords, and it is with reference to this property that the Seidenberg and McClelland model may be said to lack a lexicon (cf. Seidenberg's Footnote 3).

However, this is not the whole story. Although the system has the capacity to encode nonwords as well as words, its actual state, after training has been completed, is determined by its experience with the material with which it was trained, that is, words. Consequently the patterns of connectivity at the various levels reflect exclusively lexical knowledge. In this sense, then, the orthographic and phonological levels in the model are lexica, and the hidden units represent correspondence relations between them.

So the conclusion is that the Seidenberg and McClelland model does have what may properly be called a lexicon, but that this lexicon has the somewhat paradoxical property that it can encode not only words but also nonwords.

However, this is not as paradoxical as it seems at first glance. Indeed, it reflects a general characteristic of the Seidenberg and McClelland approach: The model is constructed according to functional principles that are not particular to reading but may be applied to stimulus recognition and response generation in general. For example, the basic architecture of the model could be applied to object naming (orthographic encoding would have to be substituted by encoding in terms of object features) or to computing a hand movement to grasp an object (phonological encoding would have to be substituted by encoding in terms of movement characteristics).

In some sense, there are lexica for objects and for types of movements, but it is obvious that in these cases there cannot be a sharp distinction in the style of the word/nonword dichotomy. Systems for object recognition must be able to deal with objects not encountered before, and systems for action control must be able to produce new movements and movement sequences, a requirement that has often been modeled by some kind of schema concept (e.g., Rumelhart et al., 1987; Schmidt, 1982). Seidenberg and McClelland's model extends this functional principle to word recognition.

In my view, this is a very plausible extension. The idea of a lexicon that distinguishes acutely between words and nonwords makes sense linguistically, but hardly psychologically. Within a language conceived as a sign system, a letter sequence is either a word or it isn't. In reading, the borderline is much more blurred. For example, readers encounter proper names and technical terms, which they regard as words even when they see them for the first time, rare words and foreign words may look more or less word-like, and so forth. In short, words do not seem to be different from other stimuli in that their recognition is based on a familiarity continuum rather than on the outcome of a search process that either finds or does not find a matching entry.

Although it is plausible as a general approach to nonword processing, the Seidenberg and McClelland model does not seem to do a good job in actually dealing with nonwords, that is, in computing their pronunciation. This is one of Besner's strongest arguments against the model. However, as with the model's other shortcomings, it is unclear whether this is a general weakness of the approach or a limitation of the present implementation. One limitation that might account for the poor performance is the lack of parsing mechanisms. The model is restricted to four-letter words, which it treats as entities. It is likely that, in humans, the transfer from experience with words to performance in nonword pronunciation is at least partially based on spelling patterns at subword levels. An extension of the model to longer and morphemically complex words would probably require some kind of parsing. It would be interesting to see how such an extension would affect the model's performance with nonwords.

Conclusion

I have reviewed, and commented upon, four challenges against the standard model as they appear in this section's chapters. They involve doubts about the measurement of lexical access, about lexical access as a theoretical concept, about the structural interpretation of priming effects, and finally, about the very notion of a mental lexicon.

Taken together, these doubts mark a theoretical situation that may well lead to the rapid demise of the standard model. The cornerstones of the standard model were, first, several appealing metaphors (e.g., a lexicon organized like a computer file, activation spreading like an electrical charge) and, second, methods that seemed to be ideally tailored to measuring lexical access time (e.g., the lexical decision task). The metaphors have turned out to be shaky, and the methods now look much less trustworthy than they did initially. Although it would be premature to predict what kind of new standard model will emerge in the future – perhaps its general style is foreshadowed in Seidenberg's chapter –, such a situation of transition invites some reflections on what was wrong with the incumbent standard model.

THE COMPUTER HARDWARE METAPHOR AND SOME OF ITS CONSEQUENCES

Although the ultimate justification for abandoning a model is (or at least should be) its empirical disconfirmation, the crisis of an approach that has previously dominated research often points to conceptual and methodological difficulties that were overlooked, or not taken seriously, as long as the approach was empirically successful. In the case of the standard model of lexical access, some of these problems are particularly interesting because they exemplify more general aspects of the traditional information-processing approach. One of its theoretical foundations has been the computer metaphor in its various variants (see, e.g., Carello, Turvey, Kugler, & Shaw, 1984; Massaro, 1986; Neumann, 1985; Scheerer, 1988). Of these, especially the hardware variant – despite its venerable age – seems to have been the cause of many of the problems and deficiencies of the standard model. One central problem is the relation between structure and function, to which the main portion of this section is devoted. At the end, I will briefly mention some further, less central consequences of the hardware metaphor.

Structure and Function

The topic of structure versus function has been one of the red threads throughout this chapter. This is not surprising, as a particular view of the relationship between structure and function has been one of the main features of the standard model.

The basic assumption is that there are functional findings that reflect in a relatively direct manner the structural properties of the system, whereas there are others for which this is not the case. Instead, they depend on the task and/or on other contextual factors. The first type of functions are often labeled automatic, whereas the latter are said to be of a strategic nature or under the subject's voluntary control (for overviews of this two-process assumption see, e.g., Humphreys, 1985; Jonides, Naveh-Benjamin, & Palmer, 1985; Neumann, 1984, 1989).

Under the premise that the basic research interest is to disclose the system's structure, the methodological consequence of this distinction has usually been that we must somehow neutralize the effect of the latter factors in order to study the former.[2] Unfortunately, this has proven to be a hard task. To recapitulate two examples, it has turned out that priming is not only caused by spreading activation but may also be due to active prediction, postlexical meaning integration, and so on (see de Groot's chapter). Similarly, lexical decision latency depends not only on lexical access time but also on the duration of discrimination and decision processes, and so forth (see Balota's and Seidenberg's chapters). In both cases, it seems that these factors have strong effects. As Balota and de Groot show, they most likely account for many findings that were originally believed to exclusively reflect lexical access or automatic spreading activation.

Researchers differ in their reaction to this problem. It seems that Balota's skepticism about the concept of lexical access has at least in part been provoked by these difficulties, whereas de Groot's chapter is an ingenious effort to master some of them. But can they be mastered at all? Perhaps there is no methodological solution to this problem because it is not really a methodological problem but a conceptual one. The premise that there are indeed functions that give us relatively direct, uncontaminated information about the system's structure (provided we can isolate them) need not necessarily be true.

This premise is based on an idea that seems to date back to the beginnings of the information-processing approach, when psychological models were strongly influenced by the communication line metaphor, soon to be followed by the computer hardware metaphor. Based on these metaphors, there was a natural tendency to put primary research emphasis on disclosing the structural architecture of the human processing system, that is, to find out its components and the pathways that connect them. The researchers' task, then, was to isolate functions that were associated with specific structural constituents of the system and to devise experimental tasks that tapped these functions. The lexical decision paradigm illustrates this. Here, the structural components are the lexicon and the pathway(s) to it, the function is lexical access, and lexical decision latency is the purported operationalization of this function.

Toward the end of the 1960s, the theoretical situation became more complicated. Theorists began to realize that what happens in an experiment depends not only on the system's structure but also on task variables. Starting with Atkinson and Shiffrin (1968), and culminating

---

[2] Of course, there has also been some interest in control processes as a topic of study in its own right. Some of the research on strategic processes in word recognition has been summarized by Coltheart (1978).

in the two-process theories of the late 1970s (e.g., Posner & Snyder, 1975; Shiffrin & Schneider, 1977), the effect of task variables was accounted for by adding control processes to the automatic machinery. In a way, a software (or software-plus-programmer) metaphor was annexed to the hardware metaphor. As often in the history of science, it was easier to add new assumptions to an existing belief than to give it up altogether.

This preservation of the hardware metaphor under the cloak of the two-process notion has had a noteworthy effect: The assumption that there are processes which directly reflect the structure of the system, that is, that are independent of task context, has continued to be taken for granted, although there is hardly any evidence to support it. Indeed, as I have shown elsewhere (Neumann, 1984, 1989), this assumption is extremely difficult to test, and the difficulty of testing it has usually been vastly underestimated.[3]

It seems fair to say that there is, at least, a huge discrepancy between the strength of the belief in the existence of task-independent processes and the shaky evidence that has been put forward to support it. We simply do not know whether purely structurally based processes exist at all. The belief in their existence has to a large extent been the consequence of a metaphor, not a conclusion from empirical observations.

Perhaps this assumption has rarely been questioned until recently, because there has been a feeling that abandoning it would cut the ground from under our feet. This feeling was perhaps justified as long as there was no attractive alternative to the various computer metaphors. Now the situation has changed. The connectionist alternative, as exemplified by Seidenberg's chapter, has entered the scene. And indeed it offers a different view on the relation between structure and function, a view that does not necessarily imply the existence of task-independent processes.

According to this view, the system's structure – the pattern of weights between units – may be considered as one set of constraints on its pattern of activity, with other constraints coming from the input into the system. Although Seidenberg considers mainly stimulus input, top-down influences from control processes can in a similar way be modeled as a source of constraining input into a subsystem (e.g., Schneider & Detweiler, 1987). The consequence of this view is that the system will never show a behavior (a pattern of activity and the output that results from it) which directly mirrors its structural properties. A

---

[3] To summarize, none of the usual criteria of automaticity actually demonstrates task-independent processing. For example, findings such as a lack of interference in dual tasks and parallel processing in search tasks speak to the capacity issue but do not tell us anything about task independence. The intrusion of irrelevant information in Stroop-type tasks demonstrates that under certain conditions it may be difficult to ignore stimuli, but it does not at all prove that the processing of these stimuli is task-independent. Priming by masked stimuli demonstrates the processing of these stimuli without awareness, but again this does not imply in any way that their processing is task-independent. For a full discussion see Neumann (1989).

subsystem with a given structure will behave differently with different input, both from stimuli and from other subsystems that are sensitive to the task context. If this is true, then isolating processes that are uncontaminated by task factors and by the subject's intentions is not just a difficult endeavor. It is an impossible endeavor, because such processes do not exist.[4]

With respect to lexical access, the implication is that the lexical decision task or the pronunciation task cannot be considered to be just methods to study lexical access as such. Instead, they should be viewed as functional contexts (actions) in which lexical knowledge is used but in possibly different ways. In particular, we should exercise great caution in generalizing from these tasks to ordinary text-reading situations.

Balota makes this point with respect to the role of meaning in word recognition, which may be larger in reading for comprehension than in these less conceptually driven tasks. However, I would not quite follow his conclusion that, to develop "adequate models of word recognition", we should therefore prefer the former type of task, particularly the study of eye movements. It all depends on what we want to know. Balota's argument is valid if we wish to study word recognition in the context of text comprehension. To study word recognition in the functional context of the visual control of speaking in oral reading, a word-pronunciation task may be more adequate than an eye-movement study. If we want to use word recognition as a tool to find out how people discriminate between familiar and unfamiliar stimuli, then the lexical decision task may be the most appropriate method. There is no best task to study word recognition, because there is – I believe – no task-independent word recognition to be studied.

Some Further Consequences of the Hardware Metaphor

Computers do not have a history of biographical experience, at least as far as their hardware is concerned. One consequence of the hardware metaphor has therefore been an emphasis on analyzing the working of mechanisms with little emphasis on how they are acquired and modified through practice. Work on reading that was done in this research context sometimes reminds one of the 19th century neuroanatomical charts that exhibited a reading center in the cortex, implying that nature's wisdom provided the human brain with an anatomical area that, unfortunately, lay waste for millions of years until, finally, a modest proportion of modern mankind has been able to use it! Somewhat similarly, reading has often been analyzed as if its functional basis consisted of a fixed set of mechanisms, endowed to us by nature.

Once again, it seems that connectionism offers a fresh perspective. Whereas early connectionist models of reading (e.g., McClelland &

---

[4] I am referring to processes that are interesting in a discussion of lexical access. Of course, I do not deny that there may be very low-level processes in the CNS that are largely context-independent. See Neumann (1989), for a more detailed discussion.

recent models have relied more and more on equipping the system with an efficient learning rule and having it develop its structure through extended contact with representative material. The model that Seidenberg describes is a good example.

One interesting aspect of this new kind of modeling is that the distinction between episodic and semantic memory becomes blurred. Semantic memory gets to be viewed as the result of an accumulation of episodic experiences, rather than being conceptualized as a different storage system. Balota describes a model of Hintzman (1986) that nicely illustrates this. As mentioned earlier, de Groot suggests a similar idea, namely that the links along which activation spreads are acquired through episodes in which attention was directed to the corresponding semantic relation.

Another shortcoming of the research dominated by the computer metaphor is perhaps somewhat less likely to be overcome by (most current versions of) connectionism. It is a lack of what may be called functional analysis (Neumann, 1985), that is, of a theoretical framework that considers a system's tasks and the constraints to which it is subjected, and interprets its mechanisms with respect to their function in accomplishing the tasks, given the constraints. Examples of functional analyses in this sense are what Marr (1982) has called a computational theory and what Grossberg (1980) has termed the analysis of minimum requirements. This is a kind of analysis that is commonplace in other brain sciences but that seems to have been conspicuously absent from most psychological theorizing under the auspices of the computer metaphor.

Though there are no fully developed examples of this type of analysis in this section's chapters, I imagine to sense something of its spirit in two of them. First, Balota's plea to bring meaning back into word recognition emphasizes the function of word recognition for the comprehension process. The second chapter to mention is that of Pollatsek and Rayner. I have had to say comparatively little about it throughout this essay. The reason is that it does not suffer from the problems and difficulties that have been my main topic. At the surface, one may attribute this to the more ecologically valid paradigm – eye movement registration during reading a text – on which most of their argument is based. However, I think there is a deeper reason, which is related to functional analysis.

What makes the Pollatsek and Rayner chapter special in my view is the kind of questions that it asks. Many of the questions that I have commented on in this chapter are of the "what is the nature of . . .?" kind. What is the nature of lexical access? (for example, does it or doesn't it precede meaning analysis?); what is the nature of the lexicon? (for example, does it or doesn't it have the capacity to encode nonwords as well as words?); what is the nature of priming (for example, is it located at the lexical or the semantic level?); and so on. Questions of this kind are not unlike the binary oppositions (e.g., features vs. templates, exhaustive vs. self-terminating search) that Newell (1973) has commented on in his classical "Twenty questions" article. Newell's pessimistic appraisal of this research style is worth remembering:

". . . far from providing the rungs of a ladder by which psychology gradually climbs to clarity, this form of conceptual structure leads rather to an ever increasing pile of issues, which we weary of or become diverted from, but never really settle" (p. 289).

Almost two decades later, the truth of this assessment can be evaluated by considering what has become of *features vs. templates* and *exhaustive vs. self-terminating search*, both central research issues in 1973!

Pollatsek and Rayner ask a different kind of question, a question of the type "how is . . . achieved?" In reading continuous text, the system must decide when to start a saccade and where to direct it. The question is, how does it do this? For example, which role does lexical access play in this process? How is the decision where to move related to the decision when to move? Answers to questions of this type will usually not result from "crucial experiments" that (purportedly) decide between binary oppositions. Rather, they emerge from putting together evidence from many sources, from building models that combine mechanisms at different levels (from visual attention and motor control to lexical access to text integration), and – last but not least – from plausibility considerations about what kind of mechanism would be functionally useful. In my judgment, Pollatsek and Rayner's chapter is a beautiful example of this style of theorizing.

It is one of the two styles of theorizing that I consider promising. The other is, of course, connectionist modeling. It would be nice if some combination of these approaches were visible on the horizon. At present, this does not seem to be the case. However, functional analysis and connectionist modeling might indeed complement each other.

Besides their obvious power to explain a system's behavior as emerging from a few simple, functionally plausible principles, the most promising potential of connectionist models is, in my view, what I have earlier called experimental modeling, that is, finding out which changes in a model lead to which consequences in its behavior. But this very asset highlights what may be the biggest danger in connectionism – the almost infinite adaptability of its models. As Massaro (1988) has put it, the approach may simply be too powerful. Perhaps this is why a decade of connectionist work has yielded many magnificent models but has provoked relatively little new empirical research. Possibly, connectionist modeling is less a substitute for empirically constrained, function-oriented theorizing in the style of Pollatsek and Rayner's chapter than a powerful tool for sharpening and refining functional explanations and for testing their implications.

ACKNOWLEDGMENT

This chapter was drafted while I was a Fellow at the Netherlands Institute for Advanced Study in the Humanities and Social Sciences (NIAS) at Wassenaar, The Netherlands. I am deeply grateful to the NIAS for its splendid hospitality and to the members of the "Reading" group for many stimulating discussions.

REFERENCES

Atkinson, R. C., & Shiffrin, R. M. (1968). Human memory: A proposed system and its control processes. In K. W. Spence & J. T. Spence (Eds.), *The psychology of learning and motivation: Advances in research and theory* (Vol. 2, pp. 90 - 195). New York: Academic Press.

Balota, D., & Chumbley, J. (1984). Are lexical decisions a good measure of lexical access? The role of word frequency in the neglected decision stage. *Journal of Experimental Psychology: Human Perception and Performance, 10*, 340 - 357.

Becker, C. A. (1976). Allocation of attention during visual word recognition. *Journal of Experimental Psychology: Human Perception and Performance, 2*, 556 - 566.

Carello, C., Turvey, M. T., Kugler, P. N., & Shaw, R. E. (1984). Inadequacies of the computer metaphor. In M. S. Gazzaniga (Ed.), *Handbook of cognitive neuroscience* (pp. 229 - 248). New York: Plenum.

Collins, A. M., & Loftus, E. F. (1975). A spreading-activation theory of semantic processing. *Psychological Review, 82*, 407 - 428.

Coltheart, M. (1978). Lexical access in simple reading tasks. In G. Underwood (Ed.), *Strategies of information processing* (pp. 151 - 216). New York: Academic Press.

Donders, F. C. (1868). Die Schnelligkeit psychischer Prozesse. [The speed of mental processes]. *Reichert's und du Bois-Reymond's Archiv für Anatomie und Physiologie und wissenschaftliche Medicin*, 657 - 681.

Forster, K. I. (1979). Levels of processing and the structure of the language processor. In W. E. Cooper & E. C. T. Walker (Eds.), *Sentence processing: Psycholinguistic studies presented to Merrill Garrett* (pp. 27 - 85). Hillsdale, NJ: Lawrence Erlbaum Associates.

Gibson, J. J. (1979). *The ecological approach to visual perception*. Boston: Houghton Mifflin.

Grossberg, S. (1980). How does the brain build a cognitive code? *Psychological Review, 87*, 1 - 51.

Hintzman, D. L. (1986). "Schema abstraction" in a multiple-trace memory model. *Psychological Review, 93*, 411 - 428.

Holender, D. (1986). Semantic activation without conscious identification in dichotic listening, parafoveal vision, and visual masking: A survey and appraisal. *Behavioral and Brain Sciences, 9*, 1 - 66.

Hörmann, H. (1976). *Meinen und Verstehen. Grundzüge einer psychologischen Semantik*. [To mean and to understand]. Frankfurt/Main: Suhrkamp.

Humphreys, G. W. (1985). Attention, automaticity, and autonomy in visual word processing. In D. Besner, T. G. Waller, & G. E. MacKinnon (Eds.), *Reading research: Advances in theory and practice* (Vol. 5, pp. 253 - 310). Orlando, FL: Academic Press.

Humphreys, G. W., Evett, L. J., & Taylor, D. E. T. (1982). Automatic phonological priming in visual word recognition. *Memory & Cognition, 10*, 576 - 590.

Jonides, J., Naveh-Benjamin, M., & Palmer, J. (1985). Assessing automaticity. *Acta Psychologica, 60*, 157 - 171.

Marr, D. (1982). *Vision.* San Francisco: Freeman.

Massaro, D. W. (1986). The computer as a metaphor for psychological inquiry: Considerations and recommendations. *Behavior Research Methods, Instruments, and Computers, 18*, 73 - 92.

Massaro, D. W. (1988). Some criticisms of connectionist models of human performance. *Journal of Memory and Language, 27*, 213 - 234.

McClelland, J. L., & Rumelhart, D. E. (1981). An interactive activation model of context effects in letter perception: Part 1. An account of basic findings. *Psychological Review, 88*, 375 - 407.

Meyer, D. E., & Schvaneveldt, R. (1971). Facilitation in recognizing pairs of words: Evidence of a dependence between retrieval operations. *Journal of Experimental Psychology, 90*, 227 - 234.

Meyer, D. E., Schvaneveldt, R. W., & Ruddy, M. G. (1975). Loci of contextual effects on visual word-recognition. In P. M. A. Rabbitt & S. Dornic (Eds.), *Attention and performance V* (pp. 98 - 118). London: Academic Press.

Morton, J. (1969). The interaction of information in word recognition. *Psychological Review, 76*, 165 - 178.

Neely, J. H. (1977). Semantic priming and retrieval from memory: Roles of inhibition-less spreading activation and limited-capacity attention. *Journal of Experimental Psychology: General, 106*, 226 - 254.

Neisser, U. (1976). *Cognition and reality.* San Francisco: Freeman.

Neumann, O. (1984). Automatic processing: A review of recent findings and a plea for an old theory. In W. Prinz & A. F. Sanders (Eds.), *Cognition and motor processes* (pp. 255 - 293). Berlin: Springer.

Neumann, O. (1985). Informationsverarbeitung, Künstliche Intelligenz und die Perspektiven der Kognitionspsychologie. [Information processing, artificial intelligence, and the perspectives of cognitive psychology]. In O. Neumann (Ed.), *Perspektiven der Kognitionspsychologie* (pp. 3 - 37). Berlin: Springer.

Neumann, O. (1989). On the origins and status of the concept of automatic processing. *Zeitschrift für Psychologie, 197*, 411 - 428.

Newell, A. (1973). You can't play 20 questions with nature and win: Projective comments on the papers of this symposium. In W. G. Chase (Ed.), *Visual information processing* (pp. 283 - 308). New York: Academic Press.

Norris, D. (1986). Word recognition: Context effects without priming. *Cognition, 22*, 93 - 136.

Posner, M. I., & Snyder, C. R. R. (1975). Attention and cognitive control. In R. L. Solso (Ed.), *Information processing and cognition: The Loyola symposium* (pp. 55 - 85). Hillsdale, NJ: Lawrence Erlbaum Associates.

Rubenstein, H., Garfield, L., & Millikan, J. A. (1970). Homographic entries in the internal lexicon. *Journal of Verbal Learning and Verbal Behavior, 9*, 487 - 494.

Rumelhart, D. E., Smolensky, P., McClelland, J. L., & Hinton, G. E. (1987). Schemata and sequential thought processes in PDP models. In J. L. McClelland & D. E.

Rumelhart, & the PDP research group (Eds.), *Parallel distributed processing: Explorations in the microstructure of cognition: Vol. 2. Psychological and biological models* (pp. 7 - 57). Cambridge, MA: MIT Press.

Sanders, A. F. (1980). Stage analysis of reaction processes. In G. E. Stelmach & J. Requin (Ed.), *Tutorials in motor behavior* (pp. 331 - 354). Amsterdam: North-Holland.

Scheerer, E. (1988). Towards a history of cognitive science. *International Science Journal, 115,* 7 - 19.

Schmidt, R. A. (1982). The schema concept. In J. A. S. Kelso (Ed.), *Human motor behavior: An introduction* (pp. 219 - 235). Hillsdale, NJ: Lawrence Erlbaum Associates.

Schneider, W., & Detweiler, M. (1987). A connectionist/control architecture for working memory. In G. H. Bower (Ed.), *The psychology of learning and motivation.* (Vol. 21, pp. 53 - 119). New York: Academic Press.

Seidenberg, M. S. (1985). The time course of information activation and utilization in visual word recognition. In D. Besner, T. G. Waller, & G. E. MacKinnon (Eds.), *Reading research: Advances in theory and practice* (Vol. 5, pp. 199 - 252). New York: Academic Press.

Seidenberg, M. S., & McClelland, J. L. (1989). A distributed, developmental model of word recognition and naming. *Psychological Review, 96,* 523 - 568.

Shiffrin, R. M., & Schneider, W. (1977). Controlled and automatic information processing: II. Perceptual learning, automatic attending, and a general theory. *Psychological Review, 84,* 127 - 190.

Sternberg, S. (1969). The discovery of processing stages: Extensions of Donders' method. In W. G. Koster (Ed.), *Attention and performance II* (pp. 276 - 315). Amsterdam: North-Holland.

Treisman, A. M. (1960). Contextual cues in selective listening. *Quarterly Journal of Experimental Psychology, 12,* 242 - 248.

Wundt, W. (1903). *Grundzüge der physiologischen Psychologie.* [Fundamentals of physiological psychology] (5th ed.). Leipzig: Engelmann.

9

WHAT'S IN A WORD? LEVELS OF REPRESENTATION AND WORD RECOGNITION

Patrick T.W. Hudson

University of Leiden

INTRODUCTION

There are many ways to examine the process of understanding linguistic material, whether presented as speech or as written material. These different points of view can be seen in terms of a number of different levels of representation, stretching from meaning to sound or print. One can, at the top level, look at meaning as it is conveyed by large regions of text or by individual sentences and distinguish literal meaning from intended interpretations simply within the level of meaning. Lower down, one may examine sentence syntax and how syntax and semantics operate within sentences at the level of the clause. Words form the point where semantics and the conceptual level are related to syntactic roles, all of which are mapped onto single entities we call words. Under the word level we can distinguish different levels which are linguistically significant and often undervalued in the study of written language comprehension. These are the levels of morphology and phonology and their interactions.

My intention in this discussion on word processes is to structure the argument around the different levels of representation. The word level, or at least the recognition of words, is the subject of this section and an understanding of what a word is, or might be, is important if we want to develop adequate models which can be applied to the higher levels. Interestingly, all the chapters in this section attacked different issues. This suggests not only that the organizers had selected carefully, but also that there may be no consensus about which are *the* issues to be considered.

Besner asks if we need a distinct lexicon to explain the relationship between graphical spelling and phonological representation. He attacks the parallel distributed processing (PDP) view advocated by Seidenberg that a single routine PDP model, without an explicit lexicon, is sufficient to explain the ways in which naming can be performed from print. Here, the focus of attention is on the phonological level (the term *phonological* should be used with considerable caution, it usually only means sound and makes no commitment to the abstract organization of such a level) and the consequences differential experimental effects should have on constraining possible models of word representation and processing.

Schreuder, Grendel, Poulisse, Roelofs, and van de Voort, one level higher, ask whether morphologically complex words are to be represented uniquely or in terms of their constituents. This level is interesting because here the notion *word*, as a single entity, itself becomes difficult to keep in focus. In a sense, the question builds on the previous one by asking which form the representations of words take in the lexicon, independent of whether they are spoken or written, for input or for output.

Balota's chapter shifts the ground to the level of word meaning. He makes a plea for its reinstatement as an important factor in studies of word recognition. He combines this with his attack on the notion of the magic moment in word recognition; the idea that there is a moment in time at which word recognition has been accomplished, when the goodies become available. The goodies in question are the information used for higher levels of representation, such as the semantic and syntactic levels, and Balota suggests that such information may become simultaneously available. In any case, he attacks the notion that word recognition is a simple progression up the levels of representation which can be tapped at specific moments in that progress by various experimental tasks.

De Groot's chapter ties in to Balota's by examining the phenomenon of semantic priming, asking whether it is purely semantic. Given that most studies have actually confused the linguistic notion *semantic* with that of *association*, she asks at which level of representation this effect takes place. Is an associative relationship between words at a purely lexical level sufficient to explain priming effects? Or is an associative relationship between the concepts a word refers to also necessary or even sufficient?

Pollatsek and Rayner's chapter, in contrast to the others, is more concerned with a methodological issue of great importance and interest. What inferences can we draw from the eye-movement record as it progresses across a text? This is an interesting question in itself, but its form suggests we can ask what inferences can we draw from different types of experiments in the field of word recognition in general? Their chapter itself is less concerned with the process of word recognition. Rather, it places constraints on the process of lexical access, which they argue is a major determinant of eye movements in reading. As such, there is little for a commentator in the word recognition field to say except to admire and note the arguments and data.

The chapters here not only cover most of the range of levels of representation appropriate to words, they also cover a wide range of tasks, or at least make reference to them, using a wide range of experimental manipulations. They are also cast within a variety of different modeling paradigms. All of this suggests, to a commentator, that the field of word recognition, despite a long history since Pillsbury (1897) and Huey (1908/1968), has still to settle on any form of consensus. If this is the case in an area as central and crucial to linguistic processing as word recognition, we may have to wait even longer for certainty in areas which depend upon understanding what words are and how they are processed. How, after all, can we reasonably express models of syntactic and semantic processing when we are still unsure as to the nature of the representations being used as the input data to such processes?

WHAT PROBLEMS UNDERLIE THE PAPERS?

Morphology and the Notion Word

A word is the point at which all the different levels of representation seem to converge. Individual morphemes may be defined as the minimal units for carrying meaning (Matthews, 1974), but they have to come together to define the meaning of a word and its syntactic status. The notion *morpheme* is one which refers to an underlying theoretical entity, not to a word as such, although the morpheme and the word may often appear identical. A word, unlike its constituent morphemes, represents the point in the hierarchy of levels at which a meaning (or meanings in the case of ambiguous words) becomes fixed, the specific syntactic class (Noun or Verb, etc.) is defined, and the values (singular or plural; person and tense) within that class are set. Schreuder et al.'s chapter is one of a series which have appeared since the early work of Taft and Forster (1975). The issue is whether affixed words are represented as words in the lexicon, thereby ignoring their morphological structure, or are decomposed and represented as morphemes. In the latter extreme case, we assume that words are not actually represented, which forces us to explain how words made up of morpheme combinations can be represented given that their meanings may not be directly deducible from the meanings of their constituent morphemes. In intermediate cases (Caramazza, Laudanna, & Romani, 1988), models are proposed in which both combined and decomposed forms are represented in the lexicon. The problem here is that, whatever evidence you find, you are left with a situation which appears to ignore the existence of well-motivated and distinct levels of representation. We would not, for instance, expect to shove syntactic and semantic information together, or phonological and morphological, so why model the mental lexicon as riding roughshod over the lexical - morphological distinction by either ignoring the morphological level (the full-entry hypothesis of

Butterworth, 1983), by ignoring the lexical level (fully decomposed lexicons), or by effectively ignoring the distinction altogether (Caramazza's
AAM model)?

Meaning and Magic Moments

The question phrased by Balota refers to an attempt to understand
how it might be that meaning may *precede* other information and how
that and all the other information may become available gradually,
rather than suddenly at one particular magic moment. The paradox
seems to be that meaning is only (logically) capable of being made
available *after* the word has first been accessed, so getting meaning *before* evidence of access seems to make us infer that our logical analysis
must itself be illogical. What lies behind such analyses is the assumption that the recognition process moves up the levels, so that meaning
access necessarily follows on access at the lexical level just because the
level of meaning is higher than that of words.

The magic moment problem is one which, as treated here, means
that the relationship between the time of a response and internal sequences of processing may be even more indirect that we would like.
A great deal happens between stimulus and response, and stage models of processing, which assume little or no feedback between processes,
make strong assumptions about process time and total time. Apparently allowing semantics to influence lower level decisions means that
the stage assumptions have, at least, to be questioned and rigorously
tested. Without adequate models of task performance we may encounter
difficulties when we attempt to map orders of response latencies to types
of stimuli onto orders within the representational system as a whole.
What I mean here is that even ordinal level comparisons (RT on stimulus A > RT on stimulus B is predicted if A is-more-difficult than B)
may not necessarily be appropriate. PDP models offer ways of breaking this circuit by showing just *how* different levels can interact *during*
the process of lexical access. Such models, however, provide radically
different explanations to differences in response latency that have been
traditionally explained by reference to independent stages (McClelland,
1979; Phaf, van der Heijden, & Hudson, in press).

I asked earlier for better analyses of how the tasks are performed.
The lexical decision task has been subject to debate as to its validity
as a straightforward measure of lexical access. Yet, initially, it was seen
as just a task that necessarily required lexical access, in a way that
pronunciation did not (Forster, 1976). The issue seems not to be that
such tasks do not tap lexical access processes (although it was not so long
ago that one had to defend the idea that pronunciation was not done
purely nonlexically), but rather that a great many other processes always
take place before any response actually becomes measurable. Effects of
word frequency (Balota & Chumbley, 1984) and word length (Hudson &
Bergman, 1985) in lexical decision and pronunciation tasks, and Balota
and Chumbley's (1985) effects of word frequency on delayed naming

tasks suggest that subjects' perceptions of the demand characteristics and the necessary existence of some processing following lexical access will always affect measurement of the actual moment of access. Even a measure as pure as gaze duration will also be affected by processing determined by factors other than simple lexical access, as Pollatsek and Rayner argue, so the best we can hope for is to find correlations and explicable task-dependent variation. Schreuder et al. also find that they have problems with tasks which use nonwords, implying that results obtained with such stimuli cannot, necessarily, be generalized to words in order to increase our understanding of how the lexical system works. Such arguments have to be treated seriously, especially given how much attention is paid to such stimuli by authors like Besner and Seidenberg.

The Rules of Inference

The fact is that every task performed on words generates information that we may use to perform inferences about how the system operates and what representations it contains. The question which interests me, therefore, is what are the rules of inference we can use in this exercise? What are the facts that we really can assume to be necessarily true and which are contingent upon our theoretical stance? For instance, apparently straightforward variations in factors such as stimulus frequency, length, and lexical status regularly produce differences in performance between stimuli. We infer from a word-frequency effect, because of the way in which word frequencies should be bound to specific lexical items, that those items have been accessed in some way. We also assume that finding reliable word-nonword differences implies lexical access in, say, naming tasks. What, then, do we infer if we find the one and not the other (Hudson & Bergman, 1985, Experiments 1 and 2)? This need not be a problem if we examine the logic, but it does require us to consider exactly what we are doing. Finding a word-frequency effect implies lexical access (WF $\longrightarrow$ Access); finding a word-nonword difference implies lexical access (W–NW $\longrightarrow$ Access). But it is a well-known logical fallacy to infer the antecedent given the consequent, so there need be no inconsistency if we only allow implication between WF or W–NW and Access. If, however, our models actually require an If and Only If relationship between WF and Access or W–NW and Access, then we are in trouble. One thing I have noticed in this area is that such rules of inference have never been sufficiently well articulated for us to agree on when experimental results should really be considered damaging to theories.

Besner's chapter highlights other problems of this nature in the way he sets the classical multilexicon approach against the monolithic PDP approach advocated by McClelland and his colleagues. One question that can be identified here is: May we use the results of brain damage as a test for models of normal functioning? This is a problem I addressed earlier (Hudson, 1977) and came to the conclusion that we really need to specify not only the representations available in some detail and the processes that use them but also to define the way in which damage is supposed to have its effect. Simplistic models may well work within closely defined boundary conditions, more realistic models capable of stretching their range of application may well show unexpected results when tested, as it were, to destruction. In terms of logical rules of inference, we need to agree on which axioms we will accept before we start inferring from results, and we also need to agree whether our system of inference shall be monotonic or nonmonotonic (what status will we accord to negative results and to unknown data)?

The Single Lexical Entry: Static or Dynamic Representations

Another set of questions centers around the notion of a single lexical entry. Balota's chapter defines a word in terms of a cluster of variegated information collected around a single representation. De Groot implies a possible organization of lexical nodes, each connected to one another by a variety of links (associative, orthographic, etc.). Both proposals are essentially single-entry models, forming what we may call a monolithic lexicon. Besner, in contrast, propounds the multilexicon model with, for instance, distinct orthographic and phonological input lexicons and matching output lexicons. But is the monolithic/multilexicon split the only distinction that can or should be made? What seems to be missing in many of the discussions about the structure of the lexicon is that there are more than just representations. The existence of representations assumes the existence of processes to make use of those representations. Now the question which rises in my mind is: How many of the arguments proposed here and phrased in terms of representations, or collections of representations in lexicons, are actually supported by data that arise because of different processes? Put in another way, how far can the single lexicon notion be taken if we place all the burden in differentiation, between modalities and input or output, on the shoulders of specific processes?

If we examine the different levels of representation which we should take into account, then we need either a large number of different lexicons, perhaps separated again by modality and direction, or we can take a more subtle view of the processes involved. This may include the notion that much of the knowledge we assume to be associated with the words, as declarative knowledge, is actually represented procedurally in the processes that use and generate representations. Schreuder et al. take one strong standpoint, that all words (in Dutch) are represented individually, but then they demonstrate that with their technique one class of verbs can (and should) be separated. In one sense, they are having their cake and eating it. This result is also at strong variance with ours in Dutch (Bergman, Hudson, & Eling, 1988), where we replicated Taft's (1979) prefix effects. Bergman (1988) also found evidence for suffix stripping in derivations in a lexical-decision task with nonwords and in a syntactic category task (Monsell, 1985) with words. But many of

Schreuder et al.'s stimuli were inflected and we should perhaps regard inflectional variation as variation on the same word, whereas derivational variation creates different words from the same stem. We should regard the evidence from different, albeit apparently similar, tasks on different, but apparently similar, classes of stimuli with considerable caution. The inferences we can draw from such contradictions must be assessed carefully, because we have to decide if we want merely to reject and ignore certain results or whether we want to accept both. In the latter case we have to have some underlying models of word representation and processing that are inherently capable of showing such divergences of results. The history of word recognition is littered with total contradictions, usually involving apparently trivial task differences, yet the assumptions about single or multiple lexicons often seem to be based upon a very small number of ostensibly hard facts that may not always be as well grounded as they initially appear.

The Interaction Among Tasks, Theories, and Inferences

We do often take care with lexical decision and pronunciation as tasks but still perform inferences without paying due attention to the classes of representational system we assume to constitute the lexicon. What I mean here is that the inferences we draw from tasks and task manipulations must be drawn not only with reference to knowledge about how the task is carried out, but also to their dependency on the general model that we assume to represent the system as a whole. A more procedurally oriented approach to lexical representation and the problem of levels of representation may well be capable of subsuming evidence both for and against morphological decomposition. The predictions have to be made taking explicit account of the tasks, as de Groot does here. Static notions of lexical representation, assuming declarative representations that just sit there waiting to be called into service, have to have their properties attached to them in ways that may necessarily require them to have effects. Does word frequency, if attached to a word as its resting level of activation (Morton, 1969), really have to have an effect every time that item is accessed? How could the meaning of words affect their behavior in tasks that do not require meaning?

The answer to these questions depends on the way in which the process works. A different thresholding mechanism might only be sensitive to minimal sufficient activation levels, being independent of variation above a minimal level. In such a case, the effect of word frequency on initial access might be minimal and restricted to marginal cases, whereas the strong effects on all types of words may be due to the nature of a different process that returns to *use* attached information in, say, a spelling check (e.g., initial access – is it a word? – vs. functional access – how is it spelled? – where the latter requires the actual information to be accessed for use). De Groot uses such an approach in her chapter by forcing use of the information rather than relying on incidental contamination between associates. If we imagine actually using or accessing the representation of a word, we may wish to explain experimental variation by reference to the properties of the procedures rather than of the representation itself. Procedures may be much more sensitive to the contexts in which they are called and we can imagine, perhaps, a word as including a set of procedures for assigning a meaning representation. This set of procedures would hold some of the information we might otherwise assign to the semantic representation of the word.

In fact, if we take this line far enough, we might wonder whether we need a static representation at all or whether the procedures themselves would suffice, with the notion *word* relegated to being a label for the set of procedures. As an example, we can take an approach to representation in which all levels are treated fairly consistently in terms of a procedural representation (Hudson & Bergman, 1984; Hudson, Bergman, Houtmans & Nas, 1984). In Figure 9.1 a simple example of the fairly standard transition network representation for sentence processing is given.

This format can be used for both perception and production and is one way of representing sentence syntactic knowledge in a form that can be used by parsers. It defines the procedures to be carried out quite clearly. Figure 9.2 shows a network representation at the lexical-morphological level, which also allows for recursive representation of morphological structure. This representation is procedural and, in parallel to the sentence representations, could also allow semantic information to be attached to various nodes in the system or for actions to be taken predicated upon the context in which the network is trying to function.

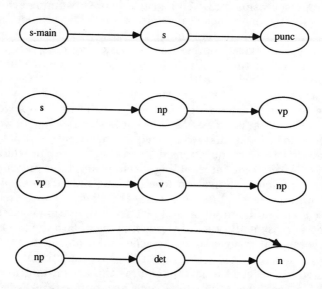

FIGURE 9.1. A simple example of a Transition Network which can be used to parse sentences. The formalism not only represents *what* is grammatical, it can also be used procedurally to parse sentences and assign grammatical structures.

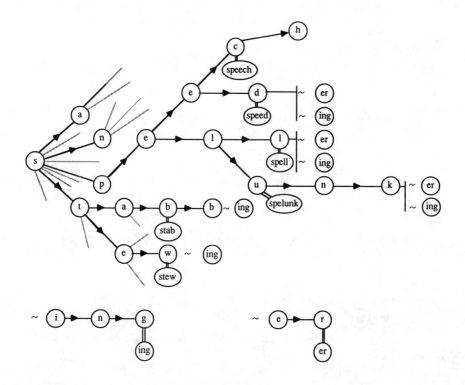

FIGURE 9.2. A fragment of a network representation of a lexicon based upon the model in Hudson et al. (1984). Morphemes are represented as sub-networks in much the same way as *np* and *vp* are sub-networks to the sentence parsing transition network in Figure 9.1.

Finally, Figure 9.3 shows networks at the lower levels of graphemic and phonemic representations and also how relations among elements, substrings, and whole words could be subsumed under mappings between the two networks. I do not wish to impose such an approach here but merely provide it as an example of how a procedural approach could be considered that would be consistent across the levels of representation.

WHAT ARE CORE QUESTIONS
IN WORD RECOGNITION?

The Scope of Explanations in Word Recognition

All the chapters, taken together, raise a series of questions. These may form the central issues in the research field of word recognition and are ordered in terms of descending scope.

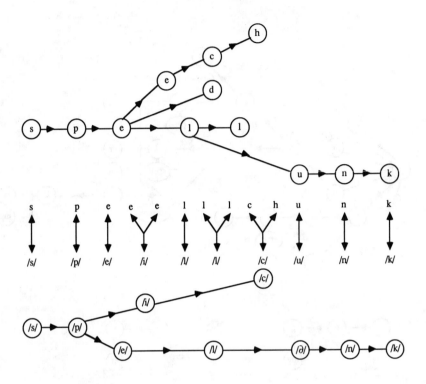

FIGURE 9.3. Fragments of graphemic (upper) and phonemic (lower) networks in the lexicon. By using a consistent notation we can express graphemic-phonemic correspondences as mappings between networks (middle).

1. What type of system for representation of lexical knowledge is implied and being used? Is it a boxtype system with many boxes each labeled as a lexicon with vague arrowed constraints between boxes or is it one that concentrates on a particular process? Is it a system that makes the underlying assumption that there is a single monolithic lexicon, or are multiple lexicons assumed, such that the notion of a single mental lexicon is only regarded as some sum of the individual lexica? If it is a process model, what information is presumed to be represented in the process and what is assumed to be stored in the products to which the process is applied?
2. What is the range of operation for the model? Under which conditions is it expected to represent a valid model? To what extent is a model constructed for linguistic processing in normal individuals expected or supposed to be applicable to, for instance, the effects of brain damage? To what extent is learning of importance, or is the model only intended to represent a final state?

3. What theoretical consequences have to be drawn from the results obtained with different tasks such as lexical-decision, pronunciation, or threshold tasks? Given that all these and similar tasks are different, is there any way of defining, a priori, which inferences we can draw? What, for instance, can we deduce from finding differences between words and nonwords in all of these tasks – can and should we draw the same conclusion in all cases? What exactly should we infer from task-dependent differences in the *size* of frequency effects?
4. What inferences can be drawn from the selection of different experimental manipulations within tasks? What are the consequences of manipulating stimulus selections, CaSe MiXiNg, repetition of stimuli, stimulus frequency, and the use of nonwords? Is it not the case that logical consequences have to be considered in light of the tasks, the area of application, and the modeling paradigm, in other words, all the previous questions?

All these questions can be found here. What one notices is that more attention is always paid to later questions. The more fundamental questions, not surprisingly, are left unanswered and their consequences often left ignored. What this means is that we have important features that are often implicit. The first two questions, concerning the type of system presupposed and the range of application, are often conflated. Neuropsychological research tends to concentrate upon *what* is lost or damaged (cf. Coltheart, Patterson, & Marshall, 1980; Coltheart, Sartori, & Job, 1987; Patterson, Marshall, & Coltheart, 1985) with very little attention paid to the details of *how* the system progresses between one representation and another (see Seidenberg, 1988, for a cogent criticism of this lack of specification of the processes). Learning, on the other hand, tends to concentrate more upon the *how* issues. The problems associated with developmental dyslexia may, among others, be related to the incompatibility among modeling approaches, which it highlights by intersecting two fields of radically different complexion and temperament.

We can distinguish two different general classes of how words and the like are represented. They are not really distinguished by absolute qualitative differences, but more by the degree of attention they pay to either representational or process issues. One class, *boxology* models, represents different classes of information in distinct boxes, usually called by such names as orthographic input lexicon. What this latter means is that some knowledge about all the words in the language is deemed to be collected together in one functioning subsystem that can be identified on logical grounds and because certain brain damaged patients can be explained by reference to damage to such a system only. The other class of model is more interested in the details of the different codes used to progress from one type of representation to another. In both we can readily distinguish one or more actual representations that are said to stand for individual words and we can also see processes that enable us to translate and progress between those representations.

What is usually missing is any serious detail of just what a representation might actually look like and how processes might lead to and from it. If we want to simulate such a system, the computational details will require both representations and processes to be sufficiently well specified to allow a system that could be capable of actually performing according to the specifications. Vague promises that turn out often to be mere rephrasings of symptoms or experimental results are not usually sufficient to build or simulate a system.

Two Questions About Theories: Representations and Their Processes

This section of the book is concerned with the mental lexicon and, therefore, with the two detailed issues arising from the first question identified earlier. These organizational questions have to be tackled because without a clear understanding we may not even be able to understand what our experiments actually mean. These are: (a) How are all the different levels of representation which have to be accounted for represented? and (b) What, in detail, are the processes that mediate between these levels? One approach is to ask whether the information that is presupposed to be represented is actually stored or is computed on the fly. In the latter case, we have to assume that the knowledge that constrains the operation of some part of the system is represented not statically but in and constraining the procedures which together constitute the process. For instance, we do not assume that all possible interpretations or semantic representations of sentences are actually stored in advance. This is not only unlikely, it is essentially impossible (Chomsky, 1957). So we accept that those representations are computed on-line. This implies that our syntactic and semantic knowledge, as linguistic systems in their own right at their various levels of representation, have to be stored in the procedures and not separately. We accept that peoples' syntactic knowledge is compiled rather than interpreted so that they might have little access to their knowledge as such except by using it. This does not, of course, mean that there are no specific and serious constraints on what that knowledge is. At the other end of the linguistic system we expect to find the same applied to our knowledge of phonology (although that knowledge is underrepresented as a source by those concentrating on the visual modality). Here again, we can accept that the facts of phonology, like those of syntax and combinatorial semantics, are in a sense inaccessible because they are compiled.

Two levels stand out differently from the rest. These are the lexical and morphological levels, because here we can point to individual items about which we can talk and which a linguistic system can use *as objects*. To these we could add a semantic/conceptual level as studied by de Groot to make a small number of levels at which the information represented might be considered to be stored rather than compiled. But if we accept that some of these levels are best regarded as procedural and compiled, why should we not consider all levels to be the same, or is there something special about the lexical levels which distinguishes them from the others? Earlier, I suggested that we could conceive of words as collections of procedures, but now we can see that we have to consider what consequences this might have for the way we would perform and understand experiments. What would this mean for word frequency, structural factors such as word length, the differences between tasks, and whether a magic moment is a good idea in a system which would, essentially constitute parallel procedures all running at their own particular levels?

If we accept the discussion about representations and processes and about which levels might be stored and which might be seen only in processes, then we can see why the chapters here are simultaneously interesting and unsatisfying. On the one hand, the models that are developed are, for the most part, so underspecified as to make answers to (a) and (b) impossible. On the other hand, the results of the experiments are all too often only capable of interpretation in terms of a specific type of model which may not be appropriate. The PDP models provide an interesting and new way of coming to grips with the problems sketched here. Not, I add, because of their supposed ability to do away with rules (Fodor & Pylyshyn, 1988; Lachter & Bever, 1988; Pinker & Prince, 1988) but because of the general attributes which they presuppose as computational devices. These are that the basic computational processes should be very simple and essentially the same everywhere. There are principles of, for instance, summation of excitation and inhibition and mutual inhibition of elements at the same level in the system (McClelland & Rumelhart, 1981). What these show is that qualitatively different behaviors *can* arise from the same system depending upon the context of operation in which it finds itself as a whole. PDP models also show that many constraints upon operation can be hidden as part of the system in, for instance, the weights to and from layers of hidden units. Such constraints can often only be seen to apply when the system is actually in operation. This is neutral with respect to whether simple PDP systems can easily learn rule-governed behaviors, which seems not to be the case in linguistically interesting applications, but it rather stresses that they can represent such constraints, which can only be described by reference to rules in a process-oriented way.

The proposal I am beginning to put forward here may well offer a compromise between the positions of Besner and the PDP proponents. What I suggest is that lexical representations at any one level of representation be seen as procedures for handling information at that level for specific uses. This naturally subsumes the requirements for differentiation between input and output and among the different modalities, insofar as each has different processing requirements. What may vanish is any notion of a monolithic lexicon, the repository of all information, because the lexicon becomes the totality of all the processing systems that use lexical knowledge. This is not the same as the PDP approach when it assumes a single layer of actual lexical representations, because that is a monolithic representation. It is much closer to Seidenberg's proposal for hidden units representing mappings between different lexicons. The latter are, however, still static and similar to the classical input and output lexicons.

In conclusion, I look at the chapters and find that some of them are attacking questions which are more fundamental but that the lack of an organized understanding of what those questions are makes it difficult to see exactly what the consequences of experiments and theoretical analyses are. I have suggested a radical model of representation, more as a counter to the prevailing models, in order to allow us to see that many of the questions we ask are in fact determined by our theoretical context. Only when we understand what words are and how they are processed will we be able to understand what is happening during a single fixation in a piece of text.

REFERENCES

Balota, D. A., & Chumbley, J. I. (1984). Are lexical decisions a good measure of lexical access? The role of word frequency in the neglected decision stage. *Journal of Experimental Psychology: Human Perception and Performance, 10*, 340 - 357.

Balota, D. A., & Chumbley, J. I. (1985). The locus of word frequency effects in the pronunciation task: Lexical access and/or production? *Journal of Memory and Language, 24*, 89 - 106.

Bergman, M. W. (1988). *The visual recognition of word structure: Left-to-right processing of derivational morphology.* Unpublished doctoral dissertation, University of Nijmegen, The Netherlands.

Bergman, M. W., Hudson, P. T. W., & Eling, P. A. T. M. (1988). How simple complex words can be: Morphological processing and word representations. *Quarterly Journal of Experimental Psychology, 40A*, 41 - 72.

Butterworth, B. (1983). Lexical representation. In B. Butterworth (Ed.), *Language production* (Vol. II, pp. 257 - 294). London: Academic Press.

Caramazza, A., Laudanna, A., & Romani, C. (1988). Lexical access and inflectional morphology. *Cognition, 28*, 297 - 332.

Chomsky, N. (1957). *Syntactic structures.* The Hague: Mouton.

Coltheart, M., Patterson, K., & Marshall, J. C. (1980). *Deep dyslexia.* London: Routledge & Kegan Paul.

Coltheart, M., Sartori, G., & Job, R. (Eds.). (1987). *The cognitive neuropsychology of language.* London: Lawrence Erlbaum Associates.

Fodor, J. A. & Pylyshyn, Z. W. (1988). Connectionism and cognitive architecture: A critical analysis. *Cognition, 28*, 3 - 71.

Forster, K. I. (1976). Accessing the mental lexicon. In E. Walker & R. J. Wales (Eds.), *New approaches to language mechanisms: A collection of psycholinguistic studies* (pp. 257 - 287). Amsterdam: North-Holland.

Hudson, P. T. W. (1977). *Cerebral dominance and language: An experimental and theoretical investigation.* Unpublished doctoral dissertation, University of St. Andrews, Scotland.

Hudson, P. T. W., & Bergman, M. W. (1984). Van spelling naar klank: modellen voor het hardop lezen van woorden. [From spelling to sound: Models for reading words aloud]. In A. J. W. M. Thomassen, L. G. M. Noordman, & P. A. T. M. Eling (Eds.), *Het Leesproces* (pp. 79 - 92). Lisse: Swets & Zeitlinger.

Hudson, P. T. W., & Bergman, M. W. (1985). Lexical knowledge in word recognition: Word length and word frequency in naming and lexical decision tasks. *Journal of Memory and Language, 24,* 46 - 58.

Hudson, P. T. W., Bergman, M. W., Houtmans, M. J. M., & Nas, G. L. J. (1984). De bestudering van woordherkenning als basis voor het lezen. [The study of word recognition as a basis for reading]. In A. J. W. M. Thomassen, L. G. M. Noordman, & P. A. T. M. Eling (Eds.), *Het Leesproces* (pp. 27 - 52). Lisse: Swets & Zeitlinger.

Huey, E. G. (1908). *The psychology and pedagogy of reading.* Cambridge, MA: MIT Press. (Reprinted 1968).

Lachter, J., & Bever, T. G. (1988). The relation between linguistic structure and associative theories of language learning – A constructive critique of some connectionist learning models. *Cognition, 28,* 195 - 247.

Matthews, P. H. (1974). *Morphology: An introduction to the theory of word structure.* London: Cambridge University Press.

McClelland, J. L. (1979). On the time relations of mental processes: An examination of systems of processes in cascade. *Psychological Review, 86,* 287 - 330.

McClelland, J. L., & Rumelhart, D. E. (1981). An interactive activation model of context effects in letter perception: Part 1. An account of basic findings. *Psychological Review, 88,* 375 - 407.

Monsell, S. (1985). Repetition and the lexicon. In A. W. Ellis (Ed.), *Progress in the psychology of language* (Vol. 2, pp. 147 - 195). London: Lawrence Erlbaum Associates.

Morton, J. (1969). The interaction of information in word recognition. *Psychological Review, 76,* 165 - 178.

Patterson, K. E., Marshall, J. C., & Coltheart, M. (1985). *Surface dyslexia.* London: Lawrence Erlbaum Associates.

Phaf, R. H., van der Heijden, A. H. C., & Hudson, P. T. W. (in press). SLAM: A connectionist model for attention in visual selection tasks. *Cognitive Psychology.*

Pillsbury, W. B. (1897). A study in apperception. *American Journal of Psychology, 8,* 315 - 393.

Pinker, S., & Prince, A. (1988). On language and connectionism: Analysis of a parallel distributed processing model of language acquisition. *Cognition, 28,* 73 - 193.

Seidenberg, M. S. (1988). Cognitive neuropsychology and language: The state of the art. *Cognitive Neuropsychology, 5,* 403 - 426.

Taft, M. (1976). *Morphological and syllabic analysis in word recognition.* Unpublished doctoral dissertation, Monash University, Clayton, Victoria.

Taft, M. (1979). Recognition of affixed words and the word frequency effect. *Memory & Cognition, 7,* 263 - 272.

Taft, M., & Forster, K. I. (1975). Lexical storage and retrieval of prefixed words. *Journal of Verbal Learning and Verbal Behavior, 14,* 638 - 647.

II

SYNTACTIC PROCESSES IN COMPREHENSION

10

THE COOPERATIVE LANGUAGE PROCESSORS: SEMANTIC INFLUENCES IN AN AUTONOMOUS SYNTAX

Charles A. Perfetti

University of Pittsburgh

INTRODUCTION

Recent research on parsing has provided a salubrious injection of syntax into our theories of comprehension. After a period in which the study of comprehension became closely identified with the analysis of higher level textual processes and in which syntactic processes typically were assumed to be either inscrutable or irrelevant, it is again credible to claim that comprehension depends in part on processes that are essentially syntactic. In parallel, after a period in which the concept of reading ability seemed to collapse around concepts of knowledge-based reasoning, use of schemata and the like, it is again reasonable to argue that reading ability, as opposed to adaptive intelligence, is largely a matter of narrow linguistic abilities rather than broadly cognitive ones (see Perfetti, 1989).

In this chapter, however, I want to raise some issues that prove to be difficult for an integrated account of comprehension, that is, for an account that attends to the connections between syntactic and semantic influences in the comprehension of sentences. The difficulty stems from two empirically plausible considerations: (a) under certain conditions, syntactic processes may produce more than one syntactic structure, and (b) under certain conditions, syntactic decisions give the appearance of being influenced by semantic and discourse factors. After developing a case for the empirical plausibility of these issues, I suggest how a syntactic processor might accommodate them without compromising its autonomy.

205

First, a broader theoretical context: I assume that a correct view of comprehension includes an autonomous syntactic process (Forster, 1979) and that the macrostructure of human comprehension includes components that do not ordinarily have unconstrained interactions. Furthermore, I take the modularity position (Fodor, 1983) to be a reasonable approximation of a functional level of cognitive organization, although I see a strong preference for either modularity or interactionism as a matter of taste, at least to some degree. Cognitive organizations that will serve language processing will include both modular cognitive components and interactive ones. The only question is the conditions that constrain the interactive components. Unconstrained interactive models, more specifically connectionist models, probably will not serve as overall architectures for a representational cognition, for reasons well articulated by Fodor and Pylyshyn (1988), and will have difficulty reflecting the subtleties of linguistic performance, as demonstrated by Pinker and Prince (1988). On the other hand, it is tempting to conceptualize specific localized portions of computational cognition as parallel and undifferentiated in the manner suggested by connectionist theories. Thus, for example, the identification of a printed word can occur as the result of connections among constituent units that are in mutual activation. Constraints on such interactions exist in the structure of the data they are able to use, that is, modules. In the case of syntax, I assume that syntactic processes constitute either a single module or a set of modules that include syntactic constituents among its data structures. This limits the contribution to syntax by sources of information that are encoded in different data structures.

Although they are relevant for this architecture question, the main issues I address here are more narrowly concerned with how parsing works in context. The general question is how determined a syntactic processor is to make a single best parse under all circumstances. On one account, it is quite determined to make a decision at each choice point, for better or worse. If later information makes it clear that the wrong decision was made, then some backtracking is necessary. Although alternatives to this degree of syntactic determinism have been proposed (e.g., Crain & Steedman, 1985; Kurtzman, 1985), the proposals that have enjoyed the most influence, and are indeed the most interesting because of their strong claims, are those that attribute to the parser a principled determination to attach each word to a partially constructed constituent tree, especially the theory put forth by Frazier (1978, 1987, this volume) and her colleagues (Rayner, Carlson, & Frazier, 1983).

The question is whether the decisiveness of the parser might be somewhat less than this proposal claims. Comprehension may include early stages of parsing in which some attachments are created tentatively and perhaps probabilistically and in which structures are sometimes left floating momentarily unattached. I emphasize "momentarily" and "sometimes" because no structures are left unattached for very long and many attachments are immediate.

To make this conjecture credible, the phenomenon of garden-pathing must be confronted. The fact that readers make incorrect parsing decisions, that is, are garden-pathed, is the central empirical phenomenon of parsing and it is the most important fact compelling acceptance of immediate decision parsers. Three prototype cases of garden-pathing are illustrated as follows from a list of such cases from Frazier (1987):

1. John hit the girl *with a book* with a bat (Rayner, Carlson, & Frazier, 1983).

2. Since Jay always jogs *a mile* seems like a short distance (Frazier & Rayner, 1982).

3. The horse *raced* past the barn *fell* (Bever, 1970; Ferreira & Clifton, 1986; Rayner et al., 1983).

The italicized portion of each sentence is a phrase whose attachment is structurally ambiguous, but which, in each case, must eventually be attached in a way that goes against the parser's initial preference – as dictated by Frazier's principle of minimal attachment in Examples 1 and 3, and by the principle of late closure in Example 2. Thus in Example 1, the parser's initial preference is to attach *with* directly to the verb phrase (VP) rather than to the noun phrase (NP) (the girl). In Example 2, the parser prefers to attach *a mile* to the already created VP rather than to begin a new clause. And in Example 3, it prefers to parse *raced* as a simple past tense verb attached to the main clause rather than as attached to a reduced relative clause. In each case, the preferred parse leads to a structure that subsequently must be abandoned.

There are at least two separable parsing issues that are addressed by garden-path phenomena. The first is whether the parser makes immediate decisions on a word-by-word basis or postpones decisions on at least some occasions. The second is whether the parser's immediate decisions are informed primarily by syntactic (or syntactic-lexical) information or whether it uses information from semantic and pragmatic sources. In each case, garden-path evidence supports the first mentioned alternative: Parsing decisions are immediately made according to syntactic principles on a word-by-word basis. I think both of these conclusions are correct in fundamental ways but may need some modification.

I propose to consider the possibility of a parser that is determined (i.e., it makes a commitment at each choice point) only for high-level constituents and local attachments triggered by syntactic features. The parser is less determined to make the full range of intermediate attachments between low-level and high-level constituents in the absence of syntactic triggers. Many questions arise concerning such a suggestion, of course: What counts as a trigger and why? What's the distinction between local (low) attachments and high attachments? These difficult questions are considered later, although they are not solved. The main goal is simply to raise the possibility for such a parser as a response to some empirical phenomena. The latter are provided by some recent experimental results, both from experiments carried out by my students and me and from the results of other research.

In each of these experiments, questions can be raised as to whether the observations are sufficiently on-line. None of these are eye-movement studies, although they all involved reading under time pressure and measures of reading time or immediate decision times. I want to suggest at least the possibility that these experiments are tapping early-occurring processes that can be confirmed by even more on-line measures. The first set of studies suggests some conditions in which multiple parses might be entertained, and the second and third sets of studies suggest some early semantic and discourse influences on parsing decisions.

IMPOVERISHED SYNTAX

Some recent studies have examined the ambiguities that accompany the impoverished syntax of newspaper headlines (Perfetti, Beverly, Bell, Rodgers, & Faux, 1987), as illustrated in Example 4:

4. Toronto Law to Protect Squirrels Hit by Mayor

This headline is ambiguous between the reading that there was some law that the Mayor criticized and the reading that there was some law aimed at bringing relief specifically to squirrels that were hit by the Mayor. We found that Example 4 took longer to read than either of its unambiguous versions 5 and 6:

5. Toronto Squirrel-Protection Law Criticized by Mayor
6. Toronto Law to Protect Squirrels that are Hit by Mayor

An important additional result was that the effect of ambiguity on headline reading time was not influenced by context. When a preceding context made clear which meaning was appropriate, unambiguous headlines were still read more quickly than ambiguous ones. Our conclusion was that syntactic principles were controlling the initial attempts to parse these headlines and that the parsing process could not be shortcut by pragmatic information provided either by plausibility or by discourse context. Even when readers knew ahead of time that they would read a headline appropriate for a story about a mayor criticizing a squirrel-protection law, the presence of the other possible structure, implausible though it might be, slowed reading time. Thus, a syntax-first process appears to have controlled comprehension even in a case in which non-syntactic information was desperately needed, a result that adds weight to the hypothesis that initial parsing operations are not penetrated by pragmatic information, as suggested by Rayner et al. (1983) and confirmed by Ferreira and Clifton (1986). What's further added by the headlines studies is that the privileged status of syntactic information is maintained even when it is clearly unreliable. Because headlines omit critical cues to syntactic structures, there would appear to be opportunity for the early use of semantic and pragmatic information and more advantage to its use.

Some of the syntactic problems of headlines are illustrated in Examples 7-9:

7. Rumors about NBA Referees Growing Ugly
8. Beirut Uprising by Ousted Leader Crushed by Militia
9. Deer Kill 130,000

Each of these headlines creates an attachment problem because of its impoverished syntax. Among other problems, the absence of *are* in Example 7 and *is* in Example 8 creates difficulties for attachment. This omission of auxiliary verbs is very typical of English headline syntax and makes attachment of the main verb or participle a problem (*growing* in Example 7, *crushed* in Example 8). In Example 9, the problem is at its most severe. There is no verb whatsoever, and the reader is tempted to parse *kill*, which normally is a verb, as the main verb.

Notice that in each case there is ample opportunity for pragmatic information to be used by the informed reader. In Example 7, a reader of the sports pages of a newspaper might expect a story concerning the officiating of basketball referees rather than one concerning their personal attractiveness. And in Example 9, most readers would be skeptical about the possibility of killer deer. Readers do indeed make use of what they know about the world when they read these headlines, but they cannot use this knowledge quickly enough to suppress the syntactic processes that are forcing other attachments to be considered.

As to the question of what the ambiguity effect implies for general parsing, we tentatively concluded that on some occasions multiple parsing possibilities were being considered and that this resulted in longer reading times. This possibility is not quite the one favored by single-choice (garden-path) parsing models. However, before concluding that the headline data favor a multiple parse process, another possibility should be considered. It may be that the ambiguity effect is restricted to those headlines whose eventual interpretation required a parse different from the one initially constructed according to some syntactic principle, such as minimal attachment, as would be expected by a garden-path model.

To illustrate how a garden-path model would handle the headline data, I repeat Example 4.

4. Toronto Law to Protect Squirrels Hit by Mayor

The first choice point comes at *to protect*. If the parser has determined that *Toronto law* is a simple NP, in accordance with the minimal attachment principle, then it ought to begin to create a VP at this point rather than an additional NP embedding the one already created. Assuming it does so, it runs into trouble three words later, where *hit* requires the construction of a reduced relative and provides the implausible reading of the headline, initiating a reparse. This is essentially the garden-path account of an ambiguity effect: An initially preferred structure is contradicted by later semantic and pragmatic information. Similarly, other cases such as Example 7, repeated here, might be explained by the principle of late closure.

7.   Rumors about NBA Referees Growing Ugly

On either reading, upon encountering *about*, the parser must create a prepositional phrase (PP) that extends at least until *growing*. However, at that point the late closure principle applies: The parser prefers to keep open the PP and can do so by attaching it to *growing ugly*. Because this turns out to be the nonpreferred reading, reanalysis must take place, again in accordance with garden-path theory. Thus, from these examples, it is conceivable to think of the parser as making commitments according to syntactic principles even for newspaper headlines that contain syntactic cues of reduced value. An ambiguity effect can be a garden-path effect in disguise.

However, there are examples among the headlines we studied in which a parsing principle such as minimal attachment or late closure was consistent with the preferred interpretation rather than inconsistent with it. For example in Sentence 10, minimal attachment favors the reading judged more plausible by our subjects, namely that there will be a trial for a defendant accused of shooting someone.

10. Court to Try Shooting Defendant

To create the bizarre reading that the court intends to shoot the defendant, the parser must violate minimal attachment by creating an additional S node under the VP. (It must also consider a sense of *try* that is not plausible following *court*.) Note that it is possible to suggest that a syntactic cue of verb stem + ing (*shooting*) causes the parser to create a full verb phrase rather than the adjectival participle required by minimal attachment. On this conjecture, one would argue that categorical cues dominate attachment cues or at least can interfere with them. It is conceivable that some of the headline ambiguity effects arise from syntactic category uncertainty rather than attachment uncertainty. Nevertheless, whether forced by categorical ambiguity or not, the parser appears to be considering alternative structures.

If the parser is delaying its decision in the case of newspaper headlines, this may be an automatic consequence of parsing difficulty caused by headline syntax. That this delay process might be general in sentence comprehension appears to be unlikely given other data (e.g., Rayner et al., 1983). However, it is possible that something similar characterizes even ordinary sentence processing under certain conditions that are explored in the next section.

SEMANTIC AND CONTEXTUAL INFLUENCES IN PARSING

A second line of research that raises doubts about how determined the parser is comes from studies of discourse and semantic influences in sentence comprehension. Ferreira and Clifton (1986) showed in a series of three experiments that structural preferences, specifically minimal attachment, governed reading times even when context supported the structurally nonpreferred reading. For example, in Sentence 11 minimal attachment causes *The editor* to be taken as a simple subject NP rather than as an embedded head of a relative clause.

11. The editor played the tape agreed the story was a big one.

Instead, the eventual reading of the sentence requires the relative clause reading. Ferreira and Clifton (1986) found that even when prior context established the existence of two editors, only one of whom listened to the tape, readers were still garden-pathed. Their first pass eye movements were longer in the disambiguating region of this sentence than in the corresponding region of a control sentence. A similar result was obtained for double preposition sentences such as 12:

12. Sam loaded the boxes on the cart onto the van.

Here, minimal attachment prefers to attach *on the cart* high in the VP rather than to modify the NP begun with *the boxes*. This preference also was found to survive a contextual manipulation that made the nonminimal reading (i.e., the boxes that were on the cart) pragmatically preferred. The evidence again was longer first pass fixation times in the disambiguating region (*onto the van*) relative to a control that permitted the minimal attachment reading to be maintained. In another experiment, Ferreira and Clifton (1986) found that this pattern of results could be obtained using subject-controlled reading times as well as eye movements.

This leads me to the Britt (1987) experiment. Britt's hypothesis was that when interpretations were sufficiently constrained by the referential semantics provided by a text, garden-path effects would be eliminated. Her experiment used sentences such as 13, 14, and 15 presented in isolation and in appropriate contexts.

13. Peter read the books on the chair instead of lying in bed.
14. Peter read the books on the chair instead of the other books.
15. Peter read the books on the war instead of the other books.

The critical attachment in each case involves the prepositional phrase *on the chair/war*. In Example 13, the eventual attachment of the phrase is the one preferred by the minimal attachment principle. In Example 14, the minimal attachment is later contradicted by the *instead* phrase, and in Example 15, minimal attachment is made immediately implausible by the word *war*, which suggests the nonminimal reading.

The context manipulation is illustrated in Table 10.1. The story (for Sentence 13) at the top of Table 10.1 makes it clear that Peter might read either while in bed or while sitting in the chair and establishes a context consistent with an immediate minimal attachment decision. The story in the middle of the Table 10.1 (for Sentence 14) makes it

TABLE 10.1

*Three Discourse Contexts for "Peter Read the Books
on the Chair". Based on Britt (1987).*

VP Attachment (Min)

Peter broke his leg very badly so he missed two weeks at school and anticipated missing two more weeks . . . His teacher had stopped by to help him make up the work he had missed. She had given him some school books and some extra books in case he got caught up. She put both sets of books on the desk. Although Peter was supposed to stay in bed, he liked to do his reading in the lounge chair. Peter hobbled to his lounge chair after deciding that he had been in bed long enough. *Peter read the books on the chair instead of lying in bed.* He hoped that he would have enough time to read all the books.

NP Attachment (NonMin)

Peter broke his leg very badly so he missed two weeks at . . . . [The teacher] had given him some school books. She also had some pleasure reading books that she knew he would like, and she had put these on the lamp table. She had put the school books on the chair near the bed so he could reach them without getting out of bed. He had to decide which books to read. *Peter read the books on the chair instead of the other books.* . . . .

NP Attachment (NonMin)

Peter broke his leg very badly so he missed two weeks at school. . . She had given him some school books. She had also given him some books on his favorite subject, the Civil war. She had put the books on his bed and told him to concentrate on the school books . . . . He looked at his homework books and got really bored. He had to decide which books to read. *Peter read the books on the war instead of the other books.* . . .

---

clear that Peter might read some books that are on the chair or he might read some other books located elsewhere, and establishes supportive context for an immediate nonminimal attachment. The story at the bottom (for Sentence 15) also establishes clear support for the nonminimal reading. Two sets of books, including one on *the war*, were available to Peter.

Britt's experiment involved self-paced word-at-a time reading. Of interest were the reading times for words from various regions of the critical sentence, i.e., the region prior to the ambiguous phrase (e.g., *Peter read*) the region containing the key ambiguous phrase (e.g., *the books on the chair*), and the region following this phrase (e.g., *instead of lying in bed/instead of the other books*). In isolation, Britt found that Example 15 took significantly longer to read than Example 13 in the region that forces a nonminimal attachment (*the war* compared with *the chair*). Comparing Example 14 to Example 13, the critical region is the phrase *instead of the other books* compared with *instead of lying in bed*, and this comparison showed a nonsignificant advantage for the minimal attachment Sentence 13. These results essentially replicate those of Rayner et al. (1983), and suggest that the reading time measure was sensitive to the structural difference between the two sentence types.

The important result, however, was that the differences favoring minimal attachment disappeared in context. When Sentences 14 and 15 occurred in their supportive contexts (Table 10.1), they took no longer to read than did Sentence 13 when it occurred in its supportive context.

The critical comparisons of Britt's experiment depended on different groups of subjects and the use of control sentences to determine expected per character reading rates. Coupled with reading times that were variable and rather long, these facts suggested some caution in interpretation of the results. However, Britt has recently replicated the experiment with some minor changes, comparing reading times of sentence types 13 and 15 in the biased contexts of Table 10.1 with their reading times in neutral contexts, in a within-subjects design that produced shorter reading times. The pattern of results supports the original conclusion. The mean per character reading times, illustrated for Sentences 13 and 15, were as follows: In neutral contexts, *Peter read the books*, the region prior to the critical phrase, produced reading times of 44 and 46 ms for the minimal attachment and nonminimal attachment versions of the sentence, respectively. For the ambiguous phrases, the times were 51 ms for *on the chair* (minimal) and 56 ms for *on the war* (nonminimal), a nonsignificant difference ($F = 1$) in the expected direction. For the following phrase, the times were 63 ms for *instead of lying in bed* (minimal) and 75 ms for *instead of the other books* (nonminimal; $F(1,63) = 7.56$, $p < .01$). Thus, in neutral contexts, nonminimal attachment sentences required more reading time in the region following the ambiguous prepositional phrase. However, in biasing contexts, this difference was completely eliminated: In the minimal attachment biasing context (Table 10.1), the per character reading time for the ambiguous phrase (*on the chair*) was 54 ms compared with 51 ms for the corresponding phrase (*on the war*) in the nonminimal sentence. For the following phrases, the times were 60 ms for the minimal attachment phrase (*instead of lying in bed*) and 62 ms for the nonminimal attachment phrase (*instead of the other books*). Neither difference is statistically reliable (both Fs < 1).

Apparently, nonminimal attachment structures of this particular kind did not create processing problems in supporting contexts. These discourse contexts provided specific referential objects that became part of the reader's discourse model. The suggestion is that the referential semantics provided by the discourse model is made quickly available to the constituent parser, as Crain and Steedman (1985) also argued.

The demonstration that at least some minimal attachment preferences might be overridden by context aligns with the results of a recent set of experiments by Taraban and McClelland (1988), who investigated exactly the kinds of structures used in the Britt experiment. Essentially, Taraban and McClelland found that the attachment preferences of structurally ambiguous prepositional phrases depended on the expectations readers have. Thus, in the case of Examples 16 and 17, the minimal attachment Version 16 is read faster than the nonminimal attachment

Version 17. However, the minimal attachment Version 18 is slower than the nonminimal attachment version 19.

16. The spy saw the cop with binoculars . . .
17. The spy saw the cop with a revolver . . .
18. The thieves stole all the paintings in the night . . .
19. The thieves stole all the paintings in the museum . . .

The difference between these two pairs is that for Examples 16 and 17, taken from Rayner et al. (1983), readers tend to expect the instrument continuation represented by Example 16 (*binoculars*) rather than the continuation represented by *revolver* in Example 17. By contrast, for pair 18 and 19 the continuation of the nonminimal 19 is more in line with readers' expectations. Taraban and McClelland found that the main controlling factors in attachment for these sentences is their conformity to expectations of case roles (e.g., instrument, location), a result also obtained by Speer, Foss, and Smith (1986), and to expectations of the specific role fillers (e.g., *revolver, binocular, museum*). [1]

Although the Britt results and the Taraban and McClelland results appear to pose some problems for an autonomous syntax, I suggest one way to solve these problems within an autonomous syntax. First, I want to discuss one more line of evidence that reinforces the problems posed by semantic and contextual factors in parsing.

Double Prepositions and Spatial Relations

In a series of experiments, Beverly Adams and I have been investigating the comprehension of sentences that ambiguously encode spatial relations, such as Example 20.

20. The pencil is on the tablet next to the watch.

This sentence can be understood to describe either of the relations illustrated in Figure 10.1. On one reading, the semantic relations can be paraphrased as *The pencil is on the tablet and next to the watch, which is also on the tablet.* On the other reading, the semantic relations can be paraphrased as *The pencil is on the tablet, which is next to the watch.* There is actually a third representation in which there are two tablets and the relations are paraphrased as *The pencil is on the tablet that is next to the watch.* The first of these semantic representations corresponds to a minimal attachment reading. The second and third correspond to nonminimal attachment readings.

---

[1] The presentation method of Taraban and McClelland was to fill the screen with blank lines and spaces, with the blank lines soon replaced by letters. Conceivably, since the blanks are viewable by the subject, active prediction processes that would not normally occur might have been encouraged by this method. More critical is that such active prediction processes cannot be general nor valuable enough to guide parsing, as Frazier (this volume) notes. Garden-path phenomena include exactly those cases in which the reader's expectations, if they could be used in time, would prevent garden-pathing.

These types of sentences allow a confrontation of two different representation principles, one semantic and one syntactic. The syntactic principle of minimal attachment seems to predict that subjects will initially prefer to encode representation (a) of Figure 10.1: *The pencil is on the tablet and so is the watch.*[2] The semantic principle is one we refer to as minimal inference and it predicts that subjects will tend to form representation (b) of Figure 10.1. To form representation (a), the reader must make an additional inference beyond the two propositions that are encoded from the sentence. That is, to the explicit propositions i. and ii. the reader must add by inference, iii.

i.   [Pencil on tablet]
ii. [Pencil next to watch]
iii. [Watch on tablet]

By contrast, representation (b) can be formed just with the two explicit propositions:

i. [Pencil on tablet]
iv. [Tablet next to watch]

The location of the watch relative to the pencil is not inferred, and, by default, it is located at any point in space off the tablet.

Our first clear result was that subjects preferred the minimal inference representation and not the minimal attachment representation (Perfetti, Adams, Weitz, & Bell, 1987). In an experiment in which subjects formed mental images of the objects mentioned in the sentence, 70% of their images corresponded to the minimal inference picture represented in (b), whereas 30% corresponded to the minimal attachment representation in (a). (They virtually never formed the double object images [e.g., two tablets] that correspond to *the pencil is on the tablet that is next to the watch.*) Imagery data, of course, reflect processes that are well off-line. However, this same preference for minimal inference over minimal attachment was found in a speeded reading time study in which subjects first read a sentence and then verified a following picture. In the illustration used here, Sentence 20 could be followed by either picture (a) or (b), as well as by the double object picture (not shown). The

---

[2] The grammar of these PPs is not totally clear, and it is at least possible that the minimal attachment reading does not have fewer attachments than the nonminimal attachment reading. One analysis *is on the tablet next to the watch* is approximately [is [on the tablet] [next to the watch]]. This corresponds to panel (a) of Figure 10.2 and is minimal attachment relative to [is [on [the tablet [next to the watch]]]], which corresponds to representation (b) of Figure 10.2. However, if the V node (*is*) cannot have two sister PPs, then the correct analysis corresponding to (a) might be something like [[is [on the tablet]] [next to the watch]]. This would have the same number of attachments as (b). This latter constituent analysis does not correspond to the intuition that the two PPs in representation (a) are semantically conjoined, however. My assumption is that the grammar of English allows the simpler structure in general, so that analysis should be tried first by the parser, according to a minimal attachment principle.

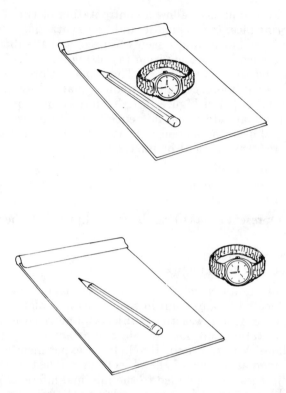

FIGURE 10.1. Two representations of *The pencil is on the tablet next to the watch.* The top panel (a) shows the representation corresponding to the constituent structure [is [*on the tablet*] [*next to the watch*]] which is nonminimal if the parser can create a single VP node with two sister PPs as indicated. (See footnote 3.) Panel (b) corresponds to [*is* [*on the tablet* [*next to the watch*]]], that is, the putatively nonminimal attachment. Not shown is a third representation containing two tablets, with the pencil on the tablet that is next to the watch. This is syntactically the same as panel (b).

times to verify were faster for minimal inference representations (b) than for minimal attachment representations (a). One might object that, in sentence - picture verification, a good deal of the processing is devoted to encoding the picture and that verification time comparisons are misleading. Our interpretation, however, is that verification time includes the time to correct a mismatch if the reader's sentence representation does not match the picture. This interpretation is supported by the rather dramatic result we obtained when we reversed the order of the prepositions in the sentences, keeping the pictures the same. For example, instead of Sentence 20, we presented Sentence 21:

20. The pencil is on the tablet next to the watch.

21. The pencil is next to the watch on the tablet.

For Sentence 21 subjects were now faster at verifying minimal attachment than minimal inference representations, completely reversing the initial result obtained for Sentence 20.

The reason for the reversal has to with the pragmatics of expressions that encode spatial relations. Some prepositions have clear ordering preferences, or dominance relations, which appear to derive from physical constraints encoded by prepositions. Thus, *next to* generally presupposes that two objects share a surface, so *next to* is dominated by *on*, because *on* asserts an object-surface relationship. Thus Sentence 20, which does not violate the dominance relationship of *on-next to* on either reading, is free to be encoded according to inferential simplicity. Sentence 21, however, violates the dominance relationship on one reading, the minimal inference reading, and so requires the minimal attachment despite the extra inference required. (See Herskovits, 1985, for an interesting account of prepositional semantics.)

These subtle issues of spatial representations and constraints on prepositions aside, the main point is that the comprehension of these simple double locative expressions is partly controlled by principles of perhaps both semantics (minimal inference) and pragmatics (expression of dominance relations). Again a caveat: This is true to the extent that results with such paradigms are general and sufficiently *on-line*. At least for now, it is interesting to assume that the results of these experiments, as well as those discussed previously, reflect early contributions of nonsyntactic factors and then to consider how a language processor with an autonomous syntax might account for them. First, there are some issues about the syntax of the structures under consideration that deserve comment.

The Syntax of Post-nominal Prepositional Phrases

In the Britt study, the Taraban and McClelland (1988) study, and the Perfetti, Adams et al. (1987) spatial relations study, there has been only one type of syntactic structure – a post-nominal prepositional phrase that is part of a verb phrase. I repeat Examples 13 from Britt and 20 from Perfetti et al. as reminders.

13. Peter read the books on the chair . . .
20. The pencil is on the tablet next to the watch.

Both sentences are ambiguous concerning the attachment of a prepositional phrase following a noun phrase. The assumption has been that the attachment of the PP directly to the VP is minimal attachment, whereas attachment of the PP to the preceding NP is nonminimal attachment.

However, it is possible that there is really no difference between these structures in the number of attachments formed. Smith (1988) has argued that neither parsing choice yields a minimal attachment. Her argument rests on a constituent analysis of NPs that expands noun modifiers directly under a nominal head, an analysis for which there is some syntactic evidence (e.g., Baker, 1978) and which happens to conform to semantic intuitions in the case of the post-nominal PPs under consideration. On this analysis, a nominal (NOM) is a constituent that includes a head NOUN plus all its post-nominal modifiers. Thus, *the books on the chair* in its NOM analysis would be DET + [N + PP], [*the* [*books on the chair*]].[3] This would be the structure for the nonminimal attachment reading with an extra node labeled NOM instead of an extra node labeled NP – an extra attachment in either case. However, if the NOM constituent is created automatically on any appearance of a DET, then even the minimal attachment alternative will create this NOM node. This is what Smith argues, and if the argument is correct, then there is no difference between the minimal and nonminimal alternatives for these post-nominal structures. Indeed, any syntactic complexity that depends on expansion of a noun will not increase the number of attachments.

Figure 10.2 illustrates what is at issue for the *chair* Sentence 13. It represents a parser that has created a VP beginning with *read* and is now faced with two alternatives for *on the chair* (or simply *on*). If it has created the structure shown in Figure 10.2 with a NOM, it can

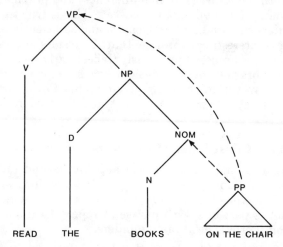

FIGURE 10.2. The possibilities for post-nominal PP attachment for *Peter read the books on the chair* on the assumption that the parser automatically creates a NOM node when it encounters a DET, as suggested by Smith (1988). Given this structure, the parser should be indifferent to whether it attaches the PP on *the chair* to the VP or to the NOM, at least on minimal attachment grounds.

---

[3] The linguistic evidence for this analysis comes from pro-form substitution. Essentially, the pro-form "one" is substituted for a constituent that corresponds to NOM rather than to one that corresponds to NP or N. For example, in "Bill read two books about the war and Sue read one", *one* substitutes for the NOM, "books about the war" rather than the NP, "the books". (Example based on Smith, 1988.)

build either the low attachment PP (the nonminimal alternative) or the high VP attached structure (the minimal alternative) at equal cost. Either one is a single attachment, as indicated by the dashed lines that represent the two parsing options.

Frazier (this volume) has pointed out some problems with this analysis, most importantly that if the NOM node is always created, the principle of late closure, for which there is independent evidence, should cause the PP to be attached low to the NOM node rather than high to the VP. Thus, the preferred reading for *read the books on the chair* should be the nonminimal [*the*] [*books on the chair*], a preference for which there is no evidence. Somehow, as Frazier argues, the parser has to decide which attachment to build: [*read* [[*the*] [*books on the chair*]]] or [*read* [*the books*] [*on the chair*]]. It is at this point that communication between a semantic representation and a syntactic representation becomes compelling.

THE COOPERATIVE
AUTONOMOUS LANGUAGE PROCESSOR

A comprehension model comprising cooperative processors, including a cooperative autonomous parser, provides for this kind of communication. It has two important features. First, it preserves an autonomous syntax. Second, it allows semantic influences very early in comprehension.

The Organization of Language Processors

The general architecture into which the cooperative autonomous parser might fit is shown in Figure 10.3. Its important feature is the existence of three kinds of functioning representations during reading: a syntactic, a semantic, and a text level. Although this scheme traces its ancestry to that introduced by Forster (1979), it contains a critical difference from Forster's: It places a short-term semantic representation in a central communicative role. This semantic representation is the part of the system that allows arrows in both directions and thus brings discourse information and syntactic information together.

The language processors, as represented in Figure 10.3, include an autonomous syntax of restricted duties – one that builds constituents free from nonsyntactic influences. They include also an immediate and shallow semantic representation, a text model, and a lexicon. The semantic representation receives referential information from the text model and information about thematic roles (verb argument structures) from the lexicon. It assigns thematic roles and referential values to the constituents it receives from the syntactic processor. Although no arrow is shown going from semantics to syntax, some attachment decisions are, in effect, informed by the thematic and referential information represented in the semantic processor. This assumption can be elaborated, with awkwardness, either by representing some duplicate constituent mechanisms in the semantics or by representing feedback of referential and thematic information to the constituent builder. In either case, the semantic influences are very restricted, and thus consistent with a one-direction arrow from syntax to semantics.

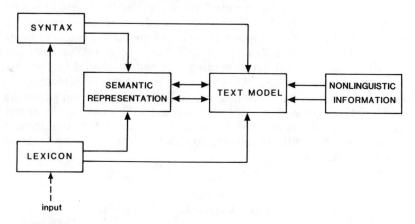

FIGURE 10.3. A schematic view of the organization of cooperative language processors.

To illustrate how a sentence might be processed by a language comprehension system organized along these lines, consider again Example 13:

13. Peter read the books on the chair . . .

The text representation is a mental model of the discourse that has both referents and relations. It is the updated representation a reader holds of a discourse world.[4]   Thus, for Sentence 13, the representation constructed when the sentence is read will depend on whether the reader decides that Peter is sitting on the chair while reading some books or whether the books that Peter is reading are those on the chair. The updated text representation depends critically on two things: (a) the semantic relations encoded from the sentence and (b) the model established up to that point.

First, assume that the reader has read the text corresponding to the reading that Peter will sit in the chair to read the books. (This is the text shown in the top of Table 10.1.) When the key sentence is encountered, the reader has a model with the following referents: Peter, Peter's teacher, some books, a bed, a lounge chair. There is also a series of relationships that comprise the history of the model (e.g., Peter broke

---

[4] There are many names for such a model. I have called it the "text model" (Perfetti, 1985) and it is similar to Johnson-Laird's (1983) mental model and Van Dijk and Kintsch's (1983) situation model. But it is perhaps less inferential than a fully elaborated mental model.

his leg) that can be ignored for present purposes. In reading the key Sentence 13, elements of the model are immediately activated as words and phrases are encountered: first *Peter*, then *the books*, and then *the chair*. As the text model includes no books on the chair, the critical attachment decision, where to attach *on the chair*, is quickly decided in favor of *read*, which, by the time the decision has to be made, has been encoded as a semantic predicate, that is, *Peter read . . .* (or, *read* [AGENT:PETER . . .]).

The question is whether the parsing decision to attach *on the chair* to *read* is made independently of the text model. The language processor illustrated in Figure 10.3 assumes that this attachment is a matter of indifference to the parser. The parser has formed local attachments (*the + books*), and has opened a verb phrase with *read*, but has no strong guidance for its final attachment of *the books*, that is, whether to close it and attach it directly to the verb phrase or to hold it as an extendable noun phrase (or NOM). The decision, however, is informed very quickly as the discourse model supplies referents for first *the books* and then *the chair*, and as the thematic roles associated with reading are confirmed: [*Peter* [*read* [*the books*] [*on the chair*]]]. This representation is what gets established in the semantic processor, which knows both what the syntactic processor has told it about likely constituent attachments and what the text model has told it about referents and their relations in the model. It also knows about the semantics of *read* (from the lexicon), including the case frames that it requires and allows, that is, its thematic constraints.

The alternative text model, in which there are two sets of books, contains these referents: Peter, Peter's teacher, a bed, a table, a chair, some books on the chair, some books on the table. In this case, when *the books* is encountered, there is momentary uncertainty, because the noun phrase does not pick out a unique referent from the discourse model. But the next few words identify the exact referent: *the books on the chair*. This putatively nonminimal reading is no more difficult to construct than the alternative. The ultimately required attachment is made very quickly because of information provided by both thematic constraints (or case frames) that are part of the representation of verbs and discourse constraints that are provided by the text model. The critical cooperative event is communication between what the parser proposes and what the semantic representation accepts from the discourse model.

There are at least two ways to understand this idea of cooperation between the syntactic and semantic processor. One is to imagine that the semantic processor, through its access to thematic role information, informs the syntactic processor concerning the viability of the candidate structures it is building according to minimal attachment and late closure principles. This is essentially the solution proposed by Frazier (this volume). An alternative is to imagine that some kinds of attachments are not made by the syntactic processor but are delayed pending quickly available information from the text model and the thematic processor. For example, local attachments involving words and their immediately dominating constituent heads are not delayed, but remote attachments involving intermediate constituents are delayed. It is not clear whether these are two different proposals or merely paraphrases of a single claim that certain semantic factors inform parsing decisions that are independently proposed by a syntactic processor.

At a more general level, notice that this language processor relies on the rapid use of information from a text model, which is incrementally built as part of comprehension. There is no required postponement of semantic analysis. On the other hand, building discourse models is mental work that is most efficiently postponed until some of the sentence has been encoded linguistically, that is, until semantic relations have been extracted. Here is where an autonomous syntax is a very handy thing to have. If syntax had to wait for discourse model influences or could somehow be easily influenced by the entire range of potential plausibility factors, comprehension would be very slow and very faulty. An autonomous syntax that ignores much of what is potentially available provides more to comprehension than a syntax that would take help promiscuously from wherever it could. In a language processor with a cooperative autonomous syntax, the syntactic processor works rapidly on its own data structures, that is, constituents, but it does not always make a deep commitment to an attachment. Its cooperativeness derives not from its seeking of help but from its postponing some attachment decisions (or, equivalently perhaps, to reconsider decisions after having made them). This, at least, is one instantiation of the idea of a cooperative autonomous syntax. Parsing carried out in pieces effectively delays just those attachments that are most likely to be informed by semantic influences.

The Pieces Parser

A pieces parser is obligated to make attachment decisions when syntactic and syntactic-lexical features trigger attachment. However, when these triggers are absent, a parsing decision is either postponed or made on some permissibility basis. There are three ways to construe permissibility here: (a) first available; (b) random; (c) multiple. In each case, the decision must be checked by semantic factors, and the initial parse therefore can be thought of either as truly delayed or as proposed very tentatively and marked as retrievable, which is rather much the same thing. These interpretations of what a less determined parser might do are merely the logical choices available to parsers. More challenging is to explain what controls the attachment decisions, or at least the decision about whether to make an attachment or to delay it.

Identifying the principles that control attachment decisions is obviously a difficult business. At this point, a well-developed theory of attachment controls based on parsing in pieces does not exist, nor can I even offer an atheoretical list of triggering devices. Instead, I suggest only the kinds of control principles that might lead to further development and illustrate how some of the examples cited earlier might be handled by them.

The main control principles are that the parser must build local constituents immediately and that, in the absence of a trigger, it can postpone remote attachments. Local constituents comprise syntactically categorized words or morphemes (terminal nodes) plus their immediately dominating constituent heads. Thus, *the books* immediately becomes a noun phrase, and *on the chair* immediately becomes a prepositional phrase. However, the remote attachment decision of whether to attach these two phrases as part of an intermediate (remote) expanded noun phrase has no trigger and is postponed. Meanwhile, top-down parsing is also proceeding automatically. Frames with high-level nodes such as S, NP, and VP (or their equivalents in an X-bar type projection theory) are always produced and are available for attachments from lower constituents.

A processing constraint is served by these assumptions, namely that the parser is sensitive to processing limitations. It must make local decisions quickly so as to avoid dealing later with unanalyzed word strings. It is helped in this task both by rapidly triggered local attachments and by automatic (resource-free) top-down frames. But, within the limits of processing and memory resources, it postpones intermediate attachment decisions, which turn out to be just the decisions that are likely to be informed by semantic analyses. An interesting effect of suggesting such control principles is that triggers open constituents, but, in effect, do not close them. Thus, the principle of late closure would be a consequence of parser with these proposed control principles.

One possible objection to this conjecture is that it appears to run up against the immediacy assumption, that is, the assumption that the information associated with each word is fully extracted during a single fixation (Just & Carpenter, 1980). On the other hand, there must be some limits to how fully information gets encoded during the reading of a single word, and the movement of the eye from a fixation cannot be postponed indefinitely. Indeed, Rayner and Pollatsek (1987) observed that there are very clear spillover effects, in which eye fixations immediately following some text feature show the effects of that text feature. Moreover, recent evidence of Frazier and Rayner (1987) shows that syntactic category decisions are delayed when a word is categorically ambiguous within its local context, for example, *warehouse fires*, where fires can be either a noun or a verb. Finally, I emphasize that the parser in fact does a lot of immediate processing. Every word is attached to something immediately, that is, a local constituent. It just isn't attached to everything immediately.

As to what counts as a trigger, closed class words (articles, prepositions, conjunctions, clausal adverbs) and bound morphemes associated with syntactic categories are reasonable candidates for the present. Such forms are bound to nondominating constituent nodes, in effect requiring (triggering) the opening of a dominating phrasal node. The idea, of course, is to develop such a proposal in a principled way, and it remains to be seen whether this can be done. The attractiveness of principles such as minimal attachment and late closure, and other purely structural principles, is their generalized scope. They are free of particular syntactic categories and even of particular levels of constituent analysis and hence are both powerful and elegant. The control principles of the pieces parser, by contrast, are of unproven generality and appear rather ungainly. But they can at least be tested on some of the cases that have provided the data previously considered.

For a concrete case, consider again *Peter reading the books on the chair* (Example 13). Suppose that there is a relatively impoverished discourse model as this sentence is encountered, as it might be in an experiment on isolated reading time. The pieces parser does the following:

1. *Peter*:   held as NOM (name, actually)
2. *read*:   NP1 closed, VP opened
3. *the*:   NP2 / NOM opened
4. *books*:   attached to *the*; NP2 remains open
5. *on*:   PP opened, PP unattached
6. *the*:   NP3 / NOM opened; attach to PP
7. *chair*:   attached to *the*; NP3 remains open
8. . (end signal): close NP3; attach PP to VP or to NP and close

The important step in this list of parsing operations is what happens at step 4. *Books* is immediately attached to the NP opened by *the*, because local attachments are obligatory. A DET is a trigger to open a NOM (or an NP or some minimal projection of N, as Frazier [this volume] suggests.) However, the NP is not closed by *books* but rather remains open until there is information about where to close it. If a discourse model has referential information concerning *chair*, this might be sufficient to cause closure at step 7. But in the isolated sentence, there is no help from a discourse model and the sentence ends abruptly with things up in the air. The parser must now assemble the pieces it has constructed. It automatically closes the current phrase and then has a choice about what to do with the two unattached pieces, the PP opened at step 5 and the NP, opened at step 3. Of course, there's really only one decision, attach PP to VP or to NP, and the NP closes automatically in either case. The parser, I suggest, simply satisfies some comprehension criterion established by the reader. In the case of an isolated sentence, this is likely to be a shallow semantics criterion.

Given a parser that does not uniformly have to make strong commitments on structural grounds, it is free to accept choices made available by sentence semantics as well as by the text model. These semantic influences include thematic frames associated with the verb and the referential semantics controlled in part by the discourse. Many parsing proposals (e.g., Ford, Bresnan, & Kaplan, 1982) and some experiments suggest a prominent role for the verb, although there is disagreement about whether the verb plays a guidance role (Tanenhaus & Carlson,

1989) or a checking role (Frazier, 1987; Mitchell, 1987). In the thematic frame selection process proposed by Rayner et al. (1983), thematic roles associated with the verb are quickly accessed to check against the constituents proposed by the constituent parser. Their proposal is the one that is adopted here.

With the pieces parser, the role of the verb would be decisive when pieces are unattached, but its role would be primarily to check structures when the parser is forced to make attachments by the local attachment triggers. Consider *Peter threw the books on the chair*, with *threw* instead of *read*. The parsing steps are as in the *read* example; in particular, *books* is attached to *the*, and the NP is not closed with *on*; however, the occurrence of *chair* at the end of the sentence now makes more available the VP attachment, and that one is more likely to be taken. This is because lexical information for *chair* includes satisfaction of the goal role that is suggested by *throw*.

What about garden-path phenomena in this model? Certain garden-path phenomena continue to be predicted because the parser will commit itself to local attachments. Thus, the reduced relative will continue to produce garden-path effects.

11. The editor played the tape agreed the story was a big one.

In Example (11), from Ferreira and Clifton (1986), the key parsing decision occurs at *played*. The pieces parser makes a NP for *the editor* and opens a VP for *played* because of the trigger provided by [verb + *ed*]. The alternative of building a reduced relative clause is never considered because there is nothing to trigger it.

Alternatively, one can capture this garden-path effect, as Frazier (1978, 1987) proposed, with a principle that avoids creating attachments, that is, minimal attachment. In the case of the reduced relative represented by Example 11, minimal attachment prohibits the construction of an embedded NP (or a second projection of N) at the very first phrase, *the editor*. This constraint, at the beginning of the sentence, seems very powerful: Avoid intermediate nonterminal nodes at the beginning of S construction; thus S $\rightarrow$ NP $\rightarrow$ NP $\rightarrow$ *the editor* is never considered and S $\rightarrow$ NP $\rightarrow$ *the editor* is the only structure built.

One curious consequence of the generality of the minimal attachment principle is that it treats this very powerful constraint against the creation of embedded nonterminal nodes at the beginning of a sentence exactly the same as the constraint against attaching a post-nominal PP to the NP rather than to the higher VP. We have already seen how weak this latter constraint is in the various experiments discussed in preceding sections. On the present account, the attachment prohibitions are just not the same in the two cases. More generally, the present account implies that minimal attachment prohibitions are simply derivative consequences of a set of parsing principles that are actually based not on attachments but on local constituent building, as suggested by the pieces parser.

This latter possibility is consistent with the fact that the reduced relatives and the more benign post-nominal PPs tend to differ in the presence of local syntactic triggers. In the reduced relatives, there tends to be a strong syntactic trigger. As observed for Example 11, *played* opens a VP that continues to get constituents for several words. There is no such syntactic trigger for the post-nominal prepositional phrases of the type discussed so far. Or, more carefully, for the post-nominal PPs, the triggers serve to initiate phrases (PPs) that survive intact no matter where else they are attached eventually.

There is, moreover, an influence of the semantic processor in the more dramatic garden-path cases. In the reduced relative (11), the semantic processor attaches *editor* to *played* – as semantic objects, for example, *played* (**AGENT:EDITOR**) – well before the syntax is played out. The plausibility of the semantic reading adds problems even on the second pass reading of the reduced relative because it is now available as a competitor to the reading that's required. This combination of influences is what makes the garden-path effect of these reduced relatives so dramatic.

Here we come to an interesting prediction. The parser commits itself in the case of reduced relatives but not in the case of prepositional phrases. This means that semantic and contextual effects will be rather readily obtained in prepositional phrase attachment but not in reduced relative attachment. Ferreira and Clifton (1986) found that sentences such as 21 showed garden-path effects even when context favored the reduced relative reading. I believe that their result will be replicated under even the most compelling contexts favoring the reduced relative reading. This would contrast, of course, with the demonstrations concerning prepositional phrases.

As I have tried to suggest, the variable results obtained with PPs, specifically the apparent preference for VP attachment in some cases but not others, are consistent with the assumptions of the pieces parser, and more generally, the proposed organization of the language processor. Verb frames will play a role, as both Speer et al. (1986) and Taraban and McClelland (1988) have shown; discourse effects will be observed, as the Britt experiment suggests; and principles from outside the syntactic processor will be able to exert themselves, as the spatial relations experiments suggest. The model suggested here to account for these observations clearly shares important basic assumptions with that of Frazier (this volume). It also shares some assumptions with the proposal of Crain and Steedman (1985), who reported experimental results similar to some of those discussed here, and who emphasized the early availability of referential information to the parsing process.

Recently, Altmann and Steedman (1988) have refined the Crain and Steedman (1985) proposal in several ways, including both a general architecture that allows semantic influences and a refined concept of referential assistance for parsing. Referential assistance comes from Altmann and Steedman's principle of referential support, which favors a noun phrase analysis that is supported by discourse referents over any analysis not so supported. The pieces parser essentially uses this principle. However, both the Crain and Steedman (1985) proposal, which holds to an autonomous syntax for descriptive but not representational purposes, and the Altmann and Steedman (1988) proposal appear to predict that all garden-pathing can be eliminated by semantics. The current proposal instead assumes a functional autonomous syntax in which the data structures and the procedural vocabulary are essentially specialized for constituent analysis. It further assumes that there are structural principles to guide the procedures of this processor, as Frazier has argued, thus predicting irreversible garden-path effects in some situations.

Finally, the data of the newspaper headline studies can be reconsidered briefly in light of the proposed model. The impoverished syntax of newspaper headlines creates difficulties for a parser, which may respond by delaying decisions about the syntactic categories of words and their attachments. Parsing occurs in a more piecemeal way than for ordinary sentences, but the normal parsing process cannot be suppressed. The parser makes attachments in the manner for which it is specialized, attachments triggered by local syntactic features, but it also presents the semantic processor with pieces that are unattached. Our original conclusion (Perfetti, Beverly et al., 1987) was that problem-solving procedures could not guide the parser, a conclusion that is correct as far as it goes. The rest of the story, consistent with the proposed organization of the cooperative language processors, is that when the syntactic processor cannot quickly provide a single, fully attached structure, then procedures that rely heavily on semantics and pragmatics have a large influence on how to assemble the pieces. Of course, the idea that final decisions are influenced by semantic factors is a conclusion to which everyone agrees regardless of the details of the syntactic processes. If nature abhors a vacuum, comprehension abhors that vacuum left by an indecisive parser. It must go about filling it quickly in whatever way it can. On this account, syntax remains autonomous but it gives up just a bit of its authority.

SUMMARY

The importance of syntax for comprehension has been correctly reasserted by recent research. The power of an autonomous syntax is a significant factor in considering how a language processor is organized. On the other hand, some studies suggest the existence of both indeterminacy and early semantic influences in comprehension. It remains possible that these effects occur after an earlier syntactic analysis that is difficult to detect with reading time measures. However, if results continue to support the plausibility of early semantic influences and indecisiveness, then some revision of the language processor along the lines suggested may be in order. The model proposed puts greater emphasis on the role of a semantically rich discourse model during the comprehension of sentences while retaining an autonomous syntax. This influence is indirect, not on the syntactic processor, but on the immediate semantic representation that is the interface between syntax and the reader's text model. The parser is autonomous but less thorough than in most proposals in that its first pass creates mainly local constituents within a higher syntactic frame. Semantic influences are early when the parser produces unattached pieces, a condition that obtains whenever attachment triggers are absent. Such a model might be developed to handle a variety of phenomena, including both garden-pathing for some structures and the overriding of garden-pathing in other structures.

ACKNOWLEDGMENTS

This chapter was prepared while the author was a fellow at the Netherlands Institute for Advanced Studies, Wassenaar. Parts of the research described in the chapter were supported by the Learning Research and Development Center, University of Pittsburgh, and the U.S. Office of Educational Research. Some of the syntactic discussions in the chapter benefited from discussion with Lyn Frazier and from her presentation to the conference.

REFERENCES

Altmann, G., & Steedman, M. (1988). Interaction with context during human sentence processing. *Cognition, 30*, 191 - 238.

Baker, C. L. (1978). *Introduction to generative-transformational syntax.* Englewood Cliffs, NJ: Prentice-Hall.

Bever, T. G. (1970). The cognitive basis for linguistic structures. In J. R. Hayes (Ed.), *Cognition and the development of language* (pp. 279 - 362). New York: Wiley.

Britt, A. (1987). *Parsing in context.* Unpublished master's thesis, University of Pittsburgh.

Crain, S., & Steedman, M. (1985). On not being led up the garden path: The use of context by the psychological syntax processor. In D. R. Dowty, L. Karttunen, & A. M. Zwicky (Eds.), *Natural language parsing: Psychological, computational, and theoretical perspectives* (pp. 320 - 358). Cambridge: Cambridge University Press.

Ferreira, F., & Clifton, C., Jr. (1986). The independence of syntactic processing. *Journal of Memory and Language, 25*, 348 - 368.

Fodor, J. A. (1983). *Modularity of mind.* Cambridge, MA: MIT Press.

Fodor, J. A., & Pylyshyn, Z. W. (1988). Connectionism and cognitive architecture: A critical analysis. *Cognition, 28*, 3 - 71.

Ford, M., Bresnan, J., & Kaplan, R. M. (1982). A competence-based theory of syntactic closure. In J. Bresnan (Ed.), *The mental representation of grammatical relations* (pp. 727 - 796). Cambridge, MA: MIT Press.

Forster, K. I. (1979). Levels of processing and the structure of the language processor. In W. E. Cooper & E. C. T. Walker (Eds.), *Sentence processing: Psycholinguistic studies presented to Merrill Garrett* (pp. 27 - 85). Hillsdale, NJ: Lawrence Erlbaum Associates.

Frazier, L. (1979). *On comprehending sentences: Syntactic parsing strategies.* Bloomington: Indiana University Linguistics Club.

Frazier, L. (1987). Sentence processing: A tutorial review. In M. Coltheart (Ed.), *Attention and performance XII: The psychology of reading* (pp. 559 - 586). Hillsdale, NJ: Lawrence Erlbaum Associates.

Frazier, L., & Rayner, K. (1982). Making and correcting errors during sentence comprehension: Eye movements in the analysis of structurally ambiguous sentences. *Cognitive Psychology, 14*, 178 - 210.

Frazier, L., & Rayner, K. (1987). Resolution of syntactic category ambiguities: Eye movements in parsing lexically ambiguous sentences. *Journal of Memory and Language, 26*, 505 - 526.

Herskovits, A. (1985). Semantics and pragmatics of locative expressions. *Cognitive Science, 9*, 341 - 378.

Johnson-Laird, P. N. (1983). *Mental models.* Cambridge, MA: Harvard University Press.

Just, M. A., & Carpenter, P. A. (1980). A theory of reading: From eye fixations to comprehension. *Psychological Review, 87*, 329 - 354.

Kurtzman, H. (1985). *Studies in syntactic ambiguity resolution.* Unpublished doctoral dissertation, Massachusetts Institute of Technology, Cambridge.

Mitchell, D. C. (1987). Lexical guidance in human parsing: Locus and processing characteristics. In M. Coltheart (Ed.), *Attention and performance XII: The psychology of reading* (pp. 601 - 618). Hillsdale, NJ: Lawrence Erlbaum Associates.

Perfetti, C. A. (1985). *Reading ability.* New York: Oxford University Press.

Perfetti, C. A. (1989). There are generalized abilities and one of them is reading. In L. Resnick (Ed.), *Knowing, learning, and instruction: Essays in honor of Robert Glaser* (pp. 307 - 334). Hillsdale, NJ: Lawrence Erlbaum Associates.

Perfetti, C. A., Adams, B., Weitz, J., & Bell, L. (1987). *Syntax and semantics in space.* Paper presented at the annual meeting of the Psychonomic Society, Seattle.

Perfetti, C. A., Beverly, S., Bell, L., Rodgers, K., & Faux, R. (1987). Comprehending newspaper headlines. *Journal of Memory and Language, 26*, 692 - 713.

Pinker, S., & Prince, A. (1988). On language and connectionism: Analysis of a parallel distributed processing model of language acquisition. *Cognition, 28*, 73 - 193.

Rayner, K., Carlson. M., & Frazier, L. (1983). The interaction of syntax and semantics during sentence processing: Eye movements in the analysis of semantically biased sentences. *Journal of Verbal Learning and Verbal Behavior, 22*, 358 - 374.

Rayner, K., & Pollatsek, A. (1987). Eye movements in reading: A tutorial review. In M. Coltheart (Ed.), *Attention and performance XII: The psychology of reading* (pp. 327 - 362). Hillsdale, NJ: Lawrence Erlbaum Associates.

Smith, C. (1988) *Structural and other factors in parsing.* Unpublished manuscript, University of Texas.

Speer, S., Foss, D., & Smith, C. (1986). *Syntactic and thematic contributions to sentence complexity.* Paper presented at the annual meeting of the Psychonomic Society, New Orleans.

Tanenhaus, M. K., & Carlson, G. N. (1989). Lexical structure and language comprehension. In W. Marslen-Wilson (Ed.), *Lexical representation and process* (pp. 529 - 561). Cambridge, MA: MIT Press.

Taraban, R., & McClelland, J. L. (1988). Constituent attachment and thematic role assignment in sentence processing: Influences of content-based expectations. *Journal of Memory and Language, 27,* 597 - 632.

Van Dijk, T. A., & Kintsch, W. (1983). *Strategies of discourse comprehension.* New York: Academic Press.

11 PARSING AND COMPREHENSION: A MULTIPLE-CONSTRAINT VIEW

Roman Taraban and James L. McClelland

Carnegie-Mellon University

INTRODUCTION

A theory of parsing must explain how sentences are processed. Specifically, it must explain how a serially presented surface string is analyzed into its underlying representation. Two central components of the underlying representation include (a) a specification of how any particular constituent is configured with other constituents, which we refer to as syntactic attachment; and (b) an assignment of semantic roles to constituents, which we refer to as thematic role assignment. This representation for a sentence generally specifies what goes with what in a sentence, as well as the semantic relations holding between one constituent and another. Constructing this representation under the limits imposed by the serial order of a sentence string constitutes a large part of what is required to read and understand a sentence.

Consider the two parse trees shown in Figure 11.1. These trees consist of the same constituents, but they differ in how the constituents attach into the tree. In the first case, *clearly* attaches to the sentence node (S), and in the second case it attaches to the verb phrase node (VP). Does this have any consequences? Certainly. The point of syntactic attachment constrains the possible thematic roles that a constituent can fill. In the example, when *clearly* is attached to S, it fills the role of a parenthetical comment of the speaker; when it is attached to VP, it modifies the verb, specifying the manner in which the writing was done (Jackendoff, 1972). Of course, constraints in the other direction may also hold. That is, the thematic role that a constituent is to fill will determine the place where it attaches onto a parse tree. Thus, if one wanted to attach a parenthetical comment into a parse tree, it would get attached to S to provide sentential context rather than to VP to specify something about the verb; if one wanted to specify something about the action expressed by the verb, like the manner in which an action was performed or the instrument that was used, then the constituent would get attached to the VP node.

A

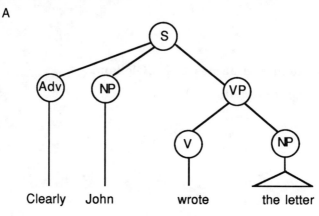

B

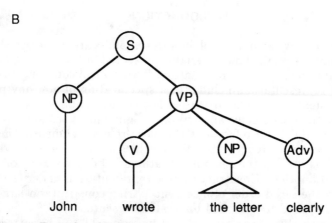

FIGURE 11.1. Examples of parse trees.

This simple example exemplifies the major theoretical concern to be tackled in this chapter, which can be summarized thus: In reading, can factors associated with thematic roles – specifically, semantic factors – constrain the initial syntactic attachment of a constituent? The reason this question is particularly important is because the initial constraints in sentence processing have often been viewed as originating in the syntax. In this chapter we question this view. We do not intend to deny the possibility that syntactic considerations may play some role. Rather, we seek evidence for the influence of semantic factors in the context of a model in which syntactic and semantic factors jointly influence the course of constructing the initial representation of a sentence.

TWO VIEWS OF PARSING

The relationship between syntax and semantics cannot be dealt with independently of a consideration of the cognitive architecture in which these potential sources of influence have their effect, that is, without a consideration of parsing models. This is because the architecture places limits on the directionality of influence within a model. For example, given the configuration shown in Figure 11.2A, Processor B could never directly influence Processor A; Processor B could only use whatever output Processor A decided to send it. If Processor B could generate a feedback signal, as shown in Figure 11.2B, then it could affect Processor A, but only after Processor A had produced some initial output and Processor B had evaluated it. Therefore, whatever contribution factors associated with Processor B might make to processing, this influence will always be with respect to the output of Processor A.

The Standard View: "Syntax Proposes and Semantics Disposes"

If we label Processor A as the *syntactic* processor and Processor B as the *semantic* processor, then Figure 11.2A and 2B schemata can be used to describe the general constraints on information flow in one class of parsers, which we will refer to as syntax-first parsers. Processor A does syntactic attachment; Processor B instantiates and evaluates the thematic roles of the attached constituents. In parsers of this class, semantic processes can filter syntactic output but cannot influence initial syntactic processing (Bresnan & Kaplan, 1982; Ford, Bresnan & Kaplan, 1982; Forster, 1979; Kaplan & Bresnan, 1982; Rayner, Carlson, & Frazier, 1983; Winograd, 1971; Woods, 1972).

The operation of the syntactic processor in syntax-first models is subject to two types of guidance, which are, by definition, in the syntax. These two types of guidance allow us to identify roughly two subclasses of syntax-first parsers.

1. *Principled.* On the one hand, the parser could be guided by general syntactic principles, that is, by a set of rules that specify the attachment of a constituent based strictly on the grammatical category of words and phrases (e.g., N V Adv NP PP VP S') and the partial configuration of the parse tree when the principle is applied. Examples of these sorts of principles are Right Association (Kimball, 1973) and the Canonical Sentoid Strategy (Fodor, Bever, & Garrett, 1974). Frazier and colleagues (Frazier, 1978; Frazier, 1987; Frazier & Fodor, 1978; Frazier & Rayner, 1982; Rayner et al., 1983) have proposed various versions of syntax-first models that are

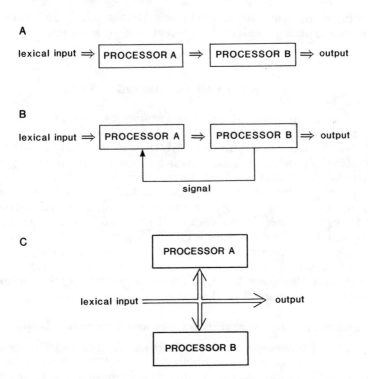

FIGURE 11.2. Syntax-first schemata (A and B) and multiple-constraint schema (C).

especially important exemplars of this subclass as the models configure phrases into a parse tree largely through guidance from principles
(e.g., Minimal Attachment and Late Closure). These principles are
presumably so powerful that the syntactic processor in these models
initially computes just a single structurally preferred analysis of a
sentence consisting of phrasal configurations specified by these general principles.

2. *Lexical.* Another subclass of syntax-first models consists of models
that use lexically specified arguments and complements associated
with heads of phrases (Bresnan & Kaplan, 1982; Chomsky, 1981;
Ford et al., 1982; Kaplan & Bresnan, 1982; Mitchell & Holmes, 1985)
– referred to here simply as subcategorization frames – in addition to
syntactic principles. Ford et al. (1982), for example, use information
about the preferred grammatical functions associated with verbs in
order to make initial decisions about syntactic attachment. These
subcategorization frames are stored in the lexicon and are activated
when the verb is initially encoded. The syntactic processor in a sense
looks at the verb and asks, What do I expect from this word syntactically? If the preferences that these frames represent are strong, they

influence initial syntactic analysis; if there are no strong lexically based preferences, default syntactic preferences direct parsing.

The Alternative View: Multiple Constraint Satisfaction

An alternative class of models consists of those in which construction of syntactic and conceptual representations occurs in parallel, with syntax and semantics exerting mutual influence on each other. For purposes of discussion, we need only extend the syntax-first schemata as shown in Figure 11.2c to illustrate that in this class of models syntactic principles, lexically encoded information about arguments and complements of heads of phrases – that is, subcategorization frames – and conceptual knowledge can influence parsing from start to finish. Models in this class include interactive models of the type proposed by Just & Carpenter (1980), MacWhinney (1986), Marslen-Wilson and Tyler (1980), McClelland (1987), St. John & McClelland (in press), Thibadeau, Just, and Carpenter (1982), and Tyler and Marslen-Wilson (1977). In these models, it is generally assumed that graded activation and competition allow information from multiple syntactic and semantic sources to work together or to compete with each other, with the interpretation that is most consistent with the information and most internally consistent winning out over other alternatives. Syntactic processes could dominate in some cases, but semantic information could dominate in other cases, depending on the relative strength of each source.

How is Comprehension Related to Parsing?

According to syntax-first models, syntactic attachment is initially done without considering semantic information. Of course, it is true that the syntactic relevance of semantic information has been noted in lexically based models and that these models incorporate into the syntax features like animacy and a few other selectional features. Detailed consideration of roles and their plausible fillers is, however, against the spirit of syntax-first proposals. Thus, we would not include within this class those models in which the actual semantic characteristics of a phrase or the thematic roles it might fill with respect to other constituents could influence the initial decisions made by the syntactic processor.

Multiple-constraint models include syntactic constraints on initial processing. A major difference is that they also include semantic constraints. The syntactic attachment of a constituent that is being read and the role that is assigned to this constituent are immediately subject to what that constituent and other constituents in the context are all about. For example, in the sentence fragment *Joe stirred the coffee with a . . .*, there is probably an expectation for an instrument that is like a spoon; if the fragment were *Joe stirred the paint with a . . .*, the expectation would probably still be for an instrument, but one that was somewhat different from a spoon. And if the fragment were *Joe chose the paint with a . . .*, the expectation for the prepositional phrase would presumably be altogether different. Thus, according to this view, comprehension and parsing cannot be separated.

THE RIGORS OF READING

The analysis of a sentence in a left-to-right serial fashion is typical of reading. Time and time again, the reader faces uncertainties about attachment and assignment because information is not yet available to force one or another decision. For instance, upon reaching *clearly* in *John clearly wrote the letter*, *clearly* could be interpreted in accord with either Figure 11.1a or 11.1b. The ambiguity could be lessened by content preceding the constituent – for example, *As the handwriting expert himself has testified, John clearly wrote the letter* – or it could be resolved by content following the ambiguity – *John clearly wrote the letter and received an A for style*. In some cases, the ambiguity encountered and manner of initial resolution lead to disastrous consequences, as in the well-known garden path sentence *The horse raced past the barn fell*. Here, the late occurring final verb is a cue that *The horse* fills the thematic role of patient rather than agent, and that *raced* is not the main verb but rather a participial form, which requires major revisions that some people are unable to grasp even after considerable thought (Warner & Glass, 1987).

Processing Expectations

What does a reader do under these conditions of uncertainty? On the one hand, it appears that readers are sensitive to the alternative constructions possible when faced with ambiguities, as discussed in the research on verb-complexity (Fodor, Garrett, & Bever, 1968; Holmes & Forster, 1972; Shapiro, Zurif, & Grimshaw, 1987). Further, readers appear biased in the initial syntactic attachment of constituents, as discussed in part in the research on verb preferences (Clifton, Frazier, & Connine, 1984; Connine, Ferreira, Jones, Clifton, & Frazier, 1984; Holmes, 1984, 1987; Mitchell & Holmes, 1985). It was our view that readers were sensitive to what a sentence was about, and the content of a sentence suggested itself as a potential source of processing preferences. It was our goal to show that the ongoing process of constituent attachment and role assignment was influenced by prior content. This content set up *expectations* for further processing and provided an important source of guidance.

Our studies centered on a particular syntactic ambiguity that has been the focus of previous studies that purported to find evidence for a syntax-first model and, in particular, for the view that initial parsing decisions are guided by general syntactic principles. Our intuitions, however, suggested to us that, in this particular construction, syntactic preferences were in fact relatively weak and that attachment and role assignment seemed more susceptible to semantic guidance based on the specific content of the sentence. We chose to study this construction as

A

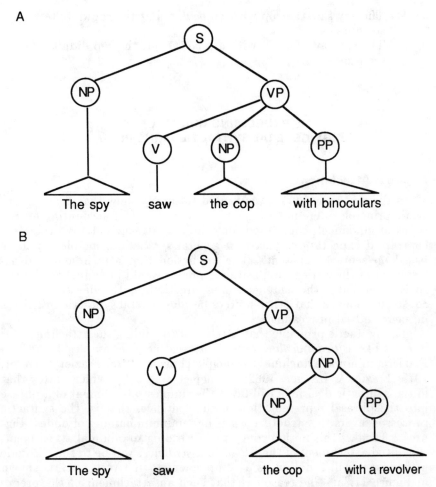

FIGURE 11.3. Examples of parse trees. A. Minimally attached prepositional phrase. B. Nonminimally attached prepositional phrase.

a test case, not because we felt that syntactic influences on processing are necessarily weak in general, but because we felt that content-based influences on initial processing would be most easily observed in the absence of strong syntactic bias.

The ambiguity in question is the ambiguity in the attachment of prepositional phrases in sentences like (1) and (2). The target constituent in both cases is the prepositional phrase (PP) that follows the object noun phrase (Object NP) in the first clause. This PP could attach either to the VP node or to the Object-NP node, as shown in Figure 11.3. As shown in Examples 1 and 2, the target phrase is followed by a conjunction signaling the beginning of a new clause.

1. The spy saw the cop with *binoculars* but the cop didn't see him.
2. The spy saw the cop with a *revolver* but the cop didn't see him.

IS PROCESSING GUIDED ONLY BY GENERAL SYNTACTIC PRINCIPLES?

Minimal Attachment

In the first experiment, we wanted to simply show that general syntactic principles were not adequate by themselves for accounting for the types of guidance people used for syntactic attachment. We therefore contrasted expectations based on general syntactic principles to those based on sentence content. The prediction that attachment and assignment of the critical prepositional phrase would be influenced by the specific content in the sentence comes directly from the view in multiple-constraint models that other sources besides general syntactic principles influence initial processing.

The syntactic principle that is relevant to guiding the attachment for phrases like *with binoculars* or *with a revolver* in Examples 1 and 2 is Frazier's minimal attachment principle (Frazier, 1978; Frazier & Fodor, 1978; Frazier & Rayner, 1982; Rayner et al., 1983), which states that initial syntactic decisions will favor the simplest attachment of a phrase into the phrasal representation of the sentence; that is, the syntactic processor favors the structure with the minimum number of nodes. Figure 11.3 makes this notion concrete. According to minimal attachment, the initial attachment of the PP *in both sentences* will be to the VP node – that is, it will function as a complement to the verb *saw*, as shown in Figure 11.3a. The reason is that such an attachment of the prepositional phrase does not, on Frazier's account, require the construction of new nodes in the syntactic tree that represents the structure of the sentence. Attachment as a constituent of a complex noun phrase – as in *the cop with a revolver* – on the other hand, does, according to Frazier, require the construction of a new node – the one that represents the complex noun phrase as a whole, under which the simple noun phrase *the cop* and the prepositional phrase are both attached, as shown in Figure 11.3b. If minimal attachment makes an implausible decision, as *with a revolver* attached to VP would be, a thematic processor can veto this decision, based on its access to likely thematic arguments of verbs and world knowledge, and could require syntactic reanalysis. This reasoning fits a syntax-first model of the Figure 11.2b type.

Experiment 1

Although results in Rayner et al. (1983) for sentences like 1 and 2 fit the predictions of minimal attachment and supported a syntax-first model, it seemed intuitively possible, and consistent with reasoning according to a multiple-constraint model, that the specific content preceding the prepositional phrase in their stimuli predisposed so-called minimal attachment. We therefore used the original pairs of matched sentences from Rayner et al. and constructed an additional set of sentence pairs for which we felt the content preceding the prepositional phrase predisposed subjects towards non-minimal attachment, as illustrated in Examples 3 and 4.[1]

3. The couple admired the house with a *friend* but knew that it was overpriced.
4. The couple admired the house with a *garden* but knew that it was overpriced.

In order to quantify subjects' expectations for either minimal or nonminimal attachment, we submitted the Rayner et al. stimuli and the Taraban and McClelland stimuli to two tests of 'expectedness.' One was a cloze task in which subjects completed sentence *frames* (that part of the test sentence up to the noun in the prepositional phrase) with the first completion that came to mind; the other test was a rating task in which subjects previewed *frames* and rated prepositional phrase completions using a scale worded in terms of 'expectations' (these completions were used in a reading task with another group of subjects). The results from both of these tests of the stimuli clearly showed that subjects' expectations for Rayner et al. frames were for minimal attachment of the prepositional phrases, whereas expectations for the Taraban and McClelland frames were for nonminimal attachment of the prepositional phrases.

We then collected word-by-word reading times for the sentences, using a self-paced task in which subjects answered a comprehension question after each sentence that they read. Our main goal was to determine the amount of guidance provided by the minimal attachment principle and the amount contributed by the specific content of the sentence, which, as noted, are two distinct sources of influence. The results for the Rayner et al. stimuli are shown in Figure 11.4a, indicating that minimally attached phrases had a significant total reading time advantage of 94 ms compared to matched nonminimally attached phrases, computed over the noun-filler and the three words that followed (e.g., *binoculars but the cop* vs. *revolver but the cop*). This replicated the major finding in the Rayner et al. study. The results for the Taraban and McClelland stimuli produced just the opposite effect on reading times,

---

[1] The complete set of stimuli for this experiment and for the next experiment, as well as a full description of the procedure and the statistical results, are provided in Taraban and McClelland (1988).

with nonminimally attached phrases showing a total significant reading time advantage of 69 ms when compared to matched minimally attached phrases, as shown in Figure 11.4b.

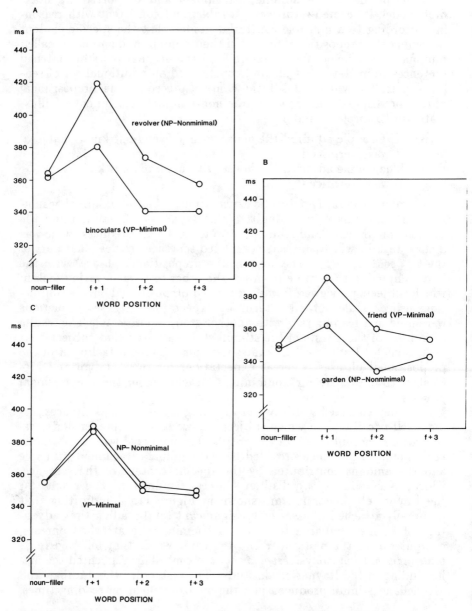

FIGURE 11.4. Experiment 1: Reading times (ms) for the noun-filler and the three words that followed for Rayner et al. stimuli (e.g., *binoculars but the cop*) (Panel A); for Taraban and McClelland stimuli (Panel B); and for minimally-attached versus nonminimally-attached stimuli (Panel C).

Content, Not General Syntactic Principles, Makes the Difference

The expectation ratings and cloze task showed that one set of sentence frames set subject's expectations to favor VP attachment of the prepositional phrase, whereas another set of sentence frames set expectations to favor Object-NP attachment. The reading times showed that these expectations were not epiphenomenal with respect to reading; rather, they produced significant differences in reading time. When attachment expectations fit the attachment required by the content of the sentence, reading times were faster compared to cases in which expectations did not fit. To determine whether there was any evidence that minimal attachment played any role in performance with these stimuli, we simply combined the results from both sentence sets and looked at the overall advantage of minimally versus nonminimally attached sentences. As shown in Figure 11.4c, the principle itself made little difference in reading times, producing an insignificant total difference of 12 ms over the four critical word positions.

Although these results do not strictly rule out the minimal attachment principle as one source of guidance, they reflect the influence of other sources besides general syntactic principles on the attachment that a subject initially expects. Specifically, subjects are influenced to expect a particular attachment for a constituent based on the specific content that precedes that constituent in the string. Thus, an important factor in the on-line processing of sentences is the degree to which the ultimate attachment of constituents in the sentence actually matches the subject's expectations for these constituents. When these expectations are violated, subjects experience difficulty relative to cases in which expectations are fulfilled. It should be noted that the particular interaction between expectations, attachment, and reading difficulty that we have reported here cannot be accounted for by *any* general syntactic principle of which we are aware – that is, by any principle that does not consider the content of the sentence – as the expectation effects occurred in sentences that differed in the content, and not the syntactic constituents, of the sentence frames. Minimal attachment may have played a small role below the level of detection possible in our design. For the remaining studies, though, we continued to focus on the role of content.

THE SEPARATE CONTRIBUTION OF THREE TYPES
OF CONTENT-BASED EXPECTATIONS

The violation of content-based expectations appears to cause processing difficulty, as we found in Experiment 1. In that experiment, we tried to quantify expectations for syntactic attachment, in accord with the specific type of prediction that minimal attachment makes. But several aspects of subject's expectations may have been violated in that experiment, because presumed violations of attachment expectations covaried with possible violations of thematic role expectations for the prepositional phrase and also with possible expectations for the noun-filler for the prepositional phrase. For example, the critical phrases in Examples 1 and 2 require different attachments, but they also receive different thematic roles (instrument of seeing in 1 and possession of the cop in 2), and these are instantiated with different noun-fillers (binoculars vs. revolver). Perhaps it was the violation of the expected thematic role of the prepositional phrase that determined processing difficulty, rather than the violation of the expected attachment per se. Or perhaps it was neither the violation of the expected attachment of the prepositional phrase nor of the expected thematic role of the prepositional phrase that produced the effects but simply a violation of a subject's expectations for a particular noun-filler. Subjects may have had a select pool of candidates, or perhaps a single candidate, in mind for the noun-filler, given the prior content of the sentence. For a verb phrase attachment, for example, and a particular role, like instrument, there are clearly better and worse instances of appropriate instruments in the context of a particular sentence. The data from Experiment 1 do not help to separate out these various sources of influence. In fact, the two conditions for the Rayner et al. and Taraban and McClelland stimuli confound all three sources. It was important to ascertain that we were indeed tapping into factors associated with syntactic attachment and role assignment, and not simply factors associated with particular noun-fillers. If processing was in fact subject to all three influences, we wanted to know their relative effects.

Experiment 2

We needed to consider, then, how to measure the effects of violations of expectations for each of these sources of influence without confounding them with the others. One way was to identify a set of sentence frames such that each one evoked a consistent expectation for an attachment and role for the prepositional phrase. We could then find four different noun-fillers for each frame, creating four different prepositional phrases. These four prepositional phrases associated with the same frame would differ according to the way in which they violated subject's expectations. The following is an example set of four sentences, with the labels used for the experimental conditions shown in parentheses:

5. The janitor cleaned the storage area with the
   a. broom (Fully Consistent)
   b. solvent (Less-Expected Filler)
   c. manager (Less-Expected Role)
   d. odor (Less-Expected Attachment)
   because of many complaints.

Phrases in the first condition are (1) consistent with subject's expectations for the attachment and role of the prepositional phrase, and (2) the particular word used for the noun-filler is actually quite good for that role and attachment. (See Taraban & McClelland, 1988, for a discussion of how thematic roles were identified.) To determine (1) we used a cloze task identical to the one in Experiment 1. The set of frames selected for the experiment showed 90% agreement between the attachment and role associated with completions in the cloze task and the attachment and role required of noun-fillers in the fully consistent condition. To determine (2) a separate group of subjects rated the expectedness of the noun-fillers, as in Experiment 1, and they additionally rated the plausibility of the fillers in the context of the sentence frames.

The sentences in the remaining conditions violated expectations for the filler; filler and role; and filler, role, and attachment, as follows. The second condition used less-expected and less-plausible noun-fillers, according to the results of the rating tasks, but fillers that were consistent with the expected attachment and role for the phrase. The sentences in the remaining conditions included the expectation violations of the previous conditions and added a new one: the thematic role of the prepositional phrases in condition (c) did not fill a role subjects were expecting; the attachment of prepositional phrases in condition (d) was not the attachment subjects were generally expecting, in addition to the roles being unexpected, as in (c). The results from the rating task for the noun-fillers showed a significant difference in expectedness and plausibility between conditions (a) and (b), and no differences between (b) and (c) or between (c) and (d), as was hoped for. As we closely matched the plausibility and expectedness of noun-fillers in conditions (b), (c), and (d), the comparison of conditions (b) and (c) in the reading task was a relatively pure indication of the processing cost of violating role expectations, and the comparison of (c) and (d) was a relatively pure indication of the processing cost of violating attachment expectations, over and above the cost of role expectation violations. A comparison of conditions (a) and (b), on the other hand, which differed in terms of the plausibility and the expectedness of the noun-fillers, indicated the effects of manipulating these factors for the noun-filler itself, while holding everything else constant.

Expectations for Thematic Roles and for Thematic Role Fillers Count for a Lot

The reading data were collected in a manner identical to Experiment 1. An examination of mean reading times by position in Figure 11.5 shows significant effects for two types of expectations. One is an expectation for the noun-filler that instantiates a thematic role. High expectedness and high plausibility for noun-fillers in the fully consistent condition and moderate expectedness and plausibility for noun-fillers in the less-expected filler condition produced a significant difference in reading time of 40 ms, summed over the noun-filler and the three words following it. That is, there was a total advantage of about 40 ms over all four words when noun-fillers were more highly expected and plausible (e.g., *broom because of many*) than when they were not (e.g., *solvent because of many*). This effect was produced in sentences that were consistent both with respect to subject's expectations for attachment of the prepositional phrase and thematic role assignment of the prepositional phrase.

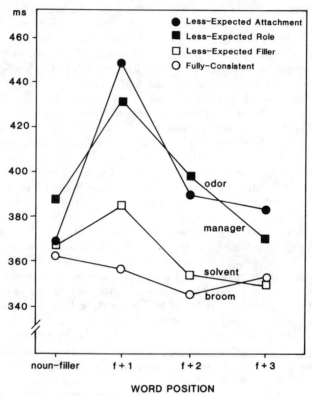

FIGURE 11.5. Experiment 2: Reading times in ms for the noun-filler and for each of the three words that followed (e.g., *broom because of many*).

The second type of expectation that was important was for the thematic role of a phrase. A violation of this expectation produced the most dramatic effect in this study. The less-expected filler condition shows reading times for sentences in which the noun-fillers disambiguated the role of the prepositional phrase in accord with subject's expectations for the thematic role of the phrase, whereas the less-expected role condition shows reading times when the role required by a sentence for the prepositional phrase was inconsistent with expectations. Attachment was held constant for sentence pairs in these conditions, and filler expectedness and plausibility were controlled. Phrases that could be assigned a role in accord with expectations (less-expected filler) produced a highly significant total advantage of about 120 ms over all four words (e.g., *solvent because of many*) compared to those phrases for which the role required by the sentence for the phrase was not in accord with role expectations (less-expected role) (e.g., *manager because of many*). Relative to on-line reading effects in general, this violation of thematic role expectations produced a substantial slowdown in processing.

Quite surprisingly, violations of subject's expectations for the syntactic attachment of prepositional phrases produced little additional processing difficulty over and above that already produced by thematic role violations. The phrases that were neither in accord with attachment expectations nor thematic role expectations (less-expected attachment) showed a nonsignificant total additional disadvantage of about 16 ms over the critical four words (e.g., *odor because of many*) compared to the condition in which attachment was in accord with expectations but the thematic role required by the sentence for the prepositional phrase was not (less-expected role) (e.g., *manager because of many*).

Semantic Violations?

The evidence so far is consistent with the view that the guidance that content provides requires comprehension processes. This is most clearly so for the instantiation of a thematic role filler, which resulted in clear differences in difficulty. Fillers like *broom* or *solvent*, for example, cannot be evaluated for their value as instruments unless one also considers what they are instruments for and who is using them. It seems that comprehension involves just these sorts of intricate webs of weightings between agents, objects, and actions.

A similar case can be made for thematic role violations. The cloze task that we used to examine subject's expectations for thematic roles gave subjects ample time to form a conceptual representation of the frame, and it is presumably on this basis that subjects provided completions in that task. The predictive value of the cloze data is clear in the reading data. This combination of data suggests that the expectations for thematic roles in the on-line reading task, like the expectations for the fillers of those roles, were activated in the course of comprehending the sentence (cf., Schank, 1972, 1975), rather than through processes that did not require comprehension, like the activation of lexical subcategorization frames.

Finally, the time course for all the violations – noun filler, thematic role, and attachment – provides additional support for the view that the effects depend on semantically based expectations that guide the first attempts at integrating the prepositional phrase into a representation for the sentence. Figure 11.5 shows that regardless of the type of violation, a slowdown in processing occurs almost immediately to some aspect of the completion that does not fit. The type of violation determines how much additional processing is required for resolution. With more accurate tracking equipment, we could perhaps find a detectable difference in the point where the various violations are noticed by the subject. But for now, the effects seem to fall primarily on the word immediately following the word that instantiates a filler and disambiguates the attachment and role assignment of the prepositional phrase. Again, it is easier to argue that what all these violations have in common is based on readers' attempts to make sense of a sentence as they go along – that is, on comprehension processes – rather than arising from lexical subcategorization frames.

THE STRONG PREDICTION OF MULTIPLE-CONSTRAINT MODELS

Lexical models and multiple-constraint models differ in how they use semantic information to guide initial processing. Multiple-constraint models allow for the influence of lexically encoded information on initial processing, but as we have stressed, they also allow for the influence of semantic information that is not easily encoded in a lexicon, like constraints arising from the interaction of specific participants and things described in a sentence. In contrast, in lexical models constituents are initially configured without semantic guidance. Specifically, information that is stored in subcategorization frames about likely arguments and complements for heads of phrases can be accessed and used in order to configure the syntactic attachment of the constituents in a sentence and, additionally, to label their thematic roles, without giving these constituents a semantic interpretation. This allows for the major work of sentence representation to be done in the syntax and reflects the rationale behind syntax-first models.

Chomsky (1981) provides the theoretical impetus for this view, by providing a strictly feed-forward connection between the lexicon and grammar that construct the syntactic representation of a sentence and that component that interprets the sentence. The Marcus (1980) parser is closely related to this sort of thinking in that syntactic representation is viewed as relatively foolproof without requiring close communication with interpretive mechanisms. The syntactic processor passes its output on to a case frame processor in a strictly feed forward manner, and any syntactic ambiguity that requires semantic resolution is handled with an interrupt to the syntactic processor. Finally, the lexical-functional grammar (LFG) parser of Kaplan and Bresnan (1982) fits a similar mold. Thematic role labels are accessed in the lexicon and are associated with the respective constituents in a representation of structure and grammatical function, but the role information is sufficiently independent of syntactic processing to be passed on and interpreted by a separate mechanism (Halvorsen, 1983). Indeed, processing in an LFG parser is intricately worked out without much concern for semantic/conceptual interaction (Bresnan & Kaplan, 1982; Ford et al., 1982; Kaplan & Bresnan, 1982).

As long as one limits one's view to verb-based subcategorization frames (cf. Ford et al., 1982), syntax-first guidance appears to be manageable yet powerful under some sort of priority ordering system for examining all possible expansions of the verb phrase. A multiple-constraint model predicts that guidance based on the words that appear in a sentence is not always that simple but may depend on the influence of constituents beyond just the verb head. Therefore, in the next experiment, we sought to demonstrate the effects of another constituent – the Object NP – on expectations for attachment and role assignment in on-line reading, as before.

Experiment 3

This experiment used the same sequence of syntactic phrases as the previous experiments, and the constituent of interest again was the post-verbal prepositional phrase but with the following difference. In this experiment, we constructed sets of four sentences that held the subject noun phrase, main verb, and preposition constant, but varied the object noun phrase, as shown in the following examples:

6. The   dictator   viewed   the   masses   from   the
       steps (verb phrase attachment in locative role;
               consistent with subject's expectations)
       city   (noun phrase attachment in source role;
               inconsistent with subject's expectations)
    but he was not very sympathetic.

7. The   dictator   viewed   the   petitions   from   the
       prisoners (noun phrase attachment in source role;
                   consistent with subject's expectations)
       podium   (verb phrase attachment in locative role;
                   inconsistent with subject's expectations)
    but he was not very sympathetic.

With one object the attachment and role for the prepositional phrase that are consistent with subject's expectations are different from the attachment and role that are consistent with the other object. For example, *masses* evokes an expectation for verb phrase attachment in the role of location, whereas *petitions* evokes an expectation for noun phrase attachment in the role of source, when used in the context of the sentence frame in the example. For each object, there were two prepositional phrase noun-fillers: one that was consistent with expectations given that particular object and one that was inconsistent with those expectations.

The goal in using these stimuli was to shift expectations from one particular attachment and role assignment for the prepositional phrase to an alternative attachment and role assignment by changing the object noun phrase. If expectations actually shift with a change in this constituent, then we should predict faster reading times in an on-line reading task for all sentences in the consistent conditions compared to those in the inconsistent conditions. A stronger test of the expectation shift would require one analysis using the sets of consistent and inconsistent sentences for which subjects are expecting verb phrase attachment

(VP-expectation) and a separate analysis using the sets of consistent and inconsistent sentences for which subjects are expecting noun phrase attachment (NP-expectation). After all, the change in the object is posited to modulate expectations for attachment regardless of the site of attachment. The VP-expectation and NP-expectation sets each provide for a test of consistency over frames that use the same verb, and could show whether there is actually only one consistent cell over the four conditions associated with a verb or whether there are truly two consistent cells, as required for a clear test of the hypothesis at hand.

Eighteen stimulus quadruples like Examples 6 and 7 were used for this experiment.[2] The sequence of pretesting and reading was identical to Experiment 2.

The Object Noun Phrase Influences Expectations and Reading Times

When we compared reading times for noun-fillers and the four words that followed in sentences in the consistent condition to those in the inconsistent condition there was a significant total net advantage of 90 ms for consistent prepositional phrases. Word-by-word reading times for the overall comparison of consistent to inconsistent sentences are shown in Figure 11.6a, and separate times for objects that evoked an expectation for prepositional phrase attachment to the verb phrase and those that evoked an expectation for prepositional phrase attachment to the Noun Phrase are shown in Figures 11.6b and 11.6c.

In the overall analysis, faster reading times could not be dependent on a single specific attachment, because the consistent conditions cross attachments. In the analysis by type of attachment expectation (VP- or NP-expectation), the advantage of consistent sentences could not depend exclusively on a particular verb frame, since the verb was held constant across the VP- and NP-expectation sets. In fact, minimal attachment and verb-based lexical models would both predict null effects for Consistency, for these reasons. Faster reading times for the consistent conditions were found though and can reasonably be attributed to the modulating effect of the particular object noun phrase on the attachment and role assignment that subjects were expecting for the prepositional phrase.

In pointing out that the object noun phrase is a source of influence on attachment and role assignment, we definitely do not want to suggest that it has this influence on its own. Although the other constituents in a frame were held constant for purposes of this demonstration it is, we believe, fairly clear that the particular objects had their influence by virtue of the other constituents that appeared with them in the frame.

---

[2] A full description of this experiment and a list of the stimuli is in Taraban (1988), and can be obtained from the first author.

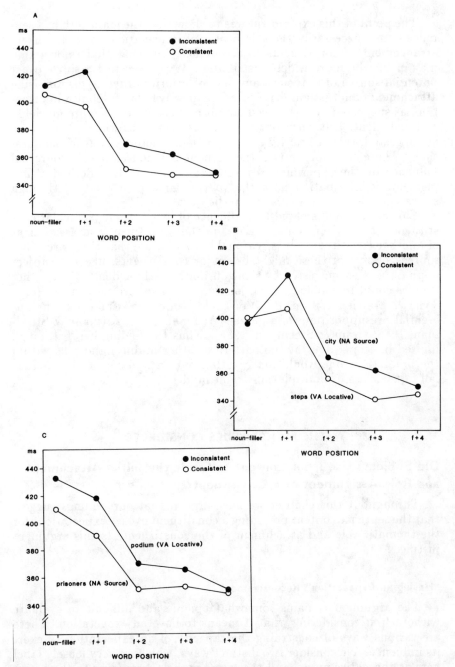

FIGURE 11.6. Experiment 3: Reading times in ms for the noun-filler and the four words that followed (e.g., *steps but he was not*) (Panel A); for sentence frames with verb phrase attachment expectations (Panel B); and for sentence frames with noun phrase attachment expectations (Panel C).

The point of this experiment was to show that the main verb in a sentence is not necessarily the sole bearer of information about the likely arrangement of constituents in a sentence, but that that information may in fact be more widely distributed. With even just a single other potential source of influence, any sort of priority ordering of promising attachments and assignments to adopt in advance of definite information, as suggested in verb-based lexical models, becomes quite unwieldy and inefficient. If it turns out that information is as widely distributed as suggested, then a priority ordering is most definitely out of the question. Therefore, not only is the verb questioned as a sole source of influence by the experimental results at hand, but the method of implementing information from that particular source, that is, through subcategorization frames, is also to be questioned.

This experiment showed the influence of just a single particular constituent – the object noun phrase – on the attachment and assignment of another constituent. It is reasonable to suppose that there are other sources. Some of these might be major constituents, like the subject noun phrase, as suggested by some off-line work by Oden (1978). Other sources could be outside the major clause in a subordinate clause (e.g., Tyler & Marslen-Wilson, 1977) or could be quite abstract, like the referential presuppositions of a phrase (Altmann, 1987; Altmann & Steedman, 1988; Crain & Steedman, 1985). Thus the finding here, although limited in scope, does fit the pattern of other findings and falls within the predictions one would make with any of a number of models that fall in the class of multiple-constraint models.

THE MAJOR ISSUES CONSIDERED

Did Subjects Use Prior Content to Guide the Initial Attachment and Role Assignment of a Constituent?

Throughout this chapter we have argued that our findings suggest that the sentence content preceding a constituent evokes expectations for the thematic role and attachment of the constituent. Is this argument justified?

"Having an Expectation" Reconsidered

The argument remains somewhat opaque and difficult to evaluate without first considering what it means to have an expectation. There are various ways of construing the capacity of an expectation to exert its influence. We consider two distinct ways, which we very loosely label here as the *active* model and the *latent* model. According to the active model, expectancies about attachment and role assignment are activated *prior* to reaching the disambiguating material that determines the fit of these expectancies with the disambiguating material.[3] When the fit is good, the pre-activated expectations and the subsequent activation of constituents composing the disambiguating material go through easily, relative to the case in which the fit is not so good. The distinguishing feature of this view is that the expectations that a person holds are activated to some degree prior to being used to process forthcoming material. In the latent model, this is not so. A person reads through the content of a sentence and only attempts to form a representation for content as it is made available. Multiple possible syntactic attachments and role assignments for constituents do not come into play until the person reaches the disambiguating material and must process it. At this point, some role assignments and attachments go through more easily than others given the particular preceding content, not because they are already active but because the preceding content affords some constructions of the constituent more readily than others.

The end result, empirically, of the active and latent models would be the same, at least in the experimental paradigm that we adopted. In both cases, processing would be slower in the region of disambiguation when the disambiguating material did not fit together very well with the way that the prior content disposed subjects to initially process it. The data that we collected do not help to distinguish between these two possibilities. In fact, it is not clear what paradigm would.

The force of the argument made in this chapter, though, does not in the end depend on which model – active or latent – most accurately describes the course of processing. The thesis is that the content prior to the disambiguating information sets people up to initially attach a constituent and assign it a role according to one set of possibilities rather than another, and all the data are consistent with this claim.

Fit of the Filler as a Possible Confound

There is a possible alternative explanation of the data that has nothing to do with expectations. As an alternative explanation would weaken the thesis, it deserves careful consideration.

Perhaps, it might be argued, we were not so much observing a violation of expected roles and attachments in the data but a difficulty in integrating the noun-filler of a prepositional phrase into the attachment and role to which it ultimately fits. To make this argument concrete, consider Sentences 8 and 9 from Experiment 1.

8. The doctor examined the patient with a stethoscope . . .
9. The doctor examined the patient with a toothache . . .

Subjects process Sentence 8 more quickly than Sentence 9, it might be argued, not so much because the prepositional phrase in 9 actually

---

[3] Kurtzman (1985) described a number of possible models of this sort, that vary according to the point and extent of activation, and the processes that are included, like the *abandonment* and reinstatement of hypotheses.

violates their expectations for role and attachment – they might test all roles and attachments in parallel without any preference for one over another – but because *toothache* fits less well into the role of modifier-of-the-patient than *stethoscope* fits into the role of instrument-of-the-verb.

This interpretation seems quite consistent with the results of Experiment 1, because in that experiment, it is possible that (on the average, anyway) the prepositional phrase noun-fillers that supposedly violated subjects' role assignment and attachment expectations fit less well into their ultimate role given the prior content of the sentence.[4] This being the case, it could well be that the difficulty subjects had with the unexpected versions of the prepositional phrases in that experiment could have reflected a difficulty finding a coherent interpretation of the entire sentence. Therefore, beginning with Experiment 2, we treated the *fit of a noun-filler* for a particular attachment and role as a factor distinct from the *fit of the attachment and role assignment* of a phrase; the first factor was quantified using expectation and plausibility ratings for the noun-fillers (e.g., *broom* vs. *solvent* vs. *manager* vs. *odor*) and the second factor was quantified using a cloze task for sentence frames (e.g., *The janitor cleaned the storage area with the __*).

In Experiment 2, we showed that noun-fillers that are judged to fit less well with the prior content result in longer reading times relative to fillers with a better fit. However, the remaining results of Experiments 2 and 3 are difficult to reconcile with the view that all we found were effects of this sort. For in these experiments, we found that prepositional phrases whose noun-fillers were matched for plausibility and indeed also for rated expectedness could still differ in the amount of slowing they produced, as a function of whether the attachment and role that the prepositional phrase was interpreted as filling matched the attachment and role that the subject expected based on the prior content of the sentence. This fit-to-expectation effect for attachment and role assignment was thereby shown to be separate from problems with integrating the noun-filler into its ultimate role and attachment.

Summary

In summary, the results of Experiments 2 and 3 are all consistent with the general conclusion that subjects generate expectations for the attachment and role assignment of upcoming constituents and use these expectations to guide the processing of those constituents. The differences we obtained between conditions in which the prepositional phrase attached and took a role as expected and those conditions in which it did not seem to indicate that the prior content of the sentence leads the

---

[4] Kurtzman (1985) provided an analysis of the Rayner et al. (1983) stimuli that is compatible with this view. In a rating study he conducted, he found that the nonminimal completions were "more unlikely, unusual, unexpected, or implausible" (p. 213) than minimal completions.

subject to set up some mental structure that is more ready to accommodate a prepositional phrase filling one attachment and role than a prepositional phrase filling another attachment and role. When a completed prepositional phrase fits these expectations – even if it does not fit it particularly well – processing goes through much more quickly than it does when the prepositional phrase requires a different attachment and role.

Did Subjects Use General Syntactic Principles for the Initial Attachment of Constituents?

The major goal in Experiment 1 was to see how much of the total processing difference between matched pairs of sentences could be accounted for by the specific content composing the test sentences. But we also wanted to see whether any effect remained to be accounted for by general syntactic principles that could arrange constituents into the ultimate configuration they would hold. Principles such as these would be useful for guiding processing. The relevant principle was Frazier's minimal attachment principle. As we showed in Experiment 1, the prediction made by this principle did not hold up to the data, specifically, the principle did not appear to play a role in guiding subjects' attachment decisions. The evidence we provided, admittedly, is only relevant to the prepositional phrase attachment at hand. Evidence for minimal attachment in other cases, or evidence for other principles, needs to be evaluated on its own merits.

What is the Locus of Content-Based Guidance?

The hypothesis that we were pursuing here suggested that the locus of content-based guidance would not be limited to the influence of the main verb in a sentence. Once one entertains the possibility that other constituents besides the verb can influence attachment and assignment expectations, one is left with a multitude of additional possible sources, for example, the subject, the object, modifiers of these phrases, or even a definite *the* vs. indefinite *a* form for these phrases. We were unable to examine the influence of each potential additional source and chose rather to attempt to show the influence of the object noun phrase. Demonstrating the influence of this constituent would at least show that the verb is not the sole source of guidance. In Experiment 3, we therefore constructed pairs of sentence frames (the content up to and including the preposition) that differed in the object used but that were otherwise identical. If the object were not a source of guidance, the same attachment and role should have been expected for both frames and that attachment and role should have outperformed other possible attachments and roles in on-line reading. We showed, however, that for these particular test sentences, it was not possible to predict which particular attachment and role would be facilitated in on-line reading by simply looking at the main verb. There are findings in the literature (Altmann, 1987; Altmann & Steedman, 1988; Crain & Steedman, 1985; Oden, 1978) indicating influences of other factors, though not all of these studies showed their effects on on-line processing.

Are Thematic Roles Assigned by the Syntax?

We know that violations of thematic role expectations produce slower processing relative to the case in which role expectations are fulfilled. This was a finding in Experiment 2. A question of major theoretical importance is whether the thematic role information had been semantically interpreted at the point when the slower processing times occurred, as an answer to this question is relevant to determining what the underlying cognitive architecture must be like.

One could place thematic role information associated with heads of phrases in the lexicon. This information as well as information about the arguments and modifiers of these lexical items could then be used to construct a structural representation of a sentence. Chomsky (1981, 1986) does so within core grammar. Kaplan and Bresnan (1982; Bresnan & Kaplan, 1982; Ford et al., 1982) use lexical entries similar to Chomsky's. In both cases, thematic role information is passed on to a semantic processor, but the thematic roles themselves can be viewed initially, at least, as part of syntax. That is, constituents are placed into a structural representation with various labels, like agent and instrument, but these labels are initially assigned without consideration for the meaning of the constituents filling these roles. According to this view, semantic interpretation is not required in order to benefit from the guidance provided by thematic role information, resulting in a model like Figure 11.2a or 11.2b.

Do the longer reading times in our data reflect a mislabeling of constituents based on a projection of role labels from individual lexical entries? It is possible, one could argue, that each lexical head could have preferred structural and thematic assignments stored with it. After a role is assigned and submitted to semantic processing, reassignment of roles may take place based on world knowledge, for example, that a *manager* is not a good instrument of cleaning in *The janitor cleaned the storage area with the manager because . . .* There are a number of problems with this view, although we will not totally reject this possibility. The implications of this view, though, are worth pondering.

In the first place, heads may have multiple sets of attachments and roles associated with them. This is evident for verbs, which often can be transitive, intransitive, or associated with sentential complements. The same could be true of noun heads in noun phrases, which could have modifiers that are likely to appear with them to one degree or another, for example, modifiers like *with a garden* for *house* or *with pepperoni* for *pizza*. Thus, the lexicon could provide information about individual items to a syntactic processor, but (a) this would most probably need to be a weighted list of possibilities, and (b) these would probably have to be evaluated in parallel in order for the processor to eventually find a mutually consistent representation for all the constituents.

The notion of a weighted list of possible expansions for heads of phrases presents a possible paradox for a lexically based, head-driven model. This is because many heads of phrases may not *in themselves* strongly support a preference but may nevertheless contribute to a strong expectation about forthcoming constituents when taken together with other information in the sentence. For example, *married*, as head of a verb phrase, allows many possible attachments and roles, so that if one were to simply look at the distribution of possibilities for *married*, there might not be a single strong contender to rely on for guidance. However, hypotheses about the right role and attachment for a *with*-PP, in advance of the complete prepositional phrase, may be strong by virtue of all the preceding constituents. In the context of *The woman married the man with* . . . the preposition reliably evokes an expectation for syntactic attachment of the prepositional phrase to the noun phrase *the man* as a descriptor of a possession, like *money* or *a Corvette*. If the verb were *beat* and the object *the man*, we might expect *with a mop*, and if the verb were *kissed* and the object *the man*, we might expect *with affection*. As is evident, these three verbs are associated with varied attachments and roles. The verb itself may in many cases constrain the possibilities for how the sentence will be elaborated. By itself, it may only weakly constrain the possibilities; in concert with the other constituents it may strongly constrain the possibilities. Complex associations between lexical items are not typically considered to be part of a lexicon so it would probably fall to the work of the syntactic processor to sort through the weighted lists for each lexical item in order to find a representation for the constituents. But facts about women liking men with Corvettes seem to be outside the purview of a syntactic processor and an associated grammar. Therefore, a model that relies on a weighted list of options for individual entries and a pure syntactic processor that uses this information would probably fail to account for the effects of conjunctions of constraints emanating from combinations of heads of phrases.

One way out of this might be to posit complex lexical entries that captured intricate weightings between agents, actions, and objects. Then, conjunctive effects of the sort we found could be attributed to these complex lexical specifications that are semantically uninterpreted. We argue here, that although possible, this sort of position is unattractive because it is tantamount to requiring that people introduce everything that they know about the world into subcategorization frames, simply for the sake of analyzing language in the syntax. A model that is consistent with our data and that is more attractive in light of these considerations is a multiple constraint satisfaction model.

Are Prepositional Phrases Arguments?

Our answer to the question "Are thematic roles in the syntax?" is that they may be, but if so, they have a tenuous existence within the syntactic processor, which, it seems, can only call on other processors to evaluate them. One objection that could be raised against us is that prepositional phrases of the sort that we have been using are not really arguments of the verb, and other mechanisms may be necessary for processing them, but that a core grammar applies to true arguments of verbs – like a PP-locative for *put* and a PP-goal for *gave*, and their thematic roles are safely "in the syntax."

One way of responding to this claim is to invoke Occam's razor and ask why one should separate verbs according to the consistency with which they take labels. If there is a mechanism or some combination of mechanisms that can do attachment and role assignment for modifiers and complements, that is, the less-intrinsic associates of a constituent why must another device be postulated for processing the more-intrinsic associates, that is, the so-called arguments? Multiple-constraint devices, as described below, can presumably make assignments for both arguments and complements, without additionally requiring any sort of preclassification of verbs.

Processing considerations do not bode well for the idea that arguments can be assigned by the syntax without input from other sources. Consider the verb *put* for example, which is oft touted as requiring NP-patient and PP-locative arguments. Can such information be applied with no concern for what the constituents mean? Sentences like 10 and 11, which follow the sequence *put NP on-PP in-PP* illustrate that it cannot. Upon reading *put* the person can reliably expect a locative argument to follow, but (a) cannot know how many potential locatives will appear, and (b) if more than one potential argument appears, cannot be positive about how to organize them. Any single PP in Sentences 10 or 11 could fill the required slot for a locative for *put*, because all the prepositions heading these phrases are capable of filling a locative role. Combinations of PPs could also fill the required slot for *put*. Therefore, although *put* seems to represent a very predictable case, this is only true for single-PP cases. It might still be argued that *put*'s lexical representation proposes an initial parse of such sentences which must then be checked by semantic processes and potentially undone when subsequent information becomes available. Further research is required to distinguish this possibility from the one that we prefer, in which we assume the processor forms a conceptual representation as it goes along and lets this influence initial decisions about constituent attachment in all cases.

10. The cook put the roast on the table in the kitchen.
11. The cook put the roast on the table in the oven.

QUESTIONS OF MODELING

What is the Right Mechanism for Modeling Thematic Role Information?

The experiments here provide a real boost for the importance of expectations for thematic roles per se in on-line reading. In order to model this influence in a computational mechanism, it would be good to get a firm grip on exactly what a thematic role is. We have handled this question throughout using no more than a handful of broad distinctions, like instrument, that have an established place in the literature. Yet it seems that language is capable of nuancing any distinction that one would care to make in a way that could influence the way we process information that falls into these categories. There are, for example, a doctor's instruments, a musician's instruments, and an aviator's instruments, and for each we may have certain beliefs that can be influenced by the particular type of action associated with them, the agent, the circumstances, and so on. The point is simply that taxonomic thematic roles may not be fine-grained enough for most of the distinctions that we commonly make, and a role for any particular constituent could be shaded by the other constituents that it appears with. There is only suggestive evidence for this view here. The fit of noun-fillers, though, in Experiment 2 has some bearing on this issue. For example, *Hanukkah* is not such a good filler in *The choir sang the carol on Hanukkah*, but it would probably be considered a good filler in *The rabbi said the prayer on Hanukkah*. In both instances, the prepositional phrase locates the action in time, though a subcategory of these temporal phrases is obviously more appropriate for the rabbi saying a prayer than for the choir singing a carol.

The intricate nature of thematic roles is evidenced in the limited success linguists have had in devising tests for the presence of any particular role. One might expect that a role like agent would be one of the easiest to handle. One claim that has been made about agency, which is discussed in Lyons (1968), is that process verbs, like *die*, cannot have agentive subjects. This may be true in Sentence 12, but as Cruse (1973) points out, it is not true in Sentence 13. Another claim is that agents are supposed to be animate. If we compare Sentences 14 and 15, neither of which has animate subjects, we see that we could accept an agency argument for *wind* in 14 but not for *stone* in 15. This is because a *stone* would most typically be used by someone to break a window, so it is more instrumental than agentive. The wind, though, could be considered agentive, because it is using its own energy in carrying out the action (Cruse, 1973). If this is true, then elaborating 15, as in 16, now gives the stone critical features of agency.

12. Christ died.
13. Christ died in order to save us from our sins.
14. The wind opened the door.
15. The stone broke the window.

16. As a result of the explosion, a stone flew across the road and broke the window.

These examples show that it may be difficult to find a small set of features that defines a thematic role like agency. What also becomes clear is that a constituent is not necessarily endowed with a thematic role by virtue of its own features but gets part of its role from features of the constituents that it appears with. A striking example of this is found in the comparison of Sentences 17 and 18, where the critical constituent is an adverb, which is not usually considered to be of much importance in terms of *governing* other constituents (see, e.g., Chomsky, 1981). Yet, here the adverb plays a critical role in modulating the thematic role structure for the sentence. In Sentence 17, the adverb *accidentally* negates critical features of agency that John might have had. In Sentence 18, *carefully* affirms John's agency (Cruse, 1973).

17. John accidentally pushed the door open.
18. John carefully pushed the door open.

Given the empirical results from our experiments demonstrating the importance of thematic role information in on-line processing, a plausible model would have to provide a mechanism for using this information early on in the process of representing a sentence. Given the kinds of subtle effects one can glean from the example sentences, this mechanism could not limit itself to the features of individual constituents in finding a role for that constituent; rather, the role for any particular constituent would emerge both from the features of the constituent itself and from the features of other constituents that it appeared with in a sentence. The appropriateness of a thematic role filler thereby becomes dependent upon an intricate interaction of the semantic features of all the constituents in a sentence. To our knowledge, the McClelland and Kawamoto (1986) model is the best to-date for amalgamating these fine distinctions from a large multitude of input features. Knowledge of which features interact with which others and the implications of these interactions is gained through exposure to sentences that describe events in the real world. Within this model, there may be gross regularities in the co-occurrence of features, one of which might be labeled the instrumental role. A finer-grained analysis could presumably reveal clusters within these broader distinctions, corresponding say, to the typical instruments of a doctor as opposed to a policeman.

A Multiple Constraint Satisfaction Network

Some years ago, Forster (1979) postulated a model of sentence processing that consisted of a linear chain of processors, with each processor accepting input from one, and only one other processor. This was an autonomy of syntax model, and Forster considered it more promising theoretically than a model in which any processor could be influenced by any other processor. As it appears from our data that syntactic processing can be influenced by thematic roles and related conceptual information, there is reason to suspect that syntax is not autonomous and further, that alternative models should be seriously considered. We think that models that have been proposed in recent years that belong to the class of multiple-constraint models provide an attractive alternative to those models in which syntax shuts itself off from higher-level sources of influence and is insensitive to the guidance that these sources of information afford.

St. John and McClelland (in press) provide one example of a multiple constraint model. The model consists of a pool of densely interconnected units, that is, a parallel distributed processing network. In the course of processing a corpus of sentences, the network eventually learns to assign thematic roles to constituents based on syntactic and semantic constraints, and is able to disambiguate ambiguous words, instantiate vague words, and elaborate implied roles. As each constituent of a sentence is encountered, the model updates its representation of the sentence as a whole, and if information early in a sentence indicates one interpretation that later proves to be incorrect based on subsequent input, the model adjusts its representation. In such cases, however, there is a more dramatic change in representation than in cases where subsequent input is consistent with the initial interpretation. Such changes take time, allowing the model to account for effects of violations of expectations on processing.

The various capabilities of the St. John and McClelland model correspond in some sense to the mutual influence of multiple sources of information on each other. Interestingly, however, the St. John and McClelland model does not in fact contain several processors which execute distinct types of rules, for example, inference rules, syntactic rules, and semantic rules. Information is encoded internally in the connections in an integrated network, and these connections allow the network to act as if it knew the rules. At first glance it may seem that such a mechanism is even less principled and structured than any that Forster might have envisioned and certainly rejected. However, the network is actually carrying out an extremely delicate and subtle weighing of the various sources of evidence. If they are all treated together, it is only because all of them are required for the network to solve the problem of finding (through learning) a set of factors that, when appropriately weighted, allow it to correctly interpret the sentences that it is asked to process. In fact, the learning procedure that governs the adjustment of connection strengths is implementing what we take to be an extremely central and basic principle: that multiple sources of information must be taken into account and appropriately weighted so that the model's interpretations of sentences are minimally discrepant from the interpretations that sentences actually have in the world. It is this principle of minimizing discrepancy, rather than some artificial principle of decomposability, that governs processing in the St. John and McClelland model.

There are encouraging signs both on experimental and computational fronts for multiple-constraint satisfaction networks. At this juncture, it seems as promising to seek out more empirical evidence for multiple constraints in sentence processing and to explore the computational aspects of these data as to hold fast to the view that syntactic processing is encapsulated from other sources of influence.

CONCLUSION: A THEORY OF PARSING NEEDS A THEORY OF READING COMPREHENSION

If the evidence actually suggested that syntax-first models were adequate, then it would be possible to develop a theory of parsing that did syntactic attachment independently of other systems. The parser would be sensitive to feedback from other processors, in the case of implausible constructions, for instance, but the parser would maintain its autonomy. Reading would consist of parsing plus something else, specifically, the additional independent outputs of conceptual and discourse processors.

The picture indicated by our data suggests something different. Parsing, in the narrow sense of constructing a syntactic representation indicating the relationship of grammatical constituents to one another, appears to keep close company with conceptual processes. Syntactic attachment is not solved autonomously from the process of constructing the conceptual representation of the sentence. Our data consistently showed that the same type of constraints that govern the final fully interpreted representation govern on-line processing. The final representation is clearly based on a consideration of real-world objects and relations. The close relation between data from two independent sources – (a) the cloze data and rating data in which subjects could fully interpret the sentences and (b) the closely monitored on-line reading times suggest that subjects are drawing on the same body of information in both cases. Therefore, it appears that the computation of syntactic structure depends on semantics.

Multiple-constraint models predict that expectations that guide processing can be generated in response to characteristics of other constituents of the sentence besides the verb, for which we have found some evidence. We expect that more evidence of this nature will be forthcoming. These models also predict guidance from pre- or extrasentential context. Therefore, it should be possible to demonstrate the effects of the discourse context in which a sentence falls on the immediate expectations subjects hold for constituents that they are in the process of representing (cf. Altmann & Steedman, 1988; Perfetti, this volume). The truism that reading is for understanding makes sense in light of a multiple-constraint model, for this model suggests that the conceptual representation for a sentence and the discourse are used by the reader to structure expectations for those parts of the sentence that remain to be encountered. If it is true that parsing draws on the kinds of information and representations that reading comprehension is all about, then to understand parsing one must also understand comprehension.

ACKNOWLEDGMENTS

We would like to thank Chuck Clifton, Keith Rayner, and G. B. Flores d'Arcais for a number of valuable clarifications of parts of this chapter. The first author wishes to thank Nelson Caro for assistance with programming the experiments. This work was supported by ONR Contract N00014-82-C-0374, NSF Grant BNS 88-12048, and by a NIMH Research Scientist Development Award MH00385 to the second author.

REFERENCES

Altmann, G. (1987). Modularity and interaction in sentence processing. In J. Garfield (Ed.), *Modularity in knowledge representation and natural language understanding* (pp. 249 - 258). Cambridge, MA: MIT Press.

Altmann, G., & Steedman, M. (1988). Interaction with context during human sentence processing. *Cognition, 30*, 191 - 238.

Bresnan, J., & Kaplan, R. M. (1982). Introduction: Grammars as mental representations of language. In J. Bresnan (Ed.), *The mental representation of grammatical relations* (pp. xvii - lii). Cambridge, MA: MIT Press.

Chomsky, N. (1981). *Lectures on government and binding*. Dordrecht: Foris.

Chomsky, N. (1986). *Knowledge of language*. New York: Praeger.

Clifton, C., Frazier, L., & Connine, C. (1984). Lexical expectations in sentence comprehension. *Journal of Verbal Learning and Verbal Behavior, 23*, 696 - 708.

Connine, C., Ferreira, F., Jones, C., Clifton, C., & Frazier, L. (1984). Verb frame preferences: Descriptive norms. *Journal of Psycholinguistic Research, 13*, 307 - 319.

Crain, S., & Steedman, M. (1985). On not being led up the garden path: The use of context by the psychological syntax parser. In D. R. Dowty, L. Karttunen, & A. M. Zwicky (Eds.), *Natural language parsing: Psychological, computational, and theoretical perspectives* (pp. 320 - 357). Cambridge: Cambridge University Press.

Cruse, D. A. (1973). Some thoughts on agentivity. *Journal of Linguistics, 9*, 11 - 23.

Fodor, J. A., Bever, T. G., & Garrett, M. F. (1974). *The psychology of language: An introduction to psycholinguistics and generative grammar*. New York: McGraw-Hill.

Fodor, J. A., Garrett, M. F., & Bever, T. G. (1968). Some syntactic determinants of sentential complexity, II: Verb structure. *Perception & Psychophysics, 3*, 453 - 461.

Ford, M., Bresnan, J., & Kaplan, R. M. (1982). A competence-based theory of syntactic closure. In J. Bresnan (Ed.), *The mental representation of grammatical relations* (pp. 727 - 796). Cambridge, MA: MIT Press.

Forster, K. I. (1979). Levels of processing and the structure of the language processor. In W. E. Cooper & E. C. T. Walker (Eds.), *Sentence processing: Psycholinguistic studies presented to Merrill Garrett* (pp. 27 - 85). Hillsdale, NJ: Lawrence Erlbaum Associates.

Frazier, L. (1978). *On comprehending sentences: Syntactic parsing strategies*. Unpublished doctoral dissertation, University of Connecticut, Storrs. (Also published by the Indiana University Linguistics Club, 1979).

Frazier, L. (1987). Theories of sentence processing. In J. Garfield (Ed.), *Modularity in knowledge representation and natural language understanding* (pp. 291 - 307). Cambridge, MA: MIT Press.

Frazier, L., & Fodor, J. D. (1978). The sausage machine: A new two-stage parsing model. *Cognition, 6*, 291 - 325.

Frazier, L., & Rayner, K. (1982). Making and correcting errors during sentence comprehension: Eye movements in the analysis of structurally ambiguous sentences. *Cognitive Psychology, 14*, 178 - 210.

Halvorsen, P. (1983). Semantics for lexical-functional grammar. *Linguistic Inquiry, 14*, 567 - 615.

Holmes, V. M. (1984). Parsing strategies and discourse context. *Journal of Psycholinguistic Research, 13*, 237 - 257.

Holmes, V. M. (1987). Syntactic parsing: In search of the garden path. In M. Coltheart (Ed.), *Attention and performance XII: The psychology of reading* (pp. 587 - 599). Hillsdale, NJ: Lawrence Erlbaum Associates.

Holmes, V. M., & Forster, K. I. (1972). Perceptual complexity and underlying sentence structure. *Journal of Verbal Learning and Verbal Behavior, 11*, 148 - 156.

Jackendoff, R. S. (1972). *Semantic interpretation in generative grammar.* Cambridge, MA: MIT Press.

Just, M. A., & Carpenter, P. A. (1980). A theory of reading: From eye fixations to comprehension. *Psychological Review, 87*, 329 - 354.

Kaplan, R. M., & Bresnan, J. (1982). Lexical-functional grammar: A formal system for grammatical representation. In J. Bresnan (Ed.), *The mental representation of grammatical relations* (pp. 173 - 281). Cambridge, MA: MIT Press.

Kimball, J. (1973). Seven principles of surface structure parsing in natural language. *Cognition, 2*, 15 - 47.

Kurtzman, H. (1985). *Studies in syntactic ambiguity resolution.* Unpublished doctoral dissertation, Massachusetts Institute of Technology. (Also published by the Indiana University Linguistics Club).

Lyons, J. (1968). *Introduction to theoretical linguistics.* Cambridge: Cambridge University Press.

MacWhinney, B. (1986). *Toward a psycholinguistically plausible parser.* Paper presented at ESCOL conference, University of Pittsburgh.

Marcus, M. P. (1980). *A theory of syntactic recognition for natural language.* Cambridge, MA: MIT Press.

Marslen-Wilson, W., & Tyler, L. K. (1980). The temporal structure of spoken language understanding. *Cognition, 8*, 1 - 71.

McClelland, J. L. (1987). The case for interactionism in language processing. In M. Coltheart (Ed.), *Attention and performance XII: The psychology of reading* (pp. 3 - 36). London: Lawrence Erlbaum Associates.

McClelland, J., & Kawamoto, A. (1986). Mechanisms of sentence processing: Assigning roles to constituents. In D. E. Rumelhart, J. L. McClelland, & the PDP research group (Eds.), *Parallel distributed processing: Explorations in the microstructure of cognition. Vol. 2: Psychological and biological models* (pp. 272 - 325). Cambridge, MA: MIT Press.

Mitchell, D. C., & Holmes, V. M. (1985). The role of specific information about the verb in parsing sentences with local structural ambiguity. *Journal of Memory and Language, 24*, 542 - 559.

Oden, G. C. (1978). Semantic constraints and judged preference for interpretations of ambiguous sentences. *Memory & Cognition, 6,* 26 - 37.

Rayner, K., Carlson, M., & Frazier, L. (1983). The interaction of syntax and semantics during sentence processing: Eye movements in the analysis of semantically biased sentences. *Journal of Verbal Learning and Verbal Behavior, 22,* 358 - 374.

Schank, R. C. (1972). Conceptual dependency: A theory of natural language understanding. *Cognitive Psychology, 3,* 552 - 631.

Schank, R. C. (1975). *Conceptual information processing.* Amsterdam: North-Holland.

Shapiro, L. P., Zurif, E., & Grimshaw, J. (1987). Sentence processing and the mental representation of verbs. *Cognition, 27,* 219 - 246.

St. John, M. F., & McClelland, J. L. (in press). Learning and applying contextual constraints in sentence comprehension. *Artificial Intelligence.*

Taraban, R. (1988). *Content-based expectations: One source of guidance for syntactic attachment and thematic role assignment in sentence processing.* Unpublished doctoral dissertation, Carnegie-Mellon University, Pittsburgh.

Taraban, R., & McClelland, J. L. (1988). Constituent attachment and thematic role assignment in sentence processing: Influences of content-based expectations. *Journal of Memory and Language, 27,* 597 - 632.

Thibadeau, R., Just, M. A., & Carpenter, P. A. (1982). A model of the time course and content of reading. *Cognitive Science, 6,* 157 - 203.

Tyler, L. K., & Marslen-Wilson, W. D. (1977). The on-line effects of semantic content on syntactic processing. *Journal of Verbal Learning and Verbal Behavior, 16,* 683 - 692.

Warner, J., & Glass, A. L. (1987). Context and distance-to-disambiguation effects in ambiguity resolution: Evidence from grammaticality judgments of garden path sentences. *Journal of Memory and Language, 26,* 714 - 738.

Winograd, T. (1971). *Procedures as a representation for data in a computer program for understanding natural language.* (Project MAC-TR 84). Massachusetts Institute of Technology, Cambridge, MA.

Woods, W. A. (1972). *The lunar sciences natural language information system.* (BBN Report No. 2378). Cambridge, MA: Bolt, Beranek and Newman.

12 COMPREHENDING SENTENCES WITH EMPTY ELEMENTS

Charles Clifton, Jr. and Marica De Vincenzi
University of Massachusetts, Amherst

INTRODUCTION

Reading, as well as listening to spoken language, requires one not only to identify words but to determine the relationships among the words and use these relationships to compose the meaning of a sentence out of the meanings of its words. Since its inception, one of the main tasks of psycholinguistics has been to fathom how a reader can determine how the words in a sentence are related to one another. One psycholinguistic tradition, dating back at least to Miller (1962), emphasizes the role grammatical knowledge plays in this process. The present chapter falls squarely in this tradition. It presents some contemporary evidence, drawn from the comprehension of English and Italian sentences, about one of the oldest topics in psycholinguistics: the processing of sentences whose words occur in an order that is different from the canonical, deep structure, order.

The first joyous discoveries of psycholinguistics included the possibility that some sentences are grammatical transformations of other forms. Early psycholinguists (Clifton & Odom, 1966; Gough, 1965; Mehler, 1963; Miller, 1962) attempted to understand how people deal with a variety of sentences thought to involve grammatical transformations. Time and study led to several conclusions, including the decision that many of these sentences do not involve transformations in interesting ways, and the realization that we had few good ideas about how the remaining sentences were processed. The best idea, after a few years, seemed to be that people attempt to parse sentences as if they were untransformed so that their words occur in their deep structure order,

and entertain a transformational analysis only when this attempt fails
(Fodor, 1978; cf. also Wanner & Maratsos, 1978). This assumption was
attractive because analyses of phrase-structure parsing were enjoying
substantial success (Frazier, 1978; Kimball, 1975). The assumption also
applied very naturally to the prototype case of transformed sentences,
sentences with *wh*-moved elements such as questions, indirect questions,
and relative clauses as illustrated in Example 1.

1a.   Which man *i* did you see —*i* last night?
1b.   I wondered which man *i* you saw —*i* last night.
1c.   That's the man who *i* you saw —*i* last night.

A reader will note that the phrase *which man* occurs in a position where
it cannot serve as an argument of any verb or other argument assigner in
the sentence, and therefore will defer relating it to other phrases in the
sentence. When the reader encounters a transitive verb such as *see*, he
or she will have the lexically based expectation that an object NP (noun
phrase) will occur and will attempt to satisfy this expectation with a
phrase from the incoming lexical string. If such a phrase fails to occur,
then the reader will pull the deferred phrase *which man* (the filler) out
of memory and assign it as the verb's argument. That is, he or she will
relate the filler to a gap in the position of the verb's argument.

This story has one crucial assumption, from our perspective. This is
that the parser prefers to find its arguments at the right time and place
in the lexical string, rather than finding arguments in moved positions.
It identifies long-distance relationships only when its attempts to find
local relationships break down. In the older terminology, it postulates
movement transformations only when it is forced to. This preference has
been described as "gap as last resort" (Fodor, 1978) or, more accurately,
"gap as second resort" (Frazier, 1987b). Fodor (1978) argued that the
preference must be tempered, or else the parser would be predicted
to miss far too many filler–gap relations (e.g., the gap after *read* in
Which book did the teacher read — to the children?). She proposed
that the human sentence parsing mechanism uses information about
the preferred argument (or subcategorization) structures of verbs and
other argument-assigners to create the expectation that an argument
will be present at a given position in a sentence. The parser expects, for
instance, to have an NP after a verb that is usually used transitively,
but not after a verb that is usually used intransitively. When such an
argument-assigner appears but is not followed by a lexical argument, the
possibility of a gap is entertained. Fodor (1978) combined the gap-as-
second-resort assumption and the assumption that information about
preferred subcategorization structures is used as the *lexical expectation
hypothesis*, which can be paraphrased as:

The parser ranks alternative subcategorization possibilities for a
given lexical item in making syntactic predictions, and, when it
makes a prediction, it ranks the option of assigning a lexical string
over the option of assigning a gap.

Recent evidence indicates that the second part of this claim about the processing of moved elements is in error, and instead, its opposite is correct. This contrary claim has been expressed as the *active filler hypothesis* (Clifton & Frazier, 1989; Frazier, 1987b; Frazier & Clifton, 1989):

> When a filler has been identified, rank the option of assigning it to a gap above all other options upon encountering the position of a potential gap.

We review the existing evidence in favor of the active filler hypothesis and present some new evidence about the processing of sentences with empty elements (gaps) in English and Italian. This evidence comes from two types of tasks, self-paced reading and acceptability judgment, and goes beyond existing work in several ways. It examines how relations between *wh*-fillers and gaps are assigned within and across clauses (Experiments 1 and 2; cf. Frazier & Clifton, 1989); it provides tests of the active filler hypothesis in Italian (Experiment 3; cf. De Vincenzi, 1989); and it extends the work to non-*wh* gaps ("little pro" gaps) in Italian (Experiments 4 and 5; cf. De Vincenzi, 1988, 1989).[1] We conclude by generalizing the active filler hypothesis to incorporate all the data, and term the generalized hypothesis the *minimal chains principle* (De Vincenzi, 1988, 1989).

READING ENGLISH SENTENCES

Experiment 1: Reading Times for Lexical NPs

One implication of the active filler hypothesis is that a lexical phrase that appears in an argument position will be read more slowly when a *wh*-filler could also have been assigned to that same position than when no *wh*-filler had been available. In a sentence like *Who did the tall man see (—) Tom with — last night?* a reader will initially assign *who* as object of *see*. (The (-) means a possible but nonexistent gap.) When *Tom* appears, the reader will have to change his or her initial assignment, taking *Tom* as the object. This should result in slow reading time for *Tom*, compared to a sentence with no *wh*-filler such as *The tall man saw Tom with my wife last night*. The gap as second resort hypothesis instead would predict that *Tom* would be the preferred object of *see* and should not be read slowly in the *wh*-question sentence.

The much-cited intuitive evidence, that one does not have repeated garden paths in sentences with multiple tempting gaps, such as *Who did Tom ask (—) Meg to persuade (—) Jill to inform (—) Ted that Bob had spoken to —?* (Fodor, 1978) appears to have led all of us astray. In fact, the more sensitive experimental evidence supports the active filler hypothesis: There *are* garden paths at the tempting gap positions.

---

[1] Experiments 1 and 2 were conducted in collaboration with Lyn Frazier. Experiments 3, 4, and 5 constitute a portion of Marica De Vincenzi's doctoral dissertation research.

Crain and Fodor (1985) were the first to have shown this, and Stowe (1986) has shown it also. These authors used word-by-word, self-paced reading tasks to show that a word like *us* is read slowly in a sentence like *My brother wanted to know who Ruth will bring (—) us home to — at Christmas* (Stowe, 1986), compared to sentences without *wh*-fillers like the word *who*.

We have collected similar data (see Frazier & Clifton, 1989, for a full report of the experiment summarized here). We had subjects read sentences like 2.

2a. Who did the housekeeper from Germany urge (—) the guests to consider —?

2b. The housekeeper from Germany urged the guests to consider the new chef.

Our readers used a self-paced, phrase-by-phrase reading procedure, which resulted in somewhat faster reading times per word than Stowe and Crain and Fodor have reported. Our results for the critical phrase following the possible gap position are summarized in Table 12.1. Although there were no differences in reading time between the sentence with a *wh*-filler and the nonfiller control sentence up through the verb *urge*, the critical phrase *the guests* was read slower in the sentence with a *wh*-filler than in the other sentence (992 vs. 770 ms). This difference persisted into the next segment (1265 vs. 932 ms) (not shown in Table 12.1). Such a finding is consistent with the claim that our readers first assigned the *wh*-filler as object of the verb *urge* and then had to reanalyze that assignment when the lexical phrase *the guests* appeared.

TABLE 12.1

Experiment 1: Self-Paced Reading Times (ms) for Lexical NP at Possible Gap Position.

Number of Clauses	Sentence Type	
	Wh-*question*	*Declarative Control*
One	992	770
Two	1122	775
Mean	1057	773

Source: Frazier and Clifton (1989).

This study manipulated whether or not a clause boundary intervened between the *wh*-filler and its gap position. No clause boundary intervened in the example already discussed. However, when it was changed into Example 3 (in which clause boundaries are indicated by square brackets):

3a. [Who did the housekeeper say [she urged the guests to consider?]]

3b. [The housekeeper said [she urged the guests to consider the new chef.]]

a clause boundary does intervene between the *wh*-filler and its gap. Clifton and Frazier (1989) speculated that in this case, the filler may become inactive, and the language-processing mechanism may revert to a gap as second resort strategy. If this is so, no difficulty should be seen in reading the phrase *the guests* when it occurs in a different clause from the *wh*-filler. It does not seem to be so, as can be seen by comparing the first and second lines of Table 12.1. Reading time for the lexical phrase was, if anything, dramatically slow in the two-clause questions, 1122 ms, whereas adding a second clause doesn't slow reading time in the declarative controls, 775 ms (resulting in an interaction which was statistically significant by subjects but not by items).

Readers certainly did not overlook the potential gap after the verb in the two-clause questions, as they should have if the filler had remained active only within its own clause. There are several possible accounts for the apparent exceptional slowness in the two-clause questions, compared to the declaratives. One account notes that some of our two-clause questions had another potential gap, after the matrix verb (say in 3a). This possible gap, though implausible in many of our sentences, may have garden pathed some readers. Another account emphasizes the fact that in current linguistic analyses the filler must be related through a complementizer position to a gap outside its own clause (Chomsky, 1977, 1981; cf. Frazier & Clifton, 1989). We return to this suggestion later.

One can raise objections to using the self-paced reading technique to support the active filler hypothesis. It may be (as Crain and Fodor suggested to us) that the technique of presenting each word or phrase one at a time, at a rather slow rate, may encourage the reader to attempt to treat the entire sentence up to the current item as a single complete constituent. This will result in the reader detecting filler-gap relations he or she would otherwise have overlooked, which would artificially provide support for the active filler hypothesis. Other techniques, however, have provided support without this qualification (e.g., the cross-modal priming technique; Clifton & Frazier, 1989; Swinney, Nicol, Frauenfelder, & Bresnan, 1987). We present later yet another source of evidence about the active filler hypothesis, using an end-of-sentence acceptability judgment task.

Experiment 2: Effects of Verb Subcategorization Preferences

The second experiment examined how the parser finds gaps in the direct object position of verbs that are generally used without a direct object, such as *whisper* or *move*. The active filler hypothesis claims that the parser, when it has identified a *wh*-filler, assigns high priority to finding a gap for the filler. Even if the potential gap is in a position where lexical subcategorization factors make a gap (or a lexical phrase) unlikely, the parser will at least entertain its existence. The gap as second resort hypothesis permits the parser to overlook the potential gap, and (in the lexical expectation hypothesis proposed by Fodor, 1978) even makes it likely that a gap after a verb that is not often used with an appropriate complement will be overlooked.

Frazier and Clifton (1989) completed several tests of this claim, with results that on balance offer strong support to the active filler hypothesis. They used a task previously shown (Clifton, Frazier, & Connine, 1984) to be sensitive to lexical subcategorization preference effects. In this task, a subject sees a sentence, word by word, at the rate of 300 ms/word, and at the end of the sentence, makes an acceptability judgment. Because subjects are pressured to make quick decisions, and to reject sentences that are unacceptable on any basis (ungrammaticality or anomaly), a large proportion of judgments of ungrammaticality are obtained when subjects find a sentence confusing. Further, the times to indicate that a sentence is acceptable tend to be slower when the sentence is confusing than when it is not.

Clifton et al. (1984) used the task to demonstrate that sentences which have a *wh*-gap after a verb whose most common usage is intransitive are harder to read than sentences which have a gap after a preferred-transitive verb (e.g., *I was impressed with what Tommy drove at the racetrack* is responded to more slowly, and rejected more often, than *I was impressed with what Tommy built at the racetrack*).[2] Similarly, sentences with no gap or lexical argument after a preferred-transitive verb are harder to read than similar sentences with a preferred-intransitive verb. These findings could either mean that readers use lexical subcategorization preferences to guide their postulation of phrases or that they use lexical information to filter and modify analyses independently built on the basis of phrase structure information (Frazier, 1987a; Frazier & Clifton, 1989).

Experiment 2 directly compared sentences with a *wh*-filler that have a true gap following a preferred-intransitive verb and sentences whose gap occurs only later. We have in mind sentences such as 4.

4a. What did your niece mutter – to Willy in the house?
4b. What did your niece mutter (–) to Willy about – in the house?

As verbs like *mutter* and the other verbs used in this experiment are generally used intransitively, the lexical expectation hypothesis predicts that the early gap in Example 4a would be overlooked. Therefore, the sentence with the late gap, 4b, would be more easily comprehended than the sentence with the early gap. The active filler hypothesis, on the other hand, denies this prediction: The early gap should be identified, and a

---

[2] Frazier and Clifton (1989) replicated this finding, using the same procedures that were used in Experiment 2, to be reported next.

sentence with an early gap should be comprehended easily. The active filler hypothesis, however, does not necessarily predict that the late gap sentence would be hard to comprehend. The word which takes the *wh*-filler as an argument in this case – "about" – obligatorily requires an argument, and this lack of ambiguity together with any tendency the preferred-intransitive verb has to filter out an object gap should make the late gap sentence easy to comprehend.

Experiment 2 had subjects read early-gap and late-gap sentences like 4 using an end-of-sentence acceptability task. Subjects also read similar sentences in which a clause boundary intervened between filler and gap, like Example 5, as a test of the possibility raised earlier that a filler would be active only within its own clause.

5a. [What did you think [your niece muttered – to Willy in the house]]?

5b. [What did you think [your niece muttered (–) to Willy about – in the house]]?

Subjects in Experiment 2 also read control sentences without *wh*-fillers. These sentences were *do*-questions, for example, *Did your niece mutter something to Willy in the house?* and *Did your niece mutter to Willy about something in the house?* Finally, Experiment 2 was replicated, presenting all sentences as *wh*-questions and eliminating the *do*-question controls.

TABLE 12.2

*Experiment 2: End of Sentence Comprehension Times (ms)
and Percentage Acceptable Judgments (in brackets).*

| Number of Clauses | Sentence Type | | | | Controls replication Wh-*question* | |
| | Wh-*question* | | Do-*question* | | | |
	Early Gap	Late Gap	Early Gap	Late Gap	Early Gap	Late Gap
One	967 (59%)	956 (62%)	1012 (65%)	1038 (66%)	957 (70%)	968 (68%)
Two	966 (46%)	929 (56%)	1021 (63%)	1031 (63%)	964 (49%)	976 (55%)

Source: Frazier and Clifton (1989).

The results, shown in Table 12.2, suggest that the lexical expectation hypothesis is wrong. Consider first the data for one-clause sentences. The advantage of late-gap sentences over early-gap sentences is very small, and thoroughly nonsignificant, both in terms of proportion *acceptable* responses (62% vs. 59%) and in terms of reaction times (956 vs.

967 ms). The replication resulted in an equally nonsignificant reversal of the direction of the apparent differences. This lack of any difference is consistent with the active filler hypothesis but not with the lexical expectation hypothesis.

In the analysis of two-clause sentences, we found the merest hint of difficulty specific to the early-gap sentences. Reaction times were nonsignificantly faster in the late gap than the early gap wh-question sentences (929 vs. 966 ms), and percentage of acceptable judgments non-significantly higher (56% vs. 46%). The response time (RT) difference disappeared in the replication (976 vs. 964 ms), whereas a difference in proportion acceptable remained but was still nonsignificant. In no case was the interaction between number of clauses and early versus late gap position significant. There appears to be very little reason to accept the suggestion that a filler is active only within its own clause.

Still, there was a clear and significant overall contrast between the one-clause and two-clause wh-questions: The latter were hard to under-stand, regardless of gap position. Considering early- and late-gap items together, our subjects made 61% acceptable judgments to the one-clause wh-questions but only 51% acceptable judgments to the two-clause wh-questions. No such difference was present for the do-questions, 65% versus 63%, resulting in a significant interaction between wh- and do-question and number of clauses. This difficulty for two-clause wh-filler sentences may have the same roots as the difficulty noted for the two-clause wh-filler sentences in Experiment 1. Again, we defer discussion until later.

COMPREHENDING ITALIAN SENTENCES

Experiment 3: Processing Wh-Words in Italian

Cross-linguistic study of sentence parsing is important for several reasons. One reason is the need to determine whether the principles identified in one language are truly principles of parsing or simply re-sponses a language user makes to the grammar of his or her language. Another reason is that different languages with different sentence struc-tures allow different tests of principles such as the one proposed in the active filler hypothesis (cf. Frazier, 1987b; Frazier & Flores d'Arcais, 1989).

De Vincenzi (1989) has studied the validity of the active filler hy-pothesis (and a generalization of it to be presented later, the minimal chain principle) in Italian. Experiment 3 relied on an ambiguity that exists in Italian but not in English. In Italian, the sequence wh-word Verb NP is ambiguous in that the wh-word can be subject and the NP object of the verb, or the wh-word can be object and the NP subject. Examples 6 and 7 (which include the English word-for-word glosses of the Italian sentences used in Experiment 3) illustrate the ambiguity.

6a. Chi / ha derubato / la banca / all'angolo / di via Fiume?
(Who robbed the bank at the corner of Fiume St?)

6b. Chi / ha derubato / il ladro / all'angolo / di via Fiume?
(Who robbed the thief at the corner of Fiume St?)

7a. Che cosa / ha spezzato / l'incantesimo/ mentre stavamo
chiaccherando / sedute nel parco?
(What broke the enchantment while we were chatting
sitting in the park?)

7b. Che cosa / ha spezzato / il giardiniere/ mentre stavamo
chiaccherando / sedute nel parco?
(What broke the gardener while we were chatting sitting in
the park?)

The (a) forms are most plausibly interpreted with the *wh*-word (*chi* or *che cosa*) as subject, whereas the (b) forms are interpreted with it as object.[3] If the *wh*-word is identified as an obligatory filler, and (following the active filler hypothesis) associated with an empty element in the first possible position in the phrase structure of the sentence, it will be initially taken as subject.[4] If later information in the sentence indicates that it must be (or most plausibly is) object, its analysis must be changed. This should result in processing difficulty for the (b) forms compared to the (a) forms.

The contrast between animate (*chi*) and inanimate (*che cosa*) *wh*-words permits us to begin testing the possibility that thematic preferences play a role in the processing of filler-gap dependencies (either by guiding the initial assignment of fillers to gaps or by facilitating the reanalysis of initial structurally based assignments; cf. Frazier, 1987a). If the parser recognizes that an animate word but generally not an inanimate word can be agent, it may be more likely to take an animate *wh*-word than an inanimate *wh*-word as agent and thus as subject. If so, the subject interpretation advantage will be greater for animate *wh*-words than for inanimate *wh*-words, so the difference between the (a) and the (b) forms will be greater for Example 6 than for Example 7.

We tested whether *wh*-words are assigned quickly to subject gaps using six pairs of sentences with animate *wh*-words like those in Example 6 and six pairs of sentences with inanimate *wh*-words like those in Example 7. Each sentence had two forms, which disambiguated it

---

[3] In some cases, the disambiguation was carried by selection restrictions (Chomsky, 1965). In other cases, the disambiguation was based simply on world knowledge.

[4] We assume that the parser must identify a preverbal NP position and interpret it as subject in these sentences. If the actual subject is postverbal, it must be analyzed as being moved from or otherwise dependent on the preverbal position. See Experiment 4 for further discussion, and Experiment 5 for a contrasting case. We also assume that the parser constructs an NP node immediately dominated by the Sentence node (i.e., the subject) when it identifies the verb, if not earlier when it identifies the *wh*-word.

using plausibility (together with number agreement in some cases) toward the subject and toward the object interpretation of the *wh*-phrase. Thirty-six college students at the University of Padova (Italy) read the sentences in a self-paced, phrase-by-phrase reading task, in which the sentences were divided into phrases as indicated by the "/" in Examples 6 and 7. Each sentence was followed by a true/false question, which tested the grammatical role of the *wh*-phrase.

The data appear in Table 12.3. These data are mean reading times for each segment, conditional upon the subject answering the question after the sentence correctly, and the proportion of correct answers to the questions.[5] The reading times for the critical disambiguating segment (segment 3) and for the following segment indicated a statistically

TABLE 12.3

Experiment 3: Self-Paced Reading Times (ms) for Critical Segments and Percentage Correct Answers to Questions, Wh-Word Sentences.

Condition	Segment [a]			Percentage Correct
	2	3	4	
Animate *wh*-subject	690	706	828	93%
Animate *wh*-object	698	1001	1044	66%
Inanimate *wh*-subject	658	844	979	93%
Inanimate *wh*-object	706	821	1023	83%

[a] Example sentence, segmented, in translation with number of segments as in Table:

/ Who / robbed / the bank / at the corner / of Fiume St?
 1   2   3   4   5

Source: De Vincenzi, 1989.

significant subject interpretation preference only for animate *wh*-words (*chi*) but not for inanimate animate *wh*-words. Accuracy on the yes-no test items after each sentence was consistently higher following subject

---

[5] The same pattern of results held for overall reading time, not conditional upon correct answers.

questions than following object questions for both animate and inanimate wh-words. The apparent difficulty of object extraction sentences with wh-words was larger for animate wh-words than for inanimate wh-words, but was significant in both at the .05 level or beyond.[6] The advantage of subject extraction over object extraction in Italian presents an interesting contrast with a result reported by Stowe (1986). Stowe found no positive evidence in a self-paced reading task that a wh-item was immediately assigned to an available subject position, whereas she did find such assignment to an available object position. Subjects were not slowed in reading an overt lexical item that appeared in subject position following a wh-word (as *Ruth* does in Example 8a), compared to the same word when it did not follow a wh-filler (as in Example 8b).

8a. My mother wanted to know who Ruth will bring home to Mom at Christmas.

8b. My mother wanted to know if Ruth will bring us home to Mom at Christmas.

8c. My mother wanted to know who Ruth will bring us home to at Christmas.

However, they were slowed when a lexical item (*us*) occurred in object position following a wh-filler, as in Example 8c. Our data show people read a postverbal subject NP slowly, indicating initial assignment of a wh-filler to subject position. We doubt that the difference is a profound difference between English and Italian. It is more likely that the difference comes from the fact that the disambiguating lexical NP occurs preverbally in English but postverbally in Italian. The occurrence of the verb between ambiguous filler and disambiguating NP in Italian gives more time for the reader to become committed to an initial analysis, as well as providing a possible semantic interpretation of the wh-word (cf. Stowe, 1986), either of which could result in larger reanalysis effects.

THE MINIMAL CHAIN PRINCIPLE

Recall that in Experiments 1 and 2 of the present chapter, readers had substantial difficulty comprehending English wh-sentences that had two clauses, far more than with two-clause non-wh-sentences. One way of understanding the difficulty is suggested by the standard linguistic analysis of long-distance movement (Chomsky, 1977, 1981), in which a single operation cannot relate a wh-phrase to an empty element at its

---

[6] De Vincenzi (1989) conducted a parallel study using wh-phrases rather than wh-words, and found that the subject interpretation advantage was reduced or eliminated. She proposed an account in terms of the structural differences between wh- words and wh-phrases (cf. Cinque, 1986), according to which only wh-words will serve as active fillers in Italian.

point of origin in a lower clause. Rather, on this analysis, the *wh*-phrase and empty element must be related in a two-step fashion, in which the *wh*-phrase is first related to the complementizer position (COMP) of the embedded clause, which in turn is related to the empty element position, as indicated in Example 9. On this assumption, the comprehension difficulty of the two-clause *wh*-filler sentences is simply a reflex of the grammatical complexity of the filler-gap dependency involved, in particular, the extra link seen in Example 9b. The contemporary linguistic notion of a chain (Chomsky, 1981), a set of co-indexed elements that share a theta role and case,[7] is useful in this context. A *wh*-filler is linked to its gap via a chain (an A-bar chain). Minimally, the chain has two members, filler and gap.

9a. Two-Member Chain (One-Clause Sentence)

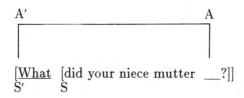

9b. Three-Member Chain (Two-Clause Sentence)

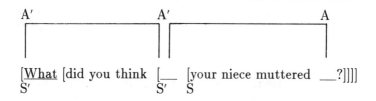

However, if a clause boundary intervenes between filler and gap, the chain must have a third member, in the COMP position of the embedded clause. We suggest that chains are sources of processing difficulty (presumably because forming each link of a chain requires computation to determine what is being linked), and specifically that the three-member chains required by our two-clause *wh*-sentences of Experiments 1 and 2 created processing difficulty relative to the two-member chains of the one-clause *wh*-sentences.

---

[7] CHAIN: set of co-indexed elements, bearing one and only one theta-role and one and only one case, where each element in the chain c-commands the next.

De Vincenzi (1988, 1989) has combined the active filler hypothesis with the claim that the parser avoids the apparently difficult act of building multi element chains, and formulated what she calls the *minimal chain principle*:

Avoid postulating unnecessary chain members at S-structure, but do not delay required chain members.

The second clause of this principle captures the core of the active filler hypothesis. When the parser identifies a *wh*-filler, it knows it has a chain and attempts to find the other end of the chain – the gap – as soon as possible. The first clause of the principle suggests that where a parse is ambiguous between a shorter and a longer chain, the parser will prefer the shorter chain. At the limit, this means that the parser will prefer to have no multiple-element chains at all.

Experiment 4: Inverted Subjects in Italian

De Vincenzi (1988, 1989) tested the minimal chain principle in Italian, capitalizing on an ambiguity not present in English. We summarize two of her experiments as Experiments 4 and 5. Experiment 4 studied the self-paced, phrase-by-phrase reading of sentences like 10:

10a. Ieri mattina/ ha chiamato il capoufficio/ per chiedergli/ un aumento/di stipendio.
   (Yesterday called the boss to ask-him a raise in pay.)
10b. Ieri mattina/ ha chiamato il capoufficio/ per offrirci/ un aumento/ di stipendio.
   (Yesterday called the boss to offer-us a raise in pay.)
10c. Ieri mattina/ ha telefonato il capoufficio/ per offrirci/ un aumento / di stipendio.
   (Yesterday telephoned the boss to offer-us a raise in pay.)

For most Italian readers, the rationale clause in Example 10a forces a reading in which *the boss* is the object of *called* and the matrix sentence has a null subject (pro). The rationale clause in Example 10b (and Example 10c, to be discussed later) forces the reading in which *the boss* is the subject, occurring in postverbal position. This latter reading requires a chain linking the postverbal position of the superficial subject with the preverbal position in which the verb assigns an argument to its subject, as can be seen in Figure 12.2. The former reading, which has a null subject, requires no chains (Figure 12.1).

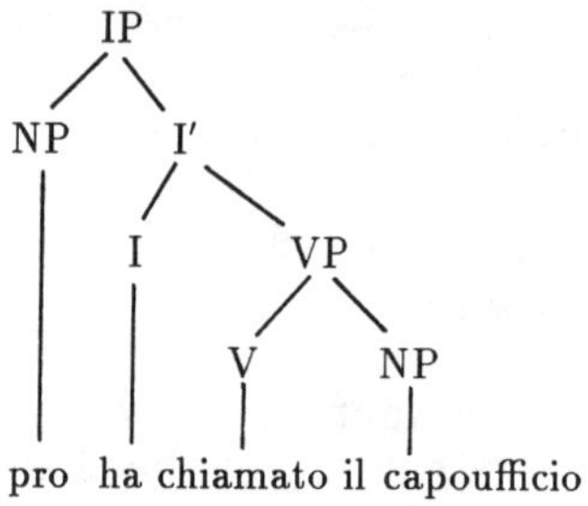

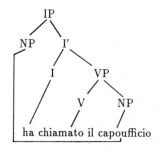

FIGURE 12.1. Diagram for null subject structure.

FIGURE 12.2. Diagram for inverted subject structure.

The minimal chain principle predicts that readers will initially prefer the null subject interpretation, and will revise it when the rationale clause pragmatically forces the inverted subject interpretation. This means that the disambiguating phrase (*per offrirci*) will be read slowly, compared to the case in which the disambiguating phrase is consistent with the initially preferred reading (*per chiedergli*).

This prediction was confirmed, as can be seen in Table 12.4, which presents the phrase-by-phrase reading times for sentences whose following questions were answered correctly (after eliminating the 15% of the subjects who systematically misunderstood the null subject sentences).[8]

The critical finding is that reading time for the disambiguating phrase was slower, 1047 versus 950 ms, when the phrase forced the inverted subject reading (which we predict to be unpreferred) than when it was consistent with the pro-subject reading (which we predict to be preferred). The difference between pro-subject and inverted-subject does not seem to be due to irrelevant differences between the disambiguating phrases. When an obligatorily intransitive verb, such as *telefonare* in Example 10c is substituted for the transitive *chiamare* of Examples 10a and 10b, eliminating the ambiguity of the postverbal NP, reading time

---

[8] This minority of subjects apparently refused to accept the null subject reading out of context – which is an intriguing observation, worth further study.

for the phrase *per offrirci* is found to be fast, 957 ms. This is as it should be, on the assumption that lexical subcategorization information is used quickly either to guide initial analyses or to filter them.[9]

TABLE 12.4

Experiment 4: Self-Paced Reading Times (ms) for Critical Segments and Percentage Correct Answers to Questions.

	Segment [a]			Percentage Correct
Condition	2	3	4	
Null subject, transitive verb (10a)	1102	950	798	66%
Inverted subject, transitive verb (10b)	1094	1047	778	72%
Inverted subject, intransitive verb (10c)	1124	957	761	93%

[a] Example sentence, segmented, in translation with segments numbered as in table:

Yesterday / called the boss / to ask - him / a raise / in pay.
　　1　　　　　2　　　　　　3　　　　　4　　　5

Source: De Vincenzi (1989).

Experiment 5: Ergative Verbs in Italian

The final experiment, Experiment 5, shows that postverbal subjects are not intrinsically hard. They are hard only when they require the postulation of a chain relating a lexical NP to an argument position. De Vincenzi (1988, 1989) assumed an analysis of Italian syntax (Belletti, 1988), illustrated in Figure 12.3, which claims that ergative verbs, like *venire* 'to come' take just one argument, in postverbal position, and their subjects get case from a postverbal position. Unergative intransitive verbs, like *esitare* 'to hesitate,' take just one argument, in preverbal

---

[9] The question of whether lexical subcategorization actually guides analysis or simply is a very effective source of information to filter and revise initial analyses is still open (Clifton et al., 1984; Frazier, 1987a; Mitchell, 1987). However, the present failure to find any slowing of reading time on the intransitive verb plus the postverbal NP, as compared to the transitive verb plus its NP, is suggestive evidence against Mitchell's claim (Mitchell, 1987; cf. Frazier, 1987b) that an initial analysis of verb plus direct object is made and then revised on the basis of subcategorization information.

position (see Figure 12.4). When a reader reads a sentence with a subject that follows an unergative verb, he or she will have to form a chain relating that subject to a preverbal subject position if the NP is to receive case and a theta role. However, if the subject follows an ergative verb, no chain need be formed; case and theta role, with the analysis we are assuming, are assigned in object position.

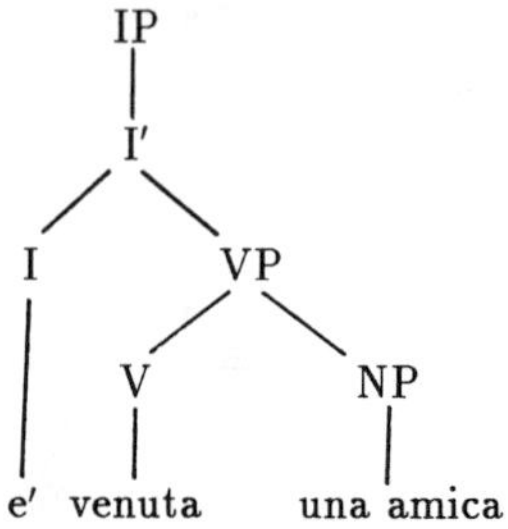

FIGURE 12.3. Diagram for ergative verb structure.

FIGURE 12.4. Diagram for unergative, inverted subject structure.

De Vincenzi had readers read sentences like 11. These sentences had ergative versus unergative verbs, and either had postverbal indefinite lexical subjects or null subjects.[10]

11a. Questa volta / è venuta una cara amica / ad aiutarci a traslocare.
      (This time a dear friend came to help us move.)
11b. Questa volta /ha esitato una cara amica / ad aiutarci a traslocare.
      (This time a dear friend hesitated to help us move.)
11c. Questa volta / è venuta / ad aiutarci a traslocare.
      (This time [she] came to help us move.)

---

[10] In the judgment of the second author, and her Italian informants, all these sentences are common, normal, acceptable sentences. (Perhaps this is less so for Example 11b, according to some native speakers, G. B. Flores d'Arcais, personal communication.)

11d. Questa volta / ha esitato / ad aiutarci a traslocare.
(This time [he/she/it] hesitated to help us move.)

Reading time should be slow for the sentences with unergative verbs compared to those with ergative verbs, at least in the inverted subject condition, because of the necessity of forming a chain in the unergative condition. This was the result, as can be seen in Table 12.5.

TABLE 12.5

Experiment 5: Self-Paced Reading Times (ms) for Critical Segments and Percentage Correct Answers to Questions.

Condition	Segment [a]			Percentage Correct
	2	3	4	
Inverted subject, Ergative verb (11a)	1043	894	893	98%
Inverted subject, Unergative verb (11b)	1300	925	881	88%
Null subject, Ergative verb (11c)	696	842	929	96%
Null subject, Unergative verb (11d)	822	872	916	95%

[a] Example sentence, segmented, in translation, with segments numbered as in table:

Yesterday / is arrived (a friend) / to greet / Luciana.
   1   2   3   4

Source: De Vincenzi (1989).

The sentences with ergative verbs were superior, in terms of time to read the relevant phrase, to the sentences with unergative verbs. The finding is not a simple reflection of some irrelevant difference between ergative and unergative verbs, because the superiority of ergatives became significantly smaller when no lexical subject was present. The finding provides support both for Belletti's analysis of the syntax of Italian ergatives and for De Vincenzi's minimal chain principle, which assumes that the parser prefers analyses that require chains of the smallest possible length.

CONCLUSIONS

We have argued that the parser prefers not to posit chains. We have further argued that if the parser is forced to posit a chain – as when it identifies a *wh*-filler in a nonargument position (in Italian, a *wh*-word filler) – it attempts to terminate the chain as quickly as possible. Both of these preferences reflect the operation of a parser that is designed to provide an analysis of a sentence as quickly as possible. If constructing chains is costly in terms of time and effort, analyses which contain no multiple-member chains will be constructed before analyses which contain a multiple-member chain, and therefore preferred over them. If a chain must be postulated, an analysis in which the chain can be terminated by assigning a filler to a gap can be made very quickly; the parser does not even have to wait and check whether a lexical item appears at the possible gap position. According to this perspective, sentences with fillers and gaps are not dealt with only when normal parsing, driven by lexical items that are present in the input, breaks down (Fodor, 1978; Wanner & Maratsos, 1978). Rather, they are parsed in a very efficient and natural fashion, following principles such as the minimal chain principle that are specifically adapted to permit the reader to deal with them easily.

ACKNOWLEDGMENT

The research reported here was supported by NIH grant HD 18708 to Charles Clifton and Lyn Frazier.

REFERENCES

Belletti, A. (1988). The case of unaccusatives. *Linguistic Inquiry, 19*, 1 - 34.

Chomsky, N. (1965). *Aspects of the theory of syntax.* Cambridge, MA: MIT Press.

Chomsky, N. (1977). On *wh*-movement. In P. W. Culicover, T. Wasow, & A. Akmajian (Eds.), *Formal syntax* (pp. 71 - 132). New York: Academic Press.

Chomsky, N. (1981). *Lectures on government and binding.* Dordrecht: Foris.

Cinque, G. (1986). Bare quantifiers, quantified NPs, and the notion of operator at S-structure. *Rivista di Grammatica Generativa, 11*, 33 - 63.

Clifton, C., Jr., & Frazier, L. (1989). Comprehending sentences with long-distance dependencies. In G. Carlson & M. Tanenhaus (Eds.), *Linguistic structure in language processing* (pp. 273 - 318). Dordrecht: Kluwer Academic.

Clifton, C., Jr., Frazier, L., & Connine, C. (1984). Lexical expectations in sentence comprehension. *Journal of Verbal Learning and Verbal Behavior, 23*, 696 - 708.

Clifton, C., Jr., & Odom, P. (1966). Similarity relations among certain English sentence constructions. *Psychological Monographs, 80*, No. 5 (Whole No. 613).

Crain, S., & Fodor, J. D. (1985). How can grammars help parsers? In D. Dowty, L. Karttunen, & A. Zwicky (Eds.), *Natural language parsing* (pp. 94 - 128). Cambridge: Cambridge University Press.

De Vincenzi, M. (1988). The minimal chain principle: A cross-linguistic study of syntactic parsing strategies. *Proceedings of the Tenth Annual Cognitive Science Society Conference* (pp. 559 - 565). Hillsdale, NJ: Lawrence Erlbaum Associates.

De Vincenzi, M. (1989). *Syntactic strategies in sentence parsing in Italian: The processing of empty elements.* Unpublished doctoral dissertation, University of Massachusetts, Amherst.

Fodor, J. D. (1978). Parsing strategies and constraints on transformations. *Linguistic Inquiry, 9*, 427 - 473.

Frazier, L. (1978). *On comprehending sentences: Syntactic parsing strategies.* Unpublished doctoral dissertation, University of Connecticut, Storrs.

Frazier, L. (1987a). Sentence processing: A tutorial review. In M. Coltheart (Ed.), *Attention and performance XII: The psychology of reading* (pp. 559 - 586). Hillsdale, NJ: Lawrence Erlbaum Associates.

Frazier, L. (1987b). Syntactic processing: Evidence from Dutch. *Natural Language and Linguistic Theory, 5*, 519 - 559.

Frazier, L., & Clifton, C., Jr. (1989). Successive cyclicity in the grammar and the parser. *Language and Cognitive Processes, 4*, 93 - 126.

Frazier, L., & Flores d'Arcais, G. B. (1989). Filler driven parsing: A study of gap filling in Dutch. *Journal of Memory and Language, 28*, 331 - 344.

Gough, P. B. (1965). Grammatical transformations and speed of understanding. *Journal of Verbal Learning and Verbal Behavior, 4*, 107 - 111.

Kimball, J. P. (1975). Predictive analysis and over-the-top parsing. In J. P. Kimball (Ed.), *Syntax and semantics 4* (pp. 155 - 179). New York: Academic Press.

Mehler, J. (1963). Some effects of grammatical transformations on the recall of English sentences. *Journal of Verbal Learning and Verbal Behavior, 2*, 250 - 262.

Miller, G. A. (1962). Some psychological studies of grammar. *American Psychologist, 17*, 748 - 762.

Mitchell, D.C. (1987). Lexical guidance in human parsing: Locus and processing characteristics. In M. Coltheart (Ed.), *Attention and performance XII: The psychology of reading* (pp. 601 - 618). Hillsdale, NJ: Lawrence Erlbaum Associates.

Stowe, L. A. (1986). Parsing wh-constructions: Evidence for on-line gap location. *Language and Cognitive Processes, 1*, 227 - 245.

Swinney, D., Nicol, N., Frauenfelder, U., & Bresnan, J. (1987, November). *The time course of co-indexation during sentence comprehension.* Paper presented at the meetings of the Psychonomic Society, Seattle.

Wanner, E., & Maratsos, M. (1978). An ATN approach to comprehension. In M. Halle, J. Bresnan, & G. A. Miller (Eds.), *Linguistic theory and psychological reality* (pp. 119 - 161). Cambridge, MA: MIT Press.

13 READING IN DIFFERENT LANGUAGES: IS THERE A UNIVERSAL MECHANISM FOR PARSING SENTENCES?

Don C. Mitchell
University of Exeter

Fernando Cuetos
University of Oviedo

Daniel Zagar
University of Dijon

INTRODUCTION

Across the world there are about 5,000 distinct languages and many more variations in dialect. *The Cambridge encyclopedia of language* (Crystal, 1987) gives brief details of about a thousand of these languages and more detailed surveys have been compiled by Voegelin and Voegelin (1977), Comrie (1981, 1987), Ruhlen (1987), and others.

A substantial minority of these languages can be written and printed and of these most can be read by at least the more educated members of their linguistic communities. This wealth and variety in written language presents a formidable problem for researchers concerned with developing a comprehensive account of the cognitive processes involved in reading. Whereas certain strategies may play an important role in a wide range of languages, there is always the possibility that some of the operations used in reading will turn out to be language-specific. This raises questions about the generality of any finding which emerges from research based on a single language or on a small group of languages. For instance we might discover little of general value about the reading process if we were to restrict our study to (say) relatively fixed-order, uninflected, alphabetic languages (like English), ignoring the vast number of other languages which happen to be constructed on different sets of principles. A genuinely comprehensive account of reading should have something to say about the processes entailed in reading a wide variety of different languages – not just one or two which are familiar in some of the richer countries of the world.

The problem of generalizing across languages emerges at all levels in the study of the reading process. Local or language-specific processes can potentially occur at the prelexical level of analysis and during word recognition, as well as during syntactic analysis and higher level aspects of textual processing. However, the implications are perhaps most serious in the process of parsing, because it is at the level of syntax that linguistic variation is arguably most marked. The world's languages display a rich and fascinating variety of conventions for coding syntactic information, and it is by no means self-evident that the mechanisms for decoding this information will be precisely the same from language to language. For this reason, the present chapter focuses on certain aspects of syntactic processing in different languages.

Before embarking on this discussion, it is perhaps worth stressing the importance of syntactic processing or parsing in the process of reading as a whole. For a start, it plays a crucial role in enabling readers to compute the appropriate relationships between the people or objects referred to in the sentence. In addition, contextual effects may in turn allow this information to play a part in word-recognition and other processes. Overall, its importance in reading for meaning is perhaps brought home most poignantly by the severe comprehension difficulties shown by agrammatic aphasic patients (see, e.g., Caplan, Baker, & Dehaut, 1985; Caramazza & Zurif, 1976).

In this chapter our approach to the issue of cross-linguistic effects in parsing is as follows. First, we give a brief overview of the work on parsing English. In doing this, we concentrate primarily on issues in which there is general consensus among different investigators. We then go on to consider the extent to which the parsers for other languages are likely to be equivalent to the mechanism used for English. Some characteristics seem likely to feature in most other systems, whereas others appear to depend upon relatively idiosyncratic grammatical details of the English language. After a brief review of the rather sparse cross-linguistic literature on this topic, we embark on a more detailed account of our own experiments on one particular aspect of the problem – the prevalence of the late closure parsing strategies in languages other than English. Finally, we discuss the viability of the notion that there is a universal human mechanism for parsing sentences.

OVERVIEW OF PARSING PROCEDURES IN ENGLISH

Over the last two decades there has been a considerable amount of work on English parsing and it is not possible to do justice to this work in a brief overview. For a more comprehensive account of this field, the reader is referred to recent reviews (e.g., Frazier, 1987a; Garnham, 1985; Mitchell, 1987a).

In general terms there are two kinds of computation that a parser has to perform. First, it has to categorize word strings in terms of preexisting structural categories or combinations of categories. Second, it has to establish appropriate dependency relationships between these units. Although there are major disagreements about how these processes are carried out, there is at the same time a good deal of consensus on certain basic issues.

For a start, it is clear that the structural description assigned to a sentence is influenced by the individual words within the sentences. It is also influenced by certain forms of punctuation that appear within the printed text (e.g., commas; Mitchell & Holmes, 1985). There is general agreement that the end-product of syntactic analysis is influenced by the detailed lexical properties of at least some of the words (e.g., the verbs; Clifton, Frazier, & Connine, 1984; Ford, Bresnan, & Kaplan, 1982; Mitchell & Holmes, 1985) and by the semantic or pragmatic context in which the constituent appears (Crain & Steedman, 1985; Rayner, Carlson, & Frazier, 1983; Tyler & Marslen-Wilson, 1977). At the time of writing, there is a fairly vigorous debate about whether these two factors influence early decisions in the parsing process or whether their effects are confined to the final stages (Altmann, 1988; Altmann & Steedman, 1988; Ferreira & Clifton, 1986; Ford & Dalrymple, 1988; Frazier, 1987a, 1988; Frazier, Clifton, & Randall, 1983; Holmes, 1987; Mitchell, 1987b). Parsing can clearly be influenced by the case, gender, and number markings of words other than verbs (e.g., the pronouns *she, her, him, his*; see Mitchell & Holmes, 1985, Type 1 sentences; *this* and *these*, Frazier & Rayner, 1987). However, marking and other similar linguistic devices have been submitted to very little investigation up to now – perhaps because they play a rather minor role in English. In addition to these lexical and contextual effects, it is quite obvious that structural assignments (e.g., cases) are influenced by the *order* in which words and constituents appear in sentences, and mechanisms for using such sequencing information are built into all theories of English parsing.

Historically, an important phenomenon within the study of parsing has been *garden-pathing* – the apparent tendency for readers and listeners to commit themselves to just one structural analysis at points in the sentence when two or more alternative interpretations are possible (i.e., at points of local structural ambiguity). According to some views (e.g., Frazier & Rayner, 1982), this commitment is more or less complete with all processing resources being assigned to a single analysis – leaving the alternatives entirely unexplored. Other theorists propose that the alternative analyses are actually pursued in parallel, albeit with heavy emphasis being placed on the preferred option (e.g., McClelland, 1987; Perfetti, this volume; Taraban & McClelland, this volume), and recently Frazier and Rayner (1987) have proposed that a complex mixture of strategies is used in different circumstances. Notwithstanding these differences of opinion about detailed questions of scheduling, there is general agreement that readers or listeners tend to show *uneven* commitment to the alternative interpretations where there is more than one potential analysis. One consequence of this is that it occasionally turns out that the structure most fully developed in the early stages of processing is one that turns out to be inappropriate. When this happens, the parser is forced to backtrack and reanalyze part of the input (on the first view) or to shift the computational emphasis from one analysis to another (on the second view) while an attempt is made to reconsider all the information which has been made available to the parser. Research over several years has shown that there are consistent patterns underlying the initial emphasis or commitment in parsing. Specifically, Frazier (1987a) has argued that the choices are usually made in such a way that they are consistent with one of two general strategies or principles: (a) *minimal attachment* – "Do not postulate any potentially unnecessary nodes" and (b) *late closure* – "attach new items into the . . . phrase or clause postulated most recently." Frazier's rationale for the prevalence of these strategies is outlined in the later section on attachment strategies.

In the broadest terms, then, the generalizations outlined in the last two paragraphs represent the major features of the parsing mechanism for English. It is conceivable that the parsers for all other languages share the same general properties, in which case we could claim to be discussing a truly universal set of procedures. However, this is a matter for empirical investigation, and in the next two sections we consider evidence that other parsers operate according to the same principles.

IS ENGLISH PARSING REPRESENTATIVE OF OTHER LANGUAGES?

In attempting to tackle this question, we are hampered by the relative paucity of information on parsing in languages other than English. Nevertheless, we attempt to consider the generality of the main features of the English system.

The Role of Agreement and Order Information

First, it seems self-evident that the parsing operations in any language must be influenced by the string of words and punctuation that make up the sentence under analysis. However, it does not follow that the outcome of syntactic analysis is necessarily driven by *all* aspects of the lexical information that can be recovered from the lexicon (e.g., by subcategorization and control properties of verbs or by the gender, number, or case markings for nouns). Moreover, if information of this kind *does* play a part in the process, it is not clear that its role will inevitably be the same as it is in English. The same observations apply to the potential effects of semantic or discourse context on syntactic analysis. Unfortunately, we know of no evidence either for contextual effects or for lexical-guidance effects in any language other than English. However, there is some evidence that parsing in at least one language (Spanish) is influenced by noun and pronoun markings. Cuetos and Mitchell (1988; Experiment IV) reported data suggesting that parsing processes were strongly influenced when potential gender mismatches were introduced into the material. This phenomenon has not yet been extensively investigated, and on present evidence it is an open question whether the processes used to handle gender are in any way compara-ble to the mechanisms that play the equivalent role in English. The range of items marked for gender in Spanish is much wider than it is in English (e.g., it includes articles and nouns as well as pronouns). The Spanish language therefore offers opportunities for gender-based parsing effects which do not exist in English. For example, there are numerous structures in which a Spanish reader will have to check for gender agreement whereas an English reader would have no correspond-ing processing commitments. Parsing effects with such materials have yet to be demonstrated empirically and until they have been properly investigated it is impossible to tell whether they would place any limi-tations on the generality of parsing mechanisms.

Turning to another aspect of the question, an important feature of the English parser is that its operations are directly controlled by the order in which its words and constituents appear in the sentence. Indeed, this feature is heavily exploited in the major formal systems for parsing English (e.g., augmented transition networks). There is good reason to believe that this emphasis on order information cannot be regarded as a universal property of parsers. MacWhinney, Bates, and Kliegl (1984) have shown that Italians pay little attention to order information when they are required to interpret sentences containing conflicting cues to syntactic structure. This argues against a universal stress on order cues. Similarly, it is inconceivable that parsers for free word-order languages like Finnish and Russian could perform their functions adequately if they were slavishly bound by the order in which the words appear. Instead, such parsers might be expected to make heavy use of case markers and other forms of inflection – none of which play an important part in English. As we point out later, these cross-linguistic differences in themselves would not necessarily rule out the possibility that there is a universal parsing mechanism. However, they do place some constraints on the kind of system such a mechanism might be.

Moving on to another well-established feature of English parsing, let us consider the strategies people use to process locally ambiguous material. We have already seen that English readers tend to show an uneven commitment to the alternative readings of such materials and that this leads to the phenomena referred to as garden-pathing and backtracking. Are structural choices of this kind treated in the same way in other languages? And do all languages therefore have similar procedures for backtracking and resuming processing when the initial decision turns out to be wrong? Again, there appears to be remarkably little evidence from languages other than English. Garden-path effects have been shown in Dutch (Frazier, 1987b) and in Spanish (Cuetos & Mitchell, 1988), indicating that at least in certain other languages there is an uneven commitment to alternative hypotheses at points of structural ambiguity. In such cases, it may be that the recovery procedures are also comparable with those employed in English. However, as before, it seems unlikely that this pattern of processing will turn out to be entirely general. Some languages (e.g., Basque) are so highly inflected that it is virtually impossible to produce locally ambiguous strings of words. It seems highly implausible that parsers for such languages will incorporate intricate and well-refined backtracking procedures that are genuinely comparable to those employed in languages where local structural ambiguity is endemic.

Finally, we turn to the question of the generality of the parsing strategies that are used to dictate the choices that are made when structural ambiguities do arise. This issue has recently been the subject of considerable debate and we therefore devote most of the rest of the chapter to it.

Are Attachment Strategies Universal?

In the discussion so far, we have concentrated primarily on the aspects of parsing concerned with assigning appropriate syntactic categories to strings of words and constituents. We now turn to the procedures used to link the various substructures within a sentence. We have already seen that a small number of simple perceptual strategies appear to play a central role in the parsing of English. It therefore seems reasonable to ask whether some of the more important strategies – particularly minimal attachment and late closure – make an equally important contribution to parsing processes in other languages. There is good reason to suggest they might. Frazier (1987a) has argued that strategies serve to improve readers' general processing efficiency by allowing people to take in new material as rapidly as possible and by enabling them to minimize the load imposed on short-term memory. Minimal attachment acts in such a way as to assign the simplest possible structure to a string of words, and as this is the configuration which is quickest and easiest to compute, the strategy ensures that processing is completed within the shortest possible time. Late closure guarantees that new constituents are immediately attached to an existing structure. This avoids the additional memory load which may otherwise be imposed when a constituent is held in isolation for a period of time before eventually being integrated with prior material.

According to Frazier's proposal, the prevalence of minimal attachment and late closure has little to do with the specific grammatical structure of English (or of any other language). Rather, these strategies predominate because they improve the general information-processing efficiency of the parser. For this reason, Frazier (1987a) has argued that we should "expect the minimal attachment and late closure strategies to be universal."

This is a bold and provocative conjecture, especially given the huge range of human languages alluded to in the opening paragraph of this chapter. As a modest step toward evaluating this proposal, two of us (Cuetos & Mitchell, 1988) recently carried out a series of experiments on the generality of one of the strategies (late closure) in a language other than English.

Experimental Evidence on the Use of Late Closure in Spanish

All of the experiments to be reported used materials in which a relative clause follows an NP incorporating a possessive phrase, as in Example 1:

1. Andrew had dinner yesterday with the niece of the teacher who belonged to the Communist party.

In sentences of this kind, there is some ambiguity about which individual is the agent of the relative clause (RC) (i.e., in this example, about who actually belonged to the Communist party). At a structural level, there are perhaps as many as four potential heads for the RC, although *dinner* can obviously be ruled out on semantic grounds. Late closure dictates that the RC should be attached to the "phrase or clause postulated most recently" (Frazier, 1987a). In this case this is the possessive phrase *of the teacher*, so the RC should be attached to *teacher* rather than *niece* or *Andrew*.

To confirm that this does indeed happen in English, we designed a questionnaire consisting of a number of sentences with a structure like Sentence 1, interwoven with a number of fillers with a variety of other structures, all of which contained one or more potential ambiguities. Each sentence was followed by a simple question (e.g., for Sentence 1: Who belonged to the Communist party?). The respondent was required to write a single word to indicate the answer. The results are shown in Table 13.1.

TABLE 13.1

English Informants: Percentage Judgments of the Head of the Ambiguous Relative Clause Following Early or Late Closure.

Early Closure (Attach to "niece")	Late Closure (Attach to "teacher")	Other or Indeterminate (Other attachment)
37.1	58.0	4.9

Overall, these results confirm that late closure predominates in English, though the substantial minority going in the other direction may raise questions about the generality of the strategy.[1]

Now, if late closure is universal, the same pattern of results should show up in other languages which employ similar possessive constructions. Spanish is one of several such languages. In fact, in Spanish literal translations of such sentences preserve the ambiguity of attachment, as in Example 2:

2.   Andrés cenó ayer con la sobrina del maestro que está en el partido comunista.

A questionnaire comparable to the English one yielded the pattern of results shown in Table 13.2.

TABLE 13.2

Spanish Informants: Percentage Judgments of the Head of the Ambiguous Relative Clause Following Early or Late Closure.

Early Closure (Attach to "sobrina")	Late Closure (Attach to "maestro")	Other or Indeterminate (Other attachment)
62.3	36.8	0.9

In other words, for Spanish subjects early closure[2] predominated over late closure. This bias was statistically reliable and clearly differs from the equally stable late closure effect for English subjects (see Cuetos & Mitchell, 1988, for further details).

In principle, a single counterexample is sufficient to show that the late closure strategy is not universal. Unfortunately, however, the question

---

[1] Frazier (this volume) and Clifton (1988) have recently carried out a similar test (in English) using sentences based on our materials. They obtained a slight bias in the opposite direction (i.e., in favor of *early* closure). The reason for the discrepancy between their results and ours is not entirely clear at the time of writing. However, we suspect that the details of their procedure may have highlighted the first potential head noun, thereby shifting the bias in the direction of high attachment. Specifically, in their questionnaire study, the probe question was always followed by the two alternative nouns with the first noun (almost) always typed above the second. It seems likely that this systematically biased prompt could have influenced the respondents' attachment decisions.

[2] The term *early closure* is used somewhat loosely here as the most obvious alternative to *late closure*. It refers to the attachment of the relative clause to the earlier noun rather than to the one immediately preceding the clause (i.e., to *sobrina* rather than to *maestro*).

cannot be resolved on the basis of questionnaire data alone. The late closure strategy only specifies the *initial* point of attachment for the ambiguous constituent. This leaves open the possibility that subjects followed the strategy faithfully on the first pass but then subsequently reassessed (and reversed) their decisions before eventually writing down their responses. The questionnaire data are suggestive, but an on-line experiment is needed to determine whether the early closure strategy predominates while the sentence is actually being read.

We carried out three experiments using a clause-by-clause, subject-paced reading task (see Cuetos & Mitchell, 1988, for procedural details). Over the different experiments, the main conditions were based on materials of the kind set out in Display 3. (The oblique line [/] marks the end of each display). In the main condition, 3a, we added an extra phrase to the basic form of the sentence used in the questionnaire study. In each case, the ambiguity in Display 2 was subsequently resolved in favor of late closure (or low attachment).[3]

3a. Alguien disparó contra el criado de la actriz / que estaba en el balcón / con su marido.

(Someone shot the male servant of the actress /who was on the balcony/ with her husband.)

In a second condition, 3b, the resolution was compatible with *either* late or early closure.

3b. Alguien disparó contra la criada ['female servant'] de la actriz/ que estaba en el balcón / con su marido.

Condition 3c was similar to 3a in that low attachment (late closure) yielded the correct reading. However, in this case the possessive phrase in Display 1 was replaced by a nonmodifying conjunction based on the same content words.

3c. Alguien disparó contra el criado y la actriz ['the male servant and the actress'] / que estaba en el balcón / con su marido.

Finally, there was an unambiguous control condition in which the possessive phrase was excluded altogether, as in Condition 3d.

3d. Alguien disparó contra la actriz / que estaba en el balcón / con su marido.

With materials of this kind, we set out to determine whether subjects initially follow the late closure strategy in Spanish. The final phrase of Condition 3d serves as a baseline, providing an indication of the reading time for the three test words in the absence of ambiguity (i.e., when

---

[3] The terms *high* and *low* refer to different attachment points on the parsing tree for the sentence. With a noun phrase like *the servant of the actress*, the noun *servant* is represented as being higher on the tree than the noun *actress*. Thus, a reader following the late closure strategy will select a *low* attachment point for the relative clause in the first instance.

there is no garden-pathing or backtracking involved). We argued that if the subjects made the "wrong" choice in the remaining (ambiguous) conditions, then the viewing time in the final display would be noticeably longer than that in the control condition. On the other hand, if the initial choice was *compatible* with the final outcome, then the response measure would not be elevated. The main results of the experiments are shown together in Table 13.3.

TABLE 13.3

Mean Reading Time (ms) for Each of the Three Displays of Sentences in Two Reading Experiments (Experiment III and Experiment IV) in Cuetos and Mitchell (1988).[a] (Numbers in parentheses refer to the example of the sentence-type given in the text.)

Experiment III

	Ambiguous	Nonmodifying Control
Display 2:		
Display 3 resolution:	LC/low (3a)	LC/low (3c)
Display 1	2623	2874
Display 2	1567	1595
Display 3	1701	1456

Experiment IV

	Unambiguous	Ambiguous	Ambiguous
Display 2:			
Display 3 resolution:	N/A (3d)	LC/low (3a)	Either (3b)
Display 1	2012	2526	2561
Display 2	1604	1552	1530
Display 3	1472	1689	1480

[a]Times are given separately for three conditions from Experiment III and two conditions from Experiment IV. A full explanation of the different conditions may be found in the main text.

The pattern of data is quite straightforward. The viewing time for Example 3 in the potentially ambiguous sentences was *not* elevated (relative to the unambiguous control) either when the conjunction *y* was used (as in 3c) or when *both* attachments were acceptable (as in 3b). This is consistent with the hypothesis that in these cases the subject made a single attachment which subsequently turned out to be compatible with the final phrase (i.e., low attachment to *actriz* in 3c and *either* low or high in 3b). In contrast with this, the viewing time was significantly *longer* with sentences like 3a when the final display dictated that the RC should end up being attached low, to the noun within the possessive phrase (i.e., to *actriz* and **not** to *criado*). This suggests, as expected, that subjects had to reverse their initial decisions on attachment.

Potential Interpretations of the Data

The current data provide clear evidence that at some point in the final display the subjects were forced to change their attachment points from high to low. As the initial attachment must have occurred before the readers reached the last display, the experimental results imply either that the early closure strategy is used during the first pass through the sentence or, alternatively, that an initial low attachment is quickly reversed before the end of the second display.

Frazier (this volume) argues for the second of these two interpretations of the data. In support of this view she has presented evidence that the second display of sentences like 4a (which is resolved in favor of low attachment) are read more quickly than the corresponding display of 4b (ultimately favoring high attachment).

4a. The doctor called in / the son of the pretty nurse who hurt herself.

4b. The doctor called in / the son of the pretty nurse who hurt himself.

On the working hypothesis that resolution is quicker when the initial and final choices are mutually consistent, Frazier (this volume) has suggested that this result can be taken as evidence that low attachment initially prevails in English. If we accept her premises and apply the same line of reasoning to the current data, it appears that we are obliged to draw the *opposite* conclusion for Spanish. For sentences where high attachment yielded an acceptable gender match (e.g., Example 3b), the viewing time for the final display was significantly *shorter* than that for sentences ultimately forcing low attachment (e.g., Example 3a). Thus, the application of Frazier's argument leaves our earlier conclusions unchanged – namely, that Spanish readers initially deviate from late closure when they deal with the structures and materials in the study. Before leaving this point it is perhaps worth noting that both Frazier's English data and our Spanish data are entirely compatible with our questionnaire findings because they demonstrated a low-attachment preference for English and a high-attachment preference for Spanish.

Further support for the view that early closure initially takes precedence in Spanish comes from comparisons between viewing time for the second display of sentences in the Spanish study (see Table 13.3). If the RC had initially been attached low (following late closure) and then reversed before the end of Display 2, then the viewing time for this display would have been longer in the potentially ambiguous conditions than in the unambiguous control. In fact, there was no significant difference. Indeed, if anything, the reading time in the unambiguous control condition (i.e., 1604 ms) was *longer* than any of the others.

Taken together the results suggest that high attachment (early closure) predominates right from the start in this particular Spanish construction. This pattern of preference could have come about in two different ways. It could be that early closure generally takes precedence in Spanish. Alternatively, it may be that late closure normally prevails and that the use of early closure here is simply a local exception to the general rule. In fact, it turns out that the first proposal can be ruled out without too much difficulty. Late closure seems to dominate in various other Spanish structures (see Cuetos & Mitchell, 1988). Thus, it seems that the particular construction used may somehow have encouraged readers to use a specially tailored strategy to select a head for the relative clause.

Why should this happen? The most obvious answer seems to be that the sequence [. . . N-possessive phrase-RC . . .] gets treated as if it were a structure in which the RC is unambiguously attached to the N. One possibility is that this sequence along with others like [. . . N-adj-RC . . .] are all categorised as structures of the form [. . . N-[modifying constituent]-RC . . .] and then treated according to conventions set up for this general structure. Now, in Spanish the vast majority of instances of this general category would be of the form [. . . N-adj-RC . . .]. Here, the noun is the only feasible head for the RC. If we assume that the strategy which evolves to handle the general form inherits the attachment preferences which are appropriate for the *adjective* subcategory, then the RC will always be attached to the first noun irrespective of the nature or content of the modifying constituent. In short, a special-purpose strategy of this kind might indeed prevail over the more general late closure strategy, but only in the very local circumstances outlined previously.

One attraction of this account is that it explains why there is less tendency to violate late closure in English, even though the surface structure of the sentence is identical to the Spanish form. In English, adjectives are used prenominally and so there would be no [. . . N-adj-RC . . .] structures to distort the attachments in the general category in favor of first-noun attachment. Thus, it may be that in most structures of the form [N-[modifying constituent]-RC . . .] the RC ends up being attached to a noun within the middle constituent. In short, on this proposal the general late closure strategy is abandoned because it is displaced by a specialized strategy produced by extensive contact with postnominal adjectival constructions.

From this it follows that comparable departures from late closure should occur in other languages in which the adjective typically follows the noun. Some confirmation of this comes from a recent questionnaire study carried out by one of us (DZ) at the University of Dijon. The results showed that, with the French equivalent of the sentence with the RC following a possessive phrase, 96% of the subjects violated the

Late Closure strategy. That is, the overwhelming majority of subjects indicated that they understood the RC to be attached to the first of the two nouns.

Clearly, several other languages would have to be tested before we could be at all confident in our generalization about early closure and adjective - noun order, but the present results are at least consistent with the conjecture. If the arguments outlined here are correct, and late closure is occasionally overridden by specialized local strategies, then it is impossible to maintain that the late closure is a truly universal strategy. The pattern of results found in English does not generalize to Spanish and may not apply more generally in other languages. On current evidence, then, it cannot be claimed that late closure predominates in *all* languages and in *all* linguistic structures. The implications of this are considered in the next section.

IS THERE A UNIVERSAL
HUMAN SENTENCE PARSING MECHANISM?

We are now almost ready to return to our original question. But before doing this it is necessary to give some consideration to the question of what would qualify as a universal parsing mechanism.

In computational terms a universal parser might be described broadly as a single program or routine that is capable of taking in strings of words in any language and using this input to compute an appropriate syntactic structure for the word sequence. To do this it would have to be capable of checking that the string conforms to the grammatical rules of the language in question. This means that there must be operations that allow the general parser to be specially configured to take account of the grammatical rules in each individual language. (Without such a facility it would not be possible to cope with numerous cross-linguistic differences such as the fact that in some languages [like English] the adjectives premodify the noun whereas others [e.g., Spanish and French] are based on postmodification.)

It would not be a trivial exercise to describe a system with this kind of flexibility. It would be necessary to devise a way in which a particular grammar could be fed into the general shell for the universal system, causing it to be reconfigured so that it could function smoothly as a parser for the language in question. However, let us leave aside for the moment the complexities of designing such a system and merely suppose that it is formally possible to do so. Assuming that it is, would a routine of this kind be an accurate description of the human sentence parsing mechanism?

A skeptic might point to some of the operations that do not appear to be universal and use this evidence to argue against the proposal. However, observations of this kind would only succeed in undermining the theory if it could be demonstrated that such variations could never emerge in different configurations of the general routine – and of course it would be very difficult to develop clear-cut arguments of this kind in the absence of a concrete and detailed specification of the hypothesized system. At the present stage of theorizing, the best we can do is to comment in general terms on each of the apparent language-specific effects referred to earlier in the chapter and attempt to assess whether they would undermine the proposition that there is a universal parser.

In order of mention these were: (a) variations in the extent to which agreement checking is called for in different languages; (b) differences in word and constituent order in well-formed sentences, and differences in the reliance on order information in different languages; (c) potential differences in garden-pathing across different languages; and (d) differences in parsing strategies.

First, a universal parser would probably not have much difficulty in accounting for cross-linguistic variations in the use of agreement matching. Where there are structures for which no overt agreement is required, it could be argued that a universal parser still carries out a test but that in these circumstances the conditions are merely met automatically. In other words, the parser might simply proceed with all of its routine checking operations even when it is dealing with a relatively uninflected language like English. Alternatively, there may be some mechanism by which the grammatical rules can be used to engage the checking operations when they are required and to disengage or switch them off when they are not. In short, cross-linguistic differences in agreement conventions need not necessarily present any difficulties for a universal parser.

Turning to differences in word and constituent order, it seems likely that this could be handled by the way in which the parser is configured by the grammars of individual languages. For example, it could be that alternative grammars cause different sets of rewrite rules (or structure-building operators) to be downloaded into the parser. As a result, languages with rules specifying that adjectives premodify nouns might readily classify the sequence [–adj–N–] as an NP and reject [–N–adj–] as ungrammatical, whereas postmodifying languages would do the reverse (using a different set of rules). Similarly, the results of studies with conflicting cues could be explained by assuming that the relative strength of different cues varies from language to language, and that this information comes to be represented more or less as if it were part of the grammar (but see MacWhinney, 1987, for alternative proposals). In making this suggestion we are conscious that we could be seen to be preserving the notion of universal parsing by interpreting all apparent cross-linguistic differences not as reflections of different parsing *mechanisms* but rather of differences in the *raw material* on which a standard device operates. We accept that this move can be questioned on the grounds that, in the absence of formal constraints on the specification of the grammar, there is a danger that it will become impossible to reject the hypothesis that there is a universal parsing mechanism. A full exploration of these issues would depend on a more detailed specification of the relative contribution of the parsing *mechanism* and its raw material (i.e., the grammar) in a system of this kind.

Next, we can move on very briefly to the suggestion that there might be cross-linguistic differences in the strategies people use for dealing with ambiguity. There is little justification for dwelling on this because such effects are only a matter of speculation at the time of writing. However, it is worth noting that if phenomena of this kind were to be demonstrated, this would represent a severe challenge to the notion of universal parsing. It is difficult to see how a truly universal mechanism could use different strategies to cope with ambiguity in different languages.

Finally, we return again to differences in parsing strategies. As discussed earlier, we are obliged to abandon the notion that at least one of the strategies (late closure) is entirely general. This has some implications for the way in which parsing theories should be formulated. It undermines the notion of universal parsing as set out by Frazier (1987a), as this proposal does not allow for the possibility that general procedures like late closure might be overridden or obscured in some way by locally applied, language-specific strategies of the kind suggested here. However, in itself, a restriction on the use of a strategy does not necessarily constitute evidence against the universality of the parsing mechanism as a whole. It is possible that the operation which determines the strength or salience of different strategies is driven by parameters or variables which can vary quite widely across languages. Thus, in the prepositional phrase structures discussed at length earlier, it may be that low attachment prevails in English because the salience of the relevant rule within the grammar is greater than that for the competing high-attachment rule. Equally, the reverse might be true in Spanish and French (for exactly the same reason). Rule-salience may be influenced by contact with related structures within the language (as suggested previously), but this does not mean that we have to postulate any changes in the hypothesized general-purpose parser – a device which uses such information to set its own processing agenda. Thus, we can preserve the notion of universal parsing provided that we weaken Frazier's (1987b) specification of the construct.

In summary, then, there do not seem to be any data which convincingly rule out the possibility that there is a universal parsing mechanism. Admittedly, it could be argued that the reason for this could be that the putative system has not been specified in enough detail here to allow it to be tested properly. It could transpire that some of the arguments outlined earlier would not turn out to be viable if an attempt were made to incorporate them into a more formal description of the parsing process. On current evidence, however, there does not seem to be any reason to dispute the proposal that there is a universal parsing mechanism for all languages – albeit one that is flexible enough to accommodate variability in parsing priorities.

If there is such a mechanism, then we are a long way from specifying how it works. In particular, we can say very little about how it would handle syntactic forms other than those which are prominent in English. A great deal of systematic cross-linguistic work will have to be carried out before we can tackle this question.

In the foregoing discussion, we have focused on grammar and syntactic processing and we have had little to say about the universality of operations at other levels in the process of reading for meaning. It would be surprising if the structural properties of different languages and writing systems did not yield language-specific effects at most other levels of processing. In this case, researchers will not be able to make confident statements about comprehension processes in reading until they have given serious attention to the relevant processes in a variety of languages other than English.

SUMMARY

Up to now the bulk of all work on the human sentence processing mechanism has been based on just one language – English. It is not clear whether the findings reflect the workings of a universal parsing mechanism or whether the principles and procedures identified up to now are tied to specific features of English. In this chapter, we compare these two views and consider how well they account for some of the major generalizations in the existing literature. We argue that whereas some of these generalizations could easily apply across a wide range of different languages, others are likely to be restricted to just a few languages. In particular, we present recent evidence that one of the perceptual strategies that appears to be fairly dominant in English (late closure) does not seem to prevail in certain structures in closely related languages (Spanish and French). Possible implications of such findings are discussed and we end by considering the viability of the proposition that there is a universal mechanism for parsing sentences.

ACKNOWLEDGMENTS

We are grateful to Chuck Clifton and Lyn Frazier for making available preliminary drafts of their reactions to our study. We also benefited from discussing some of the issues with them. However, it should be stressed that neither of them necessarily endorse all of the conclusions we have reached here.

REFERENCES

Altmann, G. (1988). Ambiguity, parsing strategies, and computational models. *Language and Cognitive Processes, 3*, 73 - 97.

Altmann, G., & Steedman, M. (1988). Interaction with context during human sentence processing. *Cognition, 30*, 191 - 238.

Caplan, D., Baker, C., & Dehaut, F. (1985). Syntactic determinants of sentence comprehension in aphasia. *Cognition, 21*, 117 - 175.

Caramazza, A., & Zurif, E. B. (1976). Dissociation of algorithmic and heuristic processes in language comprehension: Evidence from aphasia. *Brain and Language, 3*, 572 - 582.

Clifton, C., Jr. (1988). *Restrictions on late closure: Appearance and reality.* Paper presented at 6th Australian Language and Speech Conference, University of New South Wales, August 19 - 21.

Clifton, C., Jr., Frazier, L., & Connine, C. (1984). Lexical expectations in sentence comprehension. *Journal of Verbal Learning and Verbal Behavior, 23*, 696 - 708.

Comrie, B. (1981). *Language universals and linguistic typology.* Oxford: Blackwell.

Comrie, B. (1987). *The world's major languages.* London: Croom Helm.

Crain, S., & Steedman, M. (1985). On not being led up the garden-path: The use of context by the psychological syntax processor. In D. R. Dowty, L. Karttunen, & A. M. Zwicky (Eds.), *Natural language parsing: Psychological, computational, and theoretical perspectives* (pp. 320 - 358). Cambridge: Cambridge University Press.

Crystal, D. (1987). *The Cambridge encyclopedia of language.* Cambridge: Cambridge University Press.

Cuetos, F., & Mitchell, D. C. (1988). Cross-linguistic differences in parsing: Restrictions on the use of the Late Closure strategy in Spanish. *Cognition, 30*, 73 - 105.

Ferreira, F., & Clifton, C. (1986). The independence of syntactic processing. *Journal of Memory and Language, 25*, 348 - 368.

Ford, M., Bresnan, J., & Kaplan, R. M. (1982). A competence based theory of syntactic closure. In J. Bresnan (Ed.), *The mental representation of grammatical relations* (pp. 727 - 796). Cambridge, MA: MIT Press.

Ford, M., & Dalrymple, M. (1988). A note on some psychological evidence and alternative grammars. *Cognition, 29*, 63 - 71.

Frazier, L. (1987a). Sentence processing: A tutorial review. In M. Coltheart (Ed.), *Attention and performance XII: The psychology of reading* (pp. 559 - 586). Hillsdale, NJ: Lawrence Erlbaum Associates.

Frazier, L. (1987b). Syntactic processing: Evidence from Dutch. *Natural Language and Linguistic Theory, 5*, 519 - 559.

Frazier, L. (1989). Against lexical generation of syntax. In W. Marslen-Wilson (Ed.), *Lexical representation and process* (pp. 505 - 528). Cambridge, MA: MIT Press.

Frazier, L., Clifton, C., & Randall, J. (1983). Filling gaps: Decision principles and structure in sentence comprehension. *Cognition, 13*, 187 - 222.

Frazier, L., & Rayner, K. (1982). Making and correcting errors during sentence comprehension: Eye movements in the analysis of structurally ambiguous sentences. *Cognitive Psychology, 14*, 178 - 210.

Frazier, L., & Rayner, K. (1987). Resolution of syntactic category ambiguities: Eye movements in parsing lexically ambiguous sentences. *Journal of Memory and Language, 26*, 505 - 526.

Garnham, A. (1985). *Psycholinguistics: Central topics.* London: Methuen.

Holmes, V. M. (1987). Syntactic parsing: In search of the garden path. In M. Coltheart (Ed.), *Attention and performance XII: The psychology of reading* (pp. 587 - 599). Hillsdale, NJ: Lawrence Erlbaum Associates.

MacWhinney, B. (1987). Applying the competition model to bilingualism. *Applied Psycholinguistics, 8*, 315 - 327.

MacWhinney, B., Bates E., & Kliegl, R. (1984). Cue validity and sentence interpretation in English, German, and Italian. *Journal of Verbal Learning and Verbal Behavior, 23*, 127 - 150.

McClelland, J. L. (1987). The case for interactionism in language processing. In M. Coltheart (Ed.), *Attention and performance XII: The psychology of reading* (pp. 3 - 36). Hillsdale, NJ: Lawrence Erlbaum Associates.

Mitchell, D. C. (1987a). Lexical guidance in human parsing: Locus and processing characteristics. In M. Coltheart (Ed.), *Attention and performance XII: The psychology of reading* (pp. 601 - 618). Hillsdale, NJ: Lawrence Erlbaum Associates.

Mitchell, D. C. (1987b). Reading and syntactic analysis. In J. Beech & A. Colley (Eds.), *Cognitive approaches to reading* (pp. 87 - 112). Chichester: Wiley.

Mitchell, D. C., & Holmes, V. M. (1985). The role of specific information about the verb in parsing sentences with local structural ambiguity. *Journal of Memory and Language, 24*, 542 - 559.

Rayner, K., Carlson, M., & Frazier, L. (1983). The interaction of syntax and semantics during sentence processing: Eye movements in the analysis of semantically biased sentences. *Journal of Verbal Learning and Verbal Behavior, 22*, 358 - 374.

Ruhlen, M. (1987). *A guide to the world's languages: Vol. 1. Classification.* London: Edward Arnold.

Tyler, L. K. & Marslen-Wilson, W. D. (1977). The on-line effects of semantic context on syntactic processing. *Journal of Verbal Learning and Verbal Behavior, 16*, 683 - 692.

Voegelin, C. F. & Voegelin, F. M. (1977). *Classification and index of the world's languages* (Vol. 1). New York: Elsevier.

14 PARSING MODIFIERS: SPECIAL PURPOSE ROUTINES IN THE HUMAN SENTENCE PROCESSING MECHANISM?

Lyn Frazier

University of Massachusetts, Amherst

INTRODUCTION

Recently, there have been several studies which have been presented as counterexamples to the claim that the human sentence processing mechanism (HSPM) rapidly analyzes an input string of words using structural preference strategies to determine the outcome at choice points in the analysis. The studies have questioned the existence (or generality) of the late closure (Cuetos & Mitchell, 1988) and miminal attachment strategies (Abney, 1988; Smith, 1988; Speer, 1988; Speer, Foss, & Smith, 1986, Taraban & McClelland, 1988).

A variety of different issues are involved in any discussion of these studies, but what unites them is that they all involve the parsing of modifiers. To my knowledge, all other studies presenting claimed counterevidence to the miminal attachment and late closure strategies represent debates directly concerning the (non)interaction of lexical/discourse knowledge with purely structural knowledge (cf., Crain & Steedman, 1985; Ford, Bresnan, & Kaplan, 1982; Holmes, 1987, but also the discussions in Ferreira & Clifton, 1986; Frazier, in press; Mitchell, 1987).

A theory of sentence processing should attempt to identify general principles governing the analysis of sentences. The search for generality – within and across languages – will lead to a stronger theory, one capable of making predictions about new phenomena and capable of explaining already discovered generalizations. Of course, empirically it might turn out to be true that the HSPM adopts special-purpose processing routines that apply only to a particular construction or a particular processing situation, as argued by Cuetos and Mitchell. Presumably such routines, if they exist at all, are adopted in response to processing complexities associated with particular structural configurations or complexities arising from attempts to analyze such configurations using the general sentence processing routines. In short, we cannot exclude a priori the possibility of special-purpose routines. But the existence of such routines should be postulated only as a last resort, when required by robust empirical findings.

Though several solutions have been proposed for the problems concerning modifier attachment, in fact the alternatives do not hold up under close scrutiny, once the general problems faced by the HSPM are considered rather than just the problems posed by, say, prepositional phrase (PP) attachment. It is argued here that there are essentially two ways to handle the apparent counterexamples to fully general structural principles. One may assume special-purpose routines, or exceptions, apply to particular configurations involving modifiers. Alternatively, one may assume general principles apply in a modular processing system, which hides the subtle effects of minor syntactic misanalyses when they are not semantically confirmed (e.g., by thematic frame selection, cf., Clifton and Frazier, in preparation; Rayner, Carlson, & Frazier, 1983). The second option has the virtue of making stronger claims about the composition of the HSPM. It also predicts (in part) the relative complexity of revising different syntactic misanalyses. Finally, it is most consistent with the data, assuming a model of the HSPM is attempting to account for all relevant available data, not just the data from a single experiment.

PP ATTACHMENT

The empirical findings in question concern PP attachment (and one other structure discussed in the second section). Assuming the structures in Example 1 (see the following section for discussion), miminal attachment predicts Example 1a is preferred because this requires fewer nodes to be postulated.

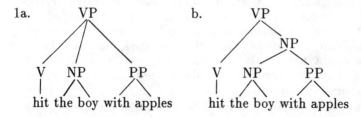

Experimental data from phoneme monitoring and self-paced reading studies fail to show a Miminal Attachment effect, at least when the preposition does not confirm or comport well with the Miminal Attachment structure (Smith, 1988 reporting data of Speer, Foss, & Smith, 1986, Speer, 1988; Taraban & McClelland, 1988). The question then is how to interpret these data? Smith (1988) proposed that the solution is to revise our assumptions about the structure of the complex noun phrase (NP) analysis shown in Example 1b (Taraban and McClelland also mention this option in passing). It is to this possibility that we turn first.

Grammatical Assumptions About the Structure of NP: Smith's Solution

Smith (1988) pointed out the well-known fact that semantically a common noun combines with its modifier before being combined with a specifier or determiner. This has often been taken as evidence in favor of the structure for complex NPs shown in Example 2, where a nominal constituent (N′) dominates the N and PP (or S′) on the assumption that a very tight syntax-semantics correspondence holds in the grammars of natural languages.

2.

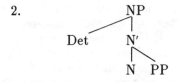

The problems with this assumption are threefold. First, purely syntactic arguments show that the structure in Example 1b must be at least one of the structures available in English. The reason is because of the existence of phrases like Example 3.

3.   The girl and the boy in the park.

Given the structure in Example 2, there is simply no place for the determiner *the* in the second NP. In other words, Example 2 predicts the PP may only appear below the level of the determiner, producing forms like *the girl and boy in the park*. As Example 3 does not require any special intonation break to interpret it as meaning that both the girl and the boy are in the park, it is ad hoc to argue that some deletion of a PP has taken place in the first of two conjoined NPs. Hence, it looks as if the structure in Example 4 is required in the grammar of English. Because the NP – PP structure is independently needed, the question is whether the N PP structure is too. It may well be. But notice now that the question for a theory of language processing is why the processor chooses a particular structure in a given circumstance (an issue to which we return).

4.

A second problem for the arguments in Smith (1988) stems from the implicit assumption that the semantic interpretation of the PP as a restrictive modifier of the common noun is only available when the PP, or other restrictive modifier (e.g., a restrictive relative clause), is attached at the level of N′. Cross-language facts suggest this strong generalization cannot be maintained. As Bach and Cooper (1978) showed several years ago, some languages (e.g., Hittite) *only* permit a relative clause at the end of the sentence (e.g., as in *The girls left who you met at the party.*). Such sentences can be semantically interpreted in an appropriate manner, despite the fact that the clause must combine with a noun phrase, not just a common noun. Hence, the assumption that the structure in Example 2 must be available in order to assign the appropriate semantic interpretation is not correct.

A third problem for the structure in Example 2 stems directly from parsing considerations. Given the structure in Example 2, a parsing theory containing a low attachment principle (late closure or right association, cf., Frazier, 1978, 1987; Kimball, 1973) will incorrectly predict that NP attachment is always preferred in cases of ambiguity (unless some principle is incorporated just to prevent this consequence). The reason is that the low (N′) attachment site will always be the lowest site available. Given that a low attachment (Late Closure) principle is independently required to account for other ambiguities (e.g., adverb attachment, conjunction preferences, complement clause vs. relative clause preferences) the structure in Example 2 makes all the wrong predictions *even* for the data Smith (1988) presented. It predicts counterfactually that NP attachments are faster than VP attachments. No general NP attachment preference has been found in any of the studies of the structure in Example 2 (Smith, 1988; Speer, 1988; Taraban & McClelland, 1988). In conclusion, simply assuming the existence of an obligatory N′ node in NPs doesn't solve the problem once we take ambiguities other than PP attachment into account and thus recognize the need for a low attachment principle.

Abney's Solution

Abney (1988) used intuitive evidence to argue for the principles in Example 5, which are applied in the order given.

5.   Abney principles
  a. Prefer θ–attachments over non-θ–attachments.
  b. Prefer attachment to verbs over attachment to nonverbs.

c. Prefer low attachment.

Principle 5a specifies that the option of parsing a phrase as a theta-marked constituted (θ–attachment) is preferred to interpretation as a non-theta-marked constituent (non-θ–attachment). He cited examples like those in 6 to support Principle 5a, for example.

6a. I saw a man with a telescope.
6b. I thought about his interest in the Volvo.
6c. The destruction of the city with a 20M-ton warhead.

The advantage of arguments (θ–attachments) over non-θ–attachments does not have to be stipulated, nor does the order of this principle with respect to other preference principles (cf., Frazier, in press). It follows automatically from the interplay of syntactic and thematic analysis. Miminal attachment will favor attachments that are appropriate for arguments and thus thematic analysis will confirm the first analysis only if the phrase does plausibly instantiate an argument listed in the thematic frame. Only θ–attachments will be confirmed by thematic frame selection because only arguments are specified in thematic frames.

Principle 5b will make the same predictions as minimal attachment in most cases including those discussed previously where recent experiments (Speer, 1988; Taraban & McClelland, 1988) have failed to find a significant VP-attachment preference. The problem with Principle 5b is that it fails to cover minimal attachment preferences in their full generality. For example, it fails to predict the preference for a postverbal noun phrase to be analyzed as the direct object of the verb rather than as the subject of a sentential complement (Frazier & Rayner, 1982; Rayner & Frazier, 1987).

Turning to Principle 5c, we have already seen evidence of the need for a low attachment (right association, or late closure) principle. The problem, however, is that this principle must be constrained by minimal attachment. Otherwise, it will incorrectly choose attachments that are low only due to the postulation of new and otherwise unnecessary nodes.[1]

---

[1] If low attachment is unconstrained by minimal attachment, then Example a is presumably preferred to Example b in the following Example, even at the point of initial attachment.

(i) Jill knew (that) at 7:30 Bill would arrive.

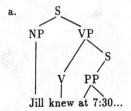

a.

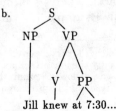

b.

Abney's solution involves apparently unnecessary stipulations (Principle 5a), it fails to cover the full set of cases where a structural preference has been documented (Principle 5b), and it leaves low attachment unconstrained by a minimal nodes principle (Principle 5c). But, limiting attention just to PP attachment and evaluating the proposal in terms of the output of the entire language comprehension system (including syntactic and thematic analysis), the proposal seems to be descriptively accurate in pointing to the importance of theta attachments – at least when the phrase attached plausibly instantiates the thematic role assigned. Abney explicitly claimed that the principles in Example 5 are syntactic, not semantic. In support of this claim, he presents examples like 7, where one is first aware of the silly or implausible interpretation of the phrase. But the examples showing an attachment preference that conflicts with semantic plausibility always involve a preference for low attachment of a nonargument, competing with an alternative nonargument analysis. In Abney's view, it is an accident that intuitive preferences favoring semantically implausible reading are restricted to situations involving a competing nonargument analysis. But in the view proposed here, this is just what we would expect: The θ–attachment preference doesn't result simply from the operation of an explicitly ordered within-module syntactic preference principle (as proposed by Abney), it results from automatic cross-module effects of selecting a thematic frame that confirms the structurally favored constituent structure.

7.   A gift to a boy in a box.

Semantically implausible θ–attachments will not be adopted because they will be quickly revised by θ–frame selection. But semantically implausible nonargument attachments will take longer to revise, because in this case (re)analysis is typically not determined by thematic frame selection. Thus, intuitions of an implausible nonargument analysis are possible because the reanalysis of this structure is not thematically guided and, therefore, is not as fast or automatic as reanalysis involving arguments.

Following Rayner et al. (1983), we may assume the most plausible thematic frame for a verb (or other head of phrase) is made available to the constituent structure processor. The selected frame supplies several types of information. First, a mismatch between the frame and the computed syntactic structure in the number or type of arguments (sisters to the head) will constitute an error signal, indicating that the first syntactic analysis is not particularly plausible. For example, the analysis in Example 1a will be confirmed only if the chosen thematic

---

[1] (cont.) Neither structure involves a theta attachment and both involve attachment into VP, so only the low attachment preference should apply. Since Example a permits the PP to attach lower (count the nodes from PP to the highest S, for example), presumably it should be preferred according to the principle in 5c.

frame for *hit* contains two internal arguments, one which can be instantiated by the NP *the boy* and one by the PP *with apples*. If the verb were, say, *wash*, then the analysis in Example 1a would be disconfirmed, because *apples*, though reasonable instruments for hitting, are not reasonable or expected instruments with which to wash boys. Second, the chosen thematic frame may guide the constituent structure processor to an alternative analysis, namely, one containing the number and type of arguments (sisters to the head) specified in the thematic frame. For example, given the string *wash the boy with apples*, choosing a frame for *wash* that contains an object (theme) but no instrument will indicate that only the NP, not the PP, is a sister to the verb. Third, during the thematic frame selection process, all phrases syntactically analyzed as sisters to a head will be evaluated for their plausibility as arguments of the head or as modifiers of an (immediately preceding) argument. We might assume that a phrase that is most plausibly interpreted as a modifier of an argument is labeled as such, for example, modifier of *x*. On this view, the syntactic processor will get considerable semantic help in sorting out the complement structure of phrases – likely arguments will be identified as well as plausible modifiers of those arguments. In sharp contrast to this, the analysis of an adjunct will not be semantically confirmed or disconfirmed by thematic frame selection, because adjuncts lie outside the domain of thematic frames. Hence, the benefits of an immediate error signal and semantic guidance of reanalysis that are automatically available to arguments simply from the evaluation of a lexical (thematic) frame are not likewise available for adjuncts or other phrases external to the last (potential) argument of a predicate. This difference will suffice to account for the relatively slow reanalysis evident in examples like 7 where *in a box* is neither an argument nor a modifier of the preceding phrase.

Taraban and McClelland's Solution

Taraban and McClelland (1988) presented evidence in a self-paced reading experiment showing that sentences semantically biased toward VP attachment take longer to read if the semantic bias is not confirmed by the continuation (i.e., if a following PP must be attached to NP rather than VP). And, crucially, sentences semantically biased toward NP attachment take longer to read if the semantic bias is not confirmed by the continuation. Counter to the predictions of minimal attachment, no significant effect of an advantage for VP attachments is observed independent of bias. To account for these effects, the investigators proposed that semantic information is assessed on a word-by-word basis and used to determine which analysis of the sentence is pursued (see Crain & Steedman, 1985, for a similar proposal). They dubbed this hypothesis content-driven processing.

There is no disagreement between the approach taken by these investigators and the structural approach with respect to the issue of ongoing semantic interpretation. That is, the idea of semantic processing proceeding immediately in parallel with syntactic analysis is proposed by both structural approaches (e.g., Rayner et al., 1983) and nonstructural approaches. What distinguishes the two views is: (a) the idea that *full* semantic interpretation of the consequences of each word takes place as each word is encountered (see Frazier & Rayner, in press, where evidence is presented in support of immediate partial interpretation); (b) that the semantic evaluation of each word occurs with respect to all possible syntactic continuations independent of whether the syntactic alternatives do or do not correspond to the analyses listed or fitting with alternative thematic frames of heads of phrases (cf., Rayner et al., 1983, for discussion), and (c) most crucial for the difference with respect to the particular issue under discussion, the idea that any semantic bias, however slight, determines on a word-by-word basis which constituent structure analysis is pursued.

To reiterate, Taraban and McClelland (1988) implied that their results are a consequence of the processor finding a bias favoring one analysis, and then pursuing that analysis. Hence, if the bias is not confirmed by subsequent items, longer reading times will result. No asymmetry is predicted favoring VP attachment. If we take the proposal seriously, it predicts, for example, that given a string like *I gave John a gift in* . . . we can simply find out whether subjects favor, say, a temporal or one of several locative interpretations of *in* for this particular context; perceivers should then be garden pathed in one of the two following sentences (8a and 8b), namely, whichever corresponds to the less preferred continuation. Intuitions do not support this prediction.

8a. I gave John a gift in March.
8b. I gave John a gift in Paris.

Perhaps there is a difficulty in parsing one of these sentences, but it just isn't large enough to be open to intuition. Alternatively, maybe Taraban and McClelland would want to argue that biases aren't immediately active but take a while to develop. But either approach to the problem of ubiquitous subtle biases favoring one analysis over another will have difficulty accounting for examples like 7, *A gift to a boy in a box.*

The impression of having analyzed this initially with *a boy in a box* corresponding to a constituent simply can't be explained on semantic grounds. Instead, it suggests when a new syntactic node must be introduced in order to achieve any analysis of a new phrase (resulting in two attachment possibilities which are equally minimal), low attachments are preferred. Only later is the semantic implausibility noted: It is noted slowly presumably because thematic frame selection does not drive the interpretation process in the case of adjuncts.

Further evidence militates against the view that processing is context-driven. Intuitions suggest that *Sally* is preferentially interpreted as patient in a phrase like Example 9a.

9a. Sally's adoption proceeded quite smoothly despite the inefficiency of the placement agency.

9b. Sally's adoption of the child proceeded quite smoothly despite the inefficiency of the placement agency.

If semantic information were used to assign an analysis on a word-by-word basis, a thematic misanalysis should occur in Example 9b, where *Sally* ultimately cannot be construed as patient, as this role ends up being instantiated by *the child*. But there is no evidence at all confirming the existence of such misanalyses (see Clifton, Seely, & Frazier, in preparation, for further discussion).

This observation is easily handled by the view that thematic frame selection is what is at stake. On this view, the processor evaluates the alternative thematic frames listed in lexical entries for heads of phrases, choosing the most plausible one. Under most circumstances, all potential arguments must be considered in order to compare alternatives. Hence, a thematic frame will be selected only at the point when the potential arguments of *adoption* have been received thereby eliminating any temptation to assign some thematic role to the specifier (*Sally*) which must be assigned to some subsequent argument (*child*).

To sum up, Taraban and McClelland's solution won't work in the general case. It predicts misanalyses for which there is no evidence (e.g., in Examples 8 and 9) and fails to account for the misanalyses that actually exist (e.g., Example 7). The HSPM is more richly structured than we are led to expect by the immediate semantic disposal view. The effect of semantics on sentence analysis is simply not as uniform or direct as the immediate semantic disposal hypothesis implies.

The Shape of the Problem

Before proceeding we should take note of several constraints on a possible solution to the PP attachment problem which have emerged from the preceding discussion. First, it should be clear that any solution will fail if it simply tries to prohibit minimal attachment from applying to PP attachment (see the earlier section on grammatical assumptions). The reason for this is that a low attachment principle (right association, late closure) is independently needed and it is minimal attachment which prevents overzealous application of that principle.

Second, the effects in question are continuously graded; they do not have the character of some special case where a new set of principles applies – principles that are not otherwise needed in a theory of language comprehension. The complexity of revising structural misanalyses is not an all or nothing effect. There are clear gradations in the difficulty of reanalyzing a structure, and gradations in the ease with which semantic biases influence the ambiguity. Examples range from the very difficult reduced relative analysis in *the horse raced past the barn fell* to the very easy to reanalyze PP attachment examples under consideration. Both types of examples are open to semantic factors in terms of ease of revision (e.g., see Carlson & Tanenhaus, in press, for discussion of open thematic roles in facilitating revision of reduced relatives). Further, a range of intermediate examples exists, where revision is more automatic and reliable than in the reduced relatives but more costly than PP attachment revision (e.g., direct object misanalyses as in *When Mary was mending the sock fell* . . . cf., Frazier & Rayner, 1982; Rayner & Frazier, 1987; Stowe, 1989; also conjunction misanalysis revisions, e.g., *John kissed Mary and her sister laughed*, Frazier, 1978; 1987).

What seems to *explain* the relative cost of these revisions and the ease with which semantic information influences this process seems to be general principles: Semantic information is available more quickly if its implicated in thematic frame selection than if it is not (see the section on a more general accounting of parsing modifiers); semantically confirmed decisions take longer to revise than semantically unconfirmed decisions (see Frazier, in press); and in a discourse context, reanalysis should be faster for modifiers of definite NPs than indefinite ones (cf. Crain & Steedman, 1985) because failure of the definite NP to refer will presumably serve as an additional error signal, speeding reanalysis.

I have suggested that the effect of general structural principles should be most open to the influence of semantics in the case of modifiers (of arguments) because semantic evaluation is required in order to choose an appropriate thematic frame for the verb (or other predicate). The consequence is that semantic information disfavoring the structurally preferred analysis, or semantic/pragmatic information favoring selection of an incompatible thematic frame, should lead to relatively automatic and presumably fast reanalysis of the first syntactic analysis because an alternative structural analysis follows almost directly from thematic labeling of a phrase as a modifier. (Indeed, the assumption that thematic frame evaluation entails modifier evaluation also explains the remarkable ability of agrammatic patients to comprehend correctly sentences that have been padded with PP modifiers, cf. Friederici & Frazier, in preparation; Schwartz, Linebarger, Saffran, & Pate, 1987.)

Given that we can explain why the predictions of very general structural principles should be most open to the influence of semantics and to automatic reanalysis in the case of modifiers (of arguments) – a matter we take up in the section on parsing modifiers – it seems at least reasonable to assume that the predicted VP attachment effect in V–NP–PP sequences is simply too subtle to be observed easily. No other solution to the PP attachment problem has been consistent with a general account of sentence processing. However, to pursue this line of reasoning we must return to questions about the structure of complex NPs and show why low attachment (late closure) does not apply in these cases.

The X-Max Solution

Major phrases obligatorily contain a head which must be of the same syntactic category as the phrase itself. The theory of phrase structure, X-bar theory (Chomsky, 1970; Jackendoff, 1977), captures this fact by viewing a phrase as a projection of its head. Thus, NP is the maximal projection of N, that is, N-max. VP is the maximal projection of the verb (V-max), and so forth. In some versions of X' theory, the number of bars or levels is fixed. For example, Jackendoff (1977) proposed a three-level system where X max is X-triple bar: X''' dominates the specifier and X''; X'' dominates X' and any restrictive modifiers; X' dominates the head (X) and its complements. On this view, every NP has three levels even if the phrase contains no specifier, modifier, or complement.

Rather than assuming a fixed bar level (i.e., that X-maximal always corresponds to a certain bar level), I simply assume that the only obligatory members of a phrase, that is, members required by X-bar theory, are the head and the maximal projection (X-max). Nodes intervening between X and X-max are required only if there is evidence requiring them to be postulated. Indeed, in some formalizations of linguistic theory (Lasnik & Kupin, 1977), the notion of immediate nonbranching self-domination is not defined. The theory simply doesn't distinguish "X-X-bar-X-max" from "X-X-max" when X-bar doesn't branch.

Given this view, a head of a phrase (e.g., noun) might be attached directly to X-max (e.g., N-max). Assuming all and only arguments appear as sister to the head of a phrase (X 0), two types of situations will constitute evidence requiring further articulation of a phrase. If a potential argument appears after the head, then N' must be postulated. If this phrase turns out to be a nonargument, then it must be sister to N' as only arguments may be sister to the head. In short, nonmaximal nodes dominating the head of a phrase will be postulated only when they are required in order to parse some input item according to the constraints of the grammar. The grammar itself does not in all cases require X to be dominated by X' and X''.

This assumption immediately solves the problem discussed earlier. Low attachment of the PP is not predicted to favor modifier interpretation of PPs for the simple reason that this requires a new node to be postulated regardless of whether the PP is attached to N-bar or N-max. So, as argued in Frazier (1978), low attachment will correctly be constrained by minimal attachment. (In fact, this was the problem with Kimball's right association principle: Unless constrained by minimal attachment, it incorrectly predicted a preference for low attachments even when they were nonminimal, cf., Frazier, 1978, Ch. 2.) Abney's proposal inherits the same problems, see discussion earlier and in Footnote 1.

In VP, phrases will initially be attached as a sister to V. However, in this case, there is no particular reason to assume a V' node is required. Arguments to the verb could be attached directly to V-max and remain sisters to V. Nonarguments must then attach as sisters to V-max, that is, adjoined to VP. In VP, attaching nonarguments (modifiers or adjuncts) outside V-max will not be problematic as the reference of the VP will not be affected. (Note in NP, a restrictive modifier must attach under a N-max to affect the reference of the phrase under the standard assumption that it is N-max which refers, not N' or N'').

To summarize, I have suggested that the processor does not enter optional (vertical) nodes into the phrase marker. Given a grammar which does not require, say, N' to be present, the parser's failure to postulate N' simply follows from minimal attachment, which specifies that nodes are postulated only when necessary. We assume an N' node will be necessary when a head noun appears with an internal argument, as in *the destruction of Rome.* As will be seen in Example 10, both late closure (low attachment) and minimal attachment guarantee that lower attachment, appropriate for arguments of the head N, will be preferred to higher attachment within the NP, which would be appropriate for modifiers.

If the analysis of the PP as an argument (sister to the head) is not grammatical or not semantically confirmed, then the PP will be reanalyzed, presumably as a restrictive modifier. If this analysis should also fail, presumably adjunction to the NP (as in Example 10d) will be necessary. This processing sequence is illustrated below Example 10, where the critical phrases are placed in sentence-initial position in order to exemplify the structures assumed for NP–PP independent of the ambiguities posed by their occurrence in postverbal position.

The minimal analysis of a determiner-common noun sequence is shown in Example 10a. The grammar does not require any additional nodes to be postulated and, therefore, no additional (nonbranching nominal) nodes are entered into the phrasemarker. When the PP is encountered in sentence initial position, it must be analyzed as a constituent of NP. Thus, the minimal attachment of the PP is that shown in Example 10b. If the N' were not postulated at this step, but instead the PP were incorporated as a daughter of N-max, hyperactive low attachment would result (in cases of ambiguity). In the sequence V–NP–PP the PP would always attach into the preceding NP by minimal attachment. Also, there would be no appropriate attachment site for modifiers (guaranteeing that they take scope over any arguments of the head).[2]

Eventually the PP may be expelled from the internal position (in Example 10b) because its argument status fails to be confirmed by thematic frame selection; in this case, because *girl* takes no arguments. Assuming

---

[2] Anything that takes scope over the head nominal must also take scope over its arguments. This is difficult to insure if the head and its arguments do not form a constituent. For example, (i) is ambiguous with respect to whether *unfair* is or is not under the scope of *second*. But on either reading we must interpret

(i) the second unfair assignment of chemistry problems

of chemistry problems under its scope. The phrase simply cannot be interpreted to mean that the second assignment of some problem was unfair and involved chemistry problems (though the first assignment did not involve chemistry problems). Notice that in several respects this argument is not parallel to that offered by Smith (1988). Her argument concerned modifiers and those constructions that ambiguously are or are not under the scope of the specifier. Here, what is at issue is the obligatory scope of arguments and how their argument status is to be recorded in the syntax.

only arguments can be sisters to the head of a phrase, this will constitute evidence that N″ must be postulated (i.e., some nominal projection dominating the head and its arguments, but dominated by the N-max). At this point, it doesn't matter if we represent the fact *girl* takes no arguments by labeling it N, dominated by N′, or just labeling it N′. To indicate that the consequence is only the claim that the head takes no internal arguments, I've annotated the head with a preceding zero (0) to emphasize what's at issue here is only the absence of any internal arguments of the head. However, at this point, Example 10c, if the analysis fails because, say, the common noun succeeds in referring without inclusion of the PP, then the PP may be analyzed as sister of X-max, indicated in Example 10d.[3]

The effect, then, is for the semantics (thematic/predicational and referential) to determine the within-phrase structure that is assigned after phrases and their heads have been identified and initially structured by constituent structure analysis.

Though this detailed analysis may appear complicated, this is more apparent than real. It results primarily from being explicit. Alternative accounts, say, Taraban and McClelland's, are considerably more complex (once their implications are made explicit) because they assume all of the analyses in Example 10 are constructed and semantically evaluated for every noun phrase *even* when the PP is truly an argument. Thus, the apparent simplicity of their proposal really rests on its vagueness, not any reduction in actual processing operations. Whether we discuss NP or S, the effect of (even temporarily) computing all structures or interpretations of a phrase under all conditions renders simple phrases as complicated to process as structurally more elaborate ones. The issues here are really no different than in the case of better studied ambiguities involving verbal arguments or clauses, with the exception that N in English rarely takes obligatory arguments and seldom takes multiple internal arguments (cf. Grimshaw, 1988).

---

[3] Though clearly related to the referential success principle of Crain and Steedman (1985), which favors referentially successful analyses of a sentence, note that the referential failure principle does not follow from that principle because both the restrictive and nonrestrictive interpretations may succeed in referring (indeed, to the same entities), the only difference being that the restrictive modification reading poses a slight violation of the brevity maxim (cf. Grice, 1968). In isolation Example a doesn't seem to permit the absolutive reading (illustrated in a″). But in a context providing a possible referent for *the students*, for example, following the sentence in (i), this reading seems at least marginally possible. See discussion in Altmann and Steedman (1988).

(i) Henrietta and Ginny are sick of being students now that most
     of their friends have dropped out.
     They never get to go to their friends' parties.
a.   The teachers pitied the students with a history exam tomorrow.
a′. With a history exam tomorrow, the teachers pitied the students.

10. A girl and a boy entered the room.
    The girl with a cough. . .

a.

b.
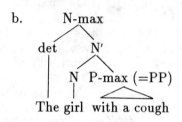

c.
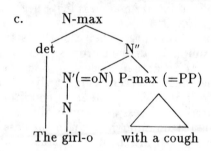

d.
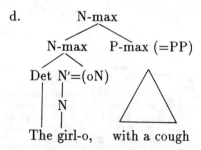

Taraban and McClelland might object to the claim that an account like theirs is more complex than the one proposed here. They might suggest, for example, that only the semantic operations of complementation, (restrictive) modification, and predication must be considered (on this account, regardless of whether the phrase is an argument or not), but the syntactic record of these operations need not be constructed.

Perhaps. But numerous problems immediately emerge. Briefly, a syntactic analysis will be required simply to identify the minimal phrases being evaluated, as well as their heads. Also, the preference-ranking of complementation, modification, and predication is not context-independent, as we see in the section on parsing modifiers (it apparently depends on whether the phrase potentially being modified is itself an argument or not). Further, simply considering these semantic operations for each phrase potentially within the complement of a verb would lead to ungrammatical analyses, for example, adjunct predications on nonfinal internal arguments (see the section on parsing modifiers). Finally, such an account would need to provide an explicit mechanism for avoiding analyses entailing crossed branches in a phrase marker (e.g., *my interest in a Volvo of yesterday with a steering wheel). Once an explicit solution is offered for these problems, I would be very surprised indeed if it turned out that any true (rather than apparent) computational savings accrued to this sort of alternative.

Summary

It has been argued that Smith's solution to PP attachment won't work because it incorrectly predicts hyperactive low attachments. Taraban and McClelland's solution has also been questioned on factual grounds: It incorrectly predicts semantic factors immediately choose *which* analysis to pursue; it also fails to explain why certain structures are more readily open to semantic influence than others (e.g., arguments vs. lower/higher attachments as a nonargument). Abney's (1988) solution is essentially correct descriptively (at least for PP attachment ambiguities), but it relies on unnecessary stipulations (of a θ-preference and its ordering with respect to other preference principles, Principle 5a) and only characterizes the final output of the entire system, not the principles underlying that output.

Instead of these solutions, I have suggested the processor postulates only required nodes, assuming that X′ theory requires only the presence of the head of a phrase (X) and its maximal projection (X-max). Immediate self-domination (e.g., X′ or X″) is possible, but these intervening nodes will be postulated only if there is evidence requiring their existence. This evidence will derive primarily from the requirements that all and only arguments are sisters to the head.

Our assumption that only required nodes are entered into the phrase marker prevents hyperactive low attachment of PPs and other modifiers. This proposal has been made in the context of a modular theory of processing where a separate thematic processor is responsible for choosing the most plausible thematic frame for heads of phrases (cf. Clifton & Frazier, in preparation; Frazier, in press; Rayner et al., 1983). Given this modular structure, the preference for argument assignments falls out as a consequence of thematic confirmation/nonconfirmation of a syntactic assignment (for VP attached arguments) and as a consequence of thematic frame selection (for ambiguous NP attached arguments). This view explains why apparent exceptions to structural preferences turn up only in particular cases like PP attachment: This simply describes the situation where an independently required aspect of semantic analysis (thematic frame selection) will fail to confirm the first constituent structure analysis. Thus, a thematic frame incompatible with the first syntactic analysis will be passed to the constituent structure module, resulting in revision that is fast, cheap, and semantically guided. We turn now to a case where the choice is between two alternative modifier analyses. We see here that the facts are quite different.

RELATIVE CLAUSE ATTACHMENT: A VIOLATION OF LATE CLOSURE?

Cuetos and Mitchell (1988) investigated the processing of potentially ambiguous Spanish sentences and argued that late closure, although it applies to some constructions or configurations in the language, does not apply to the particular configuration in Example 11. Instead, they found a preference for early closure (high attachment).

11. El periodista entrevisto a la hija del coronel que tuvo el accidente.
(The journalist interviewed the daughter of the colonel who had had an accident.)

In a self-paced reading time study, the structures in Example 12 were investigated. Reading time for the final frame of Example 12a was longer than for Example 12b or Example 12c. The structures involved are illustrated in Example 13.[4]

12a. Pedro miraba el libro de la chica / que estaba en el salon / viendo la tele.
(Peter was looking at the book of the girl who-that was in the living room watching tv.)
12b. Pedro miraba la chica / . . .
(Peter was looking at the girl / . . .)
12c. Pedro miraba el libro y la chica / . . .
(Peter was looking at the book and the girl / . . .)

Assuming the relative clause is attached low, the circled node in Example 13 will be postulated and the S' incorporated as indicated. At least this is what closure predicts. (We ignore here independent effects

---

[4] In Spanish, *de* is the form used for both *of* and *from*. Given the ambiguity, we expect low attachment of the *de* phrase as an argument to be preferred initially. Imagine, however, that a clear modifying phrase warrants postulation of N″ as sister to the determiner. attachment of a *second* modifier to that same N″-node would be preferred, by minimal attachment, over a low attachment necessitating a *new* N″-node to be constructed – if the grammar permitted N″ to dominate more than one modifier. I will tentatively assume the grammar does not permit this.

of parallelism, which are known to influence the preferred analysis of conjoined structures.) Instead, reading the final frame of sentences containing Example 12a took longer than the final frame of forms containing Example 12b or Example 12c.

13.   a.

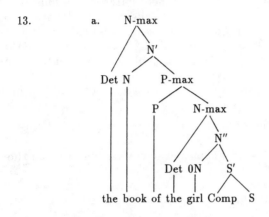

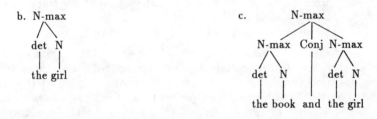

Cuetos and Mitchell pointed out that late closure must independently be assumed to apply in Spanish. Thus, the preference for N1 to be the head in Example 13a poses two problems: one concerning within language variation and one concerning cross-language variation. It suggests some special purpose routine may be at work in Spanish in parsing this structure. Cuetos and Mitchell also implied that demonstrating an exception to late closure in Spanish would suggest the strategy cannot be universal. However, given that they assume the strategy applies in Spanish, it appears that the possible existence of a special purpose routine in the HSPM is what is really at issue, not the universality of the strategy.

In the following discussion, several experiments are summarized, all of them conducted with Chuck Clifton. The first experiments demonstrate that in interpreting the structure 13a an N1 preference exists in English as well as in Spanish. They also indicate the existence of several additional factors influencing the interpretation of this structure.

Subsequent experiments explore the basis for the N1 preference and the factors influencing it.

The Phenomenon

Twenty-four ambiguous sentences were constructed based on the English equivalents of the Cuetos and Mitchell materials, as illustrated in Example 14. Several factors were varied: whether the NP appeared in object position (as in 14a, 14b and Cuetos & Mitchell's materials) or subject position 14c, 14d; the identity of the preposition – whether it was *of* (as in Cuetos & Mitchell) or had content, for example, *near* in 14b, 14d. The animacy of the NPs and the identity of the relative pronoun (*who* vs. *that* vs. *which*) was also varied, as exemplified in 14e, 14f. See Clifton (1988) for details.

14a. Someone shot the servant of the actress who was on the balcony.

14b. Someone shot the servant near the actress who was on the balcony.

14c. The servant of the actress who was on the balcony was shot.

14d. The servant near the actress who was on the balcony was shot.

14e. The suitcase of the student that was on the terrace was photographed by the detective.

14f. The detective photographed the suitcase of the student that was on the terrace.

Written test forms containing the experimental sentences (followed by a question inquiring about the identity of the head of the relative) were given to 38 subjects. The proportion of N1 responses to total responses (N1 + N2) ranged from 33% to 75%, being lowest when the animacy of the two noun phrases was equated and a lexical preposition was present, and highest when N1 was inanimate, the preposition was the case marker *of*, and the relative pronoun was *which*. The effect of the preposition (*of* vs. a preposition with lexical content) was highly significant: More N1 responses were given with *of* than with other prepositions. Also, when the relative pronoun was *which* or *that*, more N1 responses were given when N1 was nonhuman or inanimate than when it was human/animate. The effect of subject versus object position was thoroughly nonsignificant in all analyses. In short, in sentences comparable to those of Cuetos and Mitchell, an N1 preference is also observed in English. This finding is important because it suggests that – whatever its correct explanation may be – the problematic structure uncovered by Cuetos and Mitchell is somehow special in English as well as in Spanish. This in turn implies that the question at issue here is not whether strategies like late closure are universal or motivated by processing/memory efficiency considerations; instead, the issue is whether, within any given language, special purpose processing routines can be adopted.

In essence, there are two possibilities, assuming (as before) that late closure is the appropriate description of the low attachment preference. One is that the HSPM does permit exceptions, for example, Cuetos and Mitchell might assume the parser (minimally) attaches a new phrase into the current phrase except when the current phrase restricts the interpretation of a common noun. The second possibility is that some independent factor overrides or disguises the operation of late closure. Intuitively, there is such a factor. In general, the information contained in a sentence is assumed to be relevant to the sentence and discourse at hand, preferably relevant to the main assertion. In *I interviewed the daughter of the colonel . . .*, the main assertion is that x (the speaker) interviewed y (the daughter of the colonel). Hence, if a following phrase could be relevant either to y or to some other individual (not x), then we might expect a preference for the phrase to be construed with y. This *relativized relevance principle* might be cast as follows:

> Other things being equal (e.g., all interpretations are grammatical, informative, and appropriate to discourse), preferentially construe a phrase as being relevant to the main assertion of the current sentence.

The relevance principle is difficult to evaluate. It does make one prediction however. If a phrase were to modify *the colonel* (in the earlier example) but still remain relevant to y (the daughter) then the relevance principle should no longer strongly favor construing the phrase with y (the daughter) versus the colonel. Of course, there is just such a circumstance, namely, when the perceiver doesn't know who either the daughter or the colonel is without further description. Thus, by adding further identificational information to the relative clause, we might expect to reduce the pressure for the relative to modify y (the head noun of the N-of-PP phrase). Consider Example 15a for example.

15a. Julie met the friend of the man who reads news on *Saturday Night Live.*

15b. Julie met the friend of the man who was in the living room.

The sentences tested by Cuetos and Mitchell systematically had uninformative (highest) clauses in the relative (in frame two) to maintain the ambiguity between the two possible attachment sites. That is, the perceiver had to add (more) unmotivated assumptions to an implicit discourse model to imagine a situation where the relative clause could be used identificationally. Most of the materials contained locatives like that in Example 15b. The final frame of their sentences then confirmed the N2 attachment site. Descriptively, we refer to relatives like Example 15a as attributive and to those like Example 15b as locative, simply for purposes of exposition. The question is whether increasing the information conveyed by the relative that could be used to pick out a certain individual promotes the referential interpretation of the relative, rendering the analysis of the sentence consistent with the relevance principle even if the relative modifies *the colonel*, that is, some entity not mentioned in the main assertion. Nonreferential or predicational uses of the relative, where it does not identify a referent but predicates information about the head, should be most subject to the dictates of the relevance principle, because there is no loophole in this case: The only way to be relevant to the main assertion is to be directly predicated of y itself.

To test this prediction, sentences like those in Example 15 were tested in a questionnaire study. Relative clauses with simple NP heads were included as controls (e.g., *Julie met the friend who . . .*). After each sentence, subjects were asked a question like "Who reads the news on *Saturday Night Live?*". Though the effect was not huge, as expected, the proportion of N1 responses (early closure responses) was higher for locatives (70% vs. 30%) than for attributives (59% vs. 41%) in accord with the prediction derived from the relevance principle.

Reading times for the relative clause in a self-paced reading study merely showed that ambiguous sentence forms (those following N of PP structures) took longer to read than the unambiguous forms, for both locatives and attributives (and, attributives took longer than locatives, presumably because they were longer and more informative). This study thus encourages the view that a countervailing pressure, the relevance principle, disguises the effect of late closure in the structures under discussion.

The question now is whether the relevance principle governs the first attachment of the relative clause, in violation of late closure. Alternatively, late closure may in fact govern the initial attachment of the relative clause, but then the relevance principle may cause the processor to revise its first analysis, in an attempt to find the most appropriate interpretation of the sentence, that is, the interpretation consistent with Gricean constraints in general and the relevance principle in particular. The finding by Cuetos and Mitchell does not really address this question as a mild violation of a discourse constraint like the relevance principle may exhibit different effects depending on whether the sentence is grammatically unambiguous or whether it is open to more than one interpretation. In their materials, the experimental sentences were grammatically ambiguous but disambiguated by pragmatic information. The short controls were entirely unambiguous and the conjunction controls were disambiguated by subject-verb number agreement. Thus, one interpretation of Cuetos and Mitchell's results is that late closure did govern the attachment of the relative clause in all of the relative clause sentences they used. But at some point, presumably around the end of the ambiguous frame (e.g., *who was on the balcony*), the relevance principle caused a reanalysis of the ambiguous structures.[5] This analysis was

---

[5] Mitchell (personal communication) points out that the reading time on the medial frame does not differ for the ambiguous 13a, unambiguous 13b, and temporarily ambiguous 13c forms. If the ambiguous form were reanalyzed in the medial frame we might have expected a difference to appear in the associated reading times. But it is quite possible that reanalysis which is not prompted by any particular word or region of the sentence can be spread out over more than one local region. Hence, the technique used may not be appropriate for detecting this sort of reanalysis.

then incompatible with the final frame of the experimental sentences.

To test whether late closure governs the initial attachment of the relative clause, we must thus find temporarily ambiguous structures that are syntactically disambiguated. The syntactic disambiguation should prevent the relevance principle from disguising any effect of an early versus late closure preference in the attachment of the relative clause. Sentences like 16 were used for this test in a self-paced reading time experiment.

16a. The doctor called in/the son of the pretty nurse who hurt herself.
16b. The doctor called in/the son of the pretty nurse who hurt himself.
16c. Anthony hated/the boy with the pretty student who was purposely drawing attention to herself.
16d. Anthony hated/the boy with the pretty student who was purposely drawing attention to himself.

If late closure is followed, the a and c sentence forms should be read most quickly as the gender of the reflexive confirms the late closure structure. However, if early closure is followed, resulting in high attachment of the relative, then the b and d forms should be read quickly (as implied by Cuetos & Mitchell's account). The other possibility is that the processor either delays making a commitment or pursues both analyses simultaneously. In this case, no difference should emerge between the N1 and N2 sentence forms.

What we found was that N2 (late closure) forms (a, c) were read more quickly than their N1 (early closure) counterparts (b, d). This supports the view that late closure does operate here, as elsewhere in the language.

To summarize, the N of PP structure exhibits apparent violations of late closure in English, like in Spanish. But response time data in unambiguous English sentences show a response time advantage for the late closure sentence forms, suggesting that early closure interpretations result from a reanalysis process (presumably because of the relevance principle).

Before leaving this section, it should be noted that the hypothesis pursued here predicts that Spanish should be processed in accord with the same principles as English. That is, late closure would be expected to govern the initial attachment of relative clauses (as it apparently does, given the conjunction data from Cuetos & Mitchell).[6] However,

---

[6] The data from Cuetos and Mitchell argue for a low attachment preference given that reading the medial frame of the temporarily ambiguous conjoined NP structure in Example 12c took no longer than in the fully unambiguous form in Example 12b. If the relative clause were attached high, as predicted by early closure, the number marking on the verb (singular) would be incompatible with its subject, requiring the high attachment to be revised. As no reanalysis effect is observed, it appears late closure is governing the attachment of the relative in examples like 12c.

the effect of late closure in Spanish may be somewhat different from its effect in English if there are any relevant differences between the grammars of the two languages. One obvious difference is that in Spanish the meaning conveyed by the early closure (high attachment) structure cannot be conveyed by any alternative grammatical structure, unlike in English. That is, in English there is a possessive construction available which permits the head noun to be unambiguously modified: *the colonel's daughter who was on the balcony*. To my knowledge, no comparable construction exists in Spanish. The absence of any alternative means for expressing this meaning may well have the effect of strengthening the early closure preference in Spanish. Put differently, in English use of N1 of N2 *who* (= N1) may to some degree violate the conversational maxim of clarity (Be clear): The speaker would have to choose to convey a meaning with an ambiguous structure when an equally simple unambiguous alternative structure is available in the grammar. By contrast, in Spanish the speaker has no structurally provided alternative permitted by the grammar, and thus use of the ambiguous structure will not violate the Gricean maxim of clarity.

IN SEARCH OF A MORE GENERAL ACCOUNT OF PARSING MODIFIERS

A theory of parsing modifiers must account for (at least) the following phenomena:

1. The first analysis of an NP which is detected intuitively is not necessarily the semantically most plausible one (*a gift to a boy in a box*, cf. Abney, 1988).

2. Low attachment preferences are observed in NPs, but low attachment (late closure) would overapply if it were not constrained by a minimal nodes principle (minimal attachment). For example, it would incorrectly predict systematic NP attachment in all V NP PP structures, including *saw the man with binoculars* (cf. Speer, 1988; Taraban & McClelland, 1988).

3. PP attachments in V NP PP structures are elusive, not giving rise to large robust reanalysis effects, though numerical tendencies in the right direction often exist, for example, in Taraban and McClelland (1988).

Though less clearly established, (4) has also received some support:

4. High attachment of an argument seems to be easier than high attachment (reanalysis) of a nonargument (e.g., *a gift of books to a boy* vs. *a gift to a boy in a box*; assuming, perhaps incorrectly, that *to a boy* is an argument but *in a box* is not).

To account for these findings, it was assumed nodes are not postulated unless they are required. Specifically, only the head (X 0) and maximal projection (X-max) is assumed, in the absence of evidence requiring further articulation of a phrase (see earlier discussion of the X-max solution). Then minimal attachment may govern initial assignments, with late closure choosing between equally minimal attachments. When the initial constituent structure resulting from this process does not match the thematic frame that is most plausibly instantiated by the phrases in the complement of the head (e.g., the phrases following V in VP), then automatic reanalysis is possible assuming all arguments appear as sisters to their heads in constituent structure.

This account straightforwardly handles the data, assuming reanalysis can differ in its computational cost, being fastest when it results from an automatic independently required process like thematic frame selection. Hence, in the particular circumstance involving thematic frame comparison, minimal attachment effects are hardest to observe (3), reanalysis of arguments is easier than of nonarguments (4), and quick reanalysis prevents intuitive awareness of (quickly revised) assignments (e.g., *thought about his interest in the Volvo*), accounting for why examples supporting 1 derive from nonargument attachment.

This account clearly predicts a ranking in the preferred interpretation of ambiguous phrases. Arguments should be at the top of the preference list, because the first syntactic analysis will be confirmed by thematic selection in this case. Examples like 17 confirm this prediction, because intuitively one has the sense of trying to interpret the final PP as an argument of *reward*, despite the implausibility of this interpretation.

17. The teacher rewarded each child with sunshine in her eyes.
18. The government rewarded each soldier for apartheid.

Of course, *with* is the expected preposition for marking the third argument of *reward*, sentences containing some other preposition will receive less secure confirmation of the argument analysis. Nevertheless, one is intuitively aware of having taken the *for* phrase in Example 18 as an argument of *reward*, suggesting the argument preference is not limited only to phrases that potentially instantiate the most frequent thematic structure of a verb.

If analysis as an argument is not confirmed by the thematic selection process, it appears that modification of an argument is preferred. Presumably it is necessary and automatic to consider the interpretation of a PP as a potential modifier of a preceding phrase during the frame selection process. In the general case, comparing the relative plausibility of two thematic frames, for example, one with three arguments versus one with two arguments, for some NP V NP PP sequence, in essence amounts to choosing between an interpretation where the PP instantiates the third argument versus one where it modifies the second argument. I assume (as in Rayner et al., 1983) that the plausibility of the argument relative to the modifier assignment is what governs the thematic frame selection process. Hence, the analysis of a PP as a modifier of an argument should be relatively fast and easy to achieve:

consideration of this interpretation is an automatic component of thematic frame evaluation, and thematic frame selection will in essence supply the constituent structure system with the correct analysis.

This account predicts that modification gets an opportunity to bleed or take priority over (adjunct) predication. This correctly predicts the preference to interpret the PP as a modifier in the ambiguous sentence in 19.

19. The journalist couldn't look at the boy with measles.
20. The journalist couldn't look at George with measles.

In Example 20, the sentence is disambiguated toward the predication analysis of the PP as proper names usually cannot be modified. Quite clearly, the first intuitively available interpretation of Example 19 is not the interpretation parallel to the predication form in Example 20. Instead, in Example 19, *with measles* is interpreted as modifying *the boy*.

In Clifton and Frazier (in preparation), we note that identification of an adjunct predicate occurs by default, that is, because the argument (or modifier) analysis of a phrase has been rejected. This observation may help to account for the fact that adjuncts cannot occur before (internal to) the last argument of a predicate, as indicated by the ill-formedness of Example 21, for example.

21a. *John bought Ronnie sick a present.
21b. John sick bought Ronnie a present.

(That the prohibition in Example 21a does not result simply from the requirement of an adjunct predicate to be focused is suggested by the rather striking contrast between Example 21b and the complete unacceptability of Example 21a). In essence, the processor is considering adjunct predication analyses only once it has exhausted the possibilities offered by assignment as an argument or a modifier of an argument.

Turning to modifiers of adjuncts, the facts are much less clear. To my knowledge, there exist no studies focused on the processing of such phrases. My own intuitions suggest there is no preference for the modifier analysis in this case. Thus Example 22b does not give rise to intuitions of having misanalyzed the PP; and it does not seem to be noticeably harder to process than Example 22a.

22a. The patient laughed each morning with rain.
22b. The patient laughed each morning with malice.

In short, what little evidence exists suggests the preference for θ-attachments is not only to analyze a phrase as a θ-phrase (one receiving a thematic role) but also a preference for attachment to a θ-phrase rather than to an adjunct.

If anything, predication seems preferred to modification once we are outside the domain of phrases assigned a thematic role. This includes not just the modification of adjuncts (e.g., the temporal phrase in Example 22) but also the subject/external argument of bare predications, as in Example 23. In Example 23b, *in the bathtub* seems to receive a predication interpretation (see 23a which is only open to the predication analysis). It is taken to mean *Given that a man was in the bathtub ...*, which contrasts with the interpretation resulting from restrictive modification *Together with a man who was in the bathtub ...*

23a. With the sky a dark grey, it seemed safer to ...
23b. With a man in the bathtub, the heroine should have ...

At very least, it seems safe to conclude that the general preference for modification (over predication), observed when modification of a thematically marked argument is at issue, disappears once modification of other types of phrases is considered.

We have already seen that the Rayner et al. (1983) account predicts that the easiest errors to revise and the construction most quickly or readily influenced by semantic information will be those where there is competition between analyzing a phrase as an argument versus analyzing it as a modifier of an argument. This contrasts sharply with situations where the competing analyses involve competition between being an argument of the current predicate (or the head of one of its arguments) versus being an argument of some higher predicate, as in Example 24, where there is a sharp intuitive awareness accompanying the reanalysis of the PP as an argument of *put*.

24. Sally put the book that she had been reading in the library ...

It also contrasts sharply with the situation we investigated in the second section, illustrated in Example 25. Here, what is at issue is only the attachment of a modifier to one position or another – thematic frame selection is not involved.

25. The daughter of the colonel who ...

Reattachment of an adjunct to a higher argument complex also gives rise to clear intuitions of complexity, as in Example 26 where this is necessary to avoid tense-clash.

26. Everyone realized Sara will go to Rome yesterday.

In sum, parsing simply is not content-driven in any straightforward, uniform, fashion. When and how semantics influences analysis depends on the particular construction and on the type of the relation holding between competing analyses. (See also Carlson & Tanenhaus, in press; Pritchett, 1988, for discussion of thematic roles in reanalysis.)

To account for why there is reanalysis in the Cuetos and Mitchell examples, it was proposed that perceivers follow the conversational maxims of relevance. In ambiguous structures, the processor favors the analysis where a phrase is relevant to the main assertion. This principle seems reasonable and something like it seems to be required in any theory of language comprehension. For example, something like this is probably needed to exclude Example 27b, where the predicate *drunk* is taken to modify a constituent of an argument of the highest predicate rather than that argument (the head) itself. (In Example 27 the subject of *drunk* is italicized.)

27.   We met the daughter of the colonel drunk.
    a.   We met the *daughter* of the colonel drunk.
    b.   ?We met the daughter of the *colonel* drunk.

We can't account for the unacceptability of Example 27b by simply appealing to the implausibility of its meaning, because the closely comparable meaning conveyed by the (unambiguous) Example 28 is fine. And no general constraint prohibits a predicate from occurring as sister to NP (which would permit Example 27b to be excluded by c-command conditions), as shown by the at least marginal acceptability of Example 29, which achieves full acceptability once stress (or appositive intonation) is supplied.

28.   We met the daughter of the drunk colonel.
29.   The old colonel drunk was a real bastard.

So it looks as if the assumption favoring relevance to the main assertion is needed quite apart from the account of the Cuetos and Mitchell examples discussed in the last section.

Looking at the parsing of only a single structure (V-NP-PP) underdetermines the correct account of the general properties of the HSPM. Smith's (1988), Abney's (1988), or Taraban and McClelland's (1988) account seem quite appealing when we restrict our attention to just these limited data. Similarly, Cuetos and Mitchell's (1988) conclusion that languages "make use of parsing strategies in an essentially arbitrary way" doesn't seem too outlandish if we ignore the fact that the HSPM must contain subsystems beyond a constituent structure module. But what I've tried to show here is that once we step back and view the problem of modifier attachment from a perspective that takes into account the parsing of other structures and the operation of nonsyntactic subsystems, it provides us with a much different view of the principles underlying modifier attachment behavior.

ACKNOWLEDGMENT

This paper was written while I was a visitor at the Max Planck Institute for Psycholinguistics. I am extremely grateful to Chuck Clifton for extensive comments on this chapter. This work was supported by NIH grant HD-18708 to C. Clifton and L. Frazier and by NSF grant BNS-10177 to K. Rayner and L. Frazier.

REFERENCES

Abney, S. (1988). *A computational model of human parsing.* Paper presented at the First Annual CUNY Conference on Human Sentence Processing.

Altmann, G., & Steedman, M. (1988). Interaction with context during human sentence processing. *Cognition, 30,* 191 - 238.

Bach, E., & Cooper, R. (1978). The NP-S analysis of relative clauses and compositional semantics. *Linguistics & Philosophy, 2,* 145 - 150.

Carlson, G., & Tanenhaus, M. (in press). Thematic roles and language comprehension. In W. Wilkins (Ed.), *Thematic relations.* Orlando, FL: Academic Press.

Chomsky, N. (1970). Remarks on nominalization. In R. Jacobs & P. S. Rosenbaum (Eds.), *Readings in English transformational grammar* (pp. 222 - 272). Waltham, MA: Ginn & Co.

Clifton, C. (1988). *Restrictions on late closure: Appearance and reality.* Paper presented at the Sixth Australian Language and Speech Conference. Sydney, Australia.

Clifton, C., & Frazier, L. (in preparation). *Thematic constraints on adjunct interpretation.*

Clifton, C., Seely, D., & Frazier, L. (in preparation). *Thematic role assignment in nominalizations.*

Crain, S., & Steedman, M. (1985). On not being led up the garden-path: The use of context by the psychological syntax processor. In D. R. Dowty, L. Karttunen, & A. M. Zwicky (Eds.), *Natural language parsing: Psychological, computational, and theoretical perspectives* (pp. 320 - 358). Cambridge: Cambridge University Press.

Cuetos, F., & Mitchell, D. C. (1988). Cross-linguistic differences in parsing: Restrictions on the use of the late closure Strategy in Spanish. *Cognition, 30,* 73 - 105.

Ferreira, F., & Clifton, C. (1986). The independence of syntactic processing. *Journal of Memory and Language, 25,* 348 - 368.

Ford, M., Bresnan, J., & Kaplan, R. M. (1982). A competence-based theory of syntactic closure. In J. Bresnan (Ed.), *The mental representation of grammatical relations* (pp. 727 - 796). Cambridge, MA: MIT Press.

Frazier, L. (1978). *On comprehending sentences: Syntactic parsing strategies.* Unpublished doctoral dissertation, University of Connecticut, Storrs.

Frazier, L. (1987). Sentence processing: A tutorial review. In M. Coltheart (Ed.), *Attention and performance XII: The psychology of reading* (pp. 554 - 586). Hillsdale, NJ: Lawrence Erlbaum Associates.

Frazier, L. (in press). Exploring the architecture of the language processing system. In G. Altmann (Ed.), *Cognitive models on speech processing.* Cambridge, MA: MIT Press.

Frazier, L., & Rayner, K. (1982). Making and correcting errors during sentence comprehension: Eye movements in the analysis of structurally ambiguous sentences. *Cognitive Psychology, 14,* 178 - 210.

Frazier, L., & Rayner, K. (in press). Taking on semantic commitments: Processing words with multiple meanings vs. multiple senses. *Journal of Memory and Language.*

Friederici, A. D., & Frazier, L. (in preparation). *Thematic analysis in agrammatic comprehension.* Unpublished manuscript, Max-Planck-Institute for Psycholinguistics, Nijmegen.

Grice, H. P. (1968). Utterer's meaning, sentence-meaning. *Foundations of Language,* *4*, 225 - 242.

Grimshaw, J. (1988). *Adjuncts and argument structure.* MIT Center for Cognitive Science Occasional Paper 36, Cambridge, MA.

Holmes, V. M. (1987). Syntactic parsing: In search of the garden path. In M. Coltheart (Ed.), *Attention and performance XII: The psychology of reading* (pp. 587 - 599). Hillsdale, NJ: Lawrence Erlbaum Associates.

Jackendoff, R. (1977). X-Syntax: A study of phrase structure. *Linguistic Inquiry Monograph 2.* Cambridge, MA: MIT Press.

Kimball, J. (1973). Seven principles of surface structure parsing in natural language. *Cognition, 2*, 15 - 47.

Lasnik, H., & Kupin, J. J. (1977). A restrictive theory of transformational grammar. *Theoretical Linguistics, 4*, 173 - 196.

Mitchell, D. C. (1987). Lexical guidance in human parsing: Locus and processing characteristics. In M. Coltheart (Ed.), *Attention and performance XII: The psychology of reading* (pp. 601 - 618). Hillsdale, NJ: Lawrence Erlbaum Associates.

Pritchett, B. (1988). Garden path phenomenon and the grammatical basis of language processing. *Language, 64*, 539 - 576.

Rayner, K., Carlson, M., & Frazier, L. (1983). The interaction of syntax and semantics during sentence processing: Eye movements in the analysis of semantically biased sentences. *Journal of Verbal Learning and Verbal Behavior, 22*, 358 - 374.

Rayner, K., & Frazier, L. (1987). Parsing temporarily ambiguous complements. *Quarterly Journal of Experimental Psychology, 39A*, 657 - 673.

Schwartz, M. F., Linebarger, M. C., Saffran, E. M., & Pate, D. S. (1987). Syntactic transparency and sentence interpretation in aphasia. *Language and Cognitive Processes, 2*, 85 - 113.

Smith, C. (1988). *Structural and other factors in parsing.* Unpublished manuscript, University of Texas, Austin.

Speer, S. (1988). *Syntactic and thematic contributions to on-line sentence comprehension.* Unpublished doctoral dissertation, University of Texas, Austin.

Speer, S., Foss, D., & Smith, C. S. (1986). *Syntactic and thematic contributions to sentence complexity.* Paper presented at the annual meeting of the Psychonomic Society, New Orleans.

Stowe, L. (1989). Thematic structures and sentence comprehension. In G. N. Carlson & M. K. Tanenhaus (Eds.), *Linguistic structure in language processing* (pp. 319 - 357). Dordrecht: Kluwer Academic.

Taraban, R., & McClelland, J. L. (1988). Constituent attachment and thematic role assignment in sentence processing: Influences of content-guided expectations. *Journal of Memory and Language, 27*, 597 - 632.

15 CONNECTIONISM: A CASE FOR MODULARITY

Dennis Norris

MRC Applied Psychology Unit, Cambridge

INTRODUCTION

A central theme running through several of the chapters in this book concerns the question of whether syntactic and semantic processing are interactive or not. The chapters by Frazier and by Perfetti start from the conventional assumption that there are distinct syntactic and semantic processors. The question of interest then concerns how these two processes communicate with each other. The whole question of interaction has generally been based on the assumption that there are separate processors responsible for syntactic and semantic analyses. However, the strongest possible claim one could make about interaction between syntactic and semantic processing would be to argue that they were so tightly coupled that they should properly be thought of as a single integrated processing system. This is the view taken in the chapter by Taraban and McClelland. They consider that comprehension is a single, highly interactive process, which is not decomposable into sub-components. There are no separate processes of parsing or semantic interpretation. Comprehension consists of a single process in which multiple constraints from different sources are weighed together in parallel to produce a final interpretation of the sentence which minimizes the discrepancies between the various constraints. This parallel and highly interactive constraint satisfaction mechanism probably takes the form of a large connectionist network of the sort proposed by St. John and McClelland (in press). In this model, a single, undifferentiated network takes responsibility for processing operations that we would normally

331

think of as being performed by separate, but possibly interacting, processes of parsing and semantic interpretation.

Of course the claim that comprehension is a highly interactive process is not new. In particular, there have been many claims that semantic or contextual factors can influence the operation of the parser. However, in the majority of cases these theoretical claims have been made without providing an explicit account of how this interaction could come about.

Connectionism seems to provide a solution to this problem. In a constraint-satisfaction model, like the St. John and McClelland model advocated by Taraban and McClelland, there is no limit to the information that can be considered all at once in coming to an interpretation of a sentence. Indeed, it seems to be part of the nature of connectionism that processing systems should be highly interactive (rather than modular). Much of the impact of connectionist models stems from the fact that they have provided a vehicle for expressing theories of a highly interactive nature. So, if we accept the driving philosophy behind connectionism it seems almost inevitable that we are led to a view of language comprehension as a highly interactive process in which information from a variety of different sources is considered simultaneously, and where decisions at any one level can potentially influence decisions at any other level. If connectionism is the right way to go, and connectionism is so well suited to interaction, then surely this all adds further weight to the case against modularity.

If we buy the connectionist story, we might expect to see very little evidence for modularity in language processing. We might then be rather surprised to find such a wealth of experimental evidence that the parser stubbornly behaves in an autonomous fashion even when presented with potentially useful semantic or contextual information (Clifton & De Vincenzi, this volume; Ferreira & Clifton, 1986; Frazier & Rayner, 1987; Rayner, Carlson, & Frazier, 1983). However, we should remember that there really is nothing in the idea of connectionism itself that forces us to the conclusion that language processing is highly interactive. There is no reason why we should not use connectionist techniques to construct highly modular, bottom-up, psychological models. Although connectionism and interaction seem to go well together, in fact, connectionism and modularity make equally good partners. We can start from the same basic assumptions about constraint satisfaction and connectionism as Taraban and McClelland, yet come to quite the opposite conclusion about whether comprehension is highly interactive.

The extra factor that is so easily left out of the argument is the issue of learnability. We are used to thinking about problems such as autonomy and interaction in terms of the processing operations carried out by the mature individual. But connectionism, with its emphasis on learning algorithms, forces us to consider language acquisition along with processing issues. The connectionist model has to be trained to do its job. If the model can't learn, then it's no good, no matter how plausible it might seem to be as a processing model. The complexity of

learning a human language is such that if we could design a connectionist learning model that could learn language, it would have to develop
in a highly modular fashion and do most of its constraint satisfaction
within rather than between levels. In fact, if you are going to build a
connectionist language learning device, then it had better be modular.

In this chapter, I argue that connectionism should not be used as an
excuse for abandoning modularity. When we attempt to go beyond the
simple demonstration models such as that of St. John and McClelland,
we will have to face a number of problems that can only be solved
by moving away from highly interactive, undifferentiated, networks, to
networks with a far more modular architecture. The task of learning
language is simply too difficult for the simple unstructured nets in use at
present. The structure required to learn language demands a high degree
of modularity. I do not argue that the problem of learnability rules out
interaction. But connectionism cuts both ways. Not only does it give
us a potential mechanism for implementing models, but its emphasis on
the learning process forces us to consider the important issue of how to
structure a language learning device. Taraban and McClelland argue
that decomposability, that is, having separate processors for syntax and
semantics, is simply "some artificial principle". This claim could not
be further from the truth. Decomposability doesn't simply reflect some
perverse aesthetic preference for models with a large number of small
boxes rather than a small number of large boxes. Decomposability is a
necessary prerequisite for learning a language.

A second aim of this chapter is to draw attention to the fact that
connectionist models can behave in some rather strange and unfamiliar
ways. Those of us brought up in the tradition of box-model information
processing have developed some fixed ideas of how models with either
a bottom-up or top-down structure should behave. After all, the value
of labels such as bottom-up and top-down is that they are supposed to
be informative about behavior, not just architecture. However, connectionism can generate models that don't fit neatly into these conventional
categories. We can construct bottom-up connectionist models that behave exactly as we would expect top-down models to do. In other words,
thanks to connectionism, the kind of data which might once have been
taken to provide categorical evidence for top-down interaction could
now be perfectly compatible with a bottom-up model - provided it is a
connectionist one, of course.

LEARNING IN CONNECTIONIST NETS

The bulk of connectionist research at the moment uses the back-
propagation learning procedure of Rumelhart, Hinton, and Williams
(1986). Although very successful with small scale problems, particularly
with pattern recognition tasks, back-propagation suffers from some severe drawbacks. One of the most serious problems is that learning scales

poorly with network size. That is, as the network size increases, learning gets disproportionately slower. Hinton (1987) reported that learning time on a parallel machine with a separate processor for each connection is proportional to the square of the number of weights in the network. Given that back-propagation learning is slow to begin with, this is a major problem. The problem is especially serious in the case of language acquisition. Presumably the task of acquiring language would demand a very large network indeed. What chance is there that such a network would ever learn in a reasonable amount of time? In fact, the problem is even worse than this gloomy picture might suggest. There is no guarantee that the back-propagation procedure will ever learn a suitable set of weights to perform a given task. When the problem space is too big these nets just tend to thrash around and get nowhere. The problems with large nets are so great that speech researchers have recently begun to investigate ways of building networks by gluing a number of small modular networks together (Waibel, 1988).

One source of difficulty is that simple nets have no way of structuring the learning task. These nets consider all possible correlations among all parts of the input pattern all of the time. Their world really is a blooming, buzzing confusion with no structure. Solving large problems is difficult for any learning mechanism. However, simple networks are unable to adopt any of the conventional learning or problem solving strategies. For example, if the entire problem is too big to solve all at once they are unable to adopt a "divide and conquer" strategy and to break the problem down into smaller subproblems that might be solved independently. In the case of language learning, one doesn't want to try to map directly between phoneme or letter strings and meaning all in one go. The problem has to be broken down into small components over which useful generalizations can be made. In other words, a move toward a modular representational system is essential for learning large problems. That, of course, also implies that we have to construct some form of structured internal representation of the problem.

We can get a feeling for the kind of problems undifferentiated connectionist nets are likely to run into by considering how to learn a skill far simpler than language understanding. In fact, the task is so simple that it is really rather surprising that it proves so difficult.

Some individuals, often young men with limited intellectual capacities, are able to calculate the day of the week on which any date falls in a matter of only a few seconds, yet usually have only limited arithmetical ability. These "phenomenal date calculators" rarely have any insight as to how they perform this task and usually have very little explicit knowledge of calendrical information. Phil Barnard and I thought that it would be interesting to see if we could train a simple network to be a date calculator. If a simple net with no inbuilt knowledge of arithmetic or calendrical information could become a date calculator, then we would no longer feel that there was anything quite so puzzling about the behavior of these individuals we call "phenomenal" date calculators.

We started by trying to train a standard back-propagation net with a single layer of hidden units. The net received training on about one fifth of the dates in a 50-year period, and we tested it to see if it could generalize to dates on which it wasn't trained. Many hours of computer time later, we gave up. Using different numbers of hidden units or different coding schemes for the input seemed to make no difference, the net simply showed no signs of generalizing, even though it usually learned to perform correctly on dates on which it was trained. The source of the net's difficulty becomes clear when we see how the problem of calculating days from dates breaks down into its components. One of the simplest ways to perform the task is to break it down into three stages.

1. For some arbitrarily chosen month (say January, 1951), learn how to compute days from date in the month.

2. For all months in the chosen year (1951), learn that there is a systematic relationship between the day on which any date falls on in the base month (January) and the day it falls on in that month. For any date, the day it falls on in February will be 3 days later than the day it falls in in January, a date in March will also be 3 days later, and a date in April will be 6 days later, and so forth. This calculation simply involves taking the output of the first stage and adding an offset, in days, determined by the month.

3. Now take the output of the first two stages combined with the month (the month is needed to handle leap years) and work out how to compute an additional offset determined by the year of the date.

The procedure for the calculation of dates now corresponds to the successive application of three rules (really three table lookup procedures). Obviously, if the task is best performed in three successive stages, then it will clearly pose problems for any net which tries to perform the mapping in a single stage. However, simply giving the net more layers, corresponding to the extra stages, won't help matters much. The net needs some help in finding out what to compute at each stage. We can solve the problem by constructing a multilayered network like that shown in Figure 15.1. However, in order to get the net to compute the correct output at each stage we have to train each subnetwork separately. Psychologically, it certainly seems plausible that anyone learning to be a date calculator would start by learning to perform part of the task (dates in a month or year) and only later learn how to perform the complete task. Similarly, we would expect a language learner to first learn about words and then simple phrases and only later to learn to produce and understand sentences. A network trained in this way performs very well. Apart from a some difficulties with January and February of leap years it has no problem generalizing from the training set to new dates, and it learns fairly quickly.

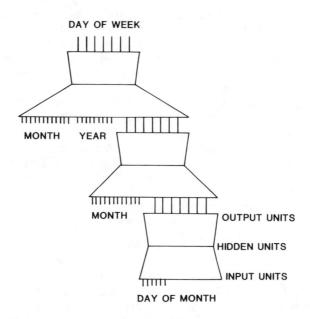

FIGURE 15.1. Multilayer date calculation network.

There are several important lessons to be learned from this simple task. The first is that a simple unstructured network finds it almost impossible to learn the task. Not only does the net not have the inbuilt structure that would help it to learn the task, but there is nothing in the learning algorithm it uses that would help it to impose structure on this task. Without structure, it has to consider all of the variables in the problem space simultaneously and gets nowhere.

The second is that even the structured multilayer net still requires some human assistance to learn the task. After the net had learned to perform the first part of the task (days in the month), learning in that part of the net was turned off before training the second stage. Once we've learned something, we want to hold onto that knowledge until circumstances change and the knowledge becomes inappropriate. If we had simply tried to train the second stage without turning learning off in the first stage (or interspersing further first-stage training with the second-stage training), the first stage would have tended to unlearn what it had already learned, despite the fact that the information it had learned was still reliable. This problem of stabilizing learning is one that has concerned Grossberg (1980) for many years and presents a serious problem for the back-propagation algorithm.

Human intervention was also required to determine which part of the network learned which part of the problem. It isn't sufficient simply to build in some structure; the net needed to be told how to use that structure. These considerations show that the problem of learning tasks that are best performed by performing a sequence of operations can't be solved simply by using multilayered nets. What we really want is a learning algorithm that can automatically determine how to allocate learning of new information to new parts of a network, and then know how to connect different parts of the network together.

Pinker and Prince (1988) drew attention to a similar problem in Rumelhart and McClelland's (1986) work on learning the past tense of verbs. Because of limitations on the learning algorithm employed, the past-tense model is unable to develop appropriate internal representations. It therefore fails to make appropriate generalization at the morphological and lexical levels.

There is an interesting question here as to whether the date-calculation network is really just an implementation of a rule based system. One of the intriguing claims made about many connectionist models is that, in some way, they operate without rules; for example see Rumelhart and McClelland's (1986) work on learning the past tense of verbs and Seidenberg's (1989) work on oral reading. Do we want to say that each stage in the network here represents a rule?

Implicit in all of this is the idea that we need a learning mechanism that develops a high degree of both representational and process autonomy. If the task has a natural structure, then we want the learning mechanism to exploit that structure. Solving a series of small problems individually is far easier than trying to solve them simultaneously as one large problem. In order to put these small solutions together, we need to develop a highly structured internal representation of the task. Linguistic structure isn't there just to keep linguists in business. Without it, language would be arbitrary, unlearnable, and unusable. As soon as we concede the advantages of a structured approach to problem solving then we automatically concede the advantages of a modular approach. When we have solved part of the problem, we need to treat that part of the solution as a stable module that can be called upon when required and is protected from interference by subsequent learning experience.

It should be noted that the issue of learnability here is rather different from questions like whether a single-layer perceptron can solve an exclusive-or problem. In such cases, we want to know whether the learning rule can generate a set of weights that can compute a particular function after exposure to all possible pairings of input and output patterns. So, for example, we know that there is no set of weights that will allow a single-layer perceptron to compute the XOR function. But with date calculation we don't want to present *all* input-output pairs for learning. We want the net to generalize on the basis of exposure to a limited subset of input-output pairs. With language understanding we simply can't present all possible inputs for learning. The language and the learning device must both be structured such that the relevant rules, or generalizations, can be induced after exposure to a small sample of the potentially infinite input patterns.

BOTTOM-UP MODELS AND TOP-DOWN EFFECTS

What I want to do next is look at how the idea of constraint satisfaction in connectionist networks relates to conventional ways of classifying psychological models as top-down, bottom-up, interactive, and so forth. To do this I will present a very simple connectionist model of word recognition. I don't want to make any strong claims for the psychological plausibility of this model, but it provides a clear demonstration of how a connectionist model that has a bottom-up flow of information can actually produce the kind of behavior which we would normally associate with a top-down interactive model.

The first connectionist models to have an impact on psycholinguistics were the hard-wired interactive activation models of visual and spoken word recognition (McClelland & Elman, 1986; McClelland & Rumelhart, 1981; Rumelhart & McClelland, 1982). These early models were hard-wired in the sense that they had no learning mechanism. The weights in the networks were set by hand. These models have largely been superseded by learning models such as the Seidenberg and McClelland (1989) model. However, the interesting feature of current learning models is that they are essentially bottom-up in structure. There are none of the feedback circuits that were present in the interactive activation models. Processing takes place in a single forward pass through the network. In the interactive activation models, processing each stimulus requires about 50 cycles through the network. Feedback is possible in learning networks. For example, there is feedback in the memory units in the St. John and McClelland model. However, these models are very powerful computational devices even in their most basic feed-forward form. A question arises, though, as to whether they are so powerful that we no longer need interaction.

The architecture of the model I want to present is very simple. It is simply a straightforward back-propagation net with a single layer of hidden units. The net receives input in the form of a set of binary features and learns to identify the words and the letters present in the input. As with Rumelhart and McClelland's interactive activation model, the net only deals with words of a fixed length and it uses position specific letter nodes. However, the net differs in a number of crucial respects from the interactive activation models. First, the net does not have the usual hierarchical structure associated with word-recognition models. In the interactive activation model, nodes in successive layers of the net correspond to features, letters, and words. In this net, the input layer corresponds to features, but the output layer is responsible for identifying both words and letters. Letters and words are at the same level in the net. It is as if letters are simply treated as single-letter words. The hidden units correspond to some intermediate level of representation that has to subserve both word and letter identification. Because this is a learning model rather than a hard-wired model, the kind of representations formed at this intermediate level will depend specifically on the set of stimuli that the model is trained on.

As a simple demonstration experiment, a net such as that shown in Figure 15.2 was trained on a set of 50 words and 50 nonwords. The net received two kinds of training that alternated with each other on successive training cycles. In one kind of training, the net was presented with only the words and was trained to activate the corresponding word node in response to each input word. The letter nodes were treated as a "don't care" condition. That is, whatever output the net produced at the letter nodes, it was told that it had produced the correct output. In the second kind of training, the net was presented with both the word and the nonword inputs. This time the word nodes were treated as a "don't care" condition while the net was taught to identify the letters in the input. Overall, the net was therefore taught how to classify half of the stimuli as words and was given equal training on identifying the letters in both words and nonwords.

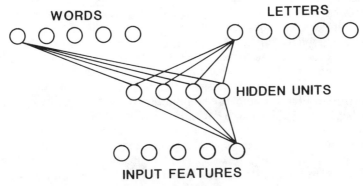

FIGURE 15.2. Simple network for recognizing words and letters.

At the end of the training procedure, the net was found to be able to identify letters in words better than it could identify letters in nonwords. This word-superiority effect still held even when the experiment was repeated with assignment of stimuli to the word and nonword categories reversed. Whatever the basis of this result, it is clearly not due to the nature of the particular stimuli employed in the word and nonword conditions.

A similar experiment was performed using a set of word and nonword stimuli and a set of letter stimuli. The net was trained to identify the words and trained to identify the letters only in the letter stimuli. Subsequent testing revealed that the net was able to identify letters in stimuli it had learned to classify as words better than in nonwords. (In this case, the net had never been exposed to nonwords during training.) In this experiment, the word superiority effect still held despite the fact that the net had never been taught to identify letters in either the words or the nonwords used in testing.

How can such a simple bottom-up model show what appears to be a strong top-down effect of lexical information? The answer to this question lies in the fact that all back-propagation nets have a top-down flow of information during learning. During the process of recognizing a word or letter, the information flow will be completely bottom up. In contrast to the interactive activation models, there is no continuous feedback from higher to lower levels during recognition. However, after each forward pass of information through the net, there is a backward pass in which the error is propagated back down the net in order to update the weights and make the net learn. This means that the success of the net in identifying both letters and words will influence the weights in both layers of the net. Errors in identifying words will alter the weights from the hidden units to the word units and also from the input units to the hidden units. The weights from the input units will also be influenced by errors in letter identification. The first layer of weights therefore has to subserve both word identification and letter identification. These weights have to be optimized so that they will perform the tasks of word and letter identification simultaneously. This is the source of the top-down effect.

If the net had sufficient capacity and learning experience it could potentially learn to perform both tasks independently. For example, it might be possible for the net to allocate one subset of the hidden units (and the weights from the input units to the hidden units) exclusively to word identification and the remainder to letter identification. Letter identification would then be totally unaffected by whether the letters appeared in words or nonwords. In fact, increasing the number of hidden units, or making the letters easier to discriminate, does tend to reduce or even eliminate the word-superiority effect. However, with smaller numbers of hidden units the need to satisfy the constraints imposed by having to identify both words and letters leads the net to develop a set of weights that are better suited to identify letters in words than letters in nonwords. Even though the net is never trained to identify a word and the letters in a word simultaneously, it still has to develop a set of weights that are suited to both tasks.

The behavior of this simple net presents an interesting contrast to the interactive activation models or the network architecture employed by St. John and McClelland. These nets use constraint satisfaction between levels during processing. The current net uses constraint satisfaction between tasks at the same level in the network. The constraints are wired into the net by the learning algorithm in such a way that no interaction between levels is required during processing. During the recognition of a single word the information flow in the present net is always bottom-up. But the interesting behavior that the net exhibits is a product of the top-down flow of information during learning. Quite clearly, this net does not fall neatly into the standard categories of top-down and bottom-up. During processing it is one thing, during learning it is another. It is also rather difficult to determine whether the net is interactive or not. We usually think of interaction as involving a feedback loop. Well, like all back-propagation nets, this net does have feedback. But there is no feedback during the processing of any individual word.

Processing simply involves a single forward pass through the net. How you decide to label this net therefore seems largely a matter of personal preference. However, if we want to compare this model to interactive activation models or, other, more traditional, psychological models which have no capacity to learn, we should really ignore the learning phase and just consider the processing component. In that case, the model is most definitely bottom-up. So, far from adding to the weight of evidence against bottom-up models, connectionism actually gives us a new and more powerful class of bottom-up models that are capable of accounting for what seem to be strongly top-down effects.

CONCLUSION

Connectionism seems to supply the missing ingredient in interactive models of language comprehension. It provides a mechanism that is ideally suited to implementing highly interactive models. Using a single connectionist network, constraints at many different levels can be satisfied in parallel. If one really does believe that these constraints are satisfied in parallel, then to try and combine all of the constraint-satisfaction processes into one large network seems the natural move to make. However, although the ease with which simple connectionist nets can combine information from different sources makes them appear particularly suitable for constructing highly interactive processing models, that very same property makes them poor candidates for language-learning devices. The task of learning a language is simply too massive a problem to be solved by a single unstructured network. Once we begin the process of structuring the learning problem we immediately move away from nondecomposable models, such as that of St. John and McClelland, toward more traditional models. In these models, the functional architecture comes to reflect the structural properties of the language.

Of course, we must be careful not to take the learnability argument too far. If a modular architecture is essential for initial learning of a language, then this is no guarantee that the system will not develop in such a way that it becomes more and more interactive once this initial hurdle is overcome. But it seems rather implausible that modularity is just a phase we have to go through.

We might have hoped that connectionism would go some way to simplifying the debate over interaction. Unfortunately, the great power of connectionist models has actually complicated matters. The simple bottom-up word-recognition network described here behaves in precisely the way we expect highly interactive models to behave. A slightly more elaborate version of the model applied to spoken word recognition can account for the results of recent work by Elman and McClelland (1988), which seemed to have provided categorical evidence for a lexical influence on phoneme perception.

The idea that reading, or even perception as a whole, is a constraint satisfaction process is perhaps one of the few things we can all agree on. However, one reason why we can all so readily agree on this point is that it doesn't in itself answer any of the interesting questions. For example, agreeing that comprehension is a constraint-satisfaction process tells us very little about parsing or the relation between syntax and semantics. The controversial issue is not whether there are constraints, but what are the effective constraints, and how and when are they satisfied? In other words, the question is still the same as it always has been: What is the nature of the comprehension process, and what information is brought to bear at each stage in the process?

REFERENCES

Elman, J. L., & McClelland, J. L. (1988). Cognitive penetration of the mechanisms of perception: Compensation for coarticulation of lexically restored phonemes. *Journal of Memory and Language, 27*, 143 - 165.

Ferreira, F., & Clifton, C. (1986). The independence of syntactic processing. *Journal of Memory and Language, 25*, 348 - 368.

Frazier, L., & Rayner, K. (1987). Resolution of syntactic category ambiguities: Eye movements in parsing lexically ambiguous sentences. *Journal of Memory and Language, 26*, 505 - 526.

Grossberg, S. (1980). How does the brain build a cognitive code? *Psychological Review, 87*, 1 - 51.

Hinton, G. E. (1987). *Connectionist learning procedures.* (Technical Report CMU-CS-87-115). Pittsburgh: Carnegie-Mellon University.

McClelland, J. L., & Elman, J. L. (1986). The TRACE model of speech perception. *Cognitive Psychology, 18*, 1 - 86.

McClelland, J. L., & Rumelhart, D. E. (1981). An interactive activation model of context effects in letter perception: Part 1. An account of basic findings. *Psychological Review, 88*, 375 - 407.

Pinker, S., & Prince, A. (1988). On language and connectionism: Analysis of a parallel distributed processing model of language acquisition. *Cognition, 28*, 73 - 193.

Rayner, K., Carlson, M., & Frazier, L. (1983). The interaction of syntax and semantics during sentence processing: Eye movements in the analysis of semantically biased sentences. *Journal of Verbal Learning and Verbal Behavior, 22*, 358 - 374.

Rumelhart, D. E., Hinton, G. E., & Williams, R. J. (1986). Learning internal representations by error propagation. In D. E. Rumelhart, J. L. McClelland, & the PDP research group (Eds.), *Parallel distributed processing: Explorations in the microstructure of cognition: Vol. 1. Foundations* (pp. 318 - 364). Cambridge, MA: MIT Press.

Rumelhart, D. E., & McClelland, J. L. (1982). An interactive activation model of context effects in letter perception: Part 2. The contextual enhancement effect and some tests and extensions of the model. *Psychological Review, 89*, 60 - 94.

Rumelhart, D. E., & McClelland, J. L. (1986). On learning the past tenses of English verbs. In J. L. McClelland, D. E. Rumelhart, & the PDP research group (Eds.),

Parallel distributed processing: Explorations in the microstructure of cognition: Vol. 2. Psychological and biological models (pp. 216 - 271). Cambridge, MA: MIT Press.

Seidenberg, M. (1989). Visual word recognition and pronounciation: A computational model and its implications. In W. Marslen-Wilson (Ed.), *Lexical representation and process* (pp. 25 - 74). Cambridge, MA: MIT Press.

Seidenberg, M. S., & McClelland, J. L. (1989). A distributed, developmental model of visual word recognition and naming. *Psychological Review, 96*, 523 - 568.

St. John, M. F., & McClelland, J. (in press). Learning and applying contextual constraints in sentence comprehension. *Artificial Intelligence.*

Waibel, A. (1988). *Modular construction of phonetic neural networks.* Paper presented at the ATR Workshop on Neural Networks and Parallel Distributed Processing, ATR Laboratories, Osaka, Japan.

16

PARSING PRINCIPLES AND LANGUAGE COMPREHENSION DURING READING

Giovanni B. Flores d'Arcais

Max Planck Institute for Psycholinguistics
and *University of Leiden*

INTRODUCTION

The chapters in this section deal with a number of extremely important and debated issues concerning syntactic processing during reading. Among the questions asked in the various chapters, the following are probably the most central: How is a parser structured and what kind of operation principles does it use? Is there an autonomous syntactic processor? Are parsing principles universal?

The current debate between connectionist positions and the autonomy modular point of view is also central in the domain of syntactic parsing, as the Taraban and McClelland chapter shows.

In this chapter, I comment on three of the issues that emerge in the contributions to this section, namely the nature of parsing principles, the notion of autonomy of syntactic analysis during reading, and finally, the universality of the parsing principles. Given the extensive comment on the connectionistic approach provided in the chapter by Norris, I will avoid this debate.

DOES SYNTACTIC ANALYSIS TAKE PLACE DURING READING?

Is a section on syntactic processing justified in a book on comprehension processes during reading? After all, what we do when reading is try to understand what is written in the text, and in most cases we care very little about the form and the structure of the text. Except when reading a piece of literary prose or a poem, meaning is probably all that we are looking for.

There is no doubt that in understanding a sentence we have to use grammatical knowledge and a lexicon. At some point during the process of language comprehension we construct a representation that includes relations among lexical elements. Without syntax, such relations would not exist. On the other hand, we can question whether the construction of an *explicit* syntactic structure is a necessary step for language comprehension during reading. Of course, there are two distinct aspects of this question. The first is to decide whether language comprehension requires syntactic analysis. The second is to decide if we have to submit the content of a text to a full syntactic analysis in order to understand it during reading.

The two questions are related but independent. Understanding a written text *is* understanding language, but, at least in fast silent reading, it is not self-evident that the comprehension system adopts the same cues and the same procedures as those used for understanding spoken language or for getting the meaning out of a written text. A system designed for comprehending the meaning of a text may be programmed to use every possible means to reach this understanding, provided these means are economical and minimize both processing effort and the risk of erroneous interpretation. If carrying out a full syntactic analysis turned out to be more time and energy demanding than some so-called dirty procedures or short cuts, a language comprehension system may quickly learn to rely on such procedures, perhaps at some cost of precision but with the advantage of speed and processing economy.

As to the first question, there are various interesting models of text comprehension and efficient language comprehension simulation programs without much syntax or that even claim to use no syntax at all. Wilks' (1978) program is one of this type, and so are some parsers developed within the conceptual dependency framework (Schank, 1972). In the most radical types, input elements are projected directly onto representations that consist of lexical elements, their thematic role, and the relationships among them. Many such models make use of a number of key words isolated on the basis of a preliminary analysis and rely on a considerable knowledge of the world. De Jong's parser FRUMP (1979, 1982) is a typical example of this approach. Several of these parsers are successful in producing appropriate paraphrases of texts, an indication that these programs are capable of successfully extracting the meaning of the text.

As to the second question, from the scanning behavior of newspaper readers or from speed readers, it is rather obvious that people are capable of extracting at least some meaning out of a text without performing (a full) syntactic analysis. A rapid glance at a page allows the reader to extract few words capable of giving information about a given issue. Also, in a very rapid search through the pages of a book or through the latest issue of a journal, a reader is likely to be able to get much useful information apparently without much syntactic analysis. At this level of reading, all that matters is the identification of a few key words or, at most, very short constituents.

Is syntactic parsing, then, necessary at all? The suggestion has repeatedly been made (e.g., Wilks, 1978) that a parser can successfully perform text analysis without necessarily requiring an explicit syntactic computation. On the other hand, there is more and more evidence that syntactic analysis is taking place obligatorily when reading, even when the reader could, apparently without much syntactic work, comprehend the text (e.g., Flores d'Arcais, 1982). Thus, it seems clear that syntactic information is essential for comprehension and that obtaining a structural description is an obligatory step at some point during the process of language comprehension.

The problem at issue, therefore, is not whether syntactic analysis is taking place during reading, but what kinds of operations are involved, what principles are guiding the comprehension system during reading, and how is the structural analysis of the text being performed. Interest in syntactic processes during reading has increased during recent years, and the evidence available is becoming more articulated and more precise. Psycholinguistics has recently offered a number of interesting models and valuable evidence for the study of processes of syntactic analysis during reading. The contributions to this section represent excellent examples of this trend.

THE NATURE OF PARSING PRINCIPLES IN READING

The end result of the comprehension of a text is a mental representation of the content of the text. The process which brings the reader to this end must include, among others, the extraction of appropriate lexical units, the computation of syntactic structures, and the assignment of thematic roles to phrases. The latter can also be expressed as the assignment of cases to the various lexical units isolated in the sentence.

The mechanism responsible for structural analysis, at various levels, during reading (as well as during spoken language comprehension) is the parser. Thus, in the language comprehension system the parser is the specific device which carries out structural analysis and produces a grammatical structure. How does such a device operate?

The form of the output of the parsing mechanism depends on the organization and the operating principles of the parser. This output can consist of a detailed linguistic structural description or of some structure in which the main relations among lexical units are specified, without a full structural description.

The means to reach this end vary. A parser can operate algorithmically, by fully exploiting the system of rules of a given language, or it can work on the basis of various heuristics. Many of the psychologically most interesting parsers operate on the basis of a number of heuristics or strategies. These offer guidance to the parser in determining the structure of the sentence and in attaching each element to the structure being built.

Various strategies have been proposed in psycholinguistics, linguistics, and artificial intelligence, some being very specific, some rather general. In psycholinguistics, the first to introduce the notion of strategies was Bever (1970), and among the first linguists to propose psycholinguistically interesting strategies one has to mention Kimball (1973). Some, such as the canonical sentoid strategy by Fodor, Bever, and Garrett (1974), are essentially agrammatic heuristics, while others are procedures used to construct explicit syntactic representations, such as Frazier's (1979) principles.

Work in recent years (see, e.g., Frazier, 1987a) has emphasized the use of phrase structure rules in sentence processing, showing how a few simple strategies allow the parser to select a given phrase structure analysis.

The most general of these strategies are minimal attachment and late closure (Frazier, 1979, 1987a) of which most or all other strategies can be shown to be special or specific cases. For example, main clause analysis in Bever's (1970) classic sentence (1) is an example of minimal attachment.

1.   The horse raced past the barn fell.

This is not a place to review again the various types of parsers and discuss their limitations and their respective merits. For a brief presentation of the main classes of parsers relevant for the psychology of reading, see Mitchell (1987b); for a critical discussion of syntactic analysis during parsing, see especially Frazier (1987a), Ferreira and Clifton (1986), Crain and Steedman (1985), and Altmann and Steedman (1988).

What is the nature of these strategies? These heuristics can be considered like the principles proposed by Gestalt Psychology to account for the perceptual results one obtains with visual configurations. In visual perception, principles such as closure, common fate, or similarity explain how different perceptual configurations are obtained from a given stimulus event. Computationally, these principles can be taken as procedures for perceptual analysis. Thus, given a visual input, the principles governing the perceptual result are instructions like the following:

2. Other things being equal, attach perceptually a given element to the closest element or to the one which is physically most similar;

or

    . . . to the ones together with which it forms a better or more regular configuration.

Thus, principles such as Frazier's minimal attachment, late closure (1979, 1987a) or Kimball's (1973) closure and right association are essentially procedures for the parser, which can take a form such as (3):

3. Attach the next lexical item to the lowest node so far constructed.

During reading, the different words of a lexical string can be attached in various ways. According to the minimal attachment principle, perceivers incorporate each word of an input lexical string into a constituent structure using the fewest syntactic nodes possible. Minimal attachment has been shown in a variety of studies to function as a powerful strategy for the construction of constituent structure representation (Frazier & Rayner, 1987; Rayner, Carlson, & Frazier, 1983). Late closure, which instructs the parser to attach each new incoming item into the phrase being constructed and processed, has also been shown to account for a variety of results (Frazier, 1987a). Both late closure and minimal attachment offer considerable processing advantages, thereby requiring the lowest possible load on working memory.

Through use of these strategies a structure is created as soon as possible, minimizing processing load and maximizing processing efficiency. In several cases, the language comprehension system will be led down a garden-path, but this is compensated by the system's efficiency. Thus, strategies such as minimal attachment or late closure sometimes induce structural assignments that later turn out to be incorrect. For example, Frazier, Clifton, and Randall's (1983) results indicate that the processor initially assigns the most recent filler to the first gap encountered, even when this later turns out to be incorrect.

The contributions of Frazier and of Clifton and De Vincenzi in this book add valuable new evidence to the available findings on syntactic parsing. The strategy proposed by Clifton and De Vincenzi in their chapter and by De Vincenzi (1989) concerning minimal chain as a powerful parsing principle in Italian, is an important addition to our knowledge about parsing. This contribution is also extremely valuable for the question of universality of the parser, which is discussed shortly.

How committed is the parser? A parser capable of making serious commitments as early as possible, at every moment, presents both advantages and disadvantages. The advantages consist of a minimum demand of processing resources and a minimal load on working memory. A blind, committed parser has reached a high level of automaticity and works at virtually no costs. The disadvantages are obvious: In many cases the parser will produce a contextually wrong analysis and will have to backtrack or redo the analysis.

Whether the functioning of the parser has come into existence through some kind of trade-off between accuracy on the one hand and ease and costs on the other is difficult to say. It is probably hard to estimate the consequences of a trade-off between processing costs and accuracy. It is unlikely that a blind and stupid parser would have established itself in a central position in a language comprehension system if the low costs were accompanied by a high proportion of erroneous analysis. At any rate, a parser that is determined, stupid, and blind, but fast and cheap in operation, is likely to have survived only if the trade-off between costs and accuracy does not result in a high rate of erroneous analysis. Of course, the commitment of such a parser does not necessarily mean a definitive commitment. As Perfetti proposes in his chapter, there can be early stages of parsing in which certain attachments are only tentative and provisory and in which elements are still momentarily unattached.

Questions about the moment and the way semantic and discourse factors affect the working of the parser are questions concerning the old issue of autonomy, which is dealt with in the next section.

THE AUTONOMY OF SYNTAX

An important issue concerning the nature and the functioning of the parsing mechanism pervades, explicitly or implicitly, in most chapters of this section of the volume. It is the classic issue of autonomy. Are the syntactic processes of the parser affected by semantic and discourse factors?

Of course, no one would deny that language comprehension during reading includes semantic and discourse processes. The question is whether semantic or pragmatic factors affect the *initial* syntactic analysis of a sentence in a word-by-word fashion. A syntactic parser that delivers the output of its initial work to a semantic and to a discourse language comprehension component is autonomous. A parser that has to wait for instructions from semantic and discourse processing units before proceeding further, and that is computationally sensitive to information coming from these units, is not autonomous.

Whether explicitly formulated or debated as such — as during the last fifteen years or so – or only implicitly taken, the issue has been a central one since the beginning of contemporary cognitive psycholinguistics. Even in early psycholinguistic experiments, such as Slobin (1966) and Herriot (1967), the question was asked whether semantic and pragmatic factors would affect the comprehension of passive sentences. Early evidence supporting an autonomous syntax was scarce. The clearest data in this respect were reported by Forster and Ryder (1971) and Forster and Olbrei (1973). On the other hand, there was considerable evidence that was also taken as support for an interactive position (see especially Marslen-Wilson, 1975; Marslen-Wilson & Tyler, 1980).

It is only rather recently that a consistent, clearly interpretable body of experimental data has been collected that gives strong support to an autonomous position (e.g., Clifton, Frazier & Connine, 1984; Ferreira & Clifton, 1986; Frazier, 1979; Frazier & Rayner, 1982, 1987; Rayner et al., 1983; Rayner & Frazier, 1987). The contributions in this book by Frazier, Clifton and De Vincenzi, and even the results of the headline study by Perfetti represent new, strong evidence along the same line. On the other hand, there is again evidence for semantic and discourse influence on rather early stages of syntactic analysis, such as Altmann and Steedman (1988), Crain and Steedman (1985), Taraban and McClelland (1988), Taraban and McClelland (this volume), Britt (quoted by Perfetti in his chapter), and even some of the Perfetti results reported in his chapter. As Norris (1987) has claimed, the available evidence is not completely conclusive either for an interactive or for a purely autonomous position.

What is the solution? One possible answer is provided by Perfetti in his chapter. If the parser is willing to become patient and cooperative, it may be able to save its autonomy. Whether the solution proposed by Perfetti is more than a compromise, and whether his cooperative autonomous syntax will prove a robust and empirically realistic component of the language comprehension system, is difficult to answer.

The other solution is to accept a weak form of the interaction hypothesis. It may turn out that these two positions are equivalent. Becoming cooperative may mean that the parser accepts some form of interaction.

It is unlikely that we will reach a definitive conclusion by waiting for more experimental evidence. However impressive the evidence in favor of the autonomous position can be, the results of a single experiment will be enough to challenge its purity. So, it is not likely that the question will be settled by simple hypothesis testing. Although it is very difficult to determine exactly at which moment in the comprehension process the different components begin and end their action, and precisely where in the comprehension mechanism they work, it is probably more important to try to specify further in the models the locus and the type of action of the nonstructural information during processing, rather than collect more evidence in favor of or against the autonomy hypothesis. The chapters in this section all provide, in different ways, elements for further debate on this issue.

ARE PARSING PRINCIPLES UNIVERSAL?

Principles such as minimal attachment and late closure allow the parser to deliver quickly and efficiently a structure that can be further interpreted. As we have seen, one of the advantages of these principles is their low processing cost. For this reason, as Frazier (1987a) has argued, such principles should be universal. This claim has not remained unchallenged (see e.g., Cuetos & Mitchell, 1988; Mitchell, 1987a, 1987b), and is one of the important issues debated in the chapters of this section. In challenging Frazier's claim about universality, Cuetos and Mitchell (1988) introduced a distinction between *process generated* strategies and *arbitrary* or *unsystematic* ones. Whereas the former have developed as a result of processing advantages, strategies of the latter type would have evolved rather arbitrarily and for some reasons would have been established in the language comprehension system of the users of a given language. According to Cuetos and Mitchell, only strategies of the first type can claim universality, whereas arbitrary strategies would be, almost by definition, language specific. These authors also suggested that minimal attachment could plausibly be a process-generated strategy, ergo possibly universal, whereas late closure would be arbitrary and unsystematically generated. Essentially the same argument is made by Mitchell et al. in this volume.

This distinction, interesting as it may be, seems logically independent of the universality issue and is only to some extent relevant to it. A process-generated strategy can, in principle, be very language specific, in the sense that it can be a very economical and efficient operating principle for a language A but not for language B. In order to be taken as a serious candidate for universality, a strategy must be general enough to be valid across specific language differences.

A different, possibly interesting distinction I would like to propose is between two forms of the universality hypothesis, a strong and a weak form. According to a strong form of the universality hypothesis, the *same* principles should hold across languages. This should be true at least for languages of the same type, for example, for head-initial languages, in which the phrasal heads precede the complements (Frazier, 1987a). According to a weak form of the hypothesis, on the other hand, in all languages the parser would adopt the first constituent structure which becomes available, but the specific parsing devices used to obtain this could be different from language to language, provided that they produce a structure consistent with the grammatical constraints of a given language.

These two forms of the universality hypothesis make different predictions concerning the specific form of the parsing principles. According to the strong form, the parsing principles would have been identical across languages. In the weak account, for each language there would be the same tendency, but specific parsing principles might take a different form. They would be functionally similar in the sense that they would allow the parser to obtain the same results, for example, allowing, within the constraints posed by the grammar of a given language, high attachment. Thus, the issue would become not whether a given parsing principle is universal, but whether, depending on the structure of a language, one can find the same general principles underlying different specific parsing procedures.

How much evidence is available concerning the universality hypothesis? Evidence is still sparse and not very abundant. Most parsing work has been done in English and with English material, and it is only recently that genuine comparative data have become available. Late closure and minimal attachment have been formulated for a head-initial language such as English. Would they also operate in head-final languages? A question faced by De Vincenzi (1989) in her dissertation and in the Clifton and De Vincenzi chapter of this section is whether minimal attachment applies in Italian in cases of null subject. De Vincenzi proposes a general principle, minimal chain, which allows avoiding postulating unnecessary chain members at S-structures but does not delay required chain membership, a result clearly within minimal attachment.

Results of experiments with head-final embedded clauses in Dutch (Frazier, 1987b) are consistent with the operation of minimal attachment and so are data from another study with Dutch sentences and with German (Bayer, unpublished data). Minimal attachment seems to function also for a left-branching language such as Japanese (Ueda, cited in Frazier, 1987a). Thus, minimal attachment seems to be a consistent strategy both for head-final clauses in normally head-initial languages and for languages typologically distinct from English, evidence in favor of the universality hypothesis.

Evidence in favor of late closure from languages other than English is available, among few others, from a study on Dutch (Flores d'Arcais, unpublished data). This included two experiments, one with a word-by-word reading task (subject paced) and one with eye-fixation recording. The study investigated readers' comprehension of sentences of the type

4. *Jan zag Anneke lopend op het strand.*
    (John saw Anneke (while) running on the beach.)

The sentence is ambiguous in the sense that it can be either Jan or Anneke who is running on the beach. In the study, the sentences were disambiguated by a following clause, as in Sentence 4a and 4b.

4a. *Jan zag Anneke lopend op het strand; hij was moe.*
    (John saw Anneke running on the beach; he was tired.)

4b. *Jan zag Anneke lopend op het strand; ze was moe.*
    (John saw Anneke running on the beach; she was tired.)

In the first experiment, reading time for the initial pronoun of the second clause (*he* or *she*, respectively) and the following word, was higher for *he* than for *she*. The eye-fixation data also pointed in the same direction, and both results are clearly consistent with late closure.

Are the Mitchell et al. results in this book evidence for early closure, which would undermine the claim of universality of late closure? Frazier gives an elegant demonstration – with English material – of the possibility of getting results which on the surface can be explained as being due to early closure but which, interpreted more correctly, point to the action of another principle following late closure, namely a relevance principle.

The question of universality of parsing in language comprehension has been discussed earlier by the proponents of the competition model (Bates, McNew, MacWhinney, DeVescovi, & Smith, 1982; MacWhinney, 1987). According to these authors, this approach would pose problems for the notion of separation between syntax and semantics and for the claim of universality of the priority of one type of sentential information over others. Thus, evidence from research within the competition model could make a challenge both to the autonomy hypothesis and for the universality hypothesis. The former would be because claims of independence between syntax and semantics based on empirical results in one language would not be valid for another language. As for the latter, the claim for universal strategies in parsing would also not be granted, in the sense that processing principles of users of different languages would be based on differential use of *cues*.

There is an essential difference between cues and parsing principles. Cues are elements in the linguistic input which are potential carriers of critical linguistic information for the listener/reader, but they are not procedures for linguistic analysis. Differential use of linguistic cues in different languages represents an interesting ecological phenomenon. It indicates sensitivity of the language comprehension system to those elements that are likely to offer valid information for language comprehension. The existence of elements capable of signaling important structural features in a given language is without question. In a language characterized by a rich system of cases functioning as word suffixes, it would be surprising indeed if the language comprehension system would not give particular weight to the word endings as being capable of signaling essential morphological and syntactic elements. But does the use of such cues mean that the parsing principles we are considering are not operating in the same way? Is this evidence against the universality hypothesis?

The fact that English speakers rely on word-order information more than Italian speakers is an indication of sensitivity to ecologically valid linguistic information, but it does not say anything substantial about probable differences in parsing strategies. Claims against the universality hypothesis of parsing should come from specific evidence consisting, for example, of clear processing differences with material which, according to a given parsing principle, should result in corresponding structures in two languages. Interesting as they may be, cross-linguistic data obtained within the framework of the competition model are not directly critical for an evaluation of the universality hypothesis of parsing.

Admittedly, the cross-linguistic evidence available is still very scarce. And here, as for many other fundamental psycholinguistic issues, the need for experimental data from languages other than English is very strong. The contributions in this section of the book offer some important evidence concerning the theoretical debate on this issue, which had scarcely been discussed previously.

CONCLUSIONS

The contributions of this section give a representative and realistic picture of the type of work on syntactic analysis during reading presently being carried out in psycholinguistics and in the area of reading research. Although there are some points of disagreement among the contributions, the reader can quite safely accept some conclusions. What are the main points one can draw based on the work presented here?

The first concerns the nature of parsing principles. The evidence presented in Frazier's and in Clifton and De Vincenzi's chapters and in some of Perfetti's data, such as the headline study, is consistent with the view of an autonomous parser that operates on the basis of simple, economical principles such as minimal attachment. The degree of autonomy of the parser might still be a point of debate, the precise locus and the moment at which semantic and discourse factors begin affecting the on-line processing is also a matter still to be settled, but the basic notion of an autonomous parser seems confirmed rather than weakened by the evidence and the discussion of the contributions of this section.

A second point concerns the universality of the parsing principles. The claim that general principles such as minimal attachment and late closure that allow the parser to operate quickly and efficiently with a minimum of processing load are universal is not inconsistent with the available experimental evidence. Given the scarcity of genuine cross-linguistic studies relevant to this specific issue, however, this conclusion might have to be changed in the light of new evidence.

As Rayner mentions in his introduction to the present volume, the scope of the conclusions about parsing mechanisms extends beyond the domain of reading research and is valid for the comprehension of both written and spoken language. This does not, of course, diminish the interest of these contributions for the specific domain to which the book is addressed, namely the processes of comprehension during reading. It is hardly possible to think of a comprehensive theory about reading that does not include an accurate explanation of the processes of linguistic analysis that eventually produce a mental representation of the content of the text.

REFERENCES

Altmann, G., & Steedman, M. (1988). Interaction with context in human sentence processing. *Cognition, 30*, 191 - 238.

Bates, E., McNew, S., MacWhinney, B., DeVescovi, A., & Smith, S. (1982). Functional constraints on sentence processing: A cross-linguistic study. *Cognition, 11*, 245 - 299.

Bever, T. G. (1970). The cognitive basis for linguistic structures. In J. R. Hayes (Ed.), *Cognition and the development of language* (pp. 279 - 362). New York: Wiley.

Clifton, C., Frazier, L., & Connine, C. (1984). Lexical expectations in sentence comprehension. *Journal of Verbal Learning and Verbal Behavior, 23*, 696 - 708.

Crain, S., & Steedman, M. (1985). On not being led up the garden path: The use of context by the psychological syntax processor. In D. R. Dowty, L. Karttunen, & A. M. Zwicky (Eds.), *Natural language parsing: Psychological, computational, and theoretical perspectives* (pp. 320 - 358). Cambridge: Cambridge University Press.

Cuetos, F., & Mitchell, D. C. (1988). Cross-linguistic differences in parsing: Restrictions on the use of the late closure strategy in Spanish. *Cognition, 30*, 73 - 105.

De Jong, G. (1979). *Skimming stories in real time: An experiment in integrated understanding.* (Research Report 158). New Haven, CT: Yale University, Computer Science Department.

De Jong, G. (1982). An overview of the FRUMP system. In W. G. Lehnert & M. H. Ringle (Eds.), *Strategies for natural language parsing* (149 - 176). Hillsdale, NJ: Lawrence Erlbaum Associates.

De Vincenzi, M. (1989). *Syntactic parsing strategies in a null subject language.* Unpublished doctoral dissertation, University of Massachusetts, Amherst.

Ferreira, F., & Clifton, C. (1986). The independence of syntactic processing. *Journal of Memory and Language, 25,* 348 - 368.

Flores d'Arcais, G. B. (1982). Automatic syntactic computation and use of semantic information during sentence comprehension. *Psychological Research, 44,* 231 - 242.

Fodor, J. A., Bever, T. G., & Garrett, M. F. (1974). *The psychology of language: An introduction to psycholinguistic and generative grammar.* New York: McGraw-Hill.

Forster, K. I., & Ryder, L. A. (1971). Perceiving the structure and meaning of sentences. *Journal of Verbal Learning and Verbal Behavior, 9,* 285 - 296.

Forster, K. I., & Olbrei, I. (1973). Semantic heuristics and syntactic analysis. *Cognition, 2,* 319 - 347.

Frazier, L. (1979). *On comprehending sentences: Syntactic parsing strategies.* Bloomington: Indiana University Linguistics Club.

Frazier, L. (1987a). Sentence processing: A tutorial review. In M. Coltheart (Ed.), *Attention and performance XII: The psychology of reading* (pp. 559 - 586). Hillsdale, NJ: Lawrence Erlbaum Associates.

Frazier, L. (1987b). Syntactic processing: Evidence from Dutch. *Natural Language and Linguistic Theory, 5,* 519 - 560.

Frazier, L. (1989). Against lexical generation of syntax. In W. Marslen-Wilson (Ed.), *Lexical representation and process* (pp. 505 - 528). Cambridge, MA: MIT Press.

Frazier, L., Clifton, C., & Randall, J. (1983). Filling gaps: Decision principles and structure in sentence comprehension. *Cognition, 13,* 187 - 222.

Frazier, L., & Rayner, K. (1982). Making and correcting errors during sentence comprehension: Eye movements in the analysis of structurally ambiguous sentences. *Cognitive Psychology, 14,* 178 - 210.

Frazier, L., & Rayner, K. (1987). Resolution of syntactic category ambiguities: Eye movements in parsing lexically ambiguous sentences. *Journal of Memory and Language, 26,* 505 - 526.

Herriot, P. (1967). The comprehension of active and passive sentences as a function of pragmatic expectations. *Journal of Verbal Learning and Verbal Behavior, 6,* 166 - 169.

Kimball, J. (1973). Seven principles of surface structure parsing in natural language. *Cognition, 2,* 15 - 47.

MacWhinney, B. (1987). The competition model. In B. MacWhinney (Ed.), *Mechanisms of language acquisition* (pp. 249 - 308). Hillsdale, NJ: Lawrence Erlbaum Associates.

Marslen-Wilson, W. D. (1975). Sentence perception as an interactive parallel process. *Science, 189,* 226 - 228.

Marslen-Wilson, W., & Tyler, L. K. (1980). The temporal structure of spoken language understanding. *Cognition, 8,* 1 - 71.

Mitchell, D. C. (1987a). Lexical guidance in human parsing: Locus and processing characteristics. In M. Coltheart (Ed.), *Attention and performance XII: The psychology of reading* (pp. 601 - 618). Hillsdale, NJ: Lawrence Erlbaum Associates.

Mitchell, D. C. (1987b). Reading and syntactic analysis. In J. Beech & A. Colley (Eds.), *Cognitive approaches to reading* (pp. 87 - 112). Chichester: Wiley.

Norris, D. (1987). Syntax, semantics, and garden paths. In A. W. Ellis (Ed.), *Progress in the psychology of language* (pp. 233 - 252). London: Lawrence Erlbaum Associates.

Rayner, K., Carlson, M., & Frazier, L. (1983). The interaction of syntax and semantics during sentence processing: Eye movements in the analysis of semantically biased sentences. *Journal of Verbal Learning and Verbal Behavior, 22*, 358 - 374.

Rayner, K., & Frazier, L. (1987). Parsing temporarily ambiguous complements. *Quarterly Journal of Experimental Psychology, 39A*, 657 - 673.

Schank, R. C. (1972). Conceptual dependency: A theory of natural language understanding. *Cognitive Psychology, 3*, 552 - 631.

Slobin, D. E. (1966). Grammatical transformations and sentence comprehension in childhood and adulthood. *Journal of Verbal Learning and Verbal Behavior, 5*, 219 - 227.

Taraban, R., & McClelland, J. L. (1988). Constituent attachment and thematic role assignment in sentence processing: Influences of content-based expectations. *Journal of Memory and Language, 27*, 597 - 632.

Wilks, Y. (1978). Computational models for language processing. *Cognitive psychology: Language*. Milton Keynes: Open University Press.

III COMPREHENSION OF DISCOURSE

17 CAUSAL RELATEDNESS AND TEXT COMPREHENSION

Jerome L. Myers

University of Massachusetts, Amherst

INTRODUCTION

The comprehension of a text must involve something more than the recognition of words and the parsing of sentences into propositional units. Presumably, the representation constructed by a reader involves not only explicit text propositions but inferences based upon those propositions and the reader's knowledge of the world. These inferences may link propositions and concepts that are widely separated in the physical text. Much recent research on text comprehension focuses on what inferences are drawn and what connections exist among the propositions that are represented in the reader's memory of a text.

Attempting to answer such questions, several theorists recently have emphasized causal inferences, arguing that the causal structures of texts influence how they are processed. This is not very surprising; common sense suggests that comprehension involves building linkages among sentences and that, particularly in narratives, such linkages will often be causal. The issue is the nature of the processing of causal information and of the resulting memory representation. What information is foregrounded by readers as they move through the text? Under what conditions do readers search their memory of the text to seek causes for current inputs? Are all possible causes of some event connected to it in the final representation, or only some subset? These are but a few of the questions we might ask about causal comprehension.

At the very least, readers respond to causal breaks in text. If the immediately preceding text fails to provide a cause for an action contained in the sentence just read, the reader reviews earlier segments of the text in memory and, if necessary, uses world knowledge to generate bridging inferences between the current sentence and sentences read earlier. This claim is supported by several studies showing that reading time increases with decreased causal coherence (Haberlandt & Bingham, 1978; Keenan, Baillet, & Brown, 1984; Myers, Shinjo, & Duffy, 1987; O'Brien & Myers, 1985). Such variation in reading time is also accompanied by variation in memory for the text. When it is difficult to generate a causal inference, memory is poor; however, when a causal inference can readily be drawn in response to a coherence break, text memory is actually better than in texts in which there is no coherence break (Keenan et al., 1984; Myers & Duffy, in press; Myers et al., 1987; O'Brien & Myers, 1985).

At one extreme, we can conceive of a model of the comprehension process in which the reader is viewed as relatively passive; causal linkages are sought and constructed only in response to coherence breaks. At the other extreme, we can conceive of a much more active processor, one that constructs a richly interconnected network of causal links among the protagonist's goals, the events of the story, and its outcome. This second type of text representation is presented in several recent articles by Trabasso and his colleagues (Trabasso & van den Broek, 1985; Trabasso & Sperry, 1985). It is consistent with the viewpoint of several other investigators of text memory (e.g. Black & Bower, 1980; Graesser, 1981). I begin by reviewing the Trabasso model, the relevant data, and the implications for processing causal relations in text. Then I discuss a model proposed by Fletcher and Bloom (1988), in which the reader is assumed to be a less active processor. One of the issues inherent in the contrast between these two models, and central in any discussion of causal processing, is the status of information about the protagonist's goal. Is it maintained in working memory as the text is read? Is it connected to many different actions and events? I conclude this chapter by describing some recent experiments in my lab which begin to address these questions.

TRABASSO'S MODEL OF CAUSAL STRUCTURE

Analysis of Narrative Text

Trabasso's analysis of a text's causal structure begins by parsing the text into statements of events, corresponding roughly to clauses. All pairs of statements are considered and one event, A, is said to cause another, B, if in the context of the story B would not have occurred if A had not occurred. Enablement, motivation, and physical and psychological causes all provide the basis for causal links among events.

Figure 17.1 presents an example of a causal structure. The nodes in this structure may be distinguished with respect to two properties. First, the number of paths to or from a node varies. For example, node 6 has three connections, whereas node 8 has five. Recall of a statement has been shown to increase with the number of connections (Trabasso

& van den Broek, 1985). Second, nodes are either on or off the causal chain between the opening statement and the closing statement. Nodes that are not on the chain, such as nodes 9, 11, 12, and 14, are less well remembered than those that are on the chain (Trabasso & van den Broek, 1985). Importance ratings (Trabasso & Sperry, 1985) and frequency of inclusion in summaries (van den Broek & Trabasso, 1986) have also been shown to correlate significantly with these two properties of the network.

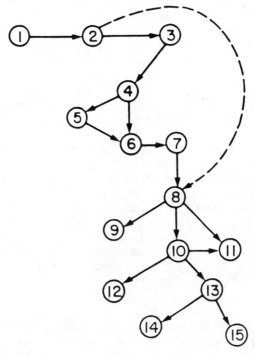

FIGURE 17.1. A possible representation of items at different levels of causal related-ness.

Retrieval Times

These effects of causal structures of texts may reflect comprehension processes operating during reading; however, they may also be a func-tion of reconstructive processes operating at a later time when recall is required. In an attempt to obtain more direct evidence of the nature of the representation, O'Brien and I (O'Brien & Myers, 1987) analyzed the effects of causal structure upon reading times and recall times ob-tained immediately after reading. Time to read a statement containing an anaphoric reference to an antecedent in the text decreased as the number of causal connections to the statement containing the anaphor increased. Time to produce the antecedent word in answer to a ques-tion (e.g., "What was the stolen object?") was measured in a subsequent study; the anaphoric reference was dropped from the text. These recall times were a function of the length of the shortest causal path from the setting information in the passage to the statement containing the targeted word.

In summary, patterns of causal connections clearly influence retrieval times. However, the critical aspect of the pattern–causal connectivity or distance–depends on the nature of the retrieval task. We assume this is because reinstatement and recall searches of the long-term memory representation start from different points. Recall involves a spread of activation along causal links, beginning at the first proposition encountered. In such a search, the shortest path dominates and therefore path length is a critical variable in determining recall times. On the other hand, reinstatement searches initiated by an anaphoric reference are assumed to start from nodes corresponding to propositions in a buffer (Kintsch & van Dijk, 1978). These propositions come from different parts of the passage and, therefore, are more likely to make contact with a targeted proposition that lies on many different causal paths; that is, one with many connections.

We should also emphasize that variables other than those derived from the analysis of the causal structure of text had no effect in either the analysis of reinstatement or recall times. In particular, we found that retrieval times were uncorrelated with variables derived from the Kintsch and van Dijk model. This is consistent with results reported by Fletcher (1986) and Fletcher and Bloom (1988). In addition, when we adjusted for causal effects, neither the time spent reading the targeted propositions, nor their rated importance, contributed significant variability.

Summary

Measures of memory obtained both during and at various times after reading support Trabasso and Sperry's "assumption that causal inferences underlie the construction of a story representation in memory." (p. 609). However, I have some reservations because many of the results rest upon regression analyses and the conclusions are therefore sensitive to (a) correlations among predictors, (b) sample size relative to the number of predictors, (c) which predictors have been included, and (d) specific strategies for assessing the contributions of predictors. Nevertheless, the pattern of results is consistent across studies. It seems clear that an adequate model of text comprehension should produce a representation consistent with these results. However, many process models should be capable of doing this. In particular, although the results are consistent with the representation proposed by Trabasso and his colleagues, they would also be predicted by many models that assumed a subset of the links and, accordingly, a less active processor than that implied by Trabasso's model. One such alternative has been proposed and is considered next.

FLETCHER AND BLOOM'S CURRENT-STATE MODEL

Table 17.1 presents a text used in a study by Bloom, Fletcher, van den Broek, Reitz, and Shapiro (1990). Each sentence has been partitioned into statements using two rules. First, a sentence boundary always terminates a statement. Second, a clause boundary terminates a statement only if it separates statements having different causal antecedents or consequences. Figure 17.2 diagrams the representation of the text in Table 17.1. The nodes represent statements and the arrows represent causal connections according to the Trabasso and Sperry text analysis.

Considering all the arrows, both solid and dashed, it should be clear that the Trabasso representation implies an active processor that must maintain many propositions in an active state or undertake frequent searches of long-term memory in order to connect current inputs to distant causal antecedents or both. The solid arrows represent a subset of connections based on a processing model proposed by Fletcher and Bloom (1988). This is essentially the Kintsch and van Dijk (1978) model but with the leading-edge strategy replaced by the assumption that the most recent statement connected to an antecedent, but not to a consequence, is held in a buffer. Fletcher and Bloom referred to this as the current-state selection strategy. As an example of this strategy, when the reader processes the first statement, a link is formed from Statement 2 to Statement 1; seeing the Bike causes Danny to want it. Statement 1 is held in the buffer as the second sentence is processed and is causally linked to Statement 4; wanting to have the bike is causally related to wanting to buy it.

Fletcher and Bloom found that propositional recall correlated significantly with the number of cycles in the buffer and the number of causal connections derived from the current-state strategy; the relevant connections are indicated by the solid arrows of Figure 17.2. Their model accounted for more of the variance (31%) of propositional recall than both the Kintsch and van Dijk model and a model closer to Trabasso's position (the most recent goal statement was held in the buffer in addition to the statements dictated by the current-state model).

A more direct comparison of the current-state and Trabasso models is provided by reading times obtained by Bloom et al. (1990). They assumed (a) that time is required to connect statements, (b) that causal connections between statements in the same sentence (sentence links) will be made more rapidly than connections between a new statement and one currently in working memory (working memory connections), and (c) that when no causal antecedent is available, a search of long-term memory is required. They also distinguished between allowable (solid lines of Figure 17.2) and potential (dashed lines of Figure 17.2) causal links. Ordinarily, a potential link will not be accompanied by increased reading time. The exception occurs when reinstatement searches occur. Bloom et al. predicted such searches under three conditions: (a)

TABLE 17.1

Passage from Bloom et al. called Danny's New Bike.

1. Danny wanted to have the red bike
2. that he saw in the window of the neighborhood bike shop.
3. Danny knew that first he had to have $50
4. to buy the bike.
5. He asked his parents if they would give him the money.
6. His parents denied his request.
7. They suggested that Danny earn the money himself
8. by getting a job.
9. Danny was mad at his parents
10. for not giving him the money,
11. but he was determined to get the money somehow.
12. He knew he would have to find a job,
13. so he called the newspaper
14. and asked for a paper route.
15. He started delivering papers in the neighborhood the next week
16. and earned ten dollars a week.
17. With this job,
18. Danny had $50 within a few weeks.
19. He took his hard-earned money to the shop,
20. bought the bike,
21. and rode happily home.

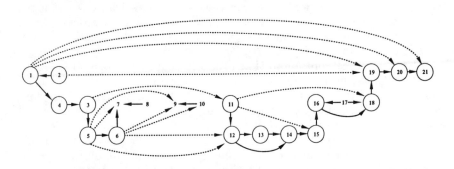

FIGURE 17.2. Bloom et al.'s representation of Danny's New Bike text.

when a sentence has no causal connection in short-term memory (coherence break), (b) when a statement satisfies a goal no longer in short-term memory (goal satisfaction), or (c) when a statement frustrates a goal no longer in short-term memory. Table 17.2 presents a summary of the results of a regression analysis performed on the average reading time per word for each statement. Only significant predictors are included.

The results are consistent with Bloom et al.'s predictions. Potential links do not have an effect upon reading time except when they link a goal to a statement satisfying it, or when there is a coherence break.

On the other hand, sentence links and working memory links apparently do require time to construct. The only exception to the authors' predictions is that goal-frustration statements were not read more slowly than other statements which were not expected to have an effect. In short, the model gives a good account of the reading time data. Furthermore, the relative magnitudes of the slope coefficients accord well with assumptions about the underlying processes. In contrast with the Trabasso model, in which all potential links are encoded, the current-state model's assumptions about the processor seem more consistent with response time data that suggest that subjects draw inferences only when required to maintain text coherence or when instructed to do so (Duffy, 1986; O'Brien, Shank, Myers, & Rayner, 1988; Potts, Keenan, & Golding, 1988; Singer & Ferreira, 1983).

TABLE 17.2

Multiple Regression Analysis on Mean Word Reading Time Per Clause.

R^2	Slope coefficient	Proportion unique variance
Predictor		
Full Model (R^2) = .53)		
Sentence Links	63	.10
Working Memory Links	115	.32
Coherence Break	1037	.08
Potential Links		
x	27	.02
Goal Satisfaction		

Source: Bloom et al., 1990.

Despite its success in accounting for reading times, the model is in an early stage of development; not surprisingly, there are still problems to be addressed. Some of these problems, such as the description of inferences readers generate, are common to all text processing models, and seem impossible to overcome. Others are specific to the basic strategy of holding a statement for another processing cycle only if it has an antecedent cause but no consequence in the previously read text. In apparent contradiction of this strategy, the results of a series of experiments by Duffy (1986) suggest that events that lack a causal antecedent in the preceding text are very likely to be held in working memory. These are events that might be characterized as script deviations. For example, Duffy used a story of someone eating in a train's dining car; in one version of the story, without apparent cause, "the train came to a screeching halt." Duffy's conclusion that this sentence is held in working memory seems quite reasonable; when some action occurs that has no obvious cause, we focus on it and search the following text for a cause or consequence to which it can be connected. This would seem to be a necessary addendum to the current-state strategy.

Another model-specific problem is related to the assumption that reading a goal-satisfying statement initiates a search of long-term memory. This assumption is supported by the reading time data. For example, the potential link between Statements 1 (wanting the bike) and 20 (buying the bike) in the example (Table 17.1 and Figure 17.2) increases reading time more than other potential links which do not connect goal-satisfaction statements. The issue, however, is how do readers recognize that some action satisfies the protagonist's goal? One possibility is that they do so by initiating a check of each new event against information in long-term memory. However, this assumption of frequent long-term memory searches defeats the primary intent of the current-state model. Furthermore, it is contradicted by the finding that potential links (with the exceptions assumed by the current-state model) do not contribute to increases in reading times.

Two other explanations appear difficult to decide between on the basis of the available data. The first is that the increased reading time for Statement 20 has nothing to do with its relation to the goal but instead reflects a search to find the antecedent of the anaphor, *the bike*. The bike has been backgrounded by 16 intervening statements (see Table 17.1) in the example provided by Bloom et al., and we would expect some increase in reading time (Ehrlich & Rayner, 1983; Lesgold, Roth, & Curtis, 1979). One way to further analyze this possibility might be to design passages in which the degree of backgrounding is held constant but the anaphor (e.g., the bike) is either part of a goal-satisfaction statement or not.

The other possible explanation of the effects of the goal-satisfaction statement is that goal information is maintained in working memory during the reading of the text and is available for connection to the goal-satisfaction sentence. Under this assumption, the slight increase in reading times for goal-satisfaction statements (relative to statements whose links are not allowed by the current-state model) may reflect time required to wrap-up the story, to further integrate the diverse elements of the representation. Fletcher and Bloom rejected this assumption of goal maintenance because a current-state + goal model did not account for more of the variance in recall of propositions than did the current-state (without goal) model. A more direct experimental test of goal maintenance would be more convincing.

It is to Fletcher and Bloom's credit that their model is well enough specified so that we can question its assumptions. The problems I have raised suggest that the next step is to obtain more direct measures of on-line processes and the resulting representation. We need to determine what is held in working memory at each point in the text and what connections are established in long-term memory. Because goals are well-defined causes of subsequent events, and because they have a central role in theories such as those I have considered, Stephen Dopkins and I have begun to investigate how readers process and represent goal information. Some preliminary findings are considered next.

The Accessibility of Information About Goals

Both Trabasso and van den Broek (1985) and Fletcher and Bloom (1988) would predict that a concept will be more accessible in long-term memory when it is part of a statement that defines a goal than when it is not part of such a statement. This is because such a goal statement typically will have more connections than other statements and will also be on the causal chain. The exact processing mechanism underlying this effect has not been specified by these authors but spreading-activation theories predict effects of causal connectivity (Bradshaw & Anderson, 1982; Myers, O'Brien, Balota, & Toyofuku, 1984; O'Brien & Myers, 1987). Dopkins and I designed our first experiments to verify whether goal information was more accessible in long-term memory. Our subjects read one of two versions of each of 28 passages with 56 filler passages interspersed. An example of the goal and control versions of one passage is presented in Table 17.3. The goal version contains a goal-setting sentence (*They looked for a hostage . . .*) whereas that goal has been met in the control version (*They grabbed a hostage . . .*). To test for the accessibility of the goal word (*hostage*), we used McKoon and Ratcliff's (1984) item-recognition procedure. Subjects read each line at their own pace and, when the last line was completed, the goal word (or some other word after filler passages) was presented. According to various models of causal linkage, the goal word should be recognized more quickly in the goal than in the control condition because in the goal condition the goal-setting (causal) statement presumably has been reinstated and linked to the goal-satisfaction statement (*Al crept up quickly behind the warden*), thus making the goal word more accessible.

In designing the critical passages, we intentionally wrote the goal statement so that the target noun (the goal word, *hostage* in the example) was a category whose membership is not well defined. This permits us to avoid strong lexical associations between the goal word and its subsequent instantiation (*warden*); such associations would operate in both versions and might obscure an advantage for the goal condition. We also avoided anaphoric references to the target in the last (goal-satisfaction) sentence. Therefore, if the target was recognized faster in goal than in control versions, we could rule out the possibility that it was because of a direct reference to the target word in the goal version. Finally, we equated the wording of the two versions as much as possible to minimize any differences in lexical associations to the target word.

In the first of two experiments, the probe immediately followed the last sentence. Because we were concerned with long-term memory retrieval, we also ran the experiment with a 10 second delay of probe; the subject counted backward by threes during the delay to increase the likelihood that retrieval was from long-term memory. In both Experiments

TABLE 17.3

Sample Passage from Dopkins and Myers (1989)
(Probe is HOSTAGE)

Goal Version

Al and Dave were in the process of breaking
out of the state pen. With snarls on
their faces, they raced down a corridor.
They looked for a hostage to improve
their bargaining position. When
the warden appeared, Al crept up quickly behind him.

Control Version

Al and Dave were in the process of breaking
out of the state pen. With snarls on
their faces, they raced down a corridor.
They grabbed a hostage to improve
their bargaining position. When
the warden appeared, Al told him to keep back.

1 and 2, the target word (e.g., *hostage*) was recognized approximately
100 ms faster in the goal than in the control condition.

There are many possible reasons for the effect we obtained. Three of
these do not reflect greater accessibility in memory. One, lexical priming, we view as extremely unlikely because our materials were written
so that the words in the goal and control conditions should not differ
in lexical relatedness to the probe word. A second possible explanation
of our result is that there are spillover effects associated with the control passages; for reasons that are unclear, subjects still may have been
processing the last sentence of the control passage when the probe was
presented, and therefore would respond more slowly to probes of control
passages. We tested this hypothesis by rerunning the experiment with a
neutral word from the text as a probe, reasoning that if the effect is due
to processing spillover, it should depend on the nature of the passage,
not on the test word. Recognition times for the goal version were 57
ms slower than for the control version and its error rate was .04 lower;
neither of these differences even approached significance.

A third possibility is that the test word fits the general context of
the goal passage better than that of the control version. To test this
context-checking hypothesis, we revised the early part of the passages
so the probe word did not appear; for example, there was no mention of
wanting to obtain (goal version) or having obtained (control version) a
hostage. This leaves the context of the last sentences. Thus, if subjects

in our initial experiments were faster to recognize *hostage* because it fit better with creeping up behind the warden than with telling the warden to stay back, negative response times should be slower in the revised goal version than in the revised control version. The response times were 1166 and 1162 ms for the goal and control versions, and the error rates were both .05. Thus there is no support for the context checking interpretation of the data.

These control experiments support the general position that a word is more accessible in memory when it is part of a goal statement than it otherwise would be. One possible reason for this is that readers recognize a sentence as setting the protagonist's goal and that sentence receives more attention than other nongoal sentences. Therefore, the node containing the goal concept would be stronger in the goal than in the control version. To test this, we truncated our original passages after the sentence containing the goal word. Subjects were required to count backward by threes to minimize the contribution of short-term memory, and then viewed the probe word. If the target received more attention when it was part of a statement of a goal than when it was part of a statement describing accomplishment of a goal, it would be recognized more quickly in the goal than in the control condition. Responses were 37 ms faster in the goal condition but error rates were .02 higher; neither effect even approached significance. We conclude that differences in attention to the sentence mentioning the goal do not account for the difference in recognition time in the goal and control conditions. The effect obtained in the initial experiments appears to require the presence of the goal-satisfaction sentence.

The results of our experiments support the position that a connection is established during reading between the goal word (e.g., *hostage*) and its instantiation (e.g., *warden*), but only in the condition in which a goal has been set (the goal condition). We assume that this connection resulted in increased activation of the goal word and, therefore, faster recognition. If this were the case, we should be able to obtain more direct evidence of the link between the goal word and its instantiation. In an attempt to do so, we presented the subject with word pairs, such as *hostage-warden*, after every two passages. They were required to respond positively only if both words had appeared anywhere in the preceding two passages; the two words did not have to come from the same passage. Foils were from earlier passages. Responses were significantly faster when the two words came from a goal passage than when they came from a control passage; the difference was 80 ms. In short, using the same word pairs and controlling the distance between the two words in the text, we found significantly faster recognition when the second member of the pair satisfied the goal represented by the first word.

We next considered the reason for the establishment of connections between the goal word and its instantiation. One possible basis for the connection is an active attempt by the reader to anticipate subsequent text events. In our example, the reader might infer that Al crept up behind the warden to make him a hostage. This seems unlikely in the face of many studies that have failed to demonstrate forward inferencing (e.g., Duffy, 1986; Potts et al., 1988). An alternative mechanism is suggested by Garrod and Sanford's (1977) discussion of the comprehension of anaphors. They hypothesized that when the reader encounters a reference to an object or individual, the reference must be checked against locations in memory in order to store the new information. Within this framework, we assumed that the warden is checked against the hostage and, in the goal version, this test is passed. Incorporating Garrod and Sanford's assumption that "each individual is represented at the most specific level possible" (p. 88), we hypothesized that if the warden had been mentioned earlier in the text, the information about the warden would be attached to that node rather than to the hostage node.

To test this hypothesis, we designed an experiment in which the goal instantiation was also an anaphoric reference to an earlier occurrence of the same word. In the example of Table 17.3, the following sentence was inserted (in both versions) just after the first sentence: *They wanted to bust out just to spite the cruel warden.* We hypothesized that the warden mentioned in the last sentence of the goal passage would now be attached to its antecedent rather than to *hostage.* There were four within-subject conditions: The subject was tested on the goal word (*hostage*) following the revised goal or control version, or the subject was tested on the adjective that had been used to describe the antecedent (ambitious) following either the goal version or a control requiring neither an anaphoric or causal connection. Using the item-recognition procedure, we obtained a 100 ms advantage for the adjective in the anaphoric condition over its control condition. Therefore, we conclude that the anaphoric connection between *the warden* in the last sentence and *the cruel warden* mentioned earlier has been made. However, recognition times were a nonsignificant 30 ms faster for the goal word in the goal than in the control version. In other words, *hostage* is not recognized significantly more quickly in the goal version when the recently mentioned *warden* can be tied to the earlier mention of *warden.*

These results are consistent with the idea that comprehension involves connecting new information to the memory representation. The search for an anaphoric antecedent is a first response in that process and, if the resulting representation is coherent, no further connections are made. The results of this last experiment also serve as further evidence against the assumption that the recognition advantage observed for the goal condition in our initial experiments was due to context checking. In these revised versions, the relation of the probe to the context in goal and control versions is essentially unchanged but we no longer observe a significant advantage for the goal condition. Similar reasoning argues that different lexical relations in the two passage versions are not a factor in the effects we have obtained.

Our results seem to support the position that goal-satisfying statements are linked to statements initially setting the goal (e.g., Bloom et al., 1990; Fletcher & Bloom, 1988; Trabasso & van den Broek, 1985).

However, we do not view the establishment of this connection as the result of an active problem-solving process in which the reader seeks causal relations between current input and previously read propositions. Nor do we believe the connection between goal-setting statements and goal-satisfaction statements occurs as generally as suggested by Bloom et al. (1990). It will occur if there is an anaphoric connection between the two statements or if there is no better place to locate concepts introduced in the goal-satisfaction statement. The reader's goal is not to establish a richly interconnected causal representation but rather to maintain what McKoon and Ratcliff (1986) have labeled minimal local coherence. In the last experiment we described, this was done by linking the current mention of the warden to the earlier mention of warden and therefore the warden was never linked to the hostage.

CONCLUDING REMARKS

Both common sense and data tell us that the processing of causal relations in text must be an important part of the comprehension process. Unfortunately, most of the results published so far tell us very little about such details of the process as which links are constructed, and at what point during the reading of the text this occurs. Much of the problem resides in our methods. The majority of studies of causal comprehension have used very indirect measures of the comprehension process – recall scores, importance ratings, frequency of inclusion in summaries. Such measures seem particularly susceptible to factors that may have their influence after the text has been read. At best, they demonstrate that there are effects of causal relations. To establish what processes underlie the effects will require more research with on-line measures of comprehension.

Fletcher and Bloom's current-state model is an important step in the right direction. Although its generality may be limited, and the assumed strategy may require modification, it has the virtue of making testable predictions about the contents of both long-term and working memory at various points in the text. Reading time data have provided some validation of its process assumptions. However, although reading times enable us to test our ideas about when processing difficulties should occur, they only indirectly reflect the contents of memory. Further tests of the current-state model should entail probes of memory at various points in the text and priming studies designed to test whether hypothesized connections are present in memory.

In summary, Trabasso and Sperry (1985) are undoubtedly correct in their general claim that causal structure underlies the construction of the memory representation of a story. Fletcher and Bloom (1988) have made an important contribution by formulating a process model that is open to on-line tests; such tests have led them to hypothesize a less active process than that implied by Trabasso and his colleagues. One central issue in understanding how causal relations are comprehended is how readers process information about goals. Although Dopkins and I have made a modest start in investigating this question, much remains to be done. We need to define the processing issues more precisely and focus our research efforts on these. I also would urge less reliance on regression analyses and more on experiments in which several versions of a text are carefully constructed and the response to some part of the text is targeted for analysis. This approach involves the risk of drawing overly general conclusions from arbitrarily constructed, perhaps unrepresentative, texts. We have to bear this risk in mind, but I believe that such a modular approach to research on text comprehension is the most promising route to the development of an adequate general model.

ACKNOWLEDGMENT

This research was supported by National Science Foundation grant BNS83-17900 and National Institute of Mental Health grant 1 RO1 MH 40029. I wish to thank Stephen Dopkins, Susan A. Duffy, and Nancy A. Myers for helpful discussions of this work, and Stephen Dopkins and Nancy A. Myers for their comments on the manuscript.

REFERENCES

Anderson, J. R. (1983). A spreading activation theory of memory. *Journal of Verbal Learning and Verbal Behavior, 22*, 261 - 295.

Black, J. B., & Bower, G. H. (1980). Story understanding as problem solving. *Poetics, 9*, 223 - 250.

Bloom, C. P., Fletcher, C. R., van den Broek, P., Reitz, L., & Shapiro, B. P. (1990). An on-line assessment of causal reasoning during comprehension. *Memory & Cognition, 18*, 65 - 71.

Bradshaw, G. L., & Anderson, J. R. (1982). Elaborative encoding as an explanation of levels of processing. *Journal of Verbal Learning and Verbal Behavior, 21*, 165 - 174.

Dopkins, S., & Myers, J. L. (1989). *Goal relationships during the processing of text.* Unpublished manuscript, University of Massachusetts, Amherst.

Duffy, S. A. (1986). Role of expectations in sentence integration. *Journal of Experimental Psychology: Learning, Memory, and Cognition, 12*, 208 - 219.

Ehrlich, K., & Rayner, K. (1983). Pronoun assignment and semantic integration during reading: Eye movements and immediacy of processing. *Journal of Verbal Learning and Verbal Behavior, 22*, 75 - 87.

Fletcher, C. R. (1986). Strategies for the allocation of short-term memory during comprehension. *Journal of Memory and Language, 25*, 43 - 58.

Fletcher, C. R., & Bloom, C. P. (1988). Causal reasoning in the comprehension of simple narrative texts. *Journal of Memory and Language, 27*, 235 - 244.

Garrod, S., & Sanford, A. (1977). Interpreting anaphoric relations: The integration of semantic information while reading. *Journal of Verbal Learning and Verbal Behavior, 16*, 77 - 90.

Graesser, A. C. (1981). *Prose comprehension beyond the word.* New York: Springer.

Haberlandt, K., & Bingham, G. (1978). Verbs contribute to the coherence of brief narratives: Reading related and unrelated sentence triples. *Journal of Verbal Learning and Verbal Behavior, 17*, 419 - 425.

Keenan, J. M., Baillet, S. D., & Brown, P. (1984). The effects of causal cohesion on comprehension and memory. *Journal of Verbal Learning and Verbal Behavior, 23*, 115 - 126.

Kintsch, W., & van Dijk, T. A. (1978). Toward a model of text comprehension and production. *Psychological Review, 85*, 363 - 394.

Lesgold, A. M., Roth, S. F., & Curtis, M. E. (1979). Foregrounding effects in discourse comprehension. *Journal of Verbal Learning and Verbal Behavior, 18*, 291 - 308.

McKoon, G., & Ratcliff, R. (1984). Priming and on-line text comprehension. In D. E. Kieras & M. A. Just (Eds.), *New methods in reading comprehension research* (pp. 119 - 128). Hillsdale, NJ: Lawrence Erlbaum Associates.

McKoon, G., & Ratcliff, R. (1986). Inferences about predictable events. *Journal of Experimental Psychology: Learning, Memory, and Cognition, 12*, 82 - 91.

Myers, J. L., & Duffy, S. A. (in press). Causal inferences and text memory. In A. C. Graesser & G. H. Bower (Eds.), *The psychology of learning and motivation* (Vol. 25). Orlando, FL: Academic Press.

Myers, J. L., O'Brien, E. J., Balota, D. A., & Toyofuku, M. L. (1984). Memory search without interference: The role of integration. *Cognitive Psychology, 16*, 217 - 242.

Myers, J. L., Shinjo, M., & Duffy, S. A. (1987). Degree of causal relatedness and memory. *Journal of Memory and Language, 26*, 453 - 465.

O'Brien, E. J. (1987). Antecedent search processes and the structure of text. *Journal of Experimental Psychology: Learning, Memory, and Cognition, 13*, 278 - 290.

O'Brien, E. J., & Myers, J. L. (1985). When comprehension difficulty improves memory for text. *Journal of Experimental Psychology: Learning, Memory, and Cognition, 11*, 12 - 21.

O'Brien, E. J., & Myers, J. L. (1987). The role of causal connections in the retrieval of text. *Memory & Cognition, 15*, 419 - 427.

O'Brien, E. J., Shank, D. M., Myers, J. L., & Rayner, K. (1988). Elaborative inference during reading: Do they occur on-line? *Journal of Experimental Psychology: Learning, Memory, and Cognition, 14*, 410 - 420.

Potts, G. R., Keenan, J. M., & Golding, J. M. (1988). Assessing the occurrences of elaborative inferences: Lexical decision versus naming. *Journal of Memory and Language, 27*, 399 - 415.

Singer, M., & Ferreira, F. (1983). Inferring consequences in story comprehension. *Journal of Verbal Learning and Verbal Behavior, 22*, 437 - 448.

Trabasso, T., & Sperry, L. L. (1985). Causal relatedness and importance of story events. *Journal of Memory and Language, 24*, 595 - 611.

Trabasso, T., & van den Broek, P. (1985). Causal thinking and the representation of narrative events. *Journal of Memory and Language, 24*, 612 - 630.

van den Broek, P., & Trabasso, T. (1986). Causal networks versus goal hierarchies in summarizing text. *Discourse Processes, 9*, 1 - 13.

18

WHICH ELABORATIVE INFERENCES ARE DRAWN DURING READING? A QUESTION OF METHODOLOGIES

Janice M. Keenan, George R. Potts,
University of Denver

Jonathan M. Golding,
University of Kentucky

Tracy M. Jennings
University of Denver

INTRODUCTION

It is well known that speakers and writers cannot make explicit everything that they want to communicate. Nor do they need to. Instead, they rely on their listeners or readers to fill in whatever gaps may exist in the message; in other words, they rely on their audience to make inferences. The question confronting researchers of language comprehension is: Which inferences can people be counted on to reliably draw? This question is particularly important for reading research because the reader, unlike most listeners, is not in a position to ask for assistance in gap-filling from the author. If we can answer this question of which inferences are likely to be drawn, not only will writers (like us) be able to write more comprehensible texts, but we will be well on our way to a general theory of language comprehension. And it is only when this question is answered that we will be able to solve such practical problems as designing machines that we can converse with.

The question of which inferences are drawn during reading usually refers to a class of inferences called elaborative inferences (or forward inferences). Elaborative inferences are contrasted with bridging inferences (or backward inferences). The distinction is not based on the type of information inferred but rather what motivates the inference. If the inference is drawn in order to establish coherence between the present piece of text and the preceding text, then it is a bridging inference. If an inference is not needed for coherence, but is simply drawn to embellish the textual information, then it is an elaborative inference. There are many possible elaborations one can make in a text. Consequently, research is needed to determine which, if any, of these many possible elaborative inferences are drawn.

Research on inferencing is relatively recent in the history of reading and psycholinguistic research. But despite the infancy of this research, or perhaps because of it, there are a large number of paradigms in use to detect inferences. Not only are there a variety of paradigms, but there are also a variety of times during which inferencing is tested. These times range from testing while a person is reading, to testing them immediately after reading, to testing them long after they have read.

Until quite recently, researchers rarely provided a rationale for either their choice of paradigm or their choice of testing time. It was generally believed that the main question to be asked is which inferences are drawn. The methods used to answer that question were thought to be comparable, or at least sufficiently comparable that one did not need to worry about them until after the more important question of which inferences are drawn was answered.

This may have seemed a reasonable approach to take because the field was in its infancy. Furthermore, if the different methods had yielded similar answers, the approach would have been lauded for providing converging evidence across a wide spectrum of methodologies. As it turns out, however, different methods often result in different answers to the question of whether an inference is drawn. And with the focus being on the type of inference drawn rather than the methodology, the differences between studies are often incorrectly attributed to the types of inferences drawn rather than to the methods used to detect them.

For example, there is a tendency to believe that people infer the referents of general terms (e.g., infer that the general term *animal* refers to a cow in the statement, *she was milking the animal*) but that they do not make instrument inferences (e.g., infer *knife* when reading *he stabbed the intruder*). The evidence cited to support this often comes from methodologies as diverse as a recognition test given long after the passage is read for the referent inferences (McKoon & Ratcliff, 1989a) and a Stroop task given immediately after reading for the instrument inferences (Dosher & Corbett, 1982). Consequently, it is unclear whether the differences between the studies are due to the type of inference, as is generally believed, or to the different requirements of the tasks, or when the test was presented.

The use of different methodologies is a problem not only in comparing different types of inferences but also within a given inference type. The result is that it is difficult to say for any single inference type whether readers typically draw that inference, because frequently there are almost as many studies answering the question affirmatively as negatively. This can be seen in Table 18.1, which summarizes the results of studies examining three main types of elaborative inferences: instrument inferences, instantiations of general terms, and inferences about the likely consequences of events (such as inferring from the fact that someone threw a delicate porcelain vase against a wall, that the vase broke).

Many simplifications have been adopted in constructing this table. First, not every inference study is included; rather, we selected representative studies to show the variety of tasks that have been used. Second, for the purpose of easy viewing, the classification of testing time is simplified. Any study that tested for the inference either while reading the inference sentence or immediately after it is classified as an immediate test. Any study that had some intervening material between the inference sentence and the test, be it from the same text or a different text, is classified as a delayed test. Third, the inferences summarized are always the most probable instruments (e.g., *hammer* rather than *mallet*) or the dominant exemplars (*cow* rather than *goat* for milking animal).

The point of Table 18.1 is to show the variety of testing procedures used to detect inferences and to show that for each inference type, there is no consensus as to whether the inference is typically drawn. Furthermore, it is hard to know if the different answers are due to the different requirements of the tasks or to the different testing times. Also complicating the picture is the fact that tasks and test times tend to be confounded. For example, cued recall is always used after a long delay, whereas activation measures (lexical decision, Stroop, naming) tend to be used either immediately or after a very short delay.

There are, of course, other differences among the studies in Table 18.1 besides the tasks and test times. Most notable are differences in materials, especially the context in which the inference is presented. For example, some studies used single sentences, whereas others used short paragraphs. Some paragraphs had previous mention of the inference concept, and some had highly constraining contexts. When making comparisons across studies, these text differences certainly may play a role in accounting for the discrepancy in answers to the question of whether the inference is drawn (cf. Lucas, Tanenhaus, & Carlson, 1987; O'Brien, Shank, Myers, & Rayner, 1988; Whitney, 1986). However, a number of the entries in Table 18.1 show that even within the domain of a single study, when materials are controlled, differences in the tasks and testing time yield different results.

Consider, for example, the instrument inference studies in Table 18.1. Although the studies listed are almost evenly split on the question of whether these inferences are typically drawn, the predominant view is that instrument inferences are not drawn. This view is based on dismissing the cued recall data as flawed and summarizing the others as showing that instruments are not inferred unless the instrument has been previously mentioned in the text, as in the McKoon and Ratcliff

TABLE 18.1

*Inference Studies Classified by Type of Task or Measure Used to
Detect the Inference, Time of Testing, and Type of Inference Drawn.*

	Task or Measure	Test Time	Is Inference Drawn?
Instrument Inferences (e.g., infer *spoon* from *stir the soup*)			
Dosher & Corbett (1982)	Stroop	Immediate	NO
Lucas et al. (1987)	Lexical decision	Immediate	DC*
	Naming	Immediate	NO
McKoon & Ratcliff (1981)	Recognition	Immediate	YES
Paris & Lindauer (1976)	Cued recall	Delay	YES
Singer (1979)	Reading time	Immediate	NO
Instantiations of General Terms (e.g., infer *cow* from *milk the animal*)			
Anderson & Ortony (1975)	Cued recall	Delay	YES
Garrod & Sanford (1977)	Reading time	Immediate	NO
McKoon (1988)	Lexical decision	Immediate	NO
	Recognition	Delay	YES
O'Brien et al. (1988)	Fixation duration	Immediate	DC*
Whitney (1986)	Stroop	Immediate	YES
Likely Consequences of Events (e.g., infer *cut* from *stepped on a jagged piece of glass*)			
Duffy (1986)	Continuation judgment	Immediate	YES
	Recognition	Immediate	NO
McKoon & Ratcliff (1986)	Cued recall	Delay	YES
speeded recognition–no prime		Delay	NO
speeded recognition–prime		Delay	YES
McKoon & Ratcliff (1988)	Recognition	Immediate	NO
		Delay	YES
Potts et al. (1988)	Lexical decision	Delay	YES
	Naming	Delay	NO
Singer & Ferreira (1983)	Verification	Immediate	NO

DC* = Depends on context.

(1981) study. However, a recent study by Lucas et al. (1987) showed that the situation is not that simple; methodological factors are paramount. In their study, all texts had previous mention of the instrument and all tests were administered immediately, yet the answer to the question of whether the inference was drawn depended on the particular task used to assess it.

Much of the research on instantiations of general terms suggests that when the inference is highly predictable, it is likely to be drawn. Yet here too, methodology ultimately determines the answer. Consider McKoon's (1988) study. Her immediate lexical decision task suggested the inferences were not drawn whereas her delayed recognition test suggested they were. Of course, in this case it is hard to know whether the controlling factor was task or delay, because the two were confounded. Nonetheless, it is clear that methodological factors are important in determining whether one concludes that these inferences are drawn or not.

Studies of inferences concerning the likely consequences of events are evenly divided on the question of whether they are typically drawn. Even within the same paradigm, one arrives at different conclusions depending on when the test is administered (McKoon & Ratcliff, 1989b) or whether the test item is primed by another item from the text (McKoon & Ratcliff, 1986). And even when delay and priming are controlled, the answer to the question of whether consequent inferences are drawn depends on the task (Duffy, 1986; Potts, Keenan, & Golding, 1988).

In sum, Table 18.1 provides clear evidence that the procedures used to assess inferences seem to be at least as important as the type of inference in determining whether inferences are drawn. Why don't the various tasks used to detect inferences yield comparable results? What are the differences between the tasks that are responsible for the different results? What effect does the time of test have on the results? The purpose of this chapter is to try and answer these questions.

MEASURES OF INFERENCING AND THE DEBATE OVER WHAT CONSTITUTES AN INFERENCE

Measures of inferencing other than reading time measures can be divided into two classes: memory measures and activation measures. Memory measures require subjects to access their representation of the text to see if the inferential information is part of the text's representation. They include cued recall, sentence verification, question answering, and recognition measures. Activation measures, on the other hand, do not require subjects to evaluate their representation of the text. Instead, they detect inferences by seeing whether an inference concept is primed, that is, if it is more activated after reading an inference version of a text versus a no inference control version. The notion is that if an inference has been drawn, then that information will be activated as part of constructing the text's representation. Tasks used to assess priming include naming, lexical decision, and the modified Stroop task.

There are two ways in which an inference concept can be activated. One is through intralexical associations as a result of reading related words in the text; we refer to this as word-based priming. The other is by actually drawing the inference based on one's knowledge about the situation described in the text. Many researchers are not inclined to consider word-based priming as drawing an inference; so, they control for intralexical activations and focus on knowledge-based activations in assessing inferencing (see Keenan, Golding, Potts, Jennings, & Aman, in press; McKoon & Ratcliff, 1986).

The decision to use a memory measure versus an activation measure is often governed by one's theory of what constitutes an inference. At issue is whether one considers simply activating an inference concept as a legitimate case of drawing an inference. Those who reject an activated concept as constituting an inference prefer memory measures to activation measures. There are two reasons for this preference, and these correspond to two dimensions involved in defining an inference.

One dimension is the unit of inferencing. It can range from an activated concept, to a set of concepts constituting a proposition, to a set of propositions constituting a higher order knowledge structure such as a schema. Some researchers' belief that only a proposition or a set of propositions constitutes an inference has led them to reject measures that test the activation level of a single concept. We wish to point out, however, that if a subject constructs a proposition, this process will involve activating concepts. Hence, measures of activation can be sensitive to all units of inferencing.

Another dimension defining an inference is the level to which an inference is processed. This can range from simple activation, to selection for maintenance in working memory, to incorporating the inference into the long-term representation of the text (see Kintsch, 1988). Some researchers believe that what should count as an inference is only what gets incorporated into the final representation of the text. Consequently, these researchers prefer memory measures that require subjects to access their representation of the text over activation measures. We wish to point out, however, that memory measures are also sensitive to activation. So, unless the test is sufficiently delayed to allow for activation to dissipate (and no one yet knows what factors govern the dissipation of activation in text comprehension), a memory test may be measuring activation as well as, or instead of, incorporation.

In sum, although memory measures have sometimes been preferred on the grounds that they measure a higher level of inferencing and can detect incorporation into the text base, these arguments are open to criticisms. In addition, memory measures suffer from another serious problem. Namely, these measures do not allow one to determine whether the inference occurred during comprehension or as a result of the test. That is because whenever the task requires the subject to go back to the text and process it, the subject is given another opportunity to draw the inference. Consequently, it is difficult to determine whether any apparent evidence for the inference was due to processes occurring at encoding or processing at the time of test. Note that having the test occur on-line as opposed to delayed (as in cued recall) is not enough to prevent the problem. In other words, testing during comprehension may be preferable to testing long after the text has been read because it minimizes reconstruction. But as long as the measure involves accessing the text, there is no guarantee that the inferences detected were drawn when the text was read. We develop this point more as we discuss each measure.

A CRITICAL ANALYSIS OF TASKS USED TO DETECT INFERENCES

Cued Recall

One of the earliest techniques used to detect the occurrence of elaborative inferences was cued recall. In this paradigm, subjects read sentences in which some information, such as the instrument of the action, is either left implicit or made explicit. An example from Corbett and Dosher (1978) is:

Explicit: The athlete cut out an article with scissors for his friend.
Implicit: The athlete cut out an article for his friend.

After reading a set of such sentences, the instruments (e.g., *scissors*) are then given as cues to recall the sentences. Paris and Lindauer (1976) found that an instrument is just as effective a retrieval cue when it is implicit as when it is explicit. Based on this, they concluded that the instrument must have been inferred during encoding.

Singer (1978) challenged this conclusion by providing evidence that suggested that cued recall reflects reconstructive processes occurring during retrieval rather than inferences at encoding. He used sentences containing actions, such as *stir the soup*, for which the possible instruments, ladle and spoon, are asymmetrically related to the action. There is a strong forward association between *stir the soup* and *spoon* but a rather weak backward association from *spoon* to *stir the soup*. On the other hand, there is a weak forward association between *stir the soup* and *ladle*, but a strong backward association. If instruments are inferred during reading, then reading *stir the soup* should lead one to infer *spoon* more often than *ladle* because it is more strongly associated. Therefore, *spoon* should be a more effective retrieval cue than *ladle*. On the other hand, if cued recall reflects reconstructive processes at retrieval, then *ladle* should be a better cue than *spoon* because *ladle* is more strongly associated to *stir the soup*. Singer's results showed *ladle* to be the more effective cue, suggesting that cued recall reflects reconstruction at retrieval. A similar point was made by Corbett and Dosher (1978). As a result of findings such as these, most inference researchers abandoned the cued recall paradigm as a method of detecting inferences.

Two aspects of the cued recall paradigm could have accounted for its reflecting retrieval processes. One is that it was presented long after the sentences had been encoded; this delay meant the sentence was no longer readily retrievable and so could have encouraged reconstruction of the inference at the time of test. The other is the fact it was a memory test; because retrieval involves processing the text again, it may induce construction of information that was not part of the original encoding. When researchers abandoned the cued recall paradigm for detecting inferences, the rationale seemed to focus on the fact that it was a delayed test, and as such, it could not distinguish processes occurring at encoding from those occurring at retrieval. There was a realization that in order to assess inferences occurring at encoding, they need to be tested during encoding, that is, on-line. We examine the on-line methods that came to replace cued recall as a means of detecting inferences. But first, we need to consider another early measure of inferences – sentence verification.

Sentence Verification

The sentence verification paradigm involves having subjects read a text in either its inference version or an explicit control version. An example from Keenan and Kintsch (1974) is:

Inference: Gas leaked from a butane tank.
　　　　　　The explosion leveled a service station and a new home.
Explicit: Gas leaked from a butane tank and caused an explosion.
　　　　　　The explosion leveled a service station and a new home.

After reading, subjects are asked to respond *true* or *false* to the sentence, *A gas leak caused the explosion*. If subjects are just as fast to verify the information after having read the inference version as the control version, then it is assumed they drew the inference while reading. The preceding is an example of using sentence verification to detect backward, bridging inferences. The paradigm has also been used to detect forward inferences, such as instruments (Singer, 1979) and inferences concerning the consequences of events (Singer & Ferreira, 1983).

One obvious problem with this paradigm is that evidence for the inference involves accepting the null hypothesis. That is, evidence for the inference consists of finding no significant difference in verification time between the two versions. Of course, an insignificant difference could occur for other reasons as well, such as lack of statistical power or subjects who are just pressing buttons and not really comprehending.

As Keenan and Kintsch (1974) and McKoon and Keenan (1974) pointed out, another problem with this paradigm is that subjects' memory for the surface form of the text can hinder the ability to detect inferences. The reason for this is that the test statement has been explicitly presented in the control version but not in the inference version. Subjects' memory for the surface form of the statement can therefore facilitate or prime their processing of the test statement following the control version. Consequently, even when subjects consistently draw inferences it may appear that they are not drawn, because verification times following inference versions will be slower than those following explicit control versions as long as subjects retain the surface form of the paragraph.

Another problem arises when using this paradigm to detect forward inferences. Recall that forward inferences are not necessary; they are likely, but not necessarily true, elaborations of the text. Consequently, when one is asked to say true or false to one of these elaborations, the subject is faced with a criterion problem. The subject knows that the statement is likely to be true, but the text did not explicitly state that it was true, and it is quite possible that it is not true. For example, in Singer and Ferreira's (1983) study a forward inference version text stated that *Bob threw the report into the fire.* The test statement was: *The report burned.* Because it is possible that Bob had a poor aim or that the report smothered the fire, one cannot have 100% certainty after reading the inference version that the report burned. In contrast, after reading an explicit control version that says the report burned, one can have such certainty; as can one after reading a backward inference version that says, *The report's ashes went up the flue.* The point is that even when subjects make the forward inference, they may hesitate to endorse it as readily as when it is explicit or required for coherence. This can slow down verification times following inference versions, suggesting that the inference was not drawn when in fact it was.

Sentence Reading Times

Haviland and Clark (1974) were among the first researchers to use the sentence reading time paradigm to detect inferences. The technique involves comparing reading times for a sentence when it is in an inference version of a text versus an explicit control version. For example:

Inference Version: Herb took the picnic supplies from the car.
                        The beer was warm.
Explicit Control: Herb took the beer from the car.
                        The beer was warm.

Longer reading time for the second sentence when it is in the inference version versus the control is thought to reflect the additional time required to draw the inference.

One problem with using a control version that makes the inferred information explicit is that the control then usually contains words that can prime words in the target sentence. For example, the first sentence of the control in the preceding example contains the word, *beer*. This can prime the processing of *beer* in the target sentence, thereby making the target sentence easier to read in the control condition. Consequently, even if no inference was involved, the target sentence might be expected to be read slower in the inference version than in the explicit control.

Haviland and Clark (1974) showed that the difference in target reading time between inference and explicit control versions could not be due solely to lexical repetition in the control condition. Nonetheless, the presence of word-based priming in the control but not the inference version is a potential problem in the reading time paradigm.

The reading time paradigm works well for assessing backward, bridging inferences because evidence for the inference is an increase in reading time. Using it to detect forward, elaborative inferences is less straightforward. For example, if in the preceding example you inferred that the picnic supplies included beer while reading the first sentence (because you know Herb and you know he never picnics without beer), then the time to read the second sentence would be the same for the inference and explicit control versions because no additional time is needed to draw the inference. Consequently, evidence for an elaborative inference in this case involves accepting the null hypothesis. An additional problem is that the evidence for an elaborative inference – namely, the lack of a difference in reading times between the second sentence of the two versions – is exactly the same result that would occur if subjects failed to draw an inference in either version. So, even if one were willing to accept the null hypothesis, there would be no way of knowing that the lack of an effect was due to an elaborative inference occurring while reading rather than no inferencing at all.

One way to avoid these problems is to design the materials so that the target sentence does not confirm the elaborative inference that the reader may draw, but rather contradicts it. That way, the reader will take longer to read the target sentence if the inference is drawn.

An example from Sanford and Garrod (1981) illustrates how the sentence reading time paradigm has been used to study elaborative inferences concerning instantiations of referents. They used two versions of a paragraph which differed only in how the agent of the first sentence was referred to. For example:

(John/The teacher) was on his way to school.
The bus trundled slowly along the road.
Last week he had trouble controlling the class.

If a reader makes the elaborative inference that John is a school boy, then it will take longer to read the final sentence than if the reader had not made that inference, as in the teacher version.

Note that this example also has the word-based, associative priming problem noted earlier. The explicit control version, which contains *teacher* in the first sentence, is more likely to prime words in the target sentence, such as *class*, than the inference version, which contains *John*. Thus, differences in target sentence reading time may be expected simply on the basis of word-based priming.

The problem of confounds between inferencing and word-based priming is not unique to the reading time paradigm. All activation measures of inferencing are also subject to this problem. We have discussed the confound and possible solutions to it elsewhere (Keenan et al., in press; see also McKoon & Ratcliff, 1986). For now, it can be noted that one way to circumvent the problem is to incorporate *teacher* in the inference version as well. The following first sentences would avoid the lexical priming problem:

Inference: As John was on his way to school, he thought about what an effective teacher would be like.

Explicit   As he was on his way to school, the teacher thought
Control: about what it would be like to be effective.

In summary, the advantage of the reading time paradigm is that it detects inferences while the person is reading. Consequently, it avoids the criticism that the inferences detected are due to reconstruction, as in cued recall, or are due to the testing process, as in some of the other measures we review later. There are two potential problems with this paradigm. One is that unless the materials are properly designed, evidence for the elaborative inference may involve accepting the null hypothesis. The other is that there may be a confound with word-based priming of the target sentence in the control versions, unless the inference versions are constructed to include the same lexical items.

A disadvantage of the sentence reading time paradigm is that it does not allow one to know exactly when the inference is drawn. For example, in the Sanford and Garrod examples, longer reading time on the final sentence in the John-version of the paragraph tells us that the inference was drawn. But, whether the inference was drawn while reading the first sentence or the second sentence is unknown. This problem is easily alleviated by using less holistic measures than reading whole sentences; namely, examining word-by-word reading times with either eye movement measures (see Rayner & Pollatsek, 1989, for a review) or button presses to advance the text (Haberlandt & Graesser, 1985; Just, Carpenter, & Woolley, 1982; Mitchell & Green, 1978). Another disadvantage of the reading-time paradigm is that increased reading time of the target sentence could reflect a difference in the ease with which the target sentence can be integrated with the first sentence on grounds other than the inference, such as syntax. Because the first sentences are different, one of them might lend itself to integration with the target on syntactic grounds more easily than the other.

Perhaps the major disadvantage of the reading-time paradigm is that it does not reveal exactly what inference was drawn. For example, longer reading times in the John-version of Sanford and Garrod's materials suggest only that the reader inferred that John was somebody other than a teacher. Whether the reader inferred him to be a schoolboy or the bus driver or someone else is unknown. The remaining measures that we review all allow a better handle on what the content of the inference is.

On-line Question-Answering Methodology

The on-line question-answering methodology involves interspersing throughout the text various questions that tap the reader's developing representation of the meaning of the text to see if it contains knowledge about unspecified information such as why events have happened and what is going to happen next (Graesser & Clark, 1985; Olson, Duffy, & Mack, 1984). This technique has the advantage that it can be used at any point during reading and that it can reveal the content of inferences. The major drawback of this methodology is that even though a reader may be able to infer the queried information when asked about it, that does not mean those inferences would be drawn in the absence of the questions. In other words, just because you can give an answer to the question of what's going to happen next in the story does not mean that the representation of the text you had before being asked the question contained that information. So, the measure is invasive, perhaps causing inferences to be drawn that are not normally made while reading. We see this methodology as useful only for revealing potential inferences that a reader might draw while reading.

Recognition

Like the question-answering technique, recognition tests of inferencing require subjects to access their representation of the text. Recognition is preferable though because the test does not ask the subject to make the inference. Rather, the subject's task is to read either an inference version or a no inference control version and to determine whether a test word representing the inference occurred in the text. The logic of the paradigm is that if an inference was drawn, the concept will have been activated and incorporated into the representation of the inference version but not the control version. Consequently, if the test word did not occur in the text, it will be harder to say so because the concept is part of the representation of the text's meaning. Similarly, if the test word did occur in the text, it will be easier to say so because of the extra occurrence of the concept in the representation due to the inference.

The major problem with recognition tests is that there is no way to know whether the inferences detected were drawn while the subject read the text or during the test. The reason why the results may reflect processes occurring at the time of test is because the recognition task requires the subject to check the probe against the text. There are two ways in which this processing of the text at the time of test could result in a difference in response time and accuracy between inference and control versions even when no inference was drawn during reading.

First, while checking the probe against the text, the reader can be led to draw the inference. For example, one might not have thought of what instrument was used to stir the soup when reading; but now that the test word *spoon* is presented, one can infer that it would be an appropriate instrument. Making this inference at the time of test would slow the response time – the same result that would be expected if one had inferred *spoon* while reading and now had to say that it did not occur.

Second, the inference may not be drawn either during reading or during testing, but the greater relatedness or compatibility of the test probe to the inference text than the no inference control text can affect the speed and accuracy of the recognition decision process. Specifically, the more compatible the probe to the text, the harder to say it did not occur in the text and the easier to say it did occur. Now, it might be argued that if word-based priming is controlled, then compatibility is equated between the probe word and the two text versions. However, constructing the no inference control version so that it contains all the words in the inference version that might be related to the test word, only makes the text versions equally compatible with the probe at the word level. At the level of propositions and higher order text structures, such as schemata, the test probe will always be more compatible with the inference version than the no inference control version because by definition the probe fits with the meaning of the inference version but not the control version.

In sum, the results of a recognition test of inferences does not allow one to distinguish between: (a) inferences occurring while reading, (b) inferences occurring during testing, or (c) compatibility matching processes occurring at the time of test. McKoon and Ratcliff (1986) recommended using a deadline procedure with the recognition task in order to eliminate the possibility of subjects drawing inferences at test time. They argued that with a strict deadline, subjects do not have time for the type of strategic comparisons of the probe to the text that would produce an inference at retrieval. Consequently, the results should reflect only automatic activation of inferences encoded during reading.

We contend that while the deadline procedure may eliminate the possibility of subjects drawing inferences when they are comparing the test probe to the text, it does not eliminate the comparison process. Therefore, it does not eliminate the possibility that compatibility matching is affecting the decision process. Although the deadline procedure restricts the amount of time subjects have, it does not change the fact that recognition, by its very nature, requires subjects to perform a comparison between the test word and the text. The deadline procedure does not change this comparison, it merely prevents it from being as complete as normal. As long as this comparison process takes place, it is possible for text-probe compatibility to affect recognition latencies. Thus, a deadline procedure does not ensure that the results of a recognition test reflect inferences made during comprehension.

Activation Measures of Inferences

The best way to ensure that the results of an inference test reflect inferences occurring during comprehension is to use a test that does not require subjects to evaluate the probe against the text. Activation

measures of inferencing are designed to be just that. The logic underlying these measures is this. If the inference has just been drawn, then
the activation level of the inference concept should be elevated; if the
activation level of the inference concept is elevated, then lexical access
should be facilitated. Hence, any task that involves lexical access of the
inference concept – reading, naming, lexical decision, or Stroop – can
be used to assess whether the inference has been drawn.

Unfortunately, all of these tasks involve not just lexical access but
some other process as well. Recently, it has been recognized that in
many cases, these other processes, too, can be influenced by text factors,
making it difficult to determine the extent to which lexical access has
been primed. In other words, we now realize that it is possible for an
on-line probe task to show facilitation even when the inference concept
has not been previously activated, that is, when the inference has not
been drawn. In that case, lexical access of the inference concept is
not primed, but the relationship between the test item and the text
facilitates other postaccess processes operating on the test item (see
Balota, this volume).

For example, single word reading time or gaze duration involves the
time to do lexical access plus the time to integrate the word's meaning
with the preceding text (cf. Schustack, Ehrlich, & Rayner, 1987). If an
inference has been drawn, then lexical access of the inference word will
be primed in the inference version relative to the no inference control.
If an inference has not been drawn, then gaze duration on the inference
word could still be shorter in the inference version than the no inference
control because the postaccess process of integrating the word with the
text could be more easily accomplished in the inference version. The
gaze duration measure does not allow one to know which of these two
processes is being facilitated. With this task it may not matter that
much because either constitutes evidence for an inference. If lexical
access is being primed, then it is a forward inference; whereas if integration is facilitated, then it is a backward inference. However, with all
the other tasks used to assess activation, it does matter whether lexical
access or a postaccess process is being primed, because only priming of
lexical access constitutes evidence for an inference. We now consider
these tasks.

Lexical Decision

In lexical decision tests of inferencing, subjects read either an inference version or a control version of a text. They then decide whether or
not a letter string is a word; the strings of interest are those representing
the inferences.

The lexical decision task has two main components: lexical access
and the decision process. Because subjects have no reason to compare
the letter string to the text, it would appear that the relatedness of
the probe to the text, which could affect the decision process, would
be irrelevant and that, consequently, lexical decision would be a good

measure of priming of lexical access that is due to inferences drawn while reading. However, even though lexical decision does not require subjects to compare the test probe to the text, a number of recent studies have suggested that such a comparison nevertheless occurs (Balota & Chumbley, 1984; Chumbley & Balota, 1984; Forster, 1981; Neely, Keefe, & Ross, 1989; Seidenberg, Waters, Sanders, & Langer, 1984; West & Stanovich, 1982). These studies have shown, for example, that lexical decision latencies are affected by the probability that the prime and target are related and by the presence of a backward association between the prime and target. This context checking occurs after lexical access, ostensibly, to help the decision process; if the target is related to the text, it promotes the decision to say it is a word.

Our own studies comparing lexical decision to other measures of inferencing, such as naming and the modified Stroop task, suggest that lexical decision may overestimate the occurrence of inferences (Keenan, Potts, Jennings, & Golding, 1988; Potts et al., 1988). It can give evidence for an inference when these other measures – measures that are less susceptible to postaccess context checking – do not.

Because context checking is not inherent to lexical decision, as it is to recognition, it may be possible to eliminate it. For example, context-checking may occur in lexical decision as a way of verifying one's decision. If so, then forcing subjects to respond quickly with the use of a deadline procedure may eliminate it.

Naming

In naming, subjects are presented with the inference word after reading either an inference or a no inference control version and asked to say it out loud. Naming latencies therefore reflect the time for lexical access plus the time for articulation. Unlike the other measures, it is difficult to see how the postaccess process here – namely, articulation – could be influenced by the probe's relatedness to the text. For this reason, naming is sometimes viewed as a purer measure of lexical access and, thus, the measure of choice when trying to assess whether some variable affects lexical access (Forster, 1981; Seidenberg et al., 1984). In support of these claims are data showing that naming, unlike lexical decision, is not affected by factors such as the probability that the prime and target are related or the presence of a backward association between them (Seidenberg et al., 1984). Although Balota, Boland, and Shields (1989) have shown semantic effects on articulation, these can be viewed as spillover effects from lexical access.

Although naming may eliminate the problem of priming of postaccess processes, there are those who question its ability to detect text-based inferences. Specifically, those who hold a modular view of language processing believe that lexical access is affected only by priming from intralexical association, not text-level factors (Fodor, 1983). According to this view, an inference may be drawn during encoding and incorporated into the text representation, but it will have no effect on lexical access of the test probe because the lexicon is informationally encapsulated from top-down effects. Consequently, these researchers would argue that naming cannot detect the occurrence of inferences.

Our own research refutes this notion that naming cannot detect inferences. We have found significant effects of inferences priming naming even under conditions that controlled for word-based priming and thus eliminated the possibility that the priming was due to intralexical associations (Potts et al., 1988). Thus, in our view, naming can be used as a measure of inferences.

One possible disadvantage of naming is that it may be less sensitive than other measures. For example, even though we successfully used naming to detect bridging inferences, the effects, though significant, were quite small – only 11 and 17 ms (Potts et al., 1988). The problem is that naming is such a fast response that there is less opportunity for it to be affected by any variable, such as top-down processes (see Norris, 1986).

Another disadvantage of naming is that, in principle, it can be accomplished without going through the lexicon; namely, via grapheme-to-phoneme correspondence rules. Of course, when this happens, naming cannot reflect priming of lexical access. Even if lexical access is bypassed on only some trials, this can weaken the sensitivity of naming as a measure of inferencing.

Finally, another possible disadvantage, associated not only with naming but with any task that uses only a single probe, is that subjects might learn to anticipate what the probe is going to be; what we might call expectancy priming (cf. Neely & Keefe, 1989). In other words, instead of generating inferences as part of the normal comprehension process, subjects may be generating expectancies about the nature of the test probe. In that case, we would have the same problem as the on-line question technique – namely, the measure used to detect inferences is causing inferences to occur that might not occur in the absence of the test. We recently examined this possibility by seeing to what extent subjects could correctly anticipate the exact form of the probe word when explicitly requested to guess what it might be and when given feedback as to what it was. We found that under these most optimal guessing conditions, subjects could make correct guesses, but only about 15% of the time. So, predictive priming may be affecting probe measures of inferencing, but it is probably not the sole basis for priming effects. One advantage of the final measure that we review, the modified Stroop task, is that it seems to discourage expectancy priming because the subject's task focuses not on the probe itself but it's ink color.

Modified Stroop Task

The Stroop task involves naming the color of ink in which color words, such as *red*, are written. The modified Stroop task involves having subjects read a text and then naming the ink color of a noncolor test word (Conrad, 1974). The task allows one to determine if the test word has been primed by the text. If it has, then it takes longer to name the color of ink that the word is written in than if it has not been primed. For example, it should take longer to name the color of ink for *doctor* following a text that referred to hospitals than one about subways. This is because when the word is primed, it is harder to suppress its articulation in favor of articulating the ink color. The modified Stroop task has been used to study forward inferences concerning the instruments of actions (Dosher & Corbett, 1982), instantiations of general terms (Whitney, 1986; Whitney & Kellas, 1984) and the likely consequences of events (Keenan et al., 1988).

Like other activation measures of inferencing, the modified Stroop task assesses not only priming of lexical access of the inference concept but also other processes – in this case, ink color identification and articulation of the color name. Like naming, it is difficult to see how these other processes would be affected by the relatedness of the probe to the text. Hence, like naming, the modified Stroop task seems to be a fairly pure measure of lexical access. In fact, the modified Stroop task may not only be just as good a measure of inferencing as naming, it may be better.

First, latencies tend to be longer in the modified Stroop task than in naming (Keenan et al., 1988), thus making it more likely to avoid potential floor effects. Second, as mentioned earlier, because the task focuses on ink color rather than the probe word itself, it may discourage expectancy priming and thus reveal only inferences that naturally occur during comprehension.

Finally, and perhaps most importantly, a major advantage of the modified Stroop test for inferences is that it allows one to determine whether subjects are processing inferences at a conceptual level or at a lexical level. When a word is primed at a conceptual level, it results in the interference effect already described. Specifically, it takes longer to name the ink color of a word like *doctor* when it has been preceded by *hospital* than by an unrelated control word like *subway*. However, when a word is primed at the lexical level, it results in the opposite effect, namely, a facilitation effect (Dosher & Corbett, 1982; Whitney, 1986). For example, if *doctor* has been preceded by the explicit generation of the lexical form *doctor*, then its ink color can be identified faster than if it had been preceded by a control.

The capability of the Stroop task to distinguish levels of priming makes it a potentially powerful method for furthering our knowledge about the types of processing that occur during comprehension. We have recently used the method to determine whether the effects we observed of inferences on naming in the Potts et al. (1988) study could be amenable to an alternative explanation consistent with modularity theory (Keenan et al., 1988). Recall that according to modularity theory, naming cannot be primed by inferences because naming reflects lexical processes and the lexicon is informationally encapsulated from text-level representations like inferences. However, if subjects not only drew the inference but also said the word to themselves while read-ing, then according to modular theory, naming could be primed, not by the inference but by the articulation of the inference word. To see if subjects were in fact saying the correct inference words to themselves thereby priming the naming response, we used a modified Stroop task on the same materials. Although we found a facilitation effect on the Stroop task following versions where the inference was made explicit, no such facilitation was found for the inference versions. The inference ver-sions yielded an interference effect, suggesting that the inferences were drawn at a conceptual level, not a lexical level. We anticipate that the modified Stroop task will also prove useful in assessing the occurrence of expectancy priming, as expectancy priming ought to result in the gen-eration of explicit lexical forms more than inferences drawn as a result of normal comprehension.

In contrast to our analysis of all the other inference measures, we are unable to identify any drawbacks to using the modified Stroop task. While this may mean it is the best measure, it is also possible that this lack of criticism is due to the fact that, by comparison, the modified Stroop task has not been used very much to study inferences.

SUMMARY OF TASK ANALYSIS

Our analysis of tasks used to assess inferencing makes it clear that there are a few major issues that must be taken into account in the selection of a paradigm to test for forward inferences. They are: (a) How do you define what it means to draw an inference? (b) Do you want to be able to distinguish inferences occurring during comprehension from processes occurring at the time of test? and (c) the choice of proper controls.

Task Selection as a Function of One's Definition of an Inference

As we previously explained, there is no uniformly accepted criterion for what constitutes drawing an inference. Given this state of affairs, we think researchers ought to try to assess both activation of inference concepts as well as their incorporation into the text base. Either the modified Stroop task or naming could be used to assess activation that is due to forward inferencing. But how does one assess whether an activated inference has been incorporated into the text representation, as tasks typically used to assess incorporation fail to distinguish between encoding and retrieval processes?

Perhaps the best way at present to assess incorporation into the text base is to use a priming technique (Ratcliff & McKoon, 1978). The logic of the technique is this: If the inference has been incorporated into the text representation, then concepts to which the inference is connected in the representation should prime the inference more than if the inference is not connected to these concepts. So, one can use a delayed test of priming to see if the inference has been incorporated into the text in the inference version but not the no inference control version. If a word that occurs in both text versions primes the inference word more after reading the inference version than the control version, then it can be assumed that this is because the inference is connected to the concept in the inference version but not the control. Ratcliff and McKoon have used this delayed test of priming with a recognition task. Because of the reconstructive problems associated with recognition, we recommend using the priming technique with less problematic measures, such as naming or the modified Stroop task.

Distinguishing Inferences Occurring During Reading from Processes Occurring at Test

Given the inability of so many inference measures to distinguish inferences occurring during reading from processes occurring at test time, McKoon and Ratcliff (1988) have recently argued that trying to determine which inferences are drawn during reading is the wrong question for researchers to be asking. They argue that it is sufficient to determine the extent to which a probe is compatible with a text without trying to determine whether an inference was drawn during reading. Consequently, whereas they used to argue that recognition needed to be used with a deadline procedure in order to rule out the possibility of inferences occurring at test time (McKoon & Ratcliff, 1986), now they have gone back to using nonspeeded recognition (McKoon, 1988). Their use of a task, which by their own admission permits inferences to occur at retrieval, is clear acknowledgment of their view that it does not matter what task you use because when an inference is drawn is neither important nor decidable.

We agree that trying to determine which inferences are drawn during reading is the wrong question to ask if one is using a recognition measure of inferencing, as McKoon and Ratcliff typically do. However, we disagree that the question is neither important nor decidable. It is an important question because the only way listeners or machines will comprehend a message is if they can fill in the gaps as they occur; consequently, we need to know which types of gaps they can handle, that is which types of inferences they can draw without being prompted to do so. It is a decidable question because as we have shown, there are tasks that can detect inferences that occurred during reading. Consequently, with converging measures and the right tasks, one can draw firm conclusions.

Construction of Proper Controls

Controlling for Word-Based Priming

No matter which task one uses to assess forward inferences, performance is always compared between an inference version and a control version. A central problem in constructing control versions is the problem of differential associative or word-based priming of the inference concept across text versions. The type of problem one has with word-based priming depends on whether the control (a) makes the inferred information explicit, (b) is unrelated to the inferred information, what we have been calling a no inference control, or (c) forces the inference as a backward, bridging inference.

If the control makes the inferred information explicit, as is typically the case with the reading time paradigm, then the control will contain more words related to the inference than the inference version. This can lead to faster reaction times for the explicit control version than the inference version, making it appear that the inference is not drawn, even when it might be.

The use of a no inference control version results in the opposite problem. Whereas an explicit control can make it appear that an inference was not drawn even when it was, a no inference control can make it appear that an inference was drawn even when it was not. Because the no inference control is unrelated to the inferred information, the inference version is more likely to have more word-based priming of the test stimulus than the no inference control. The result is faster reaction times for the inference version, regardless of whether an inference was drawn.

Finally, a control version that forces the inference as a backward, bridging inference is likely to have more words in it related to the inference than the forward, inference version. For example, in order to force a backward inference that *the report burned*, Singer and Ferreira (1983) had a sentence about *the ashes* in the backward inference version. Because *ashes* was not in the forward inference version, there was differential priming of the test statement, *the report burned*, making it impossible to determine whether or not subjects drew the inference.

Our solution to the problem of differential word-based priming across text versions is twofold. First, we recommend that all text versions be constructed so that they contain all the same words that might be related to the inference (cf. McKoon & Ratcliff, 1986). We have already given an example of this in the case of Sanford and Garrod's (1981) materials in the sentence reading time section. In addition, we strongly suggest the use of more than just one type of control version. By comparing the inference version to several controls, it is possible to determine the extent to which priming is due to inferences versus intralexical associations.

The Null Hypothesis Problem

In many inference studies, a forward inference version is compared only to a backward inference version. This type of design has been most common in the sentence verification and the sentence reading time paradigms. If subjects do not make the forward inference, then reaction time is faster following the backward inference version. However, if they do make the forward inference, then equivalent reaction times are expected. This is the null hypothesis problem, namely, evidence for a forward inference constitutes accepting the null hypothesis.

Again, our solution is to use more than one type of control version. Then if the inference is truly drawn in both forward and backward inference versions, performance should be significantly faster for these versions compared to an unrelated control. If, on the other hand, the equivalent performance between forward and backward versions is due to lack of power or the fact that no inference was drawn, then both inference conditions should be no different than the unrelated control.

Controlling for Expectancy Priming

Expectancy priming is due to subjects actively anticipating the inference word on a test. It stands in contrast to inferential priming, which is due to inferences the subject draws as a result of comprehension. Expectancy priming is a potential contaminant of priming measures of inferencing such as recognition, lexical decision, and naming whenever only a single test word is used. At this point, there is insufficient research to know the extent to which expectancy priming occurs and under what conditions. It is obvious that many researchers are sensitive to the problem because they often include filler items to lower the proportion of times the test word is the inference word and thus lessen the likelihood of subjects guessing the test word. There are two other solutions to the problem that researchers might use. One is to use a task such as the modified Stroop task that does not require responding to the probe word itself. The other is to use more than one probe to make it difficult for subjects to anticipate the test items.

WHEN TO TEST FOR INFERENCES

As the data in Table 18.1 indicated, there is no simple relation between test time and whether or not an inference is detected. This is partly because the studies in this table represent such a variety of test times, ranging from interrupting the reader in mid-sentence, to testing immediately after reading the inference sentence, to testing after an intervening unrelated sentence or paragraph, to testing after a large set of intervening unrelated paragraphs. The reason for this variety is partly due to the researcher's choice of task. Accuracy measures of memory, such as cued recall, require a delay so as to avoid ceiling effects, whereas activation measures, such as lexical decision, require a fairly immediate test so as to avoid having the activation dissipate before it is tested. The other reason for the variety of test times is that not much thought had been given to the role test time might play in the ability to detect inferences. Whereas a few studies examined the time course of activation in backward, anaphoric inferences (e.g., Dell, McKoon, & Ratcliff, 1983), forward inferences tended to be tested at a time that fit the constraints of the task and was convenient.

Recently, however, it has been suggested that test time may be an important controlling factor in the detection of forward inferences (McKoon, 1988; McKoon & Ratcliff, 1988, 1989a; Till, Mross, & Kintsch, 1988). Specifically, it has been said that inferences take time to develop. Consequently, immediate tests of inferencing may yield no evidence for an inference not because subjects do not typically draw these inferences, as was often assumed, but because the inferences had yet to be made.

Although we find this to be an interesting theoretical notion, the evidence for it is far from conclusive. In the Till et al. (1988) study, paragraphs were presented one word at a time at a fixed rate of presentation, and inferencing was assessed with a lexical-decision task that interrupted the subject's reading. The temporal interval between the text and the lexical decision task varied from 200 to 1500 ms. The results showed no evidence for a forward inference until the temporal interval was 1000 ms or greater. The authors interpreted this to mean that inferences take time to develop.

Unfortunately, this study confounded delay interval and subjects' ability to prepare for and anticipate the test item. Because the temporal interval was not filled but consisted of a blank screen, when the interval was long, subjects had a blank screen for a long time, signaling that the test word would soon be presented; whereas when it was short, there was either no blank screen or a brief one. Thus, another interpretation of the results, which is just as viable as the inferences-take-time hypothesis, is that at longer delay intervals, but not shorter ones, subjects could engage in expectancy priming.

Similar problems exist in the other studies. For example, in McKoon (1988) different tasks were used for the immediate and delayed tests, and in the McKoon and Ratcliff (1989b) study different materials were used for the immediate and delayed tests. Also, in the McKoon and Ratcliff studies, the delayed tests always involved reading an intervening unrelated filler paragraph. It strikes us as very peculiar that inferences not present after reading a text would emerge while reading an unrelated text. Consequently, we suspect that the evidence for inferences found in their delayed tests is likely due to other factors, such as the confounds we pointed out.

In sum, it remains to be seen whether inferences take time to develop. Hopefully, our discussion of the problems in previous studies on this topic, together with our analysis of tasks, point the way to better approaches to this question.

The flip side of the question of whether inferences take time to develop is whether inferences dissipate over time, either as a function of time itself or as a function of receiving little or no support from the text. To our knowledge, there has been no research on this topic as of yet. Evidence for such a phenomenon would consist of immediate measures of inferencing showing evidence for inferences that were not detected by delayed tests.

SUMMARY

We began this chapter by demonstrating that the method one uses to detect inferences is at least as important as the inference itself in determining the answer to the question of whether or not an inference is drawn. Given this, we then critically evaluated each of the tasks that have been used to detect inferences. Our evaluation showed that no task is an ideal test of inferencing; in other words, every task has some problems associated with it. But some problems are insurmountable, such as the inability of some tasks to distinguish inferences occurring during reading from processes occurring during test, whereas others, such as the problem of priming from intralexical associations, are more tractable. We urged researchers to avoid using tasks that cannot distinguish between inferences that occur during reading and retrieval processes, and we urged the use of multiple tasks to assess both the activation and the incorporation of inferences. Finally, we showed the problems involved in determining the role of test time in detecting inferences. We look forward to future studies that will not have the confounds of past studies and that will use a combination of tasks to assess the time course of forward inferences.

REFERENCES

Anderson, R. C., & Ortony, A. (1975). On putting apples into bottles – A problem of polysemy. *Cognitive Psychology, 7*, 167 - 180.

Balota, D., Boland, J., & Shields, L. W. (1989). Priming in pronunciation: Beyond pattern recognition and onset latency. *Journal of Memory and Language, 28*, 14 - 36.

Balota, D. A., & Chumbley, J. I. (1984). Are lexical decisions a good measure of lexical access? The role of word frequency in the neglected decision stage. *Journal of Experimental Psychology: Human Perception and Performance, 10*, 340 - 357.

Chumbley, J. I., & Balota, D. A. (1984). A word's meaning affects the decision in lexical decision. *Memory & Cognition, 12*, 590 - 606.

Conrad, C. (1974). Context effects in sentence comprehension: A study of the subjective lexicon. *Memory & Cognition, 2*, 130 - 138.

Corbett, A. T., & Dosher, B. A. (1978). Instrument inferences in sentence encoding. *Journal of Verbal Learning and Verbal Behavior, 17*, 479 - 491.

Dell, G. S., McKoon, G., & Ratcliff, R. (1983). The activation of antecedent information during the processing of anaphoric reference in reading. *Journal of Verbal Learning and Verbal Behavior, 22*, 121 - 132.

Dosher, B. A., & Corbett, A. T. (1982). Instrument inferences and verb schemata. *Memory & Cognition, 10*, 531 - 539.

Duffy, S. A. (1986). Role of expectations in sentence integration. *Journal of Experimental Psychology: Learning, Memory, and Cognition, 12*, 208 - 219.

Fodor, J. A. (1983). *Modularity of mind.* Cambridge, MA: MIT Press.

Forster, K. I. (1981). Priming and the effects of sentence and lexical contexts on naming time: Evidence for autonomous lexical processing. *Quarterly Journal of Experimental Psychology, 33A*, 465 - 495.

Garrod, S., & Sanford, A. (1977). Interpreting anaphoric relations: The integration of semantic information while reading. *Journal of Verbal Learning and Verbal Behavior, 16*, 77 - 90.

Graesser, A. C., & Clark, L. F. (1985). *Structures and procedures of implicit knowledge.* Norwood, NJ: Ablex.

Haberlandt, K. F., & Graesser, A. C. (1985). Component processes in text comprehension and some of their interactions. *Journal of Experimental Psychology: General, 114*, 357 - 374.

Haviland, S. E., & Clark, H. H. (1974). What's new? Acquiring new information as a process in comprehension. *Journal of Verbal Learning and Verbal Behavior, 13*, 512 - 521.

Just, M. A., Carpenter, P. A., & Woolley, J. D. (1982). Paradigms and processes in reading comprehension. *Journal of Experimental Psychology: General, 111*, 228 - 238.

Keenan, J. M., Golding, J. M., Potts, G. R., Jennings, T. M., & Aman, C. J. (in press). Methodological issues in evaluating the occurrence of inferences. In A. C. Graesser & G. H. Bower (Eds.), *The psychology of learning and motivation* (Vol. 25). Orlando, FL: Academic Press.

Keenan, J. M., & Kintsch, W. (1974). The identification of explicitly and implicitly presented information. In W. Kintsch (Ed.), *The representation of meaning in memory* (pp. 153 - 166). Hillsdale, NJ: Lawrence Erlbaum Associates.

Keenan, J. M., Potts, G. R., Jennings, T. M., & Golding, J. M. (1988). *Can naming detect inferences?* Paper presented at the annual meeting of the Psychonomic Society, Chicago, IL.

Kintsch, W. (1988). The role of knowledge in discourse comprehension: A construction-integration model. *Psychological Review, 95*, 163 - 182.

Lucas, M. M., Tanenhaus, M. K., & Carlson, G. N. (1987). Inferences in sentence comprehension: The role of constructed representations. *Proceedings of the Ninth Annual Cognitive Science Society Meetings.* (pp. 566 - 574). Hillsdale, NJ: Lawrence Erlbaum Associates.

McKoon, G. (1988). *Word identification and elaborative inference.* Unpublished manuscript.

McKoon, G., & Keenan, J. M. (1974). Response latencies to explicit and implicit statements as a function of the delay between reading and test. In W. Kintsch (Ed.), *The representation of meaning in memory* (pp. 166 - 176). Hillsdale, NJ: Lawrence Erlbaum Associates.

McKoon, G., & Ratcliff, R. (1981). The comprehension processes and memory structures involved in instrumental interference. *Journal of Verbal Learning and Verbal Behavior, 20,* 671 - 682.

McKoon, G., & Ratcliff, R. (1986). Inferences about predictable events. *Journal of Experimental Psychology: Learning, Memory, and Cognition, 12,* 82 - 91.

McKoon, G., & Ratcliff, R. (1988). *Dimensions of inferences.* Paper presented at the Conference on Inference Generation During Discourse Comprehension, Memphis State University.

McKoon, G., & Ratcliff, R. (1989a). Inferences about contextually defined categories. *Journal of Experimental Psychology: Learning, Memory, and Cognition, 15,* 1134 - 1146.

McKoon, G., & Ratcliff, R. (1989b). Semantic association and elaborative inference. *Journal of Experimental Psychology: Learning, Memory, and Cognition, 15,* 326 - 338.

Mitchell, D. C., & Green, D. W. (1978). The effects of context and content on immediate processing in reading. *Quarterly Journal of Experimental Psychology, 30,* 609 - 636.

Neely, J. H., & Keefe, D. E. (1989). Semantic context effects on visual word processing: A hybrid prospective/retrospective processing theory. In G. H. Bower (Ed.), *The psychology of learning and motivation* (Vol. 23, pp. 207 - 248). Orlando, FL: Academic Press.

Neely, J. H., Keefe, D. E., & Ross, K. L. (1989). Semantic priming in the lexical decision task: Roles of prospective prime-generated expectancies and retrospective semantic matching. *Journal of Experimental Psychology: Learning, Memory, and Cognition, 15,* 1003 - 1019.

Norris, D. (1986). Word recognition: Context effects without priming. *Cognition, 22,* 93 - 136.

O'Brien, E. J., Shank, D. M., Myers, J. L., & Rayner, K. (1988). Elaborative inferences during reading: Do they occur on-line? *Journal of Experimental Psychology: Learning, Memory, and Cognition, 14,* 410 - 420.

Olson, G. M., Duffy, S. A., & Mack, R. L. (1984). Thinking-out-loud as a method for studying real-time comprehensive processes. In D. E. Kieras & M. A. Just (Eds.), *New methods in reading comprehension research* (pp. 253 - 286). Hillsdale, NJ: Lawrence Erlbaum Associates.

Paris, S. G., & Lindauer, B. K. (1976). The role of inference in children's comprehension and memory for sentences. *Cognitive Psychology, 8,* 217 - 227.

Potts, G. R., Keenan, J. M., & Golding, J. M. (1988). Assessing the occurrence of elaborative inferences: Lexical decision versus naming. *Journal of Memory and Language, 27,* 399 - 415.

Ratcliff, R., & McKoon, G. (1978). Priming in item recognition: Evidence for the propositional structure of sentences. *Journal of Verbal Learning and Verbal Behavior, 17,* 403 - 417.

Rayner, K., & Pollatsek, A. (1989). *The psychology of reading.* Englewood Cliffs, NJ: Prentice-Hall.

Sanford, A. J., & Garrod, S. C. (1981). *Understanding written language: Explorations in comprehension beyond the sentence.* New York: Wiley.

Schustack, M. W., Ehrlich, S. F., & Rayner, K. (1987). Local and global sources of contextual facilitation in reading. *Journal of Memory and Language, 26,* 322 - 340.

Seidenberg, M. S., Waters, G. S., Sanders, M., & Langer, P. (1984). Pre- and post-lexical loci of contextual effects on word recognition. *Memory & Cognition, 12,* 315 - 328.

Singer, M. (1978). *The role of explicit and implicit recall cues.* In Symposium: Implication and Inference in Language Comprehension. Paper presented at the annual meeting of the American Psychological Association, Toronto.

Singer, M. (1979). Processes of inference during sentence encoding. *Memory & Cognition, 7,* 192 - 200.

Singer, M., & Ferreira, F. (1983). Inferring consequences in story comprehension. *Journal of Verbal Learning and Verbal Behavior, 22,* 437 - 448.

Till, R. E., Mross, E. F., & Kintsch, W. (1988). Time course of priming for associate and inference words in a discourse context. *Memory & Cognition, 16,* 283 - 298.

West, R. F., & Stanovich, K. E. (1982). Automatic contextual facilitation in readers of three ages. *Child Development, 49,* 717 - 727.

Whitney, P. (1986). Processing category terms in context: Instantiations as inferences. *Memory & Cognition, 14,* 39 - 48.

Whitney, P., & Kellas, G. (1984). Processing category terms in context: Instantiation and the structure of semantic categories. *Journal of Experimental Psychology: Learning, Memory, and Cognition, 10,* 95 - 103.

19 TEXTUAL INFERENCES: MODELS AND MEASURES

Gail McKoon and Roger Ratcliff
Northwestern University

INTRODUCTION

The inferences that are made during reading stimulate intriguing questions for research. Some inference processes seem to be automatic and effortless yet they yield quite complex kinds of information. Other inference processes seem to be dependent on the goals, strategies, and contextual situations of the readers. Some inferences are concerned with the relatively small units of reading represented by words; others are concerned with much larger units like event structures or story outlines. Since about 1970, all of these kinds of inferences have been the subject of investigation, and all of these investigations have shared a common problem: finding empirical measures that can be used to investigate the processes and the products of inference. Different investigators have used different measures, but all the measures have eventually come under criticism, and as a result, progress in understanding inference has been less than impressive.

The reason all the different measures have come under criticism is that they are often viewed as just that: empirical measures. Until recently, there has been little effort to determine a theoretical basis from which to relate them to the processes and structures they are intended to measure. This situation is beginning to change. As models in the several areas that impinge on text processing become more sophisticated, accounting for wider and more complex ranges of data, we can begin to look to these models for an understanding of how specific tasks are performed. For each model in any particular area, the implications

403

that performance on some task has for conclusions about inference processes can be evaluated. Sometimes, conclusions will be the same across all the models in an area, and sometimes they will be different and model specific. Most beneficially, sometimes the models will give new interpretations or hypotheses about inference processes that would not otherwise have been considered. The important point is that, because of the possibility of different conclusions from different classes of models, it is necessary to evaluate inference processes through all available models.

The issue of relating tasks and data to models arises because the kinds of information that are involved in reading cannot be measured directly; instead, they are mapped onto tasks that require the identification of words, the comprehension of sentences, or the recognition that some piece of information was previously presented. Obviously, this mapping is not one-to-one; a word cannot be identified in isolation from its context, a sentence cannot be comprehended without the involvement of meta-level decisions, and memory for a single word from a text will be embedded in the mental representation of the text as a whole. Thus, models of word identification, sentence comprehension (including syntax and semantics), and memory retrieval become essential.

The models to be considered in this chapter are models of word identification and memory retrieval, because these models have been developed in such a way that they can be useful in evaluating tasks that have been designed to measure inference processes. Currently, there are few models of semantic processes, syntactic processes, or meta-level processes that can be used to directly understand such tasks. For example, in some models of word identification, it is clear how inference processes are supposed to impact word identification processes and, in turn, how word identification processes impact specific tasks (e.g., lexical decision). There are no equivalently specific models to show how inference processes interact with syntactic processes to affect some task that is used to measure syntactic structures. However, even without a complete set of models, progress can be made, and this chapter outlines what can and cannot be done with current models.

WORD IDENTIFICATION

Many of the measures that have been used to investigate inference processes were originally developed to investigate the identification of single words. These include lexical decision latency, naming latency, and gaze duration. The idea behind these tasks is to catch word identification processes as they occur in real time, perhaps as they are affected by perceptual variables (e.g., stimulus degradation) but more often as they are affected by contextual variables such as preceding words or sentences. Typically, a word is presented immediately after a context (i.e., on-line), and the time spent looking at the word (gaze duration in fairly normal reading), the time to decide that the string of letters is a word (lexical decision), or the time to name the word is measured. Word identification processes are also involved when a word is tested on-line for a recognition decision about whether or not it has appeared in the immediately preceding context. All of these tasks have been used to investigate inference processes under the assumption that inferences will affect word identification and therefore performance on these tasks (see McKoon, 1988, for discussion).

Models that account for how it is that inference processes affect word identification fall into two general classes. The first, older, class views word identification as a series of component processes; this class includes the models of Becker (1979), Forster (1981), and Morton, (1969) and, following Balota (this volume), can be labeled magic moment models. The second class presents a more interactive view of word identification, and includes models by Norris (1986; see also Kintsch, 1988) and Cottrell and Small (1983; see also Kawamoto, 1988). The two classes of models share some, but not all, implications for the use of word identification tasks in measurements of inference.

In the first set of models (e.g., Forster, 1981), word identification proceeds by a series of subprocesses, which can be divided into those that affect lexical access and those that occur postlexically. The subprocesses that affect lexical access occur when the context is presented, before presentation of the target word for which processing time is to be recorded. These processes can be speeded by the prior presentation in the context of the target word itself or a high associate of the target word. Access is speeded because the criterion for recognition of the target word is lowered (Morton, 1969) or because the target word is moved forward in a search list (Becker, 1979; Forster, 1981).

The important point to stress for the purposes of this chapter is that processes that affect lexical access need have nothing to do with inference processes. From the point of view of the models, lexical access effects occur in the lexicon and can occur independently of whatever might be going on in the processes of constructing a representation of the meaning of the context. For example, a context sentence about a child's birthday party might facilitate lexical access for the target word *candles*, but this would not indicate anything about the presence of the concept *candles* as an inference in the mental representation of the context sentence. Alternatively, words in the birthday party sentence might not be highly enough associated to *candles* to facilitate lexical access, but the concept *candles* might later be inferred.

In contrast, postlexical processes are processes of word identification that do not occur until after the target word has been presented (Forster, 1981; see also Balota & Lorch, 1986; Lorch, Balota, & Stamm, 1986). In Forster's model, a word to be identified (either in normal reading or in a test situation) is checked against the preceding context for its compatibility or coherence with the preceding text. Context checking is meant to be an inescapable part of word identification and so must be taken into account in any on-line test. In models proposed by Balota and Lorch (1986) and Lorch et al. (1986), postlexical processes are not mandatory but are a function of decision biases set by the conditions in an experiment.

Because postlexical processes are triggered by the presentation of the target word, they obviously cannot directly reflect inference processes that occur during reading of the context sentence (before the target is presented). For example, identification of *candles* might be facilitated by postlexical processes that found it compatible with the birthday party context, but this could happen whether or not *candles* had been inferred during reading of the sentence. However, if identification of *candles* was not facilitated by postlexical processes, then we might want to say that *candles* was not inferred during reading. The reasoning rests on the assumption that whatever relations between the target and context underlie postlexical processes, they are at least as strong as those that underlie inference processes. If the relations are not compelling enough to affect compatibility checking, then they probably are not compelling enough to generate an inference. In the example, if the relation between *candles* and the birthday party sentence does not affect word identification, then it seems unlikely that it can generate an inference.

This last point is an important difference between the class of models just reviewed and the second class (Cottrell & Small, 1983; Norris, 1986). In the second class, the relation between a target word and its context sentence can take so much time to compute that it is not available in time to affect word identification. So the absence of an effect of context on identification of a target does not necessarily indicate that the relation is not involved in inference processing.

In this second class of models, context never affects lexical access; perceptual processes produce the same candidates for identification in every context. But context does affect identification, via the decision process. In Norris's model, candidate words are checked against context and the criterion for identification of compatible words is lowered. This criterion change allows faster identification. In Cottrell and Small's model, a word is identified when the amount of evidence in favor of that word reaches a threshold. Faster identification is produced when context adds evidence towards the threshold.

The processes proposed by these models could occur either when a context sentence was presented or when the target was presented, and in fact proceed continually from presentation of context through a decision on the target. In Norris's model, the criterion for identification could be lowered either by an inference generated during reading of the context or it could be lowered only after the target word was available to relate back to the context. Similarly, in Cottrell and Small's model, context could add evidence toward a threshold as the result of an inference generated from the context or only as the result of working backward from the target. So if the relation between the sentence about the birthday party and the target word *candles* affected word identification, it might or might not reflect an inference generated by the context alone.

Both of these models contain an explicit assumption that the computations that produce context effects vary in the amount of time they require. Some, like the connections between strong associates, can be computed very quickly. Others may take more time. In fact, they may take so much time that identification of a target may be accomplished before they finish. Thus, as mentioned earlier, the absence of an effect of context on word identification is not necessarily an indication of the absence of an inferred relation.

The two classes of models taken together provide a guide to interpretation of results of experiments that use word identification tasks to investigate inference processes. Any result must be checked against all the possible explanatory mechanisms of the models. To continue the birthday party example, facilitation of the target *candles* might be due to facilitation of lexical access (Becker, 1979; Forster, 1981; Morton, 1969), postlexical context checking (Balota & Lorch, 1986; Lorch et al., 1986), or information computed when the target was presented (Cottrell & Small, 1983; Norris, 1986). In all three cases, inference processes would not be implicated. If the birthday party context did not facilitate identification of *candles*, it might be because the computation of the necessary relation was too slow (Cottrell & Small, 1983; Norris, 1986). So again, a conclusion about whether an inference was constructed from the context would not be warranted.

All of the mechanisms of the models appear to apply to all of the tasks mentioned. The pre- and postlexical processes proposed in models like Forster's (1981) were constructed for reading words in context, and apply to lexical decision, reading of single words, and recognition of single words. It has been argued that postlexical processes are less likely to be involved in naming, but more recently it appears that they can be (Balota, Boland, & Shields, 1989). The more interactive processing systems of Norris (1986) and Cottrell and Small (1983) are also intended to apply to all of the tasks.

Finally, it should be mentioned that these models are not complete. None of them explicitly allows for other kinds of information to affect tasks that measure word identification. For example, it has been shown that syntactic processes can affect the speed of word identification (cf. West & Stanovich, 1986). Target words presented in different syntactic contexts could have different response times due to differences in syntactic processing; a target presented at the end of a sentence might have faster or slower response times than a target presented in the middle of a phrase. Also, the models do not deal with such discourse effects as anaphora. To use the phrase *the clothes* to refer to some previously mentioned *clothes* might require processing to establish the joint reference even though exactly the same word, *clothes*, was repeated; there is nothing in the models to compare this kind of processing to inference processing (e.g., it might take more or less time). Neither do the models include meta-level processes. Subjects can translate their (lack of) motivation, surprise, or bewilderment into response time differences, but these variables are outside the scope of the current models.

MEMORY RETRIEVAL

In the many experiments in which inference processes have been investigated by presenting a test item immediately after a context, the relevant information is assumed to be available in a short-term or working memory. But in other experiments, the goal is to find some indication of inferred information in the memory representation of a text, and test items are presented so that the text is no longer immediately available. To interpret these latter experiments, models for retrieval of information from memory are required.

Currently, there are several such models, all impressive in the range and detail of experimental results that they can explain. Global memory theories (Gillund & Shiffrin, 1984; Hintzman, 1986; Murdock, 1982; Ratcliff, 1978; Ratcliff & McKoon, 1988a) have explained data from recognition, recall, frequency judgments, categorization, and various reaction-time paradigms. The models differ in such respects as whether they assume that there are different nodes for each concept (Gillund & Shiffrin, 1984) or assume that concepts are distributed across a number of nodes (Hintzman, 1986; Murdock, 1982), and whether they assume that information is kept separate for each item (Gillund & Shiffrin, 1984; Hintzman, 1986) or assume that all information is collapsed into a single memory trace (Murdock, 1982). But the models converge in several respects relevant to the use of memory tasks to investigate inference.

First, the models all postulate one underlying mental representation for an encoded event, the same representation to be used for all memory retrieval tasks. However, different tasks require different processes to operate on this representation. The tasks most often used in inference research are recognition and recall. For recognition, the models all assume that a decision about a test item is based on parallel (global) access to all the items stored in memory. The recognition decision reflects the overall familiarity or match of the test item to all the items in memory (Ratcliff, 1978). Recall and cued recall are assumed to be based on an iterative search that is slower than the parallel comparison used for recognition, and involves some degree of serial processing (Metcalfe & Murdock, 1981; Raaijmakers & Shiffrin, 1981). The second point of convergence of the models is that retrieval is assumed to be cue dependent (Tulving, 1974, 1983). A test item is not matched against memory in isolation but instead is matched as part of a compound of information made up from the item plus its retrieval context. Thus, a test item may match information in memory quite well in one context but poorly in another context (see Ratcliff & McKoon, 1988a, 1988b, for discussion). Finally, the models all define the familiarity or strength of retrieval of an item as a matter of degree. A test item presented for recognition or a cue presented for recall will not match other information in memory in an all-or-none fashion but instead will match that information to some degree.

Unlike the models for word identification, the memory retrieval models are in remarkable accord with respect to the general aspects of the retrieval processes that have implications for the use of memory tasks to investigate inference. Even ACT* (Anderson, 1983), which might at first glance seem very different, embodies cue dependent retrieval, global memory matching, and a distinction between recognition and recall processes. Thus, it is a relatively straightforward task to apply the models to retrieval of possibly inferred information. However, the implications of the memory models, as well as the word identification models, for research on inference processing are not necessarily obvious. The best way to make them clear is to give specific examples. The final two sections of this chapter provide case studies of application of both kinds of models to the investigation of particular kinds of inferences.

CASE STUDY I: ELABORATIVE INFERENCES

Elaborative inferences have been studied extensively since the beginning of current interest in inference processes. These inferences have been of special interest because they go beyond what is actually required to connect the explicitly stated ideas in a text, and so could begin to test the limits of inference processes. Bransford, Barclay, and Franks (1972) and Bransford and Franks (1971) argued that a reader constructs a mental model of the situation described in a text, adding information to complete the model and combining the elements of a text into an integrated whole.

For this chapter, one kind of inference from our own research has been chosen as a case study with which to examine the implications of various experimental techniques for addressing questions about the construction during reading of elaborative inferences. The kind of elaborative inference is one that we have investigated in a series of experiments, and concerns predictable events; an example is shown in Table 19.1. The predicting sentence was written to predict that the actress would die, and this inference was expressed by the test word *dead*.

TABLE 19.1

Examples of Stimuli Used in Elaborative Inference Study.

Predicting:
The director and the cameraman were ready to shoot closeups when suddenly the actress fell from the 14th story.
Test word: *dead*

Control:
Suddenly the director fell upon the cameraman, demanding closeups of the actress on the 14th story.
Test word: *dead*

The research question that has been addressed in most studies of elaborative inferences is whether or not the predictable event is inferred during reading of the predicting sentence. This question has been addressed using most of the tasks already discussed: the on-line tasks of recognition, lexical decision, and naming, and the delayed memory tasks of cued recall and recognition. Interpretations of results from these tasks can be discussed in light of the models of word identification and memory retrieval reviewed previously.

On-line Tasks

One possible experiment would be to present a predicting sentence of the kind shown in Table 19.1, and then follow it immediately with a word representing the predicted event (*dead*) for lexical decision. There would be two possible results; either the sentence could facilitate the lexical decision or the sentence could have no effect on the lexical decision (the third possibility, inhibition, seems unlikely).

According to the models of word identification, facilitation could arise for several reasons. First, there might be individual words in the predicting sentence that were highly semantically associated to the target word. These words could speed lexical access for the target (Becker, 1979; Forster, 1981; Morton, 1969), lower the threshold for identification (Norris, 1986), or increase the amount of information leading to identification of the target (Cottrell & Small, 1983). None of these mechanisms would require that an inference about the predicted event was constructed. However, these interpretations of facilitation can be ruled out by using a control sentence like that shown in Table 19.1. The sentence includes all the words from the predicting sentence that might possibly be associated to the target word, yet the sentence does not predict the target. So if facilitation in lexical decision is obtained for the predicting sentence relative to the control sentence, then it cannot be due to word-to-word associations.

A second reason that facilitation might arise according to the models would be that a relation between the target word and the predicting sentence was constructed at the time the target word was presented. This could come about through postlexical processes (e.g., Forster's model, 1981) or through criterion or threshold changes (Norris's model or Cottrell and Small's model). In neither case would facilitation indicate that information about the inference was constructed during reading of the predicting sentence.

The alternative possible result is that the predicting sentence would *not* facilitate a lexical decision on the target word. In the interactive models, this could occur if the inference was not constructed at all or if it was constructed but too slowly to affect the lexical decision. From the point of view of models of the pre- and postlexical type, lack of facilitation would indicate that the inference was not constructed, because if it were constructed it should affect postlexical processes.

The question that arises from all of these possible interpretations of different possible results is whether there is some consistent subset of them that can fit data. The answer appears to be that there are in fact two such subsets. The results of several experiments are shown in Table 19.2. When presentation of the predicting sentence is slow (or a number of words intervene between the target word and the point in the predicting sentence where the inference could be generated), then facilitation is observed. When presentation is faster and no extra words intervene, then there is no facilitation. This pattern of data is observed both for lexical decision and for recognition.

TABLE 19.2

Results from On-line Experiments with Elaborative Inference.

Lexical Decision (Slow); (Potts, Keenan, & Golding, 1988).

Predicting	980 ms (3%)	
Control	1034 ms (11%)	sig.

Lexical Decision (Fast); (McKoon, 1988).

Predicting	651 ms (4%)	
Control	645 ms (6%)	n.s.

Recognition (Slow); (McKoon & Ratcliff, 1986).

Predicting	883 ms (7%)	
Control	853 ms (6%)	sig.

Recognition (Fast); (McKoon & Ratcliff, 1989c)[1]

Predicting	768 ms (18%)	
Control	748 ms (16%)	n.s.

Naming latency (Slow); (Potts, Keenan, & Golding, 1988).

Predicting	423 ms	
Control	422 ms	n.s.

Note: Slow and Fast refer to the amount of time available for generating the inference between presentation of context material and test. Response times and error rates are both shown; *sig.* indicates that results of analyses of variance were significant for at least one of the measures.

[1] The same result was obtained by Till, Mross, & Kintsch, 1988.

One way to look at this whole pattern of data and the models is to argue that the pattern is consistent with the interactive models and the assumption that the inferences are relatively slow to generate. The slow inferences affect decisions when there is enough time before the target word, and they do not affect decisions when the target is presented too quickly. This way of looking at the data would not be consistent with the pre- and postlexical models; if postlexical processes were operating with slow presentation, then they should also be operating with fast presentation. These models could be made consistent with the data by adding an assumption that inferences are slow to generate, but unlike the interactive models, they currently have no mechanism by which to implement such an assumption.

The data from naming latency could be fit into this pattern if it were assumed that lexical information enters a naming production system faster than it is available for the other tasks, and enters production without the benefit of slower, constructed, semantic kinds of information (Seidenberg, this volume). In this way, naming latencies could be free from any effects of inferred information. As an aside, it should be noted that there is one case where facilitation of naming was obtained for a target word that represented an inference (Potts, Keenan, & Golding, 1988). In this case, the target word was preceded by two sentences, a predicting sentence and a second sentence that required the target inference. With the second sentence, very specific information about the inference could have been constructed, and so an effect on naming latency might be expected. The information might have been articulatory (the subject "saying" the target word), or it might have been only conceptual (in which case it might not affect performance on a Stroop task; see Keenan, Potts, Golding, & Jennings, this volume).

So far, one way of looking at the pattern of data illustrated in Table 19.2 has been discussed; this way involved assuming that the target inferences are generated in response to the predicting sentences. A second way to look at the pattern of data is to suppose that the elaborative inferences are not generated during reading of the predicting sentences at all. The positive results in lexical decision and recognition would be due to postlexical processes (e.g., Forster, 1981) or to relations between the target word and predicting sentence computed when the target was presented (Cottrell & Small, 1983; Norris, 1986). The absence of facilitation with fast presentation would be a problem for the postlexical processes models, but they could add an assumption that these processes require more time than available with fast presentation.

Obviously, these two ways of viewing the data are contradictory; one assumes that elaborative inferences are generated during reading (albeit slowly) and the other assumes that they are not. The conclusion therefore is that some other method of investigating these kinds of inferences is needed. Later, it is argued that a memory task, speeded recognition, can provide such a method.

Memory Tasks

To investigate whether the inference represented by *dead* is included in the mental representation of the predicting sentence, subjects could be asked (among other tasks) to recall the sentence without a cue (free recall), recall the sentence given the cue *dead*, or decide whether the word *dead* had appeared in the sentence (recognition). Global memory models suggest interpretations for possible results in each case.

In cued recall, a list of sentences, some predicting and some control, is presented. Then after the end of the list, single word cues are given and the subject's task is to produce a studied sentence for each cue. According to the models, the cue is used to generate an iterative search of memory, a process that may take some time. If the cue word, *dead*, was encoded with the predicting text, then at some point in the search process, the text should be retrieved. However, even if the cue word was not encoded with the text, it could still be the case that self-generated cues from the meaning of the word *dead* would be used to probe memory and eventually produce the text (cf. Corbett & Dosher, 1978; McKoon & Ratcliff, 1986). Thus, according to the models, if the target word was a better cue for the predicting than the control sentence (as shown in Table 19.3), it could be either because the inference was generated and encoded during reading of the predicting sentence or because it was generated later as part of the memory retrieval process.

TABLE 19.3

Results from Delayed Memory Experiments with Elaborative Inference.

Cued Recall; (McKoon & Ratcliff, 1986).

Correct recall rate:	Predicting	23%	
	Control	4%	sig.

Speeded Recognition; (McKoon & Ratcliff, 1986).[1]

Error rate:			
Neutral Prime	Predicting	36%	
	Control	27%	n.s.
Prime from Text	Predicting	56%	
	Control	24%	sig.

[1] This pattern of data has been replicated in McKoon, 1988, and McKoon and Ratcliff, 1989a, 1989b, 1989c.

In free recall, the same list of sentences could be presented and then subjects could be asked to recall as many as they remembered, without experimenter-provided cues. An experiment like this with materials of the type shown in Table 19.1 has not been done. Interpretation of results would not be straightforward because of the possibility of all kinds of inferential processes that might take place during recall, as retrieval of some information led to the retrieval and generation of more information. Whether information inferred during reading would be produced at retrieval is not clearly predictable from the models; they have been formulated only to deal with explicitly presented information.

Recognition can be tested either by allowing subjects to respond in their own time or by giving them a deadline to require them to respond quickly. In the first case, processing may become slow enough that the mechanisms are the same as in cued recall, and any evidence of inferences could be due to generation of the inference information at the time of the test.

If recognition is speeded, with response times around 600 ms or less, then according to the models, the recognition decision is based on a global parallel match between the target word in its context and all information in memory. The models assume a fast parallel matching process because of direct empirical evidence about the time course of retrieval (Dosher, 1982, 1984; Gronlund & Ratcliff, 1989; Ratcliff & McKoon, 1982, 1989; Reed, 1973; Wickelgren, Corbett, & Dosher, 1980) and because of indirect evidence that such a process is required to account for large ranges of data. The parallel matching process produces a goodness of match value that determines the speed and accuracy of the decision. For a target word that represents an inference, a positive match must be based on a relation between the target word and information encoded when the predicting text was read. The global parallel match process would not allow for the generation of new information in the 600 ms before a response (neither would the spreading activation/production system of ACT*). If there is a positive match between the target and memory for the predicting text, a correct (negative) decision will tend to be more difficult.

The global memory models stress the cue dependent nature of recognition, and the recognition of targets representing elaborative inferences exhibits this cue dependence. In Table 19.3, when the target is primed by a word from the studied sentence, the match between the target and the predicting sentence is large enough to inhibit the decision process, relative to the control condition. But when the target is presented by itself, with only a neutral word for a prime, the decision process is not inhibited. This pattern of results can be interpreted as showing some degree of partial match or partial encoding of the inference (see McKoon & Ratcliff, 1986, 1988, 1989b, 1989c, in press, for discussion).

An alternative interpretation of this pattern of results was proposed recently by Potts et al. (1988). They suggested that a prime from a predicting sentence activates the predicting sentence, and then compatibility is computed between the target word and the activated sentence.

If the target word is compatible, then the response to it will be inhibited, even though no inference about it was made during reading. This proposal can be rejected on several grounds. First, the computation of compatibility within 600 ms is not consistent with a large body of data on the time course of information processing in recognition (cf. Dosher, 1984; Gronlund & Ratcliff, 1989; Ratcliff & McKoon, 1982, 1989); all of these data show that information about relations among items, information similar to what would be needed for the computation of inferences, is not available early enough in processing to affect speeded recognition. Second, McKoon and Ratcliff (1989a) have shown that recognition performance is not predicted by compatibility ratings in the way the compatibility hypothesis would require. According to the compatibility hypothesis, ratings should be more highly correlated with recognition performance in the condition with a prime from the text than in the neutral condition, because the prime from the text makes it more likely that compatibility will be calculated against the correct one of the several studied texts. In fact, ratings did not correlate more highly in the condition with the prime from the text. Finally, McKoon and Ratcliff (1989a) showed that there are inference target words that are compatible with their predicting texts but that do not show inhibition in speeded recognition. For all these reasons, the compatibility hypothesis cannot account for recognition data of the kind shown in Table 19.3.

Summary

The pattern of data in Table 19.3 can be made consistent with models of word identification and models of memory retrieval if it is assumed that elaborative inferences are partially encoded during reading and that the encoding is a relatively slow process. The inferences were not encoded to such a high degree that they were equally available under all retrieval conditions (see the neutral vs. prime from text conditions in Table 19.3), but they must have been encoded to some degree because they did inhibit recognition when combined with a cue from their text. This evidence from the memory tasks rules out one interpretation of the on-line data in Table 19.2, the interpretation that the inferences were not encoded at all. As a consequence, the remaining interpretation of the on-line data, slow processing, is supported (see McKoon & Ratcliff, 1986, 1988, 1989b, 1989c, in press, for further discussion).

CASE STUDY II: ANAPHORIC REFERENCES

The conclusion from the case study of elaborative inference is that progress is made by the method of combining converging empirical results with careful consideration of all possible theoretical accounts of the results. This is the same conclusion that can be drawn from recent work on anaphoric reference. Examples in this section are limited to work from our laboratory on category names used as anaphors, but the empirical and theoretical points are based also on work by Corbett and Chang (1983).

The questions that have been raised in this work concern, first, the process of connecting an anaphor to its antecedent, and second, the time course of this inference process. These questions can be illustrated using the example text shown in Table 19.4. In the first version of the text, the final sentence contains the anaphor *the criminal*, which should be connected by inference to its referent *burglar*. The second version of the text ends with a control sentence that mentions some word that is not supposed to refer to the burglar mentioned in the first sentence. To investigate whether *criminal* is understood to refer to *burglar*, both on-line and memory tasks can be used.

TABLE 19.4

Examples of Texts Used in Anaphoric Reference.

Version 1
A burglar surveyed the garage set back from the street.
Several milk bottles were piled at the curb.
The banker and her husband were on vacation.
The criminal slipped away from the streetlamp.

Version 2
A burglar surveyed the garage set back from the street.
Several milk bottles were piled at the curb.
The banker and her husband were on vacation.
A cat slipped away from the streetlamp.

Test words:
Referent - *bottles*
From the same proposition as burglar - *garage*
Control word - *bottles*

One way to test whether *the criminal* is understood to refer to *the burglar* might be to present the target word *burglar* both before and after the referent, and compare response times (this has been suggested by O'Brien, Duffy, & Myers, 1986). The idea would be that response times to the target would be speeded for the after test relative to the before test, because the target concept would be processed as part of the inference connecting the anaphor to the referent. However, this possible test has problems. If the target concept were in short-term memory, then response times might be at floor even in the before test. And if response times were reduced in the after condition, it could be because of syntactic effects on decision times (as previously mentioned, even though word identification models do not address the interaction of syntactic and lexical processes directly, they would still allow them to affect response times). For example, the before position is in the middle of a noun phrase and might have slow response times relative to the after position, which is at the end of a noun phrase.

Another way to test whether *the criminal* is understood to be the same person as *the burglar* might be to present the anaphoric and control texts for reading, and then immediately after the final sentences, present the word *burglar* for test. If the inference connecting *criminal* to *burglar* was constructed during reading of the final sentence of the anaphoric text, then a decision about the test word *burglar* should be facilitated. However, this facilitation could have several alternative interpretations other than that the inference was constructed during reading of the anaphoric sentence. The facilitation could have come about because the preexisting semantic relation between *burglar* and *criminal* speeded lexical access for *burglar*. Or, it could be that the facilitation was the result of a more compatible relation (constructed when the target was presented) between the target word and the anaphoric text than between the target word and the control text. In neither of these cases would inference processes during reading of the anaphoric sentence be implicated.

These alternative interpretations are all dependent on the preexisting relation between *criminal* and *burglar*. So to rule out these interpretations, a test word without such a relation is required. One such target is *garage*. If *the criminal* is connected to *burglar* by some inference process, then this process might also connect propositions about *criminal* and *burglar* and so involve other concepts in the propositions, such as *garage*. Then response times for *garage* would be facilitated after the anaphoric sentence relative to the control sentence. Because there are no preexisting semantic relations between *criminal* and *garage*, the facilitation could not be due to a speed up of lexical access for *garage*. Furthermore, the relations that could be computed between the target *garage* and the anaphoric sentence do not seem more compatible than those that could be computed between the target and the control sentence.

Using *garage* as a target word rules out the alternative interpretations most obviously suggested by word identification models. However, there might be other kinds of processes, at the syntactic or discourse levels, that differed between the anaphoric and control texts. Instead of speculating about what these possible differences might be, it is easier to measure them by the use of a control target word. In the example in Table 19.4, the word *bottles* has no particular relation to either *the criminal* or *a cat*, so response times to *bottles* used as a target should be the same whether it is tested with the anaphoric sentence or the control sentence. If response times for *bottles* were not the same in these two conditions, it would be an indication that the two sentences were different in some way that had nothing to do with the anaphor. Then response times for the target of interest, *garage*, would have to be evaluated against the response times for *bottles*.

The logic outlined here was followed by McKoon and Ratcliff (1980) and Dell, McKoon, and Ratcliff (1983). Using on-line recognition, they showed that both the target words *burglar* and *garage* were facilitated by the anaphoric sentence relative to the control and that response times for the control word, *bottles*, did not differ for the two sentences. Thus, it seems reasonable to suppose that an inference about the relation between *the criminal* and *burglar* was constructed during reading of the anaphoric sentence. Additional evidence that the inference was constructed during reading was provided by a recognition memory experiment that showed that responses to a word from the same proposition as *the criminal, streetlamp,* were facilitated by the prime *burglar* when the anaphoric sentence had been read relative to when the control sentence had been read.

This case study shows the power of using models as guides to experimental design. With anaphors of the type examined here, all of the mechanisms proposed by the models to be involved in word identification can be taken into consideration, and sources of facilitation for a target word that are not due to inference processes can be eliminated. Additionally, the memory models allow recognition data to confirm the results of the on-line experiments.

CONCLUSIONS

The aim of this chapter has been to illustrate how essential theoretical models are in the interpretation of data from empirical tasks. None of the tasks that has been used to investigate inference can be taken as an unequivocal measure of inference processes. Only when both theory and experimental design converge can conclusions be ventured and progress toward an understanding of inference be claimed.

ACKNOWLEDGMENT

This research was supported by NSF grant 85-16350 to Gail McKoon and NSF grant 85-10361 to Roger Ratcliff.

REFERENCES

Anderson, J. R. (1983). *The architecture of cognition.* Cambridge, MA: Harvard University Press.

Balota, D., Boland, J., & Shields, L. W. (1989). Priming in pronunciation: Beyond pattern recognition and onset latency. *Journal of Memory and Language, 28,* 14 - 36.

Balota, D. A., & Lorch, R. F. (1986). Depth of automatic spreading activation: Mediated priming effects in pronunciation but not in lexical decision. *Journal of Experimental Psychology: Learning, Memory, and Cognition, 12,* 336 - 345.

Becker, C. A. (1979). Semantic context and word frequency effects in visual word recognition. *Journal of Experimental Psychology: Human Perception and Performance, 5,* 252 - 259.

Bransford, J. D., Barclay, J. R., & Franks, J. J. (1972). Sentence memory: A constructive versus interpretive approach. *Cognitive Psychology, 3,* 193 - 209.

Bransford, J. D., & Franks, J. J. (1971). The abstraction of linguistic ideas. *Cognitive Psychology, 2,* 331 - 350.

Corbett, A. T., & Chang, F. R. (1983). Pronoun disambiguation: Accessing potential antecedents. *Memory & Cognition, 11,* 283 - 294.

Corbett, A. T., & Dosher, B. A. (1978). Instrument inferences in sentence encoding. *Journal of Verbal Learning and Verbal Behavior, 17,* 479 - 491.

Cottrell, G. W., & Small, S. (1983). A connectionist scheme for modeling word sense disambiguation. *Cognition and Brain Theory, 6,* 89 - 120.

Dell, G. S., McKoon, G., & Ratcliff, R. (1983). The activation of antecedent information during the processing of anaphoric reference in reading. *Journal of Verbal Learning and Verbal Behavior, 22,* 121 - 132.

Dosher, B. A. (1982). Effect of sentence size and network distance on retrieval speed. *Journal of Experimental Psychology: Learning, Memory, and Cognition, 8,* 173 - 207.

Dosher, B. A. (1984). Discriminating preexperimental (semantic) from learned (episodic) associations: A speed-accuracy study. *Cognitive Psychology, 16,* 519 - 555.

Forster, K. I. (1981). Priming and the effects of sentence and lexical contexts on naming time: Evidence for autonomous lexical processing. *Quarterly Journal of Experimental Psychology, 33A,* 465 - 495.

Gillund, G., & Shiffrin, R. M. (1984). A retrieval model for both recognition and recall. *Psychological Review, 91,* 1 - 67.

Gronlund, S. D., & Ratcliff, R. (1989). Time course of item and associative information: Implications for global memory models. *Journal of Experimental Psychology: Learning, Memory, and Cognition, 15,* 846 - 858.

Hintzman, D. L. (1986). "Schema abstraction" in a multiple-trace memory model. *Psychological Review, 93,* 411 - 428.

Kawamoto, A. H. (1988). Distributed representations of ambiguous words and their resolution in a connectionist network. In S. Small, G. Cottrell, & M. Tanenhaus (Eds.), *Lexical ambiguity resolution in the comprehension of human language* (pp. 195 - 228). San Mateo, CA: Morgan Kaufman.

Kintsch, W. (1988). The role of knowledge in discourse comprehension: A construction-integration model. *Psychological Review, 95,* 163 - 182.

Lorch, R. F., Balota, D. A., & Stamm, E. G. (1986). Locus of inhibition effects in the priming of lexical decisions: Pre- or postlexical access? *Memory & Cognition, 14,* 95 - 103.

McKoon, G. (1988). *Word identification and elaborative inference: The relation between theory and empirical measurement.* Unpublished manuscript.

McKoon, G., & Ratcliff, R. (1980). The comprehension processes and memory structures involved in anaphoric reference. *Journal of Verbal Learning and Verbal Behavior, 19,* 668 - 682.

McKoon, G., & Ratcliff, R. (1986). Inferences about predictable events. *Journal of Experimental Psychology: Learning, Memory, and Cognition, 12,* 82 - 91.

McKoon, G., & Ratcliff, R. (1988). Contextually relevant aspects of meaning. *Journal of Experimental Psychology: Learning, Memory, and Cognition, 14,* 331 - 343.

McKoon, G., & Ratcliff, R. (1989a). Assessing the occurrence of elaborative inference with recognition: Compatibility checking vs. compound cue theory. *Journal of Memory and Language, 28,* 547 - 563.

McKoon, G., & Ratcliff, R. (1989b). Inferences about contextually-defined categories. *Journal of Experimental Psychology: Learning, Memory, and Cognition, 15,* 1134 - 1146.

McKoon, G., & Ratcliff, R. (1989c). Semantic association and elaborative inference. *Journal of Experimental Psychology: Learning, Memory, and Cognition, 15,* 326 - 338.

McKoon, G., & Ratcliff, R. (in press). Dimensions of inference. In A. C. Graesser & G. H. Bower (Eds.), *The psychology of learning and motivation* (Vol. 25). Orlando, FL: Academic Press.

Metcalfe, J., & Murdock, B. B. (1981). An encoding and retrieval model of single-trial free recall. *Journal of Verbal Learning and Verbal Behavior, 20,* 161 - 189.

Morton, J. (1969). The interaction of information in word recognition. *Psychological Review, 76,* 165 - 178.

Murdock, B. B. (1982). A theory for the storage and retrieval of item and associative information. *Psychological Review, 89,* 609 - 626.

Norris, D. (1986). Word recognition: Context effects without priming. *Cognition, 22,* 93 - 136.

O'Brien, E. J., Duffy, S. A., & Myers, J. L. (1986). Anaphoric inference during reading. *Journal of Experimental Psychology: Learning, Memory, and Cognition, 12,* 346 - 352.

Potts, G. R., Keenan, J. M., & Golding, J. M. (1988). Assessing the occurrence of elaborative inferences: Lexical decision versus naming. *Journal of Memory and Language, 27,* 399 - 415.

Raaijmakers, J. G. W., & Shiffrin, R. M. (1981). Search of associative memory. *Psychological Review, 88,* 93 - 134.

Ratcliff, R. (1978). A theory of memory retrieval. *Psychological Review, 85,* 59 - 108.

Ratcliff, R., & McKoon, G. (1982). Speed and accuracy in the processing of false statements about semantic information. *Journal of Experimental Psychology: Human Learning and Memory, 8,* 16 - 36.

Ratcliff, R., & McKoon, G. (1988a). Memory models, text processing, and cue-dependent retrieval. In F. I. M. Craik & H. L. Roediger (Eds.), *Varieties of memory and consciousness: Essays in honour of Endel Tulving* (pp. 73 - 92). Hillsdale, NJ: Lawrence Erlbaum Associates.

Ratcliff, R., & McKoon, G. (1988b). A retrieval theory of priming in memory. *Psychological Review, 95,* 385 - 408.

Ratcliff, R., & McKoon, G. (1989). Similarity information versus relational information: Differences in the time course of retrieval. *Cognitive Psychology, 21,* 139 - 155.

Reed, A. V. (1973). Speed-accuracy trade-off in recognition memory. *Science, 181,* 574 - 576.

Till, R. E., Mross, E. F., & Kintsch, W. (1988). Time course of priming for associate and inference words in a discourse context. *Memory & Cognition, 16,* 283 - 298.

Tulving, E. (1974). Cue-dependent forgetting. *American Scientist, 62,* 74 - 82.

Tulving, E. (1983). *Elements of episodic memory.* New York: Oxford University Press.

West, R. F., & Stanovich, K. E. (1986). Robust effects of syntactic structure on visual word processing. *Memory & Cognition, 14,* 104 - 112.

Wickelgren, W. A., Corbett, A. T., & Dosher, B. A. (1980). Priming and retrieval from short-term memory: A speed accuracy trade-off analysis. *Journal of Verbal Learning and Verbal Behavior, 19,* 387 - 404.

20

THE CAUSAL INFERENCE MAKER: TOWARDS A PROCESS MODEL OF INFERENCE GENERATION IN TEXT COMPREHENSION

Paul van den Broek
University of Minnesota

INTRODUCTION

A central component of successful reading is the construction of a functional, coherent representation of the text in memory. This representation reflects the reader's understanding of the individual events in the text and of the relationships among these events. The construction of a representation may be viewed as a problem-solving process in which the reader infers relationships among the ideas, events, and states that are described in the text. Although various kinds of relations may be inferred, causal dependencies have been found to play an especially central role (Black & Bower, 1980; Graesser, 1981; Graesser & Clark, 1985; Trabasso, Secco & van den Broek, 1984; see also the chapters by Keenan, Potts, Golding, and Jennings, by McKoon and Ratcliff, and by Myers in the present volume). That is, the reader draws upon prior knowledge about psychological and physical causality to find causes and consequences of focal events. These causal relations result in the perception of coherence in the text.

A comprehensive theory of discourse comprehension should describe both the properties of memory representations of texts and the inferential processes that lead to such representations. This chapter presents an outline of a theory that achieves these goals. The first section of the chapter provides a model for representing texts as networks of causally related statements. The second section contains a review of the empirical evidence for the psychological validity of the representational model. The third section proposes a model of the inferential processes that take

423

place during reading. This process model, the causal inference maker (CIM), incorporates aspects of the representational model and of recent research on limitations of the human information-processing system in reading. It predicts *under what conditions* the inferential process is initiated, what *types* of inferences will be made, and what the *constraints on the content* of the inferences are. This section also presents preliminary evidence for the process model.

THE REPRESENTATION OF TEXT IN MEMORY

Most recent theories of discourse comprehension emphasize the role that causal relations play in the structure of a text. Story grammars (Mandler & Johnson, 1977; Rumelhart, 1975; Stein & Glenn, 1979; Thorndyke, 1977), causal-chain theories (Black & Bower, 1980; Omanson, 1982), and inferential taxonomies (Nicholas & Trabasso, 1981) propose that causal dependencies provide coherence to narrative texts. They are the cement of the textual universe (to paraphrase David Hume).

Although these theories have advanced our understanding of discourse processes, they are lacking in at least two respects. First, they do not provide clear criteria for what constitutes a causal relation. This is an important issue because, as philosophers (Hart & Honore, 1985; Mackie, 1980) and psychologists (e.g., Bindra, Clarke, & Shultz, 1980; Einhorn & Hogarth, 1986; Michotte, 1963; Tversky & Kahneman, 1982) have pointed out, many properties of the relationship of two events contribute to the perception of causality. These properties can augment as well as diminish one another (Van den Broek, in press). It therefore is important for a psychological theory of causal reasoning to distinguish among them. A second problem with the current theories of discourse processing is that they do not specify how the relationships between *pairs* of idea units are to be combined into a single representation of the *entire* text.

These limitations led to the development of a network theory of discourse representation (Trabasso & Sperry, 1985; Trabasso & Van den Broek, 1985). The theory provides a set of formal criteria for the identification of the causal relations in a text and for the assembly of the events and their interrelations into a *network* representation of the text. The resulting network captures the complex causal structure of the text.

The theory proposes four criteria for deciding whether a causal relation exists between two events. The criteria are based on philosophical and legal theories of causality (Hart & Honore, 1985; Hospers, 1973; Lewis, 1976; Mackie, 1980). According to the criterion of *temporal priority*, a cause never occurs after the consequence. According to the criterion of *operativity*, a cause is active when the consequence occurs. The *necessity in the circumstances* criterion reflects the fact that if the cause had not happened then the consequence would not have taken place, given the circumstances of the story. The *sufficiency in the circumstances* criterion indicates that if the cause occurs, then the consequence will likely occur as well, given the circumstances of the story (see Van den Broek, in press, for a more extensive discussion).

The contribution of each of the four criteria to the strength of a causal relation can be expressed mathematically (Van den Broek, in press; cf. Einhorn & Hogarth, 1986):

$$1. \ C = TO(\mathbf{N} + \mathbf{S})/2$$

where C represents the strength of the causal relationship (with range between 0 and 1), T indicates whether the candidate cause occurred before (1) or after (0) the consequence, O indicates whether the candidate cause was operative (1) or not operative (0) when the consequence occurred, and N and S stand for necessity and sufficiency in the circumstances, respectively (both varying from 0 to 1). The criteria of temporal priority and operativity are either met or not met by a candidate cause-and-effect pair. If they are, then a causal relation is possible. If one of them is not met, then no causal relation can exist. Temporal priority and operativity are therefore *required* for a causal relation. Necessity and sufficiency can be present in varying degrees. If neither of the two criteria are met, then no causal relation can exist. In all other cases, a causal relation may exist. In these cases, the extent to which necessity and/or sufficiency are met determines the *strength* of the relation.

In order to identify the causal relations among the events in a text, one applies the four criteria to all pairs of events. This procedure yields a list of the causal relations that exist in the text.

The theory also provides a method for describing the causal structure of the text *as a whole* by assuming transitivity of relations: If event A causes event B, and event B causes event C, then events A, B, and C are causally connected, A → B → C. As the strength of each of the two steps in this chain is likely to be less than 1, the strength of the A → C connection will be less than that of either A → B or B → C.

The application of the notion of transitivity to all previously identified relations results in their assembly into a *network*, which captures the causal structure of the story. Consider the story in Table 20.1 (from Van den Broek, in press). The relations among the events in this story have been identified using the causal criteria. Figure 20.1 graphically represents the causal relations among the events in the story, with the nodes depicting the individual events and the arcs capturing the causal connections.

In summary, the network theory allows one to describe the causal structure of a text. The application of the causal criteria and of the rule of transitivity results in the representation of the text as a formal network of interrelated nodes. An important question is whether these formal networks resemble the actual memory representations that are constructed by readers.

TABLE 20.1

Sample Text for Illustrating Causal Structure

1. There once was a boy named Jimmy,
2. who wanted to buy a bike.
3. He called a bike store to ask for prices.
4. He counted his money.
5. The money was not enough for a bike.
6. He put his piggy bank back on the top shelf of his closet.
7. and covered it with clothes.
8. Jimmy wanted to get some money
9. so he asked his mother for some.
10. His mother said "no, you should earn your own."
11. Jimmy decided to get a paper route.
12. He called the newspaper agency
13. and asked about a route.
14. The secretary told him to come in.
15. Jimmy talked to the manager
16. and got his job.
17. He worked very hard on his job
18. and earned a lot of tips.
19. Pretty soon he had earned $200.
20. He went to a bike store
21. and bought a beautiful bike.
22. He was the happiest kid in town.

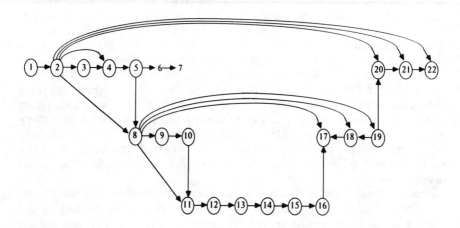

FIGURE 20.1. Causal network representation of example story (based on Van den Broek, in press).

EMPIRICAL EVIDENCE FOR NETWORK REPRESENTATIONS

Research on the psychological validity of the network representations has focused on three aspects: the extent to which the criteria capture people's intuitive notions of causality, the existence of individual causal relations in a memory representation of a text, and the importance of the causal role that events play in the network as a whole.

First, evidence that the network theory's formal criteria for identifying causal relations are consistent with readers' implicit notions of causality comes from a series of studies by Trabasso, Van den Broek, and Suh (1989). These authors presented subjects with a set of stories and asked them to judge the strength of the causal relations between selected pairs of events. The pairs of events differed with respect to the variables of temporal priority, necessity, and sufficiency in the circumstances. The results showed that the judged strength of relations was very high when all criteria were met. In agreement with Equation 1, the strength decreased when one of the criteria was not satisfied. Thus, each of the criteria contributes to the strength of a causal relation. Interestingly, however, the loss of temporal priority affected the strength much more than did the loss of either sufficiency or necessity. In fact, the relations among events that lacked temporal priority *alone* were judged to be almost as weak as those among events that lacked *both* temporal priority and one of the other causal properties. This result is in agreement with the model's assumption that temporal priority is required for a causal relation.

Trabasso et al. (1989) also provided evidence for the notion of transitivity. Subjects judged two events that were connected through a series of causal relations to be more strongly related than two unrelated events even when the latter were closer in the surface structure of the text. Also, the strength of the relation between two causally related events declined as the number of intervening causal steps increased. These findings support the notion that events can be related indirectly via transitivity and that the resulting relation is likely to be weaker than more direct relations. They held true even after the effects of other potential variables, referential overlap and surface distance, were statistically removed. The research discussed indicates that readers do agree with the formal model with respect to the strength of a causal relation between two events in a story. This suggests that the model's causal criteria capture the intuitive notions of causality held by readers.

Second, evidence that causal relations are incorporated in the memory representation of the text comes from performance on priming tasks. If the causal networks share properties with the memory representation of a story, then one would expect that reminding a reader of one event speeds up recognition of another, causally related event. Van den Broek and Lorch (1989) showed this to be the case. They found that events that were not adjacent in the surface structure of the text primed target events as much as did adjacent events, provided that the nonadjacent events satisfied the criteria for causality posited by the network model.

Nonadjacent events that did not meet the criteria did not prime the target events. Thus, the individual relations that are identified by the procedures of the network theory are indeed incorporated in the mental representation of the text.

Third, the network representation of stories has implications that go beyond those for relations between pairs of events. The networks describe how individual events differ with respect to their role in a text as a whole. Two properties of events, causal-chain status and number of causal relations to other events, are of particular interest. First, a causal chain of events connects the beginning and the end of a story. Events on this chain provide coherence to the text, whereas events that are not part of the causal chain have no relevance to the ultimate outcome of the story and therefore are peripheral (Black & Bower, 1980; Omanson, 1982; Schank & Abelson, 1977; Trabasso et al., 1984). For example, in Figure 20.1 a causal chain can be identified by finding the path from the beginning of the story (1) to its end (22). The events on the causal chain are marked by circles. Events not on the causal chain are unmarked. They are labeled *dead ends*. For example, Jimmy's talking to the newspaper manager (15) is on the causal chain because it has consequences that eventually lead to resolution of the major goal. In contrast, Jimmy's putting his piggy bank on the shelf (6) is a dead end because it is not on the chain of events that lead to the resolution of the goal.

The distinction between causal-chain and dead-end events has been tested in empirical studies. Trabasso et al. (1984) compared the probability of recall for causal-chain and dead-end events. Figure 20.2 contains the results for immediate and delayed recall. In each task, events that are part of the causal chain were better remembered than those that are dead end. In addition, the two types of events had different memory-loss rates. Over the one-week interval, the frequency of recall declined more rapidly for dead-end events than for causal-chain events. Trabasso and Van den Broek (1985; Trabasso & Sperry, 1985; Van den Broek & Trabasso, 1986) replicated these findings and, in addition, found that causal-chain events were included in summaries more often and rated as more important than dead-end events. Using statistical means, they ruled out other variables such as referential overlap, story-grammar properties, concreteness, and surface order. Thus, the psychological validity of the distinction between events that are part of the causal chain and those that are not is demonstrated in a wide range of tasks.

The second central property of an event in a network representation is the number of causal connections it has to other events. Events with a large number of connections have many causal consequences and/or antecedents and therefore play an important role in maintaining the coherence of a text. This role should be reflected in subjects' performance on various measures of text comprehension. For example, an event that has many connections has a high likelihood that at least one pathway is found to that event during retrieval. As a result it will be recalled more

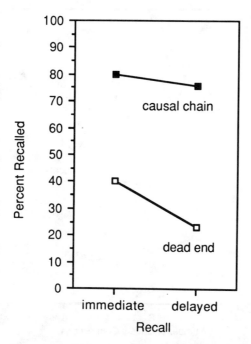

FIGURE 20.2. Percent recall of statements as a function of causal-chain status (based on Trabasso et al., 1984).

frequently than an event with fewer connections. Correlational studies show that this is indeed the case. Figure 20.3 shows the recall data reported by Trabasso and Van den Broek (1985). Events with many connections were recalled more often than events with few connections. Similar results have been reported by Fletcher and Bloom (1988), Goldman and Varnhagen (1986), and Trabasso et al. (1984).

Performance on other tasks mirrors these results. Highly connected events are more often included in summaries (Trabasso & Van den Broek, 1985; Van den Broek & Trabasso, 1986), rated as more important (Trabasso & Sperry, 1985; Trabasso & Van den Broek, 1985; Van den Broek, 1988), and retrieved more quickly (O'Brien & Myers, 1987) than events with few causal connections.

Experimental evidence for the effect of an event's number of connections is provided by Van den Broek (1988). Van den Broek systematically varied the number of connections of events while holding their content constant. Subjects judged the importance of these events on a 7-point scale. Figure 20.4 presents the results. As predicted, an event was judged as considerably more important when it had many connections than when it had only a few connections.

The effects of an event's number of connections on readers' performance are quite robust. They were observed across a variety of tasks

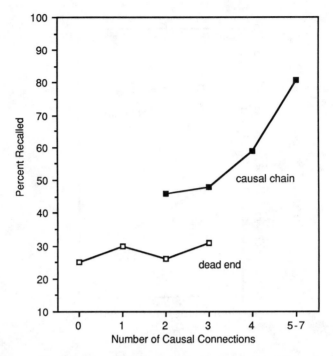

FIGURE 20.3. Percentage recall of statements as a function of number of causal connections (based on Trabasso & Van den Broek, 1985).

and in correlational as well as experimental designs. As with causal-chain status, other variables such as referential properties, story-grammar properties, concreteness, surface order (Trabasso & Van den Broek, 1985), and hierarchical position (Van den Broek, 1988) were ruled out as alternative explanations.

The studies discussed demonstrate the psychological validity of the network theory. They show that the theory's criteria describe people's intuitions about causality and that the resulting causal network captures important properties of a reader's memory representation of a text.

A PROCESS MODEL OF INFERENCE GENERATION

The studies presented support the notion that a readers' mental representation of the information in a text resembles a network of interrelated nodes. The model does not specify, however, what the *processes* are by which the reader arrives at this representation. In addition, the reader's actual mental representation may depart somewhat from the network representation of a text because the latter is idealized and limited to events that are explicitly mentioned in the text. On the one hand, it is likely that a reader infers only a subset of the relationships that are postulated by the theory. One reason for this is that limitations in attentional or short-term memory capacity may prevent the reader from identifying all possible relations. On the other hand, a reader may add events and connections that are not included in the theoretical networks. This is especially likely to happen when a text does not state explicitly all the information required for comprehension. In order to address these issues, one needs to consider the on-line inferential processes that lead to the memory representation of a text.

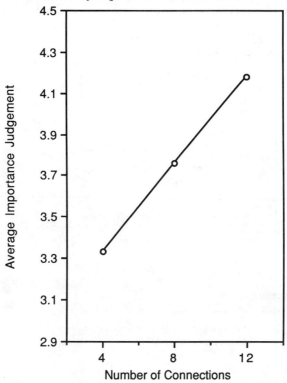

FIGURE 20.4. Average importance rating as a function of number of causal connections with content held constant (based on Van den Broek, 1988).

Several investigators have studied directly whether people make causal inferences during reading (e.g., Keenan, Baillet, & Brown, 1984; McKoon & Ratcliff, 1986, 1989; Myers & Duffy, in press; Myers, Shinjo, & Duffy, 1987; Potts, Keenan, & Golding, 1988). The results of these studies vary and sometimes contradict each other. The difficulties in interpretation arise, in part, from the need for a definition of a causal relation, from the frequent comparison of different types of inferences, and from methodological concerns.

This section presents a process model of inference generation that provides a framework for addressing these issues. The model, the causal inference maker (CIM), integrates two lines of research. First, it incorporates the central notions of the representational model already described.

In particular, it adopts the criteria for causality as the principles that guide the inferential process. Second, the model builds on recent research concerning the role of the human information-processing system in reading comprehension. Specifically, it assumes that limitations in the capacity of short-term memory or in attentional resources may restrict how much information from the prior text the reader considers

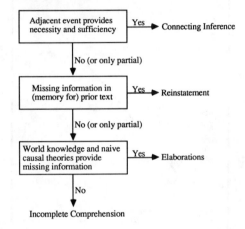

A. Backward Inferences

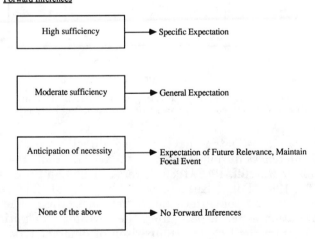

B. Forward Inferences

Note: In order to simplify the depiction of the model, it is assumed that the candidate inference fulfills the criteria of temporal order and operativity.

FIGURE 20.5. Inferential processes in the causal inference maker (CIM).

when reading a focal event. The causal criteria and the processing limitations determine the content and the type of inferences made, and hence form the conceptual and procedural *constraints* that operate on the inferential process.

The inferential process has as its starting point the newly read or focal event. Inferences may occur in a backward or in a forward direction. Each kind of inference has several subtypes. Figure 20.5 summarizes the various types of inferences as well as the conditions under which each occurs.

Backward Inferences

Backward inferences connect a focal event to prior events. The goal of the inference is to establish and maintain causal coherence in the representation of a narrative text. The model's description of backward inferences assumes a *minimalist* reader who makes only those inferences that are required to maintain local, that is, between-individual-events, coherence. Many readers may not be satisfied with this level of comprehension and others may be incapable of establishing even local coherence, but the description of a modal, minimalist reader lays the groundwork for study of these other categories of comprehenders as well.

At least two types of constraints operate on the inferential process. First, as described in Equation 1, causal coherence is maintained if the antecedents to a focal event fulfill the criteria of temporal priority, operativity, necessity, and sufficiency. If one of the criteria is not met, then additional inferences that provide the missing information are required. Second, as a result of short-term memory or attentional limitations, relevant causal information may not be readily available to the reader. The availability of information determines what kind of inference is required to attain coherence. The two types of constraints suggest the following hypothetical account of backward-inference generation. As the reader encounters an event, he or she attempts to find adequate causal justification for it. The first event to be considered is the immediately preceding or causally most recent one, because it is likely to still be activated (Fletcher & Bloom, 1988). If this event fulfills all criteria, no further explanation is necessary and the inferential process stops.[1] The inference that connects a focal event to the immediately preceding event

---

[1] The model does not assume, of course, that the reader explicitly poses necessity and sufficiency questions. Instead, the two formal criteria are analytic *tools* that capture the implications of the presence or absence of one event for the *likelihood* of another event. Thus, if A is highly necessary for B (e.g., intercourse is necessary for pregnancy), then knowledge of nonA (no intercourse) strongly suggests nonB (no pregnancy), and the occurrence of B (pregnancy) suggests A (there was intercourse). If A is sufficient for B (e.g., the delicate vase's falling is sufficient for its breaking), then A (falling) suggests B (the vase broke), whereas nonB (the vase is intact) suggests nonA (the vase did not fall). Together, necessity and sufficiency describe if and how knowledge about one event constrains expectations concerning another event. It is the awareness of these mutual implications rather than of the criteria that describe them that is likely to have psychological validity.

is called a *connecting* inference. Consider the diagram of a hypothetical story in Figure 20.6. Suppose that Statement 3 adequately explains Statement 4 (i.e., is both necessary and sufficient). When the reader encounters Statement 4 the only inference that is required is the one that explicitly connects that statement to Statement 3.

If the most recent antecedent event does not fulfill all criteria, then a *coherence* break occurs. This is likely to result in a search for information that fulfills the unsatisfied criteria. There are two potential sources for this information. The first source is the *reinstatement* of one or more prior events. That is, the reader may reactivate information from an earlier part of the text in order to meet the causal requirements. The reinstatement search is assumed to terminate at an event that provides the missing information. Consider Statement 8 in Figure 20.6. Four antecedents (Statements 4, 5, 6, and 7) each are necessary and jointly are sufficient for Statement 8. When Statement 8 is read, the reader will attempt to connect it to Statement 7. As indicated by the arcs leading to Statement 8, Statement 7 is not sufficient for Statement 8, so the reader searches backward and reinstates Statement 6 (and, time and motivation permitting, Statement 5). An example of this process can be found in narratives. These texts often revolve around goal-directed actions on the part of the protagonist. The goal itself is usually mentioned early in the story. The actions that occur later in the text cannot be understood adequately unless this goal is reinstated. For this reason the present theory predicts that, in stories, reinstatements frequently involve goal statements. Note that the reason for this prediction is not that they are goals per se but rather that they tend to be required to provide sufficiency information for later actions.

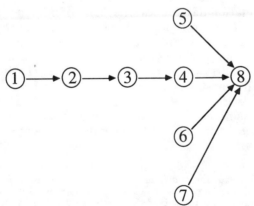

FIGURE 20.6. Diagram of a hypothetical story.

A second source of information for resolving a coherence break is that of *elaborations*. If the text itself does not provide information that meets the causal criteria or if such information is too far removed from the focal event to be reinstated readily, then the reader may infer events

that are not explicitly stated in the text. Elaborations are likely to
be constrained in several ways. First, they must provide the causal
information that is missing. Second, they must be compatible with the
causal information that is already available to the reader. Third, they
have to be compatible with the immediate context (the circumstances)
of the focal event. Fourth, they draw upon and are constrained by the
reader's knowledge about the events and about causality in general.

Elaborative inferences can either intervene between or conjoin with
explicit events. Consider Figure 20.6, and assume that Statements 3
and 5 were not included in the text. In order to adequately understand
Statement 4, the reader will have to make a bridging inference that
provides information similar to that in Statement 3 and thereby connects
Statements 2 and 4. In order to understand Statement 8, the reader
has to add information similar to that provided in Statement 5. This
elaboration will conjoin with Statements 4, 6 and 7 to fulfill the criteria
for Statement 8.

In summary, CIM describes the backward inferences that a reader
may generate in order to maintain minimal coherence. It is assumed that
the reader first tries to achieve this goal via a connecting inference to the
immediately preceding event. If the preceding event does not meet the
four properties of causality then a coherence break occurs. The reader
resolves the break by means of reinstating and/or elaborating inferences.
Which of these types of inferences takes place depends on the presence
of the missing information in the text and on processing limitations in
the reader. In either case, the content of the resulting inferences meets
the unfulfilled requirements.

Empirical Evidence for Backward Inferences

Little research has directly investigated the inferential model as a
whole, but empirical evidence on each of the types of backward inferences is available. Events that are stated explicitly in the text are related
by means of connecting and reinstatement inferences. Evidence for these
inferences comes from several sources. Van den Broek and Lorch (1989)
observed that previously read events were recognized faster when they
were preceded by an antecedent event that fulfilled the causal criteria
than when they were preceded by an unrelated event. This pattern
was observed for both adjacent and nonadjacent events, which suggests
that both connecting and reinstating inferences are incorporated into
the mental representation of the text. It is unlikely that the differences
in priming were due to time-of-test processes such as context checking
(cf. Keenan & Golding, in press) as contrasts were based on identical
pairs in various conditions. Thus, it appears that these inferences were
made *during* reading and not at retrieval.

Reading-time studies by Bloom, Fletcher, Van den Broek, Reitz,
and Shapiro (1990) provide convergent evidence for the conclusion that
connecting and reinstatement inferences are generated and that they are
generated during reading. They found that reading time for a clause

increased (a) as the number of causal relations between the clause and the prior statement increased, (b) when a coherence break occurred, that is, there was no causal link to the prior statement, and (c) when the clause contained an outcome that satisfied a goal.

These results can be interpreted readily in the framework of the causal inference maker. The first set of results concerns an event's relation to the causally prior statement. In CIM's terminology, these relations are identified through connecting inferences. The finding that the reading time of a clause increases linearly with the number of these inferences suggests that they are made at the time that the focal event is read. The second and third sets of findings concern situations where reinstatement searches are required for adequate comprehension. According to CIM, a coherence break occurs when neither sufficiency nor necessity is satisfied. In this situation, no causal relation exists between the focal event and the immediately prior text. CIM predicts that a reinstatement search will be initiated to establish a causal relation to the prior text. As a result, reading is expected to slow down. The second set of results shows that this prediction is accurate. Finally, the third set of results concerns outcome statements. As was discussed, these statements lack sufficiency without the corresponding goal and hence may initiate a reinstatement search, thereby slowing down reading. Again, the results support the model's prediction. It appears from these data that CIM accurately predicts when connecting and reinstatement inferences are made.

The causal inference maker model hypothesizes that the reinstatement search stops when the missing information is located. If this hypothesis is correct, then the missing information should be readily available after it has been reinstated. Further, the search should take longer as the missing information is farther removed in the text. The first hypothesis is supported by Suh (1989), who found that people recognize previously encountered goal information faster immediately after a reinstatement of that information was required than at other points in the text. The second hypothesis is supported by Bloom et al. (1990), who found that the amount of slowing down of reading when a reinstatement search is predicted is linearly related to the causal distance between the focal event and the missing information. Thus, once initiated, the reinstatement search appears to proceed backward through the text and to terminate at the information that restores the causal coherence (cf. O'Brien & Myers, 1987).

The studies discussed provide evidence that both connecting and reinstatement inferences are made and that this happens *during* reading. They also indicate that reinstatement searches begin when sufficiency and/or necessity are not satisfied and stop when the missing information is located.

In contrast to connecting and reinstatement inferences, elaborative inferences concern relations to events that are added by the reader. Evidence for the distinction between elaborating and connecting inferences comes from cued-recall data gathered by Myers et al. (1987). Subjects read pairs of statements that varied in the strength of their causal relationship. They then received a cued-recall task with one member of the pair serving as cue, the other as target. Figure 20.7 contains the results. Somewhat counterintuitively, the probability of recall was a curvilinear function of the strength of the causal relation between the members of the pairs. Myers et al. (1987) speculated that the relative decline in cued recall for the pairs with the strongest relation was due to the fact that these pairs do not allow elaborations and hence give rise to a weaker memory trace. A causal analysis of their materials supports this account and suggests why these pairs may not have evoked elaborative processing (Van den Broek, in press). The decrease in the judged strength of the relation between two events is accompanied by a gradual loss of necessity and/or sufficiency of the antecedent for the consequent. The most strongly related pairs fulfill both the necessity and sufficiency criteria, and therefore can be related via a connecting inference. The remaining pairs lack sufficiency and/or necessity, and thus require elaborations in order to be coherent. The finding that the pairs requiring a connecting inference showed less cued recall than those that require minimal elaborations, despite the fact that the latter are lacking in causal strength, supports the causal theory's distinction between the two types of inferences.

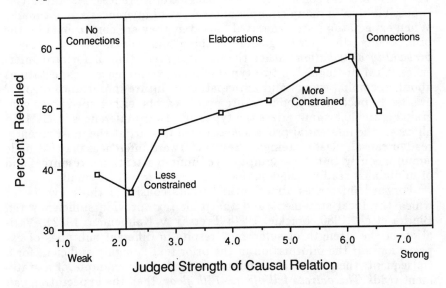

FIGURE 20.7. The effect of strength of causal relation on probability of cued recall (based on Myers et al., 1987, and Van den Broek, in press).

These findings also indicate that necessity and sufficiency play an important role in determining which inferences are made. An analysis of all the pairs that required elaborative inferences provides further evidence for this role. The pairs varied in the extent to which necessity and sufficiency were present. CIM's account of inference generation implies that as sufficiency and necessity decline, the constraints on the required elaborative inferences become weaker. The inferences become increasingly difficult to make and the relations in the memory representation of the two events will weaken. The cued-recall probabilities reflect the hypothesized decline. Thus, necessity and sufficiency affect what type of inference the reader will make, as well as how strong the resulting relation will be.

In conclusion, backward inferences occur as predicted by the causal inference maker. Connecting inferences are generated when a focal event's antecedents satisfy necessity and sufficiency. Reinstatement searches are initiated when one or both of these criteria are not met. They continue in a backward fashion until information that fulfills the criteria is located. If no explicit statements provide this information, then the reader may add events through elaborative inferences.

Forward Inferences

Forward inferences generate expectations about what will happen next in the text. They are not required for comprehension, but they may facilitate processing of later events (cf. Rayner & Pollatsek, 1989). They also are less constrained than backward inferences. As a result, it is possible that in many circumstances forward inferences are not made. When expectations are generated, however, they are constrained by the prior events. In describing some of these constraints, CIM provides a *probability distribution* rather than a firm prediction of forward inferences. CIM distinguishes two types of forward inferences: expectations about upcoming events and anticipation of future importance of prior events. Expectations about future events can be either specific or general. Figure 20.5 summarizes the types of forward inferences in CIM. In all cases, the inferential process is assumed to start at the most recently read or causally last statement. Several forward inferences may be made simultaneously, but the assumptions of limited attentional resources and of minimalist reading suggest that their number will be small.

Forward inferences about future events consist of those events for which the focal statement and the prior text provide sufficiency (cf. Bindra et al., 1980; Mackie, 1980; Tversky & Kahneman, 1982). Variation in the strength of sufficiency results in different subtypes of expectations. If the information in the prior text is highly sufficient for a consequent, then a specific inference is made. For example, if a statement reads *The actress fell off the 14th floor*, then the expectation can be specific, for example, *the actress died.* If sufficiency is moderate, then a general expectation is generated. The statement *The actress fell out of the window* suggests some bodily harm but not the extent or type of injury. Thus, the degree of sufficiency determines the specificity of the inference.

A somewhat different type of forward inference concerns expectations about the role that prior events will play in subsequent text. Here,

CIM proposes that the reader may anticipate that certain statements will be *necessary* for future, unspecified events (cf. Duffy, 1986). For example, a goal statement in the beginning of a narrative suggests that the protagonist will do something to attain this goal in the remainder of the story. Or, in detective stories, mentioning of details such as the time at which a character leaves home is likely to become important. In both cases, CIM assumes that the reader attempts to maintain this information in anticipation of its subsequent relevance. Conventions about the structure of texts and about good writing play a central role in the generation of these expectations.

Note that this account of forward inferences concerns expectations about what events will take place in the world described by the text, not about what events will actually be stated explicitly in the text. With respect to the latter, knowledge about the conventions of good writing are likely to play a major role. For example, readers usually assume that an author leaves out obvious events (Grice, 1975) and includes events that provide novel information (Rayner & Pollatsek, 1989). Thus, the events in subsequent statements are expected to be causally dependent on but not totally predictable from the focal event. For this reason, necessity of the focal event is likely to be a more important constraint on possible continuation statements than sufficiency (Van den Broek, in press). For example, consider the statement *The fragile porcelain vase fell from the 14th floor*. The information in this statement is in most circumstances sufficient as well as necessary for the vase's breaking. In contrast, it is necessary but not sufficient for, let's say, the vase's falling on top of an as of yet unmentioned car. CIM proposes that readers expect actual continuation statements to add information and therefore to be more often of the second than of the first kind.[2]

Empirical Evidence for Forward Inferences

The causal inference maker model's account of forward inferences has not been tested directly, but it is consistent with several findings in the literature. Using speeded-recognition techniques, McKoon and Ratcliff (1986, 1989; cf. Potts et al., 1988) have provided evidence that readers make specific predictive inferences but that they do so only minimally. In particular, they concluded that forward inferences are only encoded as specific events when they are highly constrained by the previous text. When they are moderately constrained, then the inference is encoded weakly or as a set of possible events. These conclusions are compatible with CIM's predictions that strong sufficiency is conducive to the generation of specific inferences, whereas weak sufficiency is likely to give rise to general inferences.

---

[2] Notice that CIM's expectations about what is *described* next differ from those about what *happens* next.

Evidence that readers generate expectations about the possible future relevance of events that they have read comes from Duffy (1986). Here, subjects judged whether a test sentence was a possible continuation to a short text. Responses were quicker when the test sentence could be expected on the basis of the prior text than when it was unrelated or contradictory to the preceding information. Control experiments suggested that these results were not due to the generation of specific inferences but rather to continued attention to potentially relevant statements from the prior text. Thus, readers appear to maintain or have ready access to information that is likely to be relevant in the subsequent text (cf. Myers, this volume).

These results suggest that specific and general inferences as well as expectations about the future role of statements occur, and that this happens under the circumstances proposed in the causal inference maker model. It should be pointed out, however, that none of the mentioned studies employed criteria of necessity and sufficiency to classify possible inferences. Therefore, their results provide only circumstantial evidence for the causal inference maker's account of forward inference generation. Precise testing of the CIM's predictions is necessary before any definitive conclusions about the psychological validity of this aspect of the model can be drawn.

Finally, Van den Broek, Fletcher, and Marsolek (1989) provided evidence that expectations about what events will actually be included in the text are more constrained by necessity than by sufficiency. In this study, subjects provided continuation sentences to story stems. The vast majority of the continuations (94%) were causally related to the focal event. Of these, 46% adhered to both sufficiency and necessity, 46% adhered only to necessity and 1% adhered only to sufficiency. Thus, causal properties, in particular necessity, have a strong influence on readers' expectations about events in upcoming statements.

In summary, the causal inference maker gives a hypothetical account of the generation of backward and forward inferences during reading. It distinguishes among subtypes within each category and specifies the conditions under which each occurs. In doing so, it provides testable predictions about the inferential process. Empirical support is already available for several of these predictions, whereas others await experimental investigation.

DISCUSSION

This chapter outlines a process model of reading comprehension. The model, the causal inference maker, specifies how the reader builds a functional, coherent mental representation of the text by means of backward and, possibly, forward causal inferences. Central to the model is the notion that constraints direct the generation of inferences. The model includes two types of constraints. One type is conceptual: Knowledge about one event may provide the reader information about the likelihood of the occurrence of another event. Various types of conceptual constraints may affect the mental representation of a text, but causal dependencies play a special role in narrative texts. Several causal properties, such as temporal priority, operativity, and necessity and sufficiency in the circumstances, contribute to the strength of a causal dependency. A second type of constraint is procedural and consists of limitations of the human information processing system. These limitations affect the availability of information to the reader and hence give rise to different types of inferences. Together, the conceptual and procedural constraints determine under which circumstances causal inferences are made, what kind of inferences are made, and what their content is.

The emphasis on constraints and dependencies among events suggests that the reading process can be conceived as the gradual building of a situation model or constraint-propagation network (cf. Collins, Brown, & Larkin, 1980; Van Dijk & Kintsch, 1983). This conceptualization of the reading process shares properties with other current models of cognitive functioning. For example, the description of the mental representation of a text as a constraint-propagation network fits recent trends to use connectionist architectures to capture cognitive processes. The present model also is compatible with the construction-integration model of text comprehension described by Kintsch (1988). Kintsch's model posits that a promiscuous inference generator activates large numbers of potential inferences. The potential inferences are then pruned to yield a selection of inferences that are retained in the mental representation. The construction-integration model does not specify the principles that guide the selection process. The causal inference maker describes the causal constraints that operate on the generation or selection of inferences, and thereby may provide an important mechanism for pruning promiscuous associations.

The causal inference maker model makes specific predictions concerning the inferential processes during reading, several of which have received empirical support. The model also suggests a number of directions for future research on inference generation. One question concerns the time course of the inferential process. For example, the various types of backward inferences may be generated in sequence, with reinstating inferences being produced only after connecting inferences have failed to provide adequate causal coherence (and elaborating inferences occurring after all possible reinstatements have been considered). An alternative is that of a race model, where two or more types of inferences are attempted in parallel but only the first one to establish coherence will actually be made. A second question is whether forward inferences are indeed made, and, if so, whether forward and backward inferences interact. For example, it is plausible that forward inferences, when made, affect the time course of subsequent backward inferences. Finally, the present version of CIM contains an immediacy assumption, that is, it assumes that inferences are made when the focal event is read (cf. Just

& Carpenter, 1987). An alternative possibility is that an event continues to generate inferences after subsequent statements have been read.

It is important to note that several conditions need to be met in order for the reader to be able to construct a coherent mental representation of a text. *First*, the construction of a memory representation of a text depends on the successful completion of several basic processes. Individual symbols on a paper or screen must be recognized as letters. Letters must be combined to form words. The function and meaning of words need to be identified and the words need to be combined to form a sentence or proposition. It is only after these tasks have been achieved that the reader can come to understand the relations among the individual events portrayed in the sentences. In focusing on the last of these processes, inferential theories assume that the reader has reached high levels of performance in the more basic processes. *Second*, in order to be able to identify the relations between events and ideas the reader needs to have access to the information that is necessary to make the required inferences. This information may be provided in the text itself or it may come from the reader's prior knowledge about the events that are portrayed. *Third*, the reader needs to have the resources to recognize and construct the connections between text elements. These resources vary as a result of developmental and individual differences (Van den Broek, 1989). They include, for example, understanding of causality and adequate attentional and short-term memory capacity. *Fourth*, the reader must have the opportunity and time to make the required inferences. External constraints such as time limitations, instructions not to look back, and distractions may interfere with the inferential process. Several experimental paradigms in reading research impose such limitations, for example, by requiring speeded reading. Studies that employ these paradigms may underestimate the extent to which inferences, in particular those that span a long distance or require some time, are generated during reading. *Fifth*, readers differ in their motivation to arrive at a coherent representation of the text. Some readers may not be interested in identifying even local relations, others may be motivated to infer global coherence such as themes, morals, genre, and so forth.

These conditions set the stage for the inferential processes that underlie the comprehension of a text as a whole. In describing these processes, the causal inference maker may provide a fruitful starting point for the systematic investigation of inference generation in reading comprehension.

ACKNOWLEDGMENTS

I am grateful to Elisabeth Husebye, Richard Thurlow and to the editors of this volume for their helpful comments on an earlier draft of this chapter, and to Randy Fletcher for many stimulating discussions. This research is supported in part by the Center for Research in Learning, Perception, and Cognition and the National Institute of Child Health and Human Development (HD-07151).

REFERENCES

Bindra, D., Clarke, K. A., & Shultz, T. R. (1980). Understanding predictive relations of necessity and sufficiency in formally equivalent "causal" and "logical" problems. *Journal of Experimental Psychology: General, 109*, 422 - 443.

Black, J. B., & Bower, G. H. (1980). Story understanding as problem solving. *Poetics, 9*, 223 - 250.

Bloom, C. P., Fletcher, C. R., Van den Broek, P., Reitz, L., & Shapiro, B. P. (1990). An on-line assessment of causal reasoning during comprehension. *Memory & Cognition, 18*, 65 - 71.

Collins, A., Brown, J. S., & Larkin, K. M. (1980). Inference in text understanding. In R. J. Spiro, B. C. Bruce, & W. F. Brewer (Eds.), *Theoretical issues in reading comprehension* (pp. 385 - 407). Hillsdale, NJ: Lawrence Erlbaum Associates.

Duffy, S. A. (1986). Role of expectations in sentence integration. *Journal of Experimental Psychology: Learning, Memory, and Cognition, 12*, 208 - 219.

Einhorn, H. J., & Hogarth, R. M. (1986). Judging probable cause. *Psychological Bulletin, 99*, 3 - 19.

Fletcher, C. R., & Bloom, C. P. (1988). Causal reasoning in the comprehension of simple narrative texts. *Journal of Memory and Language, 27*, 235 - 244.

Goldman S. R., & Varnhagen, C. K. (1986). Memory for embedded and sequential story structures. *Journal of Memory and Language, 25*, 401 - 418.

Graesser, A. C. (1981). *Prose comprehension beyond the word.* New York: Springer.

Graesser, A. C., & Clark, L. F. (1985). *The structures and procedures of implicit knowledge.* Norwood, NJ: Ablex.

Grice, H. P. (1975). William James Lectures, Harvard University, 1967. Published in part as Logic and conversation. In P. Cole & J. L. Morgan (Eds.), *Syntax and semantics: Vol. 3. Speech acts* (pp. 41 - 58). New York: Academic Press.

Hart, M. L. A., & Honore, A. M. (1985). *Causation in the Law.* Oxford: Clarendon.

Hospers, J. (1973). *An introduction to philosophical analyses.* Englewood Cliffs, NJ: Prentice-Hall.

Just, M. A., & Carpenter, P. A. (1987). *The psychology of reading and language comprehension.* Boston, MA: Allyn & Bacon.

Keenan, J. M., Baillet, S. D., & Brown, P. (1984). The effects of causal cohesion on comprehension and memory. *Journal of Verbal Learning and Verbal Behavior, 23*, 115 - 126.

Keenan, J. M., & Golding, J. M. (in press). Methodological issues in evaluating the occurrence of inferences. In A. C. Graesser & G. H. Bower (Eds.), *The psychology of learning and motivation* (Vol. 25). Orlando, FL: Academic Press.

Kintsch, W. (1988). The role of knowledge in discourse comprehension: A construction-integration model. *Psychological Review, 95*, 163 - 182.

Lewis, D. K. (1976). *Counterfactuals.* Cambridge, MA: Harvard University Press.

Mackie, J. L. (1980). *The cement of the universe.* Oxford: Clarendon.

Mandler, J. M., & Johnson, N. S. (1977). Remembrance of things parsed: Story structure and recall. *Cognitive Psychology, 9*, 111 - 151.

McKoon, G., & Ratcliff, R. (1986). Inferences about predictable events. *Journal of Experimental Psychology: Learning, Memory, and Cognition, 12*, 82 - 91.

McKoon, G., & Ratcliff, R. (1989). Semantic associations and elaborative inferences. *Journal of Experimental Psychology: Learning, Memory and Cognition, 15*, 326 - 338.

Michotte, A. (1963). *The perception of causality.* London: Methuen.

Myers, J. L., & Duffy, S. A. (in press). Causal inferences and text memory. In A. C. Graesser & G. H. Bower (Eds.), *The psychology of learning and motivation* (Vol. 25). Orlando, FL: Academic Press.

Myers, J. L., Shinjo, M., & Duffy, S. A. (1987). Degree of causal relatedness and memory. *Journal of Memory and Language, 26*, 453 - 465.

Nicholas, D. W., & Trabasso, T. (1981). Toward a taxonomy of inferences. In F. Wilkening & J. Becker (Eds.), *Information integration by children* (pp. 243 - 265). Hillsdale, NJ: Lawrence Erlbaum Associates.

O'Brien, E. J., & Myers, J. L. (1987). The role of causal connections in the retrieval of text. *Memory & Cognition, 15*, 419 - 427.

Omanson, R. C. (1982). The relation between centrality and story category variation. *Journal of Verbal Learning and Verbal Behavior, 21*, 326 - 337.

Potts, G. R., Keenan, J. M., & Golding, J. M. (1988). Assessing the occurrence of elaborative inferences: Lexical decision versus naming. *Journal of Memory and Language, 27*, 399 - 415.

Rayner, K., & Pollatsek, A. (1989). *The psychology of reading.* Englewood Cliffs, NJ: Prentice-Hall.

Rumelhart, D. E. (1975). Notes on a schema for stories. In D. Bobrow & A. Collins (Eds.), *Representation and understanding: Studies in cognitive science* (pp. 211 - 235). New York: Academic Press.

Schank, R. G., & Abelson, R. P. (1977). *Scripts, plans, goals, and understanding.* Hillsdale, NJ: Lawrence Erlbaum Associates.

Stein, N. L., & Glenn, C. G. (1979). An analysis of story comprehension in elementary school children. In R. O. Freedle (Ed.), *New directions in discourse processing: Vol. 2. Advances in discourse processes* (pp. 53 - 120). Norwood, NJ: Ablex.

Suh, S. Y. (1989). *Causal inferences during text comprehension.* Unpublished doctoral dissertation, University of Chicago.

Thorndyke, P. W. (1977). Cognitive structures in comprehension and memory of narrative discourse. *Cognitive Psychology, 9*, 77 - 110.

Trabasso, T., Secco, T., & Van den Broek, P. (1984). Causal cohesion and story coherence. In H. Mandl, N. L. Stein, & T. Trabasso (Eds.), *Learning and comprehension of text* (pp. 83 - 111). Hillsdale, NJ: Lawrence Erlbaum Associates.

Trabasso, T., & Sperry, L. L. (1985). Causal relatedness and importance of story events. *Journal of Memory and Language, 24*, 595 - 611.

Trabasso, T., & Van den Broek, P. (1985). Causal thinking and the representation of narrative events. *Journal of Memory and Language, 24*, 612 - 630.

Trabasso, T., Van den Broek, P., & Suh, S. Y. (1989). Logical necessity and transitivity of causal relations in stories. *Discourse Processes, 12*, 1 - 25.

Tversky, A., & Kahneman, D. (1982). Causal schemas in judgments under uncertainty. In D. Kahneman, P. Slovic, & A. Tversky (Eds.), *Judgment under uncertainty: Heuristics and biases* (pp. 117 - 128). Cambridge: Cambridge University Press.

Van den Broek, P. (1988). The effects of causal relations and hierarchical position on the importance of story statements. *Journal of Memory and Language, 27*, 1 - 22.

Van den Broek, P. (1989). Causal reasoning and inference making in judging the importance of story Statements. *Child Development, 60*, 286 - 297.

Van den Broek, P. (in press). Causal inferences and the comprehension of narrative texts. In A. C. Graesser & G. H. Bower (Eds.), *The psychology of learning and motivation* (Vol. 25). Orlando, FL: Academic Press.

Van den Broek, P., Fletcher, C. R., & Marsolek, C. J. (1989). *Cognitive processes in the composition of narrative texts: The role of causal reasoning.* Paper presented at the annual meeting of the American Educational Research Association, San Francisco.

Van den Broek, P., & Lorch, R. F., Jr. (1989). *The representation of causal relations in memory for narrative text: Evidence from primed recognition.* Unpublisehed manuscript.

Van den Broek, P., & Trabasso, T. (1986). Causal networks versus goal hierarchies in summarizing text. *Discourse Processes, 9*, 1 - 15.

Van Dijk, T. A., & Kintsch, W. (1983). *Strategies of discourse comprehension.* New York: Academic Press.

21 ON THE CONTROL OF INFERENCES IN TEXT UNDERSTANDING

Wietske Vonk
*Max Planck Institute for Psycholinguistics and
University of Nijmegen*

and

Leo G.M. Noordman
University of Tilburg

INTRODUCTION

Text understanding is constructing a coherent representation of the information in a text. A text contains more information than what is explicitly expressed. The representation also contains information that is implied by the text: information that the writer supposes the reader will compute from the text and that the writer therefore leaves implicit. The computation of the implicit information is referred to as inferencing.

The general question addressed in this chapter is what inferences are made during reading. Two extreme positions with respect to inferences are certainly not true. One position is that all inferences are made that are allowed by the text. This leads to an inferential explosion. The other extreme position is that no inferences are made because of cognitive economy. This implies a parsimonious or minimal processing of the text. In our opinion, inferences steer a middle course between these two extreme positions. But how are inferences controlled so as to keep that middle course?

Assuming that inferences are time-consuming processes, what does the reader motivate to make inferences? The reason for making inferences may be related to the nature of the inferences as well as to characteristics of the reader.

Inferences may serve different functions and may have different properties which will result in different probabilities that inferencing occurs during reading. Indeed a great variety of inferences can be distinguished. The answer to the question whether inferences are made on-line is probably not the same for all kinds of inference. Therefore, it is important to be more specific with respect to the notion of inference.

The first part of the chapter deals with the classification of inferences in terms of their necessity. Inferences will be described from two text-related perspectives: whether the inferences can be deduced from the text and what they contribute to the text representation.

In the second part, five experiments are discussed that deal with on-line inference processes. It will be demonstrated that some inferences that, according to the classification, are expected to be made are not made on-line (Experiments 1 and 2). Whether inferences are made during reading also depends on characteristics of the reader. It will be demonstrated that two factors are important in this respect: the reader's knowledge and the reader's purpose in reading. If a reader has much knowledge about the topic of the text, it is conceivable that inferences are more likely be made, as the reader will presumably need less effort to make them (Experiment 5). On the other hand, information that is more relevant for the reader's purpose is likely to be processed more deeply in the sense that more integrative computations are performed, as the reader is willing to spend more effort in processing the information. This will increase the number of inferences (Experiments 3 and 4).

ON THE NECESSITY OF INFERENCES

There is no consensus in the psycholinguistic literature about how to classify inferences. A distinction is frequently made between inferences that are necessary for comprehension and inferences that are not necessary, but just elaborations (e.g., Just & Carpenter, 1987; O'Brien, Shank, Myers, & Rayner, 1988). This distinction is problematic, however. What does it mean to be necessary for comprehension? Comprehension is not a monolithic notion but a graded concept. A text can be understood in many ways, depending, among other factors, on the amount of inferences that are made. But then the notion of comprehension cannot be treated as the criterion to define necessary inferences. If one wants to investigate which inferences are made during comprehension, one should have a way of characterizing inferences that is independent of the comprehension process. Given that the notion of necessary inferences plays an important role in classifying inferences, the question is with respect to which criteria an inference is considered as necessary. We classify inferences with respect to their function in the text. The criteria are not related to psychological processes in the reader but to characteristics of the inference that can be identified by analyzing the information that is inferred from the text. In this sense we classify inferences from a text-analytic point of view.

From this point of view two dimensions can be distinguished for classifying inferences. One refers to the deducibility of the inference from the text, the other refers to the contribution of the inference to the text representation. Examples of the resulting four classes are given in Table 21.1.

The first dimension is the extent to which inferences are authorized by the text. The question is whether inferences are valid deductions from the text or not. According to this dimension, inferences can be classified as necessary inferences versus possible inferences. Necessary inferences are necessarily true implications of sentences in the text. Negation of the inference leads to an inconsistency. Possible inferences are probably true implications of the sentences in the text. They are more or less likely to be true given the state of affairs in the world. Negation does not lead to an inconsistency.

TABLE 21.1

Classification of Inferences on Two Dimensions.

Deduction	Type of Contribution to Representation	
	Coherence	Completeness
Necessary	John is a linguist, but he knows statistics $\longrightarrow$ (a)	A is taller than B, and B is taller than C $\longrightarrow$ (b)
Possible	Joey went playing. The next day he was covered with bruises $\longrightarrow$ (c)	John slipped. He dropped the delicate pitcher $\longrightarrow$ (d)

Inferences:

(a) Linguists in general don't know statistics
(b) A is taller than C
(c) The bruises were due to the playing
(d) John broke the delicate pitcher

Examples of necessary inferences are presuppositions (from *John forgot to let the dog out* follows that the dog was supposed to be out, Just & Clark, 1973) and entailments (from *Dick is a father* follows that Dick has one or more children) but also conventional implications (from *John is a linguist, but he knows much about statistics* follows that, according to the speaker, linguists in general do not know much about statistics) and transitive inferences (from *Alan is taller than Bill; Bill is taller than Chris* follows that Alan is taller than Chris, cf. Potts, 1972).

Possible inferences are also called invited inferences or pragmatic inferences (Brewer, 1977; Harris, 1974; Harris & Monaco, 1978; Hildyard & Olson, 1978). Examples are the inferences that the old lady is rich from *The little old lady stepped into the chauffeur driven Cadillac* (Hildyard & Olson, 1978) and that John broke the pitcher from *John slipped on a wet spot. He dropped the delicate glass pitcher on the floor* (Johnson, Bransford, & Solomon, 1973), and the causal relation that connects the sentences in the sequence *Joey went to a neighbor's house to play. The next day his body was covered with bruises* (Keenan, Baillet, & Brown, 1984).

The second dimension is what the inference contributes to the representation of the text. This dimension allows a distinction between a contribution to the coherence versus a contribution to the elaborateness or completeness of the representation. It is this dimension that quite a lot of authors have in mind when they talk about inferences that are necessary for comprehension versus inferences that are only possible elaborations (Garnham, 1982, 1985; Hildyard & Olson, 1978; O'Brien et al., 1988). The assumption of these authors is that coherence of the discourse representation is a prerequisite for the comprehension of a text. However, we do not like to claim that comprehension requires the construction of a coherent representation: It is an empirical question how coherent a representation one constructs in reading a text. Therefore, we define the second dimension not with respect to the reader's understanding but with respect to the representation the text allows for.

Examples of inferences that contribute to the coherence of the representation are the frequently studied inferences in identifying the antecedent of an anaphoric expression. For example, in *We checked the picnic supplies. The beer was warm* the antecedent of *the beer* has to be computed (Haviland & Clark, 1974), or in *A burglar surveyed the garage set back from the street. . . The criminal slipped away . . .* it has to be established that the burglar is the antecedent of the criminal (McKoon & Ratcliff, 1980). (See also, Clark & Sengul, 1979; Garrod & Sanford, 1977; Lesgold, Roth, & Curtis, 1979; Vonk, 1985.) In the earlier example *John is a linguist, but he knows much about statistics* the inference "linguists in general do not know much about statistics" is also an inference that contributes to the coherence: The inference accounts for the contrastive relation between the two sentences that is implied by *but.* Other examples of inferences that contribute to coherence are inferences involved in establishing a causal relation between two described events, as in the earlier-mentioned sequence *Joey went to a neighbor's house to play. The next day his body was covered with bruises.*

Inferences that contribute to the completeness of the representation are such that without them the representation is coherent, but less elaborated. An example is the earlier mentioned inference that Alan is taller than Chris from *Alan is taller than Bill; Bill is taller than Chris.* Another example is the inference from the earlier mentioned sequence *John slipped on a wet spot. He dropped the delicate glass pitcher on the floor.*

The application of this dimension requires a theory of discourse coherence or at least a definition of coherence. Such a theory is not yet
available, but some requirements of such a theory can be formulated.
A theory of discourse coherence has ultimately to account for the intuitions of language users concerning the relations and dependencies
among discourse units. By a coherent representation we mean that the
representation indicates how the propositions in the discourse are related to one another. If one considers words, such as definite articles or
conjunctions, as procedures that have to be executed on the discourse
context, then the representation is not coherent if such a procedure is
not executed. For example, the definite noun phrase can express that
the entity that is referred to should have occurred – implicitly or explicitly – in the previous discourse. If that entity is not found, the
representation is not coherent. Similarly, conjunctions such as *because*
and *but* express that a particular relation between propositions has to
be accounted for, in this case a causal or a contrastive relation. If that
account is not made, the representation is not coherent.

The confusion with respect to the classification of inferences is not
only due to the ambiguous use of the word *necessary*, as has been indicated, but also to an inadequate application of the differentiating dimensions. For example, Hildyard and Olson (1978) define three kinds
of inferences: propositional inferences, enabling inferences, and possible
inferences. But each class is defined with respect to another dimension. Propositional inferences are necessarily true implications of explicit propositions. Enabling inferences are essential to the coherence.
Pragmatic inferences are defined as inferences that are not essential for
the interpretation of the sentences or text. At least the first and second
classes are defined with respect to different dimensions. The third class
is defined with respect to still another dimension, unless "interpretation"
is defined with respect to the coherence of the representation.

A distinction that some authors (e.g., Just & Carpenter, 1987) relate to the necessity of the inference is between forward and backward
inferences. Backward inferences relate the current information to previous information in the discourse context. Forward inferences relate
the current information to possible subsequent information, or rather,
they anticipate subsequent information (Duffy, 1986; Singer & Ferreira,
1983). Forward inferences are sometimes considered as elaborative inferences that embellish the representation; they are considered as optional
and not essential to comprehension, making the representation richer
and more complete (Just & Carpenter, 1987). However, one should be
careful in relating the distinction between backward and forward inferences to the necessity of the inferences. On the one hand, if one defines
necessary in terms of the contribution to the coherence, it seems likely
that backward inferences are necessary: They contribute in general to
the coherence of the representation. On the other hand, if one defines
necessary in terms of deducibility from the text, forward inferences can
be necessary, as may be illustrated by lexical entailments.

452 VONK AND NOORDMAN

The classification of inferences using the dimensions deducibility from the text – necessary versus optional – and contribution to the representation – to its coherence versus to its completeness – does not a priori say anything about whether the inferences are made during reading. It is an empirical question whether the text-analytic differences between inferences affect the probability that the inferences are made on-line during text comprehension.

Results from quite a lot of experimental research suggest that the characterization of inferences in terms of their contribution to the discourse representation is an important factor in predicting which inferences are made. Inferences that are involved in establishing co-reference relations between two parts in a discourse tend to be made. For example, Haviland and Clark (1974) demonstrated that inferences that identify the antecedent of an anaphoric expression are made on-line and require time. Garrod and Sanford (1981) demonstrated that similar kinds of inference are made, but showed that they do not necessarily require time. Inferences involved in recognizing that two words refer to the same entity are made on-line (McKoon & Ratcliff, 1980). Furthermore, causal inferences that establish the coherence between two sentences tend to be made on-line (Keenan et al., 1984; Singer & Ferreira, 1983). Inferences that do not contribute to the coherence of the representation but to its completeness tend not to be made on-line. For example, during the encoding of the sentence *The boy cleared the snow from the stairs* an instrumental inference is not made (Corbett & Dosher, 1978; Singer, 1979).

On the basis of this kind of data it is hypothesized that the text-analytic classification predicts whether inferences are made, and, in particular, that those inferences are made during reading that are necessary deductions from the text and that contribute to the coherence of the representation. That hypothesis is tested in the present study with respect to inferences in understanding causal and contrastive conjunctions.

INFERENCES IN CAUSAL AND CONTRASTIVE RELATIONS

The presence of a causal or a contrastive conjunction requires adding particular propositions that account for the causal or contrastive interpretation. For example, the conjunction *but* in *John is a linguist, but he knows much about statistics* is a signal to predicate the property "not knowing much about statistics" to "linguists". This kind of inference does not establish the coreference relation between two entities in different expressions in a text (identification of addresses) but attributes particular information to the entities (predication of information to an address). Related distinctions are found in discourse semantics (Seuren, 1985). Most of the inferences that have been studied belong to the former type: The inferences that consist of identifying the antecedent of an anaphoric expression, or in establishing that two words in different propositions refer to the same entity, establish addresses in the discourse representation.

The kind of inference that is investigated in the present study can be illustrated by the following example: From the sentence *Chlorine compounds are frequently used as propellants, because they do not react with other substances* (in a text on spray cans and the environment) it follows that, according to the writer, propellants do not react with other substances.

The understanding of the conjunction *because* in this sentence requires that an inference, related to the causal relation expressed in the sentence, is made. This can be made clear by analyzing the sentence into its propositions and showing how the propositions are connected with each other. Simplifying somewhat, the sentence consists of the following three propositions: (1) chlorine compounds (c) are good propellants (a); (2) chlorine compounds (c) do not react with other substances (b); (3) because (1,2). The inference consists of closing the chain of reasoning by making explicit the relation between the concept of propellants (a) and the property of not reacting with other material (b). So, the inference consists of deriving the hidden premise, that is, good propellants do not react with other substances.

How is this kind of inference to be classified with respect to the earlier discussed dimensions? With respect to the first dimension, these inferences are necessary inferences. They can validly be deduced from the propositions in the text: The inference is true according to (the writer of) the text.

What the exact content of the deduction is depends on the content of the sentences. For example, from *Burglary is a crime, because burglary does not respect private property* does not follow "a crime is an act of not respecting private property", an inference that would be analogous to the one in the chlorine compounds example.[1] What does follow is that not respecting private property is a crime. One may argue that in the crime example the inference is that the contextually relevant property of a crime is "not respecting private property", just as in the chlorine compounds example the inference is that the contextually relevant property of propellants is "not reacting with other substances". But, from another point of view, the inferences differ in an important respect: "Not reacting with other substances" is a necessary condition for being a propellant, "not respecting private property" is a sufficient condition for being a crime. So, the conjunction *because* indicates that a causal relation has to be computed, but what the exact information is that has to be computed also depends on the content of the sentence.

A similar situation is found in the use of the conjunction *but*. The contrastive relation in *The room was large, but expensive* is different

---

[1] Simon Garrod brought this example to our attention.

from the contrastive relation in *The room was large, but could not accommodate the desk* and requires different inferences (e.g., that *large* is attractive and *expensive* is not vs. that the desk is large).

With respect to the second dimension along which inferences are differentiated, these inferences contribute to the coherence of the representation. The conjunction *because* signals that there is a causal dependency between the propositions. The conjunction *because* can be considered as a signal to start a procedure that operates on the context and leads to the addition of information to the discourse representation. The conjunction requires that this information is computed. If the inference is not made, the representation lacks coherence, as it is not made clear how the interpretation of one clause depends on the interpretation of the other clause. A similar argument holds for the conjunction *but*.

The question now is how the *because* sentence is processed. There are, of course, two possibilities. The first is that the causal inference is not made. The chain of reasoning is not completed. The reader does not make the inference that propellants may not react with other material. The other possibility is that the inference is made. In that case, *because* is considered as a trigger to complete the chain of reasoning. This completion implies that a relation is found in terms of which the two clauses are causally connected with each other. This process consists of the following steps.

First, the identification of the two complex concepts, that is, the arguments in the propositions, that have to be connected. In the present example, these are indicated as (a) and (b).

Second, the relation between (a) and (b) has to be checked and to be added to the representation of the text. There are several ways in which this checking procedure can take place, depending on the availability of the relation. One possibility is that the relation is expressed in the preceding text. The information is then present in the discourse representation that is constructed so far and can be pointed to as part of the representation of the *because* sentence. If the relation is not expressed in the previous text, there are two other possibilities. The relation is retrieved from long-term memory and added to the representation or else it is derived from the text and added as new information to the discourse representation.

The assumption is that if the inference is made, the reading time for the *because* sentence depends on the availability of the causal relation. The processing of the sentence is supposed to require less time if the relation is expressed in the preceding text than if the relation has to be retrieved from long-term memory and, a fortiori, less time than when the relation has to be added as new information to the representation. Accordingly, if the *because* sentence is preceded by a sentence that expresses the relation, it is expected that the reading time for the *because* sentence is shorter than when it is not preceded by such a sentence. If no such difference is found, the inference is not made and the process starting with the first step has not been carried out: The conjunction *because* is not treated as a trigger to compute the inference. (The absence of a difference, of course, might also be obtained if the availability of the relation does not affect the reading time for the *because* sentence.)

A similar inference process can be assumed in understanding the conjunction *but*. The following example, expressing a particular kind of contrastive relation, namely, a concessive opposition, may serve as an illustration. *The room was large, but one was not allowed to make music.* Simplifying, the following three propositions are involved in the *but* sentence: (1) The room (c) was large (a); (2) No music was allowed (b) in the room (c); (3) but (1, 2). The inference implies that *but* is considered as a trigger to complete the chain of reasoning. This completion consists of checking that there is a contrastive relation in terms of which the two clauses are connected with each other. This consists of the following steps. First, there must be the identification of the complex concepts that have to be contrasted. In the present example, the concepts are *large* (a) and *no music allowed* (b). In addition, the dimension on which the concepts are contrastively evaluated has to be identified; in this case, this is the attractiveness of the room.

The second step is to check the contrastive relation and to add it to the representation of the text. This requires that the following information be checked: first "A large room (a) is attractive", and second, "No music allowed (b) is unattractive". If the required information is present in the representation of the preceding discourse, it can be pointed to as part of the representation of the *but* sentence. If the information is not found in the discourse representation constructed so far, it has to be retrieved from long-term memory or it has to be added as new information to the representation of the *but* sentence. Accordingly, if the information that has to be inferred is expressed in the previous text, the reading time for the *but* sentence should be shorter than when that information is not in the text. If no such difference is found, the inference is not made and the process starting with the first step is not carried out: *but* is not treated as a trigger to compute the inference.

On-Line Inferences?

Experiment 1

To investigate whether inferences are made during reading, texts were presented in which one of the sentences, the target sentence, was a *because* sentence, such as the previously discussed sentence on chlorine compounds and propellants in spray cans. The texts were presented in one of two conditions: In the explicit condition, the *because* sentence was preceded by the information that has to be inferred (explicit information sentence), in the implicit condition, the explicit information sentence was not presented. In order to avoid effects of word repetition, different content words were used in the explicit information sentence than in the target sentence.

In order to increase the probability that the occurrence of the inferences could be identified, expository texts were used that dealt with topics that were not familiar to the subjects. In particular, the relation that had to be inferred was not familiar to the subjects. This was checked with each subject individually for each text after the completion of the experiment. On the other hand, the texts were constructed in such a way that the relation could unambiguously be derived from the text.

The texts were presented on a display one sentence at the time. Each new sentence was added to the previous sentence(s) on the display at the moment the subject pressed a button on a response panel. The reading time per sentence was measured. The reading time was defined as the time from the onset of the sentence on the screen until the subject pressed the button.

Subjects were instructed to read the texts carefully. They were told that when they had finished reading a text, they had to verify statements with respect to the text. They had to indicate whether the statements were correct or incorrect according to the text by pressing the corresponding button on a two-button response panel. The verification latency was measured from the onset of the verification statement until the subject pressed the button. One of the verification statements was the sentence that contained the explicit information.

The subjects were 16 university students, and there were 14 experimental texts. Half of the subjects received one half of the texts in the explicit condition and the other half in the implicit condition. This was reversed for the other half of the subjects.

If the inference is made, the understanding of the *because* sentence in the implicit condition requires more processing time than in the explicit condition, where it is preceded by the explicit information. Accordingly, the reading time for the *because* sentence in the implicit condition should be longer than in the explicit condition.

In Table 21.2, the average reading time for the *because* sentences is presented for the two conditions. In the implicit condition the mean reading time was a non-significant 114 ms longer than in the explicit condition $(F1(1,14) = 1.46, p = .25; F2(1,12) = 1.00, p = .34)$. This result suggests that these inferences are not made during the reading of the target sentence.

This result was completely unexpected. Subjects were instructed to read carefully. The anticipation of a verification task was supposed to stimulate careful reading and inferencing. Moreover, the nature of the inferences was such that they very likely required extra processing that could be measured. Perhaps that last assumption is incorrect. One may claim that the inferences were made on-line but that they didn't require time. Two pieces of evidence argue against that possibility: the verification times of the present experiment as well as data from subsequent experiments in which reading times in the implicit condition are longer than in the explicit condition.

TABLE 21.2

Mean Reading Times (ms) on Target Sentences and Mean Verification Latencies (ms) on Explicit Information Statements as a Function of the Presence of the Explicit Information Sentence Under Different Tasks.

Task	Reading Information Explicit	Implicit		Verification Information Explicit	Implicit	
Comprehension (Exp. 1)	3807	3921	n.s.	2657	2955	sig.
Comprehension (Exp. 2)	3910	3934	n.s.	*	*	sig.
Specific question (Exp. 3)	4986	5473	sig.	–	–	
Inconsistency Judgment (Exp.4)	5478	6093	sig.	–	–	
Comprehension (Exp. 5)	1473	1536	sig.	2169	2198	n.s.

sig.: Significant difference.
n.s.: Non significant difference.
* see Table 21.3

If the inference is made on-line, the verification latency of the sentence that contained the explicit information should be the same in the explicit condition as in the implicit condition. If the inference is not made on-line, the reader has ultimately to make the inference at the moment of the verification in order to be able to verify the statement. If the inference is made at the moment of verification, the verification latency in the explicit condition should be shorter than in the implicit condition (Singer, 1979). This latter result was obtained (see Table 21.2). The difference was a significant 298 ms ($F1(1,14) = 6.86$, $p < .05$; $F2(1,12) = 6.41$, $p < .05$).

However, one may argue that this difference does not reflect an inference process but a matching process. In fact, the statement that has to be verified is the same sentence as the explicit information. If in the implicit condition the inference is made on-line, that inference is most probably not formulated in the same words as the explicit information but rather in an abstract form that can be considered as a paraphrase of the explicit information. So, the difference in verification time could reflect a difference between verifying a statement that is identical to a sentence in the text and a statement that is an inference or a paraphrase of a sentence in the text.

Experiment 2

In order to find out whether the difference in the verification latencies is due to an inference process or to a paraphrase-matching process, a subsequent experiment was conducted. The verification statements in this experiment did not only include the experimental statements that contained the explicit information, but also experimental statements that were identical to a particular (nontarget) sentence in the text and experimental statements that were paraphrases of that sentence. Moreover, the verification task was conducted in two conditions: a direct and a delayed condition. In the direct condition, the verifications with respect to a text were presented immediately after each text. In the delayed condition, the verifications were presented after reading all the texts. The delay was about 20 minutes.

If the difference between the explicit and the implicit conditions in verifying the explicit information sentence does indeed reflect a matching process and not an inference process, then that difference should disappear when the verification task is delayed (Keenan & Kintsch, 1974), just as the difference between identical and paraphrase verifications should disappear in the delayed condition. The reason is that after a certain delay there is no representation of the surface characteristics of the sentences anymore (Sachs, 1967).

There were 42 subjects in this experiment and 12 experimental texts. The texts were different from those in the previous experiment. A prestudy was conducted to make sure that the explicit information indeed filled the gap of the target sentence. In that study, subjects were asked to specify what should be inferred at different places in the texts. These protocols were used in formulating the explicit information sentences in the present experiment.

The reading times for the target sentences (see Table 21.2) confirmed the findings of the previous experiment. There was no difference between the mean reading times of the explicit and implicit condition.

The verification latencies are presented in Table 21.3. As expected, the verification latency for the explicit information statements in the explicit condition was significantly shorter than in the implicit condition, both in direct verification $(F1(1,252) = 7.50, p < .01)$, and in delayed verification $(F1(1,252) = 13.76, p < .001)$. There was no interaction between the presence of the explicit information and the delay of verification $(F1(1,252) < 1)$. The difference in mean verification latencies between the identical and paraphrase statements in the direct condition was of the same size as the difference between the explicit and implicit conditions for the explicit information statements in both conditions.

This difference between identical and paraphrase statements, significant in the direct condition ($F1(1,252) = 8.52$, $p < .01$), decreased, as predicted, to a nonsignificant one in the delayed condition ($F1(1,252) < 1$). There was indeed an interaction between identical and paraphrase verifications on the one hand, and the delay of verification on the other ($F1(1,252) = 4.60$, $p < .05$).

TABLE 21.3

Experiment 2. Mean Verification Latencies (ms) as a Function of Delay Condition and of the Presence of the Explicit Information Sentence for the Explicit Information Statements and of the Presence of Identical or Paraphrase Wording for the Other Statements.

	Explicit Information Statement		Other Statement	
	Explicit	Implicit	Identical	Paraphrase
Direct	3176	3512	3324	3779
Delayed	3248	3606	3879	3962

These results support the conclusion that the difference in verification latencies between the explicit condition and the implicit condition cannot be attributed to a direct match with the explicit information sentence in the explicit condition. The reading-time results in combination with the verification latencies lead to the conclusion that the inferences are not made during reading of the target sentence. However, they *can* be made, for example, if the reader has to verify the information, as in the present experiment.

To conclude, even those inferences that are necessary and that contribute to the coherence of the representation are not made on-line. The text-analytic classification of inferences does not reliably predict which inferences are made on-line. Other factors contribute to the control of inferences. We discuss two of them: the reader's purpose and the reader's knowledge.

Inferences and the Reader's Purpose

To the extent that information is more relevant for the reader, the reader is probably willing to process the information more carefully. In the next experiments the information that is supposed to be inferred is made more relevant for the reader by manipulating the reader's purpose in reading. The hypothesis is that in this case the inferences will be made on-line.

Experiment 3

In Experiment 3, the purpose of the reader was defined with respect to a particular topic. Readers were instructed to read the texts so as to be able to answer a specific question and to explain the answer. The question was related to the reasons underlying the causal relation expressed in the target sentence, but the answer was not simply the explicit information. For example, in the earlier discussed text on propellants and the environment the question was: How do spray cans work? According to the hypothesis, the target sentence should be read more thoroughly: Its reading time should increase and, more importantly, readers should make the inference. The occurrence of the inference should be evident from a longer reading time for the target sentences in the implicit condition than in the explicit condition.

Twelve texts were selected from Experiments 1 and 2. There were 34 subjects. The procedure was the same, except that before each text the specific question was asked. The answer had to be given immediately after reading the text. There was no verification task. The results were as expected (see Table 21.2). The mean reading time for the target sentences was about one second longer than in the previous experiments. More interestingly, the mean reading times for the target sentences in the implicit condition were longer than in the explicit condition $(F1(1,32) = 9.05, p < .01; F2(1,10) = 13.67, p < .01)$. This result suggests that the purpose of the reader affects the on-line inference processes: Inferences related to information that is relevant for the purpose of the reader are likely be made on-line.

Experiment 4

A second way in which the reader's purpose was manipulated was by instructing the reader to read the text and to check whether each sentence was consistent with the previous part of the text. Just and Carpenter (1978) demonstrated that this instruction can lead to more pronounced inference effects than when readers were just instructed to read the text carefully.

In experiment 4, the same texts as in Experiment 3 were used. Some experimental texts were changed so as to contain an inconsistency, and texts containing one or two inconsistencies were added as filler texts. The inconsistencies in the experimental texts were never related to a target sentence; they occurred in the texts after the target sentences. In this way the inconsistencies could not disrupt the processing of the *because* sentence.

Subjects were told that the texts contained one, two, or more sentences that were inconsistent with the meaning of the previous part of the text. With respect to each sentence, the subjects had to indicate whether the sentence was consistent or not with the meaning of the previous part of the text by pressing the corresponding button on a two-button response panel. Subjects were instructed to do their task carefully but as quickly as possible. The fact that reaction times were measured on each sentence was mentioned. The reading time of the target sentence was measured from the onset of the sentence until the subject pressed the button. There were 28 subjects.

The results (see Table 21.2) were similar to those in the previous experiment. First, the overall reading time for the target sentence was longer than in Experiment 2, in which the reader's purpose was not manipulated. Second, the reading time for the target sentence in the implicit condition was longer than in the explicit condition ($F1(1,26) = 12.00$, $p < .01$; $F2(1,10) = 8.2$, $p < .05$).

The results of these experiments show that the purpose of the reader is an important factor in controlling the on-line inference processes. A possible interpretation, in line with results of Cirilo and Foss (1980) and Goetz (1979), is that the reader identifies the relevance of the information immediately and that this affects the depth of processing.

Inferences and the Reader's Knowledge

Experiment 5

A second factor that may control the on-line inference processes is the reader's knowledge. The texts that were used in the previous experiments dealt with topics that were unfamiliar to the reader. In particular, the relations among the concepts in the target sentences were not part of the reader's knowledge. Consequently, the inferences required computations of new knowledge. One may hypothesize that the inferences that were investigated are not made in normal reading for reasons of cognitive economy, that is, inferences that are computations of new knowledge are not made, whereas inferences that are related to available knowledge are made on-line.

To test this hypothesis, an experiment was conducted with narrative texts on familiar topics. The inferences were contrastive inferences, signaled by the conjunction *but*. They were of a similar kind as those in the previous experiments: They can be deduced from the propositions conjoined by a conjunction, contribute to the coherence of the representation, and are backward inferences. The hypothesis is tested by the same experimental manipulation as in the previous experiments: In one condition, the information that has to be inferred is expressed in a preceding sentence in the text (explicit condition); in the other condition, that information is not stated (implicit condition). An example of a target sentence is *The room was large, but she was not allowed to make music in the room,* occurring in a text dealing with a person who is looking for a room to rent. The inference of interest in this experiment was related to the information in the *but* clause. In the explicit condition, the *but* sentence was preceded by the information that has to be inferred: She wanted to make music in her room.

The units of presentation were sentences or clauses containing a finite verb. The dependent variable was the reading time for the *but* clause.

The subjects were 32 students. There were 12 experimental texts and 24 filler texts. The procedure was the same as in Experiments 1 and 2.

If the inference is made, the reading time for the *but* clause should be longer in the implicit condition than in the explicit condition. Furthermore, there should be no difference between conditions for the verification of the explicit information after reading the text.

The results (see Table 21.2) confirmed the predictions. The mean reading time was longer in the implicit condition than in the explicit condition ($F1(1,28) = 4.25$, $p < .05$; $F2(1,11) = 5.14$, $p < .05$). In addition, there was no difference in the mean verification latencies on the explicit information statement between the explicit and the implicit conditions ($F1(1,28) < 1$; $F2(1,11) < 1$). Both results suggest that the inferences were indeed made during the reading of the target sentence. This is in agreement with the hypothesis that the on-line inferences are controlled by the reader's knowledge: Inferences that are related to available knowledge are made on-line.

The texts in Experiment 5 differ from those in the previous experiments with respect to the reader's familiarity with the topics of the texts. It should be noted, however, that other differences may play a role as well, for example, the difference between expository and narrative texts. But perhaps part of the difference between expository and narrative texts can be accounted for in terms of more or less available knowledge structures.

CONCLUSION

The results can be summarized as follows. The text-analytic characteristics of inferences do not lead to clear predictions about whether the inferences are made on-line. Even backward, necessary inferences that contribute to the coherence of the discourse representation are not always made during reading. Apparently, readers have a tendency to satisfy themselves with rather shallow processing.

The control of inferences depends to a considerable extent on the reader's purpose and the reader's knowledge. Inferences are made on-line if they are related to information that is relevant to the reader's purpose, and inferences are more likely to be made if they deal with familiar topics.

These results suggest that reading is a process in which a balance between costs and benefits is achieved. The benefits consist of the information extracted from the text; the costs are related to the extra mental processes that this requires. The reader seems to be rather parsimonious in processing. This is indicated by the absence of the inferences in normal reading expository text (Experiments 1 and 2). If the information is more relevant to the reader's purpose, the benefits are higher and inferences are made on-line (Experiments 3 and 4). If the inferences are related to information that is familiar to the reader, the costs may be lower, which enables on-line inferences (Experiment 5). It should be noted that the interpretation of the latter result is not that these inferences are made because they do not require time. They do, in fact. Readers engage in inference processes because the costs are relatively low when the inferences are related to available knowledge.

A rather speculative interpretation is that readers have a kind of integration device that regulates the degree of integration to be achieved. A higher degree of integration is envisaged if the information is more related to the reader's purpose in reading and if the reader has more knowledge of the topic of the text.

ACKNOWLEDGMENT

This research was partly supported by a Psychon-Grant (15-21-20) of the Netherlands Organization for Scientific Research (NWO) awarded to both authors. We are grateful to Henk J. Kempff for his cooperation in the research and for running Experiments 1 through 4 and Ellen W. M. Aarts for running Experiment 5.

REFERENCES

Brewer, W. F. (1977). Memory for the pragmatic implications of sentences. *Memory & Cognition, 5*, 673 - 678.

Cirilo, R. K., & Foss, D. J. (1980). Text structure and reading time for sentences. *Journal of Verbal Learning and Verbal Behavior, 19*, 96 - 109.

Clark, H. H., & Sengul, C. J. (1979). In search of referents for nouns and pronouns. *Memory & Cognition, 7*, 35 - 41.

Corbett, A. T., & Dosher, B. A. (1978). Instrumental inferences in sentence encoding. *Journal of Verbal Learning and Verbal Behavior, 17*, 479 - 491.

Duffy, S. A. (1986). Role of expectations in sentence integration. *Journal of Experimental Psychology: Learning, Memory, and Cognition, 12*, 208 - 219.

Garnham, A. (1982). Testing psychological theories about inference making. *Memory & Cognition, 10*, 341 - 349.

Garnham, A. (1985). *Psycholinguistics: Central topics.* London: Methuen.

Garrod, S., & Sanford, A. (1977). Interpreting anaphoric relations: The integration of semantic information while reading. *Journal of Verbal Learning and Verbal Behavior, 16*, 77 - 90.

Garrod, S., & Sanford, A. (1981). Bridging inferences and the extended domain of reference. In J. Long & A. Baddeley (Eds.), *Attention and performance IX* (pp. 331 - 346). Hillsdale, NJ: Lawrence Erlbaum Associates.

Goetz, E. T. (1979). Inferring from text: Some factors influencing which inferences will be made. *Discourse Processes, 2*, 179 - 195.

Harris, R. J. (1974). Memory and comprehension of implications and inferences of complex sentences. *Journal of Verbal Learning and Verbal Behavior, 13*, 626 - 637.

Harris, R. J., & Monaco, G. E. (1978). Psychology of pragmatic implication: Information processing between the lines. *Journal of Experimental Psychology: General, 107*, 1 - 22.

Haviland, S. E., & Clark, H. H. (1974). What's new? Acquiring new information as a process in comprehension. *Journal of Verbal Learning and Verbal Behavior, 13*, 512 - 521.

Hildyard, A., & Olson, D. R. (1978). Memory and inference in the comprehension of oral and written discourse. *Discourse Processes, 1*, 91 - 117.

Johnson, M. K., Bransford, J. D., & Solomon, S. (1973). Memory for tacit implications of sentences. *Journal of Experimental Psychology, 98*, 203 - 205.

Just, M. A., & Carpenter, P. A. (1978). Inference processes during reading: Reflections from eye fixations. In J. W. Senders, D. F. Fisher, & R. A. Monty (Eds.), *Eye movements and the higher psychological functions* (pp. 157 - 174). Hillsdale, NJ: Lawrence Erlbaum Associates.

Just, M. A., & Carpenter, P. A. (1987). *The psychology of reading and language comprehension*. Newton, MA: Allyn & Bacon.

Just, M. A., & Clark, H. H. (1973). Drawing inferences from the presuppositions and implications of affirmative and negative sentences. *Journal of Verbal Learning and Verbal Behavior, 12*, 21 - 31.

Keenan, J. M., Baillet, S. D., & Brown, P. (1984). The effects of causal cohesion on comprehension and memory. *Journal of Verbal Learning and Verbal Behavior, 23*, 115 - 126.

Keenan, J. M., & Kintsch, W. (1974). The identification of explicitly and implicitly presented information. In W. Kintsch (Ed.), *The representation of meaning in memory* (pp. 153 - 166). Hillsdale, NJ: Lawrence Erlbaum Associates.

Lesgold, A. M., Roth, S. F., & Curtis, M. E. (1979). Foregrounding effects in discourse comprehension. *Journal of Verbal Learning and Verbal Behavior, 18*, 291 - 308.

McKoon, G., & Ratcliff, R. (1980). The comprehension processes and memory structures involved in anaphoric reference. *Journal of Verbal Learning and Verbal Behavior, 19*, 668 - 682.

O'Brien, E. J., Shank, D. M., Myers, J. L., & Rayner, K. (1988). Elaborative inferences during reading: Do they occur on-line? *Journal of Experimental Psychology: Learning, Memory, and Cognition, 14*, 410 - 420.

Potts, G. R. (1972). Information processing strategies used in the encoding of linear orderings. *Journal of Verbal Learning and Verbal Behavior, 11*, 727 - 740.

Sachs, J. (1967). Recognition memory for syntactic and semantic aspects of connected discourse. *Perception & Psychophysics, 2*, 437 - 442.

Seuren, P. A. M. (1985). *Discourse semantics*. Oxford: Blackwell.

Singer, M. (1979). Temporal locus of inference in the comprehension of brief passages: Recognizing and verifying implications about instruments. *Perceptual and Motor Skills, 49*, 539 - 550.

Singer, M., & Ferreira, F. (1983). Inferring consequences in story comprehension. *Journal of Verbal Learning and Verbal Behavior, 22*, 437 - 448.

Vonk, W. (1985). The immediacy of inferences in the understanding of pronouns. In G. Rickheit & H. Strohner (Eds.), *Inferences in text processing* (pp. 205 - 218). Amsterdam: Elsevier Science.

22

REFERENTIAL PROCESSES IN READING: FOCUSING ON ROLES AND INDIVIDUALS

Simon Garrod and Anthony Sanford

University of Glasgow

In ordinary "realistic" fiction–what Stevenson
called subjective fiction–the writer's intent is
to let the reader fall through the page into the
scene represented.

John Gardner, *The Art of Fiction*, 1983.

INTRODUCTION

It is fair to say that any complete account of the reading process
will have to explain how a reader is able to form a coherent mental representation of the text as a whole – a representation that goes beyond
the sum of the sentences. A key ingredient of such an account will be
an explanation of the referential processes which enable the reader to
establish links between different sentences in the text mediated through
common reference. The importance of this has been recognized in most
recent theories of reading (e.g., Just & Carpenter, 1980; Kintsch & Van
Dijk, 1978). However, it is still not clear to what extent referential processes viewed purely in terms of recognizing intersentential coreference
relations can explain how a skilled reader can fulfill the writer's intent
and fall through the page into the scene represented. In this chapter,
we argue for a richer account of what needs to be represented about
text characters and a richer account of how different referential devices
interact with these different forms of representation.

The account depends upon a distinction between two types of information that the reader may draw on to individuate the characters portrayed in a story: entity-individuating information and role-individuating information. We start by explaining this distinction. We then go on to consider its bearing on the immediate interpretation of different referential devices, such as pronouns and fuller definite descriptions, and finish with a general discussion of how these referential processes may be treated within an attentional framework.

ENTITIES AND ROLES IN NARRATIVE TEXT

To the extent that effective fictional writing involves conjuring up scenes, effective reading involves identifying and representing those scenes, and this puts certain minimal requirements on the process. One such requirement is that readers be able to recognize not just the characters in a narrative as individuals but also the roles that these characters are playing in the situations portrayed. Hence, in reading any narrative we seem to assign the characters to roles automatically. To illustrate this, consider the following brief text taken from Sanford and Garrod (1981):

John was on his way to school.
He was worried about the math lesson.
He hoped he could control the class today.

Presented with such a story fragment, most readers encounter difficulty with the third sentence. They take inordinately long to read it and experience even greater problems when it is followed by:

It was not a normal part of a janitor's duties.

This simple illustration suggests that a skilled reader does more than just represent *John* as a human male individual, even though that is all that has actually been presented about him. To understand the text fully, the reader also seems to have to locate *John* at the center of a situation where he is a boy on his way to school and clearly worried about the impending math lesson. *John* has to be cast in the role "schoolboy." Thus, roles anchor individuals like John to the situation portrayed and this anchoring would seem to be an essential part of our normal comprehension process.

The question therefore arises as to how these two forms of character individuation are mentally represented and made so readily available during the normal course of reading. We suggest that individuation by entity and individuation by role arise from two different components of the reader's dynamic discourse model, one concerned with keeping track of the currently relevant story characters and the other with keeping track of the currently relevant situation. In addition, we suggest that the two forms of individuation also affect the immediate interpretation of different types of anaphor. Thus, whereas pronouns seem to operate by directly identifying antecedent discourse entities, other, fuller anaphors such as definite descriptions, operate in a more general way to recover discourse roles. This difference in mode of operation may then be used to account for experimental findings that show differences in the on-line interpretation of the various types of anaphor under what seem to be similar circumstances.

However, before addressing this issue directly it is necessary to consider in a general fashion what is known about the contribution of referential processing to reading and the role of attention in these processes.

REFERENTIAL PROCESSES AND ATTENTIONAL FOCUS

One of the first demonstrations that referential processes could have a direct impact on reading came from Haviland and Clark (1974). They demonstrated that the comprehension time for a sentence depended in part on the reader's ability to recover antecedents for the definite anaphors in the sentence. For instance, they were able to demonstrate that readers spent longer on the sentence *The beer was warm* when it followed *Mary unpacked some picnic supplies* rather than *Mary unpacked some beer*. To explain the difference they argued that in the former case the reader has to draw a time-consuming bridging inference to establish a putative antecedent for the referential expression *The beer* (e.g., some *beer* associated with the *picnic* supplies) before comprehension is achieved.

Since then a number of reading time studies have been carried out to determine other factors affecting referential processes of this sort. For instance, Garrod and Sanford (1977) were able to demonstrate that the degree to which the anaphor matched the antecedent description has a systematic effect on reading time. In a similar vein, Clark and Sengul (1979) were able to demonstrate that text distance between anaphor and antecedent also affected reading time, and more recently Ehrlich and Rayner (1983) have been able to demonstrate that this effect is localized to gaze durations in the immediate vicinity of the anaphor, when it is a pronoun.

Such studies therefore lead to the general conclusion that referential processes of this sort form an integral part of the reading process and basically involve searching back through a representation of potential antecedents in order to discover one that matches. Should the representation contain no matching antecedent, one then has to be inferred. But such an account raises questions both about the matching process itself and the form of antecedent representation. One problem concerns the range of the search domain and how it can be limited to make immediate antecedent recovery possible, and it is here that a number of people have suggested that attentional factors may play an important role.

It is now widely recognized that the ease with which one can interpret certain anaphors depends upon having the antecedent in mind when the anaphor is encountered (see Chafe, 1976, on foregrounding; Grosz, 1977, on focus). So to use Grosz's terminology, focused antecedents tend to be more readily identified by anaphors than nonfocused antecedents. This leads to the idea that at any point in reading only a few candidate antecedents may be available for immediate recovery, which would explain in a general way the importance of recency as well as how it can be overridden by other factors such as topicalization.

In the next two sections we consider the role of antecedent focusing as it affects both the interpretation of pronouns and other definite descriptions. First, we look at focusing on antecedents as entities and then turn to the possibility of focusing on roles.

Entity Focusing and the Interpretation of Pronouns

As we have already indicated, there is increasing concensus on the idea that the immediacy of anaphoric interpretation depends upon the degree to which an antecedent is in the reader's attentional focus at the time of encountering the anaphor. However, recent evidence suggests that this is not equally true for all types of anaphor.

Sanford, Moar, and Garrod (1988) and Garrod and Sanford (1985) have found evidence that antecedent entity focusing only plays an important part in the interpretation of pronouns. The Sanford et al. study first established what factors affected character prominence in short text fragments by having subjects write continuation sentences which could then be scored for incidence of mention of each of two previously introduced characters. This enabled them to identify for a given set of materials the highly focused antecedents. An example of the materials used is shown in Table 22.1 with the continuation frequency scores indicated. Three antecedent factors were manipulated: primacy of mention, centrality of role, and introduction by name versus description. As can be seen from the table, only the third means of introduction had any systematic effect with these materials. Thus, rhetorical technique mirrors social custom in that introducing a character into the story by name focuses attention onto that individual.

Using these same materials, Sanford et al. then carried out a self-paced reading experiment, with the critical target sentence containing a reference to one or other character, using either a pronoun or definite description. The reading times for these targets are shown in Figure 22.1, where it can be seen that they conform to a striking pattern.

The only contextual factor that produces any effect on reading time of the target sentence is the means of introduction (name vs. definite description) – the key device for focusing attention on one antecedent over the other – and it only affects the reading time for sentences containing the pronoun. Thus, introducing a character by name has a dramatic effect on interpretation of a subsequent sentence containing a pronoun, but no effect whatsoever on sentences containing a fuller anaphoric description. Furthermore, the reading time pattern cannot be attributed

TABLE 22.1

Example of Material Used in Part One of the Sanford et al. (1988) Experiment. Percentage Responses in the Continuation Experiment as a Function of Primacy, Situation Dependence and Naming of Antecedent.

[Masie / the customer] entered the restaurant and sat down.
[Alphonso / the waiter] wearily limped over to take her order.

Order of Mention

First	Second	Neither
43%	46%	11%

Scenario Dependence

Independent	Dependent	Neither
48%	44%	8%

Means of Introduction

Proper name	Role	Neither
61%	30%*	9%

---

to other factors such as recency of mention, as these were controlled for within the study.

This study therefore confirms the findings of others on the use and interpretation of personal pronouns in spoken narrative, which suggest that they are primarily devices for maintaining reference to highly focused antecedent entities (Karmiloff-Smith, 1980; Marslen-Wilson, Levy, & Tyler, 1982). But such a sentence reading time study cannot establish the extent to which focusing affects the immediate on-line interpretation of the pronoun. A study by Garrod and Sanford (1985) suggests that it plays a crucial role.

The study employed a somewhat different technique to determine the point in reading when a pronoun or other anaphoric device had been interpreted, using a secondary task of spelling error detection. Texts like those in the top part of Figure 22.2 were constructed containing two characters, one introduced by proper name and the other by role description. These texts acted as context for one of four critical sentences that contained a spelling error on the main verb. The four associated sentences with the text are also shown in Figure 22.2.

ORDER 1
Context S1 Mr. Bloggs was dictating a letter.
Context S2 The secretary was taking shorthand.
Target Ss *He/She/Mr. Bloggs/The secretary* was feeling hungry.

ORDER 2
Context S1 The manager was dictating a letter.
Context S2 Claire was taking shorthand.
Target Ss *He/She/The manager/Claire* was feeling hungry.

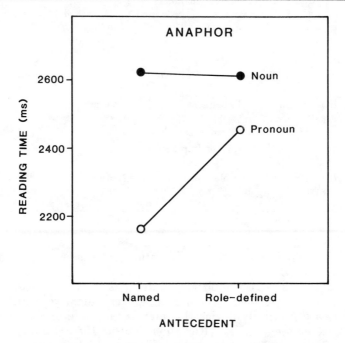

FIGURE 22.1. Target sentence reading times for the materials in Sanford, Moar, and Garrod's (1988) experiment, comparing noun anaphors with pronouns.

They were so constructed that in half the cases (e.g., in b and c) the sentence was contextually anomalous at the point of the misspelled verb. In other words, so long as the readers had established exactly who Mary and the lifeguard were, they would know that she could sink but not jump and he could jump but not sink at that point in the story. Hence, being aware of the anomaly in the verb depended upon having already interpreted the immediately preceding anaphor.

The subjects were required to read the materials one sentence at a time according to the standard self-paced reading paradigm. However, they also had the additional secondary task of pressing a key as soon as the spelling error was detected. This made it possible to determine the time to detect the critical spelling error as measured from sentence onset. The rationale for measuring detection latency came from previous studies in speech perception first carried out by Cole and Jakimik (1978, 1980) that indicated that mispronunciation detection latency is a function of the contextual consistency of the mispronounced word. So we argued by analogy that latency differences in the detection of the spelling errors in this situation should reflect a reader's synchronous knowledge of the contextual consistency of the misspelled verb, which in turn would depend upon the full interpretation of the prior anaphor. Thus, presence of a consistency effect would evidence immediate interpretation of the anaphor and absence of the effect would indicate that the anaphor had not been resolved at the point of encountering the verb.

Figure 22.2 shows the results obtained with materials of the sort illustrated containing proper name and definite description anaphors. For both types there is a clear and highly significant consistency effect (i.e., difference in detection latency for contextually consistent vs. inconsistent contexts). In this situation, with the full anaphors readers have no trouble assigning a contextual interpretation before encountering the verb. But what happens with pronouns? To test for this, the materials were slightly modified so as to ensure the unambiguous gender and number differentiation of the two antecedents and then the experiment was repeated with pronouns in place of the full anaphors.

As can be seen from Figure 22.3, this produces a very different pattern of results. In line with the previous reading-time studies, the experiment clearly indicates that readers have not interpreted the pronoun immediately in the case where it refers to an unfocused antecedent (i.e., the one not introduced by name). Again this result cannot be explained in terms of distance, as in more than half of the materials it was the unnamed character who had been mentioned most recently.

Taken together, the two studies point to a difference in the processing of pronouns as compared to other types of anaphor. In the first place, the immediate interpretation of the pronoun is shown to be heavily influenced by the degree to which the antecedent is in the reader's attentional focus. Yet there is no evidence whatsoever to indicate that attentional focus, at least at this level, has any measurable effect on the recovery of antecedents for the fuller anaphors. The studies also demonstrate that use of a proper name to introduce a character, as opposed to giving a more general role description such as "the lifeguard" or "the secretary" guarantees focus on that individual and sets up the character for subsequent pronominal reference.

So let us now turn to the question of how it may be possible to focus differentially on roles and how this might affect the interpretation of fuller definite descriptions.

A dangerous incident at the pool.

Elizabeth was a very inexperienced swimmer and wouldn't
have gone into the pool if the lifeguard hadn't been nearby.
But as soon as she was out of her depth she started to
panic and wave her hands about in a frenzy.

(a) Within seconds Elizabeth   *jumped** into the pool.
(b) Within seconds the lifeguard

(c) Within seconds Elizabeth   *sank** beneath the surface.
(d) Within seconds the lifeguard

*misspellings: jimped – senk

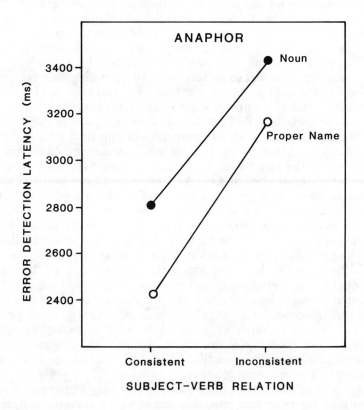

FIGURE 22.2. Time to detect verb spelling errors measured from sentence onset, for
proper name and role description anaphors.

Garrod & Sanford (1985)

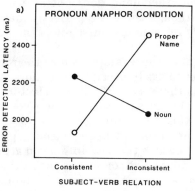

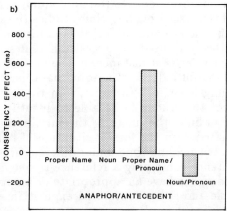

FIGURE 22.3. (a) Times to detect verb spelling errors measured from sentence on-set for pronoun anaphors. (b) Magnitude of the consistency effect (i.e. consistent-inconsistent detection latencies) for all types of anaphor and antecedent.

Focusing on Roles and Interpreting Definite Descriptions

The prior discussion tends to suggest that the ease of interpreting definite descriptions referring to antecedent roles is in no way affected by attentional focus but is only subject to constraints arising from the match between the description and the specification of the antecedent. However the situation is clearly more complicated. Consider for instance the following text fragment:

Mary usually lunches at Valentino's because she fancies the waiter there. For dinner she prefers to go to La Grande Bouffe where the food is better but *the waiter* / *he* is not nearly so handsome.

In this text, it is clear that the pronoun does not substitute for the italicized definite description as it can only identify the antecedent waiter (the one at Valentino's), hence the oddness of the example. The full description on the other hand does not attach to any antecedent discourse entity even though there is a perfectly matching one. Instead it identifies a currently relevant discourse role, "the waiter at La Grande Bouffe."

What is striking about this example is how the role identifying function of the description so easily overrides the more standard anaphoric function. Even though there is a perfectly satisfactory antecedent waiter sitting in the context, this does not seem to interfere with the situational role interpretation in this case. But clearly such a nonanaphoric interpretation will depend upon the extent to which the prior text establishes a new situational role to which the description can attach. The empirical issue is to determine under what conditions such situational role attachments will occur in the absence of explicitly introduced antecedents.

As a move in this direction, Garrod and Sanford (1982, 1983) carried out a number of self-paced reading time studies to establish the ease of such role identifications under different circumstances. In the first of these studies, titles were used to suggest different situations and hence establish different roles. For instance, in the materials shown in Figure 22.4 (Garrod & Sanford, 1983), the same basic passage could be entitled either "Telling a lie" or "In court." In the latter case, we might reasonably expect the reader to be able to identify a number of situational roles, including "the judge," "the jury," "the lawyers," and so forth, not associated with the former situation of telling a lie. The experiment contrasted reading time under different antecedent conditions for a critical sentence containing a reference to one of these characters. So the text could either have an appropriate or inappropriate title with respect to the role and either contain an explicit antecedent mention of the character or leave it implied.

As can be seen in the reading time data in Figure 22.4, readers experience no extra difficulty interpreting sentences containing a reference to a situational role in the absence of an explicit antecedent when the title is appropriate for that role, but they do have trouble otherwise (i.e., in the No-Antecedent–Inappropriate Title condition). So this study confirms the idea that immediate role identification can occur with a definite description so long as there is a clear indication of the situational setting behind the story fragment. It does not, however, establish the range of such roles afforded by any situation.

The other study reported by Garrod and Sanford (1982) gives a clearer picture of how texts may serve to identify situations that enable a reader to focus on a limited number of roles. In this study, verbs were used as a means of establishing the roles. Consider, for instance, the verb *to drive* in the sense of 'to direct a vehicle'. When such a verb occurs in sentences like *Keith drove to London*, the reader must appreciate that a vehicle of some description is involved. So according to our argument, the verb should identify a situation establishing a role for the vehicle used. In turn, this should make it possible for the reader to assign

Appropriate Topic Passage

Title: *In court*
Context S/   Fred was being questioned *(by a lawyer).*
Filler S/   He had been accused of murder.
Target S/   *The lawyer* was trying to prove his innocence.

Inappropriate Topic Passage

Title: *Telling a lie*
Context S/   Fred was being questioned *(by a lawyer).*
Filler S/   He couldn't tell the truth.
Target S/   *The lawyer* was trying to prove his innocence.

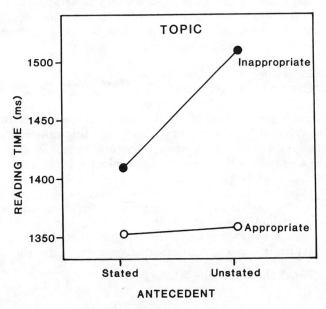

FIGURE 22.4. Examples of the materials used and the target sentence reading times for Garrod and Sanford's (1983) scenario experiment.

an immediate referential interpretation for a subsequent definite noun phrase identifying a vehicle (e.g., "the car"), as it would be immediately clear how that vehicle fits into the scene described.

Sixteen such role identifying verbs were selected on the basis of meaning definitions given by a number of independent judges. These included verb role pairings such as *buy–money, carve–knife* and *dress–clothes,* all chosen on the basis that 8 out of 15 judges included the role description in their definitions. Contrasting materials were then constructed like those in Figure 22.5 that could contain either a stated antecedent role filler or simply the role-identifying verb. At the same time two types of referential target sentence were constructed, one containing the role filler itself (e.g., *the car* as an instance of vehicle) and the other containing a definite description of something dependent on the role but not satisfying the conditions on the role itself (e.g., *the engine* which does not qualify as a vehicle but does qualify as part of one).

The critical reading time results are shown in Figure 22.5 and, as in the previous study, there is no evidence to suggest that readers encounter any problems with the target sentence in the absence of an explicitly stated antecedent role filler. But the results do indicate that indirect focusing on a role, such as "the vehicle used" in the case of the verb *drive*, is not quite the same as directly introducing an antecedent car into the context. Reading times for target sentences containing a role dependent reference were reliably longer in the implied condition than in the condition with the stated antecedents. This difference highlights the distinction between focusing on an uninstantiated role as compared to focusing on a particular entity as role filler, a difference that also might account for the problems readers encounter when confronted with a pronoun in this situation. Consider, for instance:

Keith was driving to London.
It had recently been overhauled.

Even though the content of the second sentence clearly implicates a vehicle as referent for the pronoun, the overriding impression is that London has just been overhauled and not a vehicle! So pronouns do not seem to be capable of identifying antecedent roles in the absence of entity focusing.

At first blush, the Garrod and Sanford (1982) study does seem to be at odds with previous attempts to find evidence for so-called elaborative inferences in reading (see Sanford, this volume). For instance, Singer (1979) reported some experiments that suggested that readers did not generally infer likely missing instruments for sentences like the following:

Harry cleared the snow from the stairs.
as opposed to:
Harry cleared the snow with a shovel.

Even though a high proportion of independent judges chose *shovel* as the most likely instrument for clearing snow from stairs, Singer found a reliable increase in reading time for a subsequent target sentence containing a reference to *the shovel* in the absence of an explicit antecedent, a result similar in many respects to that found earlier by Haviland and Clark (1974, see earlier discussion). This apparent conflict led Cotter (1984) to try and establish what was responsible for the difference in the

Garrod & Sanford (1982)

Stated Antecedent

Filler S/	Keith was giving a lecture in London.
Context S/	He was taking his *car* there overnight.
Target S/	*The car/the engine* had recently been overhauled.

Implied Antecedent

Filler S/	Keith was giving a lecture in London.
Context S/	He was driving there overnight.
Target S/	*The car/the engine* had recently been overhauled.

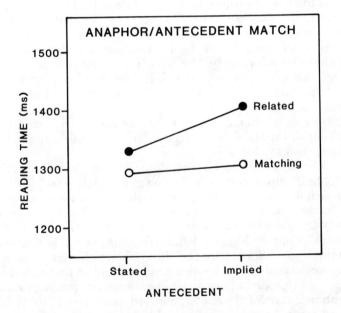

FIGURE 22.5. Examples of the materials used and the target sentence reading times for Garrod and Sanford's (1982) verb instrument experiment.

two studies, and in doing so she confirmed Garrod and Sanford's (1982) earlier speculation that it hinges on the degree to which the verb alone identifies a situation with an obligatory instrument role. Cotter began by comparing the sets of verbs associated with the two studies in terms of dictionary definitions and noted that in all 16 of the Garrod-Sanford set the instrument was either mentioned directly or subsumed under the instrument category given in the definition, whereas for the Singer materials this occurred for only half of the verbs. So, for instance, whereas *to drive* implies 'to use a vehicle', *to clear* does not imply 'to use a shovel'. Cotter was then able to replicate both the Singer results and the different Garrod-Sanford result with new materials containing the original verb phrases. Thus, this group of studies suggests that situational roles like discourse entities are subject to focusing constraints such that only a few highly relevant roles may be in focus at any time. One constraint identified here comes from the degree to which the verb alone identifies a situation that entails the role, but other more general delimitations of the boundary conditions on role focusing have yet to be established.

Summary of the Focusing Studies

The picture that emerges from both the entity-focusing and role-focusing studies is one where there is a differentiation between two objects of attention. On the one hand, readers focus attention on particular individuals who constitute the topics or thematic subjects of the scene; but on the other, readers also focus attention in a somewhat different way on the roles afforded by the situations portrayed in the text. In either case this affects the reader's ability for rapid contextually appropriate interpretation. Entity focusing plays a major part in pronominal interpretation, whereas role focusing plays a major part in interpreting fuller definite descriptions and so helps the reader to anchor newly introduced entities to the scene or recover antecedents via their previously established roles in that scene.

The attentional system is therefore instrumental in enabling the reader to build up a contextually coherent interpretation of referential expressions that can satisfy the various constraints they impose. The basic constraint imposed by a pronoun is that it should refer to a uniquely individuated entity or set of entities in the discourse model. The constraint imposed by the definite description is that it should identify a unique role afforded by the situation which may or may not be currently associated with a particular individual in that situation.

To capture this kind of relationship between referential processes and the attentional state of the reader, Sanford and Garrod (1981) proposed a memory focus framework which included two dynamic systems operating in parallel, *explicit* and *implicit focus*. In the final section of this chapter we explore how entities and roles can be represented within such a system to support efficient referential processing. First, we give a brief account of the proposed structure of explicit and implicit focus, then we discuss how the two systems relate to each other to embody a more complete model of the discourse.

THE EXPLICIT/IMPLICIT FOCUS ACCOUNT

The Overall Structure of the System

Together, explicit and implicit focus are taken to represent the reader's current working model of the discourse world. At any point in reading, explicit focus contains tokens corresponding to the relevant individuals introduced into that world, whereas implicit focus contains a scenario or mental representation of the currently relevant aspects of the scenes portrayed, including the significance of each of the roles. It is the mapping between the two systems which then defines a locally coherent model at any moment during reading, and this mapping is made possible through the situational roles represented in the scenario. Thus, the scenario in implicit focus affords roles into which the individuals represented in explicit focus may be mapped.

The system as a whole can then act as a representational substratum to support the immediate interpretation of referential expressions. The basic elements of the system are illustrated schematically in Figure 22.6. As can be seen in the figure, pronouns directly identify the discourse entity tokens in explicit focus, whereas fuller definite descriptions directly identify the discourse roles afforded by the scenario currently held in implicit focus. Hence, it is a straightforward matter to account for the immediate access of different types of antecedent information within such a framework. The key question concerns how discourse entities and situational roles are introduced into focus and maintained within the system. First, we consider some of the issues surrounding the introduction and maintenance of individuals within the explicit focus partition and then turn to the related questions about situational roles and implicit focus. Finally we explore the relationship between roles as defined in implicit focus and individuals represented in the explicit partition.

Individuals and Their Representation in Explicit Focus

As a first attempt at trying to determine the conditions for introducing entities into explicit focus, Garrod and Sanford (1982) took the strong position that explicit mention was a precondition for explicit focusing. Hence, for any entity to be represented in focus and subsequently be directly accessible by pronoun, it must at least have been explicitly referred to in the context. However, since then a number of examples have been brought to our attention which indicate that this is too strong a condition (see Bosch, 1988). For example, there seem to be circumstances associated with the use of quantified antecedents which violate this constraint. But a detailed analysis of such examples points up an interesting difference between implying the existence of a particular individual or set of individuals for subsequent pronominal reference versus implying a new situational role in the way that the verb

drive implies 'a vehicle', and so we would suggest that they do not undermine the basic distinction we are trying to draw. Let us consider two
apparent counterexamples to the explicit mention precondition.

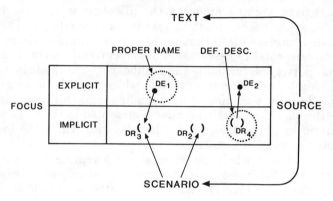

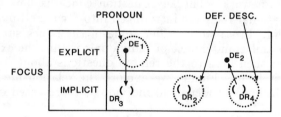

FIGURE 22.6. A schematic representation of the explicit/implicit focus model illustrating in (A) how Discourse Entities (DE_n) and Discourse Roles (DR_n) may be
introduced, and in (B) how they are accessed by different referential expressions.

The first type is associated with the use and interpretation of expressions like *few* and *only a few*. Moxey and Sanford (1987) have recently
demonstrated that these expressions can have the interesting effect of
focusing the reader's attention on discourse entities not actually referred
to by the noun phrase containing the quantifier. Consider, for instance,
your response to two slightly different ways a car salesperson might answer the question, "How reliable are the cars you sell?"

(a) A few of our cars break down within the first year of purchase.
(b) Few of our cars break down within the first year of purchase.

Most prospective buyers would be much happier to hear Sentence (b)
than Sentence (a). Yet in both cases the subject noun phrase actually
denotes the same proportion of cars – that is, if you ask subjects to

judge what proportion of a set X is denoted by *few X* they give much the same answer as for *a few X*. Moxey and Sanford argued that the difference is in the way the two expressions focus our attention. *Few of our cars . . .* focuses attention on the compliment subset of the cars denoted – the ones that do not break down – whereas *A few of our cars . . .* focuses attention on the subset of cars actually referred to – the ones which break down.

In line with this focusing effect, Moxey and Sanford found evidence that readers would regularly assign the compliment subset interpretation to a subsequent pronoun. To illustrate this, consider the difference between:

(c) Few MPs attended the meeting. They went to a film instead.
(d) ?? A few MPs attended the meeting. They went to a film instead.

In Sentence (c) the pronoun naturally attaches to an antecedent set of individuals not explicitly referred to in the prior text, whereas in Sentence (d) it does not.

Thus, certain quantified noun phrases can have the effect of focusing attention on antecedents that have not strictly been referred to in the context. A similar type of thing happens with the use of quantified adverbials, as in:

Every week the teacher gives the best pupil a prize.
She buys them in the local supermarket.

Here, the plural pronoun picks out an antecedent set not strictly introduced by the noun-phrase *a prize*. Again it seems that this type of construction is sufficient to focus attention on the set of prizes that are involved in the the iterated event described in the context.

Such examples would suggest that discourse referents can enter explicit focus both as a result of explicit mention in the text and, on special occasions, as an indirect consequence of interpreting certain forms of quantified expression. However, this latter type of introduction by implication does not seem to be associated with our knowledge of particular reference situations or scenarios. It is not knowledge of MPs and meetings or teachers giving prizes that focuses attention on the implied antecedents in the examples cited, but rather the understanding of the semantic structure of the sentences in relation to the logic of events in general. When it is indicated that *Few Xs do Y* this seems to have the rhetorical effect of highlighting the implication that many Xs do not do Y. When it is stated that some event involving an *X* occurs repeatedly, this may highlight the implication that there may be several different Xs involved across the series of events. Thus, such introduction of particular entities by implication would seem to be quite different from introducing a new role through knowledge of a particular situation referred to. To this extent, these counter-examples do not threaten the distinction we have drawn between entity individuation in explicit focus versus role individuation in implicit focus. They do, however, rule out the alternative view that it is simply the ability to identify implied antecedents that differentiates fuller definite descriptions from pronouns.

These special counterexamples notwithstanding, focus on particular discourse entities does seem to depend in general on their having been explicitly mentioned, and this in turn makes felicitous pronominal reference possible. But beyond the simple question of how discourse entities may be introduced into explicit focus, there is the vexed question of their maintenance in the system. As we have already demonstrated, sustained focus on antecedents that have not been mentioned in the very recent text seems to be a function of how the entity was first introduced. Introduction of a character by proper name produces a more stable and long-lived representation. Why should this be so? It would seem likely that the effect is semantical. As Kripke (1972) has forcefully argued, proper names have the rhetorical effect of rigidly designating their referents. When you introduce an individual as "John Smith," he and only he retains this identification throughout the narrative. This does not mean that there is in actuality only one individual with that name, which is patently false, but it does mean that within any stretch of discourse the writer is effectively committed to the fiction of rigid designation. Such rigid designation with proper names is in stark contrast to the situation with other singular noun phrases and in particular what we have called role descriptions. Thus the description *the waiter* as used in the example cited earlier is clearly seen to identify two different individuals in the two consecutive sentences. Similarly the same individual may on different occasions in the same narrative fill different roles and so be identified by different role descriptions. Thus, role descriptions only have the effect of individuating entities indirectly through the situations in which they happen to enter.

From a referential point of view, a role is a means of anchoring individuals to situations and it is mainly through definite descriptions that this is signaled. Thus, to the extent that a descriptive noun phrase, whether definite or indefinite, may serve to introduce a discourse entity into explicit focus, this entity is role dependent in the sense that its existence in the representation rests on the relevance of that role in the flux of changing situations.

So let us briefly turn to the other partition of the focus system and the corresponding questions about how roles may be established and maintained and how the two systems interrelate.

Roles and Their Representation in Implicit Focus

Whereas discourse entity representations may ultimately be traced to explicit references in the text, role representations held in Implicit focus have their origins in the reader's knowledge of the situations referred to. So any role slot will only become available as a consequence of focusing on different aspects of this referent situation or scenario. As we have already indicated, such scenarios may be cued through the use of certain types of verbs that refer to complex situations affording particular roles, or more generally as a consequence of identifying stereotypic situations of which the events described form a part. Thus, any events that the reader treats as part of a more general scenario may be sufficient to focus attention on a given role. For instance, writing about a defendant questioned in the context of a court case scenario may be sufficient to focus attention on the role "lawyer" or "judge", which would then be represented as part of implicit focus.

However, it must also be possible for such roles to be established more directly by interpretation of definite or indefinite descriptions, even though they may not immediately identify a role in the current scenario. Thus, if we encounter a reference to "the policeman" in the context of a court case, this may force the setting up of the role "policeman in the case" even though this will have to be defined locally for the actual situation being portrayed. If no such role can be established, then there is no way of representing the significance of the character in the current scenario. But in such cases we would expect the reader to take additional time incorporating the new role into the current scenario.

Finally, we are left with the question of how representations in these two systems may be related to each other. In general, entities represented in explicit focus will be mapped into roles represented in implicit focus. Hence, even though an individual might have been introduced into the narrative in a completely role independent fashion by proper name, there is nevertheless a strong tendency for the reader to assign that individual to some situational role (namely, the schoolboy passage given in the introduction). In fact it is almost inconceivable that a reader would focus on some situation in which a main protagonist did not play some role, and there is some evidence that it is focused individuals who determine the situational roles that are likely to be represented in any scenario. Thus Garrod and Sanford (1988) have argued that the tendency to focus on only one key individual at a time may reflect the fact that the reader always has to adopt a single perspective from which to represent the scenario. Highly focused individuals are the natural origin for such perspective taking.

So there is some indication that the two types of representation are intimately bound together in such a way that the representation of text individuals drives situational focus. However, much obviously has yet to be learned about the relationship between character focus and situational focus in comprehension.

SUMMARY AND CONCLUSIONS

We started this chapter by making the argument that referential processes are central to any complete account of text comprehension, as reference is crucial in achieving a cohesive and coherent representation. But we went on to argue that referential processes in reading occur against a complex and dynamic representational background. At any point in the text readers focus attention both on the individuals being written about and the situations that they enter into. These two aspects of attentional focus afford two different ways of individuating text entities, one in terms of the identification of the particular individuals themselves and the other in terms of the roles afforded by the discourse scenarios.

Allied to the representational distinction is a claim about the essential difference in function of pronouns and fuller definite descriptions. We have suggested that pronouns have a privileged status as anaphoric devices for maintaining reference to discourse individuals, whereas other definite descriptions serve the more general function of identifying discourse roles. The two arguments come together in the proposal of differential access to two systems of focus, explicit and implicit.

This proposal is very much in the spirit of the recent situational approach to meaning (cf. Barwise & Perry, 1983). On the one hand, utterances are taken to impose constraints on the situation described. On the other, attentional limitations in the reader impose constraints on the representation of those situations and the individuals involved in them. The comprehension of text is then seen as a process that is constantly attempting to reconcile these two sets of constraints with each other.

REFERENCES

Barwise, J., & Perry, J. (1983). *Situations and attitudes.* Cambridge, MA: MIT Press.

Bosch, P. (1988). Representing and accessing focused referents. *Language and Cognitive Processes, 3,* 207 - 231.

Chafe, W. L. (1976). Givenness, contrastiveness, definiteness, subjects, topics, and point of view. In C. N. Li (Ed.), *Subject and topic* (pp. 25 - 55). New York: Academic Press.

Clark, H. H., & Sengul, C. J. (1979). In search of referents for nouns and pronouns. *Memory & Cognition, 7,* 35 - 41.

Cole, R. A., & Jakimik, J. (1978). Understanding speech: How words are heard. In G. Underwood (Ed.), *Strategies of information processing* (pp. 67 - 116). London: Academic Press.

Cole, R. A., & Jakimik, J. (1980). A model of speech perception. In R. A. Cole (Ed.), *Perception and production of fluent speech* (pp. 133 - 163). Hillsdale, NJ: Lawrence Erlbaum Associates.

Cotter, C. A. (1984). Inferring indirect objects in sentences: Some implications for the semantics of verbs. *Language and Speech, 27,* 24 - 45.

Ehrlich, K., & Rayner, K. (1983). Pronoun assignment and semantic integration during reading: Eye movements and immediacy of processing. *Journal of Verbal Learning and Verbal Behavior, 22,* 75 - 87.

Garrod, S., & Sanford, A. (1977). Interpreting anaphoric relations: The integration of semantic information while reading. *Journal of Verbal Learning and Verbal Behavior, 16,* 77 - 90.

Garrod, S., & Sanford, T. (1981). Bridging inferences in the extended domain of reference. In J. Long & A. Baddeley (Eds.), *Attention and performance IX* (pp. 331 - 346). Hillsdale, NJ: Lawrence Erlbaum Associates.

Garrod, S., & Sanford, A. (1983). Topic dependent effects in language processing. In G. B. Flores d'Arcais & R. Jarvella (Eds.), *The process of language understanding* (pp. 271 - 295). Chichester: Wiley.

Garrod, S., & Sanford, A. (1985). On the real-time character of interpretation during reading. *Language and Cognitive Processes, 1*, 43 - 59.

Garrod, S. C., & Sanford, A. (1988). Thematic subjecthood and cognitive constraints on discourse structure. *Journal of Pragmatics, 12*, 519 - 534.

Grosz, B. (1977). *The representation and use of focus in dialogue understanding*. Technical Note 15. SRI International Artificial Intelligence Center, Palo Alto, CA.

Haviland, S. E., & Clark, H. H. (1974). What's new? Acquiring new information as a process in comprehension. *Journal of Verbal Learning and Verbal Behavior, 13*, 512 - 521.

Just, M. A., & Carpenter, P. A. (1980). A theory of reading: From eye fixations to comprehension. *Psychological Review, 87*, 329 - 354.

Karmiloff-Smith, A. (1980). Psychological processes underlying pronominalization and nonpronominalization in children's connected discourse. In J. Kreiman & A. E. Ojeda (Eds.), *Papers from the parasession on pronouns and anaphors* (pp. 231 - 250). Chicago: Chicago Linguistics Society.

Kintsch, W., & Van Dijk, T. (1978). Toward a model of text comprehension and production. *Psychological Review, 85*, 363 - 394.

Kripke, S. A. (1972). Naming and necessity. In D. Davidson & G. Harman (Eds.), *Semantics of natural language* (pp. 253 - 355). Dordrecht: Reidel.

Marslen-Wilson, W. D., Levy, E., & Tyler, L. K. (1982). Producing interpretable discourse: The establishment and maintenance of reference. In R. J. Jarvella & W. Klein (Eds.), *Speech, place, and action* (pp. 339 - 378). Chichester: Wiley.

Moxey, L., & Sanford, A. (1987). Quantifiers and focus. *Journal of Semantics, 5*, 189 - 207.

Sanford, A., & Garrod, S. (1981). *Understanding written language: Exploration of comprehension beyond the sentence*. Chichester: Wiley.

Sanford, A., Moar, K., & Garrod, S. C. (1988). Proper names as controllers of discourse focus. *Language and Speech, 31*, 43 - 56.

Singer, M. (1979). Processes of inference during sentence encoding. *Memory & Cognition, 7*, 192 - 200.

23

A CONNECTIONIST MODEL OF TEXT COMPREHENSION

Noel E. Sharkey

University of Exeter

INTRODUCTION

In this chapter, I will present a connectionist model that characterizes a range of processes involved in text comprehension beginning with lexical access and ending with the memory output for simple schema-based vignettes. The aim is to unify findings from disparate areas within the study of text comprehension. These include sentence processing, word recognition, and memory distortion. The various modules of the model to date are shown in Figure 23.1, but, because of space restrictions, only three of the major components are detailed here. These are: (a) a knowledge net, in which individual propositions are assembled into schemata, (b) a lexical net, in which microfeatures are assembled into lexical entries, and (c) the interface between (a) and (b), which maps microfeatures in the lexicon onto propositions in the knowledge net. The description of the model is contained in three sections which corresponds to the three components. In each section, part of the model is outlined, current data which the model must address are described, and a simulation with its predictions are presented. Context effects on single words are divided into two classes: *lexical* effects and *propositional* effects. The empirical basis of this distinction is discussed in the second major section where the lexical component of the model is described. The propositional priming effects are modeled in the third major section.

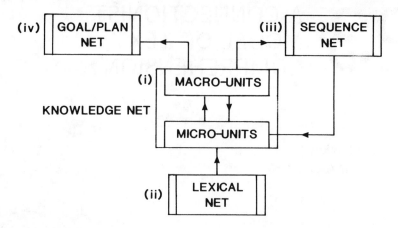

FIGURE 23.1. Modules of a connectionist model of text comprehension.

The two components of the model not described in detail in this chapter are the sequencer and the goal/plan net. The sequencer is important for language work such as paraphrase because, as would be expected in a parallel access memory, the proposition units are unordered with respect to temporal sequence. The sequential output of the system is handled by an external sequence module, which is controlled by the macro unit configuration (see N. Sharkey, 1989b, for details of the simulation). The other module, the goal/plan net, was designed to model data on goal/plan relationships (Sharkey & Bower, 1987). The goal/plan module binds characters to their appropriate goals. Later, when an action is presented to the module, it decides whether that action satisfies any of the active goals of any of the characters (see Sharkey, 1988, for details of the simulation).

THE ASSEMBLY OF WORLD KNOWLEDGE

Whenever people read a text, they are normally required to draw a number of inferences. For example, from the sentence, *All Britishers love a cup of tea in the afternoon and John was certainly British*, it can be logically inferred that John loved a cup of tea in the afternoon. In this example, the premises for the inference were explicitly mentioned in the text. However, many inferences are drawn on the basis of premises that are only implicit in a text. For example, consider the sentence, *Bob was having a wonderful meal in the restaurant until he noticed that he had forgotten his wallet*. It might be inferred from this that Bob was in trouble now and that he was probably really embarrassed. But where do the premises for these inferences come from? In this case, they come partly from knowledge about the events that routinely take place in restaurants. It is this knowledge that provides the reader with the essential premises: *people who eat in restaurants have to pay for their food before they leave.* Inferences based on such knowledge of the world are here called knowledge-based inferences.

There has been productive discussion in the literature about the nature of the inference process: whether it is automatic or strategic, whether it occurs at the time of reading or later when it is necessary (see Potts, Keenan, & Golding, 1988, for a discussion). However, this chapter is not concerned with the actual processes by which inferences are drawn but with the processes involved in assembling knowledge of the world in order to support the inference process and provide it with the necessary premises. In this section, evidence is reviewed about the structure and processes of knowledge assembly together with an examination of how the model handles the data.

Previous Research on World Knowledge

One way in which world knowledge has been modeled is in terms of preformed schemata that influence understanding (e.g., Bartlett, 1932). This notion received a new surge of attention when Schank and Abelson (1977) introduced it as the script concept. Schank and Abelson's discussion of this class of schemata has provided psychologists with a way of getting at the contents of world knowledge by suggesting a method of conducting normative studies. By constructing vignettes based on these norms, researchers have produced considerable evidence to suggest that during text comprehension, readers call upon groups of propositions or schemata to assist in understanding.

Experimentally, the script concept proved useful in predicting patterns of memory distortions. For example, in free recall, unseen actions from the script norms on which target stories were based were more likely to intrude in the recall protocols than other actions (e.g., Bower, Black, & Turner, 1979). Furthermore, unseen actions from the script norms on which a story is based are more likely to be falsely recognized than other actions (e.g., Graesser, Gordon, & Sawyer, 1979). These findings indicate that more than what is stated is remembered. It seems clear that other knowledge related to an event, but that did not occur, distorts memory of the event. But more importantly, the findings show the utility of the script concept for norm collection. From the norms it is possible to more precisely predict memory distortions for text. However, although this is useful, more is needed from a cognitive model than a means of collecting norms.

One problem with scripts is their lack of flexibility. In the original conception, scripts were essentially blocks of memory, preformed causal chains, which were loaded into active memory in response to input text. However, this was not entirely supported by the data. For example, one set of the intrusion findings from the Bower et al. study suggests that world knowledge is not in the form of prepackaged schemata such as scripts (Schank & Abelson, 1977). The Bower et al. data indicate that there are confusions among scripts that contain similar actions; therefore, actions from one script may be shared with another.

Schank (1982) responded partially to these data by developing the notion of memory organization packages that functioned to assemble something like the old script. However, even though the new system is dynamic, it still has some of the shortcomings of the older systems. For example, the structures are still prepackaged and will ignore input that is not consistent with them. Furthermore, as more detailed psychological research has been conducted, it has become clear that scripts are too limited to make the kind of processing predictions that are required. It is difficult to make empirical predictions except at the gross level of "do we have things like these in our memory and do they affect memory performance?" More detailed work on the processing of text is not explained.

A number of studies have shown that the reading time for sentences is reduced when they are preceded by materials based on script norms (e.g., Bower et al., 1979; den Uyl & van Oostendorp, 1980; Haberlandt & Bingham, 1984). These findings can be broadly predicted by the script account because the preformed causal relations in the script facilitated the process of drawing the necessary inferences to integrate the meanings of successive sentences. However, the script account cannot be used to generate more detailed predictions about where in the processing chain the facilitation occurs, for example, at the word, clause, or sentence level. This problem became clear when Sharkey and Sharkey (1987b) presented subjects with sentences split into different frames such that subject button presses initiated a new frame on a Video Display Unit (VDU). They found that schema-based priming had a greater effect on the ends of sentences than any other part of the sentence for example, clause boundaries. However, they also found evidence of inhibition/priming for words at the beginnings of sentences. The script account has no useful comment on this finding.

The results from word priming studies are even more problematic for the script account. For example, *yes* responses in a lexical decision following a script-based text are fastest when the target word is from the script norms on which the vignette was based (Sharkey & Mitchell, 1985). This is a robust finding and has been used to find out more about memory activity subsequent to reading a schema-based vignette. For example, (a) the priming which originates from reading a schema-based story *sustains* over three neutral sentences (Sharkey & Mitchell, 1985) and across five unrelated lexical decisions (A. Sharkey, 1988). (b) Priming of words by schemata appears to be activated and deactivated by control cues from the text (Sharkey & Mitchell, 1985). (c) For a short time, two distinct schemata prime at the same time (Sharkey & Mitchell, 1985). (d) Kintsch and Mross (1985) also found facilitated response time for lexical decision but claimed that it was necessary to impose a short delay between the schema-based text and the target word in order to obtain priming.

There are no mechanisms in Schank and Abelson's (1977) or Schank's (1982) account to accommodate the details of the sentence-processing or word priming data. Psychologists, then, have been left to devise their own processing accounts of their findings based broadly on the script concept. This has resulted in the development of a number of psychological models. For example, Sanford and Garrod (1981) proposed that world knowledge about events depicted in a text was held in a partition of long-term memory which they called implicit focus. This was contrasted with explicit focus, which contained the actual discourse construction. Sanford and Garrod proposed that the contents of implicit focus provide constraints on long-term memory search.

Other researchers have mainly used spreading activation accounts of their data (e.g., N. Sharkey, 1986; Sharkey & Mitchell, 1985; Sharkey & Sharkey, 1987a; Walker & Yekovich, 1987). The general mechanism underlying these accounts is quite similar: Related propositions are linked together in an associative network such that when one proposition becomes active it will activate its associates. As Sharkey and Mitchell suggested, the resulting configuration of active propositions can be thought of as an active network region. From this point the models differ slightly according to what data they are trying to explain and according to the proposed interaction with other modules in the overall account. However, none of these models gives a formal computational account to characterize the findings. Kintsch (1988) presented one of the most comprehensive accounts, but this is a mixture of computational styles (e.g., production systems, spreading activation, connectionist relaxation), which makes formal analysis of the processes difficult.

In this chapter, a different type of explanation is presented which is firmly seated within the connectionist framework and is based on the author's other connectionist work (e.g., N. Sharkey, 1989b; Sharkey & Sharkey, 1987a; Sharkey, Sutcliffe, & Wobcke, 1986). The new model is specifically designed to allow a formal global description of its computational properties. However, this model shares one important feature with the spreading activation models: There are only associative relations among the propositions. Unlike Schank and Abelson's (1977) and Schank's (1982) account, the schemata are not inferential, that is, there is no representation of causality. In the model presented here, causal relations are considered to be external to the knowledge net module and could be handled by a separate inference processor.

Dynamic Assembly of Macro-units

In the model presented here, schemata are not preformed entities; they are associated propositions that are assembled dynamically in response to textual input. At the centre of the system, as shown in Figure 23.1, are a number of propositional units called macro-units. These are so named because of their similarity to Van Dijk and Kintsch's (1983) idea of macropropositions. The macro-units are compacted representations of the lower level propositional representations. Their role is to categorize the input propositions, act as a plan for the sequencer, and interface the goal-plan module. They are the basic level of the system and may be thought of as localist summarization units.

Each macro-unit is represented as a single bit in a binary vector; when a unit is active, its corresponding vector element adopts a +1 state and when it is inactive, a 0 state. Schema assembly is then treated as a pattern completion problem. That is, when one or two macro-units are activated (a partial pattern), the system is required to activate all of the appropriate macro-units (complete the pattern). In this way, one unit will activate a pattern of other macro-units to provide, as it were, a model of the current setting: a schema. Note, however, that, unlike scripts, the schemata in the current model are self-assembling and may change in response to the input.

Each schema is installed as a minimum of an energy function E given by:

$$E = 1/2 \sum_{i \neq j} s_i w_{ij} s_j$$

where s_i is the activation level of the ith unit, w_{ij} is the weight between the ith and jth units.

Thus, schemata are treated as collections of macro-units that form stable states in the energy function (Hopfield, 1982). This provides a new formalism with which to discuss schema memory. In the past, highlighted knowledge has been discussed in terms of data-base partitioning (Hendrix, 1975) or focus (Grosz, 1977). It may now be considered as a point in an n-dimensional energy landscape created by the E function, as shown in Figure 23.2. Each learned propositional assembly is represented as a low point or basin in this landscape. Thus, the focus of the system is characterized as a point moving through energy space to relax on appropriate assemblages of knowledge.

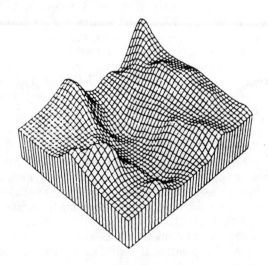

FIGURE 23.2. An n-dimensional energy landscape.

In the current system, whenever there is new text input, the current schema either assimilates it or the state of the system jumps to a high point in the energy landscape using the pulse mechanism (cf. Sharkey et al., 1986). Then Hopfield's (1982) gradient descent method is used to retrieve the schema which best fits the input constraints. Such a scheme is easy to implement on a parallel machine because an important property of Hopfield's formalism is that a given unit can locally compute the difference in energy a change in its state from 1 to 0 or vice versa will make. This is done simply by summing the total activity that a unit receives from all other active units in the network. The change in energy for a unit is given by

$$\Delta E_j = \sum_i s_i w_{ij}$$

The gradient descent rule is then simple. If the energy change results in a positive number, the unit adopts a $+1$ state, and if it results in a negative number, the unit adopts a 0 state. Eventually the system will settle in a minimum of the energy function (one of the attractor basins as shown in Figure 23.2) that is, a state that prevents the system from moving downward in energy regardless of a change of state in any of the units. When the system relaxes in one of these stable states it is said to have retrieved that state (which consists of all schema-related macro-units).

In order to install the schemata in memory attractors, the pulse mechanism was combined with an incremental least mean squares (LMS) or delta rule learning technique. A simulation of the model is described in detail in N. Sharkey (1989b). Briefly, a simple architecture was used which consisted of 25 interconnected macro-units and 25 buffer units, as shown in Figure 23.3. These were to be installed as five schemata with many shared macro-units. The buffer units were used to transfer the input to the macro-units and were themselves used as the ideal target for the learning mechanism (this is a form of autoassociation). The output values of the macro-units are compared with the values of the corresponding buffer-units to produce an error vector δ, where $\delta_i =$ (buffer-unit$_i$ – macro-unit$_i$). The change in weights between the macro-units is then given by $\Delta W = \eta \delta b$, where ΔW is the weight change matrix, η is the learning rate parameter, and b is the vector of buffer-unit values.

In Sharkey (1989b) it was shown that, with a small number of learning cycles, a set of macro-units can be installed as a schema in memory. By activating one of these macro-units, the schema which best fits the constraints will emerge as the most active pattern in the network. Using Hopfield's characterization of content addressable memory, the active schema can be described as the coordinates of a point in n-dimensional energy space, where n = the number of macro-units. With this formalism we can chart the state of memory as it moves from one stable state to another across the energy landscape. This movement from one schema to the next may be considered in the time dimension. Thus, it

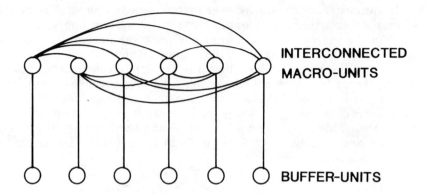

FIGURE 23.3. Architecture for interconnected macro-units and buffer units.

is possible to address the empirical findings that one schema-based sentence facilitates the reading speed of a second sentence associated in the same schema (e.g., Bower et al., 1979). It is assumed that one component of reading time is a measure of how long it takes the system to stabilize on an appropriate set of macro-units for the interpretation of the input sentence. Sentences containing propositions related to the current schema will necessitate little movement in the system; sentences containing propositions not related to the current schema will necessitate considerable movement of the system to a new schema. Other factors involved in the reading time measure are discussed next.

Proposition Units and Centrality

The next questions to be addressed are: (a) How are propositions mapped onto the appropriate macro-units? and (b) How does an assembly of macro-units activate propositions which best fit the contextual constraints of the input? As shown in Figure 23.1, the proposition layer and the macro layer interact with one another. In the first phase of processing, an active proposition unit may propagate activation to the macro-units until one of them passes a predetermined threshold. This sets the pulse mechanism into operation and the state of the system begins gradient descent toward the best fitting memory attractor. In the next phase, when the system has stabilized, activation is passed back down from the active macro-units to the appropriate proposition units. Thus, the schema pattern is also completed at the propositional level. It should be noted here that the matrix of weights between the proposition units and the macro-units replace van Dijk and Kintsch's semantic mapping rules: the macrorules. But of course the implementation here is less flexible and cannot do as much work as the macrorules.

One important psychological property which was incorporated into the present model was a typicality or centrality dimension. Galambos and Rips (1982) found that it takes less time to decide that a central proposition belongs to a routine schemata than a less central proposition. This is consistent with other work which differentiates the activation values of central versus peripheral propositions in the knowledge net (e.g., Bower et al., 1979; Walker & Yekovich, 1987). Centrality, in the current context, refers to the degree of importance of a proposition to its macro-unit (i.e., the degree of affect a proposition unit will have on its macro-unit and vice versa). For example, the most central action of the restaurant schemata would be "eating the food." Obviously, more important actions will have a high frequency of occurrence.

A Simulation of Propositional Pattern Completion

A simulation was run by first associating 72 proposition units with the 25 macro-units already established in the previous simulation. Delta rule learning was again used. Vignettes of single proposition sentences were input to the system such that each vignette was associated with one macro-unit (i.e., the macro-unit acted as the target for the learning). Centrality was built in by constructing vignettes in which some of the propositions were viewed more often than others. There were three frequency groups consisting of 25 high, 24 medium, and 23 low frequency propositions. The high frequency propositions appeared in all appropriate vignettes; the medium frequency appeared in one in three; and the low frequency appeared in one in six. Table 23.1 shows a vignette with the frequency classes and the target macro-unit.

TABLE 23.1

A Vignette and its Target Macro-Unit.

Frequency classes	Propositions
Medium	X went to the back of the line.
High	X stood in line.
Low	X moved forward.
Target: Stand in line.	

Once learning was completed the system was tested in four processing phases: (a) the input phase in which one or two single proposition sentences are presented to the system in the form of a vector of binary activations for the proposition units; (b) the initiation phase in which the states of the proposition units are propagated to the macro-units; (c) the assembly phase which occurs when one of the macro-units reaches threshold and the macro-units assemble themselves into a schema; (d) the completion phase where activation propagates back down from the macro-units to the proposition units across the same weights as the upward activation.

In two hundred test trials the system was presented with a partial schema pattern (two propositions from a single schema). On every trial it assembled the appropriate schema and always completed the pattern of proposition units which best fitted the constraints imposed by the partial input pattern. Table 23.2 illustrates a test run of the simulation. The four processing phases are shown for one vignette. The pulse operation is seen occurring for each of the three input propositions as each of these is associated with a different macro-unit.

An important point of the simulation was to find out if the dimension of centrality could be recreated by controlling the frequency with which particular propositions appeared in the vignettes during learning. This was successful. It turned out that, after the completion phase, the more central propositions were more active than the others. This effect is shown clearly in the proposition completion phase of Table 23.2. Overall, the average activation values for the three frequency classes after completion were: high 0.74, medium 0.22, and low 0.07. In this way, the continuous activity level on proposition units represents the degree of confidence of the memory that the proposition had been present.[1]

The Relation to the Data

Memory Distortions

The memory findings from recall and recognition studies are predicted in the model by utilizing the continuous values on the proposition units after completion. These values enter into a probabilistic formula ($p = 1/1+e^{-x}$, where x is a unit value) such that the higher the value of p the greater the likelihood of output. The precise formula needs to be put to empirical test; however, the model makes the qualitative prediction that propositions from the underlying routine knowledge sequence will be intruded into the recall protocols as shown in the Bower et al. (1979) and Graesser et al. (1979) data. Furthermore, as macro-units are shared by different assemblies we predict interference from one assembly to another (Bower et al., 1979). In addition, the model makes a further fine grained prediction that the more central actions will have a greater likelihood of intrusion into the recall protocols. This can be seen in Table 23.2, where a proposition that was actually in the vignette, such

---

[1] It should be noted that the completed propositions are unordered and have been arbitrarily printed by reading from left to right along the proposition vector. The memory output for paraphrase is handled by an external connectionist sequencer. This operates by using an assembly of macro-units as a contextual plan to drive the sequence. The interested reader can find the computational details in N. Sharkey (1989b).

TABLE 23.2

Output for a Three Proposition Vignette.

Input vignette $\longrightarrow$ Go to the bank, give check to bank teller, leave the bank.

Activation propagating to macro-units

Pulse operating

Active macro-units: Enter bank.

Pulse operating

Active macro-units: Enter bank, transact with bank teller.

Pulse operating

Active macro-units: Enter bank, transact with bank teller, get money.

Assembling macro-units

Stand in line
Enter bank
Write check
Transact with bank teller
Get money

Proposition completion

(The activation values are shown in parentheses)

Go to the back of the line (.22)
Stand in line (.75)
Move forward (.07)
Go to the bank (1.00)
Go into the bank (.23)
Write down the amount of money on the check (.74)
Write down the date on the check (.06)
Write signature on the check (.21)
Record the amount of money on the check (.06)
Go to the teller's window (.21)
Endorse the back of the check (.06)
Give the check to the teller (1.00)
Show identification (.06)
Receive the money (.75)
Count the money (.22)
Leave the bank (1.00)

---

as "give the check to the teller," will have a recall probability of 0.73. A proposition with high centrality, such as "stand in line," will have an intrusion probability of 0.68, and a low centrality proposition, such as "move forward," will have a probability of 0.52. These predictions have as yet to be investigated. It is not expected that the exact probabilities will be correct, but they allow qualitative predictions.

Recognition is handled in a similar way to recall. After reading a vignette, a single-proposition sentence is presented to the system and its value is summated with the value of its corresponding proposition unit. The new value can be judged to be recognized stochastically as in the probabilistic formula used in recall. This means that the system will sometimes falsely recognize propositions from the schema underlying the input proposition. The model therefore satisfies constraints imposed by the Bower et al. (1979) and Graesser et al. (1979) data. The model makes two further new predictions: (a) people should be more likely to falsely recognize propositions with higher centrality; and (b) if people are given a forced choice recognition test between an action actually seen and one from the underlying schema, they will be more likely to pick the correct proposition.

Response Time Measures

One component of sentence reading time is a measure of the movement of the system as it settles on an appropriate schema. If the system has already assembled a set of macro-units consistent with the input, there will be no movement in the system, and this component would not contribute significantly to the time measurement. If, however, the input destabilizes the system, there will be an increase in sentence reading time. These hypotheses are in keeping with the data on sentence reading times (Bower et al., 1979; den Uyl & van Oostendorp, 1980; Haberlandt & Bingham, 1984). In addition, the timing assumptions also partly account for the split sentence reading time data (Sharkey & Sharkey, 1987b). Other components which account for some of the reading time variance are discussed in the section on proposition construction and priming.

In summary, a system has been described that dynamically assembles appropriate knowledge to be used in text inferences. The model has been shown to predict the data from recognition and recall studies in such a way as to reflect centrality. In addition, the model, as described so far, captures part of the data from two of the response time measures: sentence reading time and split sentence reading time. These data are considered in more detail in the next section after the word-priming data have been discussed.

LEXICAL CONTEXT EFFECTS

Turning to the lower end of the system, details are now described about how meanings are accessed in the lexicon. Contextual effects are divided into two classes: those that occur within the lexicon (lexical effects) and those that occur postlexically (propositional effects). The class of effect is determined by the priming stimulus used. On the one hand, lexical effects are found when single-word primes are used, for example, *doctor* is used as the prime for *nurse*. On the other hand, propositional effects occur when the priming comes from textual materials, for example, the sentence, *Colonel Jones realized that he was late as he rushed into the station* is used as the prime for *bench*. The resulting effects are propositional in the sense that they rely on the construction (or activation) of related propositions. In the Colonel Jones example, *bench* is primed by propositions containing the reader's knowledge about stations that is, people waiting for trains sit on benches (Sharkey & Mitchell, 1985).

This distinction between the two types of effect may be maintained empirically as follows: The lexical effects are instantaneous (Neely, 1976) and can be disrupted by one intervening item (e.g., Foss, 1982; Gough, Alford, & Holley-Wilcox, 1981; Meyer, Schvaneveldt, & Ruddy, 1972; A. Sharkey, 1988). The propositional effects have a slow onset, i.e. they appear only after an unfilled delay (Kintsch & Mross, 1985) or a filled delay (A. Sharkey, 1988; Till, Mross, & Kintsch, 1988). In addition, propositional priming has been shown to sustain over a number of unrelated items (Foss, 1982; A. Sharkey, 1988; Sharkey & Mitchell, 1985), and is deactivated only when textual cues indicate that a new knowledge domain is in focus (Sharkey & Mitchell, 1985).

This is not an entirely new distinction, although much of the evidence is fairly recent and still coming in. For example, Foss and his colleagues (e.g., Foss, 1982; Foss & Ross, 1983) have suggested a separation between associative priming and discourse priming. They proposed that the short-lived effects were the result of associative priming whereas the sustained effects resulted from integrating the prime word into the discourse context. Although this has proved to be an extremely useful distinction, Foss did not provide a detailed process model to account for the findings, and so it has been difficult to take the distinction further. Kintsch (1988), on the other hand, made a similar proposal to Foss but fleshed it out with a more detailed model. However, the Kintsch model is parasitic on Norris' checking model to account for the word-priming effects. And, as explained in N. Sharkey (1989a), Kintsch's interpretation of the Norris model leads to problems with the data on frequency and stimulus quality. Finally, Sharkey and Mitchell (1985) separated the two types of priming in terms of their offset properties but suggested that both types were exerting their influence in the lexicon.

In the new model presented here, it is unnecessary to postulate any priming or top-down influences in the lexicon in order to account for single-word priming effects. In this section it is demonstrated how single-word-priming effects fall naturally out of the processes involved in moving through the lexicon. In the next major section, propositional priming is discussed as the postlexical process of selecting a proposition and integrating word meanings. Both initial lexical access and proposition selection are described in bottom-up terms. However, this does not imply any commitment to strict modularity. There is still significant evidence to suggest that top-down influences may be operating within the lexicon or prior to access (e.g., Blutner & Sommer, 1988; Glucksberg, Kreuz, & Rho, 1986; Keenan, Golding, Potts, Jennings, & Aman, in press; Tabossi, 1988). The evidence thus presents a muddy picture. The only thing that is really clear is that not enough is known about the exact properties of context and how they interact with parsing to be certain about the process of lexical access (e.g., Blutner & Sommer, 1988; A. Sharkey, 1988). However, regardless of these provisos, the effects of so called lexical or single-word priming are inviolably bottom-up in the present model.

Traditionally the lexicon has been considered to be a store of information about words for example, information about their meanings, syntactic class, orthography, and so on. In the current model, the lexicon consists of a set of units such that each unit corresponds to a microfeature.[2] When the lexicon is in a relaxed stable state, a short time after a word is input to the system, the activation on the lexical vector (i.e., the activation on the microfeature units) is said to be the appropriate lexical entry for that word.

The way microfeatures are used here leads to quite a different model than previous models of word recognition (cf. N. Sharkey, 1989b, for a detailed comparison). In those models, a concept, where mentioned, tended to be thought of either as a single network node or, similarly, as the contents of some addressed location in memory. The radical change here is that the concept associated with a word does not occupy a single location in memory. Instead, it is distributed across several different memory locations. Unlike the models discussed previously, each concept is composed of a number of microfeatures that represent elements of its meaning (see Sutcliffe, 1988). Meaning microfeatures may be thought of as propositional predicates (e.g., a set of microfeatures for *man* might be: is male, is tall, is strong, can't cook, likes women, etc.). In the present model, microfeatures are not simply like physical features (e.g., +male, +wings, etc.) but may represent activities or events that a word is involved in, or locations in which it may be found. Moreover, each microfeature may appear in several concepts. Thus, *doctor* shares many microfeatures with *nurse* – they are both persons and they have overlapping job roles. This distributed representation makes it difficult to maintain the old addressing metaphor because each lexical entry would occupy a number different addresses.

---

[2] This is similar to the notion of semantic features, but, as we do not wish to take on board all of the theoretical assumptions associated with feature theory, we use the new term microfeature here (Hinton, 1981).

Of course, there is more to the lexicon than meaning microfeatures. There may also be phonemic, syntactic, graphemic, and other microfeatures (e.g., Kawamoto, 1988). Meaning microfeatures are the main concern of the current model, but it is the graphemic microfeatures that are used to gain access to the lexicon.

Some Properties of the Model

Property 1: Each microfeature in the lexicon may be thought of as having an activation value. Thus a lexical entry may be characterized as a vector of microfeature activations. And, more importantly, each vector of microfeature activations may be uniquely identified as a point in n-dimensional lexical space, where n is the number of microfeatures in the lexicon.

Property 2: The lexical microfeature sets are learned using exactly the same method as described for schema access. That is, the microfeatures are autoassociated using the LMS technique in combination with the pulse mechanism. This network operates in a way similar to that of the content addressable memory proposed earlier for schema access. That is, given a partial specification of the contents of a memory, the system will stabilize in a state which represents a full specification of the contents of that memory. The transition from partial to full specification of a memory is characterized in terms of gradient descent in the energy (or goodness of fit) function E. In the lexical module, a partial memory specification is a set of graphemic microfeatures, and the full specification consists of the same graphemic microfeatures plus the set of meaning microfeatures on which the system stabilizes. The lexical representation for a word, then, is a stable state (or energy minimum) in a network.

Property 3: The relationship between the outside world and the lexicon in this model is via word units. These may be thought of as being like the outputs from McClelland and Rumelhart's (1981) interactive activation model. That is, in the simple simulation reported later, the output from the visual features of a word is represented as a single unit. The association between this unit and the graphemic microfeatures is learned using the delta rule. A property of this learning is that the weights for more frequently presented stimuli are stronger than the weights for less frequently occurring stimuli. A similar property was obtained in the centrality simulation described in the first section.

Property 4: The activation values passed between the visual features and the graphemic microfeatures are incremental and continuous. The activity on a graphemic microfeature affects the probability of it adopting the +1 state during an update in the lexicon.

Context Effects

The variable of most interest here is the distance that must be traversed in the lexicon to get from an initial state to a target state in the lexicon, where distance, d, is defined as the length between two points in n-dimensional lexical space. To make this clearer, imagine two vectors of microfeature activations in the lexical space L^n. Let these vectors represent the starting state of the system s and the required or target state r. Then the distance between the two points s and r is given by $||s - r||^{1/2}$, with length $||v|| = (v \cdot v)^{1/2}$. A major assumption of the model is that the greater the distance from an initial state to a target state, the longer will be the recognition time for a target word.

In this section, only single-word contexts of the *doctor/nurse* type is dealt with (other contextual priming is discussed in the next section). To model the experimental findings, a simulation was conducted for five pairs of related words. These were labeled *doctor/nurse*, *knife/fork*, *bread/butter*, *dog/bone*, and *foot/shoe*. This simulation was exploratory and so 10 microfeatures were arbitrarily assigned to each word in the lexicon. Four of these represented graphemic microfeatures and the other six meaning microfeatures. In addition, three of the meaning microfeatures for each word were shared with its associate, for example, *doctor* shared three meaning microfeatures with *nurse* (we do intend to gather real microfeature information for a more precise simulation of these ideas).

Once the learning had been completed (see Properties 2 and 3), the system was started in one of two initial states: either (a) a stable state resulting from the presentation of a prime word or (b) an arbitrary state resulting from the presence of a neutral prime (e.g., a row of Xs). A prime word activates a set of microfeature units and sets the system on a downward descent in the energy function until a stable minimum has been reached. This minimum will be the lexical entry for the prime word. In contrast, when the target is preceded by a neutral prime, the resulting state will be arbitrary (and it may not be a minimum of E). Now, when a target word is presented, some new graphemic units are activated, and the system begins to move from the current state to a state that best fits the input.

The model makes the correct time predictions for context effects because a target that shares a number of microfeatures with a prime (semantically related) will be closer to the prime than a word that shares no features (semantically unrelated). Thus, by definition, the state resulting from presentation of a related prime will be closer, in lexical space, to the target state than the state resulting from an unrelated prime. Figure 23.4 plots distance against energy for two pairs of words *doctor/nurse* and *doctor/fork*. For simplicity, binary activation has been used here and so the graph shows the energy of the system as it moves from the initial *doctor* state to the *nurse* and *fork* states. Note that *fork* is much further from *doctor* than *nurse* is and that there is a much steeper ascent and descent to reach *fork*. The circles indicate the state of the system after all of the graphemic microfeatures have come on and the pulse mechanism has been run. *Nurse* is still closer than *fork*.

This is a very simple and entirely bottom-up model of context effects that shows lexical priming as a measure of network distance from an initial to a decision state. The main factor in time to respond (e.g., lexical decision) is the relationship between the target and the initial state of the system. It is assumed that, overall, the target states are further away from the arbitrary neutral state than from the related prime states; but the target states may, on average, be closer to the neutral states than to the unrelated prime states.

Rate of Microfeature Activation

Before describing predictions arising from the model on the combined effects of word frequency, context, and stimulus quality, let us first look at how the rate of graphemic microfeature activation affects movement from the initial to the target state. At time t_0, just before presentation of the target, and therefore before any new graphemic units have been activated, the distance from the start state s to the required or target state r is $d = \|s-r\|^{1/2}$. At time t_1, the presentation of the target will activate the word unit vector v, and at t_2 this activation will be broadcast across the weights W using the limiting function $\text{LIMIT}[Wv] = f$, where f is the vector of new graphemic microfeature activations. The graphemic microfeatures are activated at t_3 by adding f to the initial lexical vector s. So the new state of the system, before update at t_4, will be s + f, and the distance will now be $d = \|(s + f) - r\|^{1/2}$. Thus, the magnitude[3] of the new microfeature activations, f, will affect the distance moved between the start state and the target states; the greater f, the smaller the difference between s and r. The process described in these four time cycles continues to iterate until a stable state is reached.

Stimulus Quality and Frequency Effects. Predictions concerning frequency effects rely on a property of learning to associate the visual features with the graphemic microfeatures. In delta rule learning, the weights for more frequently presented stimuli are larger than the weights for less frequently occurring stimuli. Now, as we showed previously, the distance moved by the system toward the target depends on the magnitude of f, which in turn depends on two factors: the structure of the weights W and the magnitude of word unit vector v. As frequency is encoded in W, when the stimulus quality in v is held constant, low frequency targets take longer to maximize activation on the graphemic microfeatures than do high frequency targets. In other words, the stronger the connection between a set of graphemes and their lexical representation, the greater will be the rate of microfeature activation. Thus, high frequency targets will be responded to faster than low frequency targets.

---

[3] For mathematical simplicity, it is assumed here that after initial activation, f does not change direction.

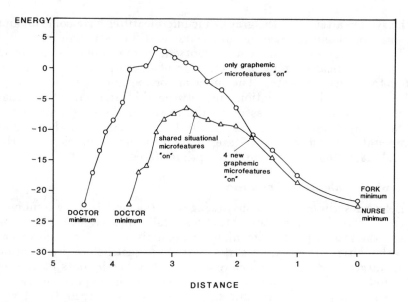

FIGURE 23.4. Energy as a function of distance for related and unrelated pairs of words.

The effect of degrading the quality of a stimulus word is simulated in the model by varying the magnitude of **v** while holding frequency constant. It should be clear from the previous analysis that the smaller the magnitude of **v** (stimulus quality), the smaller the magnitude of **f**, and consequently, the longer it will take to maximize activation on the graphemic microfeatures. Thus, the model predicts that degraded stimuli will take longer to recognize.

Combined Effects of Context, Frequency and Stimulus Quality. The model predicts that both stimulus quality and frequency will interact with context. This is because the closer the initial state **s** is to the target state **r**, the less effect the magnitude of **f** will have on the movement of the system from **s** to **r**. An initial state close to a target state will reach the target state before the microfeature activations have been maximized. Because of the nature of the update, the lexicon will in effect clean up the degraded stimulus. These predictions have been supported empirically. Becker and Killion (1977) and Becker (1979) found context by frequency interactions, and interactions of context and stimulus quality have been demonstrated by Meyer, Schvaneveldt, and Ruddy (1975) and Becker and Killion (1977). Moreover, as frequency and stimulus quality effects are brought about by changes in the magnitude of **f**, our model predicts an additive effect of stimulus quality and frequency. However, demonstrations have had mixed results. Some research has shown frequency and stimulus quality to be interactive (Stanners, Jastrzembski, & Westbrook, 1975), though the majority have found them to be additive (Becker & Killion, 1977; Norris, 1984).

It should be noted that the distance metric has parallels with the older location shifting model (e.g., Meyer et al., 1972; Posner & Snyder, 1975). Both models accurately predict that associative priming effects can be disrupted by the presentation of an unrelated item between the prime and the target (e.g., Foss, 1982; Gough et al., 1981; Meyer et al., 1972; A. Sharkey, 1988). In both models, an unrelated intervening item would move the state/location of the system to a new state/location. And it is this new state/location that would be the initial state/location before the presentation of the target. Therefore, priming of the target would be disrupted. However, because we use the computational power of a distributed representation, it is not possible, as in Posner and Snyder (1975), to speak of *the* location for a concept; it may share meanings with other concepts in more than one location. Instead, location is discussed more abstractly in terms of n-dimensional energy space and Euclidean vector distance.

In summary, it has been shown how a simple connectionist model can handle context effects and their interaction with frequency and stimulus quality. There are no hidden processes in this model and all of the associations are learned. The model provides an entirely bottom-up account of single-word priming effects. It does not rely on spreading activation to contextually related concepts, recognition threshold adjustments, plausibility checks, or shortlist search. Indeed, it does not require any special purpose mechanisms to handle context effects; the effects fall naturally out of the normal operation of the lexicon during access. If the prime word is contextually related to the target word, in the restricted definition of sharing microfeatures, the lexicon will have less distance to travel in order to stabilize on the best fitting lexical microfeatures.

PROPOSITION CONSTRUCTION AND PRIMING

In the treatment of contextual effects in the previous section, a distinction was made between lexical effects and propositional effects. This was based on a review that indicated that they could be distinguished empirically by their onset and offset characteristics. The discussion now turns to how the model works for propositional effects and how these rely on the construction of meaning elements greater than the word, that is, propositions. Before that, however, we give a description of the operation of the model and how it can account for the split sentence reading time findings (Sharkey & Sharkey, 1987b).

During reading, once lexical access has been completed, the set of lexical microfeatures are mapped onto the correct slots of a proposition.[4] This mapping is important here as it is the key to the model's

---

[4] The precise mapping will, of course, rely on syntactic information that has not yet been modeled. The next best thing is to hold syntax constant as Actor Action Object.

time predictions for priming beyond the lexicon. (The relation between the microfeatures and the proposition units is initially learned using the delta rule technique described earlier.) There are two time-varying properties of the mapping between the lexicon and the proposition net that may account for propositional facilitation. These are: (a) a selection phase, in which a unique proposition unit is found that most closely matches the constraints imposed by the lexical microfeature output (see Sutcliffe, 1988, for an alternative account of this process); and (b) an associative phase, in which the most active proposition unit is linked to the currently active lexical microfeatures. I will now discuss these phases in turn.

The Selection Phase

The job of the system in this phase is to propagate positive and/or negative activation from the microfeature units to the proposition units. The activation is incremental and continues to increase until a preset threshold has been reached by one of the proposition units (and the next process is initiated). This process of matching the lexical information with a proposition is time varying according to the current state of activation of the units in the proposition unit vector. For instance, if an appropriate proposition unit has already been activated via the macro-units as discussed in the first section, then it will reach threshold faster than other competing units that are not active. Empirical support is provided by the split sentence reading time findings of Sharkey and Sharkey (1987b). They presented subjects with short schema-based sentences on a computer screen one frame at a time (subject paced). Each frame was either the initial part of a sentence or the final part. A target word was embedded in either the first or second frame of the final sentence. For example, the target word *tip*, which was a strong schema-based word, appeared in one of the following sentences: *He then picked up \the tip* or *The tip\was on the table*. In the first position, *tip* was read no faster than a thematic substitute word *mess*, but faster than an unrelated word *hen*. In the model this is predicted because reading the short story would result in schema completion at the level of the proposition units. And there would be units among those activated which would be appropriate proposition units for *tip* or *mess*. Thus, selection would be fast. The word *hen*, on the other hand, would cause destabilization in the net as a new unit would have to be activated as its proposition. It now remains to explain the final position findings.

The Associative Phase

The second time varying process is an associative phase in which the most active proposition unit is linked to the currently active lexical microfeatures, that is, a proposition is constructed. Every time one of the proposition units reaches threshold, it is associated with the active microfeatures using the outer product learning rule to assign case structure (see N. Sharkey, 1989a). The idea is that the closer the currently active lexical microfeature set is to the microfeature set already associated with the proposition unit, the faster the association will be. This makes sense because the closer the two sets of microfeature activations are, the less weight adjustment will be required. In the most extreme case, the microfeatures already associated with the most active proposition unit will be in one to one correspondence with the currently active lexical microfeatures. Such a condition would result in no weight changes being necessary and consequently no time being required.

This time varying process fits well with the second part of the Sharkey and Sharkey (1987b) data. When strong schema-based words (e.g., *tip*) were compared with a thematic substitute word (e.g., *mess*) in the final frames of sentences, the former were read quicker. In the current model, this effect is demonstrated in the linking between the proposition unit and the microfeatures. A strong schema-based word will be a better fit to one of the active proposition units than a thematic substitute word. Therefore, the weight construction will take longer for the thematic word and will account for the differences in the response times.

Returning to the question of propositional priming effects on single words, there are three characteristics that the model must be able to account for: a delay, filled, or unfilled is required for the onset of the effect (Kintsch & Mross, 1985; A. Sharkey, 1988; Till et al., 1988); the effect sustains over a number of unrelated items or sentences (Foss, 1982; A. Sharkey, 1988; Sharkey & Mitchell, 1985); the effect has only been shown to be disrupted by indications in the text that a new knowledge domain is in focus (Sharkey & Mitchell, 1985). In the model, the onset of propositional priming is slow because, unlike lexical effects, it does not rely on specific word primes. Rather, it relies on the construction of a proposition. As already discussed, the construction of a proposition has two time-varying phases: selection and association. If a delay is imposed during reading, a proposition can be constructed and pattern completion within the knowledge net will occur, that is, proposition units related to the input will be activated. These proposition units will remain active until textual cues create a new assembly of propositions. Thus, there is a slow onset and a long sustain of priming. It only remains to be explained how the actual priming occurs. Both top-down and bottom-up variations are examined.

The Bottom-Up Account

In this view, priming emerges from the selection phase of proposition construction. That is, when a word is input, the system automatically attempts to select an appropriate proposition to later associate with the word's microfeatures. It has already been shown how this selection phase is time varying according to the current state of the knowledge net. Thus, the time taken to select the appropriate proposition unit will be reflected in the decision time for the target word. This is very similar to the account given earlier for the first part of the Sharkey and Sharkey (1987b) data. However, there is one problem here which needs to be ironed out. It concerns the question of how proposition selection can affect the time taken to recognize a word. As recognition entails finding the correct lexical entry, the lexicon must have some way of knowing that the entry has been found. Otherwise, the computation would continue in the lexicon until it relaxed on a stable state of microfeatures. Thus, there would be no facilitation.

The Top-Down Account

It is clear from the model that if people want to be able to expand or unpack a proposition unit, it is necessary to propagate activation back down into the lexicon. In this way they can decode a proposition. This may be useful, for example, in trying to understand a sentence when one of its words is unfamiliar. In order to do this, the system simply has to propagate activation back down from the proposition units to the lexical microfeatures. This is implementationally quite simple and may be used to explain propositional priming effects. In the case of sustained priming, an indeterminate number of lexical entries would be activated by the proposition units. This is more or less sympathetic with the position put forward by Sharkey and Mitchell (1985). However, the computer implementation of this model soon highlights some of the problems. For example, as activation may sustain for some time, and as the lexical microfeatures interact with one another, the lexicon would be in a continually changing and muddled state. Obviously, the computational messiness of such a model is not sufficient grounds for rejecting it. However, it must be considered as one way of comparing alternative accounts.

The Minimal Top-Down Account

The model favored here is a compromise position that brings together the best assets of both the top-down and bottom-up accounts. It is proposed here that, in the priming task, top-down activation from the active proposition units occurs only when the lexicon is destabilized. This happens whenever a new word is input and the system begins to move through lexical space to find the new appropriate minimum. If, at this point, there is additional activation in the lexicon from the proposition layer, it will increase the momentum of the lexical movement. In effect, the movement will occur in greater strides. Thus, the lexicon will be quicker to stabilize and this will show up in the decision times, as discussed in the last major section.

There is one further advantage to the minimal top-down account, which concerns ambiguity and sense selection. The time course of ambiguity resolution has been the subject of considerable psychological research (e.g., Seidenberg, Tanenhaus, Leiman, & Bienkowski, 1982; Swinney, 1979). Although this has not been central to the model presented here, in a related connectionist model, Kawamoto (1988) has shown that, because of their overlap in lexical information, homophones are close together in the energy landscape and separated by a high energy ridge. Now, before settling on the final meaning of a homophone, the system may move along the ridge between the alternative meanings. It should be closer to these alternatives than to any other minima. Thus, until the system has stabilized, both sets of microfeatures will be fairly equally available. Using the network distance metric developed in this chapter, the Kawamoto model would predict that, because of the closeness of both sets of microfeatures, both meanings of the homophone will be primed. However, soon after the system stabilizes, there will be facilitation only for words that share microfeatures with the stable configuration, that is, words related to contextually appropriate word meanings.

Kawamoto found that when there was no contextual information in the lexicon, the system would stabilize on the most frequent meaning of a word. However, when activation was added to the contextual features in his lexicon, the system settled on the contextually appropriate meaning. Thus it is possible to see the similarity with the model developed here and how disambiguation would occur. As suggested earlier, the momentum added by context moves the system faster toward the eventual stable state. However, during its movement, the state will pass close to related words including homophones. Thus, some of the microfeatures of the inappropriate sense of a homophone will be active for a while. While these microfeatures are active, if a new word comes in that shares some of them, that word will be recognized faster than unrelated words. In sum, it was shown how two time varying properties of the model address the current data on propositional priming. When these were examined in the light of some recent experimental results (Sharkey & Sharkey, 1987b), evidence was found to support the division of proposition construction into an associative and a selection phase. Moreover, three ways were shown in which propositional priming effects could be modeled in the system. A minimal top-down account was favored. In addition, the minimal top-down account was used, in combination with an analysis by Kawamoto, to explain polysemous word effects.

DISCUSSION OF THE MODEL

The goal of this chapter was to develop a unitary description for different processing accounts within the study of text comprehension. Work has been presented which attempts to uncover possible automatic or reflexive mental behaviors, ones which readers have no choice but to engage in with a particular language input. The idea has been to test the notion of automaticity by constructing computational models from which predictions can be generated and tested. This has entailed an examination of natural language from the perspective of memory. The new model is of the access to the necessary memory support for understanding. The simulations capture, in an integrated fashion, a range of phenomena from memory distortions through sentence priming to priming in word recognition. The psychological predictions of the model were derived in two ways. First, the memory output of the model, with the addition of a stochastic recall and recognition device, was shown to predict the usual pattern of false recognition, memory intrusion, and centrality findings. Second, the time-varying properties of the model were used to predict sentence reading time, split sentence reading time, and two classes of word priming.

One advantage of building a connectionist model of the text comprehension processes is that it carries with it a new set of tools for formal analysis of the characteristics of the model. These tools can be used to generate new predictions. For example, movement, distance, and energy were used to capture findings both at the lexical and the knowledge levels; an active schema or a lexical entry can be described as the coordinates of a point in n-dimensional energy space, where n is equal to the total number of potentially active units. With this formalism it is possible to chart the state of memory, in the knowledge net or in the lexicon, as it moves from one stable state to another across the energy landscape. This unitary concept can subsume Posner and Snyder's (1975) location shifting at the lexical level. That is, the connectionist metaphor can be aligned with the traditional metaphor by saying that the unique point in n-dimensional space is a location for a lexical entry and that the vector of microfeature activations is the address of that entry. Moreover, the same description of points in n-dimensional space at the propositional level can be used to capture the notions of implicit focus (Grosz, 1977; Sanford & Garrod, 1981), active network regions (Sharkey & Mitchell, 1985), scripts (Schank & Abelson, 1977), thematic subnodes (Anderson, 1983), and knowledge partitioning (Hendrix, 1975) (cf. Figure 23.2).

Finally, learning has played a significant role in the construction of our models. This has an advantage over the old semantic network research in that the links between units (or nodes) are not set by hand. Such setting can often guarantee that a model fits the data. In our model the weights were set using formal learning algorithms with well-known properties. Thus, we are forced to construct, a priori, the architecture and processing properties of the model. However, a drawback of the model is that no psychological predictions were made concerning the learning mechanism. The main reason for this is a paucity of appropriate experimental work in the area. However, research is underway in my laboratory on learning novel words in context and learning novel schemata.

In conclusion, the three components discussed here were all constructed from the same underlying principles. Thus they interfaced gracefully. The advantage is that the same mechanisms were used to explain phenomena that are generally treated as being from different areas. For example, it was shown how the same pattern completion mechanism can be used both in assembling microfeatures in the lexicon to form entries and assembling propositions in the knowledge net to form schemata. It is therefore possible to abstract the particular process mechanism from the content on which it is operating and give a more general account. Nonetheless, the exploration has only begun on the utility of possible descriptions and analyses within the formal structure of the model.

ACKNOWLEDGMENTS

I would like to thank Amanda Sharkey for incisive comments on earlier versions of this chapter, Richard Sutcliffe and Wayne Wobcke for their cooperation on earlier versions of the Schema modeling; David Balota for helpful comments, and the ESRC (Grant No C 08 25 0015) for supporting the research.

REFERENCES

Anderson, J. R. (1983). *The architecture of cognition.* Cambridge, MA: Harvard University Press.

Bartlett, F. C. (1932). *Remembering: A study in experimental and social psychology.* Cambridge: Cambridge University Press.

Becker, C. A. (1979). Semantic context and word frequency effects in visual word recognition. *Journal of Experimental Psychology: Human Perception and Performance, 5,* 252 - 259.

Becker, C. A., & Killion, T. M. (1977). Interaction of visual and cognitive effects in word recognition. *Journal of Experimental Psychology: Human Perception and Performance, 3,* 389 - 401.

Blutner, R., & Sommer, R. (1988). Sentence processing and lexical access: The influence of the focus-identifying task. *Journal of Memory and Language, 27,* 359 - 367.

Bower, G. H., Black, J. B., & Turner, T. J. (1979). Scripts in memory for text. *Cognitive Psychology, 11,* 177 - 220.

den Uyl, M., & van Oostendorp, N. (1980). The use of scripts in text comprehension. *Poetics, 9,* 275 - 294.

Foss, D. J. (1982). A discourse on semantic priming. *Cognitive Psychology, 14,* 590 - 607.

Foss, D. J., & Ross, J. R. (1983). Great expectations: Context effects during sentence processing. In G. B. Flores d'Arcais & R. J. Jarvella (Eds.), *The process of language understanding* (pp. 169 - 191). Chichester: Wiley.

Galambos, J. A., & Rips. L. J. (1982). Memory for routines. *Journal of Verbal Learning and Verbal Behavior, 21,* 260 - 281.

Glucksberg, S., Kreuz, R. J., & Rho, S. H. (1986). Context can constrain lexical access: Implications for models of language comprehension. *Journal of Experimental Psychology: Learning, Memory, and Cognition, 12,* 323 - 335.

Gough, P. B., Alford, J. A., Jr., & Holley-Wilcox, P. (1981). Words and contexts. In O. J. L. Tzeng & H. Singer (Eds.), *Perception of print: Reading research in experimental psychology* (pp. 85 - 102). Hillsdale, NJ: Lawrence Erlbaum Associates.

Graesser, A. C., Gordon, S. E., & Sawyer, J. D. (1979). Recognition memory for typical and atypical actions in scripted activities: Tests of a script pointer + tag hypothesis. *Journal of Verbal Learning and Verbal Behavior, 18*, 319 - 332.

Grosz, B. (1977). *The representation and use of focus in dialogue understanding* (Technical Note 15). Stanford, CA: Stanford Research Institute.

Haberlandt, K., & Bingham, G. (1984). The effect of input direction on the processing of script statements. *Journal of Verbal Learning and Verbal Behavior, 23*, 162 - 177.

Hendrix, G. G. (1975). *Partitioned networks for the mathematical modeling of natural language semantics* (Technical Report NL-28). Doctoral dissertation, The University of Texas at Austin, Dept. of Computer Sciences.

Hinton, G. E. (1981). Implementing semantic networks in parallel hardware. In G. E. Hinton & J. A. Anderson (Eds.), *Parallel models of associative memory* (pp. 161 - 187). Hillsdale, NJ: Lawrence Erlbaum Associates.

Hopfield, J. J. (1982). Neural networks and physical systems with emergent collective computational abilities. *Proceedings of the National Academy of Sciences, USA, 79*, 2554 - 2558.

Kawamoto, A. H. (1988). Distributed representations of ambiguous words and their resolution in a connectionist network. In S. L. Small, G. W. Cottrell, & M. K. Tanenhaus (Eds.), *Lexical ambiguity resolution in the comprehension of human language* (pp. 195 - 228). San Mateo, CA: Morgan Kaufmann.

Keenan, J. M., Golding, J. M., Potts, G. R., Jennings, T. M., & Aman, C. J. (in press). Methodological issues in evaluating the occurrence of inferences. In A. C. Graesser & G. H. Bower (Eds.), *The psychology of learning and motivation* (Vol. 25). Orlando, FL: Academic Press.

Kintsch, W. (1988). The role of knowledge in discourse comprehension: A construction-integration model. *Psychological Review, 95*, 163 - 182.

Kintsch, W., & Mross, E. F. (1985). Context effects in word identification. *Journal of Memory and Language, 24*, 336 - 349.

McClelland, J. L., & Rumelhart, D. E. (1981). An interactive activation model of context effects in letter perception: Part 1. An account of basic findings. *Psychological Review, 88*, 375 - 407.

Meyer, D. E., Schvaneveldt, R. W., & Ruddy, M. G. (1972). *Activation of lexical memory.* Paper presented to the Psychonomic Society, St. Louis, MO.

Meyer, D. E., Schvaneveldt, R. W., & Ruddy, M. G. (1975). Loci of contextual effects on visual word recognition. In P. M. A. Rabbitt & S. Dornic (Eds.), *Attention and performance V* (pp. 98 - 118). New York: Academic Press.

Neely, J. H. (1976). Semantic priming and retrieval from lexical memory: Evidence for facilitatory and inhibitory processes. *Memory & Cognition, 4*, 648 - 654.

Norris, D. (1984). The effects of frequency, repetition and stimulus quality in visual word recognition. *Quarterly Journal of Experimental Psychology, 36A*, 507 - 518.

Posner, M. I., & Snyder, C. R. R. (1975). Attention and cognitive control. In R. L. Solso (Ed.), *Information processing and cognition: The Loyola Symposium* (pp. 55 - 85). Hillsdale, NJ: Lawrence Erlbaum Associates.

Potts, G. R., Keenan, J. M., & Golding, J. M. (1988). Assessing the occurrence of elaborative inferences: Lexical decision versus naming. *Journal of Memory and Language, 27*, 399 - 415.

Sanford, A. J. & Garrod, S. (1981). *Understanding written language: Exploration of comprehension beyond the sentence.* Chichester: Wiley.

Schank, R. C. (1982). *Dynamic memory.* Cambridge: Cambridge University Press.

Schank, R. C., & Abelson, R. P. (1977). *Scripts, plans, goals, and understanding.* Hillsdale, NJ: Lawrence Erlbaum Associates.

Seidenberg, M. S., Tanenhaus, M. K., Leiman, J. M., & Bienkowski, M. (1982). Automatic access of the meanings of ambiguous words in context: Some limitations of knowledge-based processing. *Cognitive Psychology, 14,* 489 - 537.

Sharkey, A. J. C. (1988). *Contextual mechanisms of text comprehension.* Unpublished doctoral dissertation, University of Essex.

Sharkey, N. E. (1986). A model of knowledge-based expectations in text comprehension. In J. A. Galambos, R. P. Abelson, & J. B. Black (Eds.), *Knowledge structures* (pp. 49 - 70). Hillsdale, NJ: Lawrence Erlbaum Associates.

Sharkey, N. E. (1988). A PDP system for goal-plan decisions. In R. Trappl (Ed.), *Cybernetics and systems* (pp. 1031 - 1038). Dordrecht: Kluwer Academic Publishers.

Sharkey, N. E. (1989a). Fast connectionist learning: Words and case. *Artificial Intelligence Review, 3,* 33 - 47.

Sharkey, N. E. (1989b). A PDP learning approach to natural language understanding. In I. Alexander (Ed.), *Neural computing architecture* (pp. 92 - 117). London: Kogan Page.

Sharkey, N. E., & Bower, G. H. (1987). A model of memory organization for interacting goals. In P. Morris (Ed.), *Modeling cognition* (pp. 231 - 248). New York: Wiley.

Sharkey, N. E., & Mitchell D. C. (1985). Word recognition in a functional context: The use of scripts in reading. *Journal of Memory and Language, 24,* 253 - 270.

Sharkey, N. E., & Sharkey, A. J. C. (1987a). KAN: A knowledge access network model. In R. G. Reilly (Ed.), *Communication failure in dialogue and discourse* (pp. 287 - 308). Amsterdam: Elsevier, North-Holland.

Sharkey, N. E., & Sharkey, A. J. C. (1987b). What is the point of integration? The loci of knowledge-based facilitation in sentence processing. *Journal of Memory and Language, 26,* 255 - 276.

Sharkey, N. E., Sutcliffe, R. F. E., & Wobcke, W. R. (1986). Mixing binary and continuous connection schemes for knowledge access. *Proceedings of the American Association for Artificial Intelligence* (Vol. 1, pp. 262 - 266). Los Altos, CA: Kaufman.

Stanners, R. F., Jastrzembski, J. E., & Westbrook, A. (1975). Frequency and visual quality in a word-nonword classification task. *Journal of Verbal Learning and Verbal Behavior, 14,* 259 - 264.

Sutcliffe, R. F. E. (1988). *A PDP approach to the representation of knowledge for natural language understanding.* Unpublished doctoral dissertation, University of Essex.

Swinney, D. A. (1979). Lexical access during sentence comprehension: (Re)consideration of context effects. *Journal of Verbal Learning and Verbal Behavior, 18,* 645 - 659.

Tabossi, P. (1988). Accessing lexical ambiguity in different types of sentential contexts. *Journal of Memory and Language, 27,* 324 - 340.

Till, R. E., Mross, E. F., & Kintsch, W. (1988). Time course of priming for associate and inference words in a discourse context. *Memory & Cognition, 16,* 283 - 298.

Van Dijk, T.A., & Kintsch, W. (1983). *Strategies of discourse comprehension.* New York: Academic Press.

Walker, C. H., & Yekovich, F. R. (1987). Activation and use of script-based antecedents in anaphoric reference. *Journal of Memory and Language, 26,* 673 - 691.

24

ON THE NATURE
OF TEXT-DRIVEN
INFERENCE

Anthony J. Sanford

University of Glasgow

INTRODUCTION

The ubiquity of inferences in text comprehension makes the study of text comprehension look like a subset of the study of inference making. The import of inference is not in dispute. As the present group of chapters shows, attention has turned from mere demonstration of inferences to the more discriminating questions of which inferences are made at particular times during reading, and, perhaps to a more limited degree, how they are made.

Answering these questions turns out to be a difficult thing to do. There is the sheer difficulty of deciding what is the possible set of inferences that could be made over any given period of reading a discourse. Without some idea of what this set might be, an account of inference control cannot be complete. I may make taxonomic distinctions of various kinds based upon an analysis of what kinds of inferences appear to be possible. Indeed, one apparently simple distinction, used by McKoon and Ratcliff and by Keenan, Potts, Golding, and Jennings in the present volume, is to dichotomize inferences into those necessary for connecting the explicitly stated ideas in a text (necessary), and elaborative inferences, which merely fill out the picture. As with any taxonomic distinction, such a framework allows questions to be asked about which inferences are and are not made under particular circumstances. But our question must be whether or not any given distinction is useful. Indeed, Vonk and Noordman (this volume) use the term *necessary* in the sense of logic, to cover inferences that may be logically valid on the basis of a text fragment, including presupposition, entailment, and

515

conventional implicature. This sense of *necessary* is very different from the process-oriented usage of *necessary for coherence*, which Vonk and Noordman call coherence inferences and which they contrast with inferences that *contribute to completeness*. This distinction in usage understood, I will use the Keenan/McKoon/Ratcliff formulation to motivate the discussion. Putting aside the vexed issue of taxonomies, which is well discussed in the chapter by Vonk and Noordman, the root question is that of what determines which inferences are made.

One thing is clear. Linking operations are necessary even to get what is stated in a text joined together. The most well-worked of these operations is probably anaphoric reference. In the present volume, this issue is addressed by at least four of the papers and receives some attention here also. But the problem is that it is unclear how anaphoric relations are realized in the human processor. Furthermore, as I will be at pains to discuss later, the problem of how other coherence relations work is not at all clear. On the one hand, this is a theoretical question: When an inferred relation has been established, what kind of cognitive operation has taken place? On the other hand, it is a practical question: By what process can the presence of an inference be detected?

Equally clear is the fact that the inferences that I make must be in some way constrained, or so I might suppose. But dig a little deeper and it becomes unclear how I should elaborate the fact. Is it because of system constraints like computational effort? Such an argument loses some of its force now that researchers are once more taking parallel architectures on as possible realizations of processing. Is it because only relevant inferences are made? The problem with this answer is that relevance itself seems to be a very difficult thing to define and proceduralize. The present chapter embodies an attempt to give some of these issues an airing, especially in light of the other papers on the topic presented in this volume. Some original experimental data are also included.

NECESSARY AND ELABORATIVE INFERENCES
FOR TEXT UNDERSTANDING

This is perhaps the simplest intuitively appealing distinction. If only necessary inferences are made during reading, then computational effort will be minimized. Such a solution also appears to solve the relevance problem. In view of these attractive features, it is no wonder that the distinction has found favor. Closely related to the idea of the necessary is the distinction between forward and backward inferences. Both concepts may be illustrated by the following, taken from Keenan et al. (this volume). In Example 1, in order to understand what happened, it is necessary to infer that the vase broke:

1. No longer able to control his anger, the husband threw the delicate porcelain vase against the wall. It cost him well over

one hundred dollars to replace the vase.

In contrast, Example 2 can be understood without making any such inference, even though it is a likely event.

    2.   No longer able to control his anger, the husband threw the delicate porcelain vase against the wall. He had been feeling angry for weeks, but had refused to seek help.

In Example 2, the argument is that the inference would be merely elaborative and need not be made for the text to be understood. In terms of the forward/backward inference distinction, if with Example 2 the inference were drawn that the vase broke, as the first sentence was read, then one could say that a forward inference had been made. If, in contrast, the inference is not drawn with Example 2 and is drawn with Example 1 only when it transpires that the vase needed to be replaced, then it can be said that only the necessary inference was drawn (in Example 1), and that it was a backward inference. It has been argued by some that forward inferences might not occur at all (Corbett & Dosher, 1978; Singer, 1979). If this were true, then not only would there be an apparently simple way of defining what is a necessary inference (a backward inference which supports cohesion and coherence), but it would be true that only these are drawn.

Anaphora

Anaphora appears essential for cohesion and coherence and is widely recognized as an example of a situation demanding necessary inferential activity. The following serves our discussion:

    3.   John met Mary at the linguistics conference.
        He knew that his life would be bound to hers.

It is necessary to recognize that *he* and *John* corefer to the character initially denoted by the expression *John*. Much effort has been expended on the process by which such inferences are drawn, including the utilization of a wide range of cues that can serve to disambiguate logically ambiguous cases.

Work described by Garrod and Sanford (1985, this volume) suggests that anaphoric inferences of this type are made very shortly after encountering the anaphor, be it pronoun (as in Example 3), or fuller noun phrase. Other work consistent with this point of view is described later, and an expanded discussion is provided in Sanford (1989), where arguments are made in support of the view that anaphor resolution is a major, autonomous goal of the language processor.

However, even with anaphora, problems for this version of the necessary/elaborative distinction are soon encountered. For instance, in their now classic work, Haviland and Clark (1974) showed that the second sentence in Example 4 took longer to read than did the second sentence in Example 5.

4. Mary unpacked the picnic things.
   The beer was warm.
5. Mary unpacked the beer.
   The beer was warm.

The presumed inference that took the time is that *The beer* is part of *the picnic things*. It was assumed that beer was not part of the representation (the meaning of) picnic things set up on encountering Example 4, and that a time-consuming backward inference had to be made when *the beer* was encountered. There is ample demonstration of backward inferences of this sort being made. However, not all such inferences are made with equal ease. For instance, reading-time data show the speed of resolving pronominal anaphors as dependent upon a variety of variables, such as whether the antecedent entity is a main character or not (Garrod & Sanford, this volume; Sanford, Moar, & Garrod, 1988) and, more generally, the degree to which it is foregrounded (Hudson, Tanenhaus, & Dell, 1986, among many others). Thus, some of the work supporting inferences appears to be made before the anaphor is encountered. In a sense, this is elaborative, as there is no hard-and-fast way of the system knowing whether or not the appropriate reference will occur. However, it is reasonable to suppose that things that have been put into the forefront of the readers' attention will be the things to which the writer is likely to refer, so it should not surprise us that something like main characterhood might lead to processes paving the way to future anaphoric inferences. Indeed, it can be argued that all bridging inferences are a compromise between activity resulting from the current input (such as an anaphor) and the activity resulting from prior input. In light of these arguments, the clear distinction between the necessary and the elaborative becomes muddied.

Further examples of such forward activity is described in Garrod and Sanford (this volume), where a sketch of the scenario theory is given. Essentially, this account supposes that discourse serves to trigger situational representations in memory (as in Minsky, 1975). Entities that figure in these representations can then be referred to easily, as though they were given.

A practical issue raised by the scenario account is its apparent circularity. If an anaphoric reference takes no extra time under conditions that merely suggest an antecedent through a scenario, then it may be concluded that the antecedent is somehow available in the prior representation (i.e., as a scenario). But there are no independent means for checking what might be in a scenario. A good example of this problem comes from a comparison of the results of Singer (1979) with those of Garrod and Sanford (1982): Both concerned the ease with which references to implied instruments could be made. The Garrod-Sanford data fitted the view that inferences were supported by scenarios, whereas Singer's data suggested that the inferences were not made until forced by the introduction of the instruments. A subsequent experiment by

Cotter (1984), using both sets of materials, showed that the Garrod-Sanford and Singer results were replicable within the same study, ruling out spurious explanations. The difference appears to be that with the Garrod-Sanford set, the instruments are part of the meaning of the verbs (e.g., *key* is part of the meaning of *unlock*), whereas for Singer's verbs, this is not true. Cotter's experiments demonstrated not only that forward inferences were made with the Garrod-Sanford materials but also that a small set of inferences seemed to be made rapidly. In normal or self-paced reading, only forward inferences in the Garrod-Sanford set would be detectable. (A cautionary note should be sounded, however, about the idea of elements of the meaning of a verb being the only things contributing to forward inference, as similar results can be obtained with more complex scenarios [Garrod & Sanford, 1983, this volume].)

This somewhat retrospective introduction serves a number of functions. First, it shows that the necessary/elaborative distinction does not have a readily defined boundary, which must weaken its usefulness. Second, like any schema theory, the scenario account shows how one must be careful in defining what one means by an inference. In the Sanford - Garrod model, for instance, it is almost misleading to say that given *Jane unlocked the door* the inference *she used a key* is drawn. Rather, such *knowledge* becomes *accessible*.

Causes and Outcomes

Evidence for backward inferences with causal relations comes from a number of sources, including Myers (this volume) and in earlier seminal work by Keenan, Baillet, and Brown (1984) and others. For instance, Keenan et al. (1984) showed how reading time for a target sentence requiring causal integration with an earlier sentence increased with the complexity of the inferential chain that would be needed to fill the gap. This is a direct analog of the Haviland and Clark work on anaphoric bridging inferences. The question arises as to whether or not elaborative forward inferences are drawn, specifying the likely consequences of events and actions (Keenan et al.; McKoon & Ratcliff, this volume). Keenan et al. used the example reiterated in 6, where the inference "the vase broke" would conform to a likely event. Keenan et al. showed that the conclusion would seem to depend upon the means of detecting the inference (a critical issue). But there is another issue, and that is the sense in which a likely event is a likely inference. For instance, given Example 6, it would be deemed likely that the vase broke as a result:

6. Unable to control his anger, the husband threw the delicate porcelain vase against the wall.

But is this what the sentence is about? It is possible that the sentence is about the husband being unable to control his anger, a result of the topicalizing adverbial phrase which fronts the sentence. That is, the state of attentional focus brought about by the sentence is not necessarily about the vase. Furthermore, one would expect different sentences to have different foci. So it may be possible to highlight "breaking" by downplaying "anger control" through rewording.

7. The husband had been unable to control his anger, and he hurled the extremely delicate and very valuable antique porcelain vase at the brick wall.

Here, a great deal has been changed. Throwing the vase becomes a second conjoined sentence, and the initial adverbial is dropped. This alone may be enough to change focus. The verb is changed to *hurled*, which might suggest something more vigorous than a mild lob (cf. the effects of verb choice on eyewitness recollections; Loftus & Palmer, 1974). Stacking up intensifiers and adjectives must also highlight the importance of the object (Anderson, 1982; Sanford & Garrod, 1981, pp. 171 - 185). Even emphasizing that the wall was made of brick might have an effect. Now this is not to say that Keenan et al. completely blocked the possibility of the system registering that the vase probably broke, though it was by no means emphasized. Rather, the point is that unless the attentional focus initiated by a sentence is considered, just because an inference is plausible does not mean that it will be made or that it will be fully developed. On some accounts (e.g., McKoon & Ratcliff, this volume), the priming results of Keenan et al. could be taken as evidence for elaborative inferences being made that take a relatively long time to develop.

In summary, there is evidence for automatic elaborative inferential activity, and evidence that inferential activity apparently necessary for coherence establishment (anaphora, causal structuring) takes place too. I have argued that the degree to which an inferential activity is important (in focus) influences the speed and ease of backward inferences, as with anaphora. By extension, it can be argued that focus will influence forward, elaborative inferential activity, but there is less in the way of controlled investigation on this point. The presence of forward inferences reduces the utility of the necessary/elaborative distinction as stated at the outset. It certainly cannot be used as a procedural criterion for a system to use in controlling inferential activity. Basically, inferential activity should be a function of the structure of the text, of the choice of words, and of the topicalization devices used by the writer. It should not surprise anyone that elaborative inferences can be made; the questions are how the state of an inference relates to focus and how focus relates to language input.

INCOMPLETE PROCESSES

Interpretation, Cohesion, and Incompleteness

There are a number of examples which strongly suggest that processes necessary for the establishment of cohesion and subsequent coherence may be incomplete, and so care must be taken over what is meant by making an inference. For instance, answer the following question:

8. Can a man marry his widow's sister?

Most people answer in a way which indicates missing the simple fact: If you have a widow, then you are dead. Thus, the necessary process of interpreting the meaning of "the reader has a widow" was not made. Rather, the interpretation which seems to come through is something like "Can a man marry his deceased wife's sister", to which the answer is yes.

As a second example, consider the following, fuller text:

9. There was a tourist flight on its way from Vienna to Barcelona. On the last leg of the journey, it developed severe engine trouble over the Pyrenees. The pilot lost control, and it crashed, right on the border. Wreckage was equally strewn in France and Spain, and one question facing the authorities was where the survivors should be buried. What was the solution?

The solution is that there is no need to bury the survivors, which would be rather a bizarre thing to do, yet subjects do not typically realize this when the item is set as a problem-solving puzzle. Presumably, whatever computation occurs is not detailed enough to access the differences between the specifications on the role to be filled and the semantic properties of *survivor*. Erickson and Mattson (1981) suggested that it is a failure to get a match at all, rather than a failure to get a complete fit, which might trigger noticing the problem. Note, however, that as subjects are likely to argue about where people can be legally buried, the result of the mapping operations here is effectively to represent the survivors as the (dead) victims. Rather than claim that processing of particular relations is necessarily shallow, the claim is that processing can be shallow, but that whether it is or not depends upon the circumstances. For instance, consider the following version of the air disaster passage:

10. . . . Wreckage was equally strewn in France and Spain, and one question facing the local people was where the passengers who survived should be buried.

This version does not lead to misunderstandings on quite the same scale (Sanford, in preparation). One explanation is that passengers who survived, being a more surface-complex expression, affords a greater opportunity for more complete processing of the "still living" component of *survive* to occur. It is in the hands of the writer to highlight various relations through rhetorical skill.

These observations further reduce the utility of the necessary-elaborative distinction, as they show that relations which are clearly necessary for the coherence of a piece of discourse are not necessarily fully established. However, I might still argue that necessary relations are computed but that they are only partially worked out. In the case of the air disaster, the presence of a superficially suitable role filler might be enough to cause the processor to simply make a mapping between the filler and the role without an exhaustive check on adequacy.

Summarizing first with respect to the necessary/elaborative distinction: Some processes are more important than others for the integration of text into a coherent representation, although the examples given barely scratch the surface. Anaphora, role filling, temporal anaphora, and causal coherence are just some cases where the need for a link can be triggered explicitly in the text. So not only is there evidence for some kind of forward inferential activity; there is also evidence for incompleteness in backward inference making. Now this strongly undermines a straw-man rule of processing only necessary inferences. I have to weaken it and say that there are certain types of inferential activity that have to be carried out to support understanding, but that inferential activity over and above this can occur, and that the central activities may be incomplete.

Established Relations and Component Processes

If the processing of inferences is incomplete, in what way is it incomplete? Linguistic elements can fill roles that they do not really fit on the basis of partial matches. What kind of relation can be said to result? In terms of conventional AI, the role could be said to be an IS-AN-INSTANCE-OF relation. Yet this may not make much sense. With the airplane scenario, if one asks explicitly, "do you bury survivors?" subjects recognize how silly the problem was. An alternative to the full relation is that the pattern match produces the equivalent of a link, but one that does not have a semantic value (i.e., *survivors* is simply *associated* with the slot for patient). This is very different from the classical view of inference, of course, which would require the derivation of a predicate with a semantic value.

It is not just with the example given that this question arises, of course. It may be raised of any presumed inference. The following illustrates another case where it is not at all obvious which precise relation may be computed:

11. Paul wanted a new Hitachi radio.
    It was in Sears' window.

Although easily understood, it would be foolhardy to suppose that a *particular* relation has been established between what Paul wanted and what was in the window. The window could contain the very one and only the one which he wanted; a bunch of them, of which he wanted one; a bunch of them representing the class of radio of which he wanted some member, and so on. It could mean any of these things. Sometimes it might matter; oft-times it will not. I might argue that to the extent that it does matter, it would be signaled by a communicator or be settled by the receiver asking for clarification. The question is, how does one specify the relation which underlies one's initial understanding, as there surely must have been one, otherwise even local coherence could not have been established.

There are several possible answers that might be given, the two main classes of which are: (a) some specific pragmatically guided value is given to the relationship, so that an answer could be given to the question of what the relation is, or (b) the relation is not established at the level assumed in the previous discussion: rather, the relation amounts to something which is not specified, but which, if it were, would be some elaborated version of a class member relation. This verbal description is quite inadequate but is designed to indicate the possibility of a constrained but uninstantiated relation holding.

Sadly, there are no data to distinguish among these alternatives, although it may be possible to devise investigations based upon the speed of answering questions. It seems possible that under some circumstances, a particular relation could be forced, as in the following material where the likely uniqueness of the item could force one-to-one coreference:

12. John wanted a Louis XIV armchair. It was in the antique shop window.

However, such restrictions will not operate in every case, and I still need to develop techniques to assess relationships actually established and their semantic values. This question has received almost no attention, although it calls into question what inferences are in terms of content. Perhaps the inferences made in the examples given are little more than pattern-matched connections having no particular semantic value (in the sense of being a defined propositional predicate). This would be similar to the role-filler incompleteness problem described earlier.

Whereas definitive work on these problems may be hard to find, there are effects which might be and have been interpreted within the present framework. A case at hand is that studied by Sanford, Garrod, Lucas, and Henderson (1983), who investigated the curious effect of sentence pairs like the following:

13. Harry sailed to Ireland. It sank without trace.

Many people think that this has the property of sounding like it was Ireland that sank. One explanation is that when encountered, definite pronouns initiate an autonomous search for antecedent procedure, the outcome of which in this case is to find a fit between *it* and *Ireland*. The result is to give the impression that an anaphoric relation was asserted. A full argument of this type must be based on the idea that all of this happens before the information in the predicate of the second sentence is seriously analyzed, otherwise pragmatic considerations would rule out such a silly interpretation. But this assumption seems to founder in the face of the next example.

14. Harry sailed to Ireland. It seemed to be a beautiful day.

Here there is no sounds-like effect comparable with the earlier one (Sanford, 1985b). Of course, the pronoun here is not anaphoric, but under the account given earlier, the bonding should still occur, because its nonanaphoric nature could not be known until the predicate was processed. But if the predicate were processed before the assignment, there would not be a bonding effect with the first example. One solution (Sanford, 1985a, 1985b) is to suppose that some sort of relation is established between the pronoun and a suitable antecedent quite automatically, but that this relation can be thought of simply as a locus for the establishment of a relation with a defined semantic value. So, in the first case, the relation "anaphoric" is applied to the locus. In the second, it is not. It is the predicate information that brings about this further definition. So although a process that could support the development of a full-blown inference is initiated, it is only completed (in the sense of having a semantic value) when the predicate information signals this to be done. (Elsewhere, Webber, 1988, has used this type of argument, plausibly claiming a delay in the full interpretation of discourse deictics like *this* and *that*, on the basis of purely linguistic evidence).

Although these examples are by no means definitive, and the arguments by no means uncontentious, the aim here is to underline the point that because connections between parts of a discourse may occur, it does not mean that a particular semantic value can be ascribed to that connection. The situation is even more problematic if it is the timing of inferences that is at issue. One might presume that it takes time to make a full-blown (semantically interpreted) inference and that various connections of a less specified sort are made during this time (as argued earlier with the sounds-like example). In the context of anaphora, it has been argued elsewhere that experimental data provide evidence for the utilization of linguistic cue information pertinent to assignment as soon as the pronoun is encountered, but that the complete assignment is not made immediately (Ehrlich & Rayner, 1983; Vonk, 1985). Balota (this volume), asked the question of whether there is a magic moment for lexical access, the prevailing view being that this is not an appropriate way to characterize lexical access. The message of the present section is to beware believing that there is a magic moment for drawing an inference. Rather, there is a period over which activity supporting inference takes place. Indeed, in the pronoun comprehension literature, there is ample evidence that constraints on likely inferences operate continuously. Furthermore, what kind of end product occurs is far from clear: It need not necessarily be a fully instantiated semantic relationship.

The idea that inferences are the result of component activities is not in itself surprising. Indeed, McKoon and Ratcliff (this volume) made the point that certain elaborative inferences may be made relatively slowly, (consistent with Cotter's, 1984) view of forward inferences of instruments) and that they may be only partially encoded. The idea of partial encoding is not made clear, unfortunately. There seem to be two possibilities: that inferences are made fully, but are relatively inaccessible, or that only some of the inferential work has been done to produce a full inference. McKoon and Ratcliff were concerned with explaining how different tasks produce different results with respect to the apparent detection of inferences. They pointed out that different tasks have different characteristics, so that although a particular elaborative inference might not be detectable with a priming task, it can be detected with a speeded recognition task, so some encoding of the inference must have taken place. Presumably, it remains to be seen what partial encoding is, but relating task characteristics to assumed models of inferential activity is an obvious necessary step. This step is also recognized by Keenan et al. (this volume). Although they disagree with McKoon and Ratcliff regarding the detailed interpretation of the processes underlying the tasks of naming and lexical decision, their data, showing elaborative inferential activity to be detectable in priming tasks using lexical decision, but not with naming, are consistent with the view that processes that can occur rapidly will be less sensitive to relatively weak primes.

The use of priming tasks as an index of inferential activity is quite widespread, and notwithstanding the debate between McKoon and Ratcliff and Keenan et al., it is assumed that a priming effect can be taken as an indicator that an inference has been made. So, for instance, taking all of the appropriate controls into account, if a priming effect for the word broke is obtained with materials like Example 2, it would be assumed that an inference had been drawn (that the vase broke). The problem is that we cannot conclude any such thing. True, something to do with concept *break* might be activated, but whether a fully instantiated relation (BROKE, VASE) is being detected is another thing altogether. The same argument applies to any method that does not test for the whole proposition. Of course, such a relation may result at some time or it may never really emerge as a full-blown relation (a semantically instantiated relation?). It may be partially computed, in which case I want to know what its partial computation might be (simple activation?). So, although priming and related tasks can be used to detect inferential activity, they cannot necessarily be said to detect full-blown inferences. Perhaps this is uncontentious. But it does raise issues about the psychological formulation of cohesion and coherence, as inferences have traditionally been supposed to be complete predicate-argument n-tuples.

THE CONTROL OF INFERENTIAL PROCESSES

Let us return to the problem of the control of inferential processes. The argument put forward in the introduction was to the effect that inferential processes must be constrained. Taking the view that inference is to be equated with computational effort (e.g., Vonk & Noordman, this volume), it is reasonable to suppose that the number of inferences made at any time will be constrained. Because of computational limitations, a restricted number of inferences might be generated over any given time period. A second view might be that it is somehow pointless to make inferences that are not central (or relevant) to the discourse. In this view, inferential activity could be constrained by processes orientated toward certain key activities that are usually required for comprehension. Examples include anaphora and causality. A slightly different possibility is that the limiting of inference might be a function of the choice of wording on the part of the writer, bringing about various types of emphasis. Indeed, were this not the case, there could be no scientific foundation for style and rhetoric. The two views, based on limited resources and relevance are, of course, neither exhaustive nor exclusive. Each is given a cursory examination as follows.

Computational and Mental Resources

Drawing an inference utilizes computational resources, however those resources are realized within the system. For instance, the combination of premises (application of AND predicate), the further application of a rule of inference, and appending the result (at least another AND) underlies the most straightforward syllogistic inference (e.g., Wilks, 1986). The more inferences there are, the more operations there are, and so more resources are required. So, inferences cost effort, and if they are computed serially, they will use time, at least in proportion to to each inference. If they are computed in parallel, of course, they will not use time in this proportion, but they will have to be independent of each other. For these reasons, I might suppose that the number of inferences which can be made will be limited by the cognitive (computational) resources of the reader. However, we should remind ourselves that in psychology such a line of reasoning is full of problems.

For instance, it has been well demonstrated that if there is a rich background memory structure to relate facts to, then those facts are easy to remember (for expert player's memory for chess, see De Groot, 1966; for other game positions, see Eisenstadt & Kareev, 1975; and for memory for very long digit sequences, see Chase & Ericsson, 1981). Thus, at the memory level, it seems to be the richness of the background which supports memory, perhaps because there are more links between the thing to be remembered and existing memory structures. Should it take more computational effort to establish more of these links? This is an old issue and has received some experimental attention in the language setting (see Gentner, 1981, and cf. Kintsch, 1974).

Returning to the issue at hand, it would appear that connectedness correlates positively with memorability and with reading speed (e.g., Sanford & Garrod, 1981). Whereas at one level of description more computation must be involved, performance measures indicate less psychological difficulty. This kind of observation inevitably restricts arguments relating richness of connections and computational effort. The restriction may be that the brain is good at one kind of computation and poor at others. In the present context, it seems likely that the brain is poor at inference in the classic sense of making full-blown inferences but is well adapted to making simpler mappings between things. In the discourse context, the brain is good for mapping segments of discourse onto existing knowledge but is perhaps less good for generating novel inferential outcomes.

The distinction can be illustrated by the following: I can describe to you a type of problem in which you are told things like Fred is taller than Bill, Bill is shorter than John, and so on, and you recognize it as a prototype transitive inference problem. But unless you were expecting to be questioned, you would probably not have constructed the kind of inferential structure (mental model or propositional) to enable you to produce a transitive inference. I would argue that such a case shows that, for what is only a little more effort in terms of inference operations, there is a large difference in difficulty between having a representation for a transitive inference problem and knowing that a problem belongs to the transitive inference class. This serves only to highlight the fact that we know little of how to assess computational effort in terms that are psychologically meaningful. Indeed, I am not really skating on thin ice in saying this. It is undeniable that a regular AI program will be solving more inference problems in scene recognition than in solving a syllogism or material implication task, and this would be reflected in time to do the tasks or by any other resource measure. Of course, it is possible that the answer to this lies in the fact that many of the computations done in vision will be in parallel, that they probably use purpose-evolved neural apparatus in which biologically meaningful elements in the world are decoded by specific recognition systems. In general, the ease of recognizing the classes of problems and situations which one knows (cf., Sanford, 1987), compared to the slowness of overt logical inference, provides strong grounds for looking toward parallel pattern matching as a support for understanding rather than toward a uniform type of inference making. Once again, one can also question whether full-blown semantic relations are established during matching or whether associated loci for further computation, if needed, are established.

The argument that there are two kinds of inferential mechanisms, a fast pattern-matching facility and a facility corresponding to a slower, classical inference engine, is not new. In essence, the argument is basic to all schema theories of understanding (such as Schank and Abelson's, 1977, script theory) and was put forward in a psychological context by Sanford and Garrod (1981). Indeed, the process finds its natural formulation at a subsymbolic level, which studies of connectionism (see Sharkey, this volume) are beginning to make clear and which discourse psychologists would be unwise to resist. The control of operations of mapping, and the containment of possibilities, is assumed to be largely top-down, through the focus system, as described by Garrod and Sanford (this volume; Sanford & Garrod, 1981). Failures of matching are assumed to trigger more detailed analytical procedures that are both time consuming and that yield the equivalent of single inferences. The realization of scenarios within the a parallel distributed memory seems capable of overcoming the problems of knowledge modularity assumed by earlier formulations (cf. Rumelhart, Smolensky, McClelland, & Hinton, 1987; Sharkey, this volume).

Finally, there is a rather different sense in which computational factors may constrain inferential activity. Reading is usually a continuous process, and over quite small fragments of text I might argue that a number of types of inferential process are probably occurring. However, whether these processes actually get very far may depend upon what comes next. For example, if some feature of the text has a large effect at some stage, then it may weaken previous effects which were not so dominant. Such an account is appealing, but there is little evidence in the inference literature, although the sounds-like effects described earlier are being examined on this basis. Such an approach invites an analysis in terms of the devices used by writers.

Type- and Content-Based Inferential Patterns: Causality

The idea that inferential patterns may be based upon major types of activity that are likely to be important for comprehension is appealing and is similar to the idea of necessary inference. Anaphora and causality are two of the most well-worked candidates here. Sanford (1989) argued for processes of reference resolution being an automatic process triggered by appropriate linguistic cues. The present volume contains thorough descriptions of studies indicating the centrality of causal inferences (especially van den Broek, and Myers), as well as the material discussed earlier. Van den Broek presents an analysis of a sample text in which a causal structure in the form of a connected graph is produced and provides evidence that the analysis has psychological utility. The bulk of his presentation concentrates on the way in which causes are sought for focal events. The experiments he cites, and those discussed by Myers, support in detail the view that the establishment of causes, especially of the gap-filling variety, is a good candidate for a categorical activity.

Causality itself raises problems for selectivity, however. One issue is which events are likely to trigger a search for a cause. Clearly not every event will do this. The issue is complicated by the fact that states as well as events can trigger the seeking of causes. Let us begin with an example from van den Broek's own analysis. The story he uses is about a boy who wanted to buy a bike. At one stage, he asks his mother for some money, and she says "no, you should earn your own." Now, in the diagram of the causal structure, the antecedent cause was Jimmy asking his mother for money. The particular link in the graph here is as it is because the causal structure is analyzed from *the point of view of Jimmy.* His mother's remark, given the apparent semantic interpretation of the network, must be no more than "his attempt failed." A cause from his mother's point of view could be that she said what she did because she wanted him to learn about the value of money, for instance. (In this context, note the interesting results on reader purpose, described by

Vonk and Noordman, this volume, Experiment 3, which shows that the detail of a causal inference can depend rather critically on purpose).

With the van den Broek example, the question arises as to whether the processor would try to explain why Jimmy's mother said what she did. One possibility is that in simple stories like this one, the causal structuring would be built primarily around things that are relevant to the goals of the principal protagonist (Jimmy, in this case), and not around those of secondary characters. Indeed, this seems plausible in view of some recent evidence obtained by Sanford and Al-Ahmar (see Garrod & Sanford, 1988). The investigators discovered that some inferential operations were more readily carried out with respect to main characters than to secondary characters in simple narratives. To illustrate, consider the following simple description and questions:

15. Harry went into the cinema. The usherette showed him to a seat. The atmosphere was hot and sticky.

16. Did Harry find the atmosphere hot and sticky?

17. Did the usherette find the atmosphere hot and sticky?

People were more likely to answer *yes* to the first question than to the second, for which *don't know* was a popular category (see Garrod & Sanford, 1988). In an on-line reading time investigation of this, Garrod and Sanford attempted to test the theory that such *psychological atmosphere* statements would be interpreted not merely as setting information but as potentially relevant to the aims or states of the protagonists in the story. The Sanford and Al-Ahmar data suggest this and also suggest that the relevance to goal/state is biased toward the main character of a narrative, hence the bias in answers to the questions posed in Examples 16 and 17. The Garrod and Sanford (1988) study used a self-paced reading time paradigm to measure on-line aspects of this effect. The idea was to introduce main and secondary characters into a simple narrative, as in Example 15. An atmosphere sentence was presented in half of the materials that a given subject saw, followed by an action on the part of the main or secondary character that could plausibly be explained by the atmosphere sentence (e.g., *He/She mopped his/her brow.*) The results showed that when such an action was described of the secondary character, there was no effect on reading time of presence or absence of the atmosphere sentence. In contrast, reading time was slightly shorter for the main character case in the presence of an atmosphere sentence and was considerably longer than the secondary character case in the absence of the atmosphere sentence. One interpretation of these data is that if a relatively rare action is carried out by a main character (wiping his brow), and there is no a priori reason, then the processor is thrown, because it is set up to *integrate* the main characters' activities into a whole (Sanford, 1989). Secondary characters are not treated this way. Certainly, in novels, the actions of main characters are almost always explained rather directly, because intentionality is central, whereas secondary characters are not, and many of their actions are described to indicate dispositional properties. It appears therefore that the pattern of inferential processing is a function of character type.

From the point of view of narratives, this kind of selectivity makes sense and may indeed be a general principle. Inferences of all types (including elaborative activity) will be more thorough to main characters than to secondary characters. This amounts to mapping into background knowledge which serves the perspective of the main character. A knowledge-based account of understanding with this kind of restriction, or preference, would be recruiting single-perspective knowledge, which we would normally acquire as a result of our experience. (Of course, this raises the interesting question of what happens when two characters interact over a long sequence.)

Generalizing Beyond Causality

The idea that when events are encountered in discourse, causes or reasons for those events are sought as part of an automatic process, opens up a more general issue of what more general kinds of (inferential) activity might be triggered by text elements. The reality of this question is brought home by a variety of studies that try to establish what text elements bring to mind in the reader. One way that has been tried thoroughly over recent years is a simple question-asking paradigm, championed by Graesser and his colleagues (e.g., Graesser & Clark, 1985). He used a variety of stories and narratives and asked questions following statements in the texts. For instance, if a narrative contains the statement ". . . the dragon kidnapped the daughters . . .", it is possible to ask *why, how,* and *what-happened-next* questions. Furthermore, such questions can be asked immediately after the sentence is encountered or at the end of the passage. By such means, Graesser and his colleagues attempted to discover which inferences might be made. Of course, the inferences which appear to be made are restricted, yet the question of which inferences are actually drawn on-line remains unsolved, although Graesser and Clark (1985) did argue that those which are made are a subset of those unearthed by the question-answering process.

There are obvious problems with this approach. One is that by asking people questions, inferences may be being forced. The argument that inferences actually made, on-line, will be a subset of these seems like the obvious riposte, especially in light of the arguments regarding completeness. If inferential activity can be incomplete, then perhaps Graesser's observations show the distribution of processes that need not be complete. However, there is a flaw that is perhaps more serious. Many kinds of inferential activity do not seem to be foregrounded sufficiently to be revealed directly by the question-answering technique. For instance, the discovery that people think of John as being a schoolboy in Sanford and Garrod's opening example (this volume) can only be indirectly inferred from, say, continuations, and so the question answering procedure might underestimate inferential activity of certain types.

In particular, some types of presuppositional inferences are notoriously intractable to conscious access (e.g., Noordman, 1978).

Another approach being taken by Seuren and his colleagues (personal communication) is to analyze discourse as though it were designed by the writer to lead to implicit questions being asked by the reader. The writer then provides the answers. What is intriguing about this idea is that it explains intonation patterns used by people reading a text out loud. Van Kuppeveldt (1987) took a variety of texts and showed that when people read them out loud, their intonation pattern was the same as it was if an implicit question had actually been asked. This offers the potential of linking knowledge-based questions, topic comment signaling at a linguistic level, and inference management. It also suggests patterns of anticipation in reading that is not logically justified. In an implicit dialog model of reading, the writer must be actively trying to control the inference patterns of his readers and to set up the dialog according to his or her perception of the audience. This may not be news, but it has not really been taken seriously by psychologists interested in textual inference. However, as with Graesser's task, the results of Van Kuppeveldt might be tapping the most dominant, accessible complexes of inferential activity, and one should not construe the findings narrowly by supposing that only one satisfying proposition is being sought to fill a gap. Whether the hidden, presuppositional substratum of inferential activity can be tapped by such a method remains to be seen.

An interesting possibility is that at least some inferential activity is based on the detection of deviation from some norm (e.g., Kahneman & Miller, 1986; Schank & Abelson, 1977). So, any abnormal state of affairs will require some sort of inferential activity to reduce the strain of deviation. At a cognitive level, finding a cause is one way of putting this. But the argument can be made at any number of levels. At a physical level, emphasis by changing character fonts can lead to differences in subsequent interpretation. The abnormality (with respect to rest of the text) will play a role in any interpretative consequence of font shift. At a phrase-interpretation level, using adjectives (informative, with respect to noun which it qualifies) will tend to invite processes querying the significance of the adjectives (Anderson, 1982), and so on.

CONCLUSIONS

There are two extremes to the investigation of inferences. At the microscopic level, the issue is what constitutes an individual inference. Traditionally, a text has been thought of as a set of connected propositions, with inferences either filling in gaps or elaborating the structure. Either way, it makes sense to say that all inferences will be of predicate-argument form. However, it can be argued that some of the work required to produce an inference might get done without the complete inference being calculated. In using techniques to make claims about inferences one must be careful to separate *inferential activity* (that which supports the potential development of a full inference) from an *infer-ence* (a complete product). McKoon and Ratcliff's concern with relating tasks to claims seems to be a move in that direction.

The microstructural issue is important for at least three reasons. First, it is entirely possible that some relations (like referential ones) are not required at a highly specified level in order for communication and understanding to take place. (There is good evidence for this in dialogue, e.g., Garrod & Anderson, 1987.) Second, in assessing the time course of inferential activity during reading, it is important to separate completion of an activity from the recruitment of processes in support of that activity. This may be related to the third point. Of many budding inferences, only a few of them may become sufficiently developed to be serious contenders for the trophy of being full-blown inferences, yet the microprocesses may contribute to the overall pattern of focus.

At a much broader level, there is the question of the fullness of in-ferential activity. It was argued that inferential activity may depend upon a continuous checking of an indeterminate number of input sig-nals against norms for each signal type, where the norms might be deter-mined locally by the text or globally by more general knowledge-based expectations. This way of thinking about inference generation presents insurmountable problems for conventional AI modeling and seems to be naturally explicable within the connectionist frameworks now under in-tensive development. Norm violation is one thing that pattern-matching mechanisms are capable of spotting; equally important for the fabric of comprehension are the cases where matches obtain. Reference resolution seem to be reliant on such processes (e.g., Sanford, 1989), and evidence presented earlier illustrate some aspects of this.

One theme to which I have returned on several occasions is the rela-tionship between the writer's intentions in communication and the con-trol of inference. If anything, this is probably the most neglected aspect of inference control in reading. Traditionally, computational limitations have been thought of as being primary constraints on the patterns of inferences which obtain during reading. However, for many types of in-ferential activity, there is a weakness in such an argument. A very real alternative is that inference control is in the hands of the writer. So, although an inference might be highly plausible, it might be kept out of focus by the writer's choice of wording. By arranging things in this way, in advance, a writer might ensure that a less plausible inference is entertained. This suggests how communicative relevance is at the heart of inferential activity, without ruling out the view that inferential activity is limited by processing constraints. Budding inferences may never mature if they are swamped by some new, highly focusing, incom-patible input. Indeed, given the apparently insurmountable difficulties of computing a relevance index (cf. Sperber & Wilson, 1986; Wilks, 1986) to guide the choice of inference, such a data-driven limitation of inference seems to be a reasonable idea. Whatever the mechanism of inferential control, to ignore the role of rhetorical aspects of language (writer intention) is to ignore one half of the entire communicative act.

ACKNOWLEDGMENTS

Preparation of this chapter was supported by grant No. R000231492 to the author from the ESRC. Attendance at the conference upon which my commentary is based was kindly funded in part by the British Council. I am grateful to Pieter Seuren, Leo Noordman, and Wietske Vonk, with whom I have had many fruitful discussions, and I am especially indebted to Linda Moxey and Simon Garrod, who also read and commented upon earlier drafts.

REFERENCES

Anderson, A. H. (1982). *Text comprehension – The influence of temporal information on processing and reading rate.* Unpublished doctoral dissertation, University of Glasgow.

Chase, W. G., & Ericsson, K. A. (1981). Skilled memory. In J. R. Anderson (Ed.), *Cognitive skills and their acquisition* (pp. 141 - 189). Hillsdale, NJ: Lawrence Erlbaum Associates.

Corbett, A. T., & Dosher, B. A. (1978). Instrument inferences in sentence encoding. *Journal of Verbal Learning and Verbal Behavior, 17,* 479 - 491.

Cotter, C. A. (1984). Inferring indirect objects in sentences: Some implications for the semantics of verbs. *Language and Speech, 27,* 25 - 45.

De Groot, A. D. (1966). Perception and memory versus thought. In B. Kleinmuntz (Ed.), *Problem-solving: Research, method, and theory* (pp. 19 - 50). Chichester: Wiley.

Ehrlich, K., & Rayner, K. (1983). Pronoun assignment and semantic integration during reading: Eye movements and immediacy of processing. *Journal of Verbal Learning and Verbal Behavior, 22,* 75 - 87.

Eisenstadt, M., & Kareev, Y. (1975). Aspects of human problem-solving: The use of internal representations. In D. A. Norman, D. E. Rumelhart, & the LNR research group (Eds.), *Explorations in cognition* (pp. 308 - 346). San Francisco: Freeman.

Erickson, T. D., & Mattson, M. E. (1981). From words to meaning: A semantic illusion. *Journal of Verbal Learning and Verbal Behavior, 20,* 540 - 551.

Garrod, S., & Anderson, A. (1987). Saying what you mean in dialogue: A study in conceptual and semantic co-ordination. *Cognition, 27,* 181 - 218.

Garrod, S., & Sanford, T. (1982). Bridging inferences and the extended domain of reference. In J. Long & A. Baddeley (Eds.), *Attention and performance IX* (pp. 311 - 346). Hillsdale, NJ: Lawrence Erlbaum Associates.

Garrod, S., & Sanford, A. (1983). Topic dependent effects in language processing. In G. B. Flores d'Arcais & R. J. Jarvella (Eds.), *The process of language understanding* (pp. 271 - 296). Chichester: Wiley.

Garrod, S., & Sanford, A. J. (1985). On the real-time character of interpretation during reading. *Language and Cognitive Processes, 1,* 43 - 59.

Garrod, S. C., & Sanford, A. J. (1988). Thematic subjecthood and cognitive constraints on discourse structure. *Journal of Pragmatics, 12,* 519 - 534.

Gentner, D. (1981). Verb semantic structures in memory for sentences: Evidence for componential representation. *Cognitive Psychology, 13,* 56 - 83.

Graesser, A., & Clark, L. F. (1985). The generation of knowledge-based inferences during narrative comprehension. In G. Rickheit & H. Strohner (Eds.), *Inferences in text processing* (pp. 53 - 99). Amsterdam: North-Holland.

Haviland, S. E., & Clark, H. H. (1974). What's new? Acquiring new information as a process in comprehension. *Journal of Verbal Learning and Verbal Behavior, 13*, 512 - 521.

Hudson, S. B., Tanenhaus, M. K., & Dell, G. S. (1986). The effect of discourse center on the local coherence of a discourse. In C. Clifton (Ed.), *Proceedings of the Eighth Annual Conference of the Cognitive Science Society* (pp. 96 - 101). Hillsdale, NJ: Lawrence Erlbaum Associates.

Kahneman, D., & Miller, D. T. (1986). Norm theory: Comparing reality to its alternatives. *Psychological Review, 93*, 136 - 153.

Keenan, J. M., Baillet, S. D., & Brown, P. (1984). The effects of causal cohesion on comprehension and memory. *Journal of Verbal Learning and Verbal Behavior, 23*, 115 - 126.

Kintsch, W. (1974). *The representation of meaning in memory.* Hillsdale, NJ: Lawrence Erlbaum Associates.

Loftus, E. F., & Palmer, J. C. (1974). Reconstruction of automobile destruction: An example of the interaction between language and memory. *Journal of Verbal Learning and Verbal Behavior, 13*, 585 - 589.

Minsky, M. (1975). A framework for representing knowledge. In P. H. Winston (Ed.), *The psychology of computer vision* (pp. 211 - 277). New York: McGraw-Hill.

Noordman, L. M. G. (1978). Foreground and background information in reasoning. In R. N. Campbell & P. T. Smith (Eds.), *Recent advances in the psychology of language* (Vol. 4b, pp. 289 - 303). London: Plenum.

Rumelhart, D. E., Smolensky, P., McClelland, J. L., & Hinton, G. E. (1987). Schemata and sequential thought processes in PDP models. In J. L. McClelland, D. E. Rumelhart, & the PDP research group (Eds.), *Parallel distributed processing: Explorations in the microstructure of cognition: Vol. 2. Psychological and biological models* (pp. 7 - 57). Cambridge, MA: MIT Press.

Sanford, A. J. (1985a). Aspects of pronoun interpretation: Evaluation of search formulations of inference. In G. Rickheit & H. Strohner (Eds.), *Inferences in text processing* (pp. 183 - 204). Amsterdam: North-Holland.

Sanford, A. J. (1985b). Pronoun reference resolution and the bonding effect. In G. Hoppenbrouwers, P. A. M. Seuren, & A. Weijters (Eds.), *Meaning and the lexicon* (pp. 326 - 331). Dordrecht: Foris.

Sanford, A. J. (1987). *The mind of man.* New Haven: Yale University Press.

Sanford, A. J. (1989). Component processes of reference resolution in discourse. In N. Sharkey (Ed.), *Models of cognition: A review of cognitive science* (Vol. 1, pp. 113 - 140). Norwood, NJ: Ablex.

Sanford, A.J. (in preparation). Foregrounding indexed by noticing anomalies.

Sanford, A. J., & Garrod, S. C. (1981). *Understanding written language.* Chichester: Wiley.

Sanford, A. J., Garrod, S., Lucas, A., & Henderson, R. (1983). Pronouns without explicit antecedents? *Journal of Semantics, 2*, 303 - 318.

Sanford, A. J., Moar, K., & Garrod, S. C. (1988). Proper names as controllers of discourse focus. *Language and Speech, 31*, 43 - 56.

Schank, R. C., & Abelson, R. P. (1977). *Scripts, plans, goals, and understanding.* Hillsdale, NJ: Lawrence Erlbaum Associates.

Singer, M. (1979). Processes of inference during sentence encoding. *Memory & Cognition, 7,* 192 - 200.

Sperber, D., & Wilson, D. (1986). *Relevance: Communication and cognition.* Oxford: Blackwell.

Van Kuppeveldt, J. (1987). *Topic-comment determination: Explicit and implicit questions in discourse.* Paper presented at the Conference Beyond Assertion (4th International colloquium on the interdisciplinary study of the semantics of natural language), September 2 - 4, Kleve, BRD.

Vonk, W. (1985). The immediacy of inferences in understanding pronouns. In G. Rickheit & H. Strohner (Eds.), *Inferences in text processing* (pp. 205 - 218). Amsterdam: North-Holland.

Webber, B. L. (1988). *Discourse deixis and discourse processing* (Technical Report MS-CIS-88-75). Department of Computer and Information Science, University of Pennsylvania, Philadelphia.

Wilks, Y. (1986). Relevance and beliefs. In T. Myers, K. Brown, & B. McGonigle (Eds.), *Reasoning and discourse processes* (pp. 265 - 289). London: Academic Press.

IV COMPREHENSION FAILURES AND READING

25 EXPLAINING FAILURES IN SPOKEN LANGUAGE COMPREHENSION BY CHILDREN WITH READING DISABILITIES

Stephen Crain and Donald Shankweiler
University of Connecticut and
Haskins Laboratories

INTRODUCTION

For some years our research has had the broad aim of understanding the processes whereby the language apparatus, which is biologically specialized for speech, becomes adapted to accept orthographic input. Only with such basic knowledge in hand can we hope to discover why some children fail to learn to read, and only then can we meet the challenge of effective prevention and remediation. Early work of the research group at Haskins Laboratories centered on the role of awareness of phonological segments in learning to read in an alphabetic system. It soon became evident that children who are failing to learn to read have a range of problems in the phonological sphere. In addition to problems in segmental awareness, poor readers have difficulties in naming objects, in processing speech under difficult listening conditions, and they are slower and less accurate in producing tongue twisters. The co-occurrence of these problems suggested that the nature of the children's difficulty in learning to read might lie in the underlying phonological processes themselves (Liberman & Shankweiler, 1985; Liberman, Shankweiler, & Liberman, 1989).

If the fault is in phonological processes, poor readers would also be expected to have difficulties in working memory, as this form of memory relies heavily on coding based on phonological structure (Baddeley, 1966; Conrad, 1964; 1972). The memory limitations of poor readers have been noted time and again on a variety of measures that tax the phonological aspects of language processing. Some of these measure have been shown to have predictive value, singling out preschool children who will develop reading problems later. (By "poor readers" we mean those children who show a marked disparity between their measured reading skill and the level of performance that could be expected given their [normal] intelligence and opportunity for instruction. Our research compares performance by these children with age-matched controls – children who are proceeding at the expected rate in the acquisition of reading skills.)

The hypothesis that reading disability reflects a limitation in phonological processing is challenged by two findings that have emerged from the classroom as well as the laboratory. One is that some children fail to comprehend a sentence in text even when they manage to decode all the words it contains. A second challenge to a phonological explanation is the finding that some children who are poor readers fail to correctly comprehend certain sentences, in particular those with complex syntactic structure. These difficulties would seem to implicate language problems beyond the level of phonology, possibly originating in the syntactic component of language. Our recent research has taken up these challenges to the phonological explanation.

Because the question is so important, we have devoted much effort to exploring the possibility that some poor readers have underlying problems that are *not* phonological in origin. In this chapter we focus on poor readers' ability to comprehend spoken sentences. Although the findings are not wholly consistent – a few studies have failed to turn up evidence of reader group differences (e.g., Shankweiler, Smith, & Mann, 1984; Vogel, 1975) – there is evidence that good readers are significantly more accurate than age-matched poor readers in comprehension of spoken sentences with relative clauses, temporal terms, and adjectives with exceptional control properties (Byrne, 1981; Mann, Shankweiler, & Smith, 1984; Smith, Macaruso, Shankweiler, & Crain, 1990). The indications that poor readers do not always comprehend spoken sentences as well as good readers lend support to the possibility that limitations in phonological processing is only one of the barriers to comprehension.

It must be underscored that the comprehension difficulties noted in poor readers are typically restricted to sentences containing complex syntactic structures. From these observations it has often been inferred that the problem structures are absent or incompletely represented in the grammars of many poor readers (e.g., Byrne, 1981; Stein, Cairns, & Zurif, 1984). As each of these structures has been claimed to be late-emerging in the course of language development, it has been proposed that many poor readers are in some sense language delayed. Our research has sought to test a version of this hypothesis that holds that these poor readers suffer from a developmental lag in *syntactic* knowledge. We have called this the *structural lag hypothesis*.

The structural lag hypothesis has a great deal to recommend it. It explains why many children who experience difficulty learning to read also suffer in spoken language comprehension. It also explains why their comprehension difficulties are selective; poor readers should fail to comprehend those linguistic constructions that emerge late in the course of language development but should be the equals of good readers in comprehending early-appearing constructions. As these observations suggest, the structural lag hypothesis is tied to an assumption about the course of language acquisition and to an assumption about linguistic complexity. It supposes that certain linguistic structures develop before others, with the order of acquisition determined by the relative complexity of the structures.

The structural lag hypothesis draws support from some classical studies in language acquisition that find the late emergence of sentences with temporal terms, relative clauses, and adjectives, such as *easy* as in *The doll is easy to see* (C. Chomsky, 1969; Clark, 1970; Sheldon, 1974). In light of these findings from research on child language, the hypothesis can readily explain the observed differences between good and poor readers on spoken sentences involving these constructions. As we saw, comprehension problems are anticipated on late-emerging structures that are beyond the developmental level of poor readers.

It is important to recognize, however, that by allowing at least two basic deficits in poor readers the structural lag hypothesis abandons a unitary explanation of reading disability. The limitations of poor readers in comprehension of spoken sentences are seen to be independent of their deficits in analyzing phonological information. We have proposed an alternative hypothesis that attempts to explain the entire symptom complex of poor readers, including their difficulties in spoken sentence comprehension, as a consequence of deficient phonological processing. We call this the *processing limitation hypothesis* (see also Shankweiler & Crain, 1986; Shankweiler, Crain, Brady, & Macaruso, in press).

To explain how the difficulties in understanding spoken sentences might be derived from deficient phonological processing, a few remarks are in order about our conception of the architecture of the language apparatus. Within this framework it is explained how the failures of poor readers to comprehend sentences can be directly related to their limitations in processing at the phonological level. Then we turn to the laboratory to present evidence in support of the view that the differences between good and poor readers in spoken language comprehension are a manifestation of their differences in ability to process phonological structures.

COMPREHENSION AND THE LANGUAGE APPARATUS

We hold that language processing is accomplished by a biologically coherent system in isolation from other cognitive and perceptual systems. In contemporary terms, language forms a module (Fodor, 1983; Liberman & Mattingly, 1989). We extend this notion of modularity to differentiate subcomponents of the language faculty (Forster, 1979). We see the language apparatus as composed of a hierarchy of structures and processors. The structures include the phonology, the lexicon, syntax, and semantics. Each level of structure is served by a special-purpose processing mechanism, or parser. A parser consists of algorithms for accessing the rules used to assign structural representations, and it may also contain mechanisms for resolving ambiguities that may arise.

We assume that the transfer of information within the language apparatus is unidirectional, beginning at the lowest level with phonological processing and proceeding upward to the syntactic and semantic parsers. A further assumption is that, in the course of sentence processing, the entire system works on several levels in parallel, with the operations of the various components interleaved in time, rather than in strict sequence. This permits the system to function on-line. The responsibility of synchronizing the transfer of information between levels is relegated to the verbal working memory system. Given the prominent role that this system plays in explaining the symptom complex of disabled readers, it will be worthwhile to describe our conception of working memory in slightly more detail.

The Verbal Working Memory System

Along with other researchers, we envision the verbal working memory system as having two parts (e.g., Baddeley & Hitch, 1974; Daneman & Carpenter, 1980). First, there is a storage buffer, where rehearsal of phonetically coded information takes place. This buffer has the properties commonly attributed to short-term memory: It can hold linguistic input only briefly, perhaps just for a second or two, in the order of arrival, unless the material is maintained by continuous rehearsal. The limits on capacity of the buffer mean that information must be rapidly encoded in a more durable form, beginning with phonological processing, if it is to be retained for subsequent analysis at higher levels of the language apparatus.

The second component of working memory is a control mechanism, whose primary task is to relay the results of lower-level analyses of linguistic input upward through the system. To keep information flowing smoothly, the control mechanism must avoid unnecessary computation that would stall the rapid extraction of meaning. We would speculate that the language faculty has responded to limited working memory capacity by evolving special-purpose parsing mechanisms. The parsers organize information (and resolve ambiguities), which the control component of working memory then shunts upward to the next level of the system, allowing the previous contents of the parsers to be abandoned. Rapid on-line parsing, in turn, explains how individuals with drastically curtailed working memory capacity – capable of retaining only two or three items of unstructured material – are sometimes able to comprehend sentences of considerable length and complexity (Martin, 1985; Saffran, 1985).

To see what is most costly of memory resources, we have found it useful to consider situations that are amenable to straightforward transfer of information between levels (Crain, Shankweiler, Macaruso, & Bar-Shalom, 1990; Hamburger & Crain, 1987). In the simplest case: (a) each well-formed fragment of language code at lower levels of representation is associated with a single constituent of code at higher levels; (b) the fragments of code at each level can be concatenated to form the correct representation of the input; (c) the fragments can be combined in the same order that they are accessed; and (d) each fragment is processed immediately after it is formed, permitting the source code to be discarded. These four conditions form a straightforward translation process of sequential look-up-and-concatenation familiar in the compiling of programming languages. However, all these conditions are rarely met in ordinary language. And when they are not, the computations involved in reaching the target code, for example, the semantic interpretation of a sentence, could stretch the resources of verbal working memory.

We are now prepared to show how the various difficulties manifested by poor readers can be explained in terms of the functional architecture of language. A modular view of the language apparatus raises the possibility that a deficit at the level of phonology may be the source of the entire complex of language-related deficits that characterize reading disability. As the other features of the symptom complex can be seen as stemming from a phonologic-based deficiency, the task that remains is to explain how the difficulties that poor readers encounter in spoken language comprehension also implicate the phonological component.

Put simply, our account is as follows. We saw that the regulatory duties of working memory begin at the lowest level by bringing phonetic (or orthographic) input into contact with phonological rules for word-level analysis. In our view, this is the site of constriction for poor readers. One thing leads to another: A low-level deficit in processing phonological information creates a bottleneck that impedes the transfer of information to higher levels in the system. In other words, the constriction arises because in language processing the bottom-up flow of information from the phonologic buffer is impeded by the difficulties in accessing and processing phonological information. Therefore, all subsequent processes in the language system will be adversely affected. (Perfetti, 1985, presents a similar proposal.)

TESTING COMPETING HYPOTHESES ABOUT THE SOURCE OF COMPREHENSION FAILURES

Much of our recent research has centered on testing alternative explanations of the sentence comprehension problems of poor readers. Our research strategy has two components. First, we have investigated structures that are thought to emerge late in the course of normal language acquisition. Then, for each construction we designed a pair of tasks that vary memory load while keeping syntactic structure constant. If reading disability stems from a structural lag, then children who have reading problems should perform poorly on both tasks. But according to the processing limitation hypothesis, poor readers should have greater difficulty than their age-matched controls only in tasks that place heavy demands on working memory, whatever the inherent complexity of the pertinent linguistic structures. When the same test materials are presented in tasks that minimize processing load, poor readers should do as well as good readers.

The early emergence of grammatical competence by both good and poor readers follows, in part, from our adherence to the theory of Universal Grammar. Universal Grammar maintains that many basic organizational principles of linguistic structure are innately specified (N. Chomsky, 1965, 1981). In keeping with the precepts of the theory, acquisition of syntactic structures seems to be essentially complete by the time instruction in reading and writing begins. The early emergence of syntax is seen to be a consequence of the innate specification of many syntactic principles that either come prewired or are subject to rigid system-internal constraints on grammar construction (see Crain & Fodor, 1989, for a sample of empirical research). As syntactic structures are largely built into the blueprint for language acquisition, it follows that inherent complexity of grammatical structures, as such, will not be a source of reader group differences (Crain & Shankweiler, 1988). Poor readers will be at a disadvantage, however, in contexts that stress verbal working memory.

Comprehension of Temporal Terms

To illustrate how we have tested the competing hypotheses, let us consider one way that linguistic input can deviate from the simple look-up-and-concatenate procedure that is hypothesized to impose minimal demands on working memory. Recall that condition (c) of this best-case scenario would have the order of the linguistic input mirror the order in which it is composed into structural representations at higher levels. We will call a violation of this condition a *sequencing problem* (Crain, 1987). A sequencing problem arises in sentences containing temporal terms such as *before* and *after*. These terms explicitly dictate the conceptual order of events, but they may present problems of sequencing if the order in which events are mentioned conflicts with the conceptual order. This kind of conflict is illustrated in sentence (1). Note that the order in which the events are mentioned in the sentence is opposite to the order in which one would respond to the request.

1.   Push the motorcycle after you push the helicopter.

It is reasonable to suppose that sequencing problems exact a toll on the resources of working memory because both clauses must remain available long enough to enable the perceiver to formulate a response plan that represents the conceptual order. The conceptually correct response requires the formation of a two-slot template and a specification of the sequence in which the two actions are to be carried out. The information in both clauses must be held in memory long enough to put the first-mentioned action into the second slot.

There is evidence from research on language acquisition that this kind of deviation from the simple translation process is costly to working memory resources. Several studies have found that young children frequently misinterpret sentences like (1) by acting out their meanings in an order-of-mention fashion (Clark, 1970; Johnson, 1975). This response presumably reflects the simple translation process that children adopt as a default procedure for interpreting sentences that exceed their memory capacity.

An alternative explanation of the difficulties that children encounter with such sentences has been offered, however. It has been suggested that children's order-of-mention response to sentences like (1) reflects the absence in child grammar of structural knowledge that is essential to comprehension of sentences with temporal terms. This interpretation of children's errors is buttressed by the finding that they have difficulty with temporal term sentences like (1), which pose conflicts between order-of-mention and conceptual order, and not with sentences with similar meaning but with simpler syntax such as the coordinate structure sentence in (2) (Amidon & Carey, 1972).

2.   Push the motorcycle last; push the helicopter first.

However, we have questioned the assumption that sentences (1) and (2) are equivalent in meaning. Earlier studies which obtained differential responses to (1) and (2) failed to control for a presupposition that is present just in sentences like (1) (Crain, 1982; Gorrell, Crain, & Fodor, 1989). The presupposition associated with this sentence is that the hearer intends to push a helicopter. To satisfy this presupposition, the subject should have established this intention *before* the command in (1) is given. A procedure that allows subjects to establish in advance their intent to perform the action mentioned in the clause introduced by the temporal term was incorporated into a study by Crain (1982). Children are asked, before each test sentence is presented, to identify one object they want to play with in the next part of the game. The experimenter subsequently incorporates this information in the subordinate clause introduced by the temporal term. For instance, sentence (1) would have been presented only after a subject had selected the helicopter, which makes the use of the temporal term felicitous.

When young children were given this contextual support, they displayed unprecedented success in comprehending sentences with temporal terms. Thus, the mistake in research that resulted in high error rates was to present sentences like (1) in the null context, which fails to satisfy the presupposition inherent in the use of temporal terms. In the null context, un-met presuppositions must be accommodated into the listener's mental model of the discourse setting (Lewis, 1979). Compensating for un-met presuppositions requires the hearer to revise his or her current mental model (to make it match the model of the speaker). The process of revising one's model of the discourse is seen to highly tax processing resources (see Crain & Steedman, 1985; Hamburger & Crain, 1982). If this reasoning is sound, children's grammars should be exonerated from responsibility for the errors that occurred in research that failed to satisfy the presuppositions of the test sentences.

Returning to the comprehension problems of poor readers, we saw that according to the processing limitation hypothesis their performance should suffer appreciably in contexts that tax working memory. It seems reasonable to suppose, therefore, that poor reader's special limitations in working memory would cause them to have greater difficulty than good readers in processing sentences containing temporal terms *if they are presented in the null context*. However, the processing limitation hypothesis would anticipate that both good and poor readers would display a high rate of successful comprehension in felicitous contexts. The structural lag hypothesis, on the other hand, would anticipate the same differences between good and poor readers both with and without contextual support, because lightening the burdens imposed on working memory should not result in improved comprehension of a structure that is absent from a child's internal grammar.

We investigated these contrasting predictions in a figure-manipulation task in which sentences with temporal terms were auditorily presented to good and poor readers (Macaruso, Bar-Shalom, Crain, & Shankweiler, 1989). Our experiment was designed to exacerbate the processing load on both reader groups by including an additional prenominal modifier in half of the test sentences. As exemplified in (3), the main clause of these sentences contained complex NPs with an ordinal quantifier (*second*) and a superlative adjective. Adjectives combine to introduce added complexity to the plan that one must formulate in order to respond accurately to the sentence. The remaining test sentences contained simple NPs, that is, with no additional ordinal modifier in the main clause, as in (4).

3.   Push the *second smallest horse* before you push the blue car.
4.   Pick up the *largest truck* after you pick up the blue horse.

The stimuli consisted of 16 sentences with the temporal terms *before* and *after*. Four sentences were presented in which the order-of-mention of events was the same as the conceptual order, as in (3). In the remaining 12 sentences, the order of mention was opposite to the conceptual order, as in (4). Children encountered the test sentences in two contexts: one that satisfied the presupposition associated with the use of temporal terms, and one that did not (the null context).

As anticipated, poor readers performed less well overall than good readers in acting out sentences containing temporal terms. However, by satisfying the felicity conditions and thereby reducing memory demands, we obtained a significant reduction in errors for both groups combined. Moreover, the satisfaction of presuppositions benefited poor readers more than good readers. This lends credence to the hypothesis that, without contextual support, poor readers' limitations in working memory are exacerbated. However, the poor readers performed at a success rate of 82.4% when the felicity conditions were satisfied, even when half of the test sentences contained complex NPs. This calls into question the claim of the structural lag hypothesis that poor readers lag in their mastery of complex syntactic structures.

Further support for a processing interpretation of poor readers' comprehension difficulties comes from the finding that poor readers were more adversely affected by changes in NP complexity than good readers. The special problems that poor readers had with the complex NP sentences presumably reflect the fact that these sentences are more taxing on working memory resources, as discussed earlier.

Additional evidence of processing difficulty was obtained when we compared responses to the two types of sentences that present a conflict between order-of-mention and conceptual order. Notice that the presence of a temporal term in the initial clause eases the burden on working memory by indicating in advance that a two-slot template is required, as in (5). Here, the use of *before* in the initial clause delays execution. This contrasts with the corresponding sentences with *after*, such as (6), where the temporal conjunction is contained in the second clause.

5. Before you push the helicopter, push the motorcycle.
6. Push the motorcycle after you push the helicopter.

Based on the account of working memory that we have proposed, we would predict the sentences with *after* to be harder, because the subject has no warning that information should be maintained in memory while awaiting subsequent material. As expected, poor readers were least successful in responding to *after* sentences that presented a conflict between order-of-mention and conceptual order and no contextual support in the form of satisfied presuppositions. Good readers, on the other hand, were not as handicapped by the memory demands imposed by these sentences.

Taken together, the findings of the experiment by Macaruso et al. (1989) indicate that, as processing demands are increased, poor readers' performance involving temporal terms sentences is eroded much more than good readers' performance. Decreasing processing demands, either by satisfying the felicity conditions or by using less complex NPs, elevates performance by poor readers such that group differences diminish. In the best case, both reader groups perform at a high level of success.

Comprehension of Garden Path Sentences

Another way to address the question of a processing limitation versus a structural deficit is to examine the pattern of errors across constructions for each reader group. A processing limitation, and not a structural deficit, can be inferred if both reader groups reveal a similar pattern of errors across sentence types. Pursuing this research strategy, another study (Crain et al., 1990) asked how good and poor readers would respond to the kind of garden path sentences that are created when listeners follow a parsing strategy for resolving structural ambiguities, called *right association* by Kimball (1973) and *late closure* by Frazier (1978).

Late closure encourages listeners or readers to connect an incoming phrase as low as possible in the phrase marker that has been assigned to the preceding material. It seems reasonable to suppose that this parsing strategy reflects the functional architecture of the language apparatus, which has many computations to perform and little available space for their compilation and execution. Although strategies such as this may have evolved to enable the parser to circumvent the limitations of working memory, they may introduce new problems of their own, because the decision dictated by a strategy may turn out to be incorrect in light of subsequent input. Clearly, recovery from these so-called garden paths is possible only within the limits of working memory, because these limits determine whether the grammatically correct analysis is still available. Because sentences that tax working memory heavily have been found to present special difficulties for poor readers, they should be less able than good readers to recover from garden paths prompted by late closure.

We tested this prediction by asking good and poor readers to respond to several types of garden path sentences. In each of these, the parse favored by late closure tempts one to make an ungrammatical analysis, in which the extraction of the *Wh*-phrase violates a putatively innate constraint called *subjacency*. Subjacency establishes the boundary conditions on the movement of *Wh*-phrases in the formation of questions. Specifically, it prohibits movement over more than a single bounding node (NP or S in English). One consequence of subjacency is that *Wh*-phrases cannot be extracted out of complex NPs like those in the test sentences in this study, which were taken from Crain and Fodor (1986).

Three types of garden path sentences were created. These varied in severity of processing load. The subsequent examination of the error pattern by the two reader groups across sentence types was used to distinguish between the competing hypotheses about the source of comprehension difficulties in poor readers. The different syntactic constructions are illustrated in (7) - (9).

7. Prepositional Phrase (deep):
    What is Jennifer drawing a picture of a boy with?

8. Prepositional Phrase (distant):
    Who is Susan handing over the big heart-shaped card to?

9. Relative Clause:
    Who is Bill pushing the cat that is singing to?

Sentence (7) is labeled "deep" because the origin of the extracted *Wh*-phrase is a prepositional phrase that is embedded in an NP which is itself embedded in an NP. This contrasts with the "distant" case (8), in which there is only one level of embedding. Although the sentences are matched for length, we anticipated that distant prepositional phrase sentences would be easier to process than either the deep prepositional phrase sentences or relative clause sentences like (9). The depth of syntactic embedding in both relative clause and deep prepositional phrase sentences means that they deviate more than the distant sentences from the simple look-up-and-concatenate translation process.

On each trial, subjects were asked to listen carefully to a tape-recorded set of sentences that described a scene depicted in a large cartoon drawing placed in front of them. Immediately following the description, they were asked to respond to a question about some aspect of the drawing. For example, the context sentences in (10) preceded the test question (9).

10. Bill's father is waiting for Bill to bring him the cat. The cat loves to sing and has made up a song for his toy mouse.

The grammatically correct response to this question is "his father". The response "the mouse" is incorrect, because it represents an apparent violation of subjacency. The processing limitation hypothesis would argue that an examination of the pattern of errors across sentence types for each group may provide evidence that these errors are not actually violations of subjacency; instead, they are the result of the processing burdens these sentences impose on working memory. The structural lag hypothesis makes no definite predictions about the pattern of responses by good and poor readers for any of the sentence types presented in this experiment. It seems reasonable to suppose, however, that under this hypothesis we might anticipate a different response profile for good and poor readers, as these sentences incorporate exceedingly complex structures.

To reiterate, the processing limitation hypothesis predicts that both groups will manifest a similar pattern of errors across sentences of varying syntactic types, with poor readers penalized to a greater degree than good readers on sentences that are most costly to working memory resources (e.g., the deep prepositional phrase and relative clause sentences). This is exactly what we found. There was a general decrement in performance by poor readers, but both good and poor readers responded in a similar way to these different linguistic constructions (see Figure 25.1).

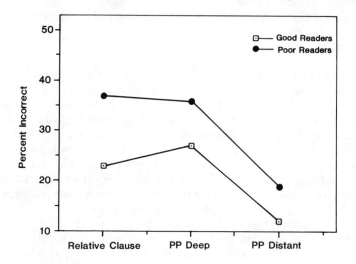

FIGURE 25.1. Percentage of incorrect responses to garden path sentences.

Detection and Correction of Ungrammatical Sentences

An experiment by Fowler (1988) deserves mention as another significant effort to disentangle structural knowledge and processing capabilities in beginning readers. Preliminary tests were administered to assess children's phonological awareness, working memory, and spoken sentence understanding. As in earlier work, there were clear-cut correlations with measures of reading. But in addition, children were compared on a grammaticality judgment task and a sentence correction task. The judgment task is presumed to place minimal demands on working memory, so it was used to establish a baseline of the subjects' structural knowledge for subsequent comparison with the correction task. The expectation that grammaticality judgments do not stress working memory is motivated in part by recent research showing that, despite severe memory limitations, agrammatic aphasic patients are able to judge the grammaticality of sentences of considerable length and syntactic complexity (Linebarger, Schwartz, & Saffran, 1983; Saffran, 1985; Shankweiler, Crain, Gorrell, & Tuller, 1989). These findings suggest that this task directly taps the syntactic analysis being assigned. In the correction task, subjects were asked to change ungrammatical sentences (taken from the judgment task) to make them grammatical. Clearly, correcting grammatical anomalies requires the ability to hold sentences in memory long enough for reanalysis.

According to the processing limitation hypothesis, both good and poor readers should do equally well on the grammaticality judgment task, but differences should occur on the correction task. This is exactly what Fowler (1988) found. Reading ability was significantly correlated with success on the correction task but not with success on the judgment task. This is further support for the view that processing complexity, and not structural complexity, is a better diagnostic of reading disability. Two additional findings bear on the competing hypotheses about the causes of reading failure. First, the level of achievement on grammaticality judgments was well above chance for both good and poor readers, even on complex syntactic structures (e.g., *Wh*-movement, and tag questions). Second, results on a test of short-term recall (with IQ partialled out) were more strongly correlated with success on the sentence correction task than with success on the judgment task.

CONCLUSION

The manner in which reading is erected on preexisting linguistic structures led us to predict that the causes of reading disability would lie within the language domain. Accordingly, seemingly normal school children who fail to make the expected progress in learning to read were found to have language-related difficulties, including problems in phonological awareness and unusual limitations in verbal working memory. As both of these problems are arguably grounded in phonology, a central concern has been to determine if all the language-related difficulties evinced by poor readers might stem from a single deficit in processing phonological information.

The observation that poor readers have difficulties in correctly interpreting some spoken sentences seemed, at first, to threaten a unitary phonological deficit account. However, in the context of our assumptions about the architecture of the language apparatus, we argued that a phonological deficit might explain this problem too. If so, this argues against attributing the comprehension difficulties of reading disabled children to a developmental lag in structural competence over and above their well-attested deficiencies in phonological processing.

In order to tease apart the alternatives, two research strategies were implemented. In one, tasks were devised to stress the language processing system in varying degrees while holding syntactic structure constant. We reviewed an experiment that followed this strategy, which yielded large differences between good and poor readers in comprehending spoken sentences in contexts that stress working memory, but much smaller differences when the same materials were presented in a way that lessened memory load. Contrary to the expectations of the structural lag hypothesis, in contexts that minimized memory demands, both reader groups achieved such a high level of accuracy that competence with the construction under investigation would seem guaranteed.

A second research strategy tested for differences between reader groups by comparing performance across a variety of linguistic structures. As anticipated by the processing limitation hypothesis, we found that both reader groups manifested a similar pattern of errors across sentences of varying syntactic types, with poor readers penalized to a greater degree than good readers on sentences that are costly to working memory resources. The absence of a reader group interaction invites the inference that the relatively inferior performance of poor readers is due to parsing pressure, rather than to ignorance of subjacency, a putatively innate constraint on syntax.

In sum, the syntactic component of the language apparatus appears to be intact in poor readers. The source of difficulties that might appear to reflect a syntactic deficiency must be sought elsewhere. It is premature at present to exclude the possibility that the comprehension problems of some poor readers are caused by a deficiency in some other component of the language apparatus (e.g., syntactic parsing). However, we can appeal to the modular architecture of the language apparatus to explain how a deficit in phonological processing may masquerade as a complex of deficits throughout the whole language system. Given the abundance of evidence attesting to poor readers' deficits in the phonological domain, there is reason to prefer the hypothesis that their comprehension problems are part and parcel of their difficulties in phonological processing. If this is correct, it would prove unnecessary to postulate additional impairments within the language system: All of the problems associated with reading ultimately spring from the same source. The possibility of providing a unitary explanation of an apparently disparate set of phenomena is a compelling reason, in our view, for adhering to a modular conception of the language apparatus.

ACKNOWLEDGMENTS

The research discussed in this chapter was supported in part by a Program Project Grant to Haskins Laboratories from the National Institute of Child Health and Human Development (HD-01994). Portions of this chapter are adapted from an earlier paper that will appear in I. G. Mattingly and M. Studdert-Kennedy (Eds.), *Modularity and the motor theory of speech perception.* Hillsdale, NJ: Lawrence Erlbaum Associates.

REFERENCES

Amidon, A., & Carey, P. (1972). Why five-year-olds cannot understand before and after. *Journal of Verbal Learning and Verbal Behavior, 11,* 417 - 423.
Baddeley, A. D. (1966). Short-term memory for word sequences as a function of acoustic, semantic and formal similarity. *Quarterly Journal of Experimental Psychology, 18,* 362 - 365.
Baddeley, A. D., & Hitch, G. (1974). Working memory. In G. H. Bower (Ed.), *The psychology of learning and motivation* (Vol. 8, pp. 47 - 89). New York: Academic Press.

Byrne, B. (1981). Deficient syntactic control in poor readers: Is a weak phonetic memory code responsible? *Applied Psycholinguistics, 2,* 201 - 212.

Chomsky, C. (1969). *The acquisition of syntax in children from 5 to 10.* Cambridge, MA: MIT Press.

Chomsky, N. (1965). *Aspects of the theory of syntax.* Cambridge, MA: MIT Press.

Chomsky, N. (1981). *Lectures on government and binding.* Dordrecht: Foris.

Clark, E. V. (1970). How young children describe events in time. In G. B. Flores d'Arcais & W. J. M. Levelt (Eds.), *Advances in psycholinguistics* (pp. 275 - 284). Amsterdam: North-Holland.

Conrad, R. (1964). Acoustic confusions in immediate memory. *British Journal of Psychology, 55,* 75 - 84.

Conrad, R. (1972). Speech and reading. In J. F. Kavanagh & I. G. Mattingly (Eds.), *Language by ear and by eye: The relationships between speech and reading* (pp. 205 - 240). Cambridge, MA: MIT Press.

Crain, S. (1982). Temporal terms: Mastery by age five. In *Papers and Reports on Child Language Development. Proceedings of the Fourteenth Annual Stanford Child Language Research Forum* (pp. 33 - 38). Stanford: Stanford University, Department of Linguistics.

Crain, S. (1987). On performability: Structure and process in language understanding. *Clinical Linguistics and Phonetics, 1,* 127 - 145.

Crain, S., & Fodor, J. D. (1986). On the innateness of subjacency. *Proceedings of the Eastern States Conference on Linguistics* (Vol. I, pp. 191 - 204). Columbus: The Ohio State University.

Crain, S., & Fodor, J. D. (1989). Competence and performance in child language. In E. Dromi (Ed.), *Language and cognition: A developmental perspective.* Norwood, NJ: Ablex.

Crain, S., & Shankweiler, D. (1988). Syntactic complexity and reading acquisition. In A. Davison & G. M. Green (Eds.), *Linguistic complexity and text comprehension: Readability issues reconsidered* (pp. 167 - 192). Hillsdale, NJ: Lawrence Erlbaum Associates.

Crain, S., Shankweiler, D., Macaruso, P., & Bar-Shalom, E. (1990). Working memory and sentence comprehension: Investigations of children with reading disorder. In G. Vallar & T. Shallice (Eds.), *Neuropsychological impairments of short-term memory* (pp. 477 - 508). Cambridge: Cambridge University Press.

Crain, S., & Steedman, M. (1985). On not being led up the garden path: The use of context by the psychological syntax processor. In D. R. Dowty, L. Karttunen, & A. M. Zwicky (Eds.), *Natural language parsing: Psychological, computational, and theoretical perspectives* (pp. 320 - 358). Cambridge: Cambridge University Press.

Daneman, M., & Carpenter, P. A. (1980). Individual differences in working memory and reading. *Journal of Verbal Learning and Verbal Behavior, 19,* 450 - 466.

Fodor, J. A. (1983). *The modularity of mind.* Cambridge, MA: MIT Press.

Forster, K. I. (1979). Levels of processing and the structure of the language processor. In W. E. Cooper & E. C. T. Walker (Eds.), *Sentence processing: Psycholinguistic studies presented to Merrill Garrett* (pp. 27 - 85). Hillsdale, NJ: Lawrence Erlbaum Associates.

Fowler, A. E. (1988). Grammaticality judgments and reading skill in grade 2. *Annals of Dyslexia, 38,* 73 - 94.

Frazier, L. (1978). *On comprehending sentences: Syntactic parsing strategies*. Unpublished doctoral dissertation, University of Connecticut, Storrs.

Gorrell, P., Crain, S., & Fodor, J. (1989). Contextual information and temporal terms. *Journal of Child Language, 16*, 623 - 632.

Hamburger, H., & Crain, S. (1982). Relative acquisition. In S. A. Kuczaj (Ed.), *Language development: Vol. 1. Syntax and Semantics* (pp. 245 - 274). Hillsdale, NJ: Lawrence Erlbaum Associates.

Hamburger, H., & Crain, S. (1987). Plans and semantics in human processing of language. *Cognitive Science, 11*, 101 - 136.

Johnson, M. L. (1975). The meaning of *before* and *after* for preschool children. *Journal of Experimental Child Psychology, 19*, 88 - 99.

Kimball, J. (1973). Seven principles of surface structure parsing in natural language. *Cognition, 2*, 15 - 47.

Lewis, D. (1979). Scorekeeping in a language game. *Journal of Philosophical Logic, 8*, 339 - 359.

Liberman, A. M., & Mattingly, I. G. (1989). A specialization for speech perception. *Science, 243*, 489 - 494.

Liberman, I. Y., & Shankweiler, D. (1985). Phonology and the problems of learning to read and write. *Remedial and Special Education, 6*, 8 - 17.

Liberman, I. Y., Shankweiler, D., & Liberman, A. M. (1989). The alphabetic principle and learning to read. In D. Shankweiler & I. Y. Liberman (Eds.), *Phonology and reading disability: Solving the reading puzzle* (IARLD Research Monograph Series). Ann Arbor: University of Michigan Press.

Linebarger, M. C., Schwartz, M. F., & Saffran, E. M. (1983). Sensitivity to grammatical structure in so-called agrammatic aphasics. *Cognition, 13*, 361 - 392.

Macaruso, P., Bar-Shalom, E., Crain, S., & Shankweiler, D. (1989). Comprehension of temporal terms by good and poor readers. *Language and Speech, 32*, 45 - 67.

Mann, V. A., Shankweiler, D., & Smith, S. T. (1984). The association between comprehension of spoken sentences and early reading ability: The role of phonetic representation. *Journal of Child Language, 11*, 627 - 643.

Martin, R. C. (1985). *The relationship between short-term memory and sentence comprehension deficits in agrammatic and conduction aphasics*. Paper presented at the annual meeting of the Academy of Aphasia, Pittsburgh, PA.

Perfetti, C. A. (1985). *Reading ability*. New York: Oxford University Press.

Saffran, E. M. (1985). *Short-term memory and sentence processing: Evidence from a case study*. Paper presented at the annual meeting of the Academy of Aphasia, Pittsburgh, PA.

Shankweiler, D., & Crain, S. (1986). Language mechanisms and reading disorder: A modular approach. *Cognition, 24*, 139 - 168.

Shankweiler, D., Crain, S., Brady, S., & Macaruso, P. (in press). Identifying the causes of reading disability. In P. B. Gough (Ed.), *Reading acquisition*. Hillsdale, NJ: Lawrence Erlbaum Associates.

Shankweiler, D., Crain, S., Gorrell, P., & Tuller, B. (1989). Reception of language in Broca's aphasia. *Language and Cognitive Processes, 4*, 1 - 33.

Shankweiler, D., Smith, S. T., & Mann, V. A. (1984). Repetition and comprehension of spoken sentences by reading-disabled children. *Brain and Language, 23*, 241 - 257.

Sheldon, A. (1974). The role of parallel function in the acquisition of relative clauses in English. *Journal of Verbal Learning and Verbal Behavior, 13*, 272 - 281.

Smith, S. T., Macaruso, P., Shankweiler, D., & Crain, S. (1990). Syntactic comprehension in young poor readers. *Applied Psycholinguistics, 11*.

Stein, C. L., Cairns, H. S., & Zurif, E. B. (1984). Sentence comprehension limitations related to syntactic deficits in reading-disabled children. *Applied Psycholinguistics, 5*, 305 - 322.

Vogel, S. A. (1975). *Syntactic abilities in normal and dyslexic children.* Baltimore, MD: University Park Press.

26 READING COMPREHENSION IN DYSLEXIC AND NORMAL READERS: A COMPONENT-SKILLS ANALYSIS

Frances A. Conners and Richard K. Olson
University of Colorado

INTRODUCTION

By definition, dyslexic children and adults have abnormally low reading skills in spite of normal educational opportunity and general intelligence (Critchley, 1970). Over the past several years, we have been studying the unexpected reading failures of dyslexic children to better understand their expression and etiology. We have examined a wide variety of component skills in reading and related cognitive processes to see which of these are uniquely deficient, and to see if the pattern of deficits varies significantly among dyslexic children (Olson, Kliegl, Davidson, & Foltz, 1985). We have explored the genetic and environmental etiology of deficits in component reading and cognitive skills by comparing the degree of similarity for identical and fraternal twins (Olson, Wise, Conners, Rack, & Fulker, 1989). For reasons that will become apparent in this chapter, most of our research has focused on deficits in word recognition and its component processes, some of which are uniquely deficient and significantly heritable in our sample of dyslexic children.

In this chapter we shift our focus to reading comprehension and its component skills. We show that printed word recognition and oral language comprehension each contributes independent variance to reading comprehension in dyslexic children. In addition, variance in each of these two components of reading comprehension is accounted for by different component skills. We argue that these points are important to understand both the reasons for reading comprehension deficits in individual dyslexic children and the appropriate methods for their re-mediation.

A number of studies have reported that word recognition (or de-coding) and general language comprehension contribute independently to differences in reading comprehension among normal readers in ele-mentary school (Curtis, 1980; Juel, Griffith, & Gough, 1986; Stanovich, Cunningham, & Feeman, 1984; Wilkinson, 1980). Developmental stud-ies suggest that the relative contributions of word recognition and lan-guage comprehension to reading comprehension change with age, such that word recognition is more important at younger ages and general language comprehension is more important at older ages (see Stanovich, 1986a, for a review).

In contrast to the pattern of independent contributions found in groups of normal readers, Curtis (1980) found that, among third- and fifth-grade poor readers, there was much common but little unique variance in reading comprehension accounted for by tasks related to word recognition and listening comprehension. Interestingly, these fifth graders turned out to be matched in both listening and reading ability to a group of skilled third grade readers. Thus, relative to skilled read-ers, the less skilled readers were no better in listening than they were in reading, providing further evidence for a strong link between the two skills among the poor readers in the Curtis sample. Comparable levels of deficit in reading and listening comprehension have also been reported by Berger (1978) for poor readers in the fifth grade and by Sticht (1979) for a group of adults in the Navy who were poor readers. The results of these studies are consistent with the view of Ceci and Baker (1989) that poor reading is associated with a broad deficit in the processing of verbal information.

It is important to note that the poor readers in the cited studies were not selected for normal-range IQ and education criteria that are traditionally required for dyslexic samples. Thus, for dyslexic read-ers, relationships between reading and listening comprehension could be quite different. If dyslexic readers' comprehension of oral language is consistent with their normal-range intelligence and educational back-ground, then their listening comprehension should be significantly higher than their word recognition, which is particularly low. In addition, if reading comprehension is partly determined by listening comprehension, dyslexics' reading comprehension should also be higher than their word recognition. These hypotheses will be tested in our first set of analyses by comparing reading skills of dyslexics with those of younger normal readers matched on word recognition.

A second set of analyses examines the contributions of listening com-prehension, word recognition, and their related skills to reading compre-hension within our dyslexic and normal samples. Although there was no evidence of independent components of reading comprehension for poor readers in the Curtis (1980) study, there are likely to be indepen-dent components within a dyslexic sample because of their characteristic dissociation of intelligence and word recognition.

Both the between- and within-group analyses are based on the same measures of component reading and language skills. We first describe models and measures of the component skills and their rationale in the next section. The between-group analyses for dyslexic and normal readers are presented in the third section, followed by within-group analyses in the fourth section, and general discussion and conclusions in the final section.

MODELS AND MEASURES OF COMPONENT SKILLS IN READING COMPREHENSION

Models

The relevant component skills are outlined in Figures 26.1 and 26.2 in the framework of hypothesized path models that are later tested in the fourth section. Following previous studies of component skills in reading comprehension, we proposed in the basic model that oral language comprehension and printed word recognition are the major components of reading comprehension (see Figure 26.1). Further, in the extended model, we specified several component skills of language comprehension and word recognition (see Figure 26.2). Consistent with the views of Hoover and Gough (1989), our models suggest that word recognition and listening comprehension are the two major components of reading comprehension and that other skills related to reading comprehension are actually components of word recognition or listening comprehension.

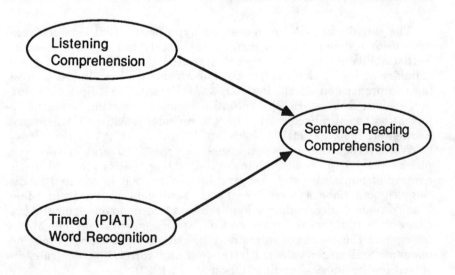

FIGURE 26.1. Hypothetical basic model of reading comprehension.

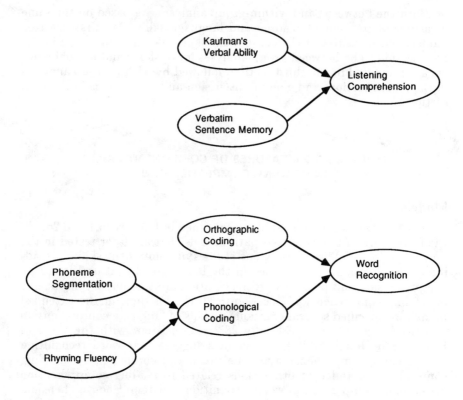

FIGURE 26.2. Hypothetical extended model of reading comprehension.

The extended model in Figure 26.2 hypothesizes that listening comprehension is dependent on general verbal ability and verbatim memory.
Verbal ability includes (among other related skills described later) vocabulary and world knowledge, both of which have been linked to reading comprehension (Beck, Perfetti, & McKeown, 1982; Spilich, Vesonder, Chiesi, & Voss, 1979). Verbatim memory involving linguistic information has also been related to reading comprehension (Daneman &
Carpenter, 1980; Perfetti & Goldman, 1976).

Word recognition is hypothesized to depend on skill in two component reading processes, phonological coding that is required in the
reading of nonwords, and orthographic coding that is required to distinguish homophones (*their, there*) and pseudohomophones (*rain, rane*).
Finally, phonological coding is hypothesized to depend on segmental language skills of rhyming fluency and phoneme segmentation. The ability
to segment the sounds of words may be critical for learning grapheme-
phoneme and larger subword letter-to-sound correspondence rules involved in phonological coding (Olson et al., 1989).

Measures

Reading Comprehension

Two measures of reading comprehension were presented. The first reading comprehension measure, the Peabody Individual Achievement Test (PIAT) for Reading Comprehension (Dunn & Markwardt, 1970), required children to read sentences silently and demonstrate comprehension by pointing to one of four pictures that represented the meaning of the sentence. Performance on this task was highly dependent on the recognition and comprehension of individual words, and probably less dependent on inference or integration of ideas. Test-retest reliability for grade-level assignment is reported to be .64.

The second measure was adapted from the Spache Diagnostic Reading Scales (Spache, 1963). Subjects read two stories aloud that consisted of approximately 200 words. The grade-level difficulty of material that each subject read was determined by his or her word-recognition grade level. After reading each story, subjects answered eight open-ended questions. The questions required memory for details in the stories. None of the questions required inferences. Spearman-Brown split-half reliability for percentage correct in this task was .71.

Listening Comprehension

Our listening comprehension test required no reading and thus may be considered a measure of general language comprehension. Children listened to two 4-minute stories, one a narrative about the life of Alexander Graham Bell and one a story about the adventures of John Colter. Following each passage, children answered eight questions that required recall of details in the stories. The questions were selected so that it was very unlikely they could be answered from the child's general knowledge. The Spearman-Brown split-half reliability for percentage correct in this task was .74.

General Verbal Ability

Two measures were included to assess skills in nonreading tasks that were hypothesized to predict subjects' performance in listening comprehension. The Kaufman verbal ability measure represents the mean performance on four subtests of the Wechsler Intelligence Scale for Children-Revised (WISC-R; Wechsler, 1974) or the Wechsler Adult Intelligence Scale-Revised (WAIS-R; Wechsler, 1981) that Kaufman (1975) found to form a verbal ability factor. The Information subtest requires subjects to answer questions considered to reflect commonly known facts, such as the names of the four seasons. The Similarities subtest requires the abstraction of common characteristics ("How are a wheel and a ball alike?"). The Comprehension subtest taps knowledge of cultural norms by asking questions such as "What are some reasons why we need police-men?" The Vocabulary subtest requires subjects to define increasingly difficult words. No reading is required in these tests. Scaled scores were averaged together to form the Kaufman verbal ability score for the path analyses. For the reading-matched comparison, however, raw score totals were used. The split-half reliabilities of the individual subtests are .85, .81, .77, and .85 respectively (Wechsler, 1974). Of all WISC-R subtests, these four correlated highest with reading and listening com-prehension within the dyslexic group.

The second measure of verbal ability that we call verbatim sentence memory was the Detroit Test of Learning Aptitude: Auditory Attention Span for Related Syllables (Baker & Leland, 1959). The test required subjects to repeat verbatim a series of sentences that increased in length until the subject made an error. The split-half reliability for this test was reported to be .81.

Word Recognition

Two reliable tests of word recognition were included so that one could be used to match older dyslexic and younger normal readers, and the other could be used to assess the validity of the match. The two word recognition measures were also used to replicate word recognition contributions to reading comprehension in the path models presented in the fourth section.

The Peabody Individual Achievement Test (PIAT) for Word Recog-nition (Dunn & Markwardt, 1970) required subjects to read aloud words increasing in difficulty. Most of the words were regularly spelled and subjects had unlimited time to read each word. Reading of the list was stopped when the subject made errors on six of the last seven words. The test-retest reliability is reported to be .89.

The timed word recognition test also required subjects to read a series of difficulty-ordered words. However, words were presented on a computer screen, and subjects had to initiate their correct oral response within 2 seconds. The test discontinued when a subject missed 10 out of the last 20 words. The correlation between this test and the PIAT word recognition test was .90 across all dyslexic and normal subjects.

Components of Word Recognition

Two measures were used to assess important component skills that were hypothesized to predict independent variance in word recognition (see Olson et al., 1989, for the rationale and detailed description of the tasks). These were phonological coding and orthographic coding.

Oral nonword reading was used to measure the phonological coding component of word recognition. Eighty-five pronounceable nonwords were read aloud as quickly as possible when they were presented indi-vidually on the computer screen. The subjects' scores were based on the first principal component of percentage correct, median time to initiate a

correct response, and phonological similarity of errors to the target nonwords. The Spearman-Brown split-half reliability was .96. Nonwords
have no prior learned relation between their whole orthographic pattern
and the desired pronunciation. Subjects must sound out the printed
nonwords by grapheme-phoneme correspondence rules or by analogy to
parts of familiar words.

A second task measured the orthographic coding component of word
recognition. Subjects designated which member of 80 word-pseudo-
homophone pairs presented on a computer (e.g., *rain, rane; sammon,
salmon*) was a word by pushing a button as quickly as possible on the
side of the word. Because phonological codes were identical for both
members of each pair, orthographic memory was necessary for a correct
response. The orthographic coding score was based on the first principal component of percentage correct and median correct response time.
The Spearman-Brown split-half reliability was .95.

Segmental Language Tasks

Two measures of segmental language skills were hypothesized to be
related to the phonological component of word recognition (see Olson
et al., 1989, for a detailed description and rationale for the tasks). In
a phoneme segmentation task similar to the children's play language
called pig latin, subjects were asked to remove the initial phoneme from
each of a series of 45 spoken words, place the phoneme at the end of the
word, and add the sound *ay*. Thus, the target word *pat* should yield the
spoken response *atpay*. The subjects' scores were based on percentage
correct on the task. The Cronbach-Alpha reliability was .90.

A second segmental language task involved rhyming. Subjects orally
generated all the words they could think of in one minute that rhymed
with the word *eel*. Their scores were based on the number of correct
responses minus the number of incorrect responses. A reliability of .83
was estimated from the correlation of scores on this test with those for
other rhyming fluency targets that were presented to a subset of our
dyslexic and normal samples.

GROUP COMPARISONS

Two groups relevant for comparison of dyslexic performance are age-
matched normal readers and reading-matched normal readers. When
our dyslexics were compared with age-matched normal readers, they
were significantly lower on all measures related to reading and language.
Comparing them with younger children reading at the same level, however, should allow detection of differences in component-skills profiles.
For example, skills that are still significantly low after matching on
reading ability may be causally related to deficits in dyslexia (Bryant
& Goswami, 1986). On the other hand, skills that are significantly low

compared to age-matched normal readers but high compared to reading-matched normal readers may be influenced by secondary effects of more serious deficits in other component reading and language skills.

Subjects

Because a central question in our research is the genetic etiology of dyslexia, most of our subjects were identical and fraternal twins drawn from 27 school districts in Colorado. Whenever possible, we also tested their parents and nontwin siblings. The initial selection of dyslexic-twin families for laboratory testing was based on school records indicating reading difficulties in at least one member of each twin pair. A normal twin sample was drawn from twins that had no indication of reading problems in their school records.

Scores from the WISC-R or WAIS-R IQ and the PIAT word recognition measure were used to finally select the samples of dyslexic and normal children for the present analyses. The dyslexic sample included any twin or nontwin sibling that read below approximately the tenth percentile for children in our sampling area on the PIAT word recognition test. Children in the dyslexic sample also met the usual exclusionary criteria, including at least 90 IQ on either the verbal or performance subscales, normal educational opportunity as assessed from school attendance, no uncorrected auditory or visual acuity deficits, and no known history of emotional, behavioral, or neurological disorders such as seizures. English was their first language. Subjects in the normal sample also met the same exclusionary criteria, and they scored above approximately the fortieth percentile for the testing area on the PIAT word recognition test. (The mean score on various standardized reading tests in our 27 Colorado school districts averages at about the sixtieth percentile on the national norms.)

The reading-matched groups consisted of 172 pairs that included one older dyslexic and one younger normal reader matched on PIAT word recognition. These two groups were also used in the path analyses that follow in the final section. Means and standard deviations for the two groups' age, IQ (WISC-R for children under 16 years and WAIS-R for subjects 16 years or older), and grade level according to the national norms on the PIAT word recognition test are presented in Table 26.1.

It should be noted that the IQ scores of the dyslexic subjects are lower than those of the normal readers. Dyslexics' poor reading probably slows the gain of knowledge by way of written material. Because performance on the Wechsler tests is dependent to a certain extent on learning from written material, the dyslexic group's lower mean IQ is to be expected (Stanovich, 1986b). However, we see later that the dyslexic subjects' performance on the Wechsler tests is generally better than expected from their word recognition.

TABLE 26.1

*Mean Age, Full-Scale IQ Scores, and Word Recognition Grade
Equivalents of Dyslexic Readers and Reading-Matched
Normal Readers.*[a]

| Variable | Reading Group | |
	Dyslexics	Normal Readers
Age	15.6 (2.7)	10.4 (1.6)
Full-Scale IQ	99.6 (9.7)	111.6 (12.2)
PIAT Word Recognition	6.5 (1.9)	6.5 (1.9)

[a] Standard deviations are in parentheses. PIAT Word Recognition Scores are grade
levels based on national norms.

Results and Discussion

Table 26.2 lists the means and standard deviations of all component
skills measures within the dyslexic and reading-matched normal groups.
Also listed for each measure is the number of standard deviation units
the dyslexic mean is from the normal readers' mean. The results are
presented in this format for comparability across the measures because of
their different types of scores (e.g., percentage correct, number correct,
principal components, raw scores).

Compared with younger normal readers, dyslexics' scores were significantly higher for some component skills, similar for some, and significantly lower for others.

Reading Comprehension

The dyslexic group performed significantly better than reading-
matched controls on PIAT reading comprehension, although the difference was not large. Difficulty in comprehending the sentences in this
task is strongly related to the decoding difficulty of words in the sentences. Based on the grade-equivalent norms for this test, the dyslexics'
mean grade level was 7.75, whereas the normals' mean grade level was
7.0. (compared to mean word recognition grade levels of 6.5 for both
groups). Dyslexics had a larger advantage over controls on Spache reading comprehension, wherein the longer text passages were selected to
compensate for subjects' skill in word recognition. This meant that the
dyslexic and normal subjects in each matched pair read the same stories.

TABLE 26.2

*Means and Standard Deviations of Component Reading Skills
for Disabled and Reading-Matched Normal Readers.*[a]

Variable	N	Dyslexic	Normal	Deviation
Timed Word Recognition	162	107.90 (34.32)	104.25 (35.12)	+.10
PIAT Reading Comprehension	172	52.33 (9.86)	49.32 (10.67)	+.28[b]
Spache Reading Comprehension	169	61.02 (19.63)	51.70 (18.81)	+.50[b]
Listening Comprehension	86	56.13 (20.49)	42.77 (22.41)	+.60[b]
Kaufman Verbal Ability	115	95.21 (12.95)	76.44 (15.96)	+1.18[b]
Verbatim Sentence Memory	172	68.55 (14.62)	66.29 (14.84)	+.15
Phonological Coding	115	-.37 (.99)	.29 (.85)	-.78[b]
Orthographic Coding	157	.21 (.85)	-.18 (1.09)	+.36[b]
Phoneme Segmentation	78	65.41 (17.40)	75.22 (17.98)	-.55[b]
Rhyming Fluency	172	4.37 (3.63)	4.52 (3.10)	-.05

[a]N = number of subject pairs. *Deviation* = position in standard deviation units of the dyslexic group mean in the normal reader distribution.

Raw scores (number of items correct) were used for Timed Word Recognition, PIAT Reading Comprehension, Kaufman Verbal Ability, Verbatim Sentence Memory, and Rhyming Fluency.

Kaufman Verbal Ability included only subjects under 16.5 years old who took the WISC-R and not the WAIS-R.

Percentage correct scores were used for Spache Reading Comprehension, Listening Comprehension, and Phoneme Segmentation.

Principle component scores were used for Phonological and Orthographic Coding.

Sample sizes vary across the measures because some tests were started later than others in the test battery, and some data were lost due to subject fatigue or equipment failure.

[b] = $p < .05$.

Together, the results for the two reading comprehension measures indicate that dyslexic readers tend to do better in reading comprehension than expected from their word recognition. The results are consistent with studies that have matched dyslexic and normal subjects on reading comprehension and then found significant deficits for the dyslexic subjects' word recognition (cf. Bruck, 1988).

Listening Comprehension

The dyslexics' largest comprehension advantage was found for our listening comprehension task. Performance on this task represents dyslexic children's comprehension skills that are independent from the direct constraints of the reading process. The results sharply distinguish our dyslexic group from other less selected groups of poor readers that show similar deficits in word recognition, reading comprehension, and listening comprehension (Berger, 1978; Curtis, 1980; Sticht, 1979).

It is important to note that although listening comprehension does not involve reading, the dyslexic group's performance was significantly low for their age. One possible reason for this deficit is that the dyslexics' long-term difficulty in gaining knowledge from print places constraints on the development of general verbal abilities that might be helpful in listening comprehension (see Stanovich, 1986b, for a related discussion of the Matthew effect in dyslexic children). The pattern of results for one of the verbal ability measures described later is at least consistent with this explanation.

General Verbal Ability

Kaufman verbal ability showed a pattern of results similar to the comprehension measures: The dyslexic group scored significantly lower than same-age normal readers, but higher than the reading-matched normal readers. As we noted earlier, dyslexic readers' IQ scores were generally lower than those of the normal readers, but their absolute level of performance on the Wechsler verbal subscales was substantially higher than expected from their word recognition. (Performance on the perceptual subscales of the WISC-R and WAIS was even higher.)

Verbatim sentence memory showed no significant difference for the reading-matched groups. Short-term memory and working memory for verbal material has often been reported to be deficient in dyslexic children (cf. Torgesen & Goldman, 1977). These types of literal memory tasks may depend on phonological coding processes (Jorm, 1983), which were uniquely deficient in the present sample (see later discussion).

Word Recognition

The reading-matched groups were not significantly different on our timed word recognition test. This result confirms the validity of the initial match of younger normal and older dyslexic readers on PIAT word recognition.

Components of Word Recognition

As described in other reports (Olson, Wise, Conners, & Rack, in press; Olson et al., 1989), a significant deficit in dyslexics was found for phonological coding and a significant advantage was found for orthographic coding. We argued that the deficit for phonological coding (and phoneme segmentation, see later discussion), relative to word recognition, suggested a causal role for phonological deficits in most dyslexic readers' problems with word recognition. A causal role was further supported by evidence from twin analyses showing that phonological coding accounted for most of the heritable variance in the dyslexic twins' word recognition deficits. The advantage of the dyslexics over reading-matched normals in orthographic coding may be related to their greater experience with text (they were much older than the normal readers).

Path models in the next major section will support the notion of independent contributions of these variables to word recognition, and through word recognition to reading comprehension.

Segmental Language Skills

The dyslexics also showed a deficit in phoneme segmentation, which was hypothesized as a component of phonological coding. Phoneme segmentation may also be causally related to dyslexia, but as discussed earlier, we hypothesize that it affects phonological coding skill, which in turn affects word recognition.

Dyslexics did not show the same degree of deficit on rhyming fluency as they did on phoneme segmentation. They performed at the same level as reading-matched normal readers on the former task. Some researchers have argued that rhyming taps different skills than those required in explicit phoneme segmentation tasks (Morais, Bertelson, Cary, & Alegria, 1986). However, rhyming does require an implicit segmentation of words in the lexicon and may be a precursor to the development of phonological skills required in reading (Bryant & Bradley, 1985). In the following path analyses, we see that both rhyming fluency and phoneme segmentation contribute to variance in phonological coding for normal but not dyslexic readers.

PATH ANALYSES

In this section, we present path analyses predicting individual differences in reading comprehension within the dyslexic and normal groups employed in the previous reading-matched comparisons. We attempted to test the general hypothesis that there is independent variance in reading comprehension contributed by listening comprehension and the word recognition measures, and that there are different component skills contributing to listening comprehension and word recognition. We also examined the similarity of models for the matched dyslexic and normal groups. Even though both groups had the same level of word recognition, we hypothesized that the dyslexic group's large discrepancy between word recognition and listening comprehension would lead to less common variance for these and related variables in the model.

Although range of performance in each group was truncated as a result of selection criteria, there was substantial within-group variance for all measures, even when age was partialled out. Though some measures contain more variance than others, the patterns were very similar for the normal and dyslexic groups. The respective dyslexic and normal standard deviations were 8.9 and 9.0 for PIAT word recognition, 34.1 and 36.2 for timed word recognition, 9.9 and 10.7 for PIAT reading comprehension, 20.5 and 23.2 for listening comprehension, 1.7 and 2.2 for Kaufman verbal ability, 14.6 and 14.8 for verbatim sentence memory, 1.0 and 1.0 for phonological coding, 0.8 and 1.1 for orthographic coding, 17.1 and 20.3 for phoneme segmentation, and 3.6 and 3.1 for rhyming fluency. Thus, differences between the groups' correlations and path structures are not likely to be due to differences in variance. Correlations for age-adjusted variables are presented in Table 26.3, with dyslexic readers above the diagonal and normal readers below.

TABLE 26.3

Correlation Among Component Reading Skills for Dyslexic (Upper Portion) and Reading-Matched Normal Readers (Lower Portion).

Reading Skill Measures	1	2	3	4	5	6	7	8	9	10
1. PIAT Word Recognition	–	.64	.43	-.01	.03	.11	.66	.47	.20	.23
2. Timed Word Recognition	.70	–	.31	.03	.09	.17	.67	.58	.32	.22
3. PIAT Reading Compreh.	.62	.63	–	.27	.27	.22	.28	.20	.14	.14
4. Listening Comprehension	.39	.41	.47	–	.42	.15	-.01	-.17	-.12	-.05
5. Kaufman Verbal Ability	.51	.55	.57	.65	–	.31	-.14	.02	.01	.18
6. Verbatim Sentence Memory	.35	.44	.40	.45	.51	–	.12	.02	.18	.13
7. Phonological Coding	.61	.51	.39	.15	.27	.19	–	.26	.48	.14
8. Orthographic Coding	.52	.53	.45	.26	.35	.23	.48	–	.02	.26
9. Phoneme Segmentation	.33	.26	.20	.05	.12	.24	.50	.15	–	.23
10. Rhyming Fluency	.49	.41	.49	.26	.38	.25	.34	.39	.22	–

Two significant constraints were placed on the path models by the measures. First was the nature of the reading comprehension test. Because the Spache reading comprehension test was adjusted for level of word recognition, it was inappropriate for addressing questions in the path analyses. Thus, we used the PIAT reading comprehension test as the dependent variable. As discussed earlier, this is a sentence-reading test, more highly dependent on ability to recognize words and their meanings than a longer passage-reading test might be. The second constraint on the path models was the reliability of the measures used. In particular, PIAT reading comprehension and listening comprehension had reliabilities of .67 and .74, respectively. These reliabilities represent the limits on the total variance in the measures that can be accounted for by the set of predictor variables.

The Basic Model

The first step in the series of path analyses was to compare the relative importance of word recognition and listening comprehension in predicting reading comprehension. If word recognition is dissociated from listening comprehension in dyslexic readers as was suggested from the reading-match comparisons in the previous section, then we would expect at least some of the two skills' variance related to reading comprehension to be independent. If a general language deficit is responsible for dyslexics' deficits in both listening comprehension and word recognition (Ceci & Baker, 1989), then we should see little independence of the two skills. Two main questions are posed in our examination of the basic model: (a) Do word recognition and listening comprehension account for independent variance in PIAT reading comprehension? (b) Are the patterns of contributions similar across groups of normal and dyslexic readers?

Multiple regression analyses were carried out within each group on age-corrected variables. Listening comprehension and word recognition (either timed word recognition or PIAT word recognition) were entered simultaneously as predictors for PIAT reading comprehension. The repetition of the analysis with two different word recognition measures served as a check on replicability. It should be noted that the basic model is considered an additive model of reading comprehension rather than a multiplicative model. Hoover and Gough (1989) maintained that the product of decoding and linguistic comprehension expresses their relationship to reading comprehension more precisely than the additive combination of their variance (see also Gough & Tunmer, 1986).

Panels A and B of Figure 26.3 show the actual contributions of word recognition and listening comprehension to PIAT reading comprehension for normal and dyslexic readers, respectively. The coefficients for the analysis involving PIAT word recognition are in parentheses. The coefficients on the straight lines are part correlations, correlations of one variable with another when all other variables (in this case, only one) are controlled. Squaring the part correlation yields the proportion of variance in PIAT reading comprehension attributed independently to a particular predictor. The coefficients on the curved lines are first-order correlations (see Biddle & Marlin, 1987, for a discussion of procedures for path modeling).

Listening comprehension and word recognition contributed significant amounts of independent variance to PIAT reading comprehension within both the dyslexic and normal groups. Word recognition was nearly twice as strong a predictor as listening comprehension in both groups, with the exception of timed word recognition in the dyslexic group. This generally stronger prediction for word recognition may have been due to the nature of the PIAT reading comprehension task, as discussed earlier. A longer, more in-depth passage reading task might be more dependent on subjects' skills in listening comprehension than in word recognition. In addition, the reliability was lower for listening comprehension (.74) than for the word recognition measures (.90). The important point is that the pattern of independent contributions was similar in both groups.

The major difference between the groups was the amount of variance common to both word recognition and listening comprehension

A. Normal Readers

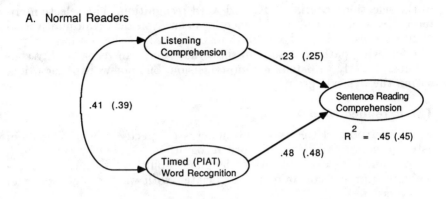

B. Dyslexic Readers

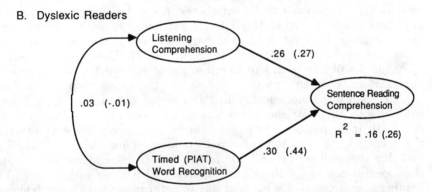

FIGURE 26.3. Results of path analysis based on the basic model of reading comprehension. Coefficients in parentheses apply to PIAT word recognition rather than timed word recognition. For all path coefficients (on straight lines), $p < .05$.

that helped to predict PIAT reading comprehension. For normal readers, 16% of the variance predicting PIAT reading comprehension was common variance. In dyslexic readers, this value was 0%. This contrast between the normal and dyslexic groups was the same for PIAT word recognition and timed word recognition (see Table 26.3). The correlations between listening comprehension and both word recognition measures were significantly different across groups (timed word recognition: Fisher's $z = 3.10$, $p < .01$; PIAT word recognition: Fisher's $z = 3.09$, $p < .01$).

The higher degree of independence for listening comprehension and word recognition within the dyslexic group may be related to the fact that the dyslexics were significantly higher in listening comprehension than would be expected from their word recognition (see Table 26.2). The discrepancy between these two skills in the dyslexic sample and their greater independence in the dyslexics' path analyses may be due to the selection criteria for IQ and word recognition. The selection criteria effectively forced a difference between dyslexics' Kaufman verbal ability scores and word recognition, compared to the normal sample. The following path analyses will show that Kaufman verbal ability contributes directly to listening comprehension, but not word recognition, within the dyslexic group.

The Extended Model

The purpose of the extended model is to specify subcomponents of listening comprehension and word recognition. Guided by this model, we examined the degree to which language abilities associated with listening comprehension were also associated with word recognition, and vice versa.

The path analyses involved a series of multiple regression analyses in which all relevant age-corrected predictor variables were entered simultaneously into the equation. All variables expressed as predictor variables anywhere in the model to the left of a particular variable were entered in the analysis for that dependent variable, even if they were not proposed to be related to it (Biddle & Marlin, 1987). This approach leaves open the possibility of unhypothesized paths emerging in the analyses. For example, even though phoneme segmentation was hypothesized as a component of phonological coding and not of word recognition, it was entered into the equation predicting word recognition, allowing a direct path from phoneme segmentation to word recognition to emerge if present. We conducted three path analyses for each group, one for listening comprehension and one for each word recognition test. Note that we did not begin these path analyses with a regression on PIAT reading comprehension. Our goal was to determine the independence of component skills in listening comprehension and the word recognition measures.

Obtained paths appear in panels A and B of Figure 26.4. Any measure whose regression weight was not significant ($p > .05$) was not pictured in the diagrams. The analyses were repeated with timed word recognition and PIAT word recognition in order to determine replicability of at least this portion of the model. Components of the model that did not replicate across the two word recognition measures cannot be considered stable within the sample, and so are not included in the diagrams of Figure 26.4.

Results for Listening Comprehension

For normal readers, Kaufman's verbal ability and verbatim sentence memory contributed significant independent variance to listening comprehension. Kaufman's verbal ability was an especially strong component. There were no significant contributions from variables hypothesized to relate to word recognition.

For dyslexic readers, Kaufman's verbal ability, orthographic coding, and phoneme segmentation contributed significant independent variance

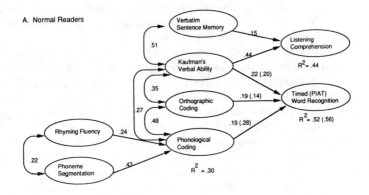

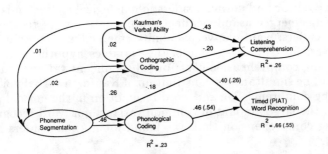

FIGURE 26.4. Results of path analysis based on the extended model of reading comprehension. Coefficients in parentheses apply to PIAT word recognition rather than timed word recognition. For all path coefficients (on straight lines), $p < .05$.

to listening comprehension. Orthographic coding and phoneme segmentation, however, showed weak but significant negative contributions, indicating that subjects who were high in either or both of these skills tended to be lower in listening comprehension. It is probably not reasonable to conclude that higher orthographic coding and phoneme segmentation actually causes lower listening comprehension. Rather, there may be selection biases in school referrals for the dyslexic sample that result in some subjects' inclusion for relatively poor comprehension processes and other subjects' inclusion for relatively poor word recognition processes. Consistent with this notion, Olson et al., (1985) reported a small but significant negative relation between Kaufman's verbal ability and phonological skill within their dyslexic sample. Perhaps the main conclusion that should be drawn from these low negative relations is that there is a substantial dissociation within dyslexic samples between variables related to reading comprehension and word recognition. See Gough and Tunmer (1986) for a related discussion.

Another interesting result pertains to the make up of variance in listening comprehension that was accounted for by the set of variables. In each group, this variance consisted partly of variance common to two or more variables (common variance) and partly of variance unique to only one variable (unique variance). More total variance was accounted for within the normal group than within the dyslexic group (44% vs 26%). However, there were similar amounts of unique variance in the two groups. The difference in total variance was attributable to differences in common variance. For normal readers about half of the variance accounted for was due to common variance (22% of 44%). For dyslexic readers, all of the variance was independently contributed (26% of 26%). This evidence falls into place with evidence from the basic model, suggesting that there is less commonality among component skills of reading comprehension among dyslexic readers than among normal readers.

Results for Word Recognition

For both dyslexic and normal readers, phonological coding and orthographic coding emerged as independent components of word recognition. For normal readers, Kaufman verbal ability emerged as a component as well. However, for dyslexics, none of the variables hypothesized to relate to listening comprehension contributed significant variance to word recognition. The simultaneous contribution of Kaufman verbal ability to both listening comprehension and word recognition in the normal group may explain the large amount of common variance for word recognition and listening comprehension that was found for normal readers in the basic model.

The balance of common and unique variance in word recognition related to orthographic and phonological coding was different in the two groups. Though there was some common variance predicting word recognition in the dyslexic group, there was less than in the normal group (16% of 55% and 27% of 66% vs. 40% of 56% and 37% of 52% for PIAT word recognition and timed word recognition in the dyslexic and normal groups, respectively). As with the dyslexics' greater discrepancy between word recognition and listening comprehension discussed earlier, their discrepancy between the phonological and orthographic coding components of word recognition (see Table 26.2) may have reduced the amount of common variance for the two variables. Elsewhere we have discussed how the development of orthographic and phonological coding should be more integrated in normal readers who do not have a phonological coding deficit (Olson et al., in press).

The phonological coding component of word recognition was predicted independently by phoneme segmentation and rhyming fluency in the normal group, but only by phoneme segmentation in the dyslexic group. The weaker relation for rhyming fluency may be due to its lower reliability and to Bertelson, Morais, De Gelder, and Tfounis's (1988) contention that rhyming taps segmental language skills that are different from those required in phoneme segmentation tasks and in phonological coding.

GENERAL DISCUSSION AND CONCLUSIONS

The picture that emerges for dyslexic readers' component skills in reading comprehension is clearly different from that for normal readers. It is also different from that for poor readers, who display a broad-ranging deficit. The between-group analyses in the third section showed that in comparison to a younger normal group matched on word recognition, the dyslexics' listening and reading comprehension were significantly higher, as was their absolute level of verbal ability measured by raw scores on WISC-R or WAIS-R tests. In contrast, their phonological coding component of word recognition and phoneme segmentation were significantly lower.

In the introduction, we cited several studies of poor readers who were equally deficient in word recognition, reading comprehension, and listening comprehension. These studies did not select their subjects according to the usual normal-range IQ and education criteria for dyslexia. Thus, the subjects in these studies may have read words and comprehended text at a level consistent with their intelligence and educational background. Results from studies that have focused on poor readers' word recognition and phonological coding skills have also varied depending on their use of selection criteria for dyslexia. In a recent meta-analysis, we found that studies of carefully defined dyslexic samples usually reported significant deficits in phonological coding relative to word recognition (Olson et al, in press), whereas studies of unselected poor readers tend not to show a phonological coding deficit. Stanovich (1988) has proposed a similar view of differences between samples of dyslexics and garden variety poor readers.

The results of the path analyses also reflected a strong dissociation between component skills in reading comprehension among dyslexic readers. Unlike previous research on poor readers (Curtis, 1980), the basic path model for dyslexics showed a clear separation of variance in PIAT reading comprehension attributable to listening comprehension and word recognition. In fact, not only was there less common variance predicting PIAT reading comprehension in the dyslexic group than the normal group, there was virtually no common variance at all.

In the extended path model, components associated with listening comprehension and with word recognition were quite distinct, particularly in the dyslexic group. Although the normal group displayed some cross-level influence of Kaufman verbal ability on word recognition, this influence was absent in the dyslexic group. The only cross-level influence within the dyslexic group was opposite in direction than would be predicted by a general verbal deficit hypothesis.

It could be argued that the striking independence of component skills in the dyslexic group is an artifact of selection criteria that forces a discrepancy between word recognition and intelligence. It is true that to some extent, as a result of these selection criteria, skills related to word recognition should be discrepant from those related to intelligence. However, two skills can still be correlated even if their general levels are different. The results for the dyslexic sample clearly show that there can be distinct and meaningful ability differences, within individuals, among different types of verbal skills that jointly contribute to variance in reading comprehension.

There are some important implications of the results for remediation of dyslexics' deficits in reading comprehension. Most of the dyslexics in our sample were uniquely deficient in word recognition, particularly in the phonological-coding component of word recognition. A first step for these subjects is to significantly improve their word recognition. Recent research with computer-based reading and speech feedback for decoding difficulties has shown substantial gains for dyslexic readers' phonological coding and word recognition (Olson & Wise, 1987; Olson et al., in press; Wise, Olson, Anstett, Andrews, Terjak, Schneider, & Kostuch, 1989).

However, the path analyses showed that word recognition accounts for only part of the variance in reading comprehension. The dyslexic group also showed less severe deficits in listening comprehension and general verbal knowledge that apparently contributed to their difficulties in reading comprehension. Improvement in these areas might come from greater access to knowledge from print that is enabled by better word recognition. But other remedial efforts that focus the development of metacognitive skills in comprehension monitoring, organization, and rehearsal should also be beneficial (Palincsar & Brown, 1984).

A final point is that the balance of remedial efforts toward decoding or comprehension skills should depend on the individual. We noted that there was considerable independent variance between the listening comprehension and word recognition portions of the path models due to individual differences within the dyslexic sample. Some dyslexics' verbal ability and listening comprehension were above normal, whereas their word recognition and phonological coding were extremely poor. A focus on the development of word decoding would be appropriate for these subjects. Other dyslexics' word recognition and phonological coding were not as severely depressed, but their listening comprehension and verbal ability were relatively low. For these subjects, the balance of remedial efforts should be directed toward the development of world knowledge and metacognitive skills for comprehension of both oral and written language.

ACKNOWLEDGMENTS

The research reported in this chapter was supported by NICHD Program Project Grant HD 11681, and Grant RO1 HD 22223 to R. Olson. We thank John DeFries, David Fulker, and Bruce Pennington for their collaboration as co-investigators on the Program Project. Barbara Wise and John Rack assisted in the analyses and commented on the manuscript. The PIAT Word Recognition, PIAT Comprehension, Verbatim Sentence Memory, Rhyming Fluency, and IQ measures were administered in DeFries' laboratory at the Institute for Behavior Genetics.

REFERENCES

Baker, H., & Leland, B. (1967). *Detroit tests of learning aptitude.* Indianapolis: Test Division of Bobbs-Merrill.

Beck, I. L., Perfetti, C. A., & McKeown, M. G. (1982). Effects of long-term vocabulary instruction on lexical access and reading comprehension. *Journal of Educational Psychology, 74,* 506 - 521.

Berger, N. (1978). Why can't John read? Perhaps he's not a good listener. *Journal of Learning Disabilities, 11,* 633 - 638.

Bertelson, P., Morais, J., De Gelder, B., & Tfouni, L. V. (1988). *Rhyme judgment and phonetic segmentation in illiterates.* Paper presented at the NIAS Conference on Comprehension Processes in Reading, Wassenaar, the Netherlands.

Biddle, B. J., & Marlin, M. M. (1987). Causality, confirmation, credulity, and structural equation modeling. *Child Development, 58,* 4 - 17.

Bruck, M. (1988). The word recognition and spelling of dyslexic children. *Reading Research Quarterly, 23,* 51 - 69.

Bryant, P. E., & Bradley, L. (1985). *Children's reading problems.* Oxford: Blackwell.

Bryant, P., & Goswami, U. (1986). Strengths and weaknesses of the reading level design: A comment on Backman, Mamen, & Ferguson. *Psychological Bulletin, 100,* 101 - 103.

Ceci, S. J., & Baker, J. G. (1989). On learning . . . more or less: A knowledge x process x context view of learning disabilities. *Journal of Learning Disabilities, 22,* 90 - 99.

Critchley, M. (1970). *The dyslexic child* (2nd ed.). London: Academic Press.

Curtis, M. E. (1980). Development of components of reading skill. *Journal of Educational Psychology, 72,* 656 - 669.

Daneman, M., & Carpenter, P. A. (1980). Individual differences in working memory and reading. *Journal of Verbal Learning and Verbal Behavior, 19,* 450 - 466.

Dunn, L. M., & Markwardt, F. C., Jr. (1970). *Peabody individual achievement test.* Circle Pines, MN: American Guidance Service.

Gough, P. B., & Tunmer, W. E. (1986). Decoding, reading, and reading disability. *Remedial and Special Education, 7,* 6 - 10.

Hoover, W. A., & Gough, P. B. (1989). *The simple view of reading.* Unpublished manuscript, Southwest Educational Development Laboratory, Austin, Texas.

Jorm, A. F. (1983). Specific reading retardation and working memory: A review. *British Journal of Psychology, 74,* 311 - 342.

Juel, C., Griffith, P. L., & Gough, P. B. (1986). Acquisition of literacy: A longitudinal study of children in first and second grade. *Journal of Educational Psychology, 78,* 243 - 255.

Kaufman, A. S. (1975). Factor analysis of the WISC-R at 11 age levels between 6 1/2 and 16 1/2 years. *Journal of Consulting and Clinical Psychology, 43,* 135 - 147.

Morais, J., Bertelson, P., Cary, L., & Alegria, J. (1986). Literacy training and speech segmentation. *Cognition, 24,* 45 - 64.

Olson, R. K., Kliegl, R., Davidson, B. J., & Foltz, G. (1985). Individual and developmental differences in reading disability. In G. E. MacKinnon & T. G. Waller (Eds.), *Reading research: Advances in theory and practice* (Vol. 4, pp. 1 - 64). New York: Academic Press.

Olson, R. K., & Wise, B. (1987). Computer speech in reading instruction. In D. Reinking (Ed.), *Computers and reading: Issues for theory and practice* (pp. 156 - 177). New York: Teachers College Press.

Olson, R. K., Wise, B. W., Conners, F. A., & Rack, J. P. (in press). Organization, heritability, and remediation of component word recognition and language skills in disabled readers. In T. H. Carr & B. A. Levy (Eds.), *Reading and its development: Component skills approaches.* Orlando, FL: Academic Press.

Olson, R., Wise, B., Conners, F., Rack, J., & Fulker, D. (1989). Specific deficits in component reading and language skills: Genetic and environmental influences. *Journal of Learning Disabilities, 22,* 339 - 355.

Palincsar, A. S., & Brown, A. L. (1984). Reciprocal teaching of comprehension-fostering and comprehension-monitoring activities. *Cognition and Instruction, 1,* 117 - 175.

Perfetti, C. A., & Goldman, S. R. (1976). Discourse memory and reading comprehension skill. *Journal of Verbal Learning and Verbal Behavior, 15,* 33 - 42.

Spache, G. D. (1963). *Diagnostic reading scales.* New York: McGraw-Hill.

Spilich, G. J., Vesonder, G. T., Chiesi, H. L., & Voss, J. F. (1979). Text processing of domain-related information for individuals with high and low domain knowledge. *Journal of Verbal Learning and Verbal Behavior, 18,* 275 - 290.

Stanovich, K. E. (1986a). Cognitive processes and the reading problems of learning-disabled children: Evaluating the assumption of specificity. In J. Torgesen & B. Wong (Eds.), *Psychological and educational perspectives on learning disabilities* (pp. 87 - 131). New York: Academic Press.

Stanovich, K. E. (1986b). Matthew effects in reading: Some consequences of individual differences in the acquisition of literacy. *Reading Research Quarterly, 21,* 360 - 406.

Stanovich, K. E. (1988). The right and wrong places to look for the cognitive locus of reading disability. *Annals of Dyslexia, 38,* 154 - 177.

Stanovich, K. E., Cunningham, A. E., & Feeman, D. J. (1984). Intelligence, cognitive skills, and early reading progress. *Reading Research Quarterly, 19,* 278 - 303.

Sticht, T. (1979). Applications of the audread model to reading evaluation and instruction. In L. B. Resnick & P. Weaver (Eds.), *Theory and practice of early reading* (pp. 209 - 226). Hillsdale, NJ: Lawrence Erlbaum Associates.

Torgesen, J., & Goldman, T. (1977). Verbal rehearsal and short-term memory in reading-disabled children. *Child Development, 48,* 56 - 60.

Wechsler, D. I. (1974). *Manual for the Wechsler intelligence scale for children-revised.* New York: The Psychological Corporation.

Wechsler, D. I. (1981). *Manual for the Wechsler adult intelligence scale-revised.* New York: The Psychological Corporation.

Wilkinson, A. C. (1980). Children's understanding in reading and listening. *Journal of Educational Psychology, 72,* 561 - 574.

Wise, B. W., Olson, R. K., Anstett, M., Andrews, L., Terjak, M., Schneider, V., & Kostuch, J. (1989). Implementing a long-term computerized remedial reading program with synthetic speech feedback: Hardware, software, and real world issues. *Behavior Research Methods, Instruments, and Computers, 21,* 173 - 180.

27

SEMANTIC PROCESSING IN DYSLEXIA

Philip H.K. Seymour
University of Dundee

INTRODUCTION

This chapter is concerned with comprehension processes in cases of developmental dyslexia. I first outline a new approach to the investigation of reading disability. This involves a merging of the experimental techniques of cognitive psychology with the single case techniques of cognitive neuropsychology. It permits the construction of more precise and differentiated cognitive descriptions of individual cases of dyslexia than has previously been possible. My aim in the later part of the chapter is to consider how the methods of individual cognitive analysis may be extended to semantic processing. It should then be possible to discuss the relationship between semantic processes and the more peripheral components of the reading process.

I deal with comprehension at the single word level (rather than at the sentence or text level). An assumption is that comprehension depends on the activity of a semantic processor module in which abstract definitions of concepts are available for representation and manipulation. I take the general view that this module is *amodal* (i.e., superordinate to a number of different sensory input channels). The involvement of the processor in reading is therefore only one aspect of a wider range of functions, including comprehension of spoken language and of objects, scenes, and social events. The semantic module is also the repository of the *intentionality* that underpins speech production and other forms of action. I assume that speech production involves a second module, the phonological processor, which contains lexical word forms, principles of word formation, and a capability for sublexical (phonemic) representation of speech.

The semantic and phonological modules predate the emergence of a specialized *orthographic* system, which is the basis of literacy. Dyslexia, narrowly defined as a disorder of reading, can be viewed as a disturbance affecting the development of the orthographic module. Disturbances of semantic or phonological processes would appear to lie somewhat outside this definition and would require the introduction of other terms (e.g., developmental agnosia, developmental dysphasia). In this view, dyslexia is defined as a disorder affecting the processing components that are specific to reading and not as a rather general and loosely defined constellation of disabilities in which a literacy disorder is only one (optional) aspect (Miles, 1983).

COGNITIVE ANALYSIS OF DYSLEXIA: AN OVERVIEW

Processing Model

The analysis of the relationship between dyslexia and semantic processing can be sharpened by making reference to an information processing model. Figure 27.1 shows a diagrammatic framework that I have found useful in developing a cognitive approach to the analysis of dyslexic disorders. The model postulates the existence of separate but interacting semantic and phonological modules. The semantic component represents concepts, possibly with more internal differentiation than is shown in the diagram (e.g., between concrete and abstract meanings, or between free and bound morphemes). The processor contains functions for comparison and evaluation of data (used in verification) and provides outputs for control of action or production of speech via the phonological processor. The latter is envisaged as containing a store of lexical forms that may be transmitted to the articulatory apparatus plus procedures for assembly of forms from phonemic (or morphemic) elements. Phonological forms may also be used to locate concepts in the semantic component.

The semantic and phonological modules are not strictly part of the *reading* system. This is represented as a *visual processor*, which is specialized for the analysis and recognition of orthography (i.e., is distinct from the *pictorial processor* involved in object recognition). The module is assumed to contain analyzers for features of letters and words, a spatially coded system for arraying abstract letter identities (ALIs); an orthographic parser for selection of vowel and consonant letter groups; and a recognition space, in which words, morphemes, and phonologically significant letter groups may be identified (cf. Seymour, 1987b for a fuller discussion). The module communicates with the higher level semantic and phonological systems via access pathways. It is assumed that the pathways may transmit morpheme identities (labeled m in the diagram) or grapheme identities (labeled g in the diagram). The model corresponds broadly to a standard three-route model (Morton & Patterson, 1980) though it differs from some other schemes in allowing for interaction of the m and g processes within the phonological processor.

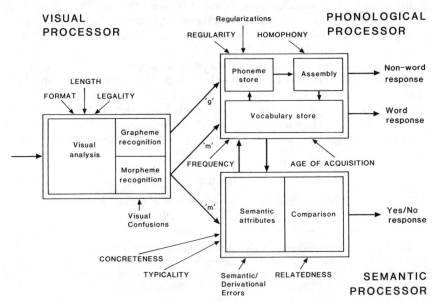

FIGURE 27.1. Schematic information-processing model showing relation of visual (orthographic) processor to semantic and phonological processors, together with suggested locations of effects and error types.

According to the strict definition, dyslexia involves a developmental impairment of the visual processor and the three access pathways. The main point here is that the modular information-processing framework allows the orthographic and semantic systems to be distinct components that are independently vulnerable to developmental impairment. What we now need to do is to turn to a consideration of the methods that can be used to probe the status of the different modules.

Cognitive Assessment Method

In earlier papers I have described a cognitive method of investigating basic reading functions in individuals (Seymour, 1986, 1987a; Seymour & MacGregor, 1984). This consists of a set of experiments that exploit techniques developed in the mainstream of experimental cognitive psychology. The experiments are automated on a microcomputer and involve measurements of both reaction time and accuracy. They are factorially designed to provide tests of linguistic and other effects.

The selection of experimental tasks and factors has been governed by the framework in Figure 27.1 with the aim of obtaining information about each of four subdomains within the reading system: (a) the visual processor, (b) route g to phonology, (c) route m to phonology, (d) route m to semantics. Table 27.1 gives an outline summary of the method.

The procedures are used to determine the general status of each component of the model. More detailed information is taken from tests of effects on reaction time or error level and from the types of error response that are produced. These interpretations depend on assumptions regarding the locus of effects and the origins of errors within the processing system, some of which have been indicated in Figure 27.1.

The argument of this section has been that the experimental methods of cognitive psychology can be adapted for use with individuals. When this methodology is combined with an information-processing framework of the kind shown in Figure 27.1 it becomes possible to describe the pattern of sparing and preservation of function that is characteristic of individual cases.

TABLE 27.1

Summary of Cognitive Assessment Procedure for Basic Reading Functions.

'g' $\longrightarrow$ *Phonology*	Non-word Vocalization – homophony
'm' $\longrightarrow$ *Phonology*	Word Vocalization – frequency – regularity – concreteness, function
'm' $\longrightarrow$ *Semantics*	Category Membership Decision – typicality, relatedness
Visual Processor	Vocalization, Decision – length – format – legality PI Matching – legality

Visual, Phonological, and Morphemic Impairments

A major question in the cognitive analysis of dyslexia concerns the nature and extent of *heterogeneity* among cases. I have investigated this issue by applying the assessment procedure to the individual members of samples of cases, including groups of young adults ($N = 6$), adolescents ($N = 15$), primary school age children ($N = 20$), and normally developing readers of age 12 years ($N = 14$) and below ($N = 80$). Only part of this work has so far been published (Seymour, 1986, 1987a). However, the analyses already completed are sufficient to establish that a radical degree of heterogeneity is apparent among cases when they are examined in detail by the cognitive method. In what follows I refer only to a few illustrative cases and follow the convention of referring to individuals by their initials.

I initially attempted to show the likely extent of the heterogeneity by presenting studies of four contrasting cases from the adult and adolescent samples (Seymour & MacGregor, 1984). The approach followed the lead given by Marshall and Newcombe (1973). This work, offering a psycholinguistic analysis of acquired dyslexia, has been the major formative influence on the establishment of the cognitive approach to developmental dyslexia.

Acquired Dyslexias

Marshall and Newcombe presented psycholinguistic analyses of six cases of acquired dyslexia (loss of reading functions in adulthood consequent upon injury to the brain). The disabilities shown by the patients were interpreted within a two-route version of the model in Figure 27.1 in which morphemic access to phonology was mediated by the semantic system (no m route to phonology). They argued that their cases exhibited three dyslexic patterns, involving: a visual processor impairment; a phonological impairment, affecting a process of nonlexical grapheme-phoneme translation; and a lexical/semantic impairment.

The cases were presented as prototypical exemplars of dyslexic types, each defined in terms of the focus of the predominant impairment, reliance on reading via the preserved system, and a characteristic pattern of error types and psycholinguistic effects, namely:

Deep dyslexia: involves loss of the phonological process (route g), preserved reading via the semantic component, the production of semantic and derivational errors, a lexical response bias, and a sensitivity to semantic variables (concreteness, syntactic function).

Surface dyslexia, results from loss of the semantic process, preserved reading via the phonological component, and the production of errors of regularization, misplaced stress, and incorrect grapheme-phoneme correspondence, plus a sensitivity to the spelling-sound regularity variable.

Visual dyslexia was considered to involve errors of letter identification but an absence of the higher order effects associated with deep and surface dyslexia. Subsequent research has revealed other patterns (Ellis, 1984; Patterson, 1982; Shallice, 1981). The most relevant of these is:

Phonological dyslexia: the phonological (grapheme-phoneme) process is impaired although many of the semantic effects associated with deep dyslexia do not occur. The major characteristic is an inability to read nonsense words which contrasts with a preserved ability to read words.

Thus, carefully designed studies of individual neurological patients have established the heterogeneity of the acquired dyslexias and have shown that the different patterns of preservation and loss of function can be interpreted within the framework of a modular information-processing model.

Developmental Dyslexias

In the Seymour and MacGregor article I attempted to treat the developmental cases in the same way, arguing that each case was a prototypical exemplar of a type of developmental dyslexia characterized by: (a) a focus of major impairment, (b) an area of relatively efficient functioning, (c) characteristic effects and error types, and (d) a hypothesized cause of the impairment of the reading system.

Phonological dyslexia. Case LT, a female science undergraduate, produced errors and major response delays when vocalizing nonwords. Word vocalization was relatively efficient and visual and semantic functions appeared quite normal. A primary impairment of the phonemic level of the phonological processor was seen as a possible cause of the dyslexia.

Visual analytic dyslexia. Case RO, a man of above average ability and a marked spelling defect, displayed approximately normal reading functions aside from reaction time delays in the matching task and a large effect of format distortion (e.g., presentation of a word as a vertical array of letters). This was considered to reflect an impairment of an analytic function of the visual processor.

Morphemic dyslexia. Case GS, an adolescent of average ability, presented with a word recognition defect, shown by errors and slow responses to words, a large effect of spelling-sound irregularity, the production of regularized error responses, and a tendency to read by a slow serial process (indexed by a word length effect in excess of 200 ms/letter). It was suggested that a cause of the problem might be an impairment of a wholistic function of the visual processor.

The discussion included a description of a fourth case, SE, a young man of average ability with an extreme spelling impairment, who presented a more complex pattern. His case was taken to support the possibility of multicomponent dyslexic disorders.

Reconsideration of the Subtype Question

I have since reported individual analyses of the full series of 21 cases contained in my adult and adolescent sample (Seymour, 1986). For each case, I constructed a cognitive description referring to the efficiency and operational mode of each of the four subdomains of the reading process. Examination of the contrasts among these descriptions convinced me that the practice of assigning prototypical status to individual cases was mistaken. The idea of a subtype entails that each postulated variety of dyslexia should be exemplified by individuals who display a characteristic *processing configuration*, involving: (a) a particular pattern of impairment and sparing over the modules and pathways involved in reading; (b) a bias in processing, usually away from the more impaired system and toward the less impaired system. According to this view, the designation *phonological dyslexia* refers to individuals who display a route *g* impairment combined with efficiency in the visual and semantic components and a bias toward lexical/semantic reading and away from grapheme-phoneme reading. The label *morphemic dyslexia* is applicable to individuals who exhibit a word recognition impairment plus serial processing plus a bias toward reading via a relatively unimpaired route *g*.

The analysis of the cases in the 1986 monograph suggested that this view was wrong in the following respects:

1. A route *g* impairment is not reliably associated with efficiency in the visual and semantic functions (cf. contrast between LT and PS).

2. A route *g* impairment does not reliably countermand a phonological bias in reading (cf. case of SB).

3. A morphemic (route *m*) impairment is not reliably associated with efficiency in route *g*.

My conclusion was that the term *dyslexia* should be considered to refer to a disorder of a specific function rather than to a complex processing configuration. Thus, *phonological dyslexia* might be taken to refer simply to an impairment of route *g* and to carry no necessary implications regarding the status of other functions or the presence of particular reading biases. The same qualifications apply to the terms *morphemic dyslexia* and *visual analytic dyslexia*. They refer to impairments of the word-recognition process or to the more peripheral functions of the visual processor and not to types of disabled readers.

Operational Definition of Impairments

The three major types of impairment can be given an operational definition. A *phonological dyslexia* is marked by a high rate of error in nonword reading and/or a widely dispersed distribution of vocal reaction times for correct responses to nonwords. An example of this pattern of reaction times is shown in the results for subject LT in Figure 27.2. Vocal reaction times to nonwords appeared widely dispersed and lacked the predominance of fast responses that occurred in word reading.

A *morphemic dyslexia* is marked by errors on *words* of lower frequency or irregular spelling-sound correspondence. The distribution of reaction times for vocal responses to words appears widely dispersed. It is usual to find large effects of word length (suggesting serial, letter-by-letter processing).

The results reported by Seymour (1986) indicate that these effects

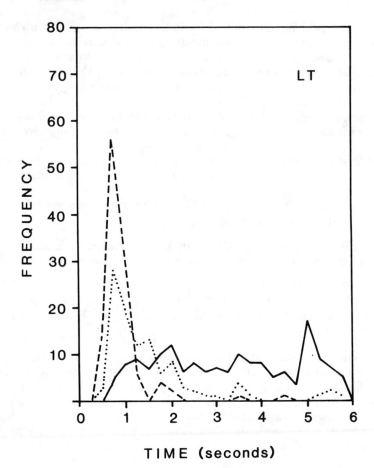

FIGURE 27.2. Distributions of vocal reaction times for reading high frequency words (dashed line), low frequency words (dotted line), and nonwords (solid line) by the phonologically dyslexic subject, LT (from Seymour, 1986).

are both present in some measure in the majority of cases. There is, nonetheless, evidence of an asymmetry in the relationship. It is possible for route *g* (nonword reading) to appear substantially more severely impaired than route *m* (word reading). A route *m* impairment on the other hand is most usually accompanied by an approximately equivalent effect on route *g*. To illustrate this point I have assembled data from subject RC, a very clear case from the primary school sample, in Figure 27.3.

The upper panels, giving results for word and nonword vocalization, show the dispersed distribution and exaggerated length effect for correct responses to words that are characteristic of a morphemic dyslexia. The length effect of over 700 ms/letter lies far outside the range encountered among normal readers (Seymour, 1987a). It appears that RC lacks a normally developed system for recognition of whole morphemes and that this forces the adoption of a serial letter-by-letter procedure (much like what occurs in acquired word-form dyslexia, Shallice, 1981).

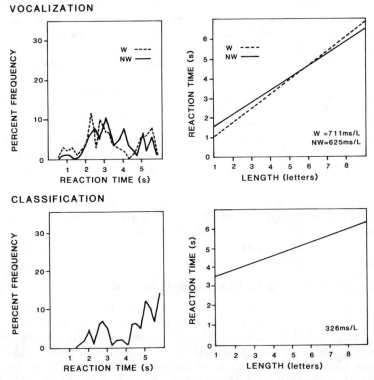

FIGURE 27.3. Reaction time distributions and length effects for the word/nonword vocalization task and the semantic decision task by the morphemic dyslexic case, RC.

Conclusion

The purpose of this section has been to present an outline of the cognitive approach to the analysis of reading disturbances in developmental dyslexia. It has been necessary to compress a large amount of complex information into a relatively brief exposition. The reader is referred to Seymour (1986) for a fuller account of the method and more detailed descriptions of cases.

The general trend of the work has been toward the establishment of operational definitions of impairments located within the visual processor and the dual (m and g) pathways by which the phonological system may be accessed. We can now turn to a consideration of the relation between these impairments and semantic processing.

SEMANTIC PROCESSING

When viewed within the framework sketched in Figure 27.1, comprehension concerns (a) the representational and comparison functions of the semantic processor and (b) access to the processor from the orthographic system. In order to discuss semantic processing (comprehension) in dyslexia, we need to consider the interaction of the semantic and orthographic components. Two general classes of relationship can be envisaged:

1. A *developmental* (causal) influence, involving an effect of the status of the semantic component on the development of the visual (orthographic) processor.

2. A *process* relationship, concerning (a) an influence of the semantic processor on visual/phonological functions or (b) consequences of an orthographic impairment for the operation of accessing semantic information from print.

A main objective is to specify the manner in which these relationships might vary, depending on which dyslexias are present and their degree of severity. As the processing issues are more tractable, I discuss them first and turn only briefly to the question of a developmental influence at the end of the chapter.

Semantic Mediation in Phonological Access

One possibility is that semantic processing might be used as a *support* for the m route to phonology. According to the theory of compensatory bias (Marshall & Newcombe, 1973), this would be most likely in cases showing a large phonological dyslexia (route g impairment). The index of this bias might be: (a) a sensitivity of vocal reading to linguistic variables associated with the semantic processor or (b) the occurrence of errors having a semantic origin.

The lists used in the 1986 study included sets of abstract and concrete words of high and low frequency and a set of high frequency functors. The assumption made was that content words of concrete reference provide a more effective basis for semantically mediated phonological retrieval than do abstract words or words having a primarily syntactic function. If so, we might expect to find a small reaction time advantage for concrete words whenever word retrieval depended on activity in both m routes. If, in addition, the semantic system was impaired, and the impairment was selective for abstract semantics (cf. Morton & Patterson's account of deep dyslexia), then we might expect to find raised reaction time and/or error levels for abstract items.

Abstract/Concrete Effect

The 1986 study provides examples of effects of abstract meaning in subjects showing strong route g impairments. Table 27.2 summarizes results from reading and spelling from subject JB. She showed large reaction time delays with abstract words and made errors in both reading and spelling. Other cases with route g impairments showed effects on reaction time only (e.g., SB: 922 ms vs. 1623 ms; JM: 1202 ms vs. 1776 ms) or showed no consistent effects at all (cases MT and LT). The effect also occurred in subjects whose primary impairment was morphemic. LH and LA read abstract words more slowly than concrete words, and GS and SM showed effects on error rate.

TABLE 27.2

Mean Response Latency (ms) and Percent Error Rates in Reading and Spelling for Concrete and Abstract Words by the Phonologically Dyslexic Case, JB.

	Concrete Words	Abstract Words
Reading		
Vocal Latency	2246	4383[a]
Percent Error	16.67	42.86[b]
Spelling		
Percent Error	23.81	59.52[c]

Note: [a] $p < .025$, [b] $p < .01$. [c] $p < .001$.

Function Word Effect

The contrast between functors and content words was generally ineffective. The exceptions were LA (balanced m and g effects) and LT (large g effect). The effect was most striking in the case of LT, who produced a widely dispersed distribution of reaction times when reading functors ($\bar{x} = 1799$ ms, $sd = 2426$ ms).

Semantic Errors

Semantic errors of the kind produced by Marshall and Newcombe's (1973) deep dyslexic patients are seldom found in developmental cases. The 1986 series produced no examples at all. Very occasional examples occurred among beginning logographic readers who had not yet developed a route g process (Seymour & Elder, 1986). Subject AT, described by Seymour and Evans (1988), presented with a genetic anomaly, a low verbal IQ, and a limited word recognition vocabulary combined with an almost total absence of the route g function (error rate in nonword reading = 95%). This boy produced some candidate semantic errors (e.g., *brooch* → "coat," *time* → "question," *ran* → "cricket," *still* → "sitting"). The errors also occurred as responses to nonwords (e.g., *smough* → "sing" via [mouth], which was produced as an error response to this target on another occasion). Some of his responses were unrelated to the target but reflected associative influences from previous responses, for example,

square ⟶ "space," here ⟶ "saucer," win ⟶ "flying".

Other responses were influenced by events external to the test, for example,

sull ⟶ "eye," bracial ⟶ "rub"

after AT had rubbed his eye.

Derivational Errors

Errors, involving preservation of a stem morpheme and alteration of an affix, are relatively common. In the 1986 series two subjects with large route g effects, LT and JB, made substantial numbers of such errors, for example,

LT: variety ⟶ "vary," crept ⟶ "creep," hunger ⟶ "hungry,"
beauty ⟶ "beautiful"
JB: heroism ⟶ "hero," loyalty ⟶ "loyal," greed ⟶ "greedy,"
these ⟶ "those," won ⟶ "win"

However, this class of error is not consistently associated with a phonological dyslexia, because some primarily phonological cases produced no examples (case MT) and because the errors also occurred among morphemic cases (SM, GS, and LH).

These effects provide evidence of semantic or syntactic mediation in word retrieval. They are not an exclusive property of phonological dyslexia because they vary from case to case and are also found in morphemic subjects. Although concreteness effects and semantic errors appear to originate in the semantic processor, the position regarding functor effects and derivational errors is less clear. Syntactic processing might be located in the semantic module (cf. Morton & Patterson, 1980) but could also be viewed as part of the assembly function of the phonological processor. It is difficult to determine the point at which the effects cease to be mere indicators of semantic involvement and suggest instead semantic reading combined with a defect of the semantic system. Very slow responses to abstract words or functors are suggestive of defects, as are frequent derivational errors and the strong semantic effects shown by AT.

Access to Semantics

A category membership decision task, involving presentation of a category name followed by an instance which was to be verified by a yes or no response, was treated as a main index of the m route to semantics. As is standard in these experiments (see Smith, Shoben, & Rips, 1974), the materials varied the typicality of the positive instances and the relatedness of the negatives. An impairment within the m route to semantics might have the effect of blocking access altogether or of introducing a *delay*, due either to the slow operation of the route or to the need to access meaning via the phonological processor.

Blocked Access

A morphemic dyslexia is a restriction on the number of words (visual morphemes) that can be recognized. In extreme cases, this will prevent access to concepts held in the semantic processor unless an alternative pathway (route *g*) is available. Subject AT (Seymour & Evans, 1988) can be cited as an illustration. As has already been noted, route *g* was not established in this case (nonwords could not be read). The word recognition system covered only a restricted vocabulary and was somewhat unstable, producing errors on some occasions but not others and different errors on different testings. AT completed the semantic decision task in both the visual and auditory modalities. Table 27.3 shows the numbers of correct and error responses for the two modalities.

TABLE 27.3

Percent Correct and Error Responses in Semantic Decisions with Visual and Auditory Presentation for Three Primary School Age Cases, AT, DK, and RC.

	Category Membership Decision				
	Visual		Auditory		
	Correct	Error	Correct	Error	
AT	50	46	81	15	sig.
DK	91	5	94	2	n.s.
RC	78	18	87	9	n.s.

It is clear that AT was able to perform the task successfully with auditory presentation but that his choices were no better than chance with visual presentation. The table also gives results from other subjects who do not show this effect. DK's nonword reading was as impaired as AT's (94% error rate) but his word recognition system was much more effective. Semantic decisions were equally accurate with visual and auditory presentation. A third subject, RC (see Figure 27.3), who had a substantial morphemic impairment, did not suffer a significant loss in the visual task. The implication is that AT demonstrates blocked semantic access due to a restriction on the scope of the logographic recognition system and the absence of a route *g*.

Delayed Access

The more usual outcome is that semantic access is *delayed* as a consequence of the morphemic dyslexia. This can be illustrated by reference to RC's results in Figure 27.3. The lower panels show that the dispersed reaction time distribution and large effect of word length that occurred in vocalization reappeared in the semantic decision task. Because visual presentation did not involve a significant loss of accuracy in this case it must be assumed that semantic access was achieved but that it was delayed as a consequence of the commitment to serial processing. This pattern was broadly repeated in the 1986 series. For example, SM and LH, two clear morphemic cases, produced dispersed distributions and serial processing in both vocalization and semantic decision. However, GS gave weaker evidence of serial processing in the semantic decision task, and this was also true of one of the subjects, RM, described by Seymour (1987a).

There is a possibility, therefore, that some subjects may demonstrate different types of processing in the phonological and semantic access tasks. The clearest demonstration occurs in the phonological cases (route g impairment as the predominant feature). Thus, LT made fast and accurate semantic decisions with a well-formed reaction time distribution and only slight effects of word length. This evidence of fully efficient processing via route $m \longrightarrow$ semantics contrasted with the mild morphemic impairments observed in word vocalization (see Figure 27.2).

I have used a procedure of loading the visual processor by variations in word length and format of presentation as a technique for investigating processing underlying access via the m routes. Words may be displayed in the vocalization or semantic decision task in a normal horizontal format or with the letters rearranged in a zigzag or vertical format, namely:

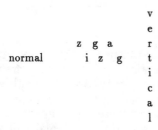

Previous research (see Seymour, 1987b) suggests that this manipulation typically produces a Length x Format interaction in which processing time per letter increases to about 200 ms/letter with the vertical distortion. In some dyslexic cases this effect is greatly exaggerated (see results for subject RO reported by Seymour & MacGregor, 1984, and by Seymour, 1986). Others show serial processing in all three formats (e.g., case SM in Seymour, 1986) or a general absence of effects (e.g., case

LT). These differing patterns provide information about the operations of the visual processor which precede word recognition and semantic or phonological access (Seymour, 1987b). The patterns observed in the vocalization and category decision tasks appear identical in some subjects, suggesting that similar processes underlie the operation of the two m routes (e.g., the visual analytic cases, MF, CE, and RO, and the morphemic cases, SM and LH), but there are exceptions (e.g., LT and GS).

These data confirm that the question of the identity of the processes underlying phonological and semantic access cannot be given a clear-cut answer. It appears possible that, in some cases at least, different access processes may be involved.

Phonologically Mediated Access

The serial processing which occurs in morphemically impaired systems might reflect the mediation of a phonological code in accessing semantics. This would occur if the $m \rightarrow$ semantics process was not functional although reading via the m and/or g routes to phonology was possible.

I used a list of 80 homophone pairs as a test for the occurrence of mediated access. Items were individually presented and the subjects were required to provide a meaning preserving association (e.g., pane $\rightarrow$ window, pain $\rightarrow$ hurt). Successful performance of this task requires orthographic discrimination. Mediated processing via the phonological representation /pein/ will result in the occurrence of homophone confusion errors (e.g., pane $\rightarrow$ "hurt") because the subject will often be unsure which of two alternative senses should be selected.

TABLE 27.4

Frequency of Correct and Homophone Confusion Associative Responses to Homophone Pairs by Cases Showing Predominant Morphemic or Phonological Impairments.

Meaningful Association (homophones)					
Morphemic Cases			Phonological Cases		
	Both Correct	Homophone Confusion		Both Correct	Homophone Confusion
SE	21	47	LT	67	5
SM	32	39	SB	46	23
GS	22	44	MT	35	34
LH	22	45	JB	43	27

Table 27.4 presents scores for (a) the number of *pairs* of homophones correctly discriminated and (b) the number of pairs involving a homophone confusion (usually assignment of both members of the pair to the same sense).

Data are shown for primarily morphemic cases and for primarily phonological cases. It is clear that whereas LT, who has a route g impairment combined with effective visual access to semantics, is able to discriminate a wide range of homophone pairs, this is not true of subjects with a word recognition impairment, such as GS and SM. For these cases, a high proportion of errors involve homophone confusions. The implication is that a morphemic dyslexia is associated with phonologically mediated access to semantics.

Conclusion

This section has been concerned with the *processing* relationship between the orthographic and semantic systems in dyslexia. The method of individual cognitive analysis makes it possible to identify instances of semantic reading in phonological access and of phonological reading in semantic access. These patterns are loosely associated with the occurrence of predominant route g or route m impairments, though the examination of a succession of cases reveals many exceptions, suggesting that the diagnostic status of the psycholinguistic effects and error types should not be overemphasized.

STATUS OF THE SEMANTIC SYSTEM

The semantic modules developed by individuals are likely to vary in efficiency. These variations are indexed in a global way by tests of general intelligence, such as the WISC-R. This section considers the possibility that the status of the semantic module might be causally related to the development of the orthographic processor. It may be noted that there is a prima-facie argument against this proposal, in that it is well established that reading disability may occur in the context of higher than average intelligence, and also that some children of low general ability develop effective basic reading functions (Ellis, 1984).

The discussion poses a general question concerning the causation of dyslexic impairments. Impaired development could be *intrinsic* to the visual module or the access pathways or could be a consequence of an impairment located in an *adjacent* system. Thus, a visual impairment might be thought to derive from an adjacent system concerned with object recognition, and a route g impairment might derive from a disturbance of the phonemic representational level of the phonological processor. Of course, if causation is assigned to defects in an adjacent system, one can ask why the adjacent system is impaired. The answer is likely to be that the impairment is intrinsic to the system. This entails an acceptance of the principle of intrinsic defects and thus allows its application to the reading processor as well as to other systems.

The experimental battery administered to the subjects in the 1986 sample included tasks that tapped the semantic processor and its capacity to generate speech output. These were the semantic decision experiments, which have already been discussed, experiments on picture naming and name-picture matching (varying age of acquisition), and experiments on associative retrieval, including an instance naming task (category name + initial letter) and the task of providing meaning preserving association to homophones. Measures of reaction time and error level were made for each of these tasks. In order to determine which subjects gave evidence of semantic system impairments, I identified the worst cases in the adult and adolescent samples (i.e., the instances in which error rate or reaction time was raised relative to the rest of the group).

One possibility is that a morphemic impairment is caused by an adjacent impairment of the semantic processor. This suggestion is not supported because some morphemic cases appeared efficient on all of the semantic tasks (SM was accurate on semantic decision and showed no large delays or inaccuracies in the other tasks). Another possibility is that phonological (route g) impairments might be associated with (or caused by) general problems of word retrieval. However, LT, who should be a clear example of any such effect, did not appear impaired on the retrieval tasks.

Table 27.5 identifies the cases from the adult and adolescent groups who stood out as having high values on the reaction time or accuracy indicators for the semantic tasks. The table also shows the lower limits of performance within each group. The two samples agree in picking out three categories of individual.

1. *Visual analytic cases.* MF and CE, who both showed delays in matching and format resolution combined with a spelling disability, stand out in terms of slow processing in the categorization experiments and effects on object naming or instance retrieval. CE produced simplified responses to pictures (*submarine* ⟶ "boat," *syringe* ⟶ "drill"). MF was sometimes unable to find the precise name for an object (*anvil* ⟶ "blacksmith's tool," *stethoscope* ⟶ "for a doctor"). She also produced an unusually large number of syntactic associations to homophones (e.g., *by* ⟶ "the way," *duel* ⟶ "carriageway," *knight* ⟶ "in shining armor").

2. *Low general intelligence.* MP and LH exhibited low verbal IQs on the Wechsler scales. They produced a large number of semantic effects, which probably reflect a generalized impairment of the semantic and phonological systems.

3. *Complex disability.* Cases SE and PS were both examples of rather complex patterns of dysfunction in reading and spelling. Both subjects also showed large response delays in the retrieval tasks. These occurred in the context of average general intelligence.

TABLE 27.5

Mean Response Latency (ms) and Percent Errors as a
Function of Task and Stimulus Type for the Adult
Cases, MF, MP, and SE, and the Adolescent Cases
CE, LH, and PS.

		Categorization		*Objects*		*Association*	
		Normal	*Format*	*Name*	*Y/N*	*Instances*	*Homophones*
Adult Cases							
MF	Latency	1673	1951	1290	887	–	–
	% Error	10	–	12	–	30	–
MP	Latency	1641	2197	1973	1085	2853	5431
	% Error	16	10	29	–	46	11
SE	Latency	2183	2086	2404	–	4699	10304
	% Error	–	–	–	–	24	12
Lower Limits							
	Latency	1150	950	1100	650	2000	3300
	% Error	2	0	5	0	12	2
Adolescent Cases							
CE	Latency	2321	3192	–	1108	4443	–
	% Error	–	–	21	–	–	–
LH	Latency	3396	3001	–	1355	–	7756
	% Error	27	18	24	10	52	13
PS	Latency	3246	2836	1795	–	5609	8865
	% Error	–	–	–	7	48	–
Lower Limits							
	Latency	1800	1400	1150	550	2500	3500
	% Error	8	4	10	0	30	6

These data tend not to support the hypothesis that semantic impairments can stand in a direct causal relation to specific impairments of the visual (orthographic) processor and its access pathways. A better interpretation is probably that intrinsic effects on the reading system may co-occur with other isolated effects, possibly varying from case to case. This would allow for a wide variety of outcomes ranging from relative isolation of the reading disturbance to co-occurrence with other difficulties.

DISCUSSION

This chapter has discussed the results that may be obtained when individual dyslexic cases are submitted to a cognitive investigation involving experimental tests of reading functions and other tasks implicating the activity of the semantic system. The discussion raises issues concerning: (a) the *method* that is likely to prove most useful in the investigation of dyslexia, (b) the types of theoretical *model* that will assist the design of studies and the interpretation of results, (c) the nature of dyslexia, and (d) the manner in which questions about the causation of dyslexia might be approached.

Methods of Investigation

The critical question here is whether researchers would be advised to persist with studies involving comparisons between undifferentiated *groups* of good and poor readers or whether it would be more sensible to concentrate on studies of *individuals*. Group studies may be justified if good and poor readers are homogeneous populations or if the variations within these groups are judged to be unimportant. The results of the work described here strongly suggest that the homogeneity assumption is unjustified. Given that the variations are complex and not easily reducible to a scheme of subtypes, it seems that there is now a good argument for looking closely at reasonably large samples of individuals.

In my research, I have found it worthwhile to attempt to exploit the full set of experimental techniques developed in cognitive psychology when attempting to analyze the processes of individual dyslexic cases. The reaction time measures are particularly helpful here. As it is now technically easy to obtain this information, I recommend that it should be treated as a standard indicator of information processing in dyslexia.

Requirements for Models

My framework for this research has been a box and arrow model, which falls within the tradition of the schemes proposed by Marshall and Newcombe (1973), Morton and Patterson (1980), and others. The additional element has been the attempt to be more explicit about the modules engaged by different tasks and the locations of particular effects and error types (see Figure 27.1). It is my view that it is difficult to talk about impaired reading systems without having some ideas about the general structure of the processing system.

Current attempts to specify the mechanisms operating within modules are described in the contribution by Seidenberg in this volume. If these theories are to prove helpful in developing an understanding of reading disability, they will need to incorporate an account of the acquisition process and a way in which different kinds of disability can emerge. It is also desirable that the models should be capable of distinguishing between processing time and error, and that they should be able to represent the full range of psycholinguistic effects.

Reading Acquisition

The models seem to start from the proposal that acquisition involves a mapping between a segmented orthography and a segmented phonology. In practice, reading starts with semantic and phonological systems in place, a phonology that is probably unsegmented, and a mapping of visual word forms onto phonological word forms, often based on partial discriminatory features (see Seymour & Elder, 1986). At this stage, the *logographic* (word recognition) process is operationally distinct from the *alphabetic* (letter-sound) process (Frith, 1985). Beginning readers produce results in word versus nonword vocalization tasks that resemble those shown by case LT in Figure 27.2. Thus, although the lexical (m) and sublexical (g) processes may well be merged in adult readers, this is not necessarily true of beginners or dyslexic individuals whose development has been arrested.

Patterns of Disability

The models need to be able to represent the distinction between the m and g processes and to show how an adverse influence on alphabetic development can produce the characteristics of phonological dyslexia (large differences between word and nonword reading). Some other intervention should be available that has the effect of limiting the development of the word recognition system and its access to semantics, and that produces letter-by-letter reading and phonologically mediated access. We need to know how these two types of intervention undermine the construction of an orthographic lexicon (i.e., a fully operational system that deals effectively with both words and nonwords).

Whether the modeling approach is capable of providing information additional to that offered by the empirical studies remains an open question. If the models do no more than mimic patterns of effects that are observed in real readers their contribution to an understanding of dyslexia may be quite limited. It might be more worthwhile to expend energy on practical efforts to modify dyslexic processing systems, using interventions of the kind described by Conners and Olson in this volume. Obviously, there would be a good case for combining such interventions with the techniques of individual cognitive assessment that have been discussed in this chapter.

Description of Dyslexia

The application of the cognitive method has proved helpful in describing the nature of dyslexia. We can now define the condition as a developmental impairment affecting the visual (orthographic) module and its pathways for accessing the phonological or semantic modules. The distribution of effects over the components of the orthographic system varies from case to case, although it will often be possible to identify a visual, morphemic (route m), or phonological (route g) impairment as a predominant feature. The relation between the g and m impairments is asymmetric. A route g impairment (marked by problems with nonword reading) may co-occur with an efficient morpheme recognition system, but a morphemic impairment (marked by errors and delays in word reading) is normally accompanied by an equivalent route g impairment.

One objective in this chapter has been to clarify the relationship between the g and m impairments and semantic (comprehension) processes. It seems that semantic processes may appear fully efficient in cases of phonological dyslexia, but that this is not always true. Thus, semantic efficiency is compatible with an impairment of route g but is not part of the narrow definition of a phonological dyslexia. A route g impairment may be accompanied by semantic reading. Morphemic dyslexia, by contrast, typically blocks or delays access to semantics and results in a bias toward phonological reading, often accompanied by slow serial processing.

Causation of Dyslexia

The second main objective of this chapter was to consider whether the semantic system played a *causal* role in the production of impairments in the orthographic systems, especially within the m routes. No clear evidence for such an effect was found. There are, of course, other (possibly more plausible) candidates for such a role, particularly visual object recognition and phonemic representation. The latter, though frequently cited, appears at best to be related by bidirectional causation to orthographic development (Bertelson, Morais, De Gelder, & Tfouni, 1988).

Although these issues are as yet unresolved, it may be worthwhile to question the presumption that disturbances of the orthographic systems have to be the result of *adjacent system* causation. It seems equally plausible that the impairments could be *intrinsic* to the systems. It might be supposed that the brain provides a neural substrate that is progressively colonized as development forces the establishment of new processing modules. The quality of this substrate may vary from one region to another and may be somewhat patchy. If a newly required module is assigned to a substandard region, a developmental impairment will occur. The results suggest the possibility of a set of effects, implicating the orthographic systems and other representational and retrieval processes, which may be isolated from more general aspects of intelligence.

REFERENCES

Bertelson, P., Morais, J., De Gelder, B., & Tfouni, L. V. (1988). *Rhyme judgment and phonetic segmentation in illiterates.* Paper presented at the NIAS Conference on Comprehension Processes in Reading, Wassenaar, The Netherlands.

Ellis, A. W. (1984). *Reading, writing, and dyslexia: A cognitive analysis.* London: Lawrence Erlbaum Associates.

Frith, U. (1985). Beneath the surface of developmental dyslexia. In K. E. Patterson, J. C. Marshall, & M. Coltheart (Eds.), *Surface dyslexia: Neuropsychological and cognitive analyses of phonological reading* (pp. 301 - 330). London: Lawrence Erlbaum Associates.

Marshall, J. C., & Newcombe, F. (1973). Patterns of paralexia: A psycholinguistic approach. *Journal of Psycholinguistic Research, 2,* 175 - 199.

Miles, T. R. (1983). *Dyslexia: The pattern of difficulties.* London: Granada.

Morton, J., & Patterson, K. (1980). A new attempt at an interpretation, or, an attempt at a new interpretation. In M. Coltheart, K. Patterson, & J. C. Marshall (Eds.), *Deep dyslexia* (pp. 91 - 118). London: Routledge & Kegan Paul.

Patterson, K. E. (1982). The relation between reading and phonological coding: Further neuropsychological observations. In A. W. Ellis (Ed.), *Normality and pathology in cognitive functioning* (pp. 77 - 111). London: Academic Press.

Seymour, P. H. K. (1986). *Cognitive analysis of dyslexia.* London: Routledge & Kegan Paul.

Seymour, P. H. K. (1987a). Individual cognitive analysis of competent and impaired reading. *British Journal of Psychology, 78,* 483 - 506.

Seymour, P. H. K. (1987b). Word recognition processes: An analysis based on format distortion effects. In J. R. Beech & A. Colley (Eds.), *Cognitive approaches to reading* (pp. 31 - 55). Chichester: Wiley.

Seymour, P. H. K., & Elder, L. (1986). Beginning reading without phonology. *Cognitive Neuropsychology, 3,* 1 - 36.

Seymour, P. H. K., & Evans, H. M. (1988). Developmental arrest at the logographic stage: Impaired literacy functions in Klinefelter's XXXY syndrome. *Journal of Reading Research, 11,* 133 - 151.

Seymour, P. H. K., & MacGregor, C. J. (1984). Developmental dyslexia: A cognitive experimental analysis of phonological, morphemic, and visual impairments. *Cognitive Neuropsychology, 1,* 43 - 82.

Shallice, T. (1981). Neurological impairment of cognitive processes. *British Medical Bulletin, 27,* 187 - 192.

Smith, E. E., Shoben, E. J., & Rips, L. J. (1974). Structure and process in semantic memory: A featural model for semantic decisions. *Psychological Review, 81,* 214 - 241.

28 COMPREHENSION PROBLEMS IN DYSLEXIA

Jan Rispens

University of Leiden

INTRODUCTION

In this chapter I review a number of studies addressing the nature of comprehension problems of dyslexic children. Children classified as dyslexic exhibit serious reading and spelling problems. From a number of studies it has become clear that these problems are difficult to overcome. As a consequence, the average achievement level in reading comprehension is 3 to 5 years behind actual grade placement upon entering the ninth grade (Gregory, Shanahan, & Walberg, 1985; Levin, Zigmond, & Birch, 1985; Miles, 1983). Even in adulthood, several of these students still suffer from their disorder, which affects the quality of their social life (Perin, 1981; Silver & Hagin, 1964; Zigmond & Thornton, 1988).

In a number of recent reviews of studies on dyslexic readers' poor performance, different interpretations of this phenomenon have been reported. Spear and Sternberg (1987) concluded that reading disabled children seem to be deficient in a number of both top-down and bottom-up processes. However, they argued that, essentially, reading disability is primarily a bottom-up type of disorder; poor comprehension is attributed to poor decoding and word recognition skills. They stated that decoding problems stem from coding problems in short-term memory.

Morrison (1987) agreed that the primary source of reading problems is at the word level. However, contrary to the Spear and Sternberg opinion, he stated that rule-learning deficits, that is, difficulties in learning the correspondence rules of the English language, are at the heart of the word-recognition difficulties. In several studies (e.g., Manis & Morrison, 1985; Szeszulski & Manis, 1987), it has been demonstrated that learning-disabled children encounter difficulties when they have to handle irregular words: they are unable to master the rules that govern their spelling.

On the other hand, there is empirical evidence in favor of the idea that there are comprehension problems independent of the level of decoding. Rabinowitz and Chi (1987) reported research supporting their premise that strategic processing is a very relevant factor contributing to reading difficulties. They argued that the lack of accessibility (and not the availability) of relevant knowledge prevents the use of adequate strategies, for example, the application of a specific content strategy, and therefore causes poor reading.

Ceci and Baker (1987) conceived of reading disabilities in terms of a general language deficit. Their observation that children with reading problems often have troubles with other language tasks as well led them to the conclusion that they have to be viewed as language-learning disabled. Therefore, comprehension problems have to be considered as deficiencies in top-down processes. They agreed with the suggestion that reading is comparable to a psycholinguistic guessing game: "at the beginning stages of reading, linguistic deficits possibly may masquerade as bottom-up deficiencies" (Ceci & Baker, 1987, p. 111).

Inconsistencies of this kind are not uncommon in dyslexia research. To a certain extent they can be attributed to controversies with respect to the definition of the condition. Due to the resulting inconsistencies in subject selection, there are many limitations in the interpretation of the data-based literature. For that reason, a summary of the outcomes of dyslexia research has to pay attention to the problem of defining and operationalizing the condition. In the following section I deal briefly with this issue.

The present review of the literature on comprehension disorders in dyslexia concentrates primarily on the question whether poor comprehension can be attributed to poor decoding. Most of the studies suggest that this is indeed the case. In the third section, I discuss a number of these studies. However, there is some evidence of the existence of comprehension problems, independent of the level of decoding. In the fourth section, I briefly review a number of these studies, addressing other aspects of poor comprehension. In the final section, I evaluate the reviewed literature.

THE CONCEPT OF DYSLEXIA

Dyslexia refers to a disorder manifested by specific (isolated) reading problems, not due to inadequate schooling, poor educational background, a lack of intelligence, or visual or hearing deficiencies (Rutter, 1978).

Since its inception, the idea of the existence of a specific reading disorder referring to a subset of the class of children with reading problems has been criticized. Indeed, several authors argue that dyslexia and poor reading are the same. Seymour (1986) stated that the idea that dyslexia represents a subtype, to be distinguished from the (larger) group of children with reading problems, is a category mistake. Even those favoring the idea that a condition like dyslexia can be recognized agree that the disorder is poorly defined (Eisenberg, 1978; Rutter, 1978). Numerous attempts to improve this situation have been undertaken but without much success (Keogh, 1986; Wong, 1986).

This inability to provide an adequate description of the condition reflects the poor state of our understanding of dyslexia. Dyslexia, poor reading, and learning disability are still poorly defined concepts. As a consequence, research samples differ widely which adds to the existing confusion. Together with other methodological flaws, this may explain part of the inconsistencies in the data.

It is interesting to note that in most studies of comprehension problems, not much attention has been paid to the issue of defining the target population. The terms *dyslexia, poor reading,* and *learning disability* are used rather loosely; it may be that most studies, although using different terms, address the same population of children with comprehension problems. For that reason I do not pay much attention to the issue of defining the population and include in my review studies of dyslexic children, poor readers, and learning-disabled children.

On the other hand, there is growing evidence that children with reading problems constitute a heterogeneous group (Stanovich, 1986). Recently, the search for subtypes has attracted much attention (Doehring, 1985; Satz & Morris, 1981). One of these subtypes could be dyslexia: a subclass of children with isolated reading and spelling problems, caused by a specific factor. Much of the research in the field of dyslexia is devoted to the identification of these specific factors (Stanovich, 1986). As it is likely that more than one specific factor may be detected, the category dyslexia itself may be constituted by a number of subtypes (Doehring, 1985). From a developmental perspective, this is an important issue that could have implications for our understanding of the development of reading skill. It may be that children belonging to different subtypes manifest a divergence of developmental course in their mastery of word recognition skill, as was demonstrated by Lovett (1984). It is interesting to note that Lovett's two subtypes (accuracy and rate disabled) although showing differences in word recognition skill, did not differ in their comprehension performance.

However, the problem of subtyping is still far from solved. This holds especially for comprehension research, which has neglected this issue to a great extent. For that reason I will not pay much attention to this topic in the present review.

WORD RECOGNITION AND COMPREHENSION

Recent theories of skilled reading highlight the importance of rapid and accurate word recognition skills as a prerequisite for comprehension (Gough & Tunmer, 1986; Perfetti, 1985; Perfetti & Lesgold, 1977; Stanovich, Nathan, & Zolman, 1988). In the simple model of reading proposed by Gough and Tunmer (1986), it is assumed that reading ability is composed of two independent factors: decoding and linguistic (listening) comprehension. Decoding skills, therefore, are of paramount importance for reading comprehension. Perfetti (1985) stated, that as a consequence of a lack of automaticity, word identification processes are still too resource demanding, at the cost of the amount of attention available for comprehension. Verbal inefficiency, manifesting itself in slower encoding and retrieval of verbal material, resulting in slower word recognition and lexical access, is therefore considered to be the main cause of the comprehension problems of poor readers.

Empirical Evidence

It is important to note, that contrary to the still widely held belief in the field of dyslexia, which states that top-down processes are by far the most important factors causing comprehension problems (Ceci & Baker, 1987), there is convincing evidence in favor of the importance of word recognition in the process of comprehension. Eye-fixation studies demonstrate that reading a text depends to a great extent on the accurate and rapid reading of words (Rayner & Pollatsek, 1987). Even skilled readers fixate most of the content words and a considerable percentage of the function words and small words. It seems safe, therefore, to assume that the word is one unit of analysis while reading a text. As a consequence, word recognition problems are of paramount importance to comprehension.

In a number of longitudinal studies, this relationship between word recognition and comprehension has been demonstrated; correlations range from .40 to .70, depending on age and reading level of the samples (Curtis, 1980; Jackson & McClelland, 1979; Stanovich, Nathan, & Vala-Rossi, 1986). In a study by Juel, Griffith, and Gough (1986), the relationship between decoding skill and comprehension was measured three times a year. Correlations ranged from .47 to .64 in Grade 1 and from .43 to .59 in Grade 2. In a path analysis the path coefficients (standardized regression coefficients) were .71 for Grade 1 and .67 for Grade 2.

An extensive Dutch study (n = 398) revealed correlation coefficients between word recognition and comprehension in Grade 1 of .47, in Grade 2 of .59, in Grade 3 of .50 and in Grade 6 of .37 (Mommers & Boland, 1987).

From a number of studies it has become clear that word recognition skills of children classified as learning disabled or dyslexic are far below

Grade level (Gregory et al., 1985). A recent Dutch investigation revealed that the mean score of a group of learning-disabled boys at the age of 12 on a 116-item word recognition test was 45.3; the mean of normal students of this age is 77.8 (van Putten, 1987).

Most of the studies on the nature of comprehension problems included in my review report poor performance on both word-recognition and comprehension tests. It seems safe, therefore, to assume that word-recognition problems are at the heart of comprehension problems of poor readers. Lesgold and Resnick (1982) even assumed a causal relation.

Absence of Text Modeling or Long Term Memory Deficiencies

In theories of skilled reading, it is assumed that based on the encoding of words, the reader constructs a text model that represents the meaning of the text (Mitchell, 1982). Several different text-modeling operations (Perfetti, 1985) play a role here, for example, schema knowledge, knowledge of prose structure, and skills such as the ability to rate the importance of ideas or the ability to generate expectancies of forthcoming ideas.

Another argument in favor of the idea that comprehension problems are caused primarily by inadequate word recognition skills is that in a number of studies it could not be demonstrated that children with comprehension problems are deficient in their text-modeling operations. Perfetti and Lesgold (1977) concluded that normal and poor readers do not differ in their sensitivity to discourse structure. Normal and poor readers were presented with pairs of sentences in which the second sentence presupposed that information is already given in the first sentence. Both groups were equally sensitive to this given-new distinction, suggesting that indeed poor comprehension performance is not due to differences in sensitivity to discourse structure. Therefore, although poor readers show less comprehension and recall than proficient readers, they seem not to be deficient in their processing of the features of the prose.

In her review of comprehension studies, Worden (1987) concluded that learning-disabled children differ from normal readers primarily in the amount of recall after reading a passage of prose. Studies of story recall and the representation of story scheme or the awareness of text structure and strategy studies, although not completely consistent in their outcomes, seem to corroborate the conclusions of Perfetti and Lesgold (1977). Worden concluded that these authors "appear to have been on the right track when they speculated that higher order features of discourse structure are not likely to be responsible for ability differences in prose processing as are bottom-up or data-driven activities" (Worden, 1987, p. 257). She also argued, that there seems to be no reason to assume that the poor comprehension performance can be attributed to defective organization of semantic memory. Several studies have shown that disabled readers perform normally on nonverbal long-term memory tasks and have an adequate long-term memory for semantic aspects of verbal material (Cohen, 1982; Jorm, 1983).

However, it is not quite clear whether Worden's conclusion holds for all children with comprehension problems. To demonstrate this problem, I discuss briefly two of her own experiments. In a typical experiment, Worden and Nakamura (1982) had learning-disabled students and a control group of normal students rate the importance of ideas in a story. Students were asked to read (aloud) a story, after which they had to rate the importance of the ideas. They were to start by indicating which ideas were least important, then which were not very important and so on (the rating scale consisted of four categories.) After about a week, they came back for a recall session; half of the students had to select recall cues before recall, the other half after recall.

The results indicated that the learning-disabled students differed from the normals in the agreement of the ratings of the ideas. This could reflect less sensitivity to the subtle nuances of a story. However, the authors favored another interpretation. They suggested that the task placed too much burden on the capacity of the memory of the learning-disabled because they had to reread the story several times and keep in memory all of the information. An interesting finding was that recall of the higher levels of importance was better then recall of the lower levels. Therefore, it seems likely that knowledge of story structure seems intact and that learning-disabled students have problems in their storage of information.

This finding was corroborated in another series of experiments (Worden, Malmgren, & Lagourie, 1982). Learning-disabled students had to recall a story they had heard the previous day. Although the learning-disabled remembered less, their pattern of recall was the same as that of the control group. Again, this suggests that they have memory problems but also have intact story structure knowledge.

Two critical remarks have to be made. First, in this experiment college students were used; their mean age was 23 years. It seems likely that they had had a lot more reading experience than younger children. (As they were college students, they may even have had formal training in the analysis of stories.) For that reason, we are not sure whether Worden's results will hold for younger children with learning problems as well. Second, it is noteworthy that both groups of students and their controls were not matched on their level of word recognition. Therefore, the possibility that differences in recall reflect differences in decoding skill cannot be excluded. For this reason, Worden's conclusion that learning-disabled children are not deficient in their knowledge of story schemas is not completely convincing. In the next section, I discuss this topic in more detail.

Some Counter Evidence

There is sufficient evidence to conclude that poor word recognition skills play an important part in comprehension problems. Some authors even suggest that it is by far the most important factor, implying more or less that other problems are no more then a derivate of the root problem: poor decoding.

However, caution is needed. In another Dutch study it was found that about 10% of the poor decoders perform better than expected (given their decoding skill) on a comprehension test (Aarnoutse, Mommers, Smits, & van Leeuwe, 1986). For that reason the authors state that decoding skill is not the only factor determining comprehension. The authors speculate about the possibility that those children performing better than expected use context information to compensate for their lack of decoding skills.

It has been argued (Stanovich, 1980) that context plays an important role in the reading performance of poor readers. Context is used to compensate for the negative effects of poor quality of word recognition. It is possible that poor readers differ widely with respect to their degree of compensation depending on their IQ, educational background, and schooling.

The study of Leu, DeGroff, and Simons (1986) provides some evidence in favor of the compensation hypothesis. They confronted poor readers with a highly predictable text that contained repetitive sentence patterns. Although their initial reading rate was below that of good readers, their comprehension was not affected. Their reading errors (e.g., substitutions) demonstrated their use of the context in order to grasp the meaning of the text. An interesting finding was that their reading speed increased in the second half of the text and was equal to that of good readers. This suggests that the repetitive pattern led them to a more automatic level of sentence reading.

On the other hand, the case of *hyperlexia* demonstrates that average or even above-average decoding skills are no guarantee for comprehension. Hyperlexia refers to a condition in which children have adequate word-recognition skills but show little comprehension. The condition is an example of the existence of isolated abilities in otherwise developmentally disordered children. Although there are a number of inconsistencies with respect to definition and cause of hyperlexia (Graziani, Brodsky, Mason, & Zager, 1983; Healy, Aram, Horwitz, & Kessler, 1982), the existence of this specific ability to decode words (and nonwords as well) in the absence of comprehension has been extensively documented.

Hyperlexia remains a strange phenomenon that is difficult to explain. Lord (1985) suggested that the failure to understand the meaning of sentences that hyperlexics can sound out stems from their lack of knowledge of the world or the inaccessibility of the knowledge that is available. Hyperlexia, therefore, may be an extreme case of deficient higher order information, such as knowledge of the world, the availability of schema knowledge, or other aspects of discourse structure. Therefore, the case of hyperlexia demonstrates that decoding is not the only factor determining comprehension; therefore, it could be that text modeling factors (Perfetti, 1985) play a role as well in the case of comprehension problems of dyslexics.

Conclusion

The studies I discussed thus far strongly support the notion that a lack of decoding skills plays a very important role in the comprehension problems of dyslexic or poor readers. However, it is not the only factor contributing to poor comprehension. The question that remains to be answered is whether dyslexic or poor readers are deficient in their higher order information-processing skills. In the next section, I discuss a number of studies addressing this problem.

COMPREHENSION AND KNOWLEDGE OF STORY STRUCTURE

The question addressed in this section is whether higher order problems contribute to the development of comprehension problems in dyslexic readers. Before discussing the outcomes of a number of studies, some preliminary remarks need to be made.

Differences in Developmental Course

Analysis of comprehension problems of dyslexic or poor readers is a much neglected issue. Most of the studies of dyslexia are devoted to the causes of poor word recognition with the implicit suggestion that comprehension problems can be reduced to poor decoding. There is a lack of studies trying to depict the problems dyslexic readers encounter when they try to grasp the meaning of a text. As a consequence, our understanding of the nature of comprehension problems is still poor. This holds especially when it comes to our insight into the heterogenity of the group of children with poor comprehension.

From my clinical experience I am familiar with intelligent, 12-15 year-old dyslexic boys who have overcome their reading problems reasonably well. Indeed, their reading is rather slow and sometimes inaccurate, but they have no special comprehension problems. When it comes to understanding texts in their natural science or biology workbooks, they perform on age level. Their problems are in the domain of spelling. Poor quality of phonological representation of the orthographic structure of words impairs their spelling performance. The acquisition of an acceptable level of spelling in second language learning produces many problems.

On the other hand, I have seen many students from the lower end of the normal IQ distribution not profiting from good educational opportunities, either at school or at home. These individuals still have very serious reading problems. Their lack of speed and, supposedly, their lack of knowledge (or the inability to apply this knowledge) of the world and maybe of story structure is a very effective hindrance to adequate comprehension.

There is some scattered evidence in the literature of this divergence of developmental course within the group of children with reading problems. Perin (1981) reported that a number of her adult dyslexics had overcome their reading problem but still exhibited poor spelling performance. However, others still had reading problems. Miles (1983) found in his large sample of 232 dyslexic children a number of children who had overcome their initial reading problems. Finally, in a number of studies devoted to the genetic aspects of dyslexia, using adult dyslexics, Pennington, McCabe, Smith, Lefly, Bookman, Kimberling, and Lubs (1986) found that some of their adult dyslexics scored reasonably well on a reading (comprehension) test, but others did not.

One of the problems of interpreting the outcomes of comprehension studies is that they do not pay attention to this problem of heterogenity of pupils classified as dyslexic and the resulting divergence in development. For that reason, it can be expected that age of subjects included in an experiment is a very relevant factor.

Explicit Awareness

Another difficulty one encounters in evaluating the research addressing higher order factors is that there is some confusion with respect to the theoretical framework. Broadly speaking, there are two different approaches. A number of researchers examine individual differences within a theory of skilled reading. Relevant topics are: knowledge of story structure, the skill to rate the importance of ideas, schema knowledge and so forth. On the other hand, a number of investigations have been undertaken to analyze the relationship between metacognitive skills and reading, focusing on topics such as knowledge of strategies or monitoring activities (Baker & Brown, 1984; Worden, 1983).

The major difference between these approaches implies awareness and control of the skills involved. Baker and Brown (1984) argued that skilled readers must have some awareness of the cognitive activities they perform during reading. However, from a number of studies it is not quite clear whether explicit awareness is involved. In most research of this type, subjects are not explicitly asked whether they use a story scheme; their recall performance is measured, and, depending on the experimental condition (e.g., presentation of the story in normal or scrambled order), the interaction between presentation and recall is considered as indicating the influence of story scheme knowledge. Explicit awareness or knowledge of story scheme has not been tested. For that reason, I will not pay attention to this distinction.

Reading and Listening Comprehension

In the simple reading model of Gough and Tunmer (1986) I briefly mentioned in the previous section, it is assumed that reading consists of two independent factors: word recognition and linguistic (listening) ability. As a consequence, it is assumed that the higher order skills and knowledge I refer to in this section play a role in both reading and listening. These skills are subsumed under the category of discourse processes, which are equally relevant for both listening and reading comprehension. In their study of comprehension and recall of passages of a story, Smiley, Oakley, Worthen, Campione, and Brown, (1977) demonstrated that listening and reading comprehension are dependent on the same basic processes. It seems to be more or less generally assumed that poor readers are poor listeners as well. Therefore, in a number of studies on reading comprehension, stories are presented orally. However, only a few studies have demonstrated that this assumption of the same underlying processes is warranted. For this reason, this issue needs further attention.

Empirical Evidence

In a number of studies it has been demonstrated that poor and normal readers differ in a number of higher orders skills. Particular attention has been paid to their knowledge and use of story schema or their sensitivity to text structure. For example, Smiley et al. (1977) presented 36 junior high school students with two stories in two conditions: listen-read or read-listen. Immediately after listening to the story or after reading the story, the students had to write their recall. The subjects were divided into two groups: children reading at or above grade level and a group reading at least 2 years below grade level. The recall protocols were analyzed using a rating scale that distinguished four levels of importance of the ideas. Good readers had a higher proportion of correct recall and they were more sensitive to the gradations in importance. This result is a replication of Brown and Smiley (1977), who used the same material and procedure with third graders. Another interesting finding is that the correlation between the reading and the listening comprehension scores was .85, suggesting that indeed the underlying processes are similar. Smiley et al. (1977) concluded that comprehension problems exist independent of decoding problems because the differential sensitivity to importance of ideas for the groups holds for both ways of presenting the stories.

A number of studies have replicated these differences in sensitivity to importance of ideas or story structure: Feagans and Short (1984); Fitzgerald (1984), with a group of fourth and sixth graders; Gold and Fleisher (1986), using fourth graders (normal readers) and sixth graders (poor readers); Rahman and Bisanz (1986); Taylor and Williams (1983), who used learning-disabled children with a mean age of 14 years and a control group matched on IQ and reading vocabulary, but not on age.

The study of Taylor and Williams (1983) is of particular interest. They compared poor readers matched to normal readers on reading level. In the first experiment, students had to write a summary or choose a title for the stories presented to them. Learning-disabled children performed equally well as normal readers. In a second experiment, deviant sentences were incorporated into the stories; some were related to the macrostructure of the paragraph, others were unrelated. Subjects had to detect whether or not a paragraph contained a deviant sentence. An interesting finding was that detection of deviant sentences depended on the position of the sentence in the paragraph: Detection is more accurate when the position is at the end of the paragraph. However, this does not hold for the poor readers: They do not use the greater amount of prior information. The authors speculated that this difference in sensitivity to text characteristics between Experiments 1 and 2 may be caused by the amount of attention learning-disabled students have to spend on lower level processes such as word recognition in the more complicated task of Experiment 2.

Wong (1982) using the same stories as in the Brown and Smiley study (1977) presented her subjects, after they had read the story, with a number of cards that contained ideas of the stories. Subjects were asked to read these cards and then select a limited number of cards which could serve as a retrieval cue if the students were asked to recall the stories. Analysis of the selection of these cues revealed a difference between the learning-disabled and the normal and gifted children. The poor readers lacked self-checking behavior and were less organized and planful in their selection of the retrieval cues. It could be that this points to a strategy deficit of poor readers.

Fitzgerald (1984) demonstrated that poor readers are less sensitive to the narrative structure of a text. Her subjects read stories and had to predict what should come next in an incomplete story or tell about the missing part of a story. Better readers were more efficient at extracting the story structure than poor readers. This finding is in line with the outcomes of the studies I discussed earlier. However, inconsistent with these findings are those of Weaver and Dickinson (1982). Using a story grammar developed by Stein and Glenn (1979), they analyzed the story recall of 26 boys attending a special school; there were two age groups, ranging from 9 to 11 years old and from 13 to 15 years old. Stories were read to the boys who were asked, after a backward counting task, to retell the story. Comparing their results with those of Stein and Glenn (1979), who used normal first and fifth graders, Weaver and Dickinson found no differences in pattern of recall between their subjects and the normal readers in the Stein and Glenn study. This holds for both the extent to which the categories of the story were recalled and the order of importance. This seems to suggest that disabled readers have intact knowledge of story structure.

However, applying another, more fine grained scoring scheme, containing nine categories of linguistic markers important to text cohesion, the recall protocols revealed a striking difference between normal and disabled students. Weaver and Dickinson therefore concluded that story grammars are an inadequate representation of story structure; their own scoring system demonstrates that the main problem of the poor readers is at the lower level of processing. They are unable to recognize surface cues to meaning; therefore, they do not choose the appropriate recognition activities. It cannot be concluded that they are deficient in their story structure knowledge.

The problem with the Weaver and Dickinson study, however, is that their original finding of no difference in story recall has not been replicated. The studies I discussed so far always found a difference in recall. Fitzgerald (1984) suggested that differences in age may be a relevant factor. However, as I already noted in my introduction, another factor may be the way of presenting the stories: In Fitzgerald's study, the children had to read themselves; in Weaver and Dickinson's study, the stories were read to the subjects.

Conclusion

Looking over the studies discussed so far, it seems safe to conclude that poor readers tend to be less sensitive to story structure than normal readers. Their recall of a story is often impoverished; they do not remember the same amount of important ideas in a text.

However, it is difficult to interpret these results. Because of the reasons outlined in the introduction to this section, firm conclusions are not warranted: The number of studies is too limited, the populations differ widely, and only a few higher order aspects have been investigated. Therefore, several questions remain unanswered.

We are not sure yet whether the differences between proficient and poor readers reflect differences in knowledge of story schema or pertain to the inability of poor readers to use their knowledge, therefore reflecting a strategy problem. A number of authors tend to accept the latter interpretation; as a consequence, they favor the application of strategy training (Gelzheiser, 1984; Hansen, 1981).

A number of studies provided some evidence in favor of the idea that knowledge of discourse features such as story structure underlies both reading and listening. The correlation between recall performance after listening to or reading a story is interpreted as an indication of this relationship. If this holds, it could mean that the impoverished recall or relative insensitivity to the main ideas of a text reflect the independence of this higher order knowledge. A lack of knowledge of story schema may then exist, independent of the level of decoding. However, not all studies replicate this finding, as was demonstrated in the Weaver and Dickinson case. Hence further research is needed.

COMPREHENSION PROBLEMS OF DYSLEXIC READERS:
A SUMMARY

Comprehension is a much neglected issue in dyslexia research. For this reason, little data are available about the dyslexic population; assumed dyslexia exists as an entity to be distinguished from poor readers in general. Therefore, I am not sure whether the research findings I presented will hold for the dyslexic population.

It is safe to conclude that a lack of decoding skill is one of the main factors contributing to poor comprehension. This has been sufficiently documented in a great number of studies. However, even if we assume a causal relationship, this does not mean that the level of decoding is the only determining factor. There is empirical evidence showing that some children have a higher level of comprehension than expected, given their decoding performance.

In a number of studies, it has been demonstrated that poor readers are less sensitive than their normal-reading age mates to the structure of a story. Their recall is impoverished and they are less able to select and remember the main ideas of a story. However, it is still unclear whether this reflects a structural deficit or an inability of these children to apply their intact knowledge of story structure. Another still undecided question pertains to the independence of these higher order skills and knowledge, although there is some evidence in favor of the idea that higher order aspects contribute to comprehension independent of the level of decoding ability.

My conclusion is that our knowledge of the comprehension problems of dyslexic readers is very poor. One of the main problems is the rather global level of the analysis of comprehension problems, especially when it concerns the impact of higher order factors. The present review suggests that we lack a firm data-based theory here.

Another much neglected issue concerns the heterogenity of the group of poor readers. To date, no distinction has been made in the several studies of poor reading children. However, it is conceivable that there are subgroups differing widely in the nature of their comprehension deficit. The most intriguing question here is whether the differences found in children with respect to the possible cause of their decoding problems are relevant for comprehension as well. Or could it be, as suggested by a number of authors, that underlying both decoding and comprehension is a unitary linguistic deficit?

The relevance of this question can easily be demonstrated. It is assumed that poor decoding is due not only to strategic processing deficits, for example, a failure to use mnemonic strategies such as chunking, but to nonstrategic processing deficits as well (Cohen, 1982; Jorm, 1983; Vellutino & Scanlon, 1985). One factor could be the apparent inability of beginning poor readers to process and utilize speech sounds. From a number of studies, using different tasks, it becomes more and more clear that poor readers have a weakness in the phonological domain

(Conners & Olson, this volume). However, not all poor readers demonstrate this problem. And, it may be that the children who manifest phonological problems differ with respect to the relationship between this coding problem and other deficiencies in the acoustic and phonetic domains. In a number of studies (e.g., Lieberman, Meskill, Chatillon, & Schupack, 1985) speech perception of dyslexics has been investigated. The clinical observation that (even adult) dyslexic readers produce errors in the identification of speech sounds led these investigators to the hypothesis that dyslexics have problems in processing and identifying specific acoustic cues or phonetic segments. Lieberman et al. argued in favor of a limited and discrete deficiency. They did not support the view that reading disorders stem from a general and pervasive difficulty of the perception of rapidly changing auditory information. However, Tallal (1980; Stark & Tallal, 1981) suggested that the inability to analyze phonological codes efficiently is caused by a basic mechanism of deficient speech perception. Phonological coding, then, is dependent on this perceptual deficiency.

Comprehension research has not paid attention to this heterogenity in the group of poor readers. As a consequence, our understanding of this phenomenon is too global. We therefore need longitudinal studies in which the development of children's comprehension is carefully matched on factors supposed to underlie their decoding problems. The outcome of this kind of study could be highly beneficial in attempts to understand the nature of poor reading comprehension.

REFERENCES

Aarnoutse, C. A. J., Mommers, M. J. C., Smits, B. W. G. M., & Van Leeuwe, J. F. J. (1986). De ontwikkeling en samenhang van technisch lezen, begrijpend lezen en spellen. [The development and coordination of technical reading, reading for comprehension, and spelling]. *Pedagogische Studiën, 63*, 97 - 110.

Baker, L., & Brown, A. L. (1984). Metacognitive skills and reading. In P. D. Pearson (Ed.), *Handbook of reading research* (pp. 353 - 395). New York: Longman.

Brown, A. L., & Smiley, S. S. (1977). Rating the importance of structural units of prose passages: A problem of metacognitive development. *Child Development, 48*, 1 - 8.

Ceci, S. J., & Baker, J. G. (1987). How shall we conceptualize the language problems of learning-disabled children. In S. J. Ceci (Ed.), *Handbook of cognitive, social, and neuropsychological aspects of learning disabilities* (Vol. II, pp. 103 - 115). Hillsdale, NJ: Lawrence Erlbaum Associates.

Cohen, R. L. (1982). Individual differences in short-term memory. In N. R. Ellis (Ed.), *International review of research in mental retardation* (Vol. 11, pp. 43 - 77). New York: Academic Press.

Curtis, M. E. (1980). Development of components of reading skill. *Journal of Educational Psychology, 72*, 656 - 669.

Doehring, D. (1985). Reading disability subtypes: Interaction of reading and nonreading deficits. In B. P. Rourke (Ed.), *Neuropsychology of learning disabilities* (pp. 133 - 147). New York: Guilford.

Eisenberg, L. (1978). Definitions of dyslexia: Their consequences for research and policy. In A. L. Benton & D. Pearl (Eds.), *Dyslexia: An appraisal of current knowledge* (pp. 29 - 43). New York: Oxford University Press.

Feagans, L., & Short, E. J. (1984). Developmental differences in the comprehension and production of narratives by reading-disabled and normally achieving children. *Child Development, 55*, 1727 - 1736.

Fitzgerald, J. (1984). The relationship between reading ability and expectations for story structures. *Discourse Processes, 7*, 21 - 41.

Gelzheiser, L. M. (1984). Generalization from categorical memory tasks to prose by learning-disabled adolescents. *Journal of Educational Psychology, 76*, 1128 - 1139.

Gold, J., & Fleisher, L. S. (1986). Comprehension breakdown with inductively organized tests: Differences between average and disabled readers. *Remedial and Special Education, 7*, 26 - 32.

Gough, P. B., & Tunmer, W. E. (1986). Decoding, reading and reading disability. *Remedial and Special Education, 7*, 6 - 10.

Graziani, L. J., Brodsky, K., Mason, J. C., & Zager, R. (1983). Variability in IQ scores and prognosis of children with hyperlexia. *Journal of the American Academy of Child Psychiatry, 22*, 441 - 443.

Gregory, J. F., Shanahan, T., & Walberg, H. (1985). Learning disabled 10th graders in mainstreamed setting: A descriptive analysis. *Remedial and Special Education, 6*, 25 - 34.

Hansen, J. (1981). The effects of inference training and practice on young children's reading comprehension. *Reading Research Quarterly, 16*, 391 - 417.

Healy, J. M., Aram, D. M., Horwitz, S. J., & Kessler, J. W. (1982). A study of hyperlexia. *Brain and Language, 17*, 1 - 23.

Jackson, M. D., & McClelland, J. L. (1979). Processing determinants of reading speed. *Journal of Experimental Psychology: General, 108*, 151 - 181.

Jorm, A. F. (1983). Specific reading retardation and working memory: A review. *British Journal of Psychology, 74*, 311 - 342.

Juel, C., Griffith, P. L., & Gough, P. B. (1986). Acquisition of literacy: A longitudinal study of children in first and second grade. *Journal of Educational Psychology, 78*, 243 - 255.

Keogh, B. K. (1986). A marker system for describing learning disability samples. In S. J. Ceci (Ed.), *Handbook of cognitive, social, and neuropsychological aspects of learning disabilities* (Vol. I, pp. 81 - 95). Hillsdale, NJ: Lawrence Erlbaum Associates.

Lesgold, A. M., & Resnick, L. B. (1982). How reading disabilities develop: Perspectives from a longitudinal study. In J. P. Das, R. Mulcaty, & A. E. Wall (Eds.), *Theory and research in learning disability* (pp. 155 - 187). New York: Plenum.

Leu, D. L, DeGroff, L. J. C., & Simons, H. D. (1986). Predictable texts and interactive-compensatory hypotheses: Evaluating individual differences in reading ability, context use, and comprehension. *Journal of Educational Psychology, 78*, 347 - 352.

Levin, E. K., Zigmond, N., & Birch, J. W. (1985). A follow up study of 52 learning-disabled adolescents. *Journal of Learning Disabilities, 18*, 2 - 7.

Lieberman, P., Meskill, R. H., Chatillon, M., & Schupack, H. (1985). Phonetic speech perception deficits in dyslexia. *Journal of Speech and Hearing Research, 28*, 480 - 486.

Lord, C. (1985). Autism and the comprehension of language. In E. Schopler & G. Mesibov (Eds.), *Communication problems in autism* (pp. 257 - 283). New York: Plenum.

Lovett, M. W. (1984). A developmental perspective on reading dysfunction: Accuracy and rate criteria in the subtyping of dyslexic children. *Brain and Language, 22*, 67 - 91.

Manis, F. R., & Morrison, F. J. (1985). Reading disability: A deficit in rule learning? In L. S. Siegel & F. J. Morrison (Eds.), *Cognitive development in atypical children* (pp. 1 - 26). New York: Springer.

Miles, T. R. (1983). *Dyslexia: The pattern of difficulties.* London: Collins.

Mitchell, D. C. (1982). *The process of reading.* Chichester: Wiley.

Mommers, M. J. C., & Boland, T. (1987). De ontwikkeling van decodeervaardigheden, begrijpend lezen en spelling. [The development of decoding skills, reading for comprehension, and spelling]. In M. J. C. Mommers (Ed.), *De ontwikkeling van de leesvaardigheid in longitudinaal perspectief* (pp. 10 - 21). Den Haag: S.V.O.

Morrison, F. J. (1987). The nature of reading disability: Toward an integrative framework. In S. J. Ceci (Ed.), *Handbook of cognitive, social, and neuropsychological aspects of learning disabilities* (Vol. II, pp. 33 - 63). Hillsdale, NJ: Lawrence Erlbaum Associates.

Pennington, B. F., McCabe, L. L., Smith, S. D., Lefly, D. L., Bookman, M. O., Kimberling, W. J., & Lubs, H. A. (1986). Spelling errors in adults with a form of familial dyslexia. *Child Development, 57*, 1001 - 1013.

Perfetti, C. A. (1985). *Reading ability.* New York: Oxford University Press.

Perfetti, C. A., & Lesgold, A. M. (1977). Discourse comprehension and sources of individual differences. In M. A. Just & P. A. Carpenter (Eds.), *Cognitive processes in comprehension* (pp. 141 - 183). Hillsdale, NJ: Lawrence Erlbaum Associates.

Perin, D. (1981). Spelling, reading, and adult illiteracy. *Psychological Research, 43*, 245 - 257.

Rabinowitz, M., & Chi, M. T. H. (1987). An interactive model of strategic processing. In S. J. Ceci (Ed.), *Handbook of cognitive, social, and neuropsychological aspects of learning disabilities* (Vol. II, pp. 83 - 103). Hillsdale, NJ: Lawrence Erlbaum Associates.

Rahman, T., & Bisanz, G. L. (1986). Reading ability and use of a story schema in recalling and reconstructing information. *Journal of Educational Psychology, 78*, 323 - 333.

Rayner, K., & Pollatsek, A. (1987). Eye movements in reading: A tutorial review. In M. Coltheart (Ed.), *Attention and performance XII: The psychology of reading* (pp. 327 - 363). Hillsdale, NJ: Lawrence Erlbaum Associates.

Rutter, M. (1978). Prevalence and types of dyslexia. In A. L. Benton & D. Pearl (Eds.), *Dyslexia: An appraisal of current knowledge* (pp. 3 - 29). New York: Oxford University Press.

Satz, P., & Morris, R. (1981). Learning disability subtypes: A review. In F. J. Pirozzolo & M. C. Wittrock (Eds.), *Neuropsychological and cognitive processes in reading* (pp. 109 - 141). New York: Academic Press.

Seymour, P. H. K. (1986). *Cognitive analysis of dyslexia.* London: Routledge & Kegan Paul.

Silver, A., & Hagin, R. (1964). Specific reading disability follow-up studies. *American Journal of Orthopsychiatry, 24,* 245 - 257.

Smiley, S. S., Oakley, D. D., Worthen, D., Campione, J. C., & Brown, A. L. (1977). Recall of thematically relevant material by adolescent good and poor readers as a function of written versus oral presentation. *Journal of Educational Psychology, 69,* 381 - 387.

Spear, L. C., & Sternberg, R. J. (1987). An information-processing framework for understanding reading disability. In S. J. Ceci (Ed.), *Handbook of cognitive, social, and neuropsychological aspects of learning disabilities* (Vol. II, pp. 3 - 33). Hillsdale, NJ: Lawrence Erlbaum Associates.

Stanovich, K. E. (1980). Toward an interactive-compensatory model of individual differences in the development of reading fluency. *Reading Research Quarterly, 16,* 32 - 71.

Stanovich, K. E. (1986). Cognitive processes and reading problems of learning-disabled children: Evaluating the assumption of specificity. In J. K. Torgesen & B. Y. L. Wong (Eds.), *Psychological and educational perspectives on learning disabilities* (pp. 87 - 133). London: Academic Press.

Stanovich, K. E., Nathan, R. G., & Vala-Rossi, M. (1986). Developmental changes in the cognitive correlates of reading ability and the developmental lag hypothesis. *Reading Research Quarterly, 21,* 267 - 283.

Stanovich, K. E., Nathan, R. G., & Zolman, J. E. (1988). The developmental lag hypothesis in reading: Longitudinal and matched reading-level comparisons. *Child Development, 59,* 71 - 86.

Stark, R. E., & Tallal, P. (1981). Selection of children with specific language deficits. *Journal of Speech and Hearing Disorders, 46,* 114 - 122.

Stein, N. L., & Glenn, C. G. (1979). An analysis of story comprehension in elementary school children. In R. O. Freedle (Ed.), *New directions in discourse processing: Vol. 2. Advances in discourse processes* (pp. 53 - 120). Norwood, NJ: Ablex.

Szeszulski, P. A., & Manis, F. R. (1987). A comparison of word recognition processes in dyslexic and normal readers at two reading-age levels. *Journal of Experimental Child Psychology, 44,* 364 - 376.

Tallal, P. (1980). Auditory temporal perception, phonics, and reading disabilities in children. *Brain and Language, 9,* 182 - 198.

Taylor, M. B., & Williams, J. P. (1983). Comprehension of learning-disabled readers: Task and text variations. *Journal of Educational Psychology, 75,* 743 - 751.

Van Putten, C. M. (1987). *Leerlingen van het individueel beroepsonderwijs nader beschouwd.* [A closer examination of pupils in the individual trade school program]. Unpublished doctoral dissertation, University of Leiden, The Netherlands.

Vellutino, F. R., & Scanlon, D. M. (1985). Verbal memory in poor and normal readers: Developmental differences in the use of linguistic codes. In D. B. Gray & J. F. Kavanagh (Eds.), *Biobehavioral measures of dyslexia* (pp. 177 - 215). Parkton: York.

Weaver, P. A., & Dickinson, D. K. (1982). Scratching below the surface structure: Exploring the usefulness of story grammars. *Discourse Processes, 5,* 225 - 243.

Wong, B. Y. L. (1982). Strategic behaviors in selecting retrieval cues in gifted, normal achieving and learning-disabled children. *Journal of Learning Disabilities, 15*, 33 - 37.

Wong, B. Y. L. (1986). Problems and issues in the definition of learning disabilities. In J. K. Torgesen & B. Y. L. Wong (Eds.), *Psychological and educational perspectives on learning disabilities* (pp. 3 - 27). London: Academic Press.

Worden, P. E. (1983). Memory strategy instruction with the learning-disabled. In M. Pressley & J. R. Levin (Eds.), *Cognitive strategies: Developmental, educational, and treatment-related issues* (pp. 129 - 149). New York: Springer.

Worden, P. E. (1987). The four M's – Memory strategies, metastrategies, monitoring, and motivation. In S. J. Ceci (Ed.), *Handbook of cognitive, social, and neuropsychological aspects of learning disabilities* (Vol. II, pp. 241 - 263). Hillsdale, NJ: Lawrence Erlbaum Associates.

Worden, P. E., Malmgren, I., & Lagourie, P. (1982). Memory for stories in learning-disabled adults. *Journal of Learning Disabilities, 15*, 145 - 152.

Worden, P. E., & Nakamura, G. V. (1982). Story comprehension and recall in learning-disabled versus normal college students. *Journal of Educational Psychology, 74*, 633 - 641.

Zigmond, N., & Thornton, H. S. (1988). Learning disabilities in adolescents and adults. In K. A. Kavale (Ed.), *Learning disabilities: State of the art and practice* (pp. 180 - 206). Boston, MA: Little, Brown and Company.

29 COMPREHENSION FAILURES

Aryan van der Leij

Free University, Amsterdam

INTRODUCTION

Reading comprehension failure is a fascinating but problematic issue in scientific research. There are many conflicting theoretical explanations, and comparison of research results is often hindered by problems concerning subject selection (e.g., heterogeneity of accompanying behavioral aspects and disturbances in underlying cognitive processes, unequal educational opportunities, differences in quality of instruction, etc.).

It is not possible to provide an account of all prevailing issues regarding comprehension failure in a commentary. Instead, my intention is to concentrate my comments on five major topics: reading comprehension and its operationalization, bottom-up versus top-down factors, developmental lag or structural deficit, individual differences, and factors contributing to comprehension failure.

READING COMPREHENSION AND ITS OPERATIONALIZATION

The chapters on comprehension failures indicate that there is no consensus in the way the ability of reading comprehension is conceived and operationalized in tasks. Seymour restricts his study to comprehension at the single-word level, assuming that comprehension depends on the activity of a semantic processor module "in which abstract definitions of concepts are available for representation and manipulation." He concludes that there is no systematic relation across subjects between status of the semantic system and reading impairment. Rispens uses the term "comprehension disorders" but does not provide a definition of this concept. Crain and Shankweiler state that reading is "largely parasitic upon primary language acquisition" and explore the possibility that poor reading is a deficit in language (and, according to their reasoning, of reading) acquisition, i.e. difficulties in accessing and processing phonological information. However, none of the studies that they present involves natural reading. Of the authors, only Conners and Olson use a test for reading comprehension, but they do not seem to have a theory of the specific characteristics of reading comprehension.

The fact that the authors in this volume do not define comprehension failures within a theory of reading comprehension reflects the state-of-the-art in research on reading problems: The focus is mainly on word decoding and word recognition. In his contribution, Rispens summarizes the evidence why this is the case: A lack of decoding skills is a primary source of comprehension problems via a bottle-neck mechanism. The possibility of deficiencies in higher order skill cannot be excluded, but he draws the conclusion that the research data are "far from convincing." Of course, the focus on bottom-up processes is the consequence of the restriction in these studies to dyslexic readers, of whom the most dominant characteristic is the laborious way they decode words. I will return to this topic later in this chapter.

One of the consequences of the prevailing emphasis of the research on dyslexia is that within the area of reading problems, very limited attention is paid to theorizing about the nature of the reading comprehension process. Comprehension of what is read seems to be defined by way of common sense. Students are given text to study and consequently asked questions about the text. This kind of operationalization of reading comprehension has face validity but can lead to conflicting results if demands of the tasks differ on relevant variables. As a result of this situation, it is not easy to discuss and validate evidence on comprehension failures in a comparative way.

To illustrate this point, data from two studies are relevant. In a longitudinal study, Aarnoutse and Van Leeuwe (1988) tested 449 normal-reading Dutch students in the third and sixth grades and reported an increasing correlation between reading comprehension and vocabulary (.52 in Grade 3, .74 in Grade 6) and a decreasing (and low) correlation between reading comprehension and word recognition (.19 in Grade 3, .11 in Grade 6). However, Conners and Olson (this volume) found in their sample of normal readers (average age by estimation at the end of Grade 4) a relatively high correlation between reading comprehension and word recognition (.48) and a low correlation between reading comprehension and listening comprehension (.23). Only 44% of listening comprehension was explained by scores on verbal tests. Therefore, according to their study, general verbal aspects of cognitive functioning do not seem to have much influence on reading comprehension scores.

It is clear that the results of Aarnoutse and van Leeuwe and of Conners and Olson differ considerably with regard to the relation between reading comprehension and general verbal ability. The discrepancy in the results seems largely to be the result of differences in the task to be predicted: reading comprehension (assuming that children in highly industrialized countries on both sides of the Atlantic Ocean have comparable abilities, an assumption which is supported by the remarks of Crain and Shankweiler on phonemic segmentation). In most tests of reading comprehension, after reading the text silently, inferences or the integration of ideas are tested. In the study of Aarnoutse and van Leeuwe, this indeed was the case. In the task used by Conners and Olson, in their own words, "performance was highly dependent on the recognition and comprehension of individual words." Possibly, the difference in the comprehension demands of the tasks explains the differences in results of the studies. Because there is evidence that in normal readers automaticity in word recognition occurs by the second or third grade (e.g., West & Stanovich, 1979) and reading comprehension continues to develop for years afterward, the correlation between these variables is expected to decrease from Grade 3 upward, at least when comprehension is defined in terms of performances at the level of phrase, sentence, or paragraph reading. This clearly is not the case in the study of Conners and Olson, indicating that the operationalization of the concept *reading comprehension* is an important issue to discuss and reach consensus about.

BOTTOM-UP VERSUS TOP-DOWN FACTORS?

In dyslexia research, the possibility of a single internal factor as a cause of dyslexia has received considerable attention. Vellutino (1979) summarizes the evidence against three such single-factor theories and defends a fourth one, his own verbal deficiency hypothesis. In line with this general idea, Crain and Shankweiler provide evidence that deficiencies in higher order skills could be rooted in lower order skills, that is, the executive component of verbal working memory, which is grounded in phonological operations. The problems poor readers face in carrying out phonological operations – well demonstrated by the research of Conners and Olson – not only cause their decoding disability but also, by way of impairments in working memory, their comprehension failure.

Like all single-factor theories of reading disability, this idea is appealing because of its simplicity. In this case, it might even account for cross-cultural data concerning reading problems in countries using different writing systems. Phonological recoding could be of less importance in writing systems like Chinese, which are not based on an alphabetic system. Still, children in such countries can be very poor readers, and suffer from reading backwardness, at least quantitatively comparable to children in countries using the alphabetic system (e.g., Stevenson, Lee, Stigler, & Lucker, 1984). According to the theory of Crain and Shankweiler, this phenomenon could be attributed to deficiencies in phonological operations in verbal working memory, which affect the reading of text in any writing system.

However, single-factor explanations are vulnerable to large individual differences, especially when a subtype of very poor readers shows up who do not seem to have deficiencies in phonological processing like the visual analytic cases demonstrated by Seymour (1986; this volume). In a later section of this comment I will return to this topic. Furthermore, the exact nature of the process which Crain and Shankweiler use to explain the deficiencies in the development of language and reading comprehension is unclear. An important issue is whether the deficit in the control system of working memory is to be conceived as a bottom-up or top-down deficit. If verbal coding or the use of phonetic coding in short-term memory is the defective process, the consensus is to define it as a deficit in bottom-up processing. If, on the other hand, the deficit is attributed to the failure to group items to aid recall, or failure to employ verbal rehearsal, or other strategic processes, the view is more top-down in nature. The terms *executive component* and *control process* used by Crain and Shankweiler suggest that they adhere to a top-down view, even though they call it a bottom-up process.

Of course, this could be a matter of the level of abstraction of the cognitive model chosen to describe the phenomenon. However, the impact of this point of view on the interpretation of the results in the perspective of prediction and treatment is quite large, especially when dyslexic readers are involved. For instance, studies show that poor readers are not impaired in the availability of strategies relevant to processing verbal information but in the use of them. In addition, training studies indicate that they can be taught to make better use of strategies (e.g., Bauer, 1987). If, on the other hand, the process is more bottom-up in nature, training is expected to be less successful in poor readers, because bottom-up processes are the core of reading disabilities (see Spear & Sternberg, 1987, for a review on this topic). The data of Conners and Olson illustrate this point: Their sample of dyslexic readers has an average chronological age of 15.6 and differs mostly from their reading-age controls in phonological coding and phoneme segmentation. With respect to prediction and treatment, it seems important to study whether the processing limitation hypothesis put forward by Crain and Shankweiler, has a more permanent influence on the development of language and reading comprehension. Because the processing limitation hypothesis strongly suggests a deficit, one gets the impression that they are in favor of such a prediction.

DEVELOPMENTAL LAG OR STRUCTURAL DEFICIT?

The lag or deficit discussion has dominated the research on reading disabilities for at least two decades now (e.g., Satz & Sparrow, 1970). In their chapter, Crain and Shankweiler contrast the structural lag hypothesis with the processing limitation hypothesis and add a new perspective to the discussion. Crain and Shankweiler are not concerned with the underlying neuropsychological structures, but with cognitive

functions which may be developmentally delayed or more or less perma-
nently impaired. Unfortunately, their results do not answer the lag or
deficit question, although they have reason to defend the processing limitation hypothesis. An experimental design which enables the researcher
to decide whether the results indicate a lag or deficit is far more complex than the one used by Crain and Shankweiler. Such a design has to
include both cross-sectional and longitudinal elements, comparing poor
readers with reading-age controls and chronological-age controls who are
matched on sex and general cognitive functioning. Furthermore, to be
sure that a specific internal factor is involved, some authors recommend
creating optimal environmental conditions through sound instruction,
and having proper control groups (e.g., chronological age and reading
age controls, see Bradley & Bryant, 1985). When a deficit is involved,
one should find that (a) significant differences in specific aspects of the
cognitive profiles show up repeatedly between poor readers and reading
age controls; (b) with increasing age, development in performance in the
investigated tasks and related task domains (e.g., spelling) is continuously affected; and (c) the deficit cannot be remediated but has to be
compensated for in one way or another. If a developmental lag is the
better explanation, one should find that (a) there are no significant differences between poor readers and reading age controls; (b) with increasing age, poor readers develop like normal readers but with a delay; and
(c) the effect of remediation on poor readers and reading-age controls
is comparable. It would be very interesting if Crain and Shankweiler in
future research test their processing limitation hypothesis using a more
conclusive design.

THE ISSUE OF INDIVIDUAL DIFFERENCES

Appealing as the issues of lag or deficit or unitary or multiple causes
in poor reading may have been in the past decades, it is possible that
a basic assumption underlying these issues is not justified by the facts.
All research projects involving group comparisons are based on the assumption that the groups are to a great extent homogeneous in their
distributions on relevant variables. The most important variables are
within the cognitive domain of functioning, not only on a general level
(intelligence) but also on more specific levels, concerning the processing
of verbal information and the act of reading itself. Unfortunately, quantitative and qualitative differences are apparent among poor readers,
most strikingly with regard to specific processes.

To escape from the obvious criticism that their results could be the
consequence of neglecting these notions (which are common knowledge
among clinicians in the dyslexic domain) many researchers have attempted to detect homogeneous subtypes within heterogeneous groups.
Most differentiations in subtypes reveal at least two main subtypes, one
linked to impairments in phonological processing and one to impairments in word recognition (e.g., Rutter, 1978). However, the chapter

of Seymour in this volume indicates that even subtyping may be an oversimplification because of the fact that it is impossible to find two subjects within any sample of dyslexics who share the same impairments in their reading processes. In his monograph of 1986, Seymour demonstrated that normal readers are not a homogeneous group either, but show considerable variability of reading function. Furthermore, formal competence is not incompatible with the occurrence of minor, localized inefficiencies. Because across subjects no clear patterns of correlations between impairments and strategic compensations can be found, Seymour proposes a model that allows for the independent impairment of each domain. This assumption diminishes the usefulness of subtyping because of the various combinations of impairments which occur. His chapter provides good examples of differences among subjects. Possibly, both lag and deficit theories (or varied combinations of the theories) may be useful explanations of the performances of some children. If this is the case, research should be directed at an individual level and not at the level of groups or subtypes, because group comparisons may obscure the heterogeneity of the subjects in specific areas of cognitive functioning.

However, the significance of the subtle variations among and within subjects is not easy to validate, at least not from an inductive point of view. It seems quite impossible to think of reading disabilities in general terms because there appear to be more exceptions than rules. Although Seymour's work is based on a solid theory of cognitive functioning, the question can be raised whether it will result in a conceptual whole that will permit the explication of laws useful for explanation and prediction, which according to Kavale and Forness (1985), is the ultimate aim of scientific research. If that deductive aim is pursued, it is necessary to interpret findings at some point in a more general way to escape from mere description of the peculiarities of single subjects.

From the clinical point of view, the way Seymour describes differences in reading processes is appealing because of its precision. Unfortunately, up until now no attempt has been made to explore the consequences in differential treatment. However, if this kind of study is carried out, it also seems inevitable that some generalizations about the research findings have to be made, for two reasons. First, because the aim of any treatment is to stimulate the development of reading skill in poor readers, which enables them to meet the demands of literacy, relevant to their age, educational level, or professional situation, it is not possible to circumvent the problem of setting criteria relative to "normal" performance. In other words, the aim of treatment often will be to bring the performance of poor or dyslexic readers within the range of variability shown by readers who can be regarded as functioning in harmony with the demands. This cannot be done on a one-by-one componential basis, and it also implies that all components of reading are mastered, or at least that the impairments are reduced to "minor localized inefficiencies," which also can occur in normal readers. For clinical use, it seems inevitable to define "normal reading" in a deductive, metacomponential way.

Second, the possible variations in treatments are relatively small. They can grossly be distinguished with respect to the stimulation of bottom-up versus top-down processes, with relevant choices to be made about the material level (letter-clusters, words, sentences, texts) and instructional methods (e.g., the use of audio support, repetition, feedback, the installment of prior knowledge). Because some choices will be made in any case (e.g., repetition and feedback) and not all combinations are useful, the variations in treatments converge on a relative few which are valid, at least at face value. Although the perspectives of remedial effectiveness and of the scientific explanation mentioned earlier need not be similar, the former also seem to call for the description of deficits in a configurational way, contrary to the view expressed by Seymour (1986; this volume).

FACTORS CONTRIBUTING TO COMPREHENSION FAILURE

To return to the central subject of this volume, it seems clear that much attention is paid to the problems of dyslexic students, who probably are a minority in the group of poor comprehenders. However, comprehension failures should not be restricted to the problems faced by children with very specific disabilities when they read texts. The first reason is described by Rispens (this volume): Not all dyslexic children seem to be affected to the same extent in their reading comprehension. Second, and more important, in our society, despite all the money that is invested in the education of reading and writing abilities, large groups of individuals are not able to understand what they read. To use a concept now widely accepted to describe these groups, one can speak of functional illiteracy.

The reasons individuals become functionally illiterate can vary considerably. There are internal factors that can be divided into specific or general factors. The papers of Conners and Olson, Seymour, Crain and Shankweiler, and Rispens are focused on specific factors that determine poor skills in reading words or sentences. However, a main source of poor comprehension, which affects far more individuals, is a general one: low intelligence. Kavale and Forness (1985) calculated a coefficient of .58 between IQ and reading comprehension for third graders (see also the data cited earlier from the study of Aarnoutse & van Leeuwe, 1988). Based on these figures, the tentative conclusion can be drawn that many school children who score low on measures of general cognitive functioning, especially verbal abilities, suffer from a poor understanding of what they read.

External factors can also play an important role, most prominently the lack of adequate educational opportunity to learn the skills of reading. Another influential factor is the quality of education in relation to the demands on literacy in the society, which seem to increase.

In industrialized countries, the issue of functional illiteracy among adults has drawn a great deal of attention lately. For example, in the report of the European community (1988), Denmark provides an estimate of 10% functionally illiterate adults, differentiated as heavily dyslexics (at least 2%), intellectually handicapped (2%), older persons who profited very little from their early education (1%), emotionally-disturbed persons who cannot use their reading skills (2%), and persons suffering from poor comprehension because of increasing social expectations of the level of literacy (at least 3%). Leaving the emotionally disturbed group out of this discussion, two out of four of the groups seem to have become functionally illiterate because of external factors: little profit from education and poor adaptation to increasing demands of society on literacy. The other two, dyslexia and intellectual handicap, represent a specific and general internal factor, respectively.

CONCLUSIONS

It would be worthwhile to direct future research on comprehension failure within a broader theoretical framework than dyslexia and to investigate, possibly on an international scale, the incidence of functional illiteracy in industrialized countries and the relative contribution of internal and external factors. As a first step, it is important to reach consensus on the operationalization of the concept of reading comprehension. Restricted to dyslexia, the possibility of a single internal factor and the issue of lag or deficit should be studied in a more conclusive way, combining longitudinal and instructional research designs. Assumptions about homogeneity of subject samples have to be considered in light of individual differences that are apparent. However, to be relevant to both explanation and treatment, it seems inevitable that it will be necessary to cope with differences between individuals.

ACKNOWLEDGMENT

The author wishes to thank Dr. Pieter Reitsma for his comments on an earlier draft of this chapter.

REFERENCES

Aarnoutse, C. A. J., & van Leeuwe, J. F. J. (1988). Het belang van technisch lezen, woordenschat en ruimtelijke intelligentie voor begrijpend lezen [The importance of decoding, vocabulary, and spatial intelligence for reading comprehension]. *Pedagogische Studiën, 65*, 49 - 59.

Bauer, R. H. (1987). Control processes as a way of understanding, diagnosing, and remediating learning disabilities. In L. Swanson (Ed.), *Advances in learning and behavioral disabilities: Supplement 2. Memory and learning disabilities* (pp. 41 - 81). Greenwich, CT: JAI.

Bradley, L., & Bryant, P. (1985). *Rhyme and reason in reading and spelling.* Ann Arbor: The University of Michigan Press.

Commission of the European Communities (1988). *Social Europe: Report on the fight against illiteracy. Supplement 2/88.* Luxembourg: Office for Official Publications of the European Communities.

Kavale, K. A., & Forness, S. R. (1985). *The science of learning disabilities.* Windsor: NFER-Nelson.

Rutter, M. (1978). Prevalence and types of dyslexia. In A. L. Benton, & D. Pearl (Eds.), *Dyslexia: An appraisal of current knowledge* (pp. 5 - 28). New York: Oxford University Press.

Satz, P., & Sparrow, S. S. (1970). Specific developmental dyslexia: A theoretical formulation. In D. J. Bakker, & P. Satz (Eds.), *Specific reading disability* (pp. 17 - 40). Rotterdam: Rotterdam University Press.

Seymour, P. H. K. (1986). *Cognitive analysis of dyslexia.* London: Routledge & Kegan Paul.

Spear, L. C., & Sternberg, R. J. (1987). An information-processing framework for understanding reading disability. In S. J. Ceci (Ed.), *Handbook of cognitive, social, and neuropsychological aspects of learning disabilities* (pp. 3 - 31). Hillsdale, NJ: Lawrence Erlbaum Associates.

Stevenson, H. W., Lee, S., Stigler, J., & Lucker, G. W. (1984). Family variables and reading: A study of mothers of poor and average readers in Japan, Taiwan, and the United States. *Journal of Learning Disabilities, 17,* 150 - 156.

Vellutino, F. R. (1979). *Dyslexia: Theory and research.* Cambridge, MA: MIT Press.

West, R. F., & Stanovich, K. E. (1979). The development of automatic word recognition skills. *Journal of Reading Behavior, 11,* 211 - 219.

30 COMPREHENSION PROCESSES IN READING: FINAL THOUGHTS

Keith Rayner
University of Massachusetts, Amherst

Giovanni B. Flores d'Arcais
Max Planck Institute, Nijmegen and University of Leiden

David A. Balota
Washington University

INTRODUCTION

During the past two decades, considerable progress has been made towards understanding the processes involved in reading (cf., Just & Carpenter, 1987; Rayner & Pollatsek, 1989). The preceding chapters have documented much of this progress. Consider for example, the progress made since Neisser's classic book *Cognitive Psychology* (1967) was published. In Neisser's book there was considerable discussion of processes tied to pattern and word recognition, and relatively little devotion to understanding processes involved in sentence and text comprehension. In addition, to further developments in understanding processes tied to simple word recognition, at least half of the present volume is devoted to higher level sentence and text processing. Our guess is that Huey would be quite pleased with the progress that has been made since his classic work (*The Psychology and Pedagogy of Reading*) was published in 1908.

Each of the four sections of the present volume deal with a particular aspect of reading. Our sense is that as we move from the chapters in Section 1 to the chapters in Section 4, we understand less well the critical processes involved. Of course, this is not terribly surprising for two reasons. First, as noted above, the work on pattern recognition and isolated word recognition has been at the center of research for a considerable period of time. Second, it is apparent that there are increasing degrees of complexity as one moves from isolated word recognition (Section 1) to syntactic parsing (Section 2) to the comprehension of text (Section 3) to the general issue of reading breakdowns (Section 4). Thus, although the progress in understanding reading has been quite impressive, it is clear that there is still much to be learned about each of the four topics, and in particular, how they are interrelated.

Our intention in this final chapter is to touch upon what we see as the key issues in this volume and, more generally, as important issues in reading research. In the introductory chapter, some global themes were identified that were present in the various chapters and sections. The four general themes identified were: (1) identifying the on-line processing activities in reading, (2) determining the appropriate measures/tasks to index such on-line processes, (3) determining the appropriate modeling framework to best facilitate our understanding of reading comprehension, and (4) specifying the relationship between word processing, parsing, and comprehension processes and breakdowns in the reading process such as those that occur in developmental dyslexia. We will now turn to a brief discussion of each of these issues.

On-line Processing Activities in Reading

If there is one thing that characterizes much of the recent research on reading, it is the desire to understand when and how various subcomponent processes are realized on a moment-to-moment basis. Some of the questions addressed in the present volume are: (1) Are there between-word semantic and within-word morphological analyses involved in lexical identification? (2) Is there a measurable point in time when the word has been recognized and meaning has not been accessed? (3) Can one point to a single aspect of eye-movement data that faithfully reflects lexical access? (4) Are text-integration processes completed while the eye is fixated on a given word in the text or do they spill over to subsequent fixations? (5) When are syntactic assignments associated with parsing made for individual words? (6) How and when is contextual information used by the human parsing mechanism in parsing sentences? (7) What types of inferences are generated during reading and precisely when are they generated?

Questions such as these, which are abundantly evident in the present volume, have been the focus of a considerable amount of attention. Clearly, in order to develop an adequate model of reading one must provide answers to these, and many more, moment-to-moment operations. We feel that although the present chapters may not have provided the ultimate answers to all, if even any, of these questions, at the very least, they have provided carefully developed frameworks for dealing with these questions in future research.

Searching for the Appropriate Measures of On-line Processing Activities

A central theme running through many of the chapters in the first three sections was related to the issue of how to best document on-line activities in reading. It is our contention that far too little attention has been paid in the area of reading research, and many other areas in Cognitive Psychology, to developing tasks that primarily tap operations related to the target behavior the researcher is attempting to better understand. For example, a researcher may develop a research program using Task A that provides some very intriguing results. In fact, based on such results, the researcher may develop a sophisticated and ingenious model of some specific aspect of reading. Unfortunately, we later find out that Task A is not simply a reflection of processes that are related to the target behavior (e.g., reading), but involves task-specific components that are producing the "intriguing" results. Hence, the researcher has developed a sophisticated and ingenious model of Task A, not the behavior which was the real object of investigation. Of course, it is not a total loss that we have an adequate model of Task A; however, the researcher did not reach the specified goal of better understanding the behavior. Because there are often reasons why one wishes to better understand a given target behavior, in this case reading, we feel that considerably more effort should be devoted to developing tasks that faithfully reflect operations involved in that behavior.

This general theme is abundantly evident in the present volume. For example, most of the chapters in Section 1 (e.g., Balota, Seidenberg, De Groot, Schreuder et al., Pollatsek & Rayner) discuss this issue. There is considerable discussion of the task-specific operations involved in lexical decision and naming performance. Researchers in this section are clearly sensitive to the limits of given tasks. For example, in an attempt to avoid some of the problems associated with these tasks, De Groot used a masked-priming paradigm, while Pollatsek and Rayner discuss the potential for the actual eye-movement record to reflect lexical access processes.

Similar concerns were abundant in the research on syntactic parsing developed in Section 2. In particular, an important issue raised in this section is whether contextual and pragmatic information have an influence on the syntactic parsing process. Some of the work discussed in this section has utilized eye-movement recording and has indicated that such information does not influence the initial parse of the sentence but primarily has an influence on the reanalysis process (Frazier). Other measures, such as self-paced reading, have suggested an early effect of contextual and pragmatic information (Perfetti and Taraban & McClelland). This, of course, is a very important issue to resolve regarding language processing in terms of modular versus interactive views. Unfortunately, there is the general confounding of theoretical position with type of on-line task used to investigate this critical issue. It is possible that characteristics of the different tasks used to investigate this issue led to this discrepancy in results. Thus, it will be interesting to determine if immediate effects of contextual and pragmatic information on sentence parsing can also be observed in the eye-movement data. If so, then one can eliminate the worry of simple task differences producing the differences in results and ultimately theoretical positions.

Turning to Section 3, one again finds concerns about the appropriate measures of on-line comprehension processes, most notably regarding the types of *inferences* that are made on-line. Traditionally, the dependent variables in this area have included reading time measures (either for a sentence or for a passage), and memory measures, e.g., cued recall, free recall, and recognition. However, such measures turn out to be rather global and in the past few years, attention has turned to developing techniques that provide some indication of more immediate processing. It's interesting in this context that Keenan et al.'s chapter (and to some extent, McKoon and Ratcliff's chapter) deals with many of the issues that researchers in word processing have been addressing. In this case, however, the question is what is the best measure of inference generation during reading? Garrod and Sanford's chapter also reflects this concern as they have moved away from the global reading time measures that they have standardly employed to a task such as *misspelling detection*. It is again abundantly clear from reading the chapters in this section that there is a general concern in the literature that researchers should be more concerned with developing measures that are more closely tied to the processes that they are trying to model.

In summary, the current state of research in the areas of word recognition, syntactic parsing, and text processing all indicate the importance of tasks analyses. We view this as a very productive endeavor in these areas, and suspect that researchers will be very innovative in the next few years in developing better tasks and will be more concerned with the validity of the measures employed. We also suspect, that Garner, Hake and Eriksen's (1956) appeal for converging operations in the development of adequate models of comprehension processes will gain a renewed commitment by researchers in these fields.

Modeling the Reading Process

Many of the chapters in the volume addressed various models of the processes associated with reading. At this point, we would argue that there is not a clearly agreed upon model of reading. The global models that currently exist of the reading process (see the relevant chapters in Just & Carpenter, 1987; Rayner & Pollatsek, 1989) all have weaknesses associated with them. Clearly, in order to develop an accurate model of reading, each of the subcomponent processes must be fully understood. In the meantime, our suspicion is that progress towards a global model of reading will be best accomplished by continued research on the various subcomponent processes of reading and the development of adequate models of these subcomponent processes. In other words, our best guess is that there will not be a major breakthrough in understanding reading that results from the development of a global, all-encompassing model of the reading process. Rather, continued progress will come as a result of further research on subcomponent processes and refinement of models of such processes. Of course, the various models will need to be integrated at some point. However, we believe that integration of less than well understood models of subcomponent processes would be premature.

The past two decades have seen the development of numerous models of the word recognition process. Although there is certainly not a consensus concerning the adequacy of these different word recognition models, it is interesting to note that some models of subcomponent processes in word recognition have been extremely successful. For example, between 1969 and 1981 the word-superiority effect virtually dominated research in the area of early visual word processing. However, the amount of research devoted to this topic came to a near standstill with the publication of the interactive activation model of McClelland and Rumelhart (1981; Rumelhart & McClelland, 1982) and the activation-verification model of Paap, Newsome, McDonald, and Schvaneveldt (1982). The reason for the decreased attention to the word-superiority effect was that these models were able to so nicely account for virtually all of the extent data relevant to the basic effect.

Currently, the major issue with respect to modeling word recognition processes is the extent to which connectionist models can accurately account for word processing. This debate is very nicely captured in the chapters by Besner and by Seidenberg, along with the commentaries by Hudson and by Neumann. Seidenberg argues that such models have tremendous potential for helping us better understand the processes associated with word recognition. However, Besner points out some potential problems with the currently implemented version of a particular connectionist model. It's certainly far too early to determine what the outcome will be concerning the activity surrounding connectionist models, but, at the very least, we do feel confident that this debate will provide the basis for self-reflection regarding theoretical predispositions. This latter outcome can only be productive.

Of course, connectionistic models aspire not only to account for the (relatively speaking) simple subcomponent process of word processing, but also for far more complex processing like parsing (see the chapter by Taraban & McClelland) and text comprehension (see the chapter by Sharkey). In his chapter, Norris makes some very telling criticisms of the currently implemented versions of connectionist models. Our own bias is that connectionist models may be better suited to account for processes that involve stored representations (like looking up the meaning of a word) than to processes associated with constructing representations (e.g., like parsing and inference generation). However, only time (and a considerable amount of research) will provide the final answer to the limits of connectionist modeling.

Within the area of sentence comprehension, the major theoretical debate has been between models of the processes that stress the modular nature of sentence parsing (chapters by Clifton & De Vincenzi and by Frazier) versus those that stress the interactive nature of sentence processing (see the chapter by Taraban & McClelland). More recently, there have been compromises between the strict autonomy approach and the highly interactive approach (see the chapter by Perfetti). The flexibility of the human sentence parsing mechanism is also related to the issue of the Universality of parsing principles. This issue is nicely addressed in the chapters by Mitchell and by Frazier and discussed in the commentary by Flores D'Arcais. Ultimately, if the emphasis on distinguishing between interactive and modular processing systems will be fruitful, there must be some agreement upon what would constitute adequate data. In this light, we find Norris' comments again quite enlightening. He indicates quite nicely that a parallel distributed processing system, typically viewed as a highly interactive system, can predict the word-superiority effect in a totally bottom-up fashion.

Within the area of text comprehension, the model proposed by Kintsch and Van Dijk (1978; Van Dijk & Kintsch, 1983) has had a major influence. However, as many of the chapters in Section 3 document (also see Kintsch, 1988), there is now considerable interest in deriving models that are more specific concerning the on-line processes than was available in the Kintsch and Van Dijk model. Thus, the chapters by Myers, McKoon and Ratcliff, Van den Broek, Vonk and Noordman, Sharkey, and Garrod and Sanford all deal with specific on-line components of the comprehension process. While the Kintsch and Van Dijk model has had a tremendous impact on the field, there appears to be a movement towards on-line models that deal with specific subcomponents of the comprehension processes involved in text processing. Of course, as noted earlier in a different context, we feel that such a change may be quite healthy, as long as there is the timely move towards integration across models of subcomponent processes.

Reading Problems

The final section of the volume deals with comprehension failures and dyslexia. The authors of the various chapters in this section touch upon most of the issues that are central in this area of research. It is interesting to note here that with the exception of the Crain and Shankweiler chapter, the chapters in this section primarily emphasize the notion that breakdowns in *word recognition skills* in large part underlie reading failures. The basic thrust is that if individuals are poor at word decoding than this will have ramifications for higher-level processes. Although this general view may be correct, it is also likely that the general emphasis on word decoding processes, may have occurred because, as noted earlier, these processes are relatively easier to empirically address, and are relatively better understood. Although the chapter by Crain and Shankweiler does not emphasize word decoding skills, these authors also point to a fundamental aspect of reading, i.e., phonologically-based working memory, as a source for higher-level (syntactic parsing of sentences) reading breakdowns. Again, the emphasis on phonological-recoding in reading has been at the heart of considerable research in reading and is an aspect of reading that is relatively well-understood. Hence, one finds a reliance on another relatively well-understood aspect of reading in accounting for breakdowns in the reading process.

One difficulty that appears to permeate this area is that researchers have looked for *the* underlying cause of dyslexia. More recently, there has been research in this area that has advocated the notion that there may not be a single cause but rather one must look at different subtypes of dyslexia and potentially different breakdowns associated with each subtype. In fact, it is possible that at least some of the conflicting results in this area may be due to different researchers having different proportions of various subtypes within their samples. (Rispens makes a similar argument regarding inconsistent results simply by noting that different studies have used different criteria for labelling an individual as dyslexic.) In this light, Seymour's chapter is quite intriguing. His work appears to suggest that there are almost as many types of dyslexia as there are dyslexics! Of course, we're being a bit facetious here – it's undoubtedly the case that some groupings can take place and, as in the acquired dyslexia research, has the potential for yielding some interesting generalizations, as Seymour nicely demonstrates.

FINAL THOUGHTS

One reaction some critics might have to the present volume is something like: "all of the work discussed in this book is interesting, but what does it have to do with comprehension." That is, for many people, the traditional study of comprehension involves either (1) some measure of what people remember after they read text or (2) the score they achieve on some type of standardized test.

The first issue was in part addressed in the first chapter of this volume. We think there is absolutely nothing wrong with the study of the product (i.e., memory) of comprehension. Indeed, we would argue that this is a very important topic of study. Being able to characterize the processes involved in remembering what was earlier read is a highly complicated endeavor, as a century of learning and memory research has clearly documented. But, that's just the point. It is more the study of memory than the study of reading. We believe that comprehension is a *process* that utilizes and produces memory representations. In order to develop adequate models of reading, one needs to model the processes involved in comprehension. Of course, it is important to understand what the output of the comprehension process is, but, with respect to the present issues, this importance is primarily due to the insight it may provide into the comprehension process itself.

With respect to the second issue, it is possible that those interested in the traditional study of comprehension within educational circles may be initially disappointed with this volume. After all, the title of the volume has *comprehension* in it, yet nowhere in the book (with the possible exception of van der Leij's chapter) do any of the authors touch on issues that would fall within the domain of "comprehension" as defined by workers in education. However, it's interesting to note that there currently appears to be a movement within the educational testing field to develop tests that are more closely tied to models developed within basic cognitive psychological research and theory (e.g., Stanovich, 1980). In this light, we feel that the type of research and theoretical developments discussed in the present volume has important implications for the traditional study of comprehension within the field of reading education.

In conclusion, we would like to reiterate that we believe that significant strides have been undertaken in the past twenty years to understand the processes involved in reading. We would argue that the chapters in this volume characterize much of that progress, and we anticipate with considerable enthusiasm the strides that will be made in the next twenty years.

REFERENCES

Garner, W. R., Hake, H. W., & Eriksen, C. W. (1956). Operationism and the concept of perception. *Psychological Review, 63*, 149 - 159.

Huey, E. B. (1908). *The psychology and pedagogy of reading.* New York: Macmillan. (Republished: Cambridge, MA: MIT Press, 1968).

Just, M. A., & Carpenter, P. A. (1987). *The psychology of reading and language comprehension.* Newton, MA: Allyn and Bacon.

Kintsch, W. (1988). The role of knowledge in discourse comprehension: A construction-integration model. *Psychological Review, 95*, 163 - 182.

Kintsch, W., & Van Dijk, T. A. (1978). Toward a model of text comprehension and production. *Psychological Review, 85*, 336 - 349.

McClelland, J. L., & Rumelhart, D. E. (1981). An interactive activation model of context effects in letter perception: Part 1. An account of basic findings. *Psychological Review, 88*, 375 - 407.

Neisser, U. (1967). *Cognitive psychology.* New York: Appleton-Century-Crofts.

Paap, K. R., Newsome, S. L., McDonald, J. E., & Schvaneveldt, R. W. (1982). An activation-verification model for letter and word recognition: The word superiority effect. *Psychological Review, 89*, 573 - 594.

Rayner, K., & Pollatsek, A. (1989). *The psychology of reading.* Englewood Cliffs, NJ: Prentice-Hall.

Rumelhart, D. E., & McClelland, J. L. (1982). An interactive activation model of context effects in letter perception: Part 2. *Psychological Review, 89*, 60 - 94.

Stanovich, K. E. (1980). Toward an interactive-compensatory model of individual differences in the development of reading fluency. *Reading Research Quarterly, 16*, 32 - 71.

Van Dijk, T. A., & Kintsch, W. (1983). *Strategies of discourse comprehension.* New York: Academic Press.

Author Index

Subject Index